A Year

in the

NEW TESTAMENT

Meditations for Each Day of the Church Year

Douglas Bauman

D1637086

Wilfred L. Karsten

Mark W. Love

Zach McIntosh

James Meichsner

William Chancellor Weedon

CONCORDIA PUBLISHING HOUSE • SAINT LOUIS

Copyright © 2010 Concordia Publishing House
3558 S. Jefferson Avenue, St. Louis, MO 63118-3968
1-800-325-3040 · www.cph.org

Manufactured in the United States of America

Library of Congress Cataloging-in-Publication Data
A year in the New Testament : meditations for each day of the church year / Douglas Bauman ... [et al.].

   p. cm.
   ISBN 978-0-7586-2590-8
   1. Bible. N.T.—Meditations. 2. Church year meditations. 3. Devotional calendars—Lutheran Church—Missouri Synod. 4. Lutheran Church—Missouri Synod—Prayers and devotions. I. Bauman, Douglas. II. Title.

BS2341.55.Y43 2010

242'.3—dc22

2010029466

1 2 3 4 5 6 7 8 9 10   19 18 17 16 15 14 13 12 11 10

PREFACE

There is no shortage of devotional books that seek to edify the Christian reader with a personal story tied to a snippet of Scripture. Rare are the devotional book authors that, by their writing, take the reader from their experiences of daily life into the Bible. The authors of *A Year in the New Testament* do just that. There is no greater source of comfort, hope, help, and counsel than the Word of God itself. Nothing serves the Christian faith more than that to diligently and daily read and search the Holy Scriptures.

While our Lutheran tradition teaches that the head of the house is the primary teacher of faith, many parents are frustrated by their own lack of scriptural understanding. As the title suggests, *A Year in the New Testament* will guide you through reading most of the New Testament in the course of a year, and do it in a way that is encouraging and manageable. Along the way you will drink deeply of the fountain of eternal life and gain in understanding of the message of God's Word.

The daily devotions of *A Year in the New Testament* follow the seasonal movements of the Church Year in a broad, general fashion, but not in the more focused and specific way that one expects for the lessons and Holy Gospel appointed for particular Sundays and festivals of the Church Year. This is consistent with the ancient Christian precedent and practice of a *lectio continua* (i.e., a continuous reading). This approach allows Scripture to interpret itself in its own literary contexts, and thereby also to inform and shape Christian prayer and devotion over the course of time.

Scot A. Kinnaman
Editor

Brief Introduction
to the Christian Church Year

Background

The life of the Church is centered around the Church's worship. As Christians gather for worship, they do so with a strong sense of time and history. Humans have always been time conscious. Light and darkness regulate our days. Daily life is ordered by the activities of work and rest. Seasons change in a regular way from times of growth to times of death. God established this time consciousness. Genesis 1 shows the centrality of time, which God created when He instituted "evening and . . . morning, the first day" (v. 5). God set the time markers in the heavens on the fourth day "to separate the day from the night. And [to] let them be for signs and for seasons, and for days and years" (v. 14). God rested on the seventh day as a model for us (Exodus 20:8–11).

Christians retain this sense of time. Our seven-day week continues to recall God's incomparable creation of the world. Early Christians recalled the historic time-related events that were important to their faith, especially events in the life of Jesus. They realized that God entered our world "when the fullness of time had come" (Galatians 4:4). Mark tells us that Jesus' first sermon was about time: "The time is fulfilled, and the kingdom of God is at hand" (Mark 1:15). In his Gospel, Luke also reminds us of the timeliness of Christ's arrival: "In the days of Herod, king of Judea" (Luke 1:5); "This was the first registration when Quirinius was governor of Syria" (Luke 2:2). The evangelist John also reports specific historical settings for our Lord's ministry (John 10:22–23). A Sunday close to Passover is now celebrated as the feast of the Resurrection of Our Lord (Luke 24:1). The Jewish harvest festival of Pentecost is remembered now as the birthday of the Christian Church (Acts 2:1).

Christians also have added their own unique celebrations and adapted others to trinitarian understandings. Easter is the principle feast day of the Church. It is the Son's Day of Days as the Church celebrates the Resurrection of Our Lord; it is also an event by which Christians identify themselves as distinctly new creations. The Nativity of Our Lord, celebrated on December 25, is the second great Christian feast and is most clearly the Father's Day. On this day, God gives His most precious gift of life to the world in the person of His Son, Jesus. Finally, Pentecost is celebrated with a specific focus on the Holy Spirit's presence, power, and purpose. Thus Pentecost is the Spirit's Day. Celebrations of the Epiphany and the Transfiguration of Our Lord also recall Jesus' ministry in power and glory. Holy Trinity Sunday reminds us of the great controversies and struggles in the first three centuries of Christianity as the Church sought to clarify and articulate the biblical revelation of God's unity in three distinct persons. As time passed, notable Church leaders were remembered on their death day, underscoring the fact that death is actually an entrance or birth into the new life with Christ in heaven.

The Christian calendar is retained in Christian Church bodies throughout the world for several reasons. First, a regular calendar is helpful to keep the remembrances before us. Just as God commanded the Jewish people to recall how He had delivered them in the past (e.g., the Passover, Exodus 12:14; Leviticus 23:4–8), so, too, early Christians recalled the historic time-related events that were important to their faith, as Jesus had encouraged His disciples to do (Luke 22:19). Second, following their Jewish predecessors, Christians consider the regularity of the holidays as teaching moments, with the celebration of the events of Christ's life used to tell and retell the Good News. Finally, Christians recognize that this life is not an end in itself. Christ's victory over death means that daily life focuses beyond the mundane to eternity. A calendar of Christian events unites present-day believers with those of the past as well as the future.

Martin Luther sought to reform the Church's liturgical and sanctoral calendar, especially the excesses that had crept into the commemoration of saints, by eliminating the festivals and commemorations that were most distant from Christ's life and work. Yet Luther said that it is important for Christians to recall the saints because they are excellent models for our faith and life, concrete examples of following Christ. Such commemorations, then, draw together our memories so that we can express our thanks to God for His gracious Spirit, as well as receive encouragement in our own activities. Lutherans have continued to celebrate the faith of some who have joined the Church Triumphant. November 1, All Saints' Day, is central for Lutherans in this regard. The variety of festivals and commemorations on the present calendar is astounding. This variety and flexibility offers numerous opportunities for local distinctions.

SUNDAYS AND SEASONS
The Liturgical Calendar

THE TIME OF CHRISTMAS

The Savior's birth is second in importance only to His resurrection on Easter Sunday. During Christmas and its season, Christians take time to reflect on God's great and gracious gift of Himself.

ADVENT

Begins the fourth Sunday before December 25, or the Sunday closest to St. Andrew (November 30).

Ends with midday prayer on December 24.

The calendar of the Church begins with Advent (from Latin *adventus*, which means "coming into"), a four-week period of preparation before Christmas. The story of Jesus in Advent is the story of hope coming into the world. When the time was just right, God sent His Son, Jesus, into the world.

The Advent season teaches us to prepare to receive Jesus, the hope of the world. It has become common to use an Advent wreath to mark the season. An Advent wreath has four candles—one for each week in Advent. As these candles are lit each week, our anticipation mounts as we look forward to Jesus' coming.

CHRISTMAS AND ITS SEASON

Begins with evening prayer on Christmas Eve (December 24).

Ends with midday prayer on January 5.

The evening services of Christmas Eve mark the beginning of the Church's celebration of the Nativity of Our Lord. The season continues after December 25 over a period traditionally known as the twelve days of Christmas. This season includes a number of lesser festivals: The festival of St. Stephen, the first martyr, occurs on December 26. St. John, apostle and evangelist, is remembered on December 27. The death of the babies in Bethlehem (Matthew 2) is observed on December 28 as the Festival of the Holy Innocents. The circumcision and naming of Jesus on the eighth day after His birth (Luke 2:21) is celebrated on January 1.

EPIPHANY AND ITS SEASON

Begins with evening prayer on January 5.

Ends the Tuesday before Ash Wednesday.

Epiphany is one of the oldest seasons in the Christian Church Year, second only to the Easter season. This season of lights emphasizes Jesus' manifestation (or epiphany, from the Greek epiphaneia) as God and man. The earliest Christians called the feast of the Epiphany the Theophany ("revelation of God"). When the Gentile Magi came to worship Jesus, they showed that everyone now has access to God. Now all people, Jew and Gentile, can come to God's temple to worship, because Jesus is the new temple: God in the flesh. The Epiphany of Our Lord (January 6) marks the celebration of the visit of the Magi.

Epiphany may include as many as nine Sundays, depending on the date of Easter. The season is marked at its beginning and at its end by two important feasts of Christ. On the First Sunday after the Epiphany, the Church celebrates the Baptism of Our Lord. The Father had sent Jesus to bear the sins of the world. So Jesus steps down into baptismal waters so that He can soak up the sins of the world: he is baptized into our sins, so that our Baptism might be into His death and resurrection for the forgiveness of sins.

The Feast of the Transfiguration, celebrated on the last Sunday in the Epiphany season, is a significant and uniquely Lutheran contribution to the Christian calendar. This festival commemorates the moment on the Mount of Transfiguration when three of Jesus' disciples glimpsed their Lord in divine splendor, seeing Him as the center of the Law (Moses) and the Prophets (Elijah). Jesus proclaimed to His disciples, then and now, that He was the long-awaited one who had come to die for the sins of the world and be raised again in glory.

The Time of Easter

Easter celebrates the chief event in the life of Christ and was the major celebration among early Christians. Given that Easter is both a movable date and also a principal celebration of the Church Year, the date of Easter determines much of the rest of the Church Year. Generally speaking, Easter is observed on the first Sunday after the first full moon on or after the vernal equinox. The date of Easter will influence the date of Ash Wednesday, the fortieth day (not counting Sundays) before Easter; the date of the Transfiguration, the Sunday before Ash Wednesday; and the number of Sundays in Epiphany and after Pentecost.

Lent

Begins on Ash Wednesday.
Ends with midday prayer on Holy Saturday.
The resurrection of Jesus is our great salvation. To prepare to celebrate the feast of the Resurrection (Easter), the Church sets aside a period of preparation. In AD 325, the Council of Nicaea recorded the first reference to the specific number of days for Lent: forty. This forty-day preparation was first prescribed for baptismal candidates and became known as Lent (from the Old English word for "spring"). During this period, the candidates were examined in preparation for Baptism at the Easter (or Paschal) Vigil. Later, these forty days were associated with Jesus' forty days in the desert prior to His temptation (Matthew 4) and with the forty years the children of Israel spent in the wilderness (Numbers 14:34) and became a period of preparation for every Christian.

Ash Wednesday begins the observance of Lent. The placing of ashes on the forehead is a sign of penitence and a reminder of human mortality. The Sundays during this season are not "of Lent" but "in Lent." Thus the Sundays retain an Easter tone and may be less solemn than the midweek services that congregations typically offer. The observances of Lent are concrete reminders of the greater solemnity of this season, yet Lutherans emphasize the Gospel of Christ as central even to this penitential season.

HOLY WEEK

The week before Easter is called Holy Week and culminates the preparation time of Lent. This week begins on Palm Sunday and ends on Holy Saturday. During these days, we focus on the events of Jesus' life from His entrance into Jerusalem until His glorious resurrection from the dead. Palm Sunday, the first day of Holy Week, commemorates the triumphal entry of Jesus into Jerusalem (Matthew 21:9). Because the complete account of the Lord's Passion from Matthew, Mark, or Luke is often read, this Sunday is also called the Sunday of the Passion.

On Maundy Thursday, the Church gives thanks to Jesus for the institution of the Lord's Supper. The Maundy Thursday service closes with the stripping of the altar while Psalm 22—a prophecy of the crucifixion—is read or sung. This reminds us of how our Lord stripped to the waist to wash His disciples' feet—and how He was stripped and beaten before His crucifixion.

Good Friday is the most solemn of all days in the Christian Church, yet a note of joy remains, as the title of the day indicates. On Good Friday, as we remember that on account of our sin the Lord was crucified and died, we give joyful thanks to God that all sin and God's wrath over sin falls on Jesus and not on us, and that by His grace we receive the benefit of this most sacrificial act.

EASTER AND ITS SEASON

Begins with evening prayer on Holy Saturday.
Ends with midday prayer on Pentecost.

Easter is a victory celebration, a time for all Christians to proclaim boldly their faith in a risen and victorious Savior. For the early Christians, Easter was not merely one day, it was (and is) a whole season that also includes the celebration of Jesus' ascension. The fifty days between Easter and Pentecost, known as the Great Fifty Days, was the first liturgical season observed in the first three centuries of the Church. This fifty-day celebration is a week of weeks, renewed in the last decades by emphasizing the Sundays as being "of Easter." The season's length is fitting because we are dedicating one seventh of the year to the celebration of the Lord's resurrection.

The first celebration of Easter is the Easter Vigil, the evening of Holy Saturday. The Vigil includes a service of light, in which fire symbolizes Jesus as the light of the world. The service is designed to take the Christian from the solemnity of Good Friday to the predawn joy of Easter.

Easter is the richest and most lavishly celebrated festival of the Church Year. Congregations may hold a sunrise service, commemorating the surprise of the women visiting the empty tomb of Christ, as well as services that celebrate the resurrection of Jesus Christ. While not as lavish, this joyous and celebratory tone echoes down through the Sundays of the Easter season.

Forty days after Easter (Acts 1:3), the Church celebrates the Ascension of Our Lord, who ascended into heaven not only as God but also as man. The final Sunday of the Easter season, celebrated as Pentecost, was adopted by early Christians to commemorate the first great harvest of believers for Christ (Acts 2:1–41). Thus, Pentecost is the birthday of the Christian Church as the Holy Spirit came upon the disciples and they gave their compelling witness about the resurrected Lord. Pentecost is a day of joy in the gifts of the Spirit as He still reaches into our lives just as He did to the crowds on that first Pentecost: through the apostolic preaching of God's Word and Holy Baptism.

THE TIME OF THE CHURCH

Jesus told His disciples, "I am the vine; you are the branches. Whoever abides in Me and I in him, he it is that bears much fruit, for apart from Me you can do nothing" (John 15:5). We are each grafted into Jesus and made a branch of the Vine by the power of the Spirit in Holy Baptism. We stay connected to Jesus, our Vine, by hearing the preaching of God's Word and receiving Absolution and the Lord's Supper. This is how our life in Christ grows: by the power of the Spirit working in our hearts through Word and Sacrament. The Sundays after Pentecost make up the longest portion of the Church Year. This is the Time of the Church—the time we focus on growing together in the life of the Holy Trinity.

THE HOLY TRINITY

The first Sunday after Pentecost.

We are baptized into only one name, the name of God. But that name is "of the Father and of the Son and of the Holy Spirit." There is only one name, only one God—but there are three persons: the Father, the Son, and the Holy Spirit. Each person is God, and each is not the others, but there is only one God. This is the great mystery of the Holy Trinity. On the first Sunday after Pentecost, the Church celebrates Holy Trinity Sunday and teaches us to confess the mystery of God's being.

THE SEASON AFTER PENTECOST

Begins the day after Pentecost.

Ends with midday prayer on the Saturday before the First Sunday in Advent.

The Sundays of this time of the Church Year are known as Sundays after Pentecost. Picking up on Pentecost as the season of growth, the Sundays after Pentecost are often referred to as the Green Sundays. It is during this season that the Readings focus on the teachings of the Lord for the Church. We hear Jesus teaching His disciples and healing the faithful.

Because the Pentecost season is "ordinary," as the Roman Catholic Church identifies it, congregations may choose to observe some of the lesser festivals of the season. When significant saint days or commemorations fall on Sundays, worship leaders could highlight these to offer teaching moments about the breadth of the Church's life and work. These noteworthy days enable the Christian to reflect on how we worship "with angels and archangels and with all the company of heaven" (*LSB Altar Book*, p. 161).

Last Sunday of the Church Year

The Church Year began with Advent and the joyful hope and expectation of Jesus' coming to save the world through His incarnation. On the Last Sunday after Pentecost, the Church gives voice to the joyful hope of the second coming of Jesus for the resurrection of the dead and the last judgment. The end-times focus of the Last Sunday of the Church Year bears themes of hope and preparation that are similar to those of Advent, which soon follows.

This liturgical calendar was essentially complete by the end of the sixth century, though it continues to be transmuted through additions and emphases.

Feasts, Festivals, and Commemorations— The Sanctoral Calendar

The long tradition of the Church seen in the Church Year calendar provides an additional resource for worship, prayer, and piety in the form of saint days and other appropriate holy days. In addition to the three festival seasons of Easter, Pentecost, and Epiphany, a tradition began among early Christians of recalling the anniversaries of local martyrs. Congregations would each have a roll of those who had suffered and died for the faith. These would be honored, with their names read at commemorative services on the days of their martyrdom. These dates were often called the martyr's birthday into eternity.

A better term for recognizing the contributions of these faithful early Christian believers is the commemoration of the saints. A calendar of commemorations is valuable to the Christian as a way of encouraging people to examine the personal stories of certain women and men to learn of the richness and the potential of human life lived by the grace of God in Jesus Christ—people whose common denominator is simply that the grace of God worked mightily within them.

Sundays and Seasons
The Liturgical Calendar

The Time of Christmas

Advent Season
First Sunday in Advent
Second Sunday in Advent
Third Sunday in Advent
Fourth Sunday in Advent

Christmas Season
THE NATIVITY OF OUR LORD
    Christmas Eve
    Christmas Midnight
    Christmas Dawn
    Christmas Day
First Sunday after Christmas
Second Sunday after Christmas

Epiphany Season
The Epiphany of Our Lord
First Sunday after the Epiphany
    The Baptism of Our Lord
Second Sunday after the Epiphany
Third Sunday after the Epiphany
Fourth Sunday after the Epiphany
Fifth Sunday after the Epiphany
Sixth Sunday after the Epiphany ⎤
Seventh Sunday after the Epiphany   *3-Year Lect.*
Eighth Sunday after the Epiphany ⎦
Last Sunday after the Epiphany
    The Transfiguration of Our Lord

The Time of Easter

Pre-Lent Season
Septuagesima ⎤
Sexagesima   *1-Year Lect.*
Quinquagesima ⎦

Lenten Season
Ash Wednesday
First Sunday in Lent
Second Sunday in Lent
Third Sunday in Lent
Fourth Sunday in Lent
Fifth Sunday in Lent

Holy Week
Palm Sunday
    Sunday of the Passion
Monday in Holy Week
Tuesday in Holy Week
Wednesday in Holy Week
Holy (Maundy) Thursday
Good Friday
Holy Saturday

Easter Season
THE RESURRECTION OF OUR LORD
    Vigil of Easter
    Easter Sunrise
    Easter Day
    Easter Evening/Easter Monday
    Easter Tuesday
    Easter Wednesday
Second Sunday of Easter
Third Sunday of Easter
Fourth Sunday of Easter
Fifth Sunday of Easter
Sixth Sunday of Easter
The Ascension of Our Lord
Seventh Sunday of Easter

PENTECOST
    Pentecost Eve
    The Day of Pentecost
    Pentecost Evening/Pentecost Monday
    Pentecost Tuesday

The Time of the Church

The Season after Pentecost
The Holy Trinity
Second through Twenty-seventh Sunday
    after Pentecost *(3-Year lectionary)*
First through Twenty-sixth Sunday
    after Trinity *(1-Year lectionary)*
Last Sunday of the Church Year

FEASTS, FESTIVALS, AND COMMEMORATIONS
The Sanctoral Calendar

The feasts and festivals are listed in roman type. The observations listed in **boldface** are principle feasts of Christ, and when they occur on a Sunday, normally replace the regular schedule pericopes for corporate worship for that Sunday of the Church Year. The commemorations are noted in *italics*.

January
1 Circumcision and Name of Jesus
2 *J. K. Wilhelm Loehe, Pastor*
10 *Basil the Great of Caesarea, Gregory of Nazianzus, and Gregory of Nyssa, Pastors and Confessors*
18 The Confession of St. Peter
20 *Sarah*
24 St. Timothy, Pastor and Confessor
25 The Conversion of St. Paul
26 St. Titus, Pastor and Confessor
27 *John Chrysostom, Preacher*

February
2 The Purification of Mary and the Presentation of Our Lord
10 *Silas, Fellow Worker of St. Peter and St. Paul*
13 *Aquila, Priscilla, Apollos*
14 *Valentine, Martyr*
15 *Philemon and Onesimus*
16 *Philipp Melanchthon (birth), Confessor*
18 *Martin Luther, Doctor and Confessor*
23 *Polycarp of Smyrna, Pastor and Martyr*
24 St. Matthias, Apostle

March
7 *Perpetua and Felicitas, Martyrs*
17 *Patrick, Missionary to Ireland*
19 St. Joseph, Guardian of Jesus
25 The Annunciation of Our Lord
31 *Joseph, Patriarch*

April
6 *Lucas Cranach and Albrecht Duerer, Artists*
20 *Johannes Bugenhagen, Pastor*
21 *Anselm of Canterbury, Theologian*
24 *Johann Walter, Kantor*
25 St. Mark, Evangelist

May
1 St. Philip and St. James, Apostles
2 *Athanasius of Alexandria, Pastor and Confessor*
4 *Friedrich Wyneken, Pastor and Missionary*
5 *Frederick the Wise, Christian Ruler*
7 *C. F. W. Walther, Theologian*
9 *Job*
11 *Cyril and Methodius, Missionaries to the Slavs*
21 *Emperor Constantine, Christian Ruler, and Helena, Mother of Constantine*
24 *Esther*
25 *Bede the Venerable, Theologian*
31 The Visitation (3-Year Lectionary)

June
1 *Justin, Martyr*
5 *Boniface of Mainz, Missionary to the Germans*
11 St. Barnabas, Apostle
12 *The Ecumenical Council of Nicaea, AD 325*
14 *Elisha*
25 *Presentation of the Augsburg Confession*
26 *Jeremiah*
27 *Cyril of Alexandria, Pastor and Confessor*
28 *Irenaeus of Lyons, Pastor*
24 The Nativity of St. John the Baptist
29 St. Peter and St. Paul, Apostles

July

2 **The Visitation** (1-Year Lectionary)
6 *Isaiah*
16 *Ruth*
20 *Elijah*
21 *Ezekiel*
22 St. Mary Magdalene
25 St. James the Elder, Apostle
28 *Johann Sebastian Bach, Kantor*
29 *Mary, Martha, and Lazarus of Bethany*
30 *Robert Barnes, Confessor and Martyr*
31 *Joseph of Arimathea*

August

3 *Joanna, Mary, and Salome, Myrrhbearers*
10 *Lawrence, Deacon and Martyr*
15 St. Mary, Mother of Our Lord
16 *Isaac*
17 *Johann Gerhard, Theologian*
19 *Bernard of Clairvaux, Hymnwriter and Theologian*
20 *Samuel*
24 St. Bartholomew, Apostle
27 *Monica, Mother of Augustine*
28 *Augustine of Hippo, Pastor and Theologian*
29 The Martyrdom of St. John the Baptist

September

1 *Joshua*
2 *Hannah*
3 *Gregory the Great, Pastor*
4 *Moses*
5 *Zacharias and Elizabeth*
14 Holy Cross Day
16 *Cyprian of Carthage, Pastor and Martyr*
21 St. Matthew, Apostle and Evangelist
22 *Jonah*
29 St. Michael and All Angels
30 *Jerome, Translator of Holy Scripture*

October

7 *Henry Melchior Muhlenberg, Pastor*
9 *Abraham*
11 *Philip the Deacon*
17 *Ignatius of Antioch, Pastor and Martyr*
18 St. Luke, Evangelist
23 St. James of Jerusalem, Brother of Jesus and Martyr
25 *Dorcas (Tabitha), Lydia, and Phoebe, Faithful Women*
26 *Philipp Nicolai, Johann Heermann, and Paul Gerhardt, Hymnwriters*
28 St. Simon and St. Jude, Apostles
31 Reformation Day

November

1 **All Saints' Day**
8 *Johannes von Staupitz, Luther's Father Confessor*
9 *Martin Chemnitz (birth), Pastor and Confessor*
11 *Martin of Tours, Pastor*
14 *Emperor Justinian, Christian Ruler and Confessor of Christ*
19 *Elizabeth of Hungary*
23 *Clement of Rome, Pastor*
29 *Noah*
30 St. Andrew, Apostle

December

4 *John of Damascus, Theologian and Hymnwriter*
6 *Nicholas of Myra, Pastor*
7 *Ambrose of Milan, Pastor and Hymnwriter*
13 *Lucia, Martyr*
17 *Daniel the Prophet and the Three Young Men*
19 *Adam and Eve*
20 *Katharina von Bora Luther*
21 St. Thomas, Apostle
26 St. Stephen, Martyr
27 St. John, Apostle and Evangelist
28 The Holy Innocents, Martyrs
29 *David*
31 **Eve of the Circumcision and Name of Jesus**
New Year's Eve

PRAYERS

Each Prayer of the Day ends with a number in parentheses. This number indicates the source of the prayer in the various products of *Lutheran Service Book* as follows:

L01–L60 Collects of the Day—Festival (Lord's) Half

A61–A100 Collects of the Day—Non-Festival Half, Series A

B61–B100 Collects of the Day—Non-Festival Half, Series B

C61–C100 Collects of the Day—Non-Festival Half, Series C

H61–H100 Collects of the Day—Non-Festival Half, One-Year (Historic)

F01–F60 Collects of the Day—Feasts, Festivals, and Occasions

101–400 Prayers, Intercessions, and Thanksgivings (Topical Prayers)

401–500 Prayers found in the various service orders

501–700 Agenda

701–900 Pastoral Care Companion

1000–1168 Treasury of Daily Prayer

1 JANUARY

Circumcision and Name of Jesus

Psalmody: Psalm 113:1–9
Additional Psalm: Psalm 21
Old Testament Reading: Isaiah 61:1–11
New Testament Reading: Luke 1:57–80

Prayer of the Day

Lord God, You made Your beloved Son, our Savior, subject to the Law and caused Him to shed His blood on our behalf. Grant us the true circumcision of the Spirit that our hearts may be made pure from all sins; through Jesus Christ, our Lord, who lives and reigns with You and the Holy Spirit, one God, now and forever. (F07)

Circumcision and Name of Jesus

Already on the eighth day of Jesus' life, His destiny of atonement is revealed in His name and in His circumcision. At that moment His blood is first shed and Jesus receives the name given to Him by the angel: "You shall call His name Jesus, for He will save His people from their sins" (Matthew 1:21). In the circumcision of Jesus, all people are circumcised once and for all, because He represents all humanity. In the Old Testament, for the believers who look to God's promise to be fulfilled in the Messiah, the benefits of circumcision include the forgiveness of sins, justification, and incorporation into the people of God. In the New Testament, St. Paul speaks of its counterpart, Holy Baptism, as a "circumcision not done by human hands" and as "the circumcision of Christ" (Colossians 2:11).

Meditation

What joy after Elizabeth's labor! A little boy, just as the angel had said. Her neighbors rejoice with her in the miraculous babe. On the eighth day the child is to be brought into the covenant of the God of Israel and receive the mark of circumcision—a reminder of the promise to Abraham that from his seed would come one who would bring blessing to every family of the earth. Elizabeth and Zechariah must have smiled to think of it, for they knew that the Blessed One was already upon earth and in their presence—in the womb of the Virgin. The joy was overflowing in the room until the moment came for naming the child.

The rabbi was preparing to give the little one the name of his father when Elizabeth interrupted. "No, he shall be called John." John, which means Yahweh is gracious. The people in the room look at one another in amazement and the rabbi frowns: "None of your relatives is called by this name!" he exclaims. All eyes fix on the old man, Zechariah, still silent, nary a word escaping his lips since his vision in the temple. He motions for a writing tablet and writes upon it: "His name is John."

And then it stopped—as suddenly as it had started. His mouth was opened, his tongue set free, and he spoke. What did he speak? Luke strongly hints at it by saying he was "blessing God." That is, the words that we know as the Benedictus. He opens his lips in a canticle of praise to the God of Israel, who has visited and redeemed His people. What is amazing about the canticle is that most of it isn't about John at all; there was a bigger miracle in the room!

Zechariah shouts to one and all that the time of the great fulfillment foretold by the prophets was at hand. The God of Israel had visited His people to rescue them. He was showing mercy, remembering His covenant and oath to Abraham. Now all of God's people would be set free to serve God without fear in holiness and righteousness all the days of their life. And if God was now in the flesh, his beloved little John would be the prophet of the Most High, going before the Lord to prepare His way, giving light to those who sit in darkness and in the shadow of death, guiding feet into the way of peace. The people marveled and wondered at the astonishing words they heard.

2 January

J. K. Wilhelm Loehe, Pastor

Psalmody: Psalm 62:5–8, 11–12
Additional Psalm: Psalm 98
Old Testament Reading: Isaiah 62:1–12
New Testament Reading: Luke 2:1–20

Prayer of the Day

Most glorious Trinity, in Your mercy we commit to You this day our bodies and souls, all our ways and goings, all our deeds and purposes. We pray You, so open our hearts and mouths that we may praise Your name, which above all names alone is holy. And since You have created for us the praise of Your holy name, grant that our lives may be for Your honor and that we may serve You in love and fear; for You, O Father, Son, and Holy Spirit, live and reign, one God, now and forever. (1134)

J. K. Wilhelm Loehe, Pastor

Although he never left Germany, Johann Konrad Wilhelm Loehe, born in Fuerth in 1808, had a profound impact on the development of Lutheranism in North America. Serving as pastor in the Bavarian village of Neuendettelsau, he recognized the need for workers in developing lands and assisted in training emergency helpers to be sent as missionary pastors to North America, Brazil, and Australia. A number of the men he sent to the United States became founders of The Lutheran Church—Missouri Synod. Through his financial support, a theological school in Fort Wayne, Indiana, and a teachers' institute in Saginaw, Michigan were established. Loehe was known for his confessional integrity and his interest in liturgy and catechetics. His devotion to works of Christian charity led to the establishment of a deaconess training house and homes for the aged.

Meditation

John was the forerunner. He went before the Lord. So his nativity was first, but the greater nativity followed some six months later. Far away in Rome, a decree had been issued for a registration of the peoples of the empire. Little did mighty Caesar Augustus guess that his decree would bring about a fulfillment of Micah's prophecy: the Messiah would come from Bethlehem.

Mary, great with child, is forced at the end of her pregnancy to travel the distance from her hometown of Nazareth to Bethlehem, for Joseph, her betrothed, descended from King David. And while they are there, in little Bethlehem of Judah—the House of Bread—the Bread of Life is born. Because there was no room for them in the inn, she gives birth among the animals, and the Lord of the universe, through whom all things were made, is wrapped in swaddling clothes and laid in a manger—where grain is put for the animals to eat.

How Mary and Joseph must have gazed in awe and wonder at the little One, as He curled His tiny fingers around theirs. How each must have recounted again in their hearts what they had heard from the angel. Suddenly in "slow" Bethlehem, a bustle outside is heard via a bunch of shepherds crowding around. They look up, startled, but they can tell from the looks upon the faces of the shepherds; they know, too, just as Elizabeth had known. Their eyes are upon the Babe who they fall before and whisper their story.

They tell of the angel and the good news of a great joy for all people: the Savior has been born in Bethlehem, and they will find Him laid in a manger. And so they had. As Mary and Joseph continue to look upon the little One, the shepherds tell of heaven itself being opened to them and angels beyond count filling the sky and the night with their hymn: "Glory to God in the highest, and on earth peace among those with whom He is pleased!"

Mary soaks in every word. Takes it all into her heart to keep it there. She would stow away the story in safety until the day when Luke would sit before her and ask her to give to the world the events and words she had stored up in her heart.

Mary's visit to Elizabeth ended in praise. John's birth likewise. Christ's birth occasioned praise on earth and praise in heaven. The shepherds join the angels "glorifying and praising God."

3 JANUARY

Psalmody: Psalm 108:1–6, 12–13
Additional Psalm: Psalm 110
Old Testament Reading: Isaiah 63:1–14
New Testament Reading: Luke 2:21–40

Prayer of the Day

O God, our Maker and Redeemer, You wonderfully created us and in the incarnation of Your Son yet more wondrously restored our human nature. Grant that we may ever be alive in Him who made Himself to be like us; through Jesus Christ, our Lord, who lives and reigns with You and the Holy Spirit, one God, now and forever. (L09)

Meditation

After eight days, the little One receives His name—Jesus—and His blood is shed upon the earth. Did Mary and Joseph begin to see and understand that this is why He had come? To keep the Law? To shed His blood?

The child is brought to the temple 40 days later. Mary and Joseph enter. Joseph holding the turtledoves, the sacrifice of the poor. Mary holding the Babe, the true sacrifice to end all sacrifices. And they see him.

Simeon is, according to tradition, an old man. He had been waiting a lifetime for this moment. The Holy Spirit had whispered in his heart that he would not see death before he laid his eyes upon the Promised One. That day the Spirit had directed him to this young mother. He came across the temple courtyard, his eyes fixated on the Babe. Mary knew from the look that yet another of God's saints knew the secret Treasure in her arms. She let the old man hold the baby.

He began to speak. First, not to them, but to the God of Israel. Perhaps even speaking directly to the Child he held. And His words, the beautiful Nunc Dimittis (from the opening words in Latin), all amount to this: "I can die now. I can die now, because I know the death of death lives on earth. I have seen the Savior, the Light for the nations, the Glory for Israel. Lord, you can let me die right now."

At last he turns to the parents to speak some words of pain. The Child will not be universally welcomed. He will, in fact, prove a stumbling block for many people—and yet He will raise many. He looks long and hard at Mother Mary: "A sword will pierce through your own soul." Did he already see this young woman's face many years hence, upturned in agony beneath a pair of feet nailed to a tree? To Joseph he says nothing; according to tradition, Joseph will have been gathered to his people before the supreme sacrifice of the cross would be made.

Coming up at that moment, another saint: Anna. She cries in delight, and begins thanking God and speaking of the child to all who would listen. Where this One is present, praise bursts forth! He has come to restore us to thanksgiving.

Luke records nothing of the trip to Egypt. His interest lies elsewhere. Matthew and Luke agree, though, that the Child of Bethlehem is raised in Nazareth.

4 JANUARY

Psalmody: Psalm 40:6–10
Additional Psalm: Psalm 65
Old Testament Reading: Isaiah 63:15–65:7
New Testament Reading: Luke 2:41–52

Prayer of the Day

Almighty God, You have poured into our hearts the true Light of Your incarnate Word. Grant that this Light may shine forth in our lives; through the same Jesus Christ, Your Son, our Lord, who lives and reigns with You and the Holy Spirit, one God, now and forever. (L10)

Meditation

How easy it was to forget who the Child was! As He grew in years and they watched Him walk and then run, play and laugh, and grow through childhood, Mary and Joseph sometimes comfortably regarded Him as their very own.

Yet one instance that Mary never forgot reminded her forcefully that her Son was not like other children. It happened at the Passover. During this joyous feast as Jerusalem swelled to the bursting point with pilgrims from all over the land—and even the world—their caravan set out for the way back to Nazareth. Mary and Joseph saw nothing of the lad, which was not unusual. A child belonged to the whole family and He was no doubt with others. How long did it take for the growing unease to finally reach them? He's not in the caravan at all!

Back to the city they fled, hearts in their throats. They'd failed of their precious charge! Where was the Child? They searched high and low, and after three days they found Him. He was in the temple, listening to the rabbis teach and asking them questions. Everyone who heard Him was amazed at the depth of His understanding and the wisdom of His answers.

Mary is not amused. "Son, why have You treated us so? Behold, Your father and I have been searching for You in great distress!" Truly an almost teen, He answers: "Why were you looking for Me?" He is genuinely puzzled. But then He delivers the blow to their hearts: "Did you not know that I must be in My Father's house?"

"Your father and I" she had said. He says: "No, he is not My father. My Father is the One whose house this temple is." It hurt, but it hurt in a good way. It was salutary to be reminded that this 12-year-old lad was like no other 12-year-old, for this One is the Only-begotten Son of the Father, born of the Virgin. He has a calling and destiny tied to that temple (note how Luke goes back there repeatedly in his telling of the story). He had come to fulfill that of which the earthly temple was but the sign: to be the very dwelling place of God in His flesh and to offer in His flesh one last perfect and total sacrifice.

As before, Mary stored up His words. Hid them in her heart. Pondered them. We do well to follow her example.

5 JANUARY

Psalmody: Psalm 37:34–40
Additional Psalm: Psalm 10
Old Testament Reading: Isaiah 65:8–25
New Testament Reading: Luke 3:1–20

Prayer of the Day

Almighty God, through John the Baptist, the forerunner of Christ, You once proclaimed salvation. Now grant that we may know this salvation and serve You in holiness and righteousness all the days of our life; through our Lord Jesus Christ, Your Son, who lives and reigns with You and the Holy Spirit, one God, now and forever. (F20)

Meditation

Subtle he was not. The Word of the Lord came to John as a fiery power, and in the strength of that Word he began his mission. Long foretold, promised by both Isaiah and Malachi, the preparer of the Lord's way began to preach a baptism of repentance for the forgiveness of sins in Judea's wilderness.

Fiery was his message! He called those who came to him "You brood of vipers!" He challenged them to examine their hearts and told them: "Bear fruit in keeping with repentance." This was no religious game; this was a matter of eternal life or eternal death. "Even now the axe is laid to the root of the trees. Every tree therefore that does not bear good fruit will be cut down and thrown into the fire."

So in terror at his preaching of God's uncompromising law, the crowds begged him to tell them what to do. He answered each group. To the crowds in general, he told them to share their food, their clothing with the poor, that is, give alms.

The taxc ollectors were instructed to collect no more than their due—to stop lying and cheating.

The soldiers were told not to extract money by threats or false accusation and to learn to be content with their wages.

Each group heard a specific fruit that they could bear, but they all amounted to the same thing: love. Love is ever the fruit of a genuine faith, the result of a genuine conversion.

The whispering began not long after he started baptizing: "Could he be the one? Is John the promised Messiah?" John quickly disabused them of the notion. He was not the Messiah, but the Messiah was coming. John plunged them into the water, but the Messiah would plunge them into the Holy Spirit and fire; a fire to burn away all that is chaff and stubble in their lives. In the end, this Messiah would make a division between people—between those who bore fruit, the wheat, and those who did not. He would gather fruit-bearers into His barn—for their fruit is the proof that their faith was no sham. But for those without such fruit, there awaits the ultimate "subtraction" of a God-void in their lives—only the everlasting burning.

How long John preached, we are not told, but we do know that his fierce preaching of the Law set him on the wrong side of Herod, who locked him up in prison because John had told him that he could not marry his brother's wife.

The Time of Christmas

Epiphany Season

6 JANUARY

The Epiphany of Our Lord

Psalmody: Psalm 45:1–7
Additional Psalm: Psalm 72
Old Testament Reading: Isaiah 66:1–20
New Testament Reading: Luke 3:21–38

Prayer of the Day

O God, by the leading of a star You made known Your only-begotten Son to the Gentiles. Lead us, who know You by faith, to enjoy in heaven the fullness of Your divine presence; through the same Jesus Christ, our Lord, who lives and reigns with You and the Holy Spirit, one God, now and forever. (L11)

The Epiphany of Our Lord

The feast of the Epiphany of Our Lord commemorates no event, but presents an idea that assumes concrete form only through the facts of our Lord's life. The idea of Epiphany is that the Christ who was born in Bethlehem is recognized by the world as God. At Christmas, God appears as man, and at Epiphany, this man appears before the world as God. That Christ became man needed no proof. But that this man, this helpless child, is God needed proof. The manifestations of the Trinity, the signs and wonders performed by this Man, and all His miracles have the purpose of proving to men that Jesus is God. Lately, especially in the Western church, the story of the Magi has been associated with this feast day. As Gentiles who were brought to faith in Jesus Christ, the Magi represent all believers from the Gentile world.

Meditation

Before he had been born, John had confessed Christ in his mother's womb. Now the two stand face to face in the flowing waters of the Jordan. He who had no sin of His own, whose life needed no repentance, stepped into the stream to receive at His kinsman's hand a sinner's baptism. As He prays, the heavens are opened above Him and the Holy Spirit descends in bodily form as a dove. God the Father speaks from heaven: "You are My beloved Son; with You I am well-pleased." A collision of words from Psalm 2 (about the promised Davidic king) and Isaiah 42 (about the Suffering Servant of the Lord), Jesus is the fulfillment of both.

Why does our Lord receive such a Baptism? He needed nothing that it gave. To Him, heaven was never shut. From Him, the Holy Spirit had ever proceeded. In His Father's love and embrace He had lived since before the ages began. He needed nothing of what He received; but we needed it all.

From the time of Adam (note that Luke drives the genealogy of our Lord all the way back to Adam), the gate of paradise had been barred. Heaven was shut to sinful men. The Holy Spirit did not dwell in and among them (though He did come sporadically upon the prophets and saints under the old covenant). Far from being "sons of God," fallen humanity was rather what John the Baptist said in yesterday's reading: "a brood of vipers"—more colloquially, sons of snakes! Sons of the snake, of Satan. "You are of your father, the devil" Christ would one day say.

But Jesus steps into the water and receives Baptism so that all that is His, might become yours when you stand in the water with Him; even as on His cross all that is yours became His. He sanctified the water with His holy, sinless body so that it might give to you the gift of an open heaven, the gift of the Holy Spirit, and the gift of a Father who looks upon you in His Son and declares: You are My beloved child, with you I am well-pleased.

By Baptism into Jesus, you step right into the start of that genealogy once again: and in the new Adam, you also get to be "a son of God." Is it any wonder that Luther would praise Baptism as a "divine, heavenly water?"

7 January

Psalmody: Psalm 46:4–6, 8–11
Additional Psalm: Psalm 45
Old Testament Reading: Ezekiel 1:1–14, 22–28
Additional Reading: Habakkuk 1:1–3:19
New Testament Reading: Romans 1:1–17

Prayer of the Day

Heavenly Father, though we do not deserve Your goodness, still You provide for all our needs of body and soul. Grant us Your Holy Spirit that we may acknowledge Your gifts, give thanks for all Your benefits, and serve You in willing obedience; through Jesus Christ, Your Son, our Lord, who lives and reigns with You and the Holy Spirit, one God, now and forever. (B69)

Meditation

"I am not ashamed of the gospel." Paul was not ashamed of the Gospel. The Gospel is the power of God for salvation. It is through the Gospel that the righteousness of God is revealed. This righteousness is not human righteousness, for it has its origin in God. The righteousness spoken of here is not God's perfection or holiness that results in His righteous anger over sin. This is a righteousness that God imputes to His people by faith, declaring sinners righteous for the sake of His Son. We are righteous before God not because of our own efforts or works but because He who knew no sin became sin for us (2 Corinthians 5:21). This is truly Gospel, the good news. Our salvation is not a reward for our faithfulness, but results from God's grace and is received through faith, which is also a gift from God.

Paul can say with all certainty that he is not ashamed of the Gospel. Confident that the Gospel is the power of God for salvation for both Jews and Gentiles, Paul courageously proclaimed the Gospel in many lands to many people. As a result of his preaching, he was jailed, beaten, flogged, stoned, and ultimately martyred. To the very end, he believed the Gospel and confessed the Gospel wherever he went, convinced that he was doing more than imparting information; he was speaking powerful words that create and strengthen faith and bestow salvation.

This powerful Gospel has worked faith in our hearts. We have received the righteousness of Christ. We are justified. The Gospel is the power of God for our salvation. Like Paul, we can boldly confess that we are not ashamed of the Gospel.

But is this true?

Is Paul's confession our confession? Do times of silence reveal that you are ashamed of the Gospel? When you are in the presence of certain people, do you hide your Christian identity or do you find yourself reluctant to confess the saving truths of the Gospel?

Yes, too often, too many of us are ashamed of the Gospel, but Christ is not ashamed of us! As the sinless Son of God He became sin for us and died the death we deserve. Risen from the dead, He clothed us with His righteousness at Baptism so that we are now justified before God. Through the same powerful Gospel, He also empowers us to speak the Gospel word to others, so that by God's grace those who hear will be saved through faith.

8 JANUARY

Psalmody: Psalm 19:1–6, 9–11, 14
Additional Psalm: Psalm 100
Old Testament Reading: Ezekiel 2:1–3:11
New Testament Reading: Romans 1:18–32

Prayer of the Day

O Lord, mercifully receive the prayers of Your people who call upon You and grant that they both perceive and know what things they ought to do and also may have grace and power faithfully to fulfill the same; through Jesus Christ, Your Son, our Lord, who lives and reigns with You and the Holy Spirit, one God, now and forever. (L13)

Meditation

They should know better. God's invisible attributes are clearly seen. Look at the created world, and you know that God exists. Only the fool says in his heart that there is no God (Psalm 14:1). Despite what they see and perceive, they refuse to believe. Instead, they worship man-made idols, giving glory and honor to that which is created rather than the Creator.

The root of humanity's sin is idolatry. Idolatry was ultimately the cause of the original sin in the Garden of Eden. Adam and Eve were tempted to eat the fruit so that they could elevate themselves to be like God. Idolatry leads to immorality. When God and His truth are ignored, immorality increases. The unnatural is regarded as natural, that which is evil is extolled, and sin is praised rather than condemned. And the downward spiral continues. Their shameful acts only intensify. They assume they are wise when they are truly fools.

The parallels are striking between the first and the twenty-first centuries. Yes, nothing new pops up under the sun (Ecclesiastes 1:9). We are witnessing the moral decline of our nation and communities. Sexual promiscuity is the norm, homosexuality is considered a valid alternative lifestyle, and violent crimes are on the rise. However, immorality is but a symptom of the ultimate problem—idolatry. When God is no longer God, the truth is exchanged for a lie, and that which is evil is considered good.

Although this Scripture serves as an indictment of our culture, our response should not be, "Look at how immoral the world is," or "See how terrible those people are."

Every sin is a sin against the First Commandment. Every sin we commit reveals our own idolatry. Every sin exposes the truth that we do not fear, love, and trust in God above all things. If we always feared, loved, and trusted in God above all things, we would never sin. Like the unbelieving world, our own issue resides with the First Commandment. Our immorality is a direct result of our own idolatry—loving the things of this world rather than the God of love; trusting in ourselves or in our money or possessions, rather than in the Giver of every good and perfect gift. We convince ourselves that our way is better than God's way.

These words not only convict the world; they convict us. We need Jesus; we need His forgiveness; we need the Gospel, and that which we so desperately need, God has graciously supplied.

9 JANUARY

Psalmody: Psalm 62:5–12
Additional Psalm: Psalm 32
Old Testament Reading: Ezekiel 3:12–27
Additional Reading: Ezekiel 4:1–11:25
New Testament Reading: Romans 2:1–16

Meditation

God's Law is not just for unbelievers. It's not only for those who have fallen into an open and scandalous sin. It's not intended only for those who have turned away from the Lord. The Law is meant for you. The bull's-eye of the Law is directly upon your chest. God didn't give you the Law so that you could judge someone else. He intended it for you. He gave His Law to show you your sin—to uncover your pride, your selfishness, and your ingratitude. His Law reveals the feebleness of your faith in God and your lack of love for your neighbor. His Law reveals the depth of your bondage to sin.

God did not give His Law so that you would put yourself above the Law and judge others by it. Instead, God gave His Law so that you would put yourself under the Law and be led to repentance. When you assume the role of judge, you ultimately condemn yourself, for you also have fallen prey to the same sins. By appointing yourself judge, you become self-excluded from God's forgiveness, ultimately bringing God's wrath and judgment upon yourself.

God shows no partiality when it comes to sin: All sin. All need to repent. All need Christ and His salvation. Those who have the Law and those who don't have the Law both stand condemned.

The best way is always the way of repentance. God is kind and patient with you because He wants to lead you to repentance. He wants to move you beyond your self-righteous and hypocritical judging of others to look into the mirror of His Law and acknowledge that you are a sinner who needs His forgiveness and deliverance.

Just as God shows no partiality when it comes to His work of revealing sin, so God shows no partiality in gifting His forgiveness and salvation. When you confess your sins, you can be certain that you are forgiven. The blood of Jesus cleanses you from your sins. Since you belong to Christ, the Law cannot eternally condemn you, for there is no longer any condemnation for those who are in Christ Jesus (Romans 8:1).

However, like all u-turns when you're lost and going the wrong way, repentance must continue. You will sin until your dying day, so God continues to target you with His word of Law. He convicts you of sin and brings you to your knees in repentance, so He can once again exalt and restore you with His word of forgiveness.

10 January

Basil the Great of Caesarea, Gregory of Nazianzus, and Gregory of Nyssa, Pastors and Confessors

Psalmody: Psalm 85:1–4, 7–8, 10–13
Additional Psalm: Psalm 58
Old Testament Reading: Ezekiel 18:1–4, 19–32
Additional Reading: Ezekiel 19:1–24:27
New Testament Reading: Romans 2:17–29

Basil the Great of Caesarea, Gregory of Nazianzus, and Gregory of Nyssa, Pastors and Confessors

Basil and the two Gregorys, collectively known as the Cappadocian Fathers, were leaders of Christian orthodoxy in Asia Minor (modern Turkey) in the later fourth century. Basil and Gregory of Nyssa were brothers; Gregory of Nazianzus was their friend. All three were influential in shaping the theology ratified by the Council of Constantinople in AD 381, which is expressed in the Nicene Creed. Their defense of the doctrines of the Holy Spirit and Holy Trinity, together with their contributions to the liturgy of the Eastern Church, make them among the most influential Christian teachers and theologians of their time.

Meditation

I am circumcised. By God's design, these words were to provide comfort and strength for the children of Israel. Circumcision revealed that you were numbered among God's covenant people and that the one true God, the God of Abraham, Isaac, and Jacob, was your God. The outward sign was significant because it revealed what God had done in the heart of the one circumcised.

Unfortunately, for many Jews, the focus was entirely on the outward and not the inward. Instead of viewing circumcision as a gift, they saw it as an obligation, as yet another law that they had flawlessly kept.

Thus, they boasted in their circumcision. They boasted in the fact that they were God's chosen people. They boasted because they believed their knowledge and their obedience far exceeded that of the Gentiles.

Circumcision means nothing apart from faith. The outward act has no value if the heart is far from the Lord. They were trusting in themselves, in their circumcision, in their keeping of the law, in their special status as God's covenant people. They were seeking praise from others for all their works, instead of serving others for the glory of God. They assumed if a person was circumcised, he was saved. However, it is not the outward sign that saves, but faith, which receives and believes the promises of God.

The same temptations exist today. Some believe that because they are baptized they will be saved, even though they are spiritually starving themselves to death by not receiving the gifts of God in His Word and Sacraments. Others boast in the fact that they live a good life, or they try their best, or they are faithful churchgoers.

God doesn't work from the outside in; He works for the inside out. The problem is our hearts, which are corrupted by sin. Because we have sinful hearts, we do not keep God's law. Evil hearts led to evil thoughts, words, and deeds. Thus, God must give us new and clean hearts. Baptism is much more than just an outward sign; it is a washing wave of regeneration and renewal of the Holy Spirit (Titus 3:5). In Baptism, our hearts were changed. We were joined to Christ's death and resurrection. We died to sin, and we were raised to new life. Since God has transformed our hearts and minds, we do not glory in ourselves and boast in our outward words and deeds. Instead, our good works flow from hearts that have been cleansed by the blood of Christ and filled with the Spirit of God.

11 JANUARY

Psalmody: Psalm 7:1–5, 8–11
Additional Psalm: Psalm 14
Old Testament Reading: Ezekiel 33:1–20
New Testament Reading: Romans 3:1–18

Prayer of the Day

O God, the protector of all who trust in You, have mercy on us that with You as our ruler and guide we may so pass through things temporal that we lose not the things eternal; through Jesus Christ, Your Son, our Lord, who lives and reigns with You and the Holy Spirit, one God, now and forever. (A82)

Meditation

Human reason leads us to believe that if we desire God's blessing and salvation, then we must earn it, impress God with our works, and come to God before He will come to us.

You find this in all the other religions of the world. Their basic creed is: do good, and the divine being will bless you; do evil, and you will be condemned.

This thinking makes sense. It's reasonable, but it's dead wrong. There is no one righteous, not even one. No one seeks God. No one does good, not even one. Our problem is not that we don't impress God with our works; we can't impress God with our works. We are sinful. Because of our fallen nature, we are entirely corrupt. We have turned away from God, and left to ourselves we do not have the desire or the ability to turn toward Him in faith.

Our sin is great, so great that we all stand condemned by the law and unable to save ourselves by what we do. If God dealt with us as He should, we would be forever lost. But God is faithful despite our unfaithfulness. Our sin does not nullify the promises of God. God doesn't wait for us to love Him before He loves us. "God shows His love for us in that while we were still sinners, Christ died for us" (Romans 5:8). We do not earn God's grace and mercy; God is already gracious and merciful toward us for the sake of Christ. These spiritual blessings are not earned but freely given.

Christianity runs contrary to human reason. Reason says, "Try your best and God will save you." Scripture says, "No one is righteous, no, not one." Reason says, "God will only accept and bless you if you appease Him." Scripture teaches that Christ has already appeased the wrath of God by His suffering and death, and we are justified before God not by our works but by the blood of Christ.

Our righteous acts cannot save us; we need the righteousness of God. Our keeping of the law cannot deliver us from our sins; we need Christ to perfectly keep the law for us. The law condemns us; we need the gospel for salvation. We are unfaithful, but God is faithful; and thus, we are justified and heirs of eternal life.

12 JANUARY

Psalmody: Psalm 63:3–11
Additional Psalm: Psalm 59
Old Testament Reading: Ezekiel 34:1–24
New Testament Reading: Romans 3:19–31

Prayer of the Day

Almighty and most merciful God, the protector of all who trust in You, strengthen our faith and give us courage to believe that in Your love You will rescue us from all adversities; through Jesus Christ, Your Son, our Lord, who lives and reigns with You and the Holy Spirit, one God, now and forever. (B70)

Meditation

You are saved by works. Yes, that's right—you are saved by works. Immediately, you vehemently object. How can this be? Today's Scripture states that "one is justified by faith apart from works of the law" (Romans 3:28). How can anyone make the claim that we are saved by works? This statement must be false.

Truthfully, you are saved by works. Verse 24 states that "God is just." Since God is just, He cannot simply overlook sin. He cannot pretend sin doesn't exist. Where sin leaves a debt, a price must be paid. As one fallen pastor warned well before he fell, "Sin will cost you more than you want to pay." He fell, and we fall. We all fall short of the glory of God. Propitiation must be made for what we have thought, said, and done—or left undone.

You are saved by works, but not your own works! Your good works are of no avail, for even your best works are tainted by sin. However, God is not only just, He is also the justifier. He has declared you not guilty. You are saved by works, Christ's work for you. Since your Lord Jesus entered this world born of the Virgin, fulfilled the law for you by never sinning, and suffered and died on the cross as the propitiating sacrifice for your sin, you are now justified. All have sinned, but all are justified by the gift of God's grace that is ours through the redemption of Christ Jesus.

You are saved by works—Christ's work for you. His work on your behalf didn't stop on Good Friday. As your risen and exalted Savior, He continues to work for you. He speaks His word to you, the Gospel word that forgives all your sin and bestows upon you all the blessings Christ accomplished for you on Calvary's cross. He clothed you with His righteousness at your Baptism, joining you to His death and resurrection. In His Supper, He feeds you with His body and blood to forgive and strengthen you in the faith.

We are saved by works, just not our works. Since we are justified not because of what we have done, but as a result of what Christ has done for us, we have no ground to boast upon—regarding either ourselves—or our works. It's not what we do; it's about Christ and what He has done for us. Your boast is not in yourself but in Christ who has justified us by His saving work for you.

13 JANUARY

Psalmody: Psalm 32:1–7
Additional Psalm: Psalm 51
Old Testament Reading: Ezekiel 36:13–28
New Testament Reading: Romans 4:1–25

Prayer of the Day

O Lord, keep Your family the Church continually in the true faith that, relying on the hope of Your heavenly grace, we may ever be defended by Your mighty power; through Jesus Christ, Your Son, our Lord, who lives and reigns with You and the Holy Spirit, one God, now and forever. (L17)

Meditation

To reinforce that a person is justified by faith and not by circumcision, Paul uses the example of Abraham. "Abraham believed God, and it was counted to him as righteousness" (Genesis 15:6). The Scriptures say this about Abraham before he was circumcised, not after. Even when he was uncircumcised, Abraham was declared righteous.

Second, Paul notes that this righteousness was counted to him as a gift. If Abraham was saved by his works, he would have deserved this righteousness as a reward for what he had done. But there is no mention of works, only of faith. Abraham believed, and because Abraham believed, He was declared righteous.

Thus, Abraham is not only the father of those who are his natural descendants; he's the father of all believers, of all who share the faith of Abraham. This is the faith you have been given. Abraham believed the promise, the promise of the Seed through whom all nations would be blessed. Although he was well advanced in years, Abraham believed that he would be the father of many nations, and God kept His promise.

Your faith has also been counted to you as righteousness. Since you share the faith of Abraham, he is your father in the faith. In the previous chapters, Paul stressed that no one is righteous. Your works cannot save you. You are not justified before God by what you do or don't do. Instead, you are justified by faith. As it was for Abraham, so it is for you. You believe, and it is counted to you as righteousness.

But this is where the devil loves to twist and distort the truth. The devil tempts people to think that their faith is something they do, a good work they must accomplish to be saved. The devil wants you to regard faith as "your end of the deal"—Jesus died for you, but you must believe it, as if you had the power and ability to do this on your own.

As it was with righteousness, so faith also was God's gift to Abraham. Without God bestowing the gift of faith on him, Abraham would have never believed that he would father a son when he was almost a century old. Likewise, you have not only been declared righteous, but you have also been given the faith by which you are justified. Since Jesus was delivered up for your trespasses and raised again for your justification, you have been given the gift of faith by which you are now justified.

14 JANUARY

Psalmody: Psalm 104:27–30
Additional Psalm: Psalm 79
Old Testament Reading: Ezekiel 36:33–37:14
New Testament Reading: Romans 5:1–21

Prayer of the Day

Lord God, heavenly Father, Your Son, Jesus Christ, our Lord, died for the ungodly, declaring all of humanity righteous by the shedding of His blood. Grant us the free gift of faith to receive this reality for our salvation, that by Your grace, we may serve You in love and righteousness all the days of our lives; through Your Son, Jesus Christ, our Lord. (1136)

Meditation

Peace and joy. These are the fruits of justifying faith. You see, once you know that you have been declared righteous by God in Jesus Christ, that He has borne all your sins and answered for them, you have an unshakable peace. What can trouble you? Not your sins! They have been left under the blood of the Lamb of God. And so a truly odd thing begins to happen.

You can even rejoice in sufferings. Yes, rejoice! How? Because the sufferings are not God punishing you, hating you, or judging and condemning you. Rather, they are the Holy Spirit's tool to lovingly craft the image of Christ upon your life. So suffering teaches you to endure; endurance produces character, character hope, and hope never disappoints because God's love has been dumped into your heart by the Holy Spirit given to you.

Paul invites you to think of it as even when you were a rebel against God, God loved you, gave His Son for you. Now, having been declared righteous by His holy blood, will you not be saved through Him from the wrath of God? If He died to blot out your sins, He lives to apply that redemption to you. In Him and from Him proceeds overflowing joy indeed. Paul spends the remainder of the chapter pondering the likeness and dissimilarity between the first and the last Adam; the father of our fallen race and the Lord Jesus Christ. Sin and death come to us from Adam and this holds true even where folks have never heard of Moses or the law. They still sin against conscience; everyone dies. But look what comes to us through Jesus! One sin brought death to everyone and sin to everyone; so one Man's act of righteousness, His obedience to the will of His Father, brings to everyone righteousness and life everlasting.

If sin is death hiding out in our flesh and death is what sin finally looks like, then forgiveness is eternal life in hiding and eternal life is forgiveness revealed.

In Adam, all die; in Christ, all may be made alive! In Adam all stand condemned; in Christ, all are acquitted! In Adam, all partook of disobedience; in Christ, all partake of the Savior's perfect obedience on our behalf.

Yes, in Jesus there is more peace, more joy than a lifetime can hold. It will spill out to all eternity as we celebrate to the ages of ages the amazing grace of our God.

15 JANUARY

Psalmody: Psalm 29:1–4a, 8–11
Additional Psalm: Psalm 29
Old Testament Reading: Ezekiel 37:15–28
New Testament Reading: Romans 6:1–23

Prayer of the Day

O Lord, mercifully hear our prayers and having set us free from the bonds of our sins deliver us from every evil; through Jesus Christ, Your Son, our Lord, who lives and reigns with You and the Holy Spirit, one God, now and forever. (L20)

Meditation

Baptism is how God puts you into Christ to give you everything that is His. When you were plunged into the water, you were joined to Jesus in His tomb. When you came up out of the water (or as it runs off you), you were joined to Jesus in His resurrection. The action is only done once, but its gifts go on forever.

You have died. When sin would lure and snare you in the old way, you can remind sin that that old way is dead and buried with Jesus. Instead, you've been given a new life to live. A life that is Christ's own. Joined to Him, you learn to walk with Him in His unbroken "yes" to the will of the Father. The old way of saying "my will be done" has been left behind in the tomb.

"Let not sin reign in your mortal body," exhorts the apostle, "to make you obey its passions." The desires of your body are not your boss; just because it itches doesn't mean you are to scratch it. Rather, as people who have been brought back from death to life, you get to live a brand new way: "present yourselves to God as those who have been brought back from death to life, and your members to God as instruments for righteousness." Yes, as surely as you used to serve sin and death by giving into every bodily craving, so now you have been set free to serve God.

The apostle invites a reflection on the shame of the old way, the way of gratifying the passions, all the disordered desires of our sinful nature. "What fruit were you getting at that time from the things of which you are now ashamed?" The answer, of course, is misery. We reaped the fruit of misery. How could it be otherwise when "the end of those things is death."

But now you have been set free from living that way, free to be slave of God in Christ. "The wages of sin" should probably be taken as "the wage sin pays." Be a willing slave to sin, and it happily serves up death to you. Similarly "the free gift of God" should be read as "the free gift God gives" to those who seek to put to death and to serve Him. For such, God dishes up, not condemnation, but eternal life. This is yours in Christ Jesus, into whose death and resurrection your Baptism placed you.

16 January

Psalmody: Psalm 36:1–6, 10
Additional Psalm: Psalm 54
Old Testament Reading: Ezekiel 38:1–23
New Testament Reading: Romans 7:1–20

Prayer of the Day

Almighty and everlasting God, You are always more ready to hear than we to pray and always ready to give more than we either desire or deserve. Pour down on us the abundance of Your mercy; forgive us those things of which our conscience is afraid; and give us those good things for which we are not worthy to ask except by the merits and mediation of Jesus Christ, Your Son, our Lord, who lives and reigns with You and the Holy Spirit, one God, now and forever. (C83)

Meditation

The Law isn't binding on the dead. It's for those who are living. By Baptism into Christ you have died, and so through your Baptism into Him the Law has lost its condemning power over your life. Raised with Christ in Baptism, you belong to Him who was raised from the dead so that in Him you can indeed bear fruit for God. Don't let anyone pull you back into the old way, the Law way, of living; you get to serve now in the new way of the Spirit!

All of which can lead a Christian to wonder if the Law is the problem. Of course, that is not the case. The Law discloses, reveals, shines a spotlight on the problem, but in itself the Law is holy, righteous, good. Because of what the Law is, it reveals to us what we are not. Some people have suggested that Paul in Romans is only talking about the ceremonial law, not the moral law. Romans 7 shows that he means the whole of the Law. The example he uses is from the Ninth and Tenth Commandments: "You shall not covet."

Did the good Law then bring about death in us? No, death arises from sin. But the Law, the commandments, exposes the sin in our lives, shows us how sinful beyond measure we truly are, how damaged and broken. It shows us constantly why we need a Savior who has perfect kept this law for us.

This is not just something a Christian needs to begin a faith walk with God. When a Christian is in earnest about seeking to keep the Law for the love of the Crucified and Risen Lord, he soon discovers that he is a constant failure at it. Why? Because we remain simul justus et peccator, as Luther put it so famously: simultaneously [a] just [one] and sinner. It will be that way with us to the grave. "I know that nothing good dwells in me, that is, in my flesh" the apostle cries out. "For I have the desire to do what is right, but not the ability to carry it out." What Christian can't shout out a loud "Amen" to that?

As long as we live in the flesh, we have a battle before us. The old Adam always wants his way: "I want to do what I want to do when I want to do it." The new Adam always wants to do the Lord's bidding: "Thy will be done." A Christian is a conflicted personality.

17 January

Psalmody: Psalm 76:1–3, 6–9, 11–12
Additional Psalm: Psalm 137
Old Testament Reading:
Ezekiel 39:1–10, 17–29
New Testament Reading: Romans 7:21–8:17

Prayer of the Day

O God, the strength of all who trust in You, mercifully accept our prayers; and because through the weakness of our mortal nature we can do no good thing, grant us Your grace to keep Your commandments that we may please You in both will and deed; through Jesus Christ, our Lord, who lives and reigns with You and the Holy Spirit, one God, now and forever. (H61)

Meditation

There's a war on. Not out in the world (though usually there too!), but in the heart, the inner life of the Christian. It's a war of conflicting principles or laws. The true inner life of a Christian delights in the Law of God, wants to live according to it, aches for his or her entire life to be nothing but love. Yet there's another Law that wages war against this, making the Christian a captive to the Law of sin that dwells in our members.

The Christian knows this painful tugging in two directions. When the psalmist prayed: "unite my heart" he, too, was crying out from the pain of a heart torn two ways. Is there any end to this struggle? Is there any hope?

Yes, indeed. The apostle cries out: "Thanks be to God who gives us the victory through our Lord Jesus Christ!" It's amazing how being assured of final victory gives one the strength to slog on and continue the fight another day.

Despite this wretched battle we all must fight, we cling to the promise that "there is now no condemnation for those who are in Christ Jesus!" None.

The Spirit of life, the Spirit Christ poured into your heart on the day of our Baptism into Him, the Spirit who continues to come to you through the Word and the Holy Sacraments, that Spirit has set you free from the law of sin and death That Spirit constantly reminds you that your life—your true life—is Jesus Christ

Himself, who came to us in the likeness of our sinful flesh and in that flesh condemned sin by His perfect obedience.

In Him the Spirit gives us the power for the righteous requirements of the Law to begin finding fulfillment in us. It's not a perfect keeping of the Law by a long shot, but what's not perfectly kept is perfectly forgiven. Indeed, the mind-set on the Spirit is life and peace! The flesh by itself can never please God, but we don't have the flesh by itself.

In us dwells the Spirit of God who is the power that raised Jesus Christ from the dead. That's some dynamite at work in you! He will give life to your mortal body. He will enable you to put to death the deeds of the body and have that life that is the freedom of the sons of God. The Spirit witnesses to you that you are God's child, heir, and fellow heir with Christ!

18 JANUARY

The Confession of St. Peter

Psalmody: Psalm 44:1–3, 9–10, 20–23a, 26
Additional Psalm: Psalm 124
Old Testament Reading:
Ezekiel 40:1–4; 43:1–12
Additional Reading:
Ezekiel 40:5–42:20; 43:13–27
New Testament Reading: Romans 8:18–39

Prayer of the Day

Heavenly Father, You revealed to the apostle Peter the blessed truth that Your Son Jesus is the Christ. Strengthen us by the proclamation of this truth that we too may joyfully confess that there is salvation in no one else; through the same Jesus Christ, our Lord, who lives and reigns with You and the Holy Spirit, one God, now and forever. (F08)

Confession of St. Peter

The Confession of St. Peter did not arise in the imagination of Peter's heart but was revealed to him by the Father. The reason this Confession is important is seen in Jesus' response: "You are Peter [Greek Petros], and on this rock [Greek petra] I will build My Church" (Matthew 16:13–20). As the people of God in the Old Testament began with the person of Abraham—the rock from which God's people were hewn (Isaiah 51:1–2), so the people of God in the New Testament would begin with the person of Peter, whose confession is the rock on which Christ would build His Church. But Peter was not alone (the "keys" given to him in 16:19 were given to all the disciples in Matthew 18:18 and John 20:21–23). As St. Paul tells us, Peter and the other apostles take their place with the prophets as the foundation of the Church, with Christ Himself as the cornerstone (Ephesians 2:20). The confession of Peter, therefore, is the witness of the entire apostolic band and is foundational in the building of Christ's Church. Thus the Church gives thanks to God for St. Peter and the other apostles who have instructed Christ's Holy Church in His divine and saving truth.

Meditation

Paul is at pains to focus the Christian on the final outcome of the war. He wants us to learn to live from the victory that will be ours in Christ, and from that certain future to find the strength to battle on in the present. He weighs the future glory against the present sufferings and declares the future glory to win hands down. Creation is on tiptoe, eagerly waiting for that wondrous moment when it will share in the liberty of the sons of God as we are unveiled for who we really are in Jesus Christ. The creation groans, waiting for that day.

And we do too. Wonderful as the firstfruits of the Spirit are in our lives, we ache for the final victory. But the Spirit is a wondrous gift. Sometimes we are so worn out in the battle we don't even know how to pray anymore, what to say, how to ask. In such moments, the Holy Spirit raises within us intercessions too deep for words, always asking for us exactly the right thing, according to God's will. What a comfort!

But there's more. "And we know that for those who love God all things work together for good, for those who are called according to his purpose." We fight along, comforted by the Spirit praying within us, and comforted by the certainty that whatever we are passing through God is weaving together to bring us final blessing. Talk about living in triumph! To be able to face each suffering that comes into our life and realize it is our servant, to bring us good, that is peace indeed.

And there's even more. When we think of all these things, we realize that God has loved us with a love immeasurable, deep, and divine. The One who did not spare His only Son, but gave Him up for us all, with Him will surely give us all things. No one can condemn those whom God has acquitted. Jesus Himself at the right hand of the Father is constantly interceding for us. Lots of bad things can and will happen to us, but none have the power to defeat us. "We are more than conquerors through Him who loved us."

Nothing, nothing at all in creation, has the power to drive a wedge between us and the love God has given to us in His beloved Son, Jesus Christ. When we remember that, we conquer indeed!

19 January

Psalmody: Psalm 15:1–5
Additional Psalm: Psalm 126
Old Testament Reading:
Ezekiel 44:1–16, 23–29
New Testament Reading:
Romans 9:1–18

Prayer of the Day

O God, Your almighty power is made known chiefly in showing mercy. Grant us the fullness of Your grace that we may be called to repentance and made partakers of Your heavenly treasures; through Your Son, Jesus Christ, our Lord, who lives and reigns with You and the Holy Spirit, one God, now and forever. (B67)

Meditation

If nothing can separate us from the love of God in Christ Jesus, how is it that Israel, God's ancient people, could miss the blessing? Paul agonized over this mystery in Romans 9–10. Paul's love for his own people is so profound, so deep, that if he could save them by being cut off from Christ himself, he would do it. Do you see how the love of Christ has totally marked this man?

What blessings God had showered on His ancient people! Theirs were the adoption, the glory, the covenants, the giving of the Law, the worship, the promises, the patriarchs, and most of all, from their flesh, the Christ who is God over all and blessed forever. Blessings abounding for them.

Has the Word of God failed for them? No, Paul argues, for just being a descendant of Abraham has never truly made one be part of Israel. "Through Isaac shall your offspring be named." Isaac, the child of God's impossible promise; not Ishmael, the child of the flesh and human ingenuity. Similarly with Jacob and Esau. It was through Jacob, the weaker homebody, that the promised descendant, God's choice, might stand without regard to human exertion. Physical descent has never yet given birth to faith; faith is born of the promise.

Does this mean God is unfair when in the history of salvation He chooses one and rejects another? Isaac over Ishmael; Jacob over Esau; Moses and the children of Israel over Pharaoh and the Egyptians? No, the apostle declares.

God is not unfair, but He is merciful: "I will have mercy on whom I will have mercy."

How big is the mercy of God? Is it big enough for all? There have been Christians who believed that God's mercy was somehow restricted to a portion of the human race. They pointed to Paul's words here about election to justify that, missing that Paul was speaking not of personal election here, but of God's choosing the way to bring salvation into the world. Remember that the same Paul who wrote these words also wrote that God "desires all people to be saved and to come to the knowledge of the truth" (1 Timothy 2:4).

Paul here rejoices in how God works His saving purposes through history, working through the people of Israel, to bring into the flesh a Savior for them and for all people. Even His "hardening" of Pharaoh was in the service of that saving will.

20 JANUARY

Sarah

Psalmody: Psalm 117:1–2
Additional Psalm: Psalm 97
Old Testament Reading: Ezekiel 47:1–14, 21–23
New Testament Reading: Romans 9:19–33

Prayer of the Day

Lord and Father of all, You looked with favor upon Sarai in her advanced years, putting on her a new name, Sarah, and with it the promise of multitudinous blessings from her aged womb. Give us a youthful hope in the joy of our own new name, being baptized into the promised Messiah, that we, too, might be fruitful in Your kingdom, abounding in the works of Your Spirit; through Jesus Christ, our Lord, who lives and reigns with You and the Holy Spirit, one God, now and forever. (1137)

Sarah

Sarah was the wife (and half sister) of the Hebrew patriarch Abraham (Genesis 11:29; 20:12). In obedience to divine command (Genesis 12:1), she made the long and arduous journey west, along with her husband and his relatives, from Ur of the Chaldees to Haran and then finally to the land of Canaan. She remained childless until old age. Then, in keeping with God's long-standing promise, she gave birth to a son and heir of the covenant (Genesis 21:1–3). She is remembered and honored as the wife of Abraham and the mother of Isaac, the second of the three patriarchs. She is also favorably noted for her hospitality to strangers (Genesis 18:1–8). Following her death at the age of 127, she was laid to rest in the Cave of Machpelah (Gen. 49:13), where her husband was later buried.

Meditation

"Who can resist His will?" people ask. "It's obviously not my fault, but God's! He made me this way!" The apostle cuts off that escape from repentance. God has indeed made you, but He has not made your sin.

What does it mean that God "endured with much patience vessels of wrath prepared for destruction"? While "prepared" is one translation, another is "who prepared themselves." The Greek is ambiguous, but the latter seems to fit better with "endured with patience." God was ever awaiting their repentance, but they continued to fit themselves out for a destruction that He never willed. Yet His patient endurance of those who insist on destruction only shines the greater light upon the riches of His glory. What is that glory? His fathomless mercy toward those whom He has called, not only from the Jews but also from the Gentiles.

The calling of the Gentiles is no innovation of the Christians. It is planted throughout the Hebrew Scriptures as the apostle shows, bringing both Hosea and Isaiah as witnesses. God had long foretold that Gentiles would join His people and, sadly, that many of His own people would reject Him and fall away.

How did it happen? The Gentiles who didn't give a fig about righteousness—intent merely on living for pleasure—ended up attaining the righteousness of God. Jews, on the other hand, who tried with might and main to live according to the Law so that they might become righteous, end up missing righteousness altogether. What happened?

Taking us right back to the first chapter of Romans, Paul reminds us that the righteousness of God is by faith from start to finish. When the Jews, and when we, start to chase after righteousness as though it were anything other than faith in God's promises, then we end up trusting in our own works. To do so is to stumble over the rock who is Jesus Christ, the stone of stumbling that God has laid in Zion. People who try to deal with God on the basis of their own works will always fall flat because of that rock. Yet our God has laid that rock down so that "whoever believes in Him will not be put to shame." Faith builds on Christ and on Christ alone—it has no other righteousness to cling to but the perfect righteousness of God's Son.

21 JANUARY

Psalmody: Psalm 20:1–9
Additional Psalm: Psalm 13
Old Testament Reading: Joel 1:1–20
New Testament Reading: Romans 10:1–21

Prayer of the Day

O Lord, grant us the Spirit to hear Your Word and know the one thing needful that by Your Word and Spirit we may live according to Your will; through Jesus Christ, Your Son, our Lord, who lives and reigns with You and the Holy Spirit, one God, now and forever. (C69)

Meditation

Paul reveals that in the final analysis there are two kinds of righteousness. There is the righteousness that a person produces by dint of effort to conform to the law; there is the righteousness that a person receives as an undeserved, unguessed gift of God. Luther referred to the first as "active" righteousness and to the second as "passive." The Jews wanted to be righteous—a noble thing—but their zeal was directed entirely toward the first sort of righteousness, the sort a person produces within themselves by activity. And that's how they missed out on God's righteousness, which a person passively receives as a gift, for Christ is "the end of the law for righteousness to everyone who believes."

Moses writes about both kinds. The first: "the person who does the commandments shall live by them." Try it and see how far it gets you. The problem with the first sort of righteousness is that we can't produce it. We can't keep the Law as the Law itself demands; whole and entire and perfect obedience. But what we can't come up with on our own, the Lord in His gracious mercy delivers to us via promise: "The word is near you." The Word delivers to you this wondrous news: If you confess with your mouth that Jesus is Lord and believe in your heart that God raised Him from the dead, you will be saved. "Everyone who believes in Him will not be put to shame."

And that promise holds for Jews and Greeks and everyone else in this entire world. There is no distinction. The same Lord is Lord of all and delights to bestow His riches on any and everyone who calls on Him. "Everyone who calls on the name of the Lord will be saved."

Such calling on the Lord comes about only as a gift. Hence no one believes without hearing and no one hears without someone preaching to them. "Faith comes from hearing and hearing through the word of Christ." The word of Christ is the message that in Him there is perfect obedience to the will of God and that

His perfect obedience is yours as you believe it. It is a gift, pure and simple. Believing is taking, receiving the gift of Christ as your righteousness.

But didn't the unbelieving Jews hear? Yes, but mankind always retains the fearful power to say "no" to the gift of God. Mankind's "no" doesn't change the ever-held-out hands of Him who bids us receive that gift by which alone we live.

22 JANUARY

Psalmody: Psalm 69:19–23, 32–33
Additional Psalm: Psalm 121
Old Testament Reading: Joel 2:1–17
New Testament Reading: Romans 11:1–24

Prayer of the Day

O God, the strength of all who put their trust in You, mercifully grant that by Your power we may be defended against all adversity; through Jesus Christ, Your Son, our Lord, who lives and reigns with You and the Holy Spirit, one God, now and forever. (L19)

Meditation

So since God has placed all righteousness in His Son, and yet many of God's ancient people reject that gift, does it mean that He's through with them, that He has washed His hands of them, completely rejected them as His people? By no means! Paul is at pains to make his readers understand that it is not God who has rejected the Jews; it is they who have rejected Him. But even so, not all of them have rejected Him.

Paul reminds the Romans that he himself is a Jew, and that as at the time of Elijah, the Lord had His remnant, chosen by grace, so it still is. By grace, because this way of righteousness must ever be wholly a gift; it never rests on the basis of works, of anything we do or are.

So some in Israel received the gift, and some among the Gentiles were added to them, and yet many of Israel (and many among the Gentiles!) reject the gift and are hardened in their unbelief, their refusal to be given to.

The apostle sees in this sad rejection of so many in Israel a wondrous opportunity. When the Jews rejected the message, the Good News went out to the Gentiles and gave them the gift of faith, and so of righteousness. They—wild olive branches—were grafted into the native vine, joined to Abraham, Isaac, and Jacob through faith in Jesus Christ. They were privileged to inherit unexpectedly the blessings that God had deposited in Israel. But again, all boasting is excluded. A Gentile dare never say: "I got grafted in and the Jews got bumped out; God loves me more than He loves them." Rather, in humility the Gentile must note: I was grafted in only by faith, and I stand only by faith, and if I fall into pride, I can be and will be broken off just as Israel in the flesh has been.

So there is both kindness and severity in God. Kindness, provided that by faith you continue in God's kindness; severity, if you dare slip into pride as though God's gift to you were actually something you had deserved and merited. God's kindness to the Gentiles remains forever the testimony of His saving good will, that as the Gentiles have been grafted into Israel through faith in Christ, so too those who are now unbelieving Jews may be grafted back in. God is able to do so!

23 JANUARY

Psalmody: Psalm 139:1–6, 12–14
Additional Psalm: Psalm 81
Old Testament Reading: Joel 2:18–32
New Testament Reading: Romans 11:25–12:13

Prayer of the Day

Almighty God, in Your mercy guide the course of this world so that Your Church may joyfully serve You in godly peace and quietness; through Jesus Christ, Your Son, our Lord, who lives and reigns with You and the Holy Spirit, one God, now and forever. (B65)

Meditation

How, then, ought a Gentile Christian to look upon the ancient people of God? While they are enemies of the Gospel, we must nevertheless regard them as God's beloved. His gift and calling to them—as His gift and calling to us—are irrevocable. He never takes them back. What comfort there is in that! Once we were disobedient, not believing or knowing the promises. Now they are disobedient, not believing or knowing the promises fulfilled in Christ, and through their disobedience, the Gospel has come to us. What a marvel, the apostle writes: "God has consigned all to disobedience." Why? "That He may have mercy on all!" Jew or Gentile, God calls all to life in His Son!

As the apostle ponders this wisdom of God by which "all Israel"—all believers—are saved, he bursts into a hymn of praise to God, whose mind no one has known, and who took counsel with no human being when He chose to bring salvation into the world through Christ. "For from Him and through Him and to Him are all things. To Him be glory forever. Amen!" In the light of all the foregoing, Paul appeals to the Roman Christians and to you, by the very mercies you have received in Jesus Christ, to live a new life. To present your bodies to God as a living sacrifice, holy and acceptable to God in Christ Jesus. Rather than letting the world squeeze you into its mold, receive the gift of a new way of thinking in Christ so that you can know what God's will is.

God's will is never human pride. Instead, think with the sober judgment that recognizes yourself as a condemned sinner who lives solely by the gift of Christ as your righteousness by faith alone. That faith has united you to a body. You are part of the Church! The Church, with many members, is a single body. Each has gifts to be used for the blessing of all the others—that's why God gave them to you. Not for you to pride yourself on them, but to use them in whatever way you can to serve and build up others. Prophesying, serving, teaching, exhorting, contributing, leading, showing mercy—whatever your gift is, use it to build up!

God's will is always love. Love that is genuine and honors each person as a precious gift of God. Love that rejoices in hope, is patient in trouble, and constant in prayer. Love that tends the needs of God's people.

24 JANUARY

St. Timothy, Pastor and Confessor

Psalmody: Psalm 131:1–3
Additional Psalm: Psalm 84
Old Testament Reading: Joel 3:1–21
New Testament Reading: Romans 12:14–13:14

Prayer of the Day

Lord Jesus Christ, You have always given to Your Church on earth faithful shepherds such as Timothy to guide and feed Your flock. Make all pastors diligent to preach Your holy Word and administer Your means of grace, and grant Your people wisdom to follow in the way that leads to life eternal; for You live and reign with the Father and the Holy Spirit, one God, now and forever. (F09)

St. Timothy, Pastor and Confessor
St. Timothy had Christian believers in his family. His mother, Eunice, was a Christian woman and was the daughter of a Christian woman named Lois (2 Timothy 1:5). Acts records that St. Paul met Timothy on his second missionary journey and wanted Timothy to continue on with him (16:1–3). Over time, Timothy became a dear friend and close associate of Paul to whom Paul entrusted mission work in Greece and Asia Minor. Timothy was also with Paul in Rome. According to tradition, after Paul's death, Timothy went to Ephesus, where he served as bishop and was martyred there around AD 97. Timothy is best remembered as a faithful companion of Paul, one who rendered great service among the Gentile churches.

Meditation
The new life that you have through Baptism is Christ's own life. This is a life that does not seek to "pay back" others for the wrongs they do you as Christ does not "pay us back" for the wrongs we did to Him. Rather, it is a life that blesses those who make your life miserable; rejoices with those who rejoice; weeps with those who weep. It is a life of harmony where haughtiness has no place—how can it when you are but a poor sinner who lives only from the saving mercy of God in Christ? Instead of giving yourself airs, you consider what is honorable, and as far as you possibly can, live at peace with all. A person may well be your enemy in their estimation of you, but your estimation of them is that they are poor sinners in need of mercy and so you seek to serve them in any way you can. The cardinal rule of the new life is simply this: do not be overcome by evil, but overcome evil with good.

The new life in Christ also implies a new relationship with the governing authorities. You begin to see that they are instituted by God—and that they have a commission from Him to be a blessing to you. So you seek to be in subjection to them, recognizing their high honor, even if they do not recognize it themselves. (Caesar certainly didn't, when Paul wrote these words.) You even pay your taxes cheerfully as a new creature in God: you know your money supports the authorities as "ministers of God."

What if the government is not particularly worthy of honor because of unjust or corrupt ruling? Even then, toward its "hidden majesty" (Luther) you show honor. Treat the governing authorities as God created them to be.

Another facet of the new life in Christ is that it is avoids every form of indebtedness, save for the ongoing obligation to show love toward one another. Love is what all the commandments of the Law describe, and so love literally is the fulfilling of the Law.

Once more the apostle orients the Christian toward the end, the consummation of all things in Christ: "salvation is nearer to us now than when we first believed." The old ways of the works of darkness is the past; the future toward which we reach renounces those old ways and puts on the Lord Jesus Christ, making zero provision for gratifying the sinful cravings of the flesh.

25 JANUARY

The Conversion of St. Paul

Psalmody: Psalm 6:4–10
Additional Psalm: Psalm 67
Old Testament Reading: Zechariah 1:1–21
New Testament Reading: Romans 14:1–23

Prayer of the Day

Almighty God, You turned the heart of him who persecuted the Church and by his preaching caused the light of the Gospel to shine throughout the world. Grant us ever to rejoice in the saving light of Your Gospel and, following the example of the apostle Paul, to spread it to the ends of the earth; through Jesus Christ, Your Son, our Lord, who lives and reigns with You and the Holy Spirit, one God, now and forever. (F10)

The Conversion of St. Paul

St. Paul's life-changing experience on the road to Damascus is related three times in the Book of Acts (9:1–9; 22:6–11; 26:12–18). As an archenemy of Christians, Saul of Tarsus set out for Damascus to arrest and bring believers to Jerusalem for trial. While on the way, he saw a blinding light and heard the words: "Saul, Saul, why are you persecuting Me?" Saul asked, "Who are You, Lord?" The reply came, "I am Jesus, whom you are persecuting." In Damascus, where Saul was brought after being blinded, a disciple named Ananias was directed by the Lord in a vision to go to Saul to restore his sight: "Go, for he is a chosen instrument of Mine to carry My name before the Gentiles and kings and the children of Israel" (9:15). After receiving his sight, Saul was baptized and went on to become known as Paul, the great apostle.

Meditation

The new life into which we have been baptized into Christ is a life that is sensitive to the scruples of our neighbor without passing judgment on him. In Paul's day the big problem with meat from the marketplace was that it had all been offered in sacrifice to the heathen idols. Some honestly believed that to eat that meat was to participate in idol worship in some way; others knew that idols are nothing and that anything could be received as a gift from God. Some early Christians held tight to the Jewish holy days and observed them in honor of the Lord Jesus; others were convinced that was just a shadow of the reality that had come in Christ and firmly believed that every day was now holy in the Lord.

The apostle doesn't tell the Romans "these ones are right and these ones are wrong." Instead, he takes a radical new approach: in the Lord both can be received and welcomed, and without passing judgment on each other. When the Lord Jesus comes between two people, He joins them together in a brand new way of relating. "None of us lives to himself, and none of us dies to himself. If we live, we live to the Lord, and if we die, we die to the Lord. So whether we live or whether we die, we are the Lord's!"

Since we are the Lord's then, we have no business judging one another. We're His servants, and every last one of us, standing before the judgment seat of God, will have to plead for mercy. None of us has the right to stand in the Judge's seat against our neighbor. That's part of the old way of living we get to leave behind in Baptism.

The test of everything then is "am I walking in love?" It's not very loving if I know a brother or sister has scruples over eating meat offered to idols for me to make a display of my freedom by eating it in their presence. Such behavior simply misses the boat. The Kingdom isn't about eating and drinking—but it is about righteousness, peace, and joy in the Holy Spirit. By the Spirit's power I'm set free to forego my freedom for the sake of love: that's being truly free.

Paul is clear that scruples about unclean foods are unfounded; yet if the person doubts and eats anyway, he is actually sinning against his own conscience. "For whatever does not proceed from faith is sin."

26 JANUARY

St. Titus, Pastor and Confessor

Psalmody: Psalm 18:46–50
Additional Psalm: Psalm 134
Old Testament Reading: Zechariah 2:1–3:10
New Testament Reading: Romans 15:1–13

Prayer of the Day

Almighty God, You called Titus to the work of pastor and teacher. Make all shepherds of Your flock diligent in preaching Your holy Word so that the whole world may know the immeasurable riches of our Savior, Jesus Christ, who lives and reigns with You and the Holy Spirit, one God, now and forever. (F11)

St. Titus, Pastor and Confessor

St. Titus, like Timothy with whom he is often associated, was a friend and co-worker of St. Paul. Titus was a Gentile, perhaps a native of Antioch, who accompanied Paul and Barnabas to Jerusalem when they brought assistance to the Christians in Judea during a famine (Acts 11:30; Galatians 2:1). It is not known if he accompanied Paul on his first or second missionary journeys, but Titus was with him on the third one, when he helped reconcile the Corinthians to Paul (2 Corinthians 7:6–7) and assisted with the collection for the Church in Jerusalem (2 Corinthians 8:3–6). It was probably on the return to Jerusalem that Paul left Titus in Crete (Titus 1:4–5). Afterward he is found working in Dalmatia (2 Timothy 4:10). According to tradition, Titus returned to Crete where he served as bishop until he died about AD 96.

Meditation

The new life in Christ is not about pleasing ourselves, but rather pleasing our heavenly Father by bearing with the failings of the weak. That, after all, is exactly what the Lord Jesus did for you. That, then, is how you build up our neighbor.

The Scriptures (Paul was speaking of the Old Testament Scriptures, but it applies as well to the New Testament writings) were given to strengthen us in hope—to enable us to orient and live our lives toward the wondrous future of this world, where love will reign in all things at our Lord's appearing and everything that is not love will be destroyed and burned up. But that's not just something we have to wait for. Paul prays that God would grant us to begin living in that coming harmony already here and now, so that even though we are many, with a single voice we glorify the God and Father of our Lord Jesus Christ. The Church is colony of that future, an outpost of the coming age. And so the love of that future characterizes her inner life: as Christ has welcomed us, we are to welcome one another, for God's glory. Our Lord reigns, but He reigned as a servant. He was servant to both the circumcised, the Jews, and to the uncircumcised, the Gentiles. His service to the Jews fulfilled the promises God had long ago given to the Patriarch. His service to the Gentiles fulfilled the numerous prophesies that God had spoken of how the Gentiles would be brought into the unending praise and worship of God, given with God's ancient people, a certain hope. Paul keeps coming back to that hope.

It is his prayer that the God of hope—the God in whose hands is our certain future—would fill you with total joy and peace through your faith in Jesus Christ. Such total joy and peace come only from Him who is the personal joy and peace that exists eternally between the Father and the Son, that is, from the Holy Spirit. The Spirit alone can give it to you. And when He does, your life is changed from being "without hope and without God in the world" to "abounding in hope."

Our world is rapidly becoming a very "hopeless" place. People are often disillusioned and fearful as they look toward the future. We as Christians have the joy of pointing them toward the surprise ending of this world's story—the triumph of Christ, the destruction of death, the eternal feast awaiting.

27 JANUARY

John Chrysostom, Preacher

Psalmody: Psalm 1:1–6
Additional Psalm: Psalm 109
Old Testament Reading: Zechariah 4:1–5:11
New Testament Reading: Romans 15:14–33

Prayer of the Day

O God, You gave to Your servant John Chrysostom grace to proclaim the Gospel with eloquence and power. As bishop of the great congregations of Antioch and Constantinople, he fearlessly bore reproach for the honor of Your Name. Mercifully grant to all bishops and pastors such excellence in preaching and fidelity in ministering Your Word that Your people shall be partakers of the divine nature; through Jesus Christ, our Lord, who lives and reigns with you and the Holy Spirit, one God, now and forever. (1138)

John Chrysostom, Preacher

Given the added name Chrysostom, which means "golden-mouthed" in Greek, St. John was a dominant force in the fourth-century Christian Church. Born in Antioch around AD 347, John was instructed in the Christian faith by his pious mother, Anthusa. After serving in a number of Christian offices, including acolyte and lector, John was ordained a presbyter and given preaching responsibilities. His simple but direct messages found an audience well beyond his hometown. In AD 398, John Chrysostom was made patriarch of Constantinople. His determination to reform the church, court, and city brought him into conflict with established authorities. Eventually, he was exiled from his adopted city. Although removed from his parishes and people, he continued writing and preaching until the time of his death in AD

407. It is reported that his final words were "Glory be to God for all things! Amen."

Meditation

Paul, because of the grace given him to be a minister of Christ, wrote with some boldness to a Church he had neither founded nor even visited. Yet he knew he wasn't writing them anything new—it was the same Gospel that had made them Christians to begin with. It was the Good News about the forgiveness of sins through the blood of Jesus Christ, who alone is our righteousness.

Paul has a very special ministry, though, in the history of salvation, and that is to offer up the firstfruits of the Gentiles as a sacrifice pleasing to God in Christ, sanctified by the Holy Spirit. He's worked his way through the eastern half of the empire from Jerusalem to Ilyricum, preaching Christ in all those territories. Now his sights are set beyond.

It's clear that he doesn't plan on staying long in Rome, for "I make it my ambition to preach the gospel, not where Christ has already been named, lest I build on someone else's foundation." Apostles are for foundation laying; they leave it to the presbyters (the pastors) they appoint in a given location to build upon the foundation they have laid. If there's already a Church in Rome, it doesn't need an apostle like Paul to labor there.

Still, he wants to visit them and enjoy their company for a time and to receive help from the Church there to fund his further mission toward the provinces out west, even to Spain. Such is always the pattern: the Church grows by those in an area already reached funding in love a mission into an area where Christ has yet to be preached.

That's was Paul's plan, at any rate, but he knows that all human plans are rather iffy. His words suggest that he had a distinctly bad feeling about heading toward Jerusalem, with the gift for the mother Church that he has

gathered from the Gentile Churches. He seeks the prayers of the Roman Christians that he be delivered from what awaits him in Judea and that his trip may be without event, so that he may finally make his way out to Rome.

We know, of course, that is not how things ended up. The Lord did indeed want Paul to come to Rome, but he did not arrive as a free man, for a short visit, then heading off on a mission trip. He would arrive under arrest, a man in chains, awaiting trial before Caesar.

28 JANUARY

Psalmody: Psalm 12
Additional Psalm: Psalm 133
Old Testament Reading:
Zechariah 6:1–7:14
New Testament Reading:
Romans 16:17–27

Prayer of the Day

Almighty and merciful God, it is by Your grace that we live as Your people who offer acceptable service. Grant that we may walk by faith, and not by sight, in the way that leads to eternal life; through Jesus Christ, Your Son, our Lord, who lives and reigns with You and the Holy Spirit, one God, now and forever. (C72)

Meditation

Our Lord had warned that false prophets would come. Paul would warn the Ephesian elders that they'd arise from their own midst. So he warns the Romans to watch out for those who cause divisions and create obstacles by varying from the faith once delivered to the saints. Avoid such people, he urges. They are not serving Christ, but their own sinful appetites. Their smooth talk and flattery of their hearers can deceive the hearts of the naive.

They abound today. They fill television screens and radio waves and write best sellers, promising prosperity and telling people how to be positive about themselves. Paul doesn't want the Romans or you to be deceived by such. That's not the faith that the apostles of Christ have delivered to us. It comes from another source—from Satan, whom God will soon crush under your feet, the apostle promises.

Several of Paul's co-workers chime in with their greetings—Timothy, Lucius, Jason, Sosipater, Tertius (the scribe who wrote at Paul's dictation), Gaius, Erastus, and Quartus. All send their greetings to these beloved brothers and sisters in Christ in Rome that they haven't had the joy of meeting yet. No matter. Neither time nor space is a barrier to those who are one Body in Jesus Christ.

In a grand doxology the apostle wraps up his lengthiest letter. "Now to Him who is able to strengthen you according to my gospel and the preaching of Jesus Christ, according to the revelation of the mystery that was kept secret for long ages, but has now been disclosed and through the prophetic writings made known to all nations, according to the command of the eternal God, to bring about the obedience of faith—to the only wise God be glory forevermore through Jesus Christ! Amen."

Here is the whole of the Epistle in a nutshell. God strengthens through His Gospel, through the preaching of Christ, the mystery that was long hidden and is now broadcast through the length and breadth of the world to all nations. This Gospel brings about "the obedience of faith"—that is, it imparts the faith that clings to the righteousness of God so that people are rescued from the old dead-end way of living and made partakers of the living Body of the Son of God, whom they eagerly await from heaven. And for this Gospel—this joyous good news—all glory goes to the Father of Jesus Christ forever!

29 January

Psalmody: Psalm 107:1–9
Additional Psalm: Psalm 107
Old Testament Reading: Zechariah 8:1–23
New Testament Reading: 2 Timothy 1:1–18

Prayer of the Day

Almighty God, You show mercy to Your people in all their troubles. Grant us always to recognize Your goodness, give thanks for Your compassion, and praise Your holy name; through Jesus Christ, Your Son, our Lord, who lives and reigns with You and the Holy Spirit, one God, now and forever. (C81)

Meditation

Paul addresses a very personal, pointed, and pressing letter to his "beloved child" Timothy. Time cannot be wasted on sentimental reminiscences or matters that have no bearing on the crisis at hand. The situation is urgent. Paul's days on earth are numbered. Even as he longs to see Timothy again, the apostle knows that he has a role in preparing the young man to face the extreme tests that he himself has already endured. Bravado will not suffice.

While Paul holds himself up as a mentor and example to Timothy, the apostle is also quick to add that "the pattern of sound words that you have heard from me" are, in fact, not his own. The God whom they both serve is the One who gives "a spirit not of fear but of power and love and self-control."

Timothy had already received the gift of faith. Before Paul became his spiritual father, Timothy was blessed with a pious mother and an equally devoted grandmother. In addition to these positive role models, there were also negative examples. The names and memories of Phygelus and Hermogenes are sullied and shamed because they were among those in Asia who deserted Paul and—by extension—Jesus.

As we "guard the good deposit" of faith that we have received from God, the apostle's words to Timothy are valuable. No matter what we think we have already experienced, worse troubles and tests may still lie before us. Opposition to our Savior and those who follow Him will intensify as we near what Paul calls, "that Day" (v. 18). Left to our own devices we will either shrink from the task of faithful discipleship or be defeated. The Good News is that we are not left to ourselves; rather, our weaknesses and failures are overcome by the power, love, and grace of God. He saved us and "called us to a holy calling." Because He has made us His own through faith in Christ Jesus, we are victorious. The "sound words" about Jesus in Holy Scripture fortify us. The Gospel message of forgiveness and salvation through Christ is the object of faith that the Holy Spirit ignites in us and then "fans into flame" as we grow in our calling. God has put mentors and teachers into our lives who have modeled the faith for us. In turn, he gives us the opportunity to do that for others. Whether in the role of Paul or Timothy, because of Jesus we can say, "I know whom I have believed."

30 JANUARY

Psalmody: Psalm 33:18–22
Additional Psalm: Psalm 33
Old Testament Reading: Zechariah 9:1–17
New Testament Reading: 2 Timothy 2:1–26

Prayer of the Day

O God, our refuge and strength, the author of all godliness, hear the devout prayers of Your Church, especially in times of persecution, and grant that what we ask in faith we may obtain; through Jesus Christ, Your Son, our Lord, who lives and reigns with You and the Holy Spirit, one God, now and forever. (H82)

Meditation

To "stay on task" means one is devoted to the duties he has been given. Here St. Paul talks about a soldier, an athlete, and a farmer. The soldier stays on task by following orders; the athlete by competing according to rules; and the farmer by laboriously persevering in his agricultural pursuits. Paul uses these varied examples to remind Timothy and those Timothy engages to serve with him what it means to be a worker approved by God. This is no easy task. It may involve hardship, self-denial, and suffering.

Despite its difficulty, being a worker approved by God is different than any other sort of task. Worldly tasks involve an assignment demanded of us. Serving the Lord, however, involves not a chore imposed but a cross imprinted. It is not an obligation we must fulfill in order to receive reward, but an opportunity we are privileged to enjoy as sons and daughters of God. The motivating power for discipleship is our Lord. Paul says, "Remember Jesus Christ, risen from the dead." Our Savior stayed "on task" regarding the mission given to Him. He never doubted or deviated from His Father's will. He offered His life on our behalf and has risen victoriously from the grave.

Only because Jesus has first given His life to us can we now give back our lives to Him in grateful, joyful service. Although His life was perfect, ours is not. We are vessels of wood and clay (v. 20). The devil would like to make us workers disapproved by God. Satan's snares for us are the same as they were for Timothy: irreverent babble (v. 16), youthful passions (v. 22), and foolish controversies (v. 23). The Word of Truth, which first confronts us with the message of the Law and then comforts us with the promise of forgiveness in Christ, shows us when we have failed. God's Spirit works within us a recognition that "everyone who names the name of the Lord" should indeed "depart from iniquity" (v. 19). In penitence we come to the Lord admitting our wrongs, asking for His healing, empowering forgiveness. That same Word of Truth then restores us and sends us forth without guilt or shame.

Paul reminds us that "the Lord knows those who are His." We are always on His mind and in His heart. He is neither a detached chief executive nor a demanding taskmaster. His involvement with us is derived from His love for us. The God who promises us salvation also permits us to be His servants.

31 JANUARY

Psalmody: Psalm 135:1–7, 13–14
Additional Psalm: Psalm 68
Old Testament Reading: Zechariah 10:1–11:3
New Testament Reading: 2 Timothy 3:1–17

Prayer of the Day

O God, whose never-failing providence orders all things both in heaven and earth, we humbly implore You to put away from us all hurtful things and to give us those things that are profitable for us; through Jesus Christ, Your Son, our Lord, who lives and reigns with You and the Holy Spirit, one God, now and forever. (H67)

Meditation

This depiction of the last days is not pleasant to people of the present world. Even we Christians have sometimes been deceived into thinking that the future of our human existence is an alluring ascent, not a damnable descent. We hear the not-so-subtle message from the media of our day: if only we avoid international conflict, nuclear proliferation, ecological disaster, or the depletion of our natural resources this world will go on forever. Such a distortion of the coming reality fails to take into account man's relation to the Maker of heaven and earth, the most important ele-

ment in the complex equation measuring the duration of this current cosmos.

Godlessness is the truest and most significant mark of the approaching end. In this text from verse 2 onward Paul describes the moral decline with seemingly every brutally true adjective available. His summation of this despicable condition is found in verse 5, where he says that people will display "the appearance of godliness, but denying its power."

A powerless godliness is a religion without a source of authority, with no normative guide for belief and action except the distorted and capricious viewpoints of one's own conscience and desires. We see that phenomenon exhibited in today's world among those who claim to be "spiritual," but not "religious." This is only a euphemism for an outright rejection of Holy Scripture. After all, what does it matter if Scripture is "profitable for teaching" if one doesn't desire to learn from it? What impact will the "reproofing" and "correcting" characteristics of Scripture have if one refuses to acknowledge that his ways are errant? What is the benefit of being "trained in righteousness" by God's Word if one would rather be an untrained, undisciplined atheist?

Scripture does have an impact on some. It succeeds effectively so "that the man of God may be competent, equipped for every good work" (v. 17). We know the difference that the Word has made in our lives as it comes to us through preaching, teaching, reading, singing; through the Sacraments where it is combined with simple, earthly elements; but most of all, through the flesh and blood of the incarnate Savior. Having been brought to faith in Jesus by the Spirit working through the Word, we now serve our Lord in the waning days of this dark world with the Word as a lamp for our feet and a light for our path (Psalm 119:105).

1 FEBRUARY

Psalmody: Psalm 28:1–9
Additional Psalm: Psalm 48
Old Testament Reading: Zechariah 11:4–17
New Testament Reading: 2 Timothy 4:1–18

Prayer of the Day

Lord God heavenly Father, Your Son fought the good fight of faith and was obedient even unto death, even death on the cross, pouring out His blood as a peace offering between You and us. Keep us faithful unto death that we may receive the crown of righteousness that the Righteous Judge will reward us with on that day, having waited in hope and love for His appearing; through Your Son, Jesus Christ, our Lord. (1139)

Meditation

Last days, last words, and last visits all make a lasting impact. They give us a standard by which to evaluate both our loved one and our relationship with our loved one. Paul is here conscious of his last days on earth. We see a man who is comfortable with his coming fate as he writes his last words, hoping for a last visit with Timothy.

Paul can face the end of his life with tranquility because his spiritual house is in order. As a former persecutor of the Church he could have been fearful of divine retribution. But the terror of the Law had been removed because of the cross of Christ. The Lord, the righteous judge—not the angry, vindictive judge—would give him the crown of life. It was a gift, not a product of Paul's own merit. The apostle could look back with no regrets because all the regrets of the past had been paid for by the blood of Jesus and blotted from God's memory.

Being secure in his own salvation, Paul can then think of those he will be leaving behind.

He gives specific instructions to his spiritual son, Timothy, summarizing the task of a Christian pastor, while warning him of the challenges ahead.

He does this with a clear conscience, free of any malice. Paul does recall those who deserted him (v. 16), but he is quick to add, "May it not be charged against them." This is not a case of failing to forget; it is an ongoing concern for the spiritual condition of those who seem to have wandered from God's ways. Finally, Paul remains engaged. There is no intent of shrinking from any ministry opportunity. As he pleads his case, he understands that "the Lord stood by me and strengthened me, so that through me the message might be fully proclaimed and all the Gentiles might hear it." He realizes that until his final breath, he is God's instrument.

Yes, the apostle is an example to us in all these respects. But even more than that, he points us to the final days of our Savior before His death and resurrection. More than anyone, our Lord "fought the good fight, kept the faith, and finished the faith." Had He failed, our final goodbye to this world would be filled with terror and desperation instead of comfort and hope. Whether it is our last day, or any of the days before it, like Paul, the Lord will stand by us and give us strength.

2 FEBRUARY

The Purification of Mary and the Presentation of Our Lord

Psalmody: Psalm 75:1–10
Additional Psalm: Psalm 104
Old Testament Reading: Zechariah 12:1–13:9
New Testament Reading: Titus 1:1–2:6

Purification of Mary and the Presentation of Our Lord

Thirty-two days after Jesus' circumcision and seventy weeks after the announcement of John's birth to Zechariah by the angel Gabriel, the Lord comes to His temple to fulfill the Torah (Luke 2:22–38). The days are indeed fulfilled with the presentation. Jesus' parents keep the Torah and fulfill it by bringing Jesus to His true home. Also, Jesus' parents offer the alternative sacrifice of two turtledoves or two pigeons. Leviticus 12:8 allows this instead of a lamb, since not everyone could afford a lamb (showing the poverty and humility of Joseph and Mary). And yet no lamb was necessary because already here at forty days old, Jesus is the Lamb brought to His temple for sacrifice. Simeon's Nunc Dimittis is a beautiful example of the immediate response to this inauguration of God's consolation and redemption in the Christ Child. Speaking to Mary, Simeon also prophesies about the destiny of the Child.

Meditation

Paul is nearing the end of his earthly life. Soon he will be martyred for proclaiming Christ. He writes to Titus, the pastor on the island of Crete, to encourage and strengthen him in his ministry.

Paul's words revolve around two major themes: teaching and Christian living. Titus is encouraged to teach in accord with sound doctrine. He is to sharply rebuke those who are teaching contrary to the truth, particularly those of the circumcision party who were insisting on circumcision's necessity for salvation. Titus must not tolerate false doctrine in the Church; he must silence all heresy.

In conjunction with the teaching of the word in its truth and purity, the overseers are to adorn their office with godly lives. Paul charges Titus to appoint elders in every city, pastors who will preach, teach, baptize, and commune God's people. However, not any warm body will do. Candidates are to be above reproach and the husband of but one wife. They are to be lovers of good, self-controlled, upright, holy, and disciplined.

The qualifications for pastors have not changed. God wants those whom He has called into the ministry to powerfully proclaim God's Word in its truth, not compromising the Word to appease itching ears or to grow the membership roster. Pastors are to call a sin a sin, expose false doctrine and rebuke those who teach it, and proclaim the precious Gospel of Christ crucified and risen. Additionally, they are to exemplify a godly life as faithful husbands and fathers and in their conversations with those both inside and outside of the Church.

Obviously, not all of the Cretan Christians appreciated when their pastor rebuked them for their sin or false teaching, and likewise the message of pastors is not always well received by the flock today. Those called to be under-shepherds of the Good Shepherd, God promises to give you the strength to fulfill your calling even in the midst of opposition. He will sustain you even when the words you speak are not eagerly received or believed. For those in the pews, God helps you to believe that what you hear from the pulpit is not man's ideas or thoughts, but the very word of God—words of Law and Gospel, judgment and mercy—spoken to you through His servant. Your pastor brings Christ to you as He speaks the Lord's word and places in your mouth His body and blood.

3 FEBRUARY

Psalmody: Psalm 47:1–9
Additional Psalm: Psalm 135
Old Testament Reading: Zechariah 14:1–21
New Testament Reading: Titus 2:7—3:15

Prayer of the Day

O Lord, we pray that Your grace may always go before and follow after us, that we may continually be given to all good works; through Jesus Christ, Your Son, our Lord, who lives and reigns with You and the Holy Spirit, one God, now and forever. (H76)

Meditation

"Be ready for every good work" (Titus 3:1b). These good works include respect and obedience to authorities. Even as Paul is about to face death at the hands of the Roman government, he urges the Christians on the island of Crete to be submissive and obedient to the governing authorities. Slaves are to obey their masters even as we are to respect and honor our employers. Living a godly life also includes avoiding sin—speaking evil of no one, avoiding foolish controversies, and those who cause division within the Church. Good works even include warning those who teach false doctrine, and if they persist in their lies, removing them from the fellowship of the Church.

God calls all Christians to be ready for every good work, and we are ready for these good works because of the work God has done for us and in us. In goodness and loving kindness, He sent Jesus to save us from our sin. In mercy, He cleansed us through Baptism, the washing of regeneration and renewal by the Holy Spirit. He justified us not because of our righteous works but as a result of His Son's righteousness so that we are now heirs of eternal life.

God has worked and continues His good work in us, and the result is we do good works.

God serves us, and we serve others. Christ willingly submitted Himself to death on the cross, so we gladly submit to those who are in authority over us. Or do we? Are we ready for every good work? Do we honor and obey government leaders, or are we quick to complain and belittle our elected officials? At work, do we respect our supervisors and employers and seek to please them, or are we quick to grumble and be subversive?

Our good works adorn the doctrine of God our Savior (Titus 2:10b). Yet often our works do the opposite. Instead of adorning the true doctrine, our unloving and sinful works cloud the good work God has done for all people through His Son, Jesus. Despite our sin, God continues to work His good work in us, forgiving our iniquities, empowering us to do good in our various vocations, and opening our eyes to see the many opportunities to serve Him by serving others. God has worked in us, and He continues to work in us until His work is brought to completion on the day of our Lord Jesus Christ.

4 FEBRUARY

Psalmody: Psalm 127:1–5
Additional Psalm: Psalm 128
Old Testament Reading: Job 1:1–22
New Testament Reading: John 1:1–18

Prayer of the Day

Almighty and everlasting God, who governs all things in heaven and on earth, mercifully hear the prayers of Your people and grant us Your peace through all our days; through Jesus Christ, Your Son, our Lord, who lives and reigns with You and the Holy Spirit, one God, now and forever. (L14)

Meditation

We live in a world filled with words.

Which word could be before time began? Only an eternal Word. What word is both with God and is God? Only a divine Word. Which word is able to be a He, a person who was present in the beginning with God? Only a fleshly Word. What word could be the only fountain from which all created things have flowed? Only an almighty Word. Which word is it that is both the reservoir and spring of life that is such a light of men that darkness cannot overcome it? Only a living Word. What word has witnesses about it? Only the revealing Word. Which word is it that comes to its own, but is not received by its own? Only the loving Word. What word is it that when received and believed in, gives the right to the believer to become a child of God, born only of God? Only the gracious Word alone. Which word is it that became flesh and dwelt among us? Only a humble Word. What word could possibly show forth the glory as of the only Son of God, full of grace and truth? The only-begotten Word from eternity. Which word has such fullness from which we all continuously receive grace upon grace? Only the crucified Word. What word is the means by which we receive and are blessed by grace and truth? Only Jesus Christ, Son of God and Son of Man.

This begs the question, what type of Word is this?

Unlike all the other words that may be found in creation, this Word presented in these first verses of the Gospel is performative. It is a Word that when spoken, does what is spoken. What reveals its performative nature better than what it did at creation. "And God said, "Let . . . and it was so" (Genesis 1). The Word's performative nature is at work in the new creation as well. "So faith comes from hearing, and hearing through the Word of Christ" (Romans 10:17). This is reflected in John the Baptist's commission to be a witness of this

Word, a testifier of this Word, so that all might believe through this Word.

In all that this performative Word does, it does so according to its two natures: Law and Gospel. While both of these two natures are the Word, each performs uniquely according to their nature when spoken. The Word of Law performs curbing, convicting, and condemning of sin and guidance in the human heart. The Word of Gospel performs forgiveness, reconciliation, rebirth, and eternal life of the person.

5 FEBRUARY

Jacob (Israel), Patriarch

Psalmody: Psalm 31:1–2, 23–24
Additional Psalm: Psalm 88
Old Testament Reading: Job 2:1–3:10
New Testament Reading: John 1:19–34

Prayer of the Day

Lord Jesus, scepter that rises out of Jacob, Lamb of God who takes away the sin of the world, rule our hearts through Your suffering cross and forgive us our sins, that we may become partakers of Your divine life; for You live and reign with the Father and the Holy Spirit, one God, now and forever. (1140)

Jacob (Israel), Patriarch

Jacob, the third of the three Hebrew patriarchs, was the younger of the twin sons of Isaac and Rebekah. After wrestling with the Angel of the Lord, Jacob, whose name means "deceiver," was renamed Israel, which means "he strives with God" (Genesis 25:26; 32:28). His family life was filled with trouble, caused by his acts of deception toward his father and his brother, Esau, and his parental favoritism toward his son Joseph. Much of his adult life was spent grieving over the death of his beloved wife Rachel and the presumed death of Joseph, who had been appointed by the Egyptian Pharaoh to be in charge of food distribution during a time of famine in the land. Prior to Jacob's death, through the blessing of his sons, God gave the promise that the Messiah would come through the line of Jacob's fourth son, Judah (Genesis 49).

Meditation

Who would John be without "this purpose"? He would likely not be someone the Jews would send priests and Levites all the way from Jerusalem to find out about. He would likely not be someone others would mistake for the Christ, Elijah, or a prophet. Very likely his name would not be recorded in Scriptures. In addition, he definitely would not be a person to whom the prophetic Word of the Lord came (Luke 3:3).

What would John be without "this purpose"? He would not be "the voice crying out in the wilderness, 'make straight the way of the Lord.'" He would not be a baptizer of repentant Jews? He would not be the prophet who proclaimed, "Behold, the Lamb of God, who takes away the sin of the world." He would not be a witness, testifying "I saw the Spirit descend from heaven like a dove, and it remained on him."

Where would John be without "this purpose"? He would likely not be out in the wilderness where there was scarcity of food and clothing. He would likely not be in Bethany giving testimony about the one who was to come after him. He would likely not be knee-deep in the waters of the Jordan.

"This purpose" was a fountain out of which flowed God's relationship to John, whom He called, and Christ's relationship to him whom He would save. From it flowed His relationship to those around him who did not know the One who stood among them. From this fountain also flowed John's vocation of believer, teacher, preacher, baptizer, catechizer, revealer, prophet, and more.

In all that "this purpose" gave to John, in all that God did through John and in all that were blessed by John, none of it could save John from who, what, and where he was conceived. John was a sinner. Like the rest of us, he was conceived and born an enemy of God. Nothing in John's divinely given purpose could save himself from himself. He, like the rest of the world would need the same Lamb of God to take away his sins.

John fulfilled "this purpose" by bearing witness to the new mightier Baptizer, who baptizes us all with the Holy Spirit and with fire (Luke 3:16). Who, what, and where are we in this baptismal purpose—the saved, the doers of good works, and in Christ.

6 FEBRUARY

Psalmody: Psalm 77:1–3, 7–12, 15
Additional Psalm: Psalm 74
Old Testament Reading: Job 3:11–26
New Testament Reading: John 1:35–51

Prayer of the Day

Almighty God, by Your grace the apostle Andrew obeyed the call of Your Son to be a disciple. Grant us also to follow the same Lord Jesus Christ in heart and life, who lives and reigns with You and the Holy Spirit, one God, now and forever. (F01)

Meditation

What is it that brings a person to Christ? What is it that creates the following of Christ? What is it that makes us want to be with Christ?

Andrew and John were standing with John the Baptist, watching the people go by. There is no coming after Jesus until John speaks the Word to them, "Behold, the Lamb of God!" There is no following of Jesus until He speaks the invitation to them, "Come and you will see." There is no remaining with Jesus until He speaks with them for a day.

Simon was doing whatever it was Simon was doing. There is no coming to Jesus until Andrew speaks the Word given to him, "We have found the Messiah." There is no following with Jesus, no want to be with Him until Jesus tells Simon, "You shall be called Cephas."

Like Simon, Philip was doing whatever it was Philip was doing. There is no coming to Jesus until Jesus comes to him. There is no following, no want to be with Jesus until Jesus tells Philip, "Follow Me."

Nathanael was under a fig tree, sitting or standing we don't know. There was no coming to Jesus until Philip told him that they had found "of whom Moses in the Law and also the prophets wrote, Jesus of Nazareth," and spoke the invitation to him to "come and see." There is no remaining with Jesus until He begins to speak of Nathanael and tell him that He saw him under the fig tree.

Through this spoken Word, the Holy Spirit called them and they were brought to Jesus, He worked in them and they followed Jesus, and He created in them a longing to be with Jesus. Through the spoken Word, the Holy Spirit worked faith in them so that they might see more than Jesus, they might see the Christ that He was.

The common thing that brought these five to Jesus, created the following of Jesus, and made them want to be with Jesus was the spoken Word. Through this Word they would see Jacob's ladder between heaven and earth replaced with a human ladder. The flesh and blood of the Son of Man would be rungs of this ladder that was affixed to a cross.

As there is no Jesus apart from the spoken Word, so also there is no faith apart from it, no

disciple of Jesus apart from the spoken Word, and no path of discipleship in Jesus apart from the spoken Word.

7 February

Psalmody: Psalm 4:1–8
Additional Psalm: Psalm 18
Old Testament Reading: Job 4:1–21
New Testament Reading: John 2:1–12

Prayer of the Day

Almighty God, You created man and woman and joined them together in holy marriage, thereby reflecting the mystical union between Christ and His bride, the Church. By Your infinite goodness, let Your blessing rest upon all husbands and wives, that they may live together in Your glory in this life and with joy may come to everlasting life; through Jesus Christ, our Lord, who lives and reigns with You and the Holy Spirit, one God, now and forever. (530)

Meditation

There is a wedding. Something is amiss. Something is not the way it should be. As the events of this wedding unfold we learn they have run out of wine, and this should not be.

Then suddenly something else runs amiss, something else suddenly becomes as it should not be. Mary does not ask Jesus to do anything about their lack of wine; she simply tells Him about it. By telling Jesus of it, she makes Him responsible for it.

His question to her is a respectful form of rebuke, like the question Jesus asked the man in the crowd who wanted Him to make his brother divide the inheritance with him (Luke 12:14). Mary, like the man, sought to make Jesus responsible for more than His Father had given Him. In this way, both seek to have Jesus run amiss of the mission and ministry His Father had given Him.

Despite the impropriety of trying to make Him responsible for such a simple thing, Jesus takes responsibility for their lack and their need. Why? Why does He assume this responsibility Mary had given Him while not assuming the one from the man in the crowd (Luke 12:14)?

First, because it was a responsibility given to Him by His mother. He who faithfully honored His heavenly Father would do no less for His earthly mother. Second, because it afforded and accomplished the purpose of feeding and nurturing the faith of His fledgling disciples.

So what were they given to feed their faith upon? Notice how Jesus accomplishes the miracle of changing the water into wine. He does not touch the water or come close to it. He only speaks. By His Word, Jesus takes responsibility for more than just the lack of wine. By His Word, the disciples learn that Jesus has taken responsibility for the servants getting the water, the water jars, the water they put in the jars, the servants giving of the water now made wine to the master, the master's confession of it being the best, and the enjoyment everyone had in drinking it.

Here Jesus fed and nurtured their faith in His Word so that they might believe that in everything He speaks, He makes Himself responsible for what He speaks, whether it is at His hour on the cross, our hour in Baptism, or the hour of feasting on His flesh and blood.

8 FEBRUARY

Psalmody: Psalm 69:1–4, 8–9, 24, 29–30
Additional Psalm: Psalm 122
Old Testament Reading: Job 5:1–27
New Testament Reading: John 2:13–25

Prayer of the Day

O God, whose glory it is always to have mercy, be gracious to all who have gone astray from Your ways and bring them again with penitent hearts and steadfast faith to embrace and hold fast the unchangeable truth of Your Word; through Jesus Christ, Your Son, our Lord, who lives and reigns with You and the Holy Spirit, one God, now and forever. (L25)

Meditation

As you read through this account of what Jesus does in the temple, is it just a matter of Jesus cleansing the temple or is Jesus doing much, much more?

Temple life had become consumed with the commercial business of monetary transactions that facilitated the people's participation in the spiritual business of the Mosaic Law. The disciples see in Jesus' actions that He has a zeal for the true and faithful purpose of God's house, which should consume any Old Testament saint.

There is even more than zeal at work in His actions. Jesus has returned to the house that He declared as a boy to be His Father's house. Now He returns as the Son of the Owner. As such, His actions testify to the fact that He has taken possession of His Father's house. Having judged it to be consumed with a business other than what His Father built it for, He executes His judgment on those who have pirated its places and purpose.

How do the Jews respond? Note that they don't argue or dispute what He has done. Why not send a detachment of the temple guards to escort Him out? Any interference done in God's name for the sake of reform or restoration of religious life in Israel was afforded the office of prophet. Everything Jesus does has the earmarks of an Old Testament prophet. They do not dispute that such acts are permissible, but they want some prophetic credentials that give Jesus the right to say and do such things. This request is not without merit as these events take place in the beginning of Jesus' ministry. His miracles to date have been few and likely distant from Jerusalem.

Jesus' response to the Jews request for a sign reveals that He has done more than taken ownership of His Father's house—He has become His Father's house, the place in which God's glory dwells. At no time did this glory dwell more fully in the house of Christ than when it was founded on the cross. On the cross, the glory of God's grace for mankind met the glory of God's Law against mankind in the house of Christ's body. In three days a glorious body was raised in which people may come and buy food without money.

In Holy Baptism, the Lord raises up a temple of the Holy Spirit in the house of our sinful bodies. The food for this temple is found in the flesh and blood of Christ and the bread of His Word.

9 FEBRUARY

Psalmody: Psalm 23:1–5
Additional Psalm: Psalm 87
Old Testament Reading: Job 6:1–13
New Testament Reading: John 3:1–21

Prayer of the Day

O God, You see that of ourselves we have no strength. By Your mighty power defend us from all adversities that may happen to the body and from all evil thoughts that may assault and hurt the soul; through Jesus Christ, Your Son, our Lord, who lives and reigns with You and the Holy Spirit, one God, now and forever. (L24)

Meditation

Has there ever been a bigger barrier to learning what we do not know than these two words: "We know" (John 3:2)? Has there ever been a greater hindrance to faith than these two words?

By stating that he and others know that Jesus has come from God, Nicodemus said something else. In dealing with Jesus according to what he and others know, Nicodemus is stating his belief that Jesus, His mission, and His teaching will fit within the confines of what he knows and his ability to know.

But what happens? Once Nicodemus utters these words, nothing Jesus says fits with what he knows or his way of knowing. His challenge to Jesus' word that one needs to be born of the water and the Spirit to see and enter the kingdom of God is all but a demand that Jesus restate things so that they fit within the confines of what he knows.

Jesus takes Nicodemus from the limitations of his knowing to faith in God and His Son. Such faith is not in what I know or my knowing, but in God, who is all-knowing and whose thoughts are not bound by our thoughts. Such is our faith in God, who is almighty and whose ways are not bound by our ways (Isaiah 55).

To make this clear, Jesus takes Nicodemus to what He knows by the Old Testament Scriptures concerning the bronze serpent. With this word, Jesus reveals that faith alone, that is the work of God alone, was the only way the people could look at a bronze serpent and be saved from the poison and power of living serpents that had bitten them.

Jesus pushes Nicodemus to understand that God's ways and Word are driven by His love for His fallen creation. So great is His love and the work that the Law demands, that it could only be given to the Son He gave in love.

Jesus contrasts the difference between faith and knowing when He speaks of people's love of darkness. Knowing turns to darkness because they know of its ability to keep others and even myself from seeing or knowing about the real, the sinful me. The faith that Jesus calls for means that I let the light come to me, expose me, and save me. Living by darkness, I live to not see what is there. Living by faith in Christ, I live to see what is there—the works of God in the blood of Jesus cleansing me from all unrighteousness.

10 FEBRUARY

(If Ash Wednesday, skip to page 68.)

Silas, Fellow Worker of St. Peter and St. Paul

Psalmody: Psalm 38:1–3, 9–11, 21–22
Additional Psalm: Psalm 38
Old Testament Reading: Job 6:14–30
New Testament Reading: John 3:22–4:6

Prayer of the Day

Almighty and everlasting God, Your servant Silas preached the Gospel alongside the apostles Peter and Paul to the peoples of Asia Minor, Greece, and Macedonia. We give You thanks for raising up in this and every land evangelists and heralds of Your kingdom, that the Church may continue to proclaim the unsearchable riches of our Savior, Jesus Christ, who lives and reigns with you and the Holy Spirit, one God, now and for ever. (1142)

Silas, Fellow Worker of St. Peter and St. Paul
Silas, a leader in the church at Jerusalem, was chosen by Paul (Acts 15:40) to accompany him on his second missionary journey from Antioch to Asia Minor and Macedonia. Silas, also known as Silvanus, was imprisoned with Paul in Philippi and experienced the riots in Thessalonica and Berea. After rejoining Paul in Corinth, Silas apparently remained there for an extended time. Sometime later he apparently joined the apostle Peter, likely serving as Peter's secretary (1 Peter 5:12). Tradition says that Silas was the first bishop at Corinth.

Meditation
"A person cannot receive even one thing unless it is given him from heaven" (John 3:27). By this response is John speaking fatalistic or faith?

This is John's response to the hyperbolic statement of his disciple, "and all are going to Him." His young disciple's statement is filled with a questioning resentment that Jesus, who had received John's Baptism, that is, submitted to John, was now doing John's work and surpassing him in volume. Jesus was making disciples of people who ought to be John's disciples.

John's response is one of faith in God—Father, Son, and Holy Spirit. Sinful pride always puts things out of their God-given place and purpose. Faith, this gift and work of God in a person, always receives things where, when, and how God would give them to be. Whether it is one's purpose, one's station, one's vocation, or one's justification, faith receives these from the Lord as His gracious gifts from above.

John expresses his faith in God's station and vocation for him when he says, "You yourselves bear me witness, that I said, 'I am not the Christ, but I have been sent before Him.'"

John affirms his faith in his God-given vocation by identifying himself as the "friend of the bridegroom." He affirms the station when he says, "The one who has the bride is the bridegroom."

John affirms his faith in his need for God's gracious justification of himself, when he said, "Whoever believes in the Son has eternal life." Through faith, John receives Jesus' testimony, Jesus' Word, and by that word he knows what has been given to Jesus from above. Even as the young disciple speaks hyperbolically in saying that "all are going to Him," John knows that these are factual and truthful words.

Having confessed Jesus to be the Lamb of God who takes way the sin of the world, John believes that everyone, even himself, will be given to Jesus. He sees what he believes in that the Father has given Jesus into our flesh, has given Him under the Law in His Baptism, has given Him all our lives to live, has given Him all our sin to suffer, has given Him the wrath of God against us all for that sin, has given Him all our dying and death, and has given Him all our graves. On the cross, Jesus was given the decrease the Law of God demands of sinners, decreased to nothing. In the resurrection we find the increase that the grace of God in Jesus Christ gives to all who believe Him, grace upon grace unto eternal life.

Where does Jesus then go, but to the woman that God will give to Him at a well, so that she might receive the living water Jesus would give to her and all through faith.

11 FEBRUARY

(If Ash Wednesday, skip to page 68.)

Psalmody: Psalm 147:1–3, 6–11
Additional Psalm: Psalm 147
Old Testament Reading: Job 7:1–21
New Testament Reading: John 4:7–26

Prayer of the Day

Lord God, heavenly Father, You have called Your Church to worship Your Son in Spirit and truth. Through the Spirit of Jesus, keep us faithful to the one who is the way, the truth, and the life, so that we may be partakers of His divine life and inherit the kingdom promised for those who drink from the water of life; through Your Son, Jesus Christ, our Lord. (1143)

Meditation

He who has come to tell us all things waits for a woman to come in hopes that she will confess her truth—seeking the greater truth that Jesus freely offers.

Jesus' petition for a drink conflicts with the truth of Jewish hatred toward Samaritans that she had experienced. She petitions Jesus to explain why He is choosing to deal with a Samaritan, and a woman at that. Forgoing His physical need for water, Jesus offers this woman spiritual water, healing water, saving water, which will cleanse and refresh her soul unto eternal life.

So He offers her better water, living spiritual water. She, however, takes Jesus literally and indignantly as she hears His offer as a denigration of the well now made sacred by the long ages it has served the descendents of Jacob. Jesus stands by His offer by differentiating what their difference could do. The effects of her water were temporal, while His would refresh the soul eternally.

Jesus has the water of life for her soul, and He wants her to drink of it. So He moves into the truth of her soul, the truth that brings her to the well at midday by telling her to go and get her husband. Blocked by a mindset of always having to focus on a literal presentation of reality, and also by the need to keep her "personal" distance, she tries to prevent His entry into the truth of her soul, claiming she has no husband.

At this point, Jesus passes through the deep well of her soul and hauls out the stagnant water of her marry-go-round relationships. He zeroes in on the truth of her parched life and soul for which there has been no well to dip from, no water to refresh and restore life.

Perceiving that Jesus is a prophet, wanting this water He offers, but still wanting to move the subject off of her personally, she shoots for a tangent of where should she worship, on the mountain or in Jerusalem?

Jesus tells her that one receives this water of life only in spirit and truth. He moves her beyond the element of a mere well. By this, Jesus states that one receives the water of life through faith (spirit) in the Word of God (truth). With His words "I who speak to you am He," Jesus tells her and everyone where to get this living water.

On the cross, Christ suffered the parchedness we rightly deserve in sin, confessing, "I thirst" (John 19:28). On that same cross, a fountain was opened in His side and from it flowed water to refresh the soul unto eternal life and blood to cleanse our sins away.

12 FEBRUARY

(If Ash Wednesday, skip to page 68.)

Psalmody: Psalm 71:1–6, 17–18
Additional Psalm: Psalm 99
Old Testament Reading: Job 8:1–22
New Testament Reading: John 4:27–45

Prayer of the Day

Lord Jesus Christ, Savior of the world, help us ever to seek You and to seek others for You, that Your harvest may be full, and we may join those from every tribe and nation at the heavenly feast where You live and reign with the Father and the Holy Spirit, one God, now and forever. (1144)

Meditation

The woman had confessed the faith of the Samaritans in what the Messiah would do when she told Jesus, "When He [Messiah] comes, He will tell us all things" (John 4:25). She had given her testimony as to what Jesus had done while with her. Her testimony brought the people to Jesus to hear His testimony. As the apostle John relayed, "So when the Samaritans came to Him, they asked Him to stay with them, and He stayed there two days. And many more believed because of His word. They said to the woman, 'It is no longer because of what you said that we believe, for we have heard for ourselves, and we know that this is indeed the Savior of the world'" (John 4:40–42).

Though grateful for the testimony of the woman, they make it plain that having heard Jesus' Word, they have been raised up from the speculation her testimony had created, to the certainty of faith that only His Word can give. Besides His works, His testimony—His Word—would be the only standard by which they would know if Jesus was the Messiah, and the woman hinted He might be.

So they come to Him, and seeing them, Jesus treats this as a time of sowing; when His Word is sown, it soon also becomes a time of harvest. Jesus sees the harvest and begins to reap in their fields as He stays with them for two days. In these days His Word is as seed and sickle—sowing the seed of the Gospel that faith might be raised up and souls harvested unto eternal life.

Notice that the disciples were as caught up in maintaining Jesus' physical needs in John 4:31, perhaps even more than the woman had been in attending to His thirst when she first came to the well. Unlike these Samaritans, the disciples were not tuning in to Jesus' words as possibly ones uttered by the Messiah, but as the words of anyone else who was thirsty or hungry. They did not envision the people coming out to Him as those who hungered and thirsted for righteousness, but treated them according to "surface" standards—as a woman, as Samaritans, a people group deemed and often "written off" as unfaithful "half-breeds" who had abandoned the true worship of God.

"I have food to eat that you do not know about," Jesus tells the disciples in John 4:32. Such was the food that Jesus consumed. His nourishment came from doing the will of His Father; in turn, in being the Living Word, He served as the Living Revelation of His Father to all people. For Jesus knew as He confessed to Satan, as He faced great hunger after fasting for 40 days, that "Man shall not live by bread alone, but by every word that comes from the mouth of God." (Matthew 4:4).

By this Word that Jesus spoke to them, the Samaritans came to know Him as the Messiah. The Samaritans were indeed a "forsaken" people. Yet Jesus identified with them. As an example to His disciples then and now, He personally presented Himself to even one deemed an outcast among outcasts—this woman at the well.

"My God, my God, why have You forsaken Me?" On the cross Jesus speaks the seven phrases that only the Messiah would say in harvesting us from the wrath of God and harvest of death. In citing Psalm 22:1, He speaks one of these phrases. As such, Jesus did more than to testify to a forsaken people; He became a forsaken person on that cross!

13 FEBRUARY

(If Ash Wednesday, skip to page 68.)

Aquila, Priscilla, Apollos

Psalmody: Psalm 95:1–7a
Additional Psalm: Psalm 70
Old Testament Reading: Job 9:1–35
New Testament Reading: John 4:46–54

Prayer of the Day

Triune God, whose very name is holy, teach us to be faithful hearers and learners of Your Word, fervent in the Spirit as Apollos was, that we may teach it correctly against those who have been led astray into falsehood and error and that we might follow the example of Aquila and Priscilla for the good of the Church You established here and entrusted into our humble care; for You, O Father, Son, and Holy Spirit, live and reign, one God, now and forever. (1144)

Aquila, Priscilla, Apollos

Aquila and his wife, Priscilla (Prisca), Jewish contemporaries of St. Paul, traveled widely. Because of persecution in Rome, they went to Corinth where they met the apostle Paul, who joined them in their trade of tentmaking (Acts 18:1–3). In turn, they joined Paul in his mission of proclaiming the Christian Gospel. The couple later traveled with Paul from Corinth to Ephesus (Acts 18:18), where the two of them established a home that served as hospitality headquarters for new converts to Christianity. Apollos was one of their numerous Jewish pupils in the faith. An eloquent man, Apollos "being fervent in spirit . . . spoke and taught accurately the things concerning Jesus" (Acts 18:25). He later traveled from Corinth to the province of Achaia, "showing by the Scriptures that the Christ was Jesus" (Acts 18:28). Aquila, Priscilla, and Apollos are all remembered and honored for their great missionary zeal.

Meditation

What is the purpose in knowing the hour? An official in Capernaum has a son who is ill. He has heard of Jesus and what He had done. Now, having heard that He had come into Galilee, the man ventures out in faith to get Jesus and bring Him back to touch and to heal his son. Jesus, however, does not applaud this man's faith, but rather chastises him and others who have such a faith.

What kind of faith did this man have, that was good enough to bring him to Jesus, but not good enough for Jesus? This man's faith is as the faith of those who went in search of Jesus after He has multiplied the loaves. He chastised them as well when He said, "Truly, truly, I say to you, you are seeking Me, not because you saw signs, but because you ate your fill of the loaves. Do not labor for the food that perishes, but for the food that endures to eternal life, which the Son of Man will give to you" (John 6:26–27). Jesus chastised the man because he sought out Jesus for merely an earthly need and not the desperate need of his own lethally sin-sick heart.

To move the man beyond such faith, Jesus sends the man back to his son with nothing but His Word that the boy will live. Therefore, the man goes back, believing Jesus' Word that his son will live. But what will he tell his wife, what will he tell the rest of his family when he gets back? "Where is He? Didn't you find Him? Why didn't He come with you?" The only response is the one Jesus gave him, gave to his dying son, "I found Jesus. He complained about my faith, and then He sent me back with only His word that our son would live." But before he has a chance to figure out what and how to tell his family what Jesus said, he experiences what Jesus said, as his servant tells him his son will live.

His question as to the hour and the answer move the man's faith from the earthly miracle Jesus might do to the blessed power of Jesus' Word and what it could do. Based upon this Word, the man knows what he shall say to his family, and by that Word given to him, he and his whole household are brought to saving faith in Jesus.

14 FEBRUARY

(If Ash Wednesday, skip to page 68.)

Valentine, Martyr

Psalmody: Psalm 119:153–160
Additional Psalm: Psalm 35
Old Testament Reading: Job 10:1–22
New Testament Reading: John 5:1–18

Prayer of the Day

Almighty and everlasting God, You kindled the flame of Your love in the heart of Your holy martyr Valentine. Grant to us, Your humble servants, a like faith and the power of love, that we who rejoice in Christ's triumph may embody His love in our lives; through Jesus Christ, our Lord, who lives and reigns with You and the Holy Spirit, one God, now and forever. (1145)

Valentine, Martyr

A physician and priest living in Rome during the rule of Emperor Claudius, Valentine became one of the noted martyrs of the third century. The commemoration of his death, which occurred in AD 270, became part of the calendar of remembrance in the Early Church of the West. Tradition suggests that on the day of his execution for his Christian faith, Valentine left a note of encouragement for a child of his jailer written on an irregularly shaped piece of paper. This greeting became a pattern for millions of written expressions of love and caring that now are the highlight of Valentine's Day in many nations.

Meditation

Who are the invalids?

Arriving in Jerusalem, Jesus attends a pool party at Bethesda. Jesus finds that many cannot get into the pool, let alone swim. Those that have gathered have done so in hopes of getting into the pool when the water began to move so that they might be healed and regain validity once again.

Jesus asks one of the long-time partyers if he wants to be healed. The man's response confesses his faith in the only means he knew of for healing. In this confession he also acknowledges that the consequences of his infirmity are such that he cannot access the healing for himself. If he is to be healed, if he is to be made valid again, it will only happen by the blessings of another doing for him what he cannot do to be healed.

Confessing the truth of his situation, Jesus speaks and moves the waters of God's grace and mercy and does for the man what he cannot do for himself. Living firmly in the validity Jesus had given him, he takes his mat and lives by the Word Jesus spoke to him.

It is here that he and we encounter a second group of invalids, not made up of the palsied but the pious. Living by Jesus' Word, this man steps in front of them on the chosen path to healing. To make themselves firm, to make themselves valid, they seek to wound this man that they might be healed. But the man will not receive their wounds or infirmity of spirit, as he confesses what Jesus said and did for him.

So great is this sin-bound infirmity of this group that it blinds them to their spiritual infirmity, and where it does not blind them to this, it definitely blinds them to their inability to heal themselves of it. This group of spiritual invalids believes their healing and validity comes by immersing themselves in the Law, which cannot heal anyone of their spiritual infirmities. According to this faith, Jesus must be gotten rid of, for His Word of healing and being the Son of God will surely empty the pool they have been immersing themselves in to validate themselves.

Nothing confessed their spiritual infirmity more than their quest to kill Jesus. Confessing this infirmity in crucifying Jesus, Jesus proceeds to do for them what they cannot do for themselves so that they might be healed through the forgiveness of their sins.

15 FEBRUARY

(If Ash Wednesday, skip to page 68.)

Philemon and Onesimus

Psalmody: Psalm 57:1–5, 8–10
Additional Psalm: Psalm 1
Old Testament Reading: Job 11:1–20
New Testament Reading: John 5:19–29

Prayer of the Day

Lord God, heavenly Father, You sent Onesimus back to Philemon as a brother in Christ, freeing him from his slavery to sin through the preaching of the apostle Paul. Cleanse the depths of sin within our souls and bid resentment cease for past offenses, that, by Your mercy, we may be reconciled to our brothers and sisters and our lives will reflect Your peace, through Jesus Christ, our Lord. (1146)

Philemon and Onesimus

Philemon was a prominent first-century Christian who owned a slave named Onesimus. Although the name Onesimus means "useful," Onesimus proved himself "useless" when he ran away from his master and perhaps even stole from him (Philemon 18). Somehow Onesimus came into contact with the apostle Paul while the latter was in prison (possibly in Rome), and through Paul's proclamation of the Gospel, he became a Christian. After confessing to the apostle that he was a runaway slave, Onesimus was directed by Paul to return to his master and become "useful" again. In order to help pave the way for Onesimus's peaceful return home, Paul sent him on his way with a letter addressed to Philemon, a letter in which he urged Philemon to forgive his slave for running away and "to receive him as you would receive me" (v. 17), "no longer as a slave but . . . as a beloved brother" (v. 16). The letter was eventually included by the Church as one of the books of the New Testament.

Meditation

How shall we consider these words of Jesus (John 5:29), lest we hear that salvation is by the good work one does?

To consider these words rightly, we need only consider what Jesus says about Himself in answer to those who object to Him making Himself equal to God. "Truly, truly I say to you, that the Son can do nothing of his own accord" (v. 19). With these words, Jesus makes it clear that everything He does is a result of what the Father has given Him. He affirms this again later in His ministry: "I am He, and . . . I do nothing on My own authority, but speak just as the Father taught Me" (John 8:28). Everything Jesus does, He does according to what the Father has given Him, and He does all things in accord with how the Father does things.

Inasmuch as all the good that the Son of God has done and the good way He has done it is from God the Father, there can be no other way by which any created person might do good. Any good that you or anyone else may do is at best an echo of the good that the Son has done to us, in us, and for us. Any good that we might do is the result of the good that God has wrought in us through faith in Jesus Christ.

To hear these words aright, we again hear more of Jesus' Word spoken just prior to these. "Whoever hears My word and believes Him who sent Me has eternal life. He does not come into judgment, but has passed from death to life" (v. 24). By these words Jesus has made it clear that resurrection to life comes through faith, not works. Jesus goes on to make it clear that such faith is not the work of man, but the work of His Word.

So different, so divine, so living, so Jesus is the Word that He speaks that it accomplishes the purpose for which He speaks it (Isaiah 55:6). As Jesus speaks, the Word is spoken, it resurrects the soul in time, and will resurrect the flesh at the end of time when He speaks again.

How shall we consider these words? As the work of the Word made flesh for us, the work of the Word crucified for us, the work of the Word resurrected for us, and the work of the Word even now interceding for us at the right hand of God the Father.

16 FEBRUARY

(If Ash Wednesday, skip to page 68.)

Philip Melanchthon (birth), Confessor

Psalmody: Psalm 91:1–6, 14–16
Additional Psalm: Psalm 119:1–8
Old Testament Reading: Job 12:1–6, 12–25
New Testament Reading: John 5:30–47

Prayer of the Day

Almighty God, we praise You for the service of Philip Melanchthon to the one, holy, catholic, and apostolic Church in the renewal of its life in fidelity to Your Word and promise. Raise up in these gray and latter days faithful teachers and pastors, inspired by Your Spirit, whose voices will give strength to Your Church and proclaim the ongoing reality of Your kingdom; through Your Son, Jesus Christ our Lord. (1147)

Philip Melanchthon, Confessor (birth date)

Philip Melanchthon (1497–1560) was a brilliant student of the classics and a humanist scholar. In 1518, he was appointed to teach along with Martin Luther at the University of Wittenberg. At Luther's urging, Melanchthon began teaching theology and Scripture in addition to his courses in classical studies. In April 1530, Emperor Charles V called an official meeting between the representatives of Lutheranism and Roman Catholicism, hoping to effect a meeting of minds between two opposing groups. Since Luther was at that time under papal excommunication and an imperial ban, Melanchthon was assigned the duty of being the chief Lutheran representative at this meeting. He is especially remembered and honored as the author of the Augsburg Confession, which was officially presented by the German princes to the emperor on June 25, 1530, as the defining document of Lutheranism within Christendom. Melanchthon died on April 19, 1560.

Meditation

Jesus says that His testimony is greater than John's and that His testimony will not be by words, but by the works the Father has given Him to accomplish.

What bears the marks of a son more than his submission to the will of his father, his doing the works of his father, his faithfully accomplishing what the father has given him charge over? The witness Jesus gives of His being sent from the Father is His willful submission to the Father's will, to what the Father does, and what the Father has given Him to accomplish.

To know and believe in Jesus and His works is to believe in what the Father has spoken of Him through the prophets, from Moses to John the Baptist. Jesus explains why the Jews refuse to receive the testimony of His works: "His voice you have not heard, His form you have never seen, and you do not have His word abiding in you." Jesus is doing exactly what the Father wills and promised in His Word. In this way, Jesus reveals that the testimony of Himself and His work is the fulfillment of

the Old Testament covenant. If one knows and believes in the covenantal promises God made, one will see and believe that Jesus and His ministry as God's keeping of those promises.

Jesus gives a name to this willful submission to the Father—He calls it the love of God. Willful submission is about choosing to be and do what the Father has chosen for you to be and do. To believe in Jesus is to believe in the works that He in love does as our prophet, our priest, and our king, for in all these is the fulfillment of what the Father has promised the Messiah would do to accomplish the salvation of the world.

To know and believe in Jesus Christ is to hear, and through that hearing to believe the Father's prophetic testimony of Him throughout the Old Testament and the living testimony Jesus offered in word and deed from His conception all the way to His bodily ascension to the right hand of the Father. In Him is the truth, the whole truth, and nothing but the truth.

17 FEBRUARY

(If Ash Wednesday, skip to page 68.)

Psalmody: Psalm 37:25–29
Additional Psalm: Psalm 77
Old Testament Reading: Job 13:1–12
New Testament Reading: John 6:1–21

Prayer of the Day

Merciful Father, You gave Your Son Jesus as the heavenly bread of life. Grant us faith to feast on Him in Your Word and Sacraments that we may be nourished unto life everlasting; through the same Jesus Christ, our Lord, who lives and reigns with You and the Holy Spirit, one God, now and forever. (B71)

Meditation

What would Jesus do? What He does in feeding the five thousand, He does again to the disciples on the lake in the middle of the night.

Seeing the growing crowd, Jesus asks Philip, "Where are we to buy bread so that these people may eat?" By this question Jesus makes all these people guests for whom He and the apostles were responsible for.

Philip immediately does a quick check on bread and announces that treating that many people as guests would far exceed the budget they are living on. Andrew quickly informs Jesus that the cupboard is all but bear, thus making it impossible for them to host so many. Both men had forgotten what happened when Jesus was asked to be the host at the wedding in Cana, where as host, He provided the best wine from water.

Jesus knew that He would be host to the dietary needs of the hungering people, even as He had been host to their physical needs in making them well. Serving as host of the feast, Jesus proceeds to feed His five thousand guests with what cannot feed five. So great is the power of His hospitality that the disciples picked up enough leftovers to feed five hundred or more.

This same hospitality is at work as He walks on the water. The disciples have gone down to their boat, to take it across their lake, under their control, the way they always have. Suddenly their boat, their way, on their lake, and under their control cannot get them where they want to go. Jesus comes walking on the water. They are scared until they hear Him say, "It is I; don't be afraid." Hearing that it was Jesus, "Then they were glad to take Him into their boat." Why were they glad to have Jesus get in the boat? Surely, by being their guest He would by His hospitality help them to do what they could not do, get their boat across their lake, His way.

Jesus' mission was to be the gracious host to all mankind, that by His hospitality He might save us who cannot save ourselves, that He might give us forgiveness of God from what was God's wrath, life with God from what is our death. Such a gracious host Jesus is to all who will believe in Him and His hospitality of grace and mercy.

18 FEBRUARY

(If Ash Wednesday, skip to page 68.)

Martin Luther, Doctor and Confessor

Psalmody: Psalm 105:1, 23, 37–43
Additional Psalm: Psalm 105
Old Testament Reading: Job 13:13–28
New Testament Reading: John 6:22–40

Prayer of the Day

O God, our refuge and our strength, You raised up Your servant Martin Luther to reform and renew Your Church in the light of Your living Word, Jesus Christ, our Lord. Defend and purify the Church in our own day, and grant that we may boldly proclaim Christ's faithfulness unto death and His vindicating resurrection, which You made known to Your servant Martin through Jesus Christ, our Savior, who lives and reigns with You and the Holy Spirit, one God, now and for ever. (1148)

Martin Luther, Doctor and Confessor

Martin Luther, born on November 10, 1483, in Eisleben, Germany, initially began studies leading toward a degree in law. However, after a close encounter with death, he switched to the study of theology, entered an Augustinian monastery, was ordained a priest in 1505, and received a doctorate in theology in 1512. As a professor at the newly established University of Wittenberg, Luther's scriptural studies led him to question many of the Church's teachings and practices, especially the selling of indulgences. His refusal to back down from his convictions resulted in his excommunication in 1521. Following a period of seclusion at the Wartburg castle, Luther returned to Wittenberg, where he spent the rest of his life preaching and teaching, translating the Scriptures, and writing hymns and numerous theological treatises. He is remembered and honored for his lifelong emphasis on the biblical truth that for Christ's sake God declares us righteous by grace through faith alone. He died on February 18, 1546, while visiting the town of his birth.

Meditation

There is bread and there is bread, but what makes bread "the bread of life"?

The bread that Jesus used to feed the five thousand was made of barley, and this bread satisfied the need of their bodies for a time. Time had passed, and that bread could no longer satisfy bodily need. So they come seeking Jesus for more of this bread and what it will do for them. Inasmuch as this bread is of the earth, its blessings cannot endure even in this earthly life.

Jesus tells them to seek a different kind of bread, a bread that endures to eternal life, a bread that is a person who has comes down from God in heaven, a bread that gives life to the world, a bread that brings resurrection, a bread that He has come to give them. Upon hearing of the effects of eating this bread, the people ask that Jesus give them this bread always.

Jesus replies with specificity to their request, "I am the bread of life; whoever comes to Me shall not hunger, and whoever believes in Me shall never thirst." Using "I am," Jesus states

that He is the bread that God has made from the seeds God had sown in the Old Testament covenant. In saying, "I am the bread of life," Jesus states that He is and will always be actively present for the purpose of being "the bread of life." This bread is not "a" bread among other breads, but "the" bread, and that there is no other.

What are the ingredients in this bread of life? Jesus' perfect doing of God the Father's will and the keeping of all those the Father has given Him. Inasmuch as Jesus has both these ingredients in Him as the Bread of Life, it is also filled with the blessed ingredients of the perfectly lived life, the perfect suffering for sin, the perfect satisfaction for sin, the perfect death of sin and death, and the resurrection over all these unto eternal life.

Unlike all other breads that are eaten of the mouth and the body, the Bread of Life is eaten of the soul through faith in Jesus, the bread of life. The work by which one may obtain the bread of life is also of faith. The having of such faith is the beneficent effect of having the bread of life offered to us.

19 February

(If Ash Wednesday, skip to page 68.)

Psalmody: Psalm 53:1–6
Additional Psalm: Psalm 30
Old Testament Reading: Job 14:1–22
New Testament Reading: John 6:41–59

Prayer of the Day

Gracious Father, Your blessed Son came down from heaven to be the true bread that gives life to the world. Grant that Christ, the bread of life, may live in us and we in Him, who lives and reigns with You and the Holy Spirit, one God, now and forever. (B72)

Meditation

"The bread that I will give for the life of the world is My flesh" (John 6:51). Yes, this bread came down from heaven; this bread is bread from God the Father. Yes, he who eats of this bread receives eternal life. Yes, to eat this bread is to believe in Jesus Christ. In these words, Jesus reveals the one ingredient in Himself, the bread of life, that will satisfy the spiritual hunger and need of every human soul is the cursed death He died on the cross.

As God the Father sent Jesus to be food and drink for us, to satisfy our hunger and our need for God, He also sent Jesus to satisfy the hunger and need of His justice upon our sins. We know that God the Father consumed Jesus' body and blood as we hear Jesus cry out, "My God, My God, why have You forsaken Me" (Mark 15:34). If one would know that the Father's hunger was satisfied, we need only hear Jesus say, "It is finished" (John 19:30). As the living Father sent Jesus to die and resurrected Him to live forever, all who feast upon Him, that is believe in Him, will live forever because of Him.

Can we have a "light" bread of life? Yes. Many offer "light," "earth friendly," or "reason friendly" bread of life varieties. The problem with these bread-of-life varieties is that none of them are "the" bread of life because they do not include the key ingredient of the cross. Such bread of life varieties are made of nothing more than the pig-food pods the prodigal son longed to fill his stomach with. As such, anyone who eats of these shall not have eternal life.

To eat of Jesus' flesh and drink of His blood is to receive what His flesh and His blood have accomplished for us according to the will of the Father. Having defined eating and drinking as faith, Jesus also defines the coming to eat and drink as faith too. Such believing comes through hearing and learning from the Father, the Word of God.

Jesus assures that through our spiritual eating and drinking of His flesh and blood, which is our believing in Him, we will abide in Him and He in us.

20 FEBRUARY

(If Ash Wednesday, skip to page 68.)

Psalmody: Psalm 16:1, 4–6, 9–11
Additional Psalm: Psalm 90
Old Testament Reading: Job 15:1–23, 30–35
New Testament Reading: John 6:60–71

Prayer of the Day

Almighty God, whom to know is everlasting life, grant us to know Your Son, Jesus, to be the way, the truth, and the life, that we may steadfastly follow His steps in the way that leads to life eternal; through Jesus Christ, our Lord, who lives and reigns with You and the Holy Spirit, one God, now and forever. (B73)

Meditation

The English states far less than what Jesus asks the grumblers in the Greek. Jesus' literal question is, "Does this trap you?" What Jesus is asking is, "Does what I have said about Myself so entrap you that if you are to continue with Me, your own way of seeing and knowing with Me will have to die?"

For the entrapped, Jesus had gone too far, making life dependent upon Himself and participation in His flesh and blood, especially flesh and blood that will suffer and die. To make eternal life dependent upon Him was one thing, but to then say that eternal life is dependent upon someone who cannot save their own flesh and blood made what He said too much for them and many others. Jesus knew what was going on in their hearts and mind: "For us to continue with You according to what you say would be the entrapment, and therefore the kill of our thinking and reason. Thus Your words catch us to the point that it kills our faith in You, and we're not sure if we should follow You." And many of His disciples did turn back.

Before they turn back, Jesus leaves no doubt who He is, what He is, and where He came from. "Then what if you see the Son of Man ascending to where He was before?" He made it clear to them that He, the Man who stood before them, was the Bread of Life that has come down out of heaven to give His flesh and blood for the life of the world.

Having laid it out clearly with this question, Jesus then tells them that if they want life, that is eternal life, it would come from the Spirit, not from the flesh, not from what the flesh could do, not from what their fleshly mind could grasp. It is almost as if Jesus was saying to them, "Yes, your thinking and reasoning are going to have to die. These things are bound by the flesh. If you are going to come to Me, follow Me, eat of My flesh and drink of My blood, you will have to do it by believing in Me and My Word."

With their thinking and reasoning held captive and dead to the Word of Christ, they continue with Him by faith as they confess, "You are the Holy One of God."

21 FEBRUARY

(If Ash Wednesday, skip to page 68.)

Psalmody: Psalm 84:1–4, 8–12
Additional Psalm: Psalm 64
Old Testament Reading: Job 16:1–22
New Testament Reading: John 7:1–13

Prayer of the Day

Lord Jesus Christ, Your time has come, for You have traveled to Jerusalem for the Passover from death to life. Help us to live knowing that the time of our redemption is at hand as You continue to dwell among us at the feast of Your very body and blood, a foretaste of the feast to come; for You live and reign with the Father and the Holy Spirit, one God, now and forever. (1149)

Meditation

How will Jesus show Himself to the world? The brothers of His earthly family are as yet unaware of whom and what Jesus really is. These brothers have heard what Jesus has said of Himself and what He has done. Now whether they are taunting Him or seeking to have Him advance an earthly agenda for their possible earthly gain, we don't know. Either way, they don't understand the why and the how of Jesus conducting ministry in Galilee of all places.

They clearly had heard enough of what Jesus has said to conclude that if He were of such stature, then He needed to be revealing that stature on a larger stage. This is Galilee of the Gentiles, and what Jewish leader would confine His ministry to this place? Jerusalem was the best stage, and the Feast of Booths was prime time to show and prove who and what He was. Jesus does not reject the need for Him to show Himself in Jerusalem. He does, however, reject the timing.

Jesus sends His brothers up to the feast because it was a time for them to show themselves for what they were, sons of Abraham who celebrated the thanksgiving feast to God for Israel's passage through the wilderness. Jesus would be going with them to publically participate in the festival.

Jesus then goes up to the festival privately, for if He shows Himself publicly, it will arouse the hatred of the Jews and alter the timing God had for Him to show Himself to the world. Also, by going privately He can show Himself less confrontationally to individuals through His teaching in the temple and the tabernacles, or booths, they had set up as their dwellings for the festival.

Six months later, Jesus showed Himself in His entry into Jerusalem the week of Passover. During the Passover, when both the Jews and Gentiles sought to get rid of Him on the cross and hide Him in a tomb, Jesus showed Himself to the world for whom and what He was.

On the cross Jesus showed Himself as the One on whom God laid the sins of the world, the death of the world, so that He might bear these away and with them the wrath of God. And then in His resurrection, God the Father showed the world who and what Jesus is—the One who overcomes the world.

22 FEBRUARY

(If Ash Wednesday, skip to page 68.)

Psalmody: Psalm 25:15–22
Additional Psalm: Psalm 114
Old Testament Reading: Job 17:1–16
New Testament Reading: John 7:14–31

Prayer of the Day

O God, on this day You once taught the hearts of Your faithful people by sending them the light of Your Holy Spirit. Grant us in our day by the same Spirit to have a right understanding in all things and evermore to rejoice in His holy consolation; through Jesus Christ, Your Son, our Lord, who lives and reigns with You and the Holy Spirit, one God, now and forever. (L50)

Meditation

What is it that makes for right judgment? The Jews had judged Jesus to be learned. The text says that they marveled, that is, they were astonished at this teaching to the point of offense. Their offensive astonishment came from the fact that He was so learned without having received such learning from them! Their question about such learning without study is not an inquiry but a judgment upon Jesus' teaching as incompetent groping for personal glory.

Jesus responds by telling them how to judge His teaching rightly. He says in so many words: "Start with the standard that's right, the will of God." In stating that they were not doing the will of God, He condemns everything they are doing in the name of Moses. His follow-up question then lays all their plotting in the light of the Law for all to see that which the leaders were planning to do in the name of Moses, albeit contrary to Moses.

The Jewish leaders judge Jesus to have a demon because He healed the man beside the pool of Bethesda on the Sabbath. Jesus takes them to circumcision, which by Mosaic Law is rightly observed on the Sabbath. Circumcision marked one as God's chosen, to whom belonged the merciful promises of God according to His covenant. Right judgment would see the healing of a man on the Sabbath not as a violation of the Commandment, but as the exercise of the Sabbath rest on the man. The carrying of His mat on that Sabbath day of His healing would not render injury of God's Law, but rather serve as an announcement that He was the living fulfillment of God's promise. Righteous judgment further says according to Mosaic Law that Jesus did not reject the Law, yet He did reject the teachings and traditions that the elders had added to the Law.

Again, the Jews judged Jesus to be lacking in being the Christ, for they knew where He came from. He tells them that to judge rightly as to where He came from, they would have to know the Father who sent Him. Inasmuch as they do not know the Father or His Law, no way exists for them to know His place of origination. Thus, they wanted to arrest Him. Yet the Father held them in check as the time had not yet come for Him to be the Christ Crucified.

23 February

(If Ash Wednesday, skip to page 68.)

Polycarp of Smyrna, Pastor and Martyr

Psalmody: Psalm 42:1–6a, 9–11
Additional Psalm: Psalm 52
Old Testament Reading: Job 18:1–21
New Testament Reading: John 7:32–53

Prayer of the Day

O God, the maker of heaven and earth, You gave boldness to confess Jesus Christ as King and Savior and steadfastness to die for the faith to Your venerable servant, the holy and gentle Polycarp. Grant us grace to follow his example in sharing the cup of Christ's suffering so that we may also share in His glorious resurrection; through Jesus Christ, our Lord, who lives and reigns with You and the Holy Spirit, one God, now and forever. (1150)

Polycarp of Smyrna, Pastor and Martyr
Born around AD 69, Polycarp was a central figure in the Early Church. A disciple of the evangelist John, he linked the first generation of believers to later Christians. After serving for many years as bishop of Smyrna, Polycarp was arrested, tried, and executed for his faith on February 23, in AD 155 or 156. An eyewitness narrative of his death, the martyrdom of Polycarp continues to encourage believers in times of persecution.

Meditation
What Jesus has taught and done among the people has liberated their faith, their hopes, and their lips to speak of Jesus as the Messiah. Being so arrested to their own traditions, the chief priests and Pharisees see a need to arrest the people's faith, hope, and their lips. To do this they must arrest their liberator.

Seeing those who would arrest Him, Jesus declares that He shall not be arrested by anyone, as He will soon return to the one who sent Him.

Then Jesus arrests those who have sought to arrest Him, both the officers and those who sent them, and He puts them into the hand of judgment. In saying that they shall seek Him and not find Him, and that where He is going they cannot come, Jesus states that their seeking will come too late. Their seeking and wanting to be where He is will be as the foolish virgins (Matthew 25:1–13). So arrested are they in sin that they have barred themselves from understanding His words.

Then on the great day of the feast, the Jewish year is arrested. Jesus offers all a liberal abundance of living water that shall never be arrested, and when drank through faith, His Spirit shall set at liberty such an abundance that shall flow by way of rivers that carry the good works that God has prepared in advance for them to do (Ephesians 2:10).

Some receive Jesus' Word and confess their liberation by naming Him the Christ. Others confess Him to be a prophet. And others are so arrested by their ignorance of where Christ has come from that they reject His liberty.

Those who were to arrest Jesus return liberated by His Word from the charge given them. So arrested were the chief priests and the Pharisees in their sin of unbelief that they condemned the very people they were to have compassion on, they condemned one of their own for calling them to deal justly with Jesus, and they ignored the fact that Jonah came from Galilee near Nazareth.

Jesus would be arrested, but even this happened according to His liberty—He allowed them to take hold of Him so that He might arrest, take hold of them and all sinful mankind, and forever arrest sin, death, the wrath of God. By His arrest, He arrests the arrested in sin and gives them the liberty of God's grace through faith.

24 FEBRUARY

(If Ash Wednesday, skip to page 68.)

St. Matthias, Apostle

Psalmody: Psalm 30:1–5, 8–12
Additional Psalm: Psalm 22
Old Testament Reading: Job 19:1–12, 21–27
New Testament Reading: John 8:1–20

Prayer of the Day

Almighty God, You chose Your servant Matthias to be numbered among the Twelve. Grant that Your Church, ever preserved from false teachers, may be taught and guided by faithful and true pastors; through Jesus Christ, our Lord, who lives and reigns with You and the Holy Spirit, one God, now and forever. (F13)

St. Matthias, Apostle

St. Matthias is one of the lesser-known apostles. According to the Early Church Fathers, Matthias was one of the seventy-two sent out by Jesus in Luke 10:1–20. After the ascension, Matthias was chosen by lot to fill the vacancy in the Twelve resulting from the death of Judas Iscariot (Acts 1:16–25). Early Church tradition places Matthias in a number of locations. Some historians suggest that he went to Ethiopia; others place him in Armenia, the first nation to adopt Christianity as a national religion. Martyred for his faith, Matthias may well have met his death at Colchis in Asia Minor, around the year AD 50. The Church of St. Matthias at Trier, Germany, claims the honor of being the final burial site for Matthias, the only one of the Twelve to be buried in Europe north of the Alps.

Meditation

You have to wonder where he is. That this woman is guilty of adultery is clear enough. John says in verse 4 that she has been "caught in the act." But there also has to be a "him." However, the man is nowhere to be found as the scribes and Pharisees drag this woman before a crowd to convict her. Such action is in sharp contrast to Old Testament Law that demands, "If a man commits adultery with the wife of his neighbor, both the adulterer and the adulteress shall surely be put to death" (Leviticus 20:10). We see the adulteress. But where is the adulterer?

The scribes and Pharisees, for all the lip service they pay to the Law of Moses (cf. v. 5), are not truly concerned with Moses' mandates. Rather, their intent is "to test [Jesus], that they might have some charge to bring against Him" (v. 6). And test Him they do. For if Jesus refuses to admit that this woman should be executed, He could be charged with disobeying Mosaic Law. Yet, if He calls for her death, He could be reported to the government for sanctioning an execution in contradiction to Roman law. And the religious leaders are not about to let Jesus weasel out of their test. They ask Him point blank: "So what do You say" (v. 5)? The Greek here is emphatic and might be translated, "You! What do You say?"

Jesus doesn't say a thing. Instead, He quietly bends down and writes in the dusty terrain of the Judean soil. Finally, after what must have been a deafening silence, Jesus renders His verdict: "Let him who is without sin among you be the first to throw a stone at her" (v. 7).

Notably, Jesus does not deny this woman's sin. Nor does He sanction or excuse it. Jesus, as "the light of the world" (v. 12) does not do such things, for His "light shines in the darkness" (John 1:5) of sin, revealing it in all its ugliness. Jesus does, however, forgive this woman's sin. "Neither do I condemn you," He says (v. 11).

We never do find out where he is. But we do finally learn where this woman is. She is with Jesus. And there is no better place to be. For with Jesus, there is forgiveness of sin. May we, like this woman, be "be found in [Christ], not having a righteousness of our own that comes from the Law, but that which comes through faith in Christ" (Philippians 3:9).

25 FEBRUARY

(If Ash Wednesday, skip to page 68.)

Psalmody: Psalm 112:1–10
Additional Psalm: Psalm 119:57–64
Old Testament Reading: Job 20:1–23, 29
New Testament Reading: John 8:21–38

Prayer of the Day

Almighty and gracious Lord, pour out Your Holy Spirit on Your faithful people. Keep us steadfast in Your grace and truth, protect and deliver us in times of temptation, defend us against all enemies, and grant to Your Church Your saving peace; through Jesus Christ, Your Son, our Lord, who lives and reigns with You and the Holy Spirit, one God, now and forever. (F33)

Meditation
The prophet Isaiah soberly expresses the breadth and depth of human sinfulness when he confesses before his God, "For our transgressions are multiplied before You, and our sins testify against us" (Isaiah 59:12).

Such an affirmation concerning the profusion of human sinfulness makes Jesus' warning in John 8:21 appear curious: "I am going away, and you will seek Me, and you will die in your sin." Notice that the word "sin" is singular. Jesus warns that some will die, not in their many sins, but in a particular sin. With so many sins from which to choose—for we all sin much—to which sin is Jesus referring?

Jesus explains: "Unless you believe that I am He you will die in your sins" (v. 24). The singular sin to which Jesus refers in verse 21 is the sin of unbelief. And this sin leads a person to die not only in one sin, but in many sins. The one sin of unbelief results in condemnation for all sins.

But it need not be this way. Jesus has come to forgive this sin—and all sins. He offers such forgiveness when He is "lifted up" (v. 28), John's indirect way to refer to Christ's crucifixion. Jesus is calling all people to believe in His death and resurrection so that they might not die in sin and sins, but rather live as His redeemed children.

Jesus' warning against unbelief and call to faith does not return void. The evangelist records, "As He was saying these things, many believed in Him" (v. 30). Blessedly, we too are included among John's "many," for we too trust in Christ. And this means that no matter how many sins we multiply before God, He forgives them all.

It is a safe bet to say that we have not sinned just once. We have sinned and will continue to sin. But it is also a safe bet to declare that Christ forgives our multiple sins, even as St. Paul happily says: "Where sin increased, grace abounded all the more" (Romans 5:20). And so we can rejoice that God's grace is sufficient for us, for His power of salvation is made perfect, even in the midst of our weakness of sin (cf. 2 Corinthians 12:9). And indeed it is. For the cross of Christ covers not just one sin or some sins, but all sins.

26 FEBRUARY

(If Ash Wednesday, skip to page 68.)

Psalmody: Psalm 3:1–8
Additional Psalm: Psalm 119:73–80
Old Testament Reading: Job 21:1–21
New Testament Reading: John 8:39–59

Prayer of the Day

Almighty and everlasting God, You have given us grace to acknowledge the glory of the eternal Trinity by the confession of a true faith and to worship the Unity in the power of the Divine Majesty. Keep us steadfast in this faith and defend us from all adversities; for You, O Father, Son, and Holy Spirit, live and reign, one God, now and forever. (L52)

Meditation

"The apple doesn't fall far from the tree." The earliest recorded instance of this old saying comes to us via pastor Johannes Mathesius, who used it in a sermon in 1554. But long before it was a pithy proverb, it was a devastating indictment, leveled by Jesus at His pharisaical opponents in John 8:44: "You are of your father the devil, and your will is to do your father's desires. He was a murderer from the beginning." Jesus charges, "The apple doesn't fall far from the tree. And your tree, O Pharisees, is the tree of the evil one. For just as your father Satan sought to bring death into the world by tempting Adam to break My Father's command and eat of the fruit of the tree of knowledge, you seek to bring death to Me by killing Me on the tree of the cross." Of course, the Pharisees don't see themselves as Satan's spawn. "Abraham is our father," they protest (v. 39). They then claim, "We have one Father—even God" (v. 41). In fact, the Pharisees become so incredulous at Jesus' accusation against them that they go so far as to question Jesus' spirituality and sanity: "Are we not right in saying that You are a Samaritan and have a demon" (v. 48)? But for all their protests, these religious leaders still manage to live up to Jesus' characterization of them as murderers. For when Jesus proclaims His relationship to Abraham and announces, "Truly, truly, I say to you, before Abraham was, I am," they pick up stones to throw at Him (vv. 58–59). They try to murder the Son of God.

In the final analysis, the Pharisees were preoccupied with to whom they were related. "We are offspring of Abraham," they clamorously claim (v. 33). Jesus, however, was focused on to whom the Pharisees belonged. "You are of [belong to] your father, the devil," He thunders (John 8:44). Genetic relatedness to Abraham does not mechanically secure membership in the family of God.

In our baptismal liturgy, we are called upon to renounce the devil, his works, and his ways. Why is this? Because in Baptism, we are "called to belong to Jesus Christ" (Romans 1:6). No matter to whom we are genetically related, whether our family tree be shameful or stately, as God's baptized children, there is no question to whom we belong: we belong to Jesus. And in this we can take great comfort.

27 FEBRUARY

(If Ash Wednesday, skip to page 68.)

Psalmody: Psalm 146:5–10
Additional Psalm: Psalm 119:89–96
Old Testament Reading: Job 30:16–31
New Testament Reading: John 9:1–23

Prayer of the Day

Almighty God, our heavenly Father, Your mercies are new every morning; and though we deserve only punishment, You receive us as Your children and provide for all our needs of body and soul. Grant that we may heartily acknowledge Your merciful goodness, give thanks for all Your benefits, and serve You in willing obedience; through Jesus Christ, Your Son, our Lord, who lives and reigns with You and the Holy Spirit, one God, now and forever. (L26)

Meditation

Our justice system declares, "If you do the crime, you do the time!" Crime and punishment go hand in hand in our society. In first-century society, too, crime and punishment went hand in hand—not only in the system of human justice, but in the system of divine justice. Just as man could punish man for his sins, sometimes using ghastly means, God could punish man for his sins, sometimes using devastating means. Indeed, the ancient rabbis taught that if a person was suffering, such suffering was punishment from God, pointing to some sin. The Jewish leaders taught that it was justified that a person could be punished not only for his own sins, but for the sins of his parents as well!

It is this view of crime and punishment that forms the backdrop for the disciples' question of Jesus upon encountering a blind man. "Rabbi," the disciples ask, "Who sinned, this man or his parents, that he was born blind" (John 9:2)? Jesus' disciples appear to be coaxing Him into settling a dispute between those rabbis who taught that a person could suffer for his parents' sins and others who maintained that a person would suffer only for his own sins. Jesus, however, rather than mediating this tired quarrel, responds, "It was not that this man sinned, or his parents, but that the works of God might be displayed in him" (v. 3). This man's suffering is not the result of this or that sin. Rather, God is up to something in this man's suffering. He is redeeming it so that He can display His work.

The Greek word for "display" is phanero'o, from the word phos, meaning "light." God, it seems, desires to bring this man darkened by blindness into the light of sight so that others, seeing his healing, might believe in God's Light of the world, Jesus Christ. And so Jesus heals this man. After making a mudpack for his eyes using His own saliva, Jesus instructs this blind man to wash it off at a pool. And the blind man sees (cf. v. 7).

As with the blind man, through us, God desires to display His works, His Word, and His mercy to others. As the apostle Paul writes of himself, "But I received mercy for this reason, that in me, as the foremost, Jesus Christ might display His perfect patience as an example to those who were to believe in Him for eternal life" (1 Timothy 1:16). May we be people through whom God displays His Gospel!

28 FEBRUARY

(If Ash Wednesday, skip to page 68.)

Psalmody: Psalm 66:8–12, 16–20
Additional Psalm: Psalm 119:169–176
Old Testament Reading: Job 31:1–12, 33–40
New Testament Reading: John 9:24–41

Prayer of the Day

Lord God, heavenly Father, as Your Son gave sight to the blind man, giving him eyes to the one who is the healer of the nations, so give us sight to see the salvation prepared for us in Him who opens our eyes in the breaking of the bread; through the same Jesus Christ, our Lord. (1151)

Meditation

The Pharisees must have been shocked by what they overheard. After the religious leaders run off a blind man who has been healed by Jesus because of his testimony about Jesus, he is found to be with Jesus. And Jesus asks, "Do you believe in the Son of Man?" The man responds, "Lord, I believe" (vv. 35, 37). But the Pharisees, who are not far away, overhear every word. And so they also hear Jesus' judgment against them: "For judgment I came into this world, that those who do not see may see, and those who see may become blind" (v. 39). The religious leaders cannot remain silent at such an indictment. They interrupt Jesus, asking, "Are we also blind" (v. 40)?

In Greek, the first word of the Pharisees' question to Jesus is *mae*, meaning "not." The Pharisees answer their own question before they ask it! A rendering of their question might read, "We're not blind, too, are we?" They refuse to believe they have anything less than unfettered spiritual clairvoyance.

Author John Godfrey Saxe is perhaps best known for his famed poem, "The Blind Men and the Elephant." In this elegy, Saxe bemoans the arrogance of six blind men who each have hold of a different part of an elephant. One believes it to be a wall as he touches the elephant's side; another believes it to be a spear as he touches its tusk; another believes it to be a snake while holding the mastodon's trunk. Saxe uses this as an allegory to critique

religious belief and to claim that no one religious system has transcendent truth. The irony of Saxe's critique, of course, is that Saxe himself claims to see the elephant and know what it truly is! Like the Pharisees, Saxe claims to see and refuses to accept his own blindness.

Jesus says of His ministry, "The Spirit of the Lord is upon Me, because He has anointed Me to proclaim good news to the poor. He has sent Me to proclaim liberty to the captives and recovering of sight to the blind" (Luke 4:18). Only Jesus can open our eyes to the things of God. Reliance on our own spiritual sight and insight just won't do, for every human eye has been blinded by sin. But with Christ, the eyes of our hearts are enlightened and we can know the hope to which we have been called and the glorious inheritance which we share (cf. Ephesians 1:18).

29 FEBRUARY

(If Ash Wednesday, skip to page 68.)

Psalmody: Psalm 23:1–6
Additional Psalm: Psalm 120
Old Testament Reading: Job 32:1–22
New Testament Reading: John 10:1–21

Prayer of the Day

Almighty God, merciful Father, since You have wakened from death the Shepherd of Your sheep, grant us Your Holy Spirit that when we hear the voice of our Shepherd we may know Him who calls us each by name and follow where He leads; through the same Jesus Christ, Your Son, our Lord, who lives and reigns with You and the Holy Spirit, one God, now and forever. (L43)

Meditation

Metaphors can be treacherous. Yes, they can add color and life to writing and speaking, but they can also be confusing, especially if you mix your metaphors. This seems to be the difficulty in John 10 as Jesus presents an extended metaphor of a Shepherd and His sheep. John comments on the confusion over Jesus' metaphor: "This figure of speech Jesus used with them, but they did not understand what He was saying to them" (v. 6). And this confusion is not surprising. After all, Jesus is mixing His metaphors.

"I am the door of the sheep," Jesus begins (v. 7). "I am the Good Shepherd," Jesus says just verses later (v. 11). Which one is it? Is Jesus the door for the sheep or the Shepherd of the sheep? Actually, He's both. As Jesus will later teach His disciples: "I am the way, and the truth, and the life. No one comes to the Father except through Me" (John 14:6). If one desires eternal life, he must go through Jesus, the door to salvation. But Jesus is not just the door to salvation, He is also the embodiment of words spoken by King David over one thousand years earlier: "The Lord is my shepherd; I shall not want" (Psalm 23:1). Jesus, the Lord, is the Shepherd of God's people. Then again, not only is Jesus the door for the sheep and the Shepherd of the sheep, He also is a sheep, as John the Baptist testifies: "Behold, the Lamb of God" (John 1:36)!

Why would Jesus mix His metaphors? The apostle Paul offers a clue: "Christ is all, and in all" (Colossians 3:11). Christ is all. That's a lot. And that means that Christ's person and work are so comprehensive that no one metaphor can cover everything. So get ready for a lot of metaphors to describe all that Christ is and has done. He is the door to salvation. He is the Shepherd of us sheep. And He is the Lamb of God.

For all of Jesus' metaphors, this much He states in baldly un-metaphorical terms: "The Good Shepherd lays down His life for the sheep" (v. 11). Again, "I lay down My life for the sheep" (v. 13). And then, "I lay down My life . . . I lay it down of My own accord . . . I have authority to lay it down" (vv. 17–18). Jesus wants us to know unambiguously that He, as God's Good Shepherd, lays down His life for us. And that's no metaphor—that's His mission. And that's our salvation.

1 MARCH

(If Ash Wednesday, skip to page 68.)

Psalmody: Psalm 82:1–8
Additional Psalm: Psalm 140
Old Testament Reading: Job 33:1–18
New Testament Reading: John 10:22–42

Prayer of the Day

Almighty and ever-living God, You fulfilled Your promise by sending the gift of the Holy Spirit to unite disciples of all nations in the cross and resurrection of Your Son, Jesus Christ. By the preaching of the Gospel spread this gift to the ends of the earth; through the same Jesus Christ, our Lord, who lives and reigns with You and the Holy Spirit, one God, now and forever. (L49)

Meditation

"Hear, O Israel: The Lord our God, the Lord are one." Wait. Check that: "The Lord is one" (Deuteronomy 6:4). In the midst of a religiously pluralistic world, this was Israel's foundational assertion of faith: there is only one God. In the words of Exodus 15:11: "Who is like You, O Lord, among the gods? Who is like You, majestic in holiness, awesome in glorious deeds, doing wonders?" The answer to this question, of course, is "No one." There is only one God. But perhaps the plural verb "are" in Deuteronomy 6:4 might be theologically appropriate, even if it's grammatically obtuse.

The Hebrew word for "one" in Deuteronomy 6:4 is *echad*, which denotes not bare numerical oneness, but singularity in essence, character, and intention. Indeed, echad can be used to describe oneness even when there is more than one! Take, for instance, God's command concerning marriage: "A man shall leave his father and his mother and hold fast to his wife, and they shall become one flesh" (Genesis 2:24). The Hebrew word for "one" is echad. Two persons—one marriage.

Theologically, oneness in marriage is a reflection of oneness in God. Although God is one, there is more to God's oneness than first meets the eye. A strange plurality continuously sneaks into God's singularity. "Let Us make man in Our image, after Our likeness," God declares at creation (Genesis 1:26). The one God uses a plural pronoun of Himself. Ancient Jewish rabbis noted the tripartite structure of Deuteronomy 6:4's confession of God: "The Lord . . . our God . . . the Lord." God is one, yet there is more to know of God than that.

In John 10, Jesus reveals the mystery of God's echad. "I and the Father are one," He declares (v. 30). With these words, Jesus alludes to Deuteronomy 6:4, except that Deuteronomy's "is" becomes Jesus' "are" as He carefully delineates the plurality of persons in the unity of the Godhead. He and the Father are echad.

How do those listening to Jesus' revelation concerning God's echad respond? "The Jews picked up stones again to stone Him" (v. 31). They scathingly accuse Jesus of blasphemy, saying, "You, being a man, make Yourself God" (v. 33). But Jesus didn't make Himself God. Jesus is God. He, along with the Father and Spirit, is God. Or is that "are God"? Three persons—one God. "Is" and "are." This is the

mystery of the Trinity. And so we worship in this name—in the name of the Father, and of the Son, and of the Holy Spirit. Amen.

2 MARCH

(If Ash Wednesday, skip to page 68.)

Psalmody: Psalm 116:1–9
Additional Psalm: Psalm 119:49–56
Old Testament Reading: Job 33:19—34:9
New Testament Reading: John 11:1–16

Prayer of the Day

O God, Your Son shines with the brightness of the true Light. Grant that as we have known the mysteries of that Light on earth we may also come to the fullness of His joys in heaven; through the same Jesus Christ, Your Son, our Lord, who lives and reigns with You and the Holy Spirit, one God, now and forever. (1152)

Meditation

King David lamented, "I walk through the valley of the shadow of death" (Psalm 23:4). Part of what makes the twenty-third Psalm so beloved is its universality. We all can relate to passing through valleys of death. When a marriage cracks under the weight of betrayal, that couple passes through a valley of death. When a parent agonizes over the decisions and life choices made by a son or daughter, those parents pass through a valley of death. When a person is diagnosed with a terminal illness, he passes through a valley of death.

It is this final case that sets the scene for John 11. The chapter opens: "Now a certain man was ill, Lazarus of Bethany" (v. 1). We are not told the nature of Lazarus's illness, but it is dire enough that Jesus hears of it. And Jesus' comments on Lazarus's state are striking: "This illness does not lead to death" (v. 4). The preposition is important. The Greek word for "to" is *pros*, denoting an endpoint, goal, or destination. The grave, Jesus says, is not Lazarus's destiny. However, Lazarus's illness does serve a purpose: "It is for the glory of God, so that the Son of God may be glorified through it." The Greek word for "through" is *dia*, related to our English word "diameter." Lazarus's illness, then, is not an end, but a means through which God will be glorified. Lazarus's illness is not a "to" infirmity, but a "through" one. Lazarus must pass through the valley of death.

Tragically, Lazarus dies. But Jesus' announcement of the death seems understated: "Our friend Lazarus," Jesus says to His disciples, "has fallen asleep" (v. 11). "Lazarus is only taking a nap," Jesus says. How can He make such an audacious claim? Because Jesus then raises Lazarus from death. He calls to His friend, "Lazarus, come out" (v. 43), and Lazarus walks forth from his tomb.

Lazarus's resurrection is a foretaste of our resurrections on the Last Day. Though we walk through valleys of death in this world, death is not our final destination. As John later writes, "We know that we have passed out of death into life" (1 John 3:14). Again, the preposition is important; we are not just headed to life, we are already in it. We have already received life in Christ through His Word, Baptism, and Communion. Salvation has already arrived. And rest assured that God's salvation is not something we pass through, it is something we are brought to. It is our endpoint, goal, and destination. Praise be to God!

3 March

(If Ash Wednesday, skip to page 68.)

Psalmody: Psalm 116:12–19
Additional Psalm: Psalm 138
Old Testament Reading: Job 34:10–33
New Testament Reading: John 11:17–37

Prayer of the Day

Almighty God, by Your great goodness mercifully look upon Your people that we may be governed and preserved evermore in body and soul; through Jesus Christ, Your Son, our Lord, who lives and reigns with You and the Holy Spirit, one God, now and forever. (L27)

Meditation

Funerals are terrible affairs. Losing a loved one invokes sorrow rarely felt in life. Such is the case at Lazarus's funeral. Lazarus's sisters, Mary and Martha, are grieving deeply. And like at most funerals, many come "to console them concerning their brother" (v. 19). I can only imagine what was said. Perhaps it was standard funeral fare. "He's in a better place now," one might have waxed. Or, "At least he's not in pain in anymore." But such pious platitudes do little to salve the sorrow death brings.

Then, Martha spots the one man who could have brought real relief to her abyss of grief. Coming down the road, Martha sees Jesus. And Martha decides she needs to have a word with Jesus concerning His absence in their time of need. So she rushes to Him and says, "Lord, if You had been here, my brother would not have died" (v. 21). Jesus responds, "Your brother will rise again" (v. 23). "Oh great," Martha must be thinking, "another pious platitude." And so she answers, "I know that he will rise again in the resurrection on the Last Day" (v. 23).

One pious platitude deserves another. Jesus speaks of the resurrection of Lazarus and Martha responds, "Yes, yes, that's fine and good. He'll rise again on the Last Day. Everyone knows that. But that doesn't help me now." But Martha misunderstands Jesus. Jesus is not in the business of doling out insipidities that might be helpful some day. Jesus continues, "I am the resurrection and the life" (v. 25). Jesus takes the future tense promise of the Last Day's resurrection and brings it into the present: "I am the resurrection and the life. Death has been put on notice. I am here to bring life!"

When I was in grade school, if one of us misbehaved, my teacher would write his or her name on the board to put that student on notice that a behavior needed correction. If the bad behavior continued, my teacher would add check marks behind that name. One check mark equaled a missed recess. Two check marks equaled staying after class. And after three check marks, you were out to the principal's office.

In John 11, death is put on notice. And later, after three days, it is out. Christ conquers death by His resurrection. As Paul writes, "Death is swallowed up in victory . . . Thanks be to God, Who gives us the victory through our Lord Jesus Christ" (1 Corinthians 15:54, 57)!

4 MARCH

(If Ash Wednesday, skip to page 68.)

Psalmody: Psalm 2:1–6, 10–12
Additional Psalm: Psalm 83
Old Testament Reading: Job 36:1–21
New Testament Reading: John 11:38–57

Prayer of the Day

Lord Jesus Christ, You raised Lazarus from the dead, giving us a glimpse of Your glorious resurrection, where You showed us what we will someday be and what we already are now through the waters of Holy Baptism. Even in the darkest hours of our lives, let the light of Your resurrection shine with the brightness of Your glory; for You live and reign with the Father and the Holy Spirit, one God, now and forever. (1153)

Meditation

When Jesus raises His voice, the dead are raised. So it was with Lazarus. In John 11, the evangelist notes that Lazarus has been dead for four days (cf. v. 39). This is no arbitrary detail. Many Jews believed a person's soul hung around its body for three days, hoping to reanimate the deceased. But now, it has been four days. Now, Lazarus's soul has taken flight. But a soul can never fly beyond the reach of Christ's command. And so, Jesus raises His voice and cries out "with a loud voice, 'Lazarus, come out' " (v. 43)! And Lazarus comes forth from his grave. When Jesus raises His voice, the dead are raised.

But not everyone is pleased with Jesus' loud voice. The chief priests and Pharisees complain, "This man performs many signs. If we let Him go on like this, everyone will believe in Him" (vv. 47–48). Their concern, of course, is none other than Satan's concern—that everyone will believe in Jesus! And so the religious leaders, under the influence of the evil one, hatch a plan "to put Him to death" (v. 53).

But then, something happens for which the religious leaders never bargained. What Jesus did at Lazarus's tomb, He does again on the cross. As Luke records: "It was now about the sixth hour, and there was darkness over the whole land until the ninth hour, while the sun's light failed . . .Then Jesus, calling out with a loud voice, said, 'Father, into Your hands I commit My spirit' " (Luke 23:44–46)! Here again is Jesus' loud voice. But this time, instead of conquering death, it introduces death: "And having said this He breathed His last" (Luke 23:46).

But Jesus' loud voice is not finished yet. Three days later, Jesus' voice roars again. And even as it has roared forth from an empty tomb, it will roar into all eternity. And all of heaven will join in loud voice to praise the One who conquered death by His loud voice. As John explains, "Then I looked, and I heard around the throne and the living creatures and the elders the voice of many angels, numbering myriads and thousands of thousands, saying with a loud voice, 'Worthy is the Lamb who was slain, to receive power and wealth and wisdom and might and honor and glory and blessing" (Revelation 5:11–12)! May we join our loud voices in praise of the One who gives us eternal life with His loud voice.

5 MARCH

(If Ash Wednesday, skip to page 68.)

Psalmody: Psalm 118:22–29
Additional Psalm: Psalm 119:41–48
Old Testament Reading: Job 37:1–24
New Testament Reading: John 12:1–19

Prayer of the Day

Almighty God, grant that in the midst of our failures and weaknesses we may be restored through the passion and intercession of Your only-begotten Son, who lives and reigns with You and the Holy Spirit, one God, now and forever. (L29)

Meditation

Quoting Scripture can be dangerous business. Not that it shouldn't be done; it's just that sometimes it is not done faithfully or well. Take, for instance, the oft-quoted axiom, "Money is the root of all evil." This is not just an axiom, of course, this is a Bible verse! Kind of. What Paul actually writes is, "The love of money is a root of all kinds of evils" (1 Timothy 6:10). Sadly, this little phrase, "the love of," is often left out when this passage is cited. But this tiny omission alters the whole meaning and intent of the apostle's warning. Paul does not think money itself is evil, but he does know that loving money breaks God's First Commandment. Loving money is tantamount to worshiping it and committing idolatry. Yes, quoting Scripture can be dangerous business.

Consider John 12. Throngs of eager crowds arrive to meet Jesus, palm branches in hand, hailing Him with a song, quoted from Psalm 118: "Hosanna! Blessed is He who comes in the name of the Lord, even the King of Israel" (v. 13)! That the crowds wave palms while they sing is no small thing. The Jews had celebrated with palms centuries earlier after the Jewish commander Judas Maccabaeus crushed the Hellenist tyrant Antiochus IV Epiphanes in the rebellion of 164 BC, thereby sealing Jewish independence. And now, palm branches appear again. Their symbolism is thick: even as Simon Maccabaeus crushed the Hellenists, Jesus will soon crush the Romans. At least, that is the hope of the crowd. And so they break out the palms.

Along with the palms, their citation of Psalm 118 also betrays an attitude of strident nationalism. They use this psalm as a battle cry. The word *Hosanna* is Hebrew for "save now!" Their request of Jesus, then, is for Him to save them now from their oppressive Roman rulers. But even as they quote the psalmist's words, they misunderstand the psalmist's intent. Psalm 118 is not about conquering Rome in order to achieve salvation. Rather, it's about Divine love so great that it moves people to receive salvation.

The psalmist opens and closes his song: "Oh give thanks to the Lord, for He is good; for His steadfast love endures forever" (Psalm 118:1, 29). It is God's steadfast love, not a people's nationalistic pride, which effects salvation. This is why Palm Sunday introduces Good Friday. It is at that cross that salvation is won. So put down your palm branches and believe in Christ's cross. There is your salvation.

6 MARCH

(If Ash Wednesday, skip to page 68.)

Psalmody: Psalm 110:1–7
Additional Psalm: Psalm 119:17–24
Old Testament Reading: Job 38:1–18
Additional Reading: Job 38:19–39:30
New Testament Reading: John 12:20–36a

Prayer of the Day

Merciful God, Your Son, Jesus Christ, was lifted high upon the cross that He might bear the sins of the world and draw all people to Himself. Grant that we who glory in His death for our redemption may faithfully heed His call to bear the cross and follow Him, who lives and reigns with You and the Holy Spirit, one God, now and forever. (F27)

Meditation

In John 12, Jesus is on His way to the cross. In the face of such a dark hour, He declares, "Now My soul is troubled" (v. 27). Jesus here quotes Psalm 6 where King David, himself in a time of trial, cries, "My soul is . . . greatly troubled" (Psalm 6:3). But even in the midst of pain, David knows he can depend on God's salvation. David prays to God, "Save me for the sake of Your steadfast love" (Psalm 6:4). But Jesus cannot quote this line of David's psalm. You don't get saved when You're the Savior. So Jesus continues, "And what shall I say? 'Father, save Me from this hour'? But for this purpose I have come to this hour" (v. 27).

Jesus' purpose is to hang on a cross— unsaved, unrighteous, unholy, and undignified. His purpose is to be condemned in our place for our sins. His purpose is not to be saved, but to save.

But the people do not understand Jesus' purpose. "We have heard from the Law that the Christ remains forever," they reply. "How can You say that the Son of Man must be lifted up" (v. 34)? The people understand that Jesus is prophesying His own execution. What they do not understand is how Jesus can be executed while also being the Messiah. After all, the Messiah "remains forever."

Though messianic expectations varied widely in this day, there was a common sentiment that the Messiah would not die. For instance, Isaiah prophesies concerning the Messiah: "For to us a Child is born, to us a Son is given; and the government shall be upon His shoulder, and His name shall be called Wonderful Counselor, Mighty God, Everlasting Father, Prince of Peace" (Isaiah 9:6). Interestingly, a Jewish targum on this verse adds that this messianic Child will live forever. The Messiah, according to the expectations of many, would not die. But here is Jesus, foretelling His death. Here is Jesus, declaring that He was born to die. Here is Jesus, inviting us to the way of the cross.

Martin Luther distinguished between two theological ways: the way of glory and the way of the cross. The way of glory expects power and exaltation. It expects a Savior who will not only save others, He will also save and exalt Himself. Conversely, the way of the cross believes that You don't get saved when

You're the Savior. You get the nail-scarred hands. You get the pierced side. You get condemnation for the world's salvation. And this Savior is our Savior.

7 MARCH

(If Ash Wednesday, skip to page 68.)

Perpetua and Felicitas, Martyrs

Psalmody: Psalm 121:1–8
Additional Psalm: Psalm 26
Old Testament Reading: Job 40:1–24
New Testament Reading: John 12:36b–50

Prayer of the Day

O God and Ruler over all our foes of body and soul, You strengthened Your servants Perpetua and Felicitas, giving them a confident and clear confession in the face of roaring beasts. Grant that we who remember their faithful martyrdom may share in their blessed assurance of victory over all earthly and spiritual enemies and hold fast to the promise of everlasting life secured for us through Jesus Christ, our Lord, who lives and reigns with You and the Holy Spirit, one God, now and forever. (1154)

Perpetua and Felicitas, Martyrs

At the beginning of the third century, the Roman emperor Septimus Severus forbade conversions to Christianity. Among those disobeying that edict were Perpetua, a young noblewoman, and her maidservant Felicitas. Both were jailed at Carthage in North Africa along with three fellow Christians. During their imprisonment, Perpetua and Felicitas witnessed to their faith with such conviction that the officer in charge became a follower of Jesus. After making arrangements for the well-being of their children, Perpetua and Felicitas were executed on March 7, 203. Tradition holds that Perpetua showed mercy to her captors by falling on a sword because they could not bear to put her to death. The story of this martyrdom has been told ever since as an encouragement to persecuted Christians.

Meditation

In John 12, Jesus has said much about His mission and ministry. But now, He has "departed and hid[den] Himself" (v. 36). And this disappearance of Jesus, says John, is a sign of God's wrath against His people. John quotes the words of Isaiah to explain: "He has blinded their eyes and hardened their heart, lest they see with their eyes, and understand with their heart, and turn, and I would heal them" (v. 40). Rather than healing for His people, God renders judgment against His people, for when Christ is concealed, the wrath of God is revealed.

Some—even some prominent authorities—believe in the revelation of God, brought in Christ (cf. v. 42). Yet, their faith is faulty because they refuse to confess it. They love "the glory that comes from man more than the glory that comes from God" (v. 43). Thus, these people, too, deserve wrath from God. They conceal their faith in the One who has come to reveal God's love.

Mercifully, even when people conceal their faith in Christ, Christ does not conceal Himself from them. By verse 44, He is already inviting people to faith once again: "Whoever believes in Me, believes not in Me but in Him Who sent Me . . . For I have not spoken on My own authority, but the Father who sent Me has Himself given Me a commandment—what to say and what to speak. And I know that His commandment is eternal life" (vv. 44,

49–50). God's desire for us, Jesus says, is not condemnation, but salvation. Indeed, God's very commandment is eternal life.

Jesus ends His public ministry with this commandment of eternal life. He then retreats privately with His disciples. The next time Jesus appears publicly is on a cross, in adherence to His Father's commandment of eternal life. It is on the cross that Jesus fulfills the requirements necessary for eternal life by dying the death we deserve. And it is on the cross that God's love is most fully revealed.

In Christ, God's love is revealed. Sadly, for far too many people, God remains concealed because they do not believe in God's Son (cf. v. 37). Pray for those who, like the crowd of John 12, refuse to trust in Jesus. And share the revelation of Christ's Gospel with them. Finally, give thanks to God that He has given you faith in Christ that, while concealing God's eternal wrath, reveals God's eternal life.

8 MARCH

(If Ash Wednesday, skip to page 68.)

Psalmody: Psalm 41:1–2, 7–13
Additional Psalm: Psalm 129
Old Testament Reading: Job 41:1–20, 31–34
New Testament Reading: John 13:1–20

Prayer of the Day

O Lord, in this wondrous Sacrament You have left us a remembrance of Your passion. Grant that we may so receive the sacred mystery of Your body and blood that the fruits of Your redemption may continually be manifest in us; for You live and reign with the Father and the Holy Spirit, one God, now and forever. (L32)

Meditation

Peter has a bad habit. He likes to boss around his Lord. In John 13, Jesus is washing His disciples' feet. But when He gets to Peter, His most heady apostle objects: "You shall never wash my feet" (v. 8). Peter believes such a menial task is beneath someone as stately as his Lord.

I can't help but think of a similar objection that Peter makes in Matthew 16 after "Jesus [begins] to show His disciples that He must go to Jerusalem and suffer many things from the elders and the chief priests and scribes, and be killed, and on the third day be raised" (Matthew 16:21). Peter rebukes his Lord: "Far be it from You, Lord! This shall never happen to You" (Matthew 16:22).

Things did not go well for Peter then. And they won't go well for Peter now. Jesus replies to Peter's objection: "If I do not wash you, you have no share with Me" (v. 8). Jesus, as the One who came to serve (cf. Mark 10:45), must serve Peter.

Of course, when given an inch, Peter takes a mile: "Lord, not my feet only but also my hands and my head" (v. 9)! But Jesus gently explains that what He does and gives is always enough and always complete: "The one who has bathed does not need to wash, except for his feet, but is completely clean" (v. 10). And then Jesus continues by exhorting His disciples: "I have given you an example, that you should also do just as I have done to you" (v. 15).

"I have given you an example." The idea that Christ would be our example has been denigrated among some. They fear that those who emphasize Christ as our example easily fall prey to spiritual snobbery as they congratulate themselves for the fine way they imitate Christ.

But notice what Christ is teaching. He is not teaching imitation toward exaltation, but imitation toward humiliation: "Truly, truly, I say to you, a servant is not greater than His

Master, nor is a messenger greater than the one who sent him" (v. 16). To imitate Christ means also to understand all the ways in which you are not Christ. Thus, for those who imitate Christ, no pats on the back are allowed for a job well done. As Christ instructs elsewhere, "When you have done everything that you were commanded, say, 'We are unworthy servants, we have only done what was our duty' " (Luke 17:10). May we rejoice in humbly imitating and serving our Lord.

9 March

(If Ash Wednesday, skip to page 68.)

Psalmody: Psalm 86:11–17
Additional Psalm: Psalm 136
Old Testament Reading: Job 42:1–17
New Testament Reading: John 13:21–38

Prayer of the Day

Merciful and everlasting God, You did not spare Your only Son but delivered Him up for us all to bear our sins on the cross. Grant that our hearts may be so fixed with steadfast faith in Him that we fear not the power of sin, death, and the devil; through the same Jesus Christ, our Lord, who lives and reigns with You and the Holy Spirit, one God, now and forever. (L31)

Meditation
Betrayals are devastating. A husband betrays a wife, and a marriage can be ruined. A citizen betrays his country, and his nation's security can be compromised. A disciple betrays his Savior, and his Lord can be crucified.

In John 13, Jesus gathers His disciples and announces, "Truly, truly, I say to you, one of you will betray Me" (v. 21). The Greek word for

"betray" is *paradidomi,* meaning "to deliver over." And this is precisely what Judas does. He comes to the chief priests and asks, "What will you give me if I deliver [Jesus] over to you" (Matthew 26:15)? And so Judas cuts a deal to deliver over his Savior for thirty pieces of silver.

Thirty pieces of silver is a paltry sum. It was the price to be paid by a bull's owner if his bull gored to death another man's slave (cf. Exodus 21:32). Judas betrays Jesus for a dead slave's ransom. Oh what a treacherous *paradidomi!*

Following Judas's delivery of Jesus to the religious leaders, Jesus' Passion continues with a series of paradidomis. The religious leaders paradidomi Jesus to Pontius Pilate: "As soon as it was morning, the chief priests held a consultation with the elders and scribes and the whole Council. And they bound Jesus and led Him away and delivered [paradidomi] Him over to Pilate" (Mark 15:1). Upon receiving Jesus, Pilate then paradidomis Jesus to a bloodthirsty crowd: "Pilate, wishing to satisfy the crowd . . . delivered [paradidomi] Him to be crucified" (Mark 15:15). Judas isn't the only betrayer in this story. Jesus is betrayed again and again on His way to the cross.

How does Jesus respond to all these paradidomis? With a paradidomi of His own! But Jesus' paradidomi is different. Whereas Judas's paradidomi was one of treachery, Jesus' paradidomi is one of salvation. The apostle Paul explains: "For I received from the Lord what I also delivered to you, that the Lord Jesus on the night when He was betrayed took bread, and when He had given thanks, He broke it, and said, 'This is My body which is for you. Do this in remembrance of Me'" (1 Corinthians 11:23–24). The Greek for "delivered" is *paradidomi.* Paul paradidomis what Jesus has first paradidomid to him: His very body and blood for the forgiveness of sin.

One paradidomi deserves another. Judas delivers his Savior to be crucified. In return, Jesus paradidomis Himself for our salvation. Oh what a glorious paradidomi!

THE TIME OF EASTER

Lenten Season

Ash Wednesday

Psalmody: Psalm 136:1–9
Additional Psalm: Psalm 90, Psalm 6
Old Testament Reading: Genesis 1:1–19
New Testament Reading: Mark 1:1–13

Prayer of the Day

Almighty and everlasting God, You despise nothing You have made and forgive the sins of all who are penitent. Create in us new and contrite hearts that lamenting our sins and acknowledging our wretchedness we may receive from You full pardon and forgiveness; through Jesus Christ, Your Son, our Lord, who lives and reigns with You and the Holy Spirit, one God, now and forever. (L22)

Lent and Ash Wednesday

During the forty days of Lent, God's baptized people cleanse their hearts through the discipline of Lent: repentance, prayer, fasting, and almsgiving. Lent is a time in which God's people prepare with joy for the Paschal Feast (Easter). It is a time in which God renews His people's zeal in faith and life. It is a time in which we pray that we may be given the fullness of grace that belongs to the children of God.

Meditation

"All . . . were going out to him" (Mark 1:5). How simple these few words, yet how descriptive of the daily path I must make in repentance and faith.

These words are my destination. I am to go "out to him," out to where he is, out to where there is a divine gift, a Baptism, a forgiveness, a kingdom laying out its boundary lines. I must go out to where he is, out into the desert, out into the place where no one lives, except the Lord, His prophet and His gift of Baptism.

But why "out" there? Pondering this, it would be well to remember that the Lord's mighty acts of salvation have always taken place—out there, outside their man-made cities and homes.

Out in the desert, out in the place where no one lives, the Lord delivered His people from Pharaoh, from starvation, from idolatry, and from their own sins by a bronze serpent. Out there, outside their city on a desolate hill is where the Lord accomplished my salvation and the salvation of all mankind.

But why out in the desert? Surely the Lord chose John's location as a messenger to me of my condition in my sin—desolate, without life. Surely this location is a revelation of my sinfulness and my total lack in this condition.

John's first going out into the desert is God's revelation that it is He who comes to me, to where I am, to what I am, and there would save me. If I would be where He is, where He calls me through John, then I must go out from the cities of illusion my sinful pride has built for me. Cities built to protect and defend me from my sin, my guilt, my desert condition.

Yet the Lord would save me not just from these illusions but also from my condition. So He calls me to repent, to turn from the illusions of my own justification, and come out into the reality of my condition in sin, for it is here alone that my God, my Savior, has come to meet me and save me.

So John calls me out, to walk in the light as He is in the light, so that I might have fellowship with John, and be cleansed of all my sin by the blood of God's Son—Jesus Christ. Amen Lord! Lead on.

THURSDAY AFTER ASH WEDNESDAY

Psalmody: Psalm 8:1–6, 9
Additional Psalm: Psalm 128, Psalm 32
Old Testament Reading: Genesis 1:20–2:3
New Testament Reading: Mark 1:14–28

Prayer of the Day

Lord Jesus, Holy One of God, You showed that the kingdom of God had come by Your healing the sick and casting out demons. Heal us in both body and soul by the medicine of immortality of Your body and blood that we may truly be Your disciples; for You live and reign with the Father and the Holy Spirit, one God, now and forever. (1001)

Meditation

The question could have been easily asked by Andrew and Simon, by James and John, and especially by Zebedee, as Jesus calls them away from their life, their livelihood: "What have you to do with us, Jesus"(Mark 1:24).

Isn't livelihood at the heart of the demon's question to Jesus? As the Holy One of God, they know Him, and He threatens their livelihood in the man they now possess. And even though they know Him, it does not stop them from assuming a higher position as evidenced by their question.

This question arises from the illusion that Jesus is beyond His bounds in dealing with them. This question challenges Jesus as having no basis for dealing with or saying anything to them. These demons make such a challenge because while they know Jesus to be the Holy One who has come to be the Messiah of mankind, they also know that Jesus has not come to be their Messiah. And if He's not going to be their Messiah, what right does He have to mess with them?

What is frightening is that I have challenged the Lord by asking this question in one form or another, when His Word calls me away from some worldly livelihood I would preserve. Don't my sinful actions challengingly state this question when I chose to do those things contrary to Him, to His Word for me?

"Have you come to destroy us?" These words confess not so much a challenge, but a pure, terrified belief that this is the one thing that Jesus could do to him. In response to this, the Holy One rebukes the demon with the words, "Be silent, and come out of him!"

As the sinner I am, I might well ask this second question too. And as I come to Jesus of Nazareth, the Holy One of God, the Messiah, He says to me, "Be silent, and come unto Me, and I will give you rest."

What destruction did the flood of Baptism ravage upon me as the Holy One of God comes to destroy me, to silence me, that I might be made alive again in Him, in His Word? Delivering destruction!

What destruction does the absolution work upon my sins to destroy their power and silence my fears? Freeing destruction!

What destruction does the blessed Meal work upon me, whereby my sins and I are exchanged for Christ and His righteousness, and I am left with the peaceful silence of being reconciled to God Almighty? Nourishing destruction!

FRIDAY AFTER ASH WEDNESDAY

Psalmody: Psalm 9:1–8
Additional Psalm: Psalm 9, Psalm 38
Old Testament Reading: Genesis 2:4–25
New Testament Reading: Mark 1:29–45

Prayer of the Day

O God, You declare Your almighty power above all in showing mercy and pity. Mercifully grant us such a measure of Your grace that we may obtain Your gracious promises and be made partakers of Your heavenly treasures; through Jesus Christ, Your Son, our Lord, who lives and reigns with You and the Holy Spirit, one God, now and forever. (H70)

Meditation

Jesus' "I will" to this leper is but the echo of His "I will" in the counsel of the Holy Trinity as the Father said to the Son, "Go!"

These two simple words confess the desire of Christ, and by the speaking of them put His desire into action. These words transform His desire into cleansing, healing, restoration, and reconciliation to a man who believed in Him.

These words, though not recorded prior to His conversation with this leper, are heard in His response to the litany of human sickness and satanic domination that came His way. Do any words so clearly testify to the desire, the want, and the activity of God to save me and all mankind?

The entire life of Christ, from His conception, to His birth, to His living, to His ministry, to His passion, His death and His burial is filled with the constant chorus of "I will."

The leper believed in the power of the Christ. What the leper did not know, and I tend so often to forget, is whether Jesus would be willing, would desire, to use that power mercifully for him, for me.

With these two words, and the healing that followed, the leper, the sinner, the outcast, the me that is lepros in sin, hears and receives the desire, the will of God for us all in Jesus Christ.

Do not these two words stand as an open invitation to me and all the world to come, to seek, and to receive the desire of God that we be healed, be cleansed, and be reconciled to Him? The fact that so many people were coming to Jesus that He couldn't openly enter a village confirms these are words of invitation.

These two words of Jesus, "I will," are the living fulfillment of two other words Jesus prayed in the Garden of Gethsemane: "Thy will." These two words, "I will," secure His silence before His accusers and during His passion and death. These same two words, "I will," drive His dialogues before His accusers and during His passion and death.

And what is the resurrection of Christ in the flesh but the Father's "Amen!" to the "I will" of Jesus. What fills the absolution with assurance of the forgiveness, but these two words of Jesus, "I will"? Nothing! What fills the blessed communion of His body and blood with wondrous comfort and resurrection but these two simple words, "I will"? Nothing!

SATURDAY AFTER ASH WEDNESDAY

Psalmody: Psalm 12:1–6
Additional Psalm: Psalm 14, Psalm 51
Old Testament Reading: Genesis 3:1–24
New Testament Reading: Mark 2:1–17

Prayer of the Day

Merciful Father, You have given Your only Son as the sacrifice for sinners. Grant us grace to receive the fruits of His redeeming work with thanksgiving and daily to follow in His way; through Jesus Christ, our Lord, who lives and reigns with You and the Holy Spirit, one God, now and forever. (B61)

Meditation

How shall I hear the fullness of what Jesus is telling this paralytic about himself and his sins? Isn't the Lord speaking to me of my spiritual paralysis in sin?

When Jesus speaks His absolution, He takes this man's sins from him, and in the taking receives them unto Himself. Jesus is declaring that He has taken our sins to Himself, and He shall deal with them and their consequences. The truth of Christ's taking both the man's sin and its consequences is found in His words setting the man free from his paralysis.

While Christ's absolution takes the paralytic's sins to Himself, it is also a petition to the paralytic and to me to let go of our sin, to believe in Him, and to let Him deal with God the Father over us and our sin.

The work of these words is done on the cross of Christ, where He petitions the Father on behalf of this man and all mankind, "Father, forgive them, for they know not what they do" (Luke 23:34). By this, Christ petitioned the Father to let Him deal with all that is rightfully due us as sinners. The events that followed our Lord's petition on the cross make it clear to all that God the Father has let Christ deal with me and my sin.

The resurrection stands as the Father's declaration of what glorious things will happen now and in eternity, to all those who believe on the Lord Jesus Christ as He deals with God the Father for them.

What richness is found in these blessed words? Here I find the Lamb of God taking away my sin as He has taken away the sin of the world. How this fills the holy absolution with Christ's declaration, "I have dealt with God the Father and His righteous wrath against you, and now you are free and have His favor."

If only I could believe in the reality that these words of Jesus are performative, that they actually do for the man, and me, what He says. If only I could remember, I could behold what is offered in the call to repentance—the Son of God inviting me and every person to come and let Him deal with me and with God the Father, so that we all may be one as Christ and the Father are one.

Blessed Spirit of the Father and the Christ, work this work in me through the Word You have inspired that I might believe.

First Sunday in Lent

Psalmody: Psalm 79:5–9
Additional Psalm: Psalm 42, Psalm 102
Old Testament Reading: Genesis 4:1–26
New Testament Reading: Mark 2:18–28

Prayer of the Day

Eternal God, Your Son Jesus Christ is our true Sabbath rest. Help us to keep each day holy by receiving His Word of comfort that we may find our rest in Him, who lives and reigns with You and the Holy Spirit, one God, now and forever. (B62)

Meditation

The commandment of God was, "Remember the Sabbath day, to keep it holy" (Exodus 20:8). Inasmuch as we are sinful from our birth, sinful from the time our mothers conceived us (Psalm 51:5), there is no keeping on our part that would not be sinful and therefore unholy.

The key to this question lies in the word remember. This activity is so much more than an intellectual enterprise by which we mentally bring to mind that on the seventh day God rested from all His labors and thus commands us rest. While there is a mental component involved in this remembrance we are to have of the Sabbath, this only serves the greater activity of remembering. God's command for us to remember the Sabbath day is a command for us to participate in His rest.

To participate in His rest is to receive His Word of promised deliverance from the laborious burden our sin has upon us.

The only way the Sabbath could be kept holy is if it were the work of God alone. All faithful remembrances of the Sabbath are participations through faith in the Word of God made flesh, the Lord Jesus Christ.

Jesus is the Word of God, and as such He is Lord of the rest. He gains this holy rest for us by participating in our sins as He is yoked to us in our flesh, yoked to us under the Law, and to our sin on the cross. Remembering that we are dust (Psalm 103:14), He participates in our burden and labors under sin and gives us rest (Matthew 11:28).

What is lawful on the Sabbath? Participation in our holy rest—Jesus Christ and Him crucified and risen for us.

How shall we participate in Sabbath? Through faith in the Lord Jesus Christ, for it is through faith in Him that He participates in our lives through the Holy Spirit, and we are given rest from our sin, rest from our dying, and restful peace with God. This rest is announced and given to us in the forgiveness of our sins.

All who would receive this rest need only come and receive His Holy Word, Baptism, Absolution, and from His body and blood where He tells us to do this by way of remembrance of me, of participation in Me, My passion, My death and My resurrection for you. Here do we understand why the Sabbath, the rest, the Lord Jesus, was made for man.

MONDAY—LENT 1

Psalmody: Psalm 2
Additional Psalm: Psalm 77, Psalm 130
Old Testament Reading: Genesis 6:1–7:5
New Testament Reading: Mark 3:1–19

Prayer of the Day

Lord Jesus, prepare us for that eternal Sabbath when You will rest in us, just as now You work in us. The rest that we shall enjoy will be Yours, just as the work that we now do is Your work done through us. But You, O Lord, are eternally at work and eternally at rest. It is not time that You see or in time that You move or in time that You rest, yet You make what we see in time. You make time itself and the repose which comes when time ceases; for You live and reign with the Father and the Holy Spirit, one God, now and forever. (1002)

Meditation

To fall down before Him was the physical response that the unclean or evil spirits made upon seeing the Son of God. After this physical response came the verbal response confessing Jesus to the Son of God.

How is it that these evil spirits both know and demonstrate so well the physical and verbal forms of true worship?

I find it striking that unclean spirits demonstrate the truest expression of worship that I as a believer can make. To worship is to bow, to bend, to prostrate the body physically as a physical confession of two things at once. The act of bowing before the Lord is my physical confession that I am the creature and He is my Creator. It is my physical confession that I am the servant and He is the master. It is my physical confession of my miserableness and His mercifulness. It is my physical confession that I am nothing in sin and He is my gracious everything. The verbal confession is an articulation of these truths.

When Son of God told the woman at the well, "The true worshipers will worship the Father in spirit and truth" (John 4:23), He made it clear that all worship is a matter of the spirit, that is, of faith. Any worship of the Son of God will flow from what one believes about Him.

What many people do not realize is that what each person really believes is most loudly confessed by what each does physically and verbally. The Lord reveals this in Isaiah 29, where He is grieved that their lips confessed one thing but their living confessed another. Having been bound before the fall of man because of their rebellion, the unclean spirits have no freedom in which to deny He who has bound them, the Son of God.

Others in this text, having seen and heard the Son of God, like we today, by the hearing were given such freedom. The Pharisees used their new freedom to worship, to physically and verbally confess themselves as they conspired how to destroy Him. The Twelve used their new freedom to physically confess their faith in Him by following His call and appointment of them as apostles.

How many worship, like the Pharisees, conditionally? "Yea Lord, as long as first You, Your church, and Your messengers must bow to my preferences as how, when, and where I will bow, will worship, I will gladly bow, gladly worship You."

TUESDAY—LENT 1

Psalmody: Psalm 104:1–9
Additional Psalm: Psalm 124, Psalm 143
Old Testament Reading: Genesis 7:11–8:12
New Testament Reading: Mark 3:20–35

Prayer of the Day

Almighty and eternal God, Your Son Jesus triumphed over the prince of demons and freed us from bondage to sin. Help us to stand firm against every assault of Satan, and enable us always to do Your will; through Jesus Christ, our Lord, who lives and reigns with You and the Holy Spirit, one God, now and forever. (B63)

Meditation

Ah, how my sinful nature would have me focus and consider the words of Christ against Satan's as his fate. Even the saint in me prays for such a division and end to Satan. Yet if I but step back and hear these words aright, my Lord has spoken of me and my daily reality.

The only word that seems out of place for me is if. If I have risen up against myself? If I am divided? If? There is no "if" for me, for I am, as St. Paul confesses himself to be, a wretched man (Romans 7:24). I cannot stand. "For I do not do what I want, but I do the very thing I hate. . . . For I do not do the good I want, but the evil I do not want is what I keep on doing. . . . I see in my members another law waging war against the law of my mind and making me captive to the law of sin that dwells in my members" (Romans 7:15, 19, 23).

Surely I am a divided kingdom, a divided house. How many times a day, even in an hour, does this division manifest itself as I arrive at my end, having fallen from those places I thought I could stand (1 Corinthians 10:12)?

Surely this division within me reveals the indisputable reality of my constant, continuous need for Christ to be my Savior. Christ alone has entered the flesh, the house of the strong man of my sin, my guilt, and my death. On the cross, even as the strong man binds my curse to Him, He by His plea for my forgiveness binds the strong man of my sin and guilt to Himself. Having bound the strong man in love, He then takes the rule and dominion of the strong man of sin into death, into its end. Having bound sin and death He plunders them for me and raises me up with Him in Baptism through His resurrection, to live in His Kingdom.

Surely these words of me and my end tell me to begin at my end, which is now Jesus Christ. Surely this is the blessed promise of God in my Baptism. "We were buried therefore with Him by baptism into death, in order that, just as

Christ was raised from the dead by the glory of the Father, we too might walk in newness of life" (Romans 6:4).

WEDNESDAY—LENT 1

Psalmody: Psalm 74:10–17
Additional Psalm: Psalm 126, Psalm 6
Old Testament Reading: Genesis 8:13–9:17
Additional Reading: Genesis 9:18–11:26
New Testament Reading: Mark 4:1–20

Prayer of the Day

Almighty and merciful God, of Your bountiful goodness keep from us all things that may hurt us that we, being ready in both body and soul, may cheerfully accomplish whatever You would have us do; through Jesus Christ, Your Son, our Lord, who lives and reigns with You and the Holy Spirit, one God, now and forever. (H79)

Meditation

What is it that could cause a person to see and yet not perceive, hear but in no way understand? Isn't this inability born of a person seeking to save themselves from the fullness of God's message, whether it be spoken openly or hidden in the parable?

Consider the parable that precedes these words. What would the fullness of this parable bring to bear upon the hearer? Wouldn't the first response of the hearer be an attempt to identify which of the types of soils one might be?

Having identified what type soil, the second response would surely be an attempt to try and figure out how one could change their situation or soil. The quest for such a hearer would turn to how one keeps Satan from devouring the seed, how one gets rid of the rocks, or how one gets rid of the weeds. And of course, if one has found themselves to be the good soil, all is well, and they need do nothing to be pleasing in God's sight.

Such a person has heard some religious words and is responding religiously. By such religious hearing, that person has saved themselves from the fullness of God's Word. Sadly, such hearing will bring no turning, no forgiveness, and no salvation.

So what would one hear if they did hear the fullness of Word of God in this parable?

First they would hear the Law that justly declares me to be all four types of soils. Or more to pointedly, I who am of the earth, am like the earth, cursed in sin. For while I may bear much fruit in one place, there are other places where nothing grows because of my busyness, my hardness of heart, or my attachment to worldly things. At this point the only thing I am left with is the Sower who sows.

Here is the good news, which reveals that this Sower has chosen to sow, and not just anywhere, but in me, in my life. Despite the paths, the rocky areas, the weed-filled areas, this Sower knows my soil, and He knows what His seed, His Word, can bring forth in and through me.

If anyone would see and perceive, hear and understand anything, it must be that everything for everyone depends upon the Sower and His seed.

THURSDAY—LENT 1

Psalmody: Psalm 107:23–32
Additional Psalm: Psalm 47, Psalm 32
Old Testament Reading: Genesis 11:27–12:20
New Testament Reading: Mark 4:21–41

Prayer of the Day

Blessed Lord, since You have caused all Holy Scriptures to be written for our learning, grant that we may so hear them, read, mark, learn, and inwardly digest them that we may embrace and ever hold fast the blessed hope of everlasting life; through Jesus Christ, Your Son, our Lord, who lives and reigns with You and the Holy Spirit, one God, now and forever. (B64)

Meditation

Hearing is a matter of receiving. By these words, the two parables and the events on the lake, Jesus is revealing in no uncertain terms, that when it comes to the kingdom of God, it is first and foremost a matter of continuous hearing or receiving it through the Word.

If I hear the full message of the first parable, I am confronted with the fact that the blessings of the kingdom of God are a matter of receiving the sown Word and harvesting what it will raise up. The kingdom of God and my place in it is not a matter my knowing the how or why of the Word, but of my receiving what this Kingdom is sowing and harvesting.

If I hear the second parable, I am confronted with the fact that the greatness of this Kingdom, and what it can raise up in those who receive it, is in no way bound to the size or greatness of the means by which God sows His Kingdom.

Oh, to have the ears to hear as the wind and the wave on that lake, for as they heard His Word, they were as He spoke to them.

And what did those who had taken Jesus in their boat, on their lake, in their part of the world have to hear? The greatness of their fear indicates that through Jesus' words to the wind and the wave they heard something that turned their world upside down. They heard, contrary to what they thought, that they were in Jesus' boat, on Jesus' lake, in Jesus' world. And such is hard to hear because it turns everything upside down with no way to right it.

With these words Jesus is revealing the only means by which things will be made right: constant and continuous hearing of the Word.

And what is the nature of God's Word? It is performative, that is, working, accomplishing, and doing what He says. Only God's Word can work the hearing He commands us to continuously do at the same moment He is speaking that Word. Such is the testimony of God in Romans 10:17: "So faith comes from hearing, and hearing through the word of Christ."

Lord, give me ears to hear, that I may be made right. Amen.

FRIDAY—LENT 1

Psalmody: Psalm 73:25–28
Additional Psalm: Psalm 133, Psalm 38
Old Testament Reading: Genesis 13:1–18
Additional Reading: Genesis 14:1–24
New Testament Reading: Mark 5:1–20

Prayer of the Day

Lord Jesus, Son of the Most High God, You freed many from their bondage to demons, demonstrating Your power over the evil one. Show us Your mercy when we are overcome by the darkness of sin, death, and the devil, and protect us by Your mighty Word that does what it says; for You live and reign with the Father and the Holy Spirit, one God, now and forever. (1003)

Meditation

Is this a man in the country of the Gerasenes? Is this a man living among the tombs? Or is this man me? Am I not a man with an unclean spirit?

Am I not a man so bound in my sin that I cannot bind myself sufficiently enough to keep me from all that is unclean? No matter the chains of discipline I may employ, I have no strength to bind or subdue myself.

Day and night, no matter where I may be, am I not this man, as I cry out in my sinful selfishness? Am I not this man as I constantly cut myself, my heart, my soul, and even my flesh in my quest to have and serve that which is unclean?

What would my hope be if Jesus, Son of the Most High God, had not chosen to cross the great sea of my sin and land on the shores of my life through Baptism? What would my hope, my peace be if Jesus, Son of the Most High God, had not chosen to have not only something, but everything to do with me?

Surely this Jesus is the one who allowed Himself to be bound to me and all mankind. What strength there must have been in His allowing Himself to be bound to the cross where He might forever subdue my sin and the wrath of God for me.

Surely this Jesus is the one who allowed Himself to be cut by cold hard stones of every sinner's heart. Yes, spike and spear may have cut His flesh, but each of these were driven and directed by the stones that have become each man's heart in sin.

Surely this Jesus is the one who cries out on the cross not for Himself but for me. Crying out for my forgiveness, that I might not be tormented, that I might be given permission to go to God the Father.

All this the Son of the Most High God comes to do to me and for me. How shall I go home, go to work, go to town, go even to church, and not tell everyone how much the Lord has done for me and for them? Shall I be silent about how merciful the Lord is to me and to all in this Jesus, Son of the Most High God? Surely not!

SATURDAY—LENT 1

Psalmody: Psalm 32:1–5
Additional Psalm: Psalm 3, Psalm 51
Old Testament Reading: Genesis 15:1–21
New Testament Reading: Mark 5:21–43

Prayer of the Day

Heavenly Father, during His earthly ministry Your Son Jesus healed the sick and raised the dead. By the healing medicine of the Word and Sacraments pour into our hearts such love toward You that we may live eternally; through the same Jesus Christ, our Lord, who lives and reigns with You and the Holy Spirit, one God, now and forever. (B66)

Meditation

A man named Jairus runs to Jesus begging help for his daughter. Jairus knows and believes that his daughter is so overcome by a sickness that it will take her life. Jairus believes himself helpless to save her from this illness. His coming to Jesus for help bears this out. But why does he come to Jesus? Does it mean he believes in Jesus so that he believes that he has nothing to lose in asking Jesus to help? We're not told this—the only thing we can be sure of is that Jairus had heard the Word about Jesus and what He was doing, and it is this that brings him to Jesus.

There is a woman in the crowd gathering around Jesus who has been vexed with a flow of blood for many years. She believed that several different physicians could free her from her affliction, only to find that her faith was misplaced and her purse was now empty. Does she come because she believes in Jesus or because He is her last best hope? In truth, due to her poverty, Jesus was her only hope. While she states what she believed, what she believes is based on the reports about Jesus. Touching Him, she receives her healing and Jesus calls her out, not to question her, but to affirm that it was through believing in Him she received her healing, not the touching of His garment.

Now word comes that Jarius's daughter is dead. Does Jairus believe that Jesus should not have delayed with that woman? Was is too late for his daughter? Such would be the thoughts of one who believes in the power of death.

While we cannot know exactly what he believed in the midst of his grief, we do know that Jesus spoke the Word of faith to him: "Do not fear, only believe." Arriving at the house, they are greeted by those who believed that nothing was more powerful than death. When Jesus speaks the reality of things because He has come, the lack of faith can be heard in the mourners' scornful laughter.

Jesus then goes in and speaks to that which death has overcome, and by His Word, death and doubt were overcome as Jairus's daughter arises to live again, and Jarius arises to eternal life through faith in Jesus Christ. Such saving faith comes only through the Word, and that Word always amazes.

SECOND SUNDAY IN LENT

Psalmody: Psalm 139:7–10
Additional Psalm: Psalm 139, Psalm 102
Old Testament Reading:
Genesis 16:1–9, 15–17:22
New Testament Reading: Mark 6:1–13

Prayer of the Day

O God, You see that of ourselves we have no strength. By Your mighty power defend us from all adversities that may happen to the body and from all evil thoughts that may assault and hurt the soul; through Jesus Christ, Your Son, our Lord, who lives and reigns with You and the Holy Spirit, one God, now and forever. (L24)

Meditation

What is it about Christ that caused and still causes a reaction to not receive a message or messenger from God? It is striking that this reaction is not born of the quality or greatness of what Jesus had given to them. They openly acknowledge the profundity of His wisdom and the mightiness of His works. This acknowledgement bears the understanding that these wondrous things had to have come from God.

So what is it that was so astonishing, so overwhelming to them that they were scandalized to the point where they took such offense and refused to receive anything from Christ?

The rhetorical questions of the people reveal what it was that caused them such offense. The first series of questions acknowledges that Jesus has received and shares great wisdom and mightiness that can only come from God. The second series of questions, acknowledge that Jesus is one of them, someone they know according to His vocation of carpentry and they know according to His family. In their minds, these two truths cannot co-exist.

Why? They believe that Jesus, due to His lowliness and familiarity, has no right to such profundity or mightiness. And inasmuch as He hasn't earned such things, surely He must have robbed God of such things (Philippians 2:6–7), for God does not so favor the humble and lowly. Thus, they were offended at Him for having and doing what He had not rightly received.

Jesus makes it plain to the apostles that as they go in lowliness and familiarity, sharing the profundity and mightiness they received from Him, certain places will not receive the gift they offer.

Isn't it striking that He, whom they were so offended at that they would not receive Him, was not so offended by our flesh He refused to receive unto Himself? Nor was He so offended by our life as servants of God and one another that He refused to receive and live it for us. Nor was He so offended by us, our guilt in sin and sinfulness, that He refused to receive us, our guilt, and the wrath of God for our guilt. Nor was He so offended by us and our death that He refused to receive even our death to save us from it. Nor was He so offended by us and our rejection of Him that He would not receive us unto Himself in His resurrection.

Oh, that the dust might not shake off the testimony of Him who has come to save us from the dust.

Monday—Lent 2

Psalmody: Psalm 91:9–16
Additional Psalm: Psalm 91, Psalm 130
Old Testament Reading: Genesis 18:1–15
Additional Reading: Genesis 18:16–20:18
New Testament Reading: Mark 6:14–34

Prayer of the Day

O Lord, You granted Your prophets strength to resist the temptations of the devil and courage to proclaim repentance. Give us pure hearts and minds to follow Your Son faithfully even into suffering and death; through the same Jesus Christ, our Lord, who lives and reigns with You and the Holy Spirit, one God, now and forever. (B68)

Meditation

Isn't this an account of two shepherds? Weren't each attempting to provide what no one else could? Weren't each attempting to provide for and protect sheep?

The basis of the first shepherd's protection of the sheep was his own guilt. The basis of the second Shepherd's protection was the guilt of the sheep. The motivation of the first's shepherd's care arose from fear. The motivation of the second Shepherd's care arose from compassion. The first shepherd exercises his position and his word to provide and protect his sheep. The second Shepherd exercises His position and His Word to provide and protect His sheep.

So who was kept safe?

For the first shepherd and his sheep, it is a sad irony. The very things he used to provide and keep his sheep safe, his position and his word, ended up being the things he had to save. And in order to save these things before men, he uses them both, and John was beheaded.

For the second Shepherd and His sheep, it is a glorious irony. The very things He used to provide and keep His sheep safe, His position and His Word, end being the things He has to lose. In order to save these sheep, He will lose both before men and be crucified. He will lose both before God and be abandoned.

Herod sought to keep John safe from other people, namely his adulterous wife. Yet in the end, Herod could not keep John safe from Herod himself. Jesus seeks to keep His sheep safe from themselves. To accomplish this, He will not keep Himself safe from the sheep or His Father.

How Jesus saw the people coming to Him, "like sheep without a shepherd," speaks an often unobserved truth. This truth is born out in Herod's attempts to be a shepherd. No person, no matter their station or vocation in life, can ever be the saving shepherd of their own life or the life of another.

In sin, in our sinfulness, we can shepherd nothing, for "All we like sheep have gone astray; we have turned—every one—to his own way; and the Lord has laid on Him the iniquity of us all" (Isaiah 53:6).

Jesus, like a shepherd, has come astray to meet us where we are in our own way. Our way is the way of sin, sorrows, and suffering that leads to the cross, and here our Good Shepherd lays down His life under the iniquity of us all, and we are saved.

The Lord is my Shepherd, I shall not want.

TUESDAY—LENT 2

Psalmody: Psalm 126
Additional Psalm: Psalm 127, Psalm 143
Old Testament Reading: Genesis 21:1–21
New Testament Reading: Mark 6:35–56

Prayer of the Day

Heavenly Father, though we do not deserve Your goodness, still You provide for all our needs of body and soul. Grant us Your Holy Spirit that we may acknowledge Your gifts, give thanks for all Your benefits, and serve You in willing obedience; through Jesus Christ, Your Son, our Lord, who lives and reigns with You and the Holy Spirit, one God, now and forever. (B69)

Meditation

Having seen the desolate place, the number of those in need, and their own needs, Jesus' disciples come and tell Him to act according to what they see and do not see. Jesus responds by telling them to go and see what they do have to meet the need. And going, all they could find was five loaves and two fish.

Jesus then tells them to go to the other side. The disciples soon see that they are virtually helpless against the wind. Jesus then goes out, not to them, but to be near them. Jesus intends to pass close to them so that they might see what they could not see they had, in meeting the needs of the crowd—the Son of God.

Yet what do they see? Not Jesus, not the Son of God, but a ghost, a disembodied spirit. So Jesus speaks a Word so that by His going and His Word, they might see who and what it was they had as their Lord.

Then once Jesus gets into the boat with them, they see the wind cease, they see that their way is clear to the other side, but they still don't see who and what they had in this Jesus, who has now made it possible for them to reach the other side.

Having gone to the other side, the people see Jesus for who and what He was, the healer of all sicknesses—not just theirs, but of anyone's He saw. So they go, calling and bringing everyone to see Jesus, that by His seeing, by His touch, they might see healing and wholeness. These people may not have seen Jesus for who and what He fully was, but the fact they brought those in need to wherever He was means that they saw in Him more than enough to deal with their needs.

The fact that hardness of heart helps the disciples from their seeing means that seeing is a matter of faith. This begs the question: "In all my goings and my seeing, what do I see?"

It is by faith I see the glorious meal He sets before me and all in this desolate place. It is by faith I see He who has come out to me on the waters of Baptism, put me in His boat of the Church. It is by faith I see Him who has come to where I am, that I might go and see where He has gone and what He has prepared for me and all who believe in Jesus Christ, Son of Man and Son of God.

Wednesday—Lent 2

Psalmody: Psalm 66:8–15
Additional Psalm: Psalm 66, Psalm 6
Old Testament Reading: Genesis 22:1–19
New Testament Reading: Mark 7:1–23

Prayer of the Day

Almighty and merciful God, defend Your Church from all false teaching and error that Your faithful people may confess You to be the only true God and rejoice in Your good gifts of life and salvation; through Jesus Christ, Your Son, our Lord, who lives and reigns with You and the Holy Spirit, one God, now and forever. (B74)

Meditation

One could erroneously begin an immediate distance test to see how near or far one is from Jesus. Once they had determined their proximity to Jesus, they would surely begin some process by which they might put themselves nearer to Jesus.

These words bespeak a deeper truth than most recognize, let alone admit. By these words, Jesus made it clear that anyone who sets aside the Word of God—is NOT where He is.

What is sadly ironic is that the agenda of the Pharisees and the Scribes was to have the people be where God is. Neither they nor the people that followed them could ever be where God is, because they sought to get there by their own vain teachings.

Why is it that the only thing that can come out of the heart of man is evil? Because such a heart is conceived and born in sin (Psalm 51); as such it is separate, aside, apart, far from God. Beginning here, any and all teachings, doctrines, and worship of God will most certainly be vain.

It is to us at this beginning that the Son of God comes in His conception and incarnation. His entire life and mission is not to call us, guide us, or instruct us on how to be where God is, but to live God "for us" where we are.

Why did the Jews have Jesus crucified? Surely it was because He was where they thought God was. What was the act of crucifying Christ, but the Jewish leaders forcing Jesus to be where God would have Him to be? Yet in all this, Jesus, the Son of God, allows us to put Him where we are— separate, aside, apart, far from God, so that He might suffer the consequences of our location and save us from it.

What is Jesus? What is all that He does and suffers, but a revelation of what is God's heart for all those who are far from Him.

While nothing outside of us can enter and defile us, thanks be to God that has Jesus entered into our flesh, our living, our sin, our rightly deserved wrath of God, and our death. By His entering into us and all that is of us, from us, and due us, we are cleansed and reborn where God is in His grace. What is Holy Baptism but a blessed invasion of Jesus Christ from outside of us so that we might be saved from what is within us and coming out of us.

Thursday—Lent 2

Psalmody: Psalm 28:6–9
Additional Psalm: Psalm 28, Psalm 32
Old Testament Reading: Genesis 24:1–31
New Testament Reading: Mark 7:24–37

Prayer of the Day

O Lord, let Your merciful ears be open to the prayers of Your humble servants and grant that what they ask may be in accord with Your gracious will; through Jesus Christ, Your Son, our Lord, who lives and reigns with You and the Holy Spirit, one God, now and forever. (B76)

Meditation

What had been opened? Yes, the man's ear was opened, as was his tongue, but before either of these could be opened, something else had to be opened. Surely it was the hearts of those involved. But this begs the question, "What was it that had so opened their hearts that they sought Jesus?"

Something had so opened Jesus to the people of Tyre and Sidon that He could not be hidden. This same thing had opened the way for the Syrophoenician woman to come and beg that Jesus cast the demon out of her daughter. It has also opened the way for the people of the Decapolis to bring the man who was deaf and mute to Jesus, that He might lay His hands upon the man to heal him.

In each case, the people are bound in sin, their bondage manifested in their affliction. The mother's bondage was that of her daughter's to the demon. The bondage of the people who brought the man who was deaf and mute, was that of his deafness and his tied tongue. Isn't the only thing that could have opened the way for them to Jesus the same thing that still opens the way to Jesus for people today? Isn't the only thing that can open the way to Jesus Jesus Himself?

Jesus alone does this because He alone gets in our way, the way of the flesh, of life in this fallen world and our bondage to sin. Jesus alone is the one who has opened Himself to all that binds us in sin, be it sin or sin's manifestation. Jesus alone is open to receiving and inviting us as we are in our bondage. "Come to Me, all who labor and are heavy laden, and I will give you rest" (Matthew 11:28).

Jesus alone allowed Himself to be opened on the cross to receive from us and God the very things that close the way to God and eternal life—our sin and God's eternal wrath against us. Jesus' prayer on the cross, "Father, forgive them, for they know not what they do" (Luke 23:34) was His way of saying to His Father, "Ephphatha! Be opened" to these people that they may receive You and in You eternal life. Jesus' resurrection is God the Father's declaration that He is open to us, and the way is open for us to Him here in time and in eternity.

In Baptism, the Lord says to us, "Ephphatha! Be opened!" and we are raised into the open favor of the Father and His grace.

FRIDAY—LENT 2

Psalmody: Psalm 118:19–24
Additional Psalm: Psalm 118, Psalm 38
Old Testament Reading:
Genesis 24:32–52, 61–67
Additional Reading: Genesis 25:1–26:35
New Testament Reading: Mark 8:1–21

Prayer of the Day

Lord Jesus, Bread of Life, in Your great compassion You fed the multitudes with a few loaves and a few fish. Feed us the holy food of Your Word broken open that hearts may burn and Your very body and blood that eyes may be opened to see You as the very Bread of heaven; for You live and reign with the Father and the Holy Spirit, one God, now and forever. (1004)

Meditation

What would such a sign do for the Pharisees who sought one from Jesus? The answer explains why Jesus refused to give them one.

Where the Pharisees wanted a sign from, heaven, indicates that they did not believe that Jesus was heaven in their midst. The most any sign would do for the Pharisees is prove that Jesus was a representative of heaven, maybe even a prophet.

Jesus and everything He does are not signs that have come down from heaven, but are signs of heaven on earth—Immanuel. Jesus speaks this reality when He said, "I have compassion on the crowd." Then He demonstrates this reality with His blessing the seven loaves and the few small fish to feed infinitely more than they were capable of in and of themselves, but heaven in the midst of all things.

The disciples' concern and discussion on the boat as to whether they had enough bread arose from the fact they didn't realize that, with Jesus, heaven was in their midst. Jesus reminds them that where He is, there heaven is at work making what they had infinitely more.

How often do I wonder whether heaven will descend into the midst of my situation, my condition, my struggle, and intervene? Oh, that the Lord would grant me to remember that my Baptism is the intrusion of Jesus into me, my sin, my life and living, and that by His earthly intervention, I might be infinitely other and more than I am in my sin. Oh, that I might remember that the Holy Absolution is heaven's intervention in the midst of my earthly and heavenly unrighteousness, that receive Christ's infinite righteousness. Make me mindful, O Lord, that in the Holy Supper Jesus comes into the midst of me, that as He comes so comes heaven, that I might be renewed in Your infinite grace.

While remembering these things, I would do even better to be mindful of the fact that, while heaven dwells with me, heaven's intervention in the things of my earthly life will happen when He who rules over heaven and earth decides the time is right. The fact that Jesus did not immediately intervene in the earthly needs of the four thousand makes this most clear. The people had been with Jesus for three days without anything to eat. It isn't until the third day that heaven in the midst intervenes, and meets their needs by taking their nothing to Himself.

SATURDAY—LENT 2

Psalmody: Psalm 2:7–9
Additional Psalm: Psalm 2, Psalm 51
Old Testament Reading: Genesis 27:1–29
New Testament Reading: Mark 8:22–38

Prayer of the Day

Almighty God, Your Son willingly endured the agony and shame of the cross for our redemption. Grant us courage to take up our cross daily and follow Him wherever He leads; through the same Jesus Christ, our Lord, who lives and reigns with You and the Holy Spirit, one God, now and forever. (A75)

Meditation

What are the things of man? This text is as filled with them as is my life and the life of each person. In the account of the blind man, the things of man are manifested in blindness: the inability to give sight to the one who is blind, the necessity of being led and brought by someone else to where one needs to be, the need for healing from outside oneself, and the need of a home.

In the confession of Jesus as the Christ, we find the things of man manifested in discipleship: erroneous confession of who Jesus really is, and the need to confess Jesus as the Christ.

In Jesus' foretelling of His death and resurrection, the things of man are found in the need to be taught, the Son of Man's need to suffer many things and be rejected by the very people who should have known Him and confessed Him to be the Christ, the killing of the Son of Man, the rebuke of Jesus; the need to be rebuked by Jesus, the ways of Satan and the setting of the mind on the things of man.

In Jesus address to the crowd, the things of man are found in the need to be called to Him: the choosing of self before all else, the refusal of the cross, the need to deny oneself, the need to lose one's life, the refusal to follow Jesus, the losing of one's life, the want to gain the whole world, the free forfeit of one's soul, the inability to give anything in return for one's soul, shame of Jesus and His words, adulterousness, and sinfulness.

In these things of man is found the Son of Man with the things of God. What might these be? Jesus Himself, hearing of petitions to touch and heal; leading to be healed, laying of His hands; speaking to the one who is being healed; healing, restoration of sight; the good confession, "You are the Christ"; teaching the truth of His mission; refusing to be rebuked from His mission; rebuking of all who would deter Him; differentiating between the things of man and the things of God; calling the crowd; losing of His life for the saving of every life, giving of His life in return for our souls, the refusal to be ashamed of us and all the things of man that are rightly ours now, and in His coming in glory.

In all these things, the greatest is that Jesus is the Christ for all the things of man and the things of God.

Psalmody: Psalm 129
Additional Psalm: Psalm 79, Psalm 102
Old Testament Reading:
Genesis 27:30–45; 28:10–22
New Testament Reading: Mark 9:1–13

Prayer of the Day

O God, whose glory it is always to have mercy, be gracious to all who have gone astray from Your ways and bring them again with penitent hearts and steadfast faith to embrace and hold fast the unchangeable truth of Your Word; through Jesus Christ, Your Son, our Lord, who lives and reigns with You and the Holy Spirit, one God, now and forever. (L25)

Meditation

In His incarnation, Jesus came to us veiled in flesh that He might be Immanuel, God with us. Here God the Father allows Peter, James, and John to see what is hidden in this world and what shall be seen in the world to come. Notice that Peter does not say that it is good that "You are here," but that "we are here." The Father reverses things so that this is a time of "us with God."

This reversal plays out again on another mount. As Jesus brought the disciples with Him to this mount, the Father brings all mankind to Jesus on Mount Calvary. As the Father lays our sins, our debts, and our guilt upon Jesus, again it is a time of "us with God." On Calvary, the Son of God is again transfigured, as both mankind and God the Father did to Jesus what pleased them. What pleased mankind was to save itself from Jesus, so we did to Him as they did to John the Baptist. What pleased God the Father was to save mankind, so He did to Jesus all that pleased the demands of His Law and His love for us all.

"Rabbi, it is good that we are here." Surely these would be my words, were I on the mount beholding the transfiguration of Christ. Surely these would be the very words of Lazarus as he was carried to the bosom of Abraham. Surely these were the words of the thief who was crucified with our Lord as he joined Christ in paradise. Surely these are the very words of every believer our Lord brought to the place He prepared for them, the place where He is.

Many might think that we will have to wait until that day before we can finally say these words. The Father tells us otherwise: "This is My beloved Son; listen to Him" (Mark 9:7). Where the Word is, there is Christ, and as we listen to Him, how shall we not say these words of Peter? Dripping wet on the shores of Baptism, how shall we not say these same words in all rejoicing? Ears ringing with the voice of Holy Absolution, how shall we not say these words in all peace? Stomachs filled with the transfigured bread and wine into the body and the blood of Christ, how shall we not say in all joy, "It is good that we are here"?

Monday—Lent 3

Psalmody: Psalm 38:13–15, 21–22
Additional Psalm: Psalm 54, Psalm 130
Old Testament Reading: Genesis 29:1–30
Additional Reading: Genesis 29:31–34:31
New Testament Reading: Mark 9:14–32

Prayer of the Day

Lord Jesus Christ, our support and defense in every need, continue to preserve Your Church in safety, govern her by Your goodness, and bless her with Your peace; for You live and reign with the Father and the Holy Spirit, one God, now and forever. (B77)

Meditation

Here we find Jesus newly returned to the rest of His disciples after His transfiguration. What does He find? Unbelief!

First, from those disputing with His disciples, perhaps some scribes for Pharisees, we find more than mere unbelief born of uncertainty, but hard-hearted refusal to believe in Jesus. Countless times, after seeing Jesus' miracles, they still refused to believe in Him.

Second, we find the disciples, those He left behind, while He took Peter, James, and John on the mount with Him to see His transfiguration. How do we know that they lacked faith, that they were unbelieving? Jesus had given these disciples the authority to cast out unclean spirits (Mark 6:7). The only reason for their inability to deal with this unclean spirit was unbelief.

Third, we have the father of the demon-possessed boy. His unbelief is found in his appeal to Jesus. His petition to Jesus, "But if you can do anything, have compassion on us and help us," testifies to the man's desperation rather than true faith in Jesus. Jesus' curt response to the man's plea makes it plain that the man lacked faith.

This short confessional plea ought to have been on the lips of all three. To fully understand this plea, we must consider the man's words prior to it, "I believe; help my unbelief." What does the man mean by these first two words? Here the man confesses what the Law has taught him. He believes in the helplessness of his son before the power of the demon. He believes in his own helplessness to save his son from the demon. He believes in his son's desperate need. Moreover, to this point, he also believed that no one could help him. All this the man believes, and over and against this, Jesus tells him that all things are possible for the one who believes.

Is it not here that the classic mistake is made about faith by many a believer? The mistake I refer to is the one of making the effectiveness of faith based on the amount of faith. This mistake leads inevitably to problem of having faith in one's faith and the amount of it, rather than in God. Jesus did not say that all things were possible with enough faith, but with God. Faith in God is a trust not only in His ability but also in His choice of the means and timing of answer to our prayers.

Jesus is Immanuel, God with us. With Him all things are possible because He has come and done all that was not possible for us, through His life, death, and resurrection.

TUESDAY—LENT 3

Psalmody: Psalm 105:5–11
Additional Psalm: Psalm 105, 143
Old Testament Reading: Genesis 35:1–29
New Testament Reading: Mark 9:33–50

Prayer of the Day

Everlasting Father, source of every blessing, mercifully direct and govern us by Your Holy Spirit that we may complete the works You have prepared for us to do; through Jesus Christ, Your Son, our Lord, who lives and reigns with You and the Holy Spirit, one God, now and forever. (B79)

Meditation

It is an interesting relationship between being last and servant. For one can be last of all by not being a servant of all, but cannot be servant of all without being last of all. How can one receive a child, that is, serve a child, unless they make themselves last after the child and his needs. Why would one object to another person doing the works of the Lord without him, unless that one put himself, his way, or the like, first for that person to follow? How could anyone knowingly cause another person to sin unless they had put themselves first before that person?

What is the meaning of Jesus' words, "causes you to sin," but another way of saying, "causes you to put yourself first"? Consider what Jesus says in terms of being last and servant: "If your hand causes you to put yourself first before another so that you deny that person the service God would do through you for them, cut it off. If your foot causes you make another last as you walk right by one whose need you could meet, cut it off. If your eye can only see what first serves you and your desires, tear it out."

Yet, this begs the question, who is this that is able to be last of all and servant of all? Who is this that is last in all things and among all people? Who is this that is servant of all things and all people? Who is it that is able to enter heaven with both hands, feet, and eyes? Who is this that has not lost His saltiness?

Surely it is Jesus Christ and Him alone, true servant of God and man. No words of Jesus better testifies to this than, "For even the Son of Man came not to be served but to serve, and to give His life as a ransom for many" (Mark 10:45). Nothing in Jesus' life better testifies to this than His passive obedience on the cross, where in service of God and man, He allowed Himself to be made last in earth and heaven. In Baptism, God unites us to Christ, and we are reborn. In this rebirth of water and the spirit, we who've lost our hands, our feet, our eyes, and our lives in sin, are given not just new hands, feet, eyes, and lives, but His crucified and resurrected hands, feet, eyes, and life.

Wednesday—Lent 3

Psalmody: Psalm 31:1–5
Additional Psalm: Psalm 31, Psalm 6
Old Testament Reading: Genesis 37:1–36
New Testament Reading: Mark 10:1–12

Prayer of the Day

Merciful Father, Your patience and loving-kindness toward us have no end. Grant that by Your Holy Spirit we may always think and do those things that are pleasing in Your sight; through Jesus Christ, Your Son, our Lord, who lives and reigns with You and the Holy Spirit, one God, now and forever. (B80)

Meditation

From the beginning, God said that it was not good for man to be alone. Why? What was wrong with man's aloneness? Let us not dabble in the notion of loneliness, for one who has never been with another cannot know what it is to be alone. Man was created in God's image; as such, man was created with the simple purpose of distributing good according to the relationships God created for him. The lack of good in man's aloneness is that it prohibited his ability to fully distribute the good that God had given him. He needed a relationship that allowed him to fulfill his created purpose to the fullest. So God created woman out of man and joined woman back to man in the first marriage. It is in this that God has taken the two and made them one. In this way, each is able to fulfill their one purpose to the fullest within the bonds of marriage.

Jesus makes it clear that the only reason Moses gave the commandment regarding divorce is that the man in the marriage had hardened his heart toward the woman and the God who gave her to him. As such, the one who wants to divorce his wife for reasons other than sexual immorality wants to stop fulfilling his created and redeemed purpose toward the woman God has given him.

As such, divorce is not only a separation of the two persons that God has made one, it is also a separation of the individuals from their created and redeemed purpose of distributing good according to the relationships God has established.

What does it mean to adulterate something? It means to make that thing impure by adding something foreign to it. Adultery is more than merely having sex with someone other than your spouse. It is to take what God has made one and join something not of God's choosing to it. The one who commits adultery seeks to both distribute and receive the good from another that God has reserved for the spousal relationship.

Who better understood adultery than Jesus? For it is He, whom God joined to us in the one flesh. It is He, whom God sent to be faithful to us the unfaithful. It is He who allowed His purity to be adulterated with our sin, so that by His blood, we, and our marital relationships, might be cleansed and purified by His grace. He suffered the loss of His oneness with the Father so that we might forever be one with Him as His bride.

Thursday—Lent 3

Psalmody: Psalm 106:44–48
Additional Psalm: Psalm 106, Psalm 32
Old Testament Reading: Genesis 39:1–23
New Testament Reading: Mark 10:13–31

Prayer of the Day

Lord Jesus Christ, whose grace always precedes and follows us, help us to forsake all trust in earthly gain and to find in You our heavenly treasure; for You live and reign with the Father and the Holy Spirit, one God, now and forever. (B81)

Meditation

In all of Jesus' dealing with those who came to Him, the rich young man is perhaps the most perplexing. Inasmuch as we are saved by grace through faith (Ephesians 2), why does Jesus direct this man to works that he might obtain heaven?

As confusing as it may seem, the answer to this question lies in Jesus' words, "You lack one thing." In light of what Jesus said after this statement, this seems rather odd. What could he lack that by making himself lack more, he would gain what he needed, the right kind of faith. This young man, like many rich, had faith, but it was a faith in what he could do via the possessions he had. What the man lacked was unbelief in himself and his riches. To sell all that he had was to give up the god he believed in.

Unbelief in self or what one has is at the heart of what Jesus meant when he told the disciples, "Whoever does not receive the kingdom of God like a child shall not enter it." A child has no real faith in themselves and their ability; all a child has is a trust in the one who has faithfully loved them and shown them that love. Why would the disciples turn the children away, unless it was because they did not believe in the children's ability to make themselves sufficiently right with Jesus, to gain eternal life.

This fact begged the question of Jesus' disciples when they asked Him, "Then who can be saved?" The rich young man got Jesus' point "with man it is impossible," and that's why he went away disheartened. Jesus seeks to clarify the issue for the disciples and for me, when he tells us that salvation is not impossible for God. "For all things are possible with God."

Of all that the young man could have said to Jesus in response to His command to sell all he had, nothing would reveal that he had gained the unbelief in himself that he lacked, more than the words, "I can't do that." Here is the confession of a child to one who could help. To all who confess this truth, the cross is Jesus' confession to all, "I can do that for you." On the cross, He who is first sold all He had to the Father and now gives it freely to the poor who are last, so that they might be first.

FRIDAY—LENT 3

Psalmody: Psalm 49:1–3, 7–10
Additional Psalm: Psalm 49, Psalm 102
Old Testament Reading: Genesis 40:1–23
New Testament Reading: Mark 10:32–52

Prayer of the Day

O God, the helper of all who call on You, have mercy on us and give us eyes of faith to see Your Son that we may follow Him on the way that leads to eternal life; through the same Jesus Christ, Your Son, our Lord, who lives and reigns with You and the Holy Spirit, one God, now and forever. (B83)

Meditation

How would you define the word *authority*? Many dictionaries today define it along the lines of power to do this or that. Yet at its core, *authority* refers more to the authorized exercise of power according to one's office than merely to power itself.

For Jesus, the purpose of exercising of authority is not how one might be over people but under them, that is, serve them. With the words, "For even the Son of Man came not to be served but to serve" Jesus clarifies the purpose of every office God has established. Any exercise of power is limited to the authorized purpose God has given each office.

Those who served as the Chief priests were authorized to exercise power according to the responsibilities of their office. Jesus makes it clear that they will exercise the power of their office in an unauthorized manner. The only way this could happen is if they authorized themselves to do as they did (Mark 7:8–9). In their petition, James and John want Jesus to exercise the power of His office to secure them the best seats in the house. Here Jesus informs them that He will not exercise His power to do what He has not been authorized to do. His response might well have been, "I have not been authorized to grant this to you."

When Jesus' calls Bartimaeus to Himself, He asks "What do you want me to do for you?" Inasmuch as Bartimaeus's request is within the limits of what Jesus has been authorized to do, He exercises His power and heals him.

When Jesus says that He came not to be served but to serve, Jesus points to the purpose for which He was authorized to exercise the divine power that had been given to Him as the only-begotten Son of God and the Son of Man (active obedience).

When Jesus says that He came also to give His life as a ransom for many, Jesus reveals that as the Son of God and the Son of man, He was not authorized to exercise this power to save Himself (passive obedience).

No place does Jesus affirm that the purpose of all authority in heaven and earth is that one might be under people rather than on the cross. Even as He was raised up on the cross, it was for the purpose of bearing up all people, not by power, but by His great love for us all. Under His authority, He gathers us up in His arms and carries us in His bosom (Isaiah 40:11).

Psalmody: Psalm 11
Additional Psalm: Psalm 118, Psalm 51
Old Testament Reading: Genesis 41:1–27
New Testament Reading: Mark 11:1–19

Prayer of the Day

God of our salvation, Your beloved Son entered the holy city to shouts of "Hosanna!" for truly He came in the name of the Lord. Give us faith to grasp the mystery of His suffering, death, and resurrection on our behalf as we journey with Him this Lenten season to the cross and, beyond that to the empty tomb; through Jesus Christ, Your Son, our Lord, who lives and reigns with You and the Holy Spirit, one God, now and forever. (1005)

Meditation

Jesus' command for His disciples to go into the village to get a colt that no one had ridden on, and His procession into Jerusalem riding that colt was a deliberate presentation of Himself as the promised Messiah.

Hosanna, the response of the people, is their public confession of faith that He is the Messiah. This plea of hosanna is a plea to save. While many cry out to Jesus to save them from the Roman domination of their promised land, Jesus proceeds to show them what they need to be saved from.

When Jesus comes to the fig tree looking for figs, he was not looking for food, as it was not the season for figs. Jesus is looking for what might be called "early figs," the physically small, not-yet-ripened fruit that would have appeared with the leaves that covered the tree. Jesus then cursed the tree, not because it didn't bear fruit, but because it symbolized the multitude of unbelieving, and therefore unfruitful within Israel. The Lord came looking for the fruit on this fig tree and found none (Jeremiah 8:13). In cursing the tree that had no fruit, Jesus is therefore revealing what the people need to be saved from: the sham displays of their own religious righteousness, a religion that bore no spiritual righteousness.

After cursing the fig tree, the only destructive miracle that Gospel writers record, Jesus proceeds immediately into the temple. In driving out the money-changers and the sellers, Jesus curses the unfruitful practices that the Jewish leaders had established. What God had established as a place where all nations might find free access to Him in His temple, the Jewish leaders re-established it as a place of access to pockets of all nations in the name of providing access to God.

By driving the money-changers and sellers out, Jesus makes it plain that He has come to save them not from the Romans but from the Jewish leaders and what they had done to people's access to God and thus the fruit He would produce through them.

Having now presented Himself as the Messiah, Jesus also presented Himself as the new temple of God. On the cross, Jesus opens up the courts of His temple, receives all nations unto Himself, and in this court, prays for them. In Him, the new temple of God, hosanna is accomplished for one and all. Access to God is purchased, not with coin or con of man, but with body and blood of God's Son.

Hosanna!

FOURTH SUNDAY IN LENT

Psalmody: Psalm 60:1, 9–12
Additional Psalm: Psalm 60, Psalm 102
Old Testament Reading: Genesis 41:28–57
New Testament Reading: Mark 11:20–33

Prayer of the Day

Almighty God, our heavenly Father, Your mercies are new every morning; and though we deserve only punishment, You receive us as Your children and provide for all our needs of body and soul. Grant that we may heartily acknowledge Your merciful goodness, give thanks for all Your benefits, and serve You in willing obedience; through Jesus Christ, Your Son, our Lord, who lives and reigns with You and the Holy Spirit, one God, now and forever. (L26)

Meditation

Why does Jesus respond to Peter's observation about the withered tree with the words, "Have faith in God" (Mark 11:22)? Well, what did Peter expect to see when he saw the fig tree? His calling attention to its witheredness indicates his surprise that it had become as Jesus' words made it: cursed. Peter's surprise at the tree's withered condition indicates that he expected to see it unaltered or unaffected by the words Jesus said to it the night before. Only a lack of faith in the ability of Jesus' words to make something or someone as He spoke them to be would cause a person to be surprised when that something or someone is as Jesus spoke them to be. So in response to Peter's surprise, Jesus calls him to faith in one for whom all things are possible: God.

To understand the role of faith in God doing great things, one must not disconnect the throwing of a mountain into the sea from Jesus exhortation, "Have faith in God." Jesus makes it clear that faith in God is faith in the infinite ability of God to do what He says. In prayer, faith is the issue, not in regards to amount, but the object of faith. The object of our faith is Jesus Christ and His life in and for us. The extent of God's ability in answering prayer is affirmed by St. Paul, "Now to Him who is able to do far more abundantly than all that we ask or think, according to the power at work within us . . ." (Ephesians 3:20). So we heed the hymn writer, "Thou art coming to a King, large petitions with thee bring" (*LSB* 779:2).

As Peter was surprised that the tree had become as Jesus had spoken to it, so also the chief priests, the scribes, and the elders of Israel were surprised that the people of Israel were becoming as Jesus had spoken. They were frustrated that their words could not keep things from becoming such. Their lack of faith is found in their surprise, but their refusal to believe is confessed in their refusal to confess the mission of John the Baptist.

Faith's primary work is one of receiving God and His work. Jesus is the object of our faith because He alone received all of God and His work on us for ourselves, our sin, our unbelief. With Jesus as the object of our faith, we receive Him, and from Him, God's good work of forgiveness and peace with God.

MONDAY—LENT 4

Psalmody: Psalm 3
Additional Psalm: Psalm 7, Psalm 130
Old Testament Reading: Genesis 42:1–34, 38
New Testament Reading: Mark 12:1–12

Prayer of the Day

Almighty God, You exalted Your Son to the place of all honor and authority. Enlighten our minds by Your Holy Spirit that, confessing Jesus as Lord, we may be led into all truth; through the same Jesus Christ, our Lord, who lives and reigns with You and the Holy Spirit, one God, now and forever. (A79)

Meditation
Jesus asks, "What will the owner of the vineyard do?" (Mark 12:9). While Jesus answers this question in detail, there is a far more basic answer that lies beyond the one Jesus gave. To hear this answer we need to step back from the individual results of the parable and look at all the events in total. In doing this, don't you find that there are only two constants throughout this parable, the owner and the vineyard? The owner owns the vineyard. He planted it, built the fence, dug the wine press, and leased it out. He keeps coming for some of the fruit. He comes and destroys the unfaithful tenants and leases the vineyard to new tenants.

A more basic answer to this question would be, "The owner of the vineyard is going to be the owner of his vineyard." As such, the owner will own his vineyard not according to the agenda of the tenants but according to his own agenda.

How could the Jewish leaders perceive that Jesus had spoken this parable against them? When He asks the question, "Have you not read . . . " and then quotes Psalm 118:22–23, He lays this parable squarely on the Jewish leaders.

What is striking on the part of the Jewish leaders is that while they feared the people's faith in the parable, they didn't believe the words of it or the promise found in Psalm 118:22–23. This is proven by the fact that they proceed to take the owner's Son and kill him outside the vineyard.

How is it possible that they did not get the implication of the words, "The stone the builders rejected has become the cornerstone; this is the Lord's doing"? With these words Jesus makes it clear to them that no matter what they do to get rid of the Son so as to possess the vineyard, the Owner will own the vineyard and His Son and will bring Him back as the tenant.

At the fall of Adam and Eve, God the Father made His Son the tenant of His now fallen vineyard. Finding no fruit in us, God the Father comes to collect His share of the fruit from His Son outside the vineyard on a cross. Here Jesus offers up the most precious of fruit as He yields up a harvest of His body and His blood. And there is peace in this vineyard as the owner re-owns us by a better fruit and new vineyard planted in His Son.

TUESDAY—LENT 4

Psalmody: Psalm 37:16–20
Additional Psalm: Psalm 37, Psalm 143
Old Testament Reading: Genesis 43:1–28
New Testament Reading: Mark 12:13–27

Prayer of the Day

Lord God heavenly Father, the God of Abraham, and the God of Isaac, and the God of Jacob, Your servant Moses proclaimed the resurrection to the children of Israel to give them hope in the midst of their darkness. As we journey to the darkness of the cross, give us hope to look beyond it to the light of the resurrection; through Jesus Christ, Your Son, our Lord. (1006)

Meditation

Do you see the Pharisees' test within their test? Having failed to do much to deter Jesus' ministry or place in the hearts of the people, the Pharisees and the Herodians hope to deter Him via the civil realm. The trap is obvious: If He refuses to pay taxes, they have grounds to hand Him over to the Romans. If, however, He endorses paying taxes, they have grounds to turn the people's hearts against Him and deal with Him as they want.

Yet, their test goes much deeper than taxes. Isn't the real test they press upon Jesus one of ego or pride? The heart of this test is found in their statement, "Teacher, we know that You are true and do not care about anyone's opinion." The question of paying taxes to Caesar is filled with danger. After setting the stage with this statement, the question about taxes was really a test to see if Jesus was as bold in rejecting the opinions, or laws, of the Romans, as He had been in rejecting their laws and traditions. They believed that either way Jesus exercised His ego or pride they would have Him.

Jesus' response to them, as to the Sadducees, turns the issue from one of opinions to one of divinely established relationships. It is God who established the civil government. Having and using this coin with Caesar's image on it testified to the privilege of such government, their subjection to it, and their responsibility to it. God's establishment of such government is for the interests of the people. Rendering to Caesar what is his is a rendering unto God according to the Fourth Commandment. Rendering unto God was Jesus' way of challenging them to recognize the divinely established relationship He had with them and the whole world, and their need to treat him accordingly. Such is what Jesus charges the Sadducees to do in regard to marriage. This relationship was established for this world, not the next.

For Jesus, faithfulness in the relationships God has created is the key in all that we render, whether it be to God, to government, or to our neighbor. In this fallen world, we live amidst broken relationships on all levels. It is into this breakage, into our brokenness on all these levels that Jesus has come. On the cross, He alone in His body is faithful to one and all, and in Him we have a new relationship that finds full faithfulness with one and all, even God our heavenly Father.

WEDNESDAY—LENT 4

Psalmody: Psalm 26:1–7
Additional Psalm: Psalm 16, Psalm 6
Old Testament Reading:
Genesis 44:1–18, 32–34
New Testament Reading: Mark 12:28–44

Prayer of the Day

Lord Jesus Christ, our great High Priest, cleanse us by the power of Your redeeming blood that in purity and peace we may worship and adore Your holy name; for You live and reign with the Father and the Holy Spirit, one God, now and forever. (B84)

Meditation

Unknown to him at the time, the scribe confessed his belief in the very mission and ministry of the kingdom of God in Jesus Christ. This is his nearness, his entrance into the kingdom would come in same way that David received it, by the Holy Spirit calling him to the faith so that he might call Jesus Lord too.

Jesus then proceeds to show who, despite all appearances, is far from the kingdom of God. What creates this distance from the kingdom of God? When anyone, whether they claim to be in the kingdom or not, is like those Jesus mentions, living to love their neighbor for themselves rather than as themselves.

Sitting opposite the treasury, what standard does Jesus use to determine the gifts that people gave? What are two copper coins compared to a denarius, a sack of gold shekels? Not much when compared apart from what one is left with. While the monetary value of what others gave far exceeds hers, what she is left with far exceeds what they are left with. They were all left with what remained of their riches and their purses, while she was left with just the kingdom of God.

So Jesus draws attention to the one who is living her faith in the kingdom of God. Jesus draws attention to the one who gave all she had to a system that had become corrupt, a system under which she likely suffered. Only her faith in the kingdom of God to provide for her could free her to live her love for God and for the very neighbors who had likely denied her the rightful care a widow was due from the Jewish priests and elders.

Jesus Christ is the love of God. By His life He lived to love God in the way we cannot—for us and for our neighbor. He let go of everything and made Himself nothing, so that He might serve us and save us (Philippians 2:7). The cross forever testifies to all that both the Father and the Son let go out of love for us. Yet in all that Jesus let go of, He held onto us so that even in our farness from the kingdom of God in our sin, we might find the kingdom of God come to save us. In love for us, God has let go of our sins that we might live in Him and His kingdom through faith in Jesus Christ.

THURSDAY—LENT 4

Psalmody: Psalm 82
Additional Psalm: Psalm 18, Psalm 32
Old Testament Reading:
Genesis 45:1–20, 24–28
New Testament Reading: Mark 13:1–23

Prayer of the Day

O Lord, by Your bountiful goodness release us from the bonds of our sins, which by reason of our weakness we have brought upon ourselves, that we may stand firm until the day of our Lord Jesus Christ, who lives and reigns with You and the Holy Spirit, one God, now and forever. (B86)

Meditation

What are the disciples to be on their guard for? What are they to watch themselves for? Is it a matter of making sure they do not get themselves wrong with councils or kings? Is it a matter of not being in the wrong place at the wrong time? Or is it a matter of having the wrong Christ?

As Jesus speaks of what will be happening to them and to the temple and to Jerusalem, He is making sure in all this, they remember something He taught them. "If anyone would come after Me, let him deny himself and take up his cross and follow Me. For whoever would save his life will lose it, but whoever loses his life for My sake and the gospel's will save it" (Mark 8:34–35).

While the four disciples asked about the signs of the coming destruction of the temple out of curiosity, they also asked out of self-preservation. Give us a timetable so that we can make sure we're not around when this happens. In answering their question, Jesus tells these four disciples far more than they asked. Jesus' answer turns the issue from one of escaping it to one of living in the midst of it and more. Even as Jesus sent into the fallen and falling of this world that He might bear witness to the love of God, so He will send His disciples into the same fallen and falling world so that they might bear witness to Him as the love of God.

In all that Jesus foretells will happen to them, none will happen until after they have happened to Him in His passion and death. For them as for Him, whether they are before councils, kin, or kings, in Jerusalem or Judea, their physical lives will be in jeopardy, and they will be put to death. All such times and places will be anxious ones; as such their hearts may turn to how they might escape so as to save themselves. Here is where they must be on their guard; for in these times, many other christs present themselves as the way of salvation from such earthly danger and death.

To be on their guard is to believe and bear witness to the Christ, who suffered and died for all that is fallen and falling, and on the third day, rose again to raise all that is fallen and built a new house built of living stones with Himself as the Chief Cornerstone.

FRIDAY—LENT 4

Psalmody: Psalm 77:11–15
Additional Psalm: Psalm 17, Psalm 38
Old Testament Reading: Genesis 47:1–31
Additional Reading: Genesis 48:1–49:28
New Testament Reading: Mark 13:24–37

Prayer of the Day

Lord Jesus Christ, so govern our hearts and minds by Your Holy Spirit that, ever mindful of Your glorious return, we may persevere in both faith and holiness of living; for You live and reign with the Father and the Holy Spirit, one God, now and forever. (B87)

93

Meditation

As Jesus continues with His prophecy concerning the coming destruction of the temple and Jerusalem, He connects this with His second coming. How are we to understand this language about the sun being darkened and the stars falling from heaven? This same kind of language was used in the Old Testament to portray the judgment of God. Ezekiel 32:7–8 speaks of the judgment of Egypt; Amos 8:9 the judgment of Northern Kingdom; and Joel 2:30–32 and 3:15 speaks of the judgment on those nations in relation to Judah's return from the Babylonian captivity. In each of these, the language portrays the great destruction that will come upon any nations under God's wrathful judgment. These words are a portrayal of the radical effect of God intervening in human events with His wrath.

Matthew 26:64 clarifies the fact that the coming of the Son of Man is a singular event as the end of time. The coming of the Son of Man shall be an ongoing event that will find its consummation at a time of the Father's choosing. The prophesied destruction of the temple and Jerusalem are simply a part of the Son's ongoing coming.

The Son of Man's coming will commence the moment the promised Holy Spirit proceeds from the Father and the Son. The gathering of the elect is precisely the work of the Holy Spirit through the Gospel.

Jesus makes it clear that in all these things He speaks of what will happen within the hearers' lifetime. While many monumental institutions, civilizations, and individuals will pass away, His words will not pass away. The parable of the man going on a journey speaks of Jesus' coming departure that the events He's spoken of may commence. He is speaking to the servants He will put in charge with the different work He will give to each (Ephesians 4:11). The work of these servants will be in service of the one thing that does not pass away, the words of Jesus, which is the Holy Gospel.

The prophetic language of the Old Testament that Jesus uses to speak of the doom that will come upon the temple and Jerusalem, He also uses to speak of what will literally happen to Him on the cross. For at that time, the sun was darkened, and Satan fell from heaven forever. Jesus' resurrection reveals the enduring nature of His words, for He is the Word made flesh, made death, and made alive forever for us.

SATURDAY—LENT 4

Psalmody: Psalm 44:1–4
Additional Psalm: Psalm 44, Psalm 51
Old Testament Reading:
Genesis 49:29–50:7, 14–26
New Testament Reading: Mark 14:1–11

Prayer of the Day

Lord Jesus Christ, Your body was anointed with holy oil by the woman at the house of Simon the leper to prepare it for burial. May Your church continue to take care of Your Body as she feeds Your people the holy food of Your very body and blood for the forgiveness of sins; for You live and reign with the Father and the Holy Spirit, one God, now and forever. (1007)

Meditation

The word *opportunity* implies a favorable time for advancement. The chief priests and the scribes are searching for an opportunity to advance their agenda of getting rid of Jesus without jeopardizing themselves and their position. The only way they can advance both parts of their agenda is if it is done in stealth or after the Passover.

In Bethany, a young woman has heard Jesus speak of His impending death. In the house of Simon the leper, she finds the opportunity to advance her want to express her deep love for Jesus, to Jesus. In taking this opportunity to express her love to Jesus, there can be no stealth in the depth of her love as the aroma of the expensive nard filled the whole house.

As this young woman takes the opportunity to express her love, others, namely Judas, object to this because it denies him the opportunity to advance his agenda of helping himself to what was to be given to the poor (John 12:4-6). As he proceeds to scold her, Jesus denies Judas any advancement of his agenda as He takes this opportunity to commend her for what she has done. Jesus uses this opportunity to further His teaching of His impending death.

With Jesus ever so committed to His advancing His messianic agenda, Judas sees that the opportunities to further the agenda of his purse will soon be gone. In the impending loss of his opportunities with Jesus, Judas sees an opportunity to advance the agenda with those whom Jesus says will kill Him.

Now the chief priests and the scribes have the means by which to advance both parts of their agenda. In Judas, they had the opportunity to get close to Jesus, to know His movements, and the stealthiest opportunity to advance their agenda. In Judas, they had the opportunity to advance their own innocence if one Jesus' own had betrayed Him, not them. In Judas, they would have the opportunity to present themselves as arbiters of God's holy law.

Yet in all the opportunities that Judas afforded them, the sinful advancement of his agenda and the chief priests', God the Father takes the opportunity to advance His agenda of saving mankind. Jesus knows that unless Judas takes the opportunity to advance his own sinful agenda, He will never have the opportunity to fulfill His messianic agenda on the cross. When Jesus said it is finished, sin and death's opportunities to separate us from God are their end.

FIFTH SUNDAY IN LENT

Psalmody: Psalm 129
Additional Psalm: Psalm 81, Psalm 102
Old Testament Reading: Exodus 1:1–22
New Testament Reading: Mark 14:12–31

Prayer of the Day

Almighty God, by Your great goodness mercifully look upon Your people that we may be governed and preserved evermore in body and soul; through Jesus Christ, Your Son, our Lord, who lives and reigns with You and the Holy Spirit, one God, now and forever. (L27)

Meditation

Surely the preparations the disciples made were for the Passover that God had instituted through Moses at the time of Israel's deliverance from Egypt. However, once the Passover meal commences, Jesus speaks in terms of when they will sacrifice Himself as the Passover Lamb of God who takes away the sin of the world.

Having participated in the Passover meal, Jesus establishes a new covenant that will subsist in Himself and His sacrificial death as the Lamb of God. In establishing a new covenant through His sacrificial death, Jesus institutes a new feast. In this feast they will still eat of the flesh of sacrificial lamb as He gives them His flesh in, with, and under the form of bread. In this meal they will be given the Lamb's blood in, with, and under the form of the wine, not to sprinkle it upon the doorposts of their homes, but to drink that it may be sprinkled upon the doorposts of their hearts.

As they head out to the Mount of Olives the time draws near to when they will prepare the Lamb of God for sacrifice. When this happens Jesus makes it clear that He will be alone as they will all abandon Him. When Peter professes his faithfulness to Jesus even unto death, Jesus tells him plainly that even before the time when they will sacrifice Him, Peter will deny Him three times.

When they sacrificed the Passover Lamb, there was only one Lamb from God that could take away the sins of the world. When they sacrificed the Passover Lamb, there was only one Lamb's blood that could be sprinkled upon us and our children that eternal death might pass over us.

What are we to make of the woe that Jesus speaks upon His betrayer? Isn't it a word of judgment upon the unbelieving one who refused to let Jesus be his Passover Lamb from God? While Judas's betrayal is most grievous, even more grievous to this Lamb of God was the fact that when He was sacrificed, Judas wanted His blood sprinkled in his purse, not on his person, not on his heart.

When they sacrificed the Passover Lamb of God on the cross, death, like the sin that brings it to all, was not allowed to pass over. When they sacrificed this Passover Lamb of God, He ate the full meal of death and swallowed it and its victory. In Him death has now become a pass-through unto eternal life. Now begins the preparation for the feast of victory.

MONDAY—LENT 5

Psalmody: Psalm 31:9–14
Additional Psalm: Psalm 116, Psalm 130
Old Testament Reading: Exodus 2:1–22
New Testament Reading: Mark 14:32–52

Prayer of the Day

Lord Jesus Christ, in the Garden of Gethsemane You suffered the agony of drinking from the cup of Your Father's wrath against our sin, being betrayed by a kiss from one of Your own. Give us strength to remain awake as we now wait and watch for Your coming again, knowing that the Father's wrath against us has been satisfied by Your bloody death and vindicating resurrection; for You live and reign with the Father and the Holy Spirit, one God, now and forever. (1008)

Meditation

How shall the crowd, with swords and clubs, capture Jesus? By what instrument, what means shall they capture and hold the Son of God? Maybe they plan to use the authority of the chief priests, or the quill and scroll of the scribes, or the wisdom of the elders.

Jesus' question and statement about their failure to seize Him in the temple questions the extreme measures they have taken to capture Him. These also mock the illusion that allows them to believe they are the captors and Jesus is the captured. Such an illusion arises from a hardened heart that has rejected the Word Jesus preached to them day after day in the temple courts.

In truth there is only one thing that captured Jesus, "Abba, Father . . . Yet not what I will, but what You will." The opening word of this prayer, *Abba*, bears the deepest movement of the heart to His Father. Jesus, Son of God and Son of Man, was captured by the love of His Father, and in that love, the will of His Father. Even as Jesus is captured by His Father's love for Him, He is also held captive to the Father's love for us. Jesus does not hide what has captured Him from the disciples, as when He told them, "As the Father has loved Me, so I have loved you" (John 15:9).

Sadly, those that came to capture Jesus failed to see that He was there to capture them so that neither they nor anyone else in fallen creation might be forever captured by sin and death. It was not the lies, the cowardice, the perverted justice, or the nails of His captors that held Jesus to the cross, but His being captive to the love of God for Him and for us. Only on the cross, only in the place of the captured could Jesus fully capture our sin and the full wrath of God against our sins and take them into death with Him. The resurrection of Christ Jesus from the dead reveals that He has also captured death.

What is our Baptism but a time of blessed captivity, our sin to the cross of Christ and our new life to the resurrection of Christ. What is the Holy Absolution but a time of captivity, our sin and guilt to the death of Christ and our new life to the forgiveness of God in Jesus Christ. What is our faith, but the blessed captivity of God's all-sufficient grace in Jesus Christ.

TUESDAY—LENT 5

Psalmody: Psalm 39:1–7
Additional Psalm: Psalm 5, Psalm 143
Old Testament Reading: Exodus 2:23—3:22
New Testament Reading: Mark 14:53–72

Prayer of the Day

Lord Jesus Christ, the temple of Your body was destroyed on the cross and three days later raised from the dead and exalted to the right hand of the Father. Visit us now with this same body, that we may not deny that we know You, but in faith hear in our ears Your life-giving voice and receive on our lips Your very body and blood to strengthen us in times of temptation; for You live and reign with the Father and the Holy Spirit, one God, now and forever. (1009)

Meditation

In reading these verses, did you catch all the testimony against? The conduct of the whole Sanhedrin is a testimony against themselves. Those who were supposed to adjudicate Jesus' guilt or innocence prosecuted Jesus by seeking out testimony against Jesus according to the measure of guilt that would justify their goal of putting Him to death.

Then Jesus provides testimony against the Sanhedrin and their agenda when says, "I am." By this simple statement Jesus testifies against their unbelief, not their accusations of what He had said. The fact that they could quote Jesus yet were still seeking to kill Him was testimony of their hardness of heart in unbelief. In quoting Jesus, they gave testimony against themselves of their unbelief.

Consider the testimony against the high priest, the Sanhedrin, and the guards as given in their reaction to Jesus' proclamation of Himself as the Christ, the Son of the Blessed. The high priest tears the high priest's garments in contemptuous rejection of the true High Priest. The high priest declares the Word of God spoken by the Word of God to be blasphemy. The Sanhedrin condemns to death the Author and Redeemer of life. Some spit on the One who offers living water. Some cover the face of the One who will cover their sin and their same. Some strike the One whose stripes will bring them healing. Some mock the prophetic office of the One whose words are life and salvation. Guards give body blows to the One whose body will guard them from the blows of sin, death, and the wrath of God.

Then there is the testimony against Peter. One of the high priest's servant girls testifies twice against Peter. First she testifies the truth against Peter, to Peter, that he was with Jesus. Then she testifies the truth against Peter to bystanders that Peter is one of Jesus' disciples. Then the bystanders testify to the truth against Peter that he was a disciple of Jesus and a Galilean.

This brings us to Peter's testimony. Peter has but one goal, to save himself from what he is and the consequences for it. Because Peter testifies against the truth about himself, it is testimony against himself. Only upon hearing the second testimony of the rooster does Peter remember Jesus' testimony against him. The testimony of Peter's breaking down and weeping reveals the verdict he rendered upon himself.

What a blessed and saving thing it is that all the testimony against Jesus convicted Him of being only what He was, the Christ. What peace there is for us in that all the testimony that there will be for or against us, Jesus testifies last, and He testifies for us.

WEDNESDAY—LENT 5

Psalmody: Psalm 18:6–7, 16–20
Additional Psalm: Psalm 23, Psalm 6
Old Testament Reading: Exodus 4:1–18
New Testament Reading: Mark 15:1–15

Prayer of the Day

Lord Jesus Christ, You released many from their bondage to sin, death, and the devil as the healer of the nations, but when it came time to release You, the crowd chose a murderer instead. Through our co-crucifixion with You in the waters of our Baptism, may we continually be released from our sins as we confess You to be our everlasting King; for You live and reign with the Father and the Son, one God, now and forever. (1010)

Meditation

Envy is far more than an emotion one may feel at the success of another. Envy lives in our sinful heart. It is the favored henchman of our sinful pride. The mission of envy arises from the mission of our sinful pride. Sinful pride seeks above all else to save us from both the realities of our sinful fallenness and God. To save us, sinful pride uses envy to destroy or tear down anyone or anything that confronts us with the truth or reality about ourselves and God.

Pilate's perception that envy had motivated the Jewish leaders to seek Jesus' death was right on the mark. Jesus presented a reality of God to the people contrary to the illusions their sinful pride created to save their position and power. Jesus presented a reality of God contrary to the illusion of God their sinful pride created to save themselves from God. Jesus was the reality of God with us, contrary to the illusion their sinful pride had created of God with them. For all this, Jesus had to be destroyed.

At this point Pilate has to choose whether he will live by this envious illusion. Pilate believes that whatever their accusations, they are made because Jesus threatens their position and power over the people. So he questions Jesus. Pilate isn't sure how to take Jesus' one response so he tries to get Jesus to challenge the illusions the Jews have cast about Him. His silence leaves Pilate with nothing to challenge the envious charges of the Jews. Wanting to save himself the potential consequential realities of his faithful fulfillment to his responsibility, such as a riot, Pilate chooses to deal with Jesus according to envy's mission and orders His crucifixion.

Nothing reveals the reality of envy's mission more than their chant in ever-increasing volume, "Crucify Him."

In light of this, consider the confession, "I, a poor miserable sinner . . . " Our sinful pride would save us from this, casting the illusion that sin only has to do with actions. Inasmuch as the Lord included the role of envy in the crucifixion of Jesus testifies to the reality of our sinfulness. We, like St. Paul must cry out, "Wretched man that I am! Who will deliver me from this body of death?" (Romans 7:24). The answer is found in the fact that our Lord's crucifixion came from our sinful heart; as such, His crucifixion also saves us from what we are. Thanks be to God (Romans 7:25).

THURSDAY—LENT 5

Psalmody: Psalm 69:33–36
Additional Psalm: Psalm 69, Psalm 32
Old Testament Reading: Exodus 4:19–31
New Testament Reading: Mark 15:16–32

Prayer of the Day

Almighty and everlasting God, You sent Your Son, our Savior Jesus Christ, to take upon Himself our flesh and to suffer death upon the cross. Mercifully grant that we may follow the example of His great humility and patience and be made partakers of His resurrection; through the same Jesus Christ, our Lord, who lives and reigns with You and the Holy Spirit, one God, now and forever. (L28)

Meditation

What does it mean to be the "direct object"? In sentence grammar it refers to that which receives the activity of the verb that is done by the subject of the sentence.

As you have read this text did you notice how many times pronoun "Him" was the direct object of various activities done by others? " . . . led Him away . . . clothed Him . . . put it (crown of thorns) on Him . . . salute Him . . . striking His head . . . spitting on Him . . . homage to Him . . . mocked Him . . . stripped Him . . . put His clothes on Him . . . led Him . . . crucify Him . . . brought Him . . . offered Him . . . crucified Him . . . crucified Him . . . derided Him . . . mocked Him . . . reviled Him."

Who is the subject, the doer of all this activity directed at Jesus? While their names are not mentioned, they are us. They are nothing more and nothing less than the voices of sin, the hostile voices of our sinful nature we are born with (Psalm 51; Romans 8:7).

Who is the direct object, the receiver of this activity, the "Him"? His name is never mentioned in this reading. Of course this is Jesus. He alone has come to be the direct object of all sinful humanity's rebellion against and rejection of God. As such, He has come to be the receiver of all our unrighteous anger, the receiver of all our hatred and murder of our neighbor, the receiver of our curse because we are cursed in sin.

Yes, Jesus willingly comes to be the direct object of all that is us and our doings in sin. For only when He has fully received all that is us and our doing, He is able to be the direct object of God's wrathful activity against us for what we are and what we do. When Jesus asks why God had forsaken Him on the cross, we can be sure that Jesus has become the direct object, the receiver of all God's wrath against us.

With Jesus as the direct object of us and the wrath of God, we are made the direct objects, the receivers of God's forgiveness and favor. "Now to Him who is able to keep you from stumbling and to present you blameless before the presence of His glory with great joy, to the only God, our Savior, through Jesus Christ our Lord, be glory, majesty, dominion, and authority, before all time and now and forever. Amen" (Jude 1:24–25).

FRIDAY—LENT 5

Psalmody: Psalm 22:1–5
Additional Psalm: Psalm 22, Psalm 38
Old Testament Reading: Exodus 5:1–6:1
New Testament Reading: Mark 15:33–47

Prayer of the Day

Merciful and everlasting God, You did not spare Your only Son but delivered Him up for us all to bear our sins on the cross. Grant that our hearts may be so fixed with steadfast faith in Him that we fear not the power of sin, death, and the devil; through the same Jesus Christ, our Lord, who lives and reigns with You and the Holy Spirit, one God, now and forever. (L31)

Meditation

Everyone is looking at the cross, but what are they looking for? Did they find it? Many were looking for Jesus' death. They found that only when breathing His last, Jesus entered into their death.

Countless others, at the cross and through Jerusalem, were looking from the sixth hour to the ninth hour for some sign of daylight in this midday darkness that covered the whole land. They found it only when Jesus entered the darkness of their sealed tomb.

At the ninth hour Jesus' cry tells us that He is looking for His God and Father who had now forsaken Him on the cross. Jesus found Him only when He had finished what the Father had given Him (John 19:30), and He commended His spirit into His Father's hands (Luke 23:46).

Bystanders were looking for Elijah to come and take Jesus down. They find what they are looking for only when Joseph of Arimathea, who later served as a missionary (prophetic office) to Gaul, came and took Jesus down.

The two Marys are looking for the time when the suffering and humiliation of their Lord would end. They find what they are looking for only when Jesus takes sin, the cause of all suffering and humiliation, with Him into death as He breathes His last.

Joseph of Arimathea was looking for the kingdom of God. He finds what he is looking for only in the corpse he took courage to ask for, in the corpse he is granted, in the corpse he buys a linen shroud for, in the corpse he took down from the cross, in the corpse he wraps in his linen, in the corpse he laid in a tomb, in a tomb he rolls a stone against.

While this text tells us of those of those participating in the events of Jesus' crucifixion and what they were looking for and what they found, does it tell us of someone else and what they found?

In Jesus' cry, "My God, My God, why have You forsaken Me?" we learn of someone else and what they were looking for. God the Father is looking for us and the only place He wants to find us is in His Son. This cry of Jesus tells us that God the Father has found us where we are. Finding us here, He deals with His Son so that in Him, we might look and find the forgiving love and favor of God for us.

SATURDAY—LENT 5

Psalmody: Psalm 78:52–55
Additional Psalm: Psalm 78, Psalm 51
Old Testament Reading: Exodus 7:1–25
New Testament Reading: Mark 16:1–20

Prayer of the Day

Almighty God, through the resurrection of Your Son You have secured peace for our troubled consciences. Grant us this peace evermore that trusting in the merit of Your Son we may come at last to the perfect peace of heaven; through the same Jesus Christ, Your Son, our Lord, who lives and reigns with You and the Holy Spirit, one God, now and forever. (L39)

Meditation

What is there to see on that first Easter morning and the days that followed it?

The women see the stone rolled away from the tomb. What is there to see in this? No stone, no guardian, and no seal could sufficiently protect the Jews, Pilate, Romans, or the world from the invasion of divinely resurrected life.

The women see a young man dressed in white sitting on the right side. What is there to see in this? Something greater and other than this world had intervened to bring resurrection to human flesh.

The women see that Jesus' body is not there, and they hear the messenger tell them that Jesus has risen from the dead. What is there to see in this? Christ's victory of death and all its causes in sin.

Mary Magdalene sees Jesus when He appears to her. What is to be seen in this? He who had cast out the seven demons that once possessed her, has now cast out her sin and death, and the sin and death of all people.

Mary Magdalene sees unbelief when she tells Jesus' disciples that He is risen. The two returning from Emmaus to tell the disciples they had seen the Lord (Luke 24:34–35), see unbelief. What is to be seen in these? Jesus tells us what He saw—hardness of heart and unbelief.

The eleven see the resurrected Jesus. What is to be seen in this? What the Holy Spirit so convinced St. Paul of: "For I am sure that neither death nor life, nor angels nor rulers, nor things present nor things to come, nor powers, nor height nor depth, nor anything else in all creation, will be able to separate us from the love of God in Christ Jesus our Lord" (Romans 8:38–39).

The eleven see the Lord ascending into heaven. What is there to be seen in this? "When He ascended on high He led a host of captives, and He gave gifts to men" (Ephesians 4:8).

The twelve, and many others, see the Lord work signs accompanying and confirming their message. What is there to be seen in these? "I am with you always, to the end of the age" (Matthew 28:20).

What is there for us to see in all this? Jesus said, "I am the resurrection and the life. Whoever believes in Me, though he die, yet shall he live, and everyone who lives and believes in Me shall never die" (John 11:25–26).

THE TIME OF EASTER
Holy Week

PALM SUNDAY

Psalmody: Psalm 71:19–24
Additional Psalm: Psalm 45, Psalm 130
Old Testament Reading: Exodus 8:1–32
Additional Reading: Psalm 118
New Testament Reading: Hebrews 1:1–14

Prayer of the Day

Almighty and everlasting God, You sent Your Son, our Savior Jesus Christ, to take upon Himself our flesh and to suffer death upon the cross. Mercifully grant that we may follow the example of His great humility and patience and be made partakers of His resurrection; through the same Jesus Christ, our Lord, who lives and reigns with You and the Holy Spirit, one God, now and forever. (L28)

Meditation

The only true God went to extreme efforts to speak to His people through His prophets in the Old Testament. Many times they refused to listen, and His prophets expressed their frustration. Jeremiah accused the people of spiritual adultery as they turned away from God. "By the waysides you have sat awaiting lovers like an Arab in the wilderness" (Jeremiah 3:2).

Though the entire Old Testament pointed to the coming of the Messiah, many Israelites did not accept Jesus of Nazareth as the Promised One. Even as He rode into Jerusalem on a donkey there were many skeptics. The writer of the Letter to the Hebrews went to extreme efforts to show the people Jesus was God's Son, the Messiah.

Today God speaks to us through His Son, His living Word. Jesus is the supreme voice of God. His voice is above every voice. People of every age, from Adam to Malachi, were clearly shown the divine plan of salvation. It reached its greatness of completeness in Jesus, the Christ. "In these last days He has spoken to us by His Son" (Hebrews 1:2).

Through His Son God created the world. Through His Son God blasts His radiance and glory to the world. Through His Son the heavenly Father protects and takes care of His creation. Paul reminds us that nothing "will be able to separate us from the love of God in Christ Jesus our Lord" (Romans 8:39).

Today, many reject Jesus as the Promised Messiah, the Savior of the world. Some are still waiting for the "real messiah," and others have turned to a "messiah" of their own making. But Jesus of Nazareth has proved to be the Messiah, the Supreme Voice of God.

We can never understand the love that brought Him to earth in human form, or the humility that took Him to the cross of sacrifice. He purged us, He cleansed us from sin, and He reconciled us by convincing God not to judge us with His wrath. He has earned the name Jesus, which means Savior. He proved the power of His words to each repentant sinner—"Your sins are forgiven."

We do not have to use superlative flamboyant words like "magnificent," "terrific," or "stupendous," to attract people to Christ. We do not have to engage entertaining or flashy types of Sunday worship to draw folks into the church. Jesus leads people to Himself through faith with the powerful proclamation of the Law and Gospel. We give thanks to Him for giving us the eternal victory.

MONDAY IN HOLY WEEK

Psalmody: Psalm 35:1–6, 9–10
Additional Psalm: Psalm 71, Psalm 143
Old Testament Reading: Exodus 9:1–28
Additional Reading: Lamentations 1:1–22
New Testament Reading: Hebrews 2:1–18

Meditation

In view of declining church membership and worship attendance in the major denominations, could the conclusion be drawn that many Americans are losing their faith? Have they developed widespread apathy toward religion, God, and church?

It appears the high standard of living has helped promote the standard of high living, in which we like to indulge and feed our sensual appetites at the cost of neglecting our souls. It is quite common that family devotions have been taken over by watching television or time on the computer. Sunday worship mainly has succumbed to recreational activities. Postmodern theologians proclaim there is no absolute objective spiritual truth, and each person may develop their own standard of morality. This greatly influences people to question biblical truths and Christian precepts.

In view of these influences, the writer to the Hebrews is encouraging Christians to hold on to their faith. With this encouragement, he asks us, "How shall we escape if we neglect such a great salvation?" (Hebrews 2:3).

It is implied that there shall be no escape if we fail to hang on to our glorious faith. Then the question comes up, how are we to avoid such a disaster? The writer has the answer: "Therefore we must pay much closer attention to what we have heard, lest we drift away from it" (Hebrews 2:1).

If we neglect the wonderful salvation in Christ that was preached to us—if we deliberately cast aside what we know to be the only way to heaven, there will be no excuse when the Lord calls us to account on the Last Day.

Satan, who accuses and tempts us day and night to forsake our salvation, also tempted our Lord. But it was in vain. In His substitutionary death, our Savior gained the final everlasting victory over the forces of darkness. He even went to hell, the very citadel of Satan, to proclaim our glorious redemption victory over the devil's power. The head of the Serpent was bruised and the Seed of the Woman has fully paid for our apostasy. Though Satan attacks us again and again with temptation, we can victoriously fight off his assaults through faith in Him, our loving, sympathizing High Priest, our dear Savior. His strength is made perfect in our weakness. His saving Word is our sure defense.

Tuesday in Holy Week

Psalmody: Psalm 88:3–9
Additional Psalm: Psalm 77, Psalm 6
Old Testament Reading: Exodus 9:29–10:20
Additional Reading: Lamentations 2:1–22
New Testament Reading: Hebrews 3:1–19

Meditation

The sacred writer calls Christians "holy brothers" (Hebrews 3:1). Indeed, Christians are holy and consecrated to God through faith. Through God's call in the Gospel we have actually secured a participation in the heavenly treasures. The scribe tells us, "Because of the hope laid up for you in heaven. Of this you have heard before in the word of truth, the gospel" (Colossians 1:5).

This helps us to realize the scope of Christ as our High Priest and the greatness of His dignity. As the bearer of the message of salvation Jesus was our High Priest and Sacrifice, not only at the altar but also on the altar of the cross. He, with superlative love assumed our sin and guilt, paying for them. This we gladly believe and confess.

It was the faithfulness of God's Son to the obedience of His Father that marked His special qualification for His high office. Moses was faithful in the congregation of the believers, but his faithfulness cannot compare with Christ's faithfulness. Christ builds, prepares, and equips the household of God, the Church.

Moses was faithful in preaching the Law that served a definite purpose in the Old Testament Church. But Christ is much more. As God's Son He is the Lord of the Church, to which we and all believers belong. We will continue to be His children as long as we remain faithful to the hope of our salvation.

This hope of all Christians is not erratic, unsteady, subject to every whim of our feelings, but it is cemented in the Lord's promises. It is a cheerful confidence that there is laid up for us a "crown of righteousness, which the Lord, the righteous judge, will award to me on that Day" (2 Timothy 4:8). It is not based on my self-sufficiency, but only on the resolute trust in God's love and power.

As we know, Christians' hearts can be hardened by rebellion against God. Therefore, a positive admonition is given us, "Exhort one another every day . . . that none of you may be hardened by the deceitfulness of sin. For we have come to share in Christ, if indeed we hold our original confidence firm to the end" (Hebrews 3:13–14).

Exhorting and encouraging one another in Christian love should be done daily in Christian congregations. Motivated by Christ's love and concern for brothers and sisters in Christ should cause us watch for such opportunities. Then, with our trust anchored in Christ, we can look forward to feasting around heaven's banquet table.

WEDNESDAY IN HOLY WEEK

Psalmody: Psalm 89:20–27
Additional Psalm: Psalm 89, Psalm 32
Old Testament Reading: Exodus 10:21–11:10
Additional Reading: Lamentations 3:1–66
New Testament Reading: Hebrews 4:1–16

Prayer of the Day

Merciful and everlasting God, You did not spare Your only Son but delivered Him up for us all to bear our sins on the cross. Grant that our hearts may be so fixed with steadfast faith in Him that we fear not the power of sin, death, and the devil; through the same Jesus Christ, our Lord, who lives and reigns with You and the Holy Spirit, one God, now and forever. (L31)

Meditation

A curbstone philosopher commented as the cars sped by, "This is typical of our age, tearing like mad to get nowhere." Everyone seems to be in a hurry, complaining they do not have time for things they should be doing. Most folks do not even get enough rest at night, let alone make time to spend with their families, or time to spend with God.

We are a restless generation. Our lifestyle seems to be cheating us out of rest. For 1,500 years, from Egypt to Christ's coming, Israel was searching for rest. But it passed them by because of a lack of faith. The children of Israel wandering in the wilderness paint a picture of humanity chasing after rest.

They failed to enter the Promised Land with its rest from their weary wanderings. This rest is the great Sabbath that God created on the seventh day of creation. It is Christ's work of redemption. It is the rest that is given to us by promise. We enter this heavenly rest by faith.

The Israelites did not enter this rest because of the hardness of their hearts. Unbelief was their downfall. Unbelief is also at the root of today's troubles. Some influential theologians claim the Bible is not infallible, historical, reliable, or authoritative. This leads to false teachings and human suppositions, such as the belief that the creation and the fall into sin is just a story Moses made up. Postmodernists deny the virgin birth of Christ, the sinful nature of man, and Christ's resurrection, among others.

With these denials Christ and His work of salvation is lost. There is no longer a need for a Savior from sin. There is no longer a need for an eternal rest because it can be found in the comforts of this life.

We have the same promise given us to enter a rest from our weary pilgrimage. We have the good news of the rest in our Lord Jesus. He replaced the ancient Sabbath that we might know rest can only be found in Him—He is our Rest! By His death, to cancel our sins, and His resurrection to guarantee the resurrection of our bodies, He gives us evidence of what real rest in God is.

Not repeating the foolishness of the Israelites who died in the wilderness without entering their rest, may we hold to our faith and the promise to enter our rest in the mansions prepared for us. "So then, there remains a Sabbath rest for the people of God" (Hebrews 4:9).

Holy (Maundy) Thursday

Psalmody: Psalm 37:1–7
Additional Psalm: Psalm 110, Psalm 38
Old Testament Reading: Exodus 12:1–28
Additional Reading: Lamentations 4:1–22
New Testament Reading: Hebrews 5:1–14
Additional Reading: Psalm 31

Prayer of the Day

O Lord, in this wondrous Sacrament You have left us a remembrance of Your passion. Grant that we may so receive the sacred mystery of Your body and blood that the fruits of Your redemption may continually be manifest in us; for You live and reign with the Father and the Holy Spirit, one God, now and forever. (L32)

Maundy Thursday

Maundy Thursday, the Day of Commandment (Dies Mandati), most properly refers to the example of service given us by our Lord and the directive to love as we have been loved (John 13:34). Yet we must not forget the command given in the words of our Lord to "do this in remembrance of Me." This day, with its commemoration of the institution of the Lord's Supper, is set off from the rest of Holy Week as a day of festive joy.

Meditation

Our Savior has the threefold office of Prophet, Priest and King. His Prophetic Office consists in speaking through those whom He sent and still speak through His Word. As a Priest, He offered up Himself as the supreme sacrifice for the sins of the world. As King, He sits at the right hand of God ruling over all in the interest of His Bride.

Jewish Christians were placing far too much emphasis upon Old Testament worship forms, believing these were necessary for a proper attitude toward God. Instead, the sacred writer launches into what Christ has accomplished as our High Priest. When using the proper forms in worship becomes the primary focus, there is a danger the doctrine of faith and salvation takes a back seat.

The Old Testament high priest was selected from men to offer sacrifices for himself and the people. In the New Testament, Jesus established the Office of the Holy Ministry, the pastoral office. The pastor represents the Lord and speaks on Christ's behalf to His Church, the people of God. He also is called into the ministry from among men.

Like the high priest, the pastor must also recognize he is a sinner. In humility, he comes before the throne of grace, confessing his sins and begging for forgiveness. Being conscious of his own sins helps him develop an attitude of gentleness in dealing with congregation members.

The high priest never took upon himself the honor of the office, and neither should any man assume the pastoral office on his own authority. He should only become a pastor by the call of God through the Church.

Sadly, today some denigrate the Holy Office by simply declaring themselves to be ministers, such as some on television whose main focus is on raising money for "their ministry" while neglecting to proclaim Christ crucified.

Jesus, as our High Priest, never sought to glorify Himself, but always brought glory to His heavenly Father. He did so by being obedient to the call of His Father. This obedience included becoming the sacrificial Lamb for the sins of the world.

On the day before He died, our sacrificial Lamb gave His Church the great mystery of His body and blood in His Supper for the forgiveness of sins to strengthen the faith of those partaking. Today, as we kneel at the altar, may we present to Him thankful hearts.

Jesus, the Good Shepherd, is the model for His pastors. May we be found faithful in praying for them.

GOOD FRIDAY

Psalmody: Psalm 135:1–4, 8–9
Additional Psalm: Psalm 136, Psalm 51
Old Testament Reading:
Exodus 12:29–32; 13:1–16
Additional Reading: Lamentations 5:1–22
New Testament Reading: Hebrews 6:1–20
Additional Reading: Psalm 22

Prayer of the Day

Almighty God, graciously behold this Your family for whom our Lord Jesus Christ was willing to be betrayed and delivered into the hands of sinful men to suffer death upon the cross; through the same Jesus Christ, Your Son, our Lord, who lives and reigns with You and the Holy Spirit, one God, now and forever. (L33)

Good Friday

Good Friday is the high point of Holy Week, but not of the Church Year—for we know that after Good Friday a day is coming when death will give way to life. If the commemoration of Good Friday was separated from Easter we would remain in our sins, and thus the ultimate word of Good Friday would be "you are condemned." Even as we stand at the foot of the cross and contemplate the price of our sin, we gather as children reconciled to God. In the services of Good Friday, the Church does not leave us in the darkness and the shadow of death but rather fills us with the certainty of victory over sin, death, and the devil, pointing us to the final victory that will be celebrated on Easter.

Meditation

On this day the serpent's head was crushed and Satan was defeated with his kingdom of evil. Jesus killed death and sin with His death. He fulfilled His mission for which He came into the world, that is, to save sinners.

As Christians, we still have our sinful nature. Its final killing will occur when we are called home to our heavenly rest. Meanwhile, we should not become weary in living out our faith.

The inspired writer warns against apostasy from the faith and encourages us to spiritual growth. Repentance and faith are fundamental for Christian life. They mark a person's turning from spiritual darkness to the light of God's grace in Christ Jesus.

It is possible to fall away, even if a person had placed his trust in Christ's salvation and anticipated the joys of eternal life. It is possible, despite the saving knowledge, by deliberately denying that knowledge. Then the return to repentance is not possible. The reason it becomes impossible to return to repentance is because the heart is hardened against the Word of God. This is meant to be a warning to all.

With the Hebrew Christians, we are called beloved to encourage us to make progress in holy living. This is shown by works of love springing from faith, such as husbands and wives showing patience, forgiving and supportive of each other; parents training and admonishing their children in kindness and love; children listening to, respecting, and obeying their parents and teachers; everyone taking advantage of opportunities to help others in time of need; pastors and congregation members respecting, praying for, and dealing gently with one another, building up the Church.

The story of Good Friday is that Jesus went to His Father. What about us? What about our death? As a rule, people die as they live. They die at peace with God because they have lived at peace with God. Or they die without faith because they lived without faith. Death does not change a person, but rather reveals where his heart and mind have been.

Like Jesus, do we know the way to the Father? We certainly can. The way to the Father is through the valley of shadows with the cross of Christ marking the way.

Each night before we die the little death of sleep, may we say Christ's words, "Father, into Your hands I commit My spirit" (Luke 23:46).

HOLY SATURDAY

Psalmody: Psalm 37:1–7
Additional Psalm: Psalm 76, Psalm 102
Old Testament Reading: Exodus 13:17–14:9
New Testament Reading: Hebrews 7:1–22

Prayer of the Day

O God, You made this most holy night to shine with the glory of the Lord's resurrection. Preserve in us the spirit of adoption which You have given so that, made alive in body and soul, we may serve You purely; through Jesus Christ, Your Son, our Lord, who lives and reigns with You and the Holy Spirit, one God, now and forever. (466)

Holy Saturday

The commemoration of Holy Saturday encompasses our Lord's rest in the tomb and His descent into hell. The descent into hell is not, however, the depth of Christ's humiliation but rather the demonstration of His complete victory over death. This day takes us out of the depths of most painful sorrow and out of the solitude of holy meditation upon Christ's Passion to the celebration of victory as we anticipate the Lord's resurrection breaking forth in all its glory on Easter.

Meditation

Of Jesus, the Christ, the sacred writer says, "You are a priest forever after the order of Melchizedek" (Hebrews 7:17). Melchizedek is a Hebrew name that is translated "king of righteousness." He was king of Salem, which means "peace." Melchizedek was by his name and his official position the "king of peace." It is most significant that righteousness and peace are important characteristic properties of the messianic kingdom.

The Levitical priesthood faded away, and God ordained and appointed our great High Priest, who was not called after the order of Aaron, did not belong to the tribe of Levi, but arose after the order of Melchizedek. The inspired writer carefully explained this so the Jewish Christians were able to come to a sound understanding of the connection to Christ.

If perfection were obtainable through the Levitical priesthood, from which the people received the law, there would be no need of another priest. If the Levitical priesthood had been able to bring people to a state of forgiveness of sins, life, and salvation through the teaching of the law and offering sacrifices, it would have been very foolish for God to appoint another priest.

Christ is the perfect High Priest. His salvation is complete in each detail. Every person that turns to Christ for salvation and places his faith in Jesus has Christ as the only way to God. There is no need of priests and sacrifices, ceremonies and special festivals, for He is our Mediator. He has opened the way to the eternal love of the Father.

We know this to be an absolute certainty. Jesus is still functioning in His office of High Priest as our Intercessor with the Father. He made the ultimate sacrifice for our sins, and today He continues to spend Himself for us and all people. He is devoted to offering eternal salvation to all through the proclamation of His mission.

Our High Priest was holy, innocent, stainless of sin, separate from sinners, and exalted to the Father's right hand. As true God and true man, Christ has fought through and defeated all the confusion, turmoil, and suffering this life brings.

The perfection of God's Son was tested by many temptations that He endured and overcame for us. It was as if we had stood the test of all these attacks. We are still sinners, but through faith we are covered with His righteousness, and that makes us sinless in His sight.

THE TIME OF EASTER

Easter Season

Easter Sunday

The Resurrection of Our Lord

Psalmody: Psalm 96:1–3, 6, 11–13
Additional Psalm: Psalm 107
Old Testament Reading: Exodus 14:10–31
New Testament Reading: Hebrews 7:23—8:13

Prayer of the Day

Almighty God the Father, through Your only-begotten Son, Jesus Christ, You have overcome death and opened the gate of everlasting life to us. Grant that we, who celebrate with joy the day of our Lord's resurrection, may be raised from the death of sin by Your life-giving Spirit; through Jesus Christ, our Lord, who lives and reigns with You and the Holy Spirit, one God, now and forever. (L36)

The Resurrection of Our Lord— Easter Sunday

Easter is the oldest and highest of all Christian festivals—the festival of festivals, the feast of feasts! On this day, when Christ first stepped triumphantly from the ranks of the dead, all our waiting is declared to be a waiting that is already completed; Christ's triumph makes all the waiting that follows in our lives of faith a building anchored on the foundation that was laid when He whom the builders rejected became the Cornerstone. Christ is risen! He is risen indeed. Alleluia!

Meditation

What joy to celebrate the Feast of the Resurrection! Jesus won the greatest victory of all. He triumphed over sin, death, and the devil. He then gives that victory to us through faith. Yes, we also have beaten sin; we have won the victory—triumphed over death.

At the first Easter dawn, women came to Jesus' tomb to apply spices to His body, as was their custom. He was not there. He had risen! They rushed back to tell the apostles, but the apostles were skeptical, for "these words seemed to them an idle tale, and they did not believe them" (Luke 24:11).

An idle tale or just plain nonsense? What did women know about such things? The whole scenario seemed too good to be true. Peter, however, sprang into action. He had to see for himself, hoping that what seemed too good to be true was true! The women were right! There was nothing there—just an empty hole in the side of the hill.

If there had been a body, there would be no salvation, no Christianity, no life after death. Satan would be dancing in victory; sin would be rejoicing in triumph; and death would be celebrating its vicious death-grip on us. The grave would forever claim its dead through eternity.

Who Christ was and everything He had done, and His invitation to believe His Word of salvation, were all based on His claim that He would rise on the third day. Skeptics claim His resurrection cannot be proved logically or demonstrated. If we were to trust in God only by what we can demonstrate, we would not be trusting in God, but only in our demonstrative ability. And that destroys the point of Christianity—trust in Christ's work of salvation.

The Christian Church, the New Testament, the apostles—none of these explain the resurrection. The resurrection explains them! Today, we do not explain Christ's resurrection, but we are explained and defined by it!

That Peter found nothing means everything to a Christian's faith. Satan is not dancing, sin is not rejoicing, death is not celebrating, and the grave must give up its dead. This victory begins with Christ and ends with fulfillment in our hearts.

This victory slices through our lives like a two-edged sword. Where the verdict of our lives constantly rules against Christ, Easter blasts at us. When we believe Christ's resurrection is our resurrection, then life makes sense, but only on God's terms. What seemed too good to be true is true!

MONDAY AFTER EASTER

Psalmody: Psalm 13
Additional Psalm: Psalm 59
Old Testament Reading: Exodus 15:1–18
New Testament Reading: Hebrews 9:1–28

Prayer of the Day

O God, in the paschal feast You restore all creation. Continue to send Your heavenly gifts upon Your people that they may walk in perfect freedom and receive eternal life; through Jesus Christ, Your Son, our Lord, who lives and reigns with You and the Holy Spirit, one God, now and forever. (L38)

The Easter Season—the Great Fifty Days

The Easter season is a fifty-day-long season of joy extending from Easter to Pentecost. During this time the Church celebrates the end of Christ's struggles and proclaims His victory over death and the reception of the benefits of His life, death, and resurrection as gracious gifts of love and mercy for all those who believe in Him. This is the Church's great season of joy! Christ is risen! He is risen indeed. Alleluia!

Meditation

The celebration of Easter would not be possible without Christ having paid the ultimate price of shedding His blood. This was the culmination of the Old Testament sacrifices of spilling the blood of multitudes of animals, all which pointed the Israelites toward the sacrifice of the High Priest.

Unthinkable blood purges have been carried out in the last century. Under Joseph Stalin, the Communist Party executed up to 60 million people to purge or cleanse the party. In Cambodia, the Khmer Rouge, the Marxist ruling party, marched the population of the capital city, Phnom Penh, out of town and executed them, the number well into the millions.

In Christianity, there is also a place for a blood purge. Its purpose and form, however, was completely different from the murderous acts of police states. It was a spiritual purge or cleansing from the death-killing disobedience against God.

Before Christians enter God's presence in worship, there is at the beginning of the Divine Service Confession and Absolution. After confessing our sins we are absolved, or forgiven. We then come to the Father's throne of grace in worship through prayer, praise, and song.

Because we sin much we cannot live without a daily purging of our conscience. No matter how painful it may be, it must be done, for our hope of heaven depends on it. Its importance is in direct proportion to us being aware of the importance of what our Savior did on Calvary.

Many times we lose the sense of sin. We often stumble into sin and pick ourselves up with a weak excuse and laugh it off. We think God will not make a fuss over trifles such as selfishness at home, little words of profanity, forgetting to pray, or worship. We may even refuse to deal with sin, hoping it will go away. Or we turn into moralists and humanists, and try to live a good life without God's help and the painful discipline of self-examination and confession.

The Messiah did not come just to convict us of our sin; He came to cleanse us from sin. This He accomplished by offering Himself as the Sacrificial Lamb—the Great Purge. This was the only payment acceptable to God.

The Great Purge made possible the lesser purges we now undergo as we confess our sins, and, in faith, receive forgiveness. This is the glory of Christianity. This is the glory of our life.

Tuesday after Easter

Psalmody: Psalm 81:1–7
Additional Psalm: Psalm 40
Old Testament Reading: Exodus 15:19–16:12
New Testament Reading: Hebrews 10:1–18

Prayer of the Day

Almighty God, through the resurrection of Your Son You have secured peace for our troubled consciences. Grant us this peace evermore that trusting in the merit of Your Son we may come at last to the perfect peace of heaven; through the same Jesus Christ, Your Son, our Lord, who lives and reigns with You and the Holy Spirit, one God, now and forever. (L39)

Meditation

The Church Year is more than just fifty-two Sundays. It is the time during which we speak the Word of God to one another; it is God's action in and through that Word; it is God telling us His will, His forgiveness, His power, and His life. Every Divine Service is a call to specific action and a power to carry it out.

We still have our selfish nature that restrains us from loving God and our neighbors as we should. This results in a guilty conscience that induces us to run from God. And if we come into His presence with other folks, we think we must wear a mask to cover our real selves. Such phoniness only adds to our guilt.

Because of Christ we do not need a mask; we can come before our heavenly Father just as we are. Jesus made the once-for-all-time sacrifice for our sins. He died as the guilty you, the guilty me. He felt the harsh sting of God's justice, which is hell, when He was forsaken by His Father. Then the perfect One went into the holy presence, and there, as our sacrifice, He took our part forever.

God, in Christ, is our Savior who has sprinkled our hearts clean from an evil conscience. He has fully atoned for our sins. We can boldly come to Him in worship, in confession and prayer, without any false front. In full assurance of faith, He forgives us and helps in every need.

To strengthen our confession of the sure hope we have in Christ we have this promise, "I will remember their sins and their lawless deeds no more" (Hebrews 10:17). God does not let go. He does not give up on us. He stays with us in our weaknesses and failures. We have His Word and the pledges of His sacraments for this.

Our power for bold, steady confession comes from our faithful Lord, since He loves us with a love that will not let us go.

There is no longer a sacrifice for sin. To say no to the perfect sacrifice means that we must bear our sins and their judgment. Therefore, to talk about another Church Year of God's grace in Christ, we are talking about the most crucial thing in our lives. May God help us to respond to His wonderful grace always with faith and a new life.

Wednesday after Easter

Psalmody: Psalm 134
Additional Psalm: Psalm 135
Old Testament Reading: Exodus 16:13–35
New Testament Reading: Hebrews 10:19–39

Prayer of the Day

Almighty God, by the glorious resurrection of Your Son, Jesus Christ, You destroyed death and brought life and immortality to light. Grant that we who have been raised with Him may abide in His presence and rejoice in the hope of eternal glory; through the same Jesus Christ, our Lord, who lives and reigns with You and the Holy Spirit, one God, now and forever. (L40)

Meditation

This section of Scripture portrays no striking figure like John the Baptist, but something that draws a striking picture. It is the picture of our natural heart. Ordinarily the human heart is not bold enough to enter into communion and fellowship with God as we know Him. If such boldness appears in an unregenerate heart, it is either under a false pretense or absurd and arrogant.

Christians are told, "We have confidence to enter the holy places by the blood of Jesus" (Hebrews 10:19). This refers to such places as the Most Holy Place in the temple in Jerusalem that only the high priest entered on the Day of Atonement. He splashed blood on the ark to make atonement for his and his family sins, and for the people's sins. That we have boldness to enter the holiest places implies we are considered priests. Christ has come into our hearts, through His Spirit, with His regenerating power. We may now enter the holiest "by the blood of Jesus, by the new and living way that He opened for us through the curtain, that is, through His flesh" (Hebrews 10:19b–20). This is the foundation for our boldness of heart.

At the death of Christ, the large heavy curtain in the temple hiding the Most Holy Place was torn in half. This signified that Jesus has opened to us the way of eternal life. We now can look directly into God's great heart of love. We have the one and only High Priest. It also means each of us is a priest before God.

Our new heart is confirmed by exercising glorious privileges. "Let us draw near with a true heart in full assurance of faith, with our hearts sprinkled clean from an evil conscience and our bodies washed with pure water" (Hebrews 10:22). Blessed privileges become glorious blessings. These glorious blessings are flowing to us as a continuous stream.

We come to the Lord not with a hypocritical heart but with a true heart and with the confidence of faith. We come with a faith that is not a matter of feeling, but is an objective certainty that clings to the Lord's promises. We come with the promise that the filth of our hearts has been washed away by Christ's blood, the cleansing water of Baptism having washed away all our sins.

Thus prepared, we are privileged to approach the heavenly temple, the new Most Holy Place, by a new and living way. We enter its inner sanctuary by faith, and present ourselves in the presence of God.

THURSDAY AFTER EASTER

Psalmody: Psalm 114
Additional Psalm: Psalm 136
Old Testament Reading: Exodus 17:1–16
New Testament Reading: Hebrews 11:1–29

Prayer of the Day

Almighty God, through Your only-begotten Son, Jesus Christ, You overcame death and opened to us the gate of everlasting life. We humbly pray that we may live before You in righteousness and purity forever; through the same Jesus Christ, our Lord, who lives and reigns with You and the Holy Spirit, one God, now and forever. (L35)

Meditation

The great heroes of faith listed in today's reading tell a wonderful story of the power of faith. Faith is a conviction of the mind concerning things for which we hope. It is the absolute certainty of things that are not seen.

Faith that trusts in Christ and His righteousness is the result of the salvation God has completed for us, and upon which we place our hope. It is the unchangeable conviction of the heart regarding those things that we cannot see, things that are impossible for our eyes and reason to understand. Faith concerns the things of the future that have their beginnings in this life. As with the heroes of faith, our faith, beginning with our Baptism, carries us through this life. It ends beyond the grave, taking us into the mansions prepared for us.

Because of sin we all must suffer death. The grave calls us and we are all dancing toward it. Christians dance toward death and the grave because we have been baptized into death with Christ. Christ has already plunged us into the grave that awaits us.

With open contempt toward that death, we confess our hope in the life to come. We can dance this life because Jesus has victoriously placed death under His feet. The victory of life over death that placed death under Christ's feet means that He is the death of death. "Death is Destroyed" should be engraved on our tombstones.

We live knowing death is dead. The world lives what it thinks is life, but in reality it is a living death. The world dances backward into a swallowing grave with the frantic steps of the desperate, of those trying to escape the dance's end. Christians can dance the dance of death with the calming and beautiful steps of a waltz, because for them, death has been destroyed.

Death was the archenemy, but now it is like a toothless dog, rendered harmless. Through Baptism we have been inoculated with Christ's death, so death is no longer death. Death cannot hold us or harm us. Only our mortal leftovers, the old skin, flesh and blood must still decay before it, too, can be renewed and follow the soul.

With an unshakable faith in Christ's death that paid for our sins, we can with the saints of old stand unmovable, firm and steadfast to the end. We can joyfully guide the dance of life toward such a death. My grave is yawning, but I fear it as little as my bed.

FRIDAY AFTER EASTER

Psalmody: Psalm 145:1–9
Additional Psalm: Psalm 94
Old Testament Reading: Exodus 18:5–27
New Testament Reading: Hebrews 12:1–24

Prayer of the Day

Almighty God, You show those in error the light of Your truth so that they may return to the way of righteousness. Grant faithfulness to all who are admitted into the fellowship of Christ's Church that they may avoid whatever is contrary to their confession and follow all such things as are pleasing to You; through Jesus Christ, Your Son, our Lord, who lives and reigns with You and the Holy Spirit, one God, now and forever. (L44)

Meditation

The inspired writer tells us, "You have come to Mount Zion and to the city of the living God, the heavenly Jerusalem" (Hebrews 12:22). These are not tricky words; they tell us we have already gone to heaven. These words help us understand we have all the blessings of heaven, even though we are still earthbound. It takes the Old Testament picture of a birthright to tell us we should hold on to our spiritual birthright, the myriad of blessings that God's love gives us through His Son.

We are to watch that we keep heaven and eternal life by faith, to remember that God, for Jesus' sake, has forgiven our sins and bridged the separation from God caused by our sins. In this watch, we are responsible for encouraging one another to remain sons of God by trusting God's love and forgiveness.

A Christian, slipping away from God, may become a stumbling block for other Christians. We prevent this when we pray for and help one another remember the Good News of Christ.

A birthright can be lost. Esau sold his birthright to be an ancestor of the Messiah, to his brother, Jacob, for a measly meal. Believers are vulnerable to temptation. Under pressure of persecution the Hebrew Christians were starting to slide back to their former man-made religion.

We also can be tempted to look away from God. We ransack our lives for a respectable and wonderful act that we hope will make us right with God. The more we search, the more uneasy we become, because we only find ourselves back at the awful mountain of God's holy Law.

No one can stand up to God's Law. His Commandments are demanding and damning, filled with trumpet blasts and flaming fire. They tell us that within ourselves we have no rights to eternal life with God.

However, we are reminded that God has already judged us. This happened when we were given eternal life through faith in Christ's death, His resurrection and ascension. The holy God judged His innocent Son for our sins. Through Him our sins have been punished; God has forgiven us.

Even now we are enjoying the blessings of heaven, and everything that belongs to God belongs to us. We have come, not to Mount Sinai, but to a higher mountain—Mount Zion, God's city, the heavenly Jerusalem. We have our spiritual birthright as His children. We are heirs to all of God's blessings.

SATURDAY AFTER EASTER

Psalmody: Psalm 30:3–12
Additional Psalm: Psalm 68
Old Testament Reading: Exodus 19:1–25
New Testament Reading: Hebrews 13:1–21

Prayer of the Day

Lord Jesus, You are the Good Shepherd, without whom nothing is secure. Rescue and preserve us that we may not be lost forever but follow You, rejoicing in the way that leads to eternal life; for You live and reign with the Father and the Holy Spirit, one God, now and forever. (C77)

Meditation

The great dividing line between Christianity and other religions is the teaching of salvation by grace alone. Other religions arise from humanity and credit sinful man with some ability to gain favor with God and being saved. Christianity alone gives all glory to God by teaching that sinful humanity is saved by the free grace of God.

When this doctrine of free grace lives in our heart, it keeps us strong so that we are not "led away by diverse and strange teachings, for it is good for the heart to be strengthened by grace" (Hebrews 13:9).

We cannot say we have kept the requirements of the Law. We know that the heart produces evil thoughts—not love, but hate; not hospitality, but cold indifference; not sympathy, but cruel condemnation; not purity, but immorality. The law is kept only by faith in and through Christ's perfect obedience.

The heart established by grace finds the way to God. The secret of this heart is a love so great that it impelled God's true Son to die that our heart might have life. This mystery of grace is a light for explaining the Scriptures.

For Martin Luther, the doctrine of salvation by grace was the touchstone of faith. By it all other teachings could be measured and tested. Today, many claiming to know the way of salvation based primarily on what we do deluge us. Their message is centered on the third use of the Law, which is a guide for living. It seems that proclaiming salvation only by God's grace is humiliating because it leaves human merit out of the picture. We may measure the teachings of all theologians by this, namely, that God has revealed Himself as a gracious God in Jesus Christ, our Lord, who has won for us freedom from sin.

The struggle to live this life in Christ is not easy. It really takes a heart established by grace to walk in His ways. Such a heart clings to Christ, whose blood purifies us from all sin. As God's children, we are to be content with the blessings God has given us. He has promised to supply all our wants of body and soul. Filled with God's love in Christ we are able to offer sacrifices pleasing to God as we are encouraged to do. "Through Him then let us continually offer up a sacrifice of praise to God, that is, the fruit of lips that acknowledge His name" (Hebrews 13:15). He has promised, "I will never leave you nor forsake you" (Hebrews 13:5).

SECOND SUNDAY OF EASTER

Psalmody: Psalm 119:9–16
Additional Psalm: Psalm 91
Old Testament Reading: Exodus 20:1–24
New Testament Reading: Luke 4:1–15

Prayer of the Day

Almighty God, grant that we who have celebrated the Lord's resurrection may by Your grace confess in our life and conversation that Jesus is Lord and God; through the same Jesus Christ, Your Son, who lives and reigns with You and the Holy Spirit, one God, now and forever. (L41)

Meditation

Satan saves his best temptations for last. Jesus has been in the desert "being tempted" for forty days. The Greek text denotes a continuous action, so that hour after hour, day after day, week after week, Satan has been tempting Jesus, hoping to whittle away His resistance to sin. And now, Satan trots out his best material.

Luke says that Jesus "was hungry" (v. 2). So Satan tempts Jesus accordingly: "If You are the Son of God, command this stone to become bread" (v. 3). But Jesus doesn't fall for Satan's allurement. A Scripture verse is enough to rebuke him: "Man shall not live by bread alone" (v. 4).

How about a temptation to power? Satan shows Jesus the world's kingdoms and promises, "To You I will give all this authority and their glory . . . If You . . . will worship me" (vv. 6–7). No dice on this temptation either. Another Bible verse rebuts him: "You shall worship the Lord your God, and Him only shall you serve" (v. 8).

So Satan tries once more. And this final temptation is an ingenious one. Satan tries to tempt Jesus, who is God, with God's own words. Satan says, "If you are the Son of God, throw Yourself down from here, for it is written, 'He will command His angels concerning you, to guard you' " (vv. 9–10). If Jesus can quote Scripture, Satan can too. A simple psalm will suffice. He says to Jesus, "You said it! Now do it!" But you can't tempt God with Himself. After all, it is written, "You shall not put the Lord your God to the test" (v. 12).

Satan's best temptation of man is when he tempts man to play God. He said to Adam and Eve in the garden, "When you eat of [this fruit] your eyes will be opened, and you will be like God" (Genesis 3:5). And Adam and Eve fall for it. They eat the fruit to try to be like God.

Likewise, Satan's best temptation of God is when he tempts God to play God. "Believe Your own psalm," Satan says to Jesus, "And throw Yourself down!" But Jesus will not play along. Jesus—who is God—is playing man to redeem man from playing God.

Satan saved his best temptations for last. He must have thought it would have been a snap to win over Jesus. After all, he won over a well-fed man in a garden. But this time, he loses to a hungry man in a desert. And that's good news.

Monday—Easter 2

Psalmody: Psalm 146
Additional Psalm: Psalm 103
Old Testament Reading: Exodus 22:20–23:13
New Testament Reading: Luke 4:16–30

Prayer of the Day

Lord God, heavenly Father, Your Son announced in the synagogue of His hometown of Nazareth that as the Messiah, His teaching and miracles demonstrated His presence in creation to release it from bondage and bring healing by making all things new. Give us faith to see that His teaching and miracles continue today in the healing medicine of Your Word and the Sacraments, which put to flight the diseases of our souls; through Jesus Christ, Your Son, our Lord. (1011)

Meditation

It's homecoming for Jesus. I suppose He must have felt much like I did the first time I returned home from college—simultaneously excited and nervous. Excited at the prospect of seeing family and friends and nervous because I wondered how much had changed since I had left. But Jesus, now an adult, returns to Nazareth. And, as a faithful Jew, He attends synagogue on the Sabbath where He has the privilege of sharing a Scripture reading from the prophet Isaiah: "The Spirit of the Lord is upon Me, because He has anointed Me to proclaim good news to the poor. He has sent Me to proclaim liberty to the captives and recovering of sight to the blind, to set at liberty those who are oppressed, to proclaim the year of the Lord's favor" (vv. 18–19). Luke then offers this important note concerning what Jesus does following His reading: "And He rolled up the scroll and gave it back to the attendant and sat down" (v. 20).

In that day, it was customary to proffer authoritative teaching while sitting down. We have vestiges of this even today. When the pope, for instance, makes an official pronouncement, he does so ex cathedra, a Latin phrase meaning, "from the chair." When Jesus sits down, "the eyes of all in the synagogue [are] fixed on Him" (v. 20); everyone knows Jesus is getting ready to say something important. And what does He say? "Today this Scripture has been fulfilled in your hearing" (v. 21). Jesus declares Himself to be the fulfillment of Isaiah 61. He is the One who has come to bring good news.

Jesus has not just come to bring good news. Jesus is Good News! He is good news for the blind He heals. He is good news for the demon-oppressed he frees. He is good news for the sinners He saves. Jesus is God's Gospel incarnate—the One who is our forgiveness of sins, life, and salvation thanks to His sacrifice on the cross. And after Jesus sacrifices Himself for us, what does He do? The preacher of Hebrews answers: "But when Christ had offered for all time a single sacrifice for sins, He sat down at the right hand of God" (Hebrews 10:12). It's authoritative. It's official. Jesus has brought God's Gospel to pass. Indeed, it's so authoritative and official that Jesus sits down upon its completion. Your salvation is as sure as the throne on which Jesus sits.

TUESDAY—EASTER 2

Psalmody: Psalm 26:1–3, 8–12
Additional Psalm: Psalm 41
Old Testament Reading: Exodus 23:14–33
New Testament Reading: Luke 4:31–44

Prayer of the Day

Lord Jesus, in Your ministry of teaching, casting out demons, and healing the sick, You proclaimed the Good News of the kingdom of God. Send us into all the world to announce that today, in You, Scripture has been fulfilled, the new creation has come, and the healing of the nations is here; for You live and reign with the Father and the Holy Spirit, one God, now and forever. (1012)

Meditation

For the folks from Capernaum who bring their sick, diseased, and demon-possessed to Jesus in Luke 4, it must have felt like early morning Black Friday. Black Friday, of course, is the day after Thanksgiving when retailers garner sales large enough to take their books from the "red" to the "black." And as the years wear on, Black Friday sales seem to begin earlier and earlier. It used to be that an "early bird" sale began at 7 a.m. Then it was 6 a.m.

Now it's 4. I have heard of some stores opening their doors at midnight's stroke on Black Friday to satisfy their bargain-hungry patrons.

"When the sun was setting . . . " (v. 40). This is the time at which people bring their infirmed to Jesus. This is significant because the day drawing to a close is a Sabbath, so no work can be done. But now the day has ended. And at sunset's stroke, the people storm Jesus. But then Jesus leaves. And so the people seek Him and come to Him.

But Jesus has further work to do. "I must preach the good news of the kingdom of God to other towns as well," Jesus says (v. 43). The Greek word for "preach the good news" is *euangelizo*, a verbal form of the noun "Gospel." Thus, Jesus must literally Gospel-ize other towns, for He has come to do the Gospel through His work on the cross. But the people at Capernaum are concerned that Jesus' travel to others will somehow result in them missing out. This is a strange fear, especially since Luke says that Jesus does His Gospel for "every one of them" (v. 40). It is not as if Jesus withholds His Gospel from anyone.

In a famed line from Charles Dickens' *A Christmas Carol*, Tiny Tim exclaims at Christmas dinner, "God bless us, every one!" This is the promise of the Gospel—that God blesses us, every one, with what His Son has done on the cross. This is why Jesus must continue His journeys so that He can Gospel-ize every one in other towns even as He has Gospel-ized every one in the town of Capernaum.

Martin Luther noted that the Gospel is only the Gospel when it is "for you." For the Gospel to do you any good, you must believe not only that Jesus died, but that Jesus died for you. And indeed He has. Jesus has died for every one. And the "every one" includes you.

Wednesday—Easter 2

Psalmody: Psalm 99:1–5
Additional Psalm: Psalm 79
Old Testament Reading: Exodus 24:1–18
New Testament Reading: Luke 5:1–16

Prayer of the Day

Lord Jesus, when Peter fell before You in repentance as a sinful man, You absolved Him of his sins by saying to him, "Fear not"; for by Your grace, He was worthy to stand in Your presence. Send us out like Peter to catch men alive, announcing to the world the forgiveness of sins that comes through You, our only Savior and Lord; for You live and reign with the Father and the Holy Spirit, one God, now and forever. (1013)

Meditation
Love/hate relationships are a part of life. We all have them. I have a love/hate relationship with my mechanic. I love his work; I hate his prices. The apostle Peter, in Luke 5, has a similarly mixed relationship with his Lord. No, he doesn't have a love/hate relationship with Jesus. He has a love/fear relationship. On the one hand, Peter loves Jesus. For even when Jesus gives Peter what must have seemed like foolish fishing advice, Peter graciously complies. "Master," Peter says, "we toiled all night and took nothing! But at Your word I will let down the nets" (v. 5). Peter addresses Jesus respectfully and heeds His guidance obediently. And when he does, they have success fishing.

It's at this point when Peter's love for Jesus melts into fear of Jesus. Peter falls on his knees and exclaims, "Depart from me, for I am a sinful man, O Lord" (v. 8). Peter's fear is straightforward: Jesus is perfect; Peter is not.

Peter knows that he is out of his league. And Peter is scared.

But then, Jesus comforts Peter: "Do not be afraid; from now on you will be catching men" (v. 10).

"Do not be afraid." This is the most common command in the Bible. It is spoken to a despondent mother named Hagar who is afraid for the well-being of her son Ishmael (cf. Genesis 21:17). It is spoken to a commander named Joshua as he prepares to fight a battle at Ai (cf. Joshua 8:1). It is spoken by an angel to shepherds who are "keeping watch over their flock by night" (Luke 2:8) when they receive word of Jesus' birth. And now, Jesus speaks this same command to Peter: "Do not be afraid."

Thankfully, Peter learns this command well. Later, when Jesus' teaching has become controversial and many disciples have begun to leave, He asks His Twelve: "Do you want to go away as well?" Peter's answer is unequivocal: "Lord, to whom shall we go? You have the words of eternal life" (John 6:67–68). Peter no longer fears Jesus because of his uncleanness. Rather, he loves Jesus because of his uncleanness. For Peter now recognizes that only Jesus offers words of eternal life to unclean people. So rather than wanting Jesus to depart from him, Peter now wishes Jesus to remain close. May we all wish the same.

Thursday—Easter 2

Psalmody: Psalm 119:25–32
Additional Psalm: Psalm 9
Old Testament Reading: Exodus 25:1–22
Additional Reading: Exodus 25:23–30:38
New Testament Reading: Luke 5:17–39

Prayer of the Day

O Lord, absolve Your people from their offenses that from the bonds of our sins, which by reason of our frailty we have brought upon ourselves, we may be delivered by Your bountiful goodness; through Jesus Christ, Your Son, our Lord, who lives and reigns with You and the Holy Spirit, one God, now and forever. (H83)

Meditation

Aesop relays the story of a wagoner who was driving a heavy load of cargo along a muddy road. The wagoner came to an especially treacherous spot where his wheels sank deep into the mire. The harder the wagoner whipped his horses to pull, the deeper he sank. Finally, the wagoner prayed to Hercules for help. Incredibly, Hercules appeared and responded: "Lazy fellow! Get up and stir yourself. Urge your horses stoutly, and put your shoulder to the wheel. Heaven helps only those who help themselves."

Hercules' final sentence, of course, is the basis for the widely known cliché: "God helps those who help themselves." Sadly, many people believe this to be true. Some even believe it to be biblical. In one survey, a majority of Christians believed Aesop's moralism to be taught by the Bible! But it is neither true nor biblical. Indeed, it teaches the precise opposite of orthodoxy. For orthodoxy believes and teaches that God helps those who can't help themselves.

In Luke 5, we meet a man who is an archetypal image of helplessness. He is a paralytic. By this point in His ministry, Jesus' reputation as a healer has already spread so far and wide that a huge crowd gathers, hoping to see another miraculous salving. But in this case, Jesus surprises everyone. Jesus says, "Man, your sins are forgiven you" (v. 20). The crowd thinks it is this man's paralysis that makes him helpless, but Jesus knows it is his sin that has left him truly helpless.

The rabbis taught that a sick man could not be healed of sickness until his sins had been forgiven. Yet, even in the face of such a tradition, the Pharisees and teachers of the Law become indignant at Jesus. "Who is this who speaks blasphemies?" they ask. "Who can forgive sins but God alone" (v. 21)? Jesus, in order to demonstrate His authority, responds, "That you may know that the Son of Man has authority on earth to forgive sins . . . I say to you, rise, pick up your bed and go home" (v. 24). And the man does! He is no longer helpless; Christ has healed and forgiven him.

The sobering pronouncement of Scripture is that we have all been made helpless by sin. And yet, God's good news is that "while we were still weak, at the right time Christ died for the ungodly" (Romans 5:6). God helps and saves us even when we can't help and save ourselves.

FRIDAY—EASTER 2

Psalmody: Psalm 92:1–9
Additional Psalm: Psalm 92
Old Testament Reading: Exodus 31:1–18
New Testament Reading: Luke 6:1–19

Prayer of the Day

Lord Jesus, our Sabbath rest, You called the twelve apostles to go out into all the world to carry on Your proclamation of the kingdom of God and Your miracles of release. May Your Church with its apostolic foundation continue to announce the Good News that in You there is healing and forgiveness; for You live and reign with the Father and the Holy Spirit, one God, now and forever. (1014)

Meditation

In Luke 6, Jesus is engaged in a series of so-called "Sabbath controversies" with the Pharisees, who accuse Him of impiously disregarding the day's rules for rest. In the second of these controversies, the Pharisees watch Jesus "to see whether He would heal on the Sabbath, so that they might find a reason to accuse Him" (v. 7). The Pharisees watch Jesus to trap Him.

To confront the Pharisees' ill-intended watching, Jesus calls to Himself a man with an atrophied hand. He asks the Pharisees, "Is it lawful on the Sabbath to do good or to do harm, to save life or to destroy it" (v. 9)? No one responds. So Jesus continues by commanding the man, "Stretch out your hand" (v. 10). And Jesus heals him. Interestingly, in this instance, Jesus does nothing Sabbath-breaking, even by the legalistic standards of the Pharisees. Jesus does not physically assist this ailing man, nor does He even touch him. He simply speaks to him: "Stretch out your hand." And speaking is surely not prohibited on the Sabbath!

Jesus does nothing to break Sabbath law. And yet, the Pharisees become enraged at Him: "They were filled with fury and discussed with one another what they might do to Jesus" (v. 11). The Greek here is instructive. The word for "fury" is *anoia*. The best way to translate this is that the Pharisees are so angry with Jesus, they literally "lose their minds."

The verdict of Scripture is that we are all, by nature, *anoia*. We are all furious with God to the point of losing our minds. As Paul writes, "The god of this world has blinded the minds of unbelievers, to keep them from seeing the light of the gospel of the glory of Christ" (2 Corinthians 4:4). This is the case with the Pharisees. No matter what Jesus does, no matter who He heals, no matter how many prophecies He fulfills, the Pharisees refuse to believe in Him, for their minds have been taken captive by Satan.

Blessedly, God gives to us new minds in Christ, able to believe in Him and perceive His work on our behalf. In this way, then, we are called to "lose our minds." We are called to lose our minds of sin and receive by faith new minds that are not antagonistic toward God, but faithful to Him. As Paul puts it, "We have the mind of Christ" (1 Corinthians 2:16).

SATURDAY—EASTER 2

Psalmody: Psalm 106:16–23
Additional Psalm: Psalm 68
Old Testament Reading: Exodus 32:1–14
New Testament Reading: Luke 6:20–38

Prayer of the Day

Almighty God, in Your mercy so guide the course of this world that we may forgive as we have been forgiven and joyfully serve You in godly peace and quietness; through Jesus Christ, Your Son, our Lord, who lives and reigns with You and the Holy Spirit, one God, now and forever. (C61)

Meditation

"Jumbo shrimp." "Genuine imitation leather." "Original copies." We have all encountered oxymorons before. Indeed, oxymorons are nearly ubiquitous, which, by the way, is an oxymoron.

Jesus' beatitudes are, at least at first glance, oxymoronic. "Blessed are you who are poor . . . Blessed are you who are hungry now . . . Blessed are you who weep now . . . Blessed are you when people hate you" (vv. 20–22). According to popular opinion, poverty, hunger, weeping, and being hated hardly qualify as blessings! But here Jesus says it: "Blessed are the unblessed."

In His pronouncements, Jesus blesses a group of people who had come to be known as the "pious poor," or in Hebrew, the *anawim*. God seems to have a special affection for these afflicted ones. Indeed, the psalmist reminds us of God's promise to them: "For the needy shall not always be forgotten, and the hope of the poor shall not perish forever" (Psalm 9:18). God watches out for His *anawim*.

It is important to understand that it is not that there is inherent virtue in being poor or afflicted, per se. However, such circumstances do often lead people to rely on God to meet their needs. Such reliance on God stands in sharp contrast to those who are self-sufficient and smug. In Jesus' kingdom, then, it is these who trust in God who are called "blessed," no matter how unblessed their external circumstances may appear.

The blessings of God often appear unimpressive and even downright ghastly. Indeed, God blesses the world through His Son's death on a cross, the very instrument of death pronounced by Old Testament Law to be "cursed." Moses writes, "If a man has committed a crime punishable by death and he is put to death, and you hang him on a tree . . . a hanged man is cursed by God" (Deuteronomy 21:22–23).

It is here that we find the great oxymoron of God. Christ was cursed by hanging on a tree; in return, we are blessed. "Blessed are we when Christ is cursed." This makes no sense! This is why the apostle Paul writes, "For the word of the cross is folly to those who are perishing, but to us who are being saved it is the power of God" (1 Corinthians 1:18). What seems to be weakness and accursedness is really power and blessing. "Blessed are we when Christ is cursed." Though it may be an oxymoron, it is also most certainly true!

THIRD SUNDAY OF EASTER

Psalmody: Psalm 119:49–56
Additional Psalm: Psalm 79
Old Testament Reading: Exodus 32:15–35
New Testament Reading: Luke 6:39–49

Prayer of the Day

O God, through the humiliation of Your Son You raised up the fallen world. Grant to Your faithful people, rescued from the peril of everlasting death, perpetual gladness and eternal joys; through Jesus Christ, our Lord, who lives and reigns with You and the Holy Spirit, one God, now and forever. (L42)

Meditation

I suppose it would have been about as easy as trying to fit a square peg into a round hole. Fitting a log into an eye is not only unlikely, it's impossible! Jesus' listeners surely must have chuckled as they heard Him ask, "Why do you see the speck that is in your brother's eye, but do not notice that log that is in your own eye" (v. 41)? A log lodged in an eye? This statement is so hyperbolic, it's ridiculous. And this is precisely Jesus' point. The sin of those who self-righteously condemn others while failing to recognize their own shortcomings is so ridiculous that it's analogous to trying to fit firewood into a cornea. It just doesn't work.

Sadly, many people misinterpret Jesus' words as a prohibition against any kind of condemnation or confrontation of sin whatsoever. Nothing could be further from the truth. Jesus continues, "You hypocrite, first take the log out of your own eye, and then you will see clearly to take out the speck that is in your brother's eye" (v. 42). Jesus' admonition to remove logs of iniquity from our eyes comes with an express purpose—that we may see clearly enough to help our brother

123

remove the specks of sin that are destroying his eyes. In other words, it is not that we should slackly sanction sin and never seek to remove a speck from our brother's eye, it is that we cannot do so with a log in our own eye because, in such a state, we cannot see our brother to help him. Thus, Jesus calls us to repent of our own sin so that we can help our brother by lovingly confronting him with his sin and calling him to repentance. Jesus wants us to be able to "go and tell him his fault, between you and him alone" (Matthew 18:15).

In Revelation, John sees "one like a son of a man" whose eyes are like "a flame of fire" (1:13–14). Such language is meant to invoke the all-seeing, all-penetrating nature of Jesus' eyes. Christ has no plank of sin in His eye. He is perfectly righteous. He sees with 20/20 clarity the horror of our sin. But happily, He desires to help us. By the planks of Calvary, Christ removes our timbers of transgression so that we may see His goodness and believe His salvation. As the psalmist prays, "Open my eyes, that I may behold wondrous things" (Psalm 119:18). Christ has opened our eyes.

Monday—Easter 3

Psalmody: Psalm 80:1–7
Additional Psalm: Psalm 27
Old Testament Reading: Exodus 33:1–23
New Testament Reading: Luke 7:1–17

Prayer of the Day

O God, by Your almighty Word You set in order all things in heaven and on earth. Put away from us all things hurtful, and give us those things that are beneficial for us; through Jesus Christ, Your Son, our Lord, who lives and reigns with You and the Holy Spirit, one God, now and forever. (C62)

Meditation

Luke likes centurions. Throughout his writings they are portrayed as faithful and godly men. At Jesus' death, it is a centurion who recognizes the injustice that has been done. "Certainly this man was innocent!" he declares (Luke 23:47). In Acts, it is a centurion who asks to hear the Gospel and leads even the apostle Peter to "understand that God shows no partiality, but in every nation anyone who fears Him and does what is right is acceptable to Him" (Acts 10:34–35). Luke likes centurions.

In Luke 7, we meet another centurion. He is a God-fearing man, concerned because one of his servants is deathly ill. So, he sends some Jewish elders to Jesus, requesting healing for his servant. These elders plead with Jesus, saying, "He is worthy to have You do this for him, for he loves our nation, and he is the one who built us our synagogue" (vv. 4–5). These Jewish elders, because of all the centurion's charitable work on behalf of the Jewish people, consider this centurion "worthy."

The centurion, however, knows better. Before Jesus even arrives, he sends an envoy to meet the Healer with this message: "Lord, do not trouble Yourself, for I am not worthy to have You come under my roof . . . But say the word, and let my servant be healed" (vv. 6–7). The Jewish elders call this centurion "worthy." This centurion confesses himself to be "not worthy," for he knows that no number of his good works can make him worthy of Jesus.

The centurion is not the only one who confesses his unworthiness. John the Baptist declares, "I baptize you with water for repentance, but He who is coming after me is mightier than I, whose sandals I am not worthy to carry" (Matthew 3:11). Likewise, Paul says, "I am the least of the apostles, unworthy to be called an apostle, because I persecuted the church of God" (1 Corinthians 15:9). Over and over again, those who seem most pious and worthy confess their unworthiness.

If even the most pious declare themselves "unworthy," who is worthy? Heaven answers, "Worthy is the Lamb who was slain, to receive power and wealth and wisdom and might and honor and glory and blessing" (Revelation 5:12)! Here is true worthiness. It is found not in the charitable works we perform, but in the Lamb who was slain. It is Jesus' worthiness in which the centurion trusts. And it is Jesus' worthiness that heals the centurion's servant. But best of all, it is Jesus' worthiness that forgives our sins.

TUESDAY—EASTER 3

Psalmody: Psalm 86:11–17
Additional Psalm: Psalm 34
Old Testament Reading: Exodus 34:1–28
New Testament Reading: Luke 7:18–35

Prayer of the Day

Lord Jesus, prepare us to receive Your very body and blood by giving us repentance to weep over our sins and then rejoice that in You the blind receive their sight, the lame walk, lepers are cleansed, the deaf hear, the dead are raised up, and the poor have Good News preached to them; for You live and reign with the Father and the Holy Spirit, one God, now and forever. (1015)

Meditation

We usually prefer that which is definite to that which is indefinite. Before we sign a contract, we read the fine print. We may even consult a lawyer. After all, we want to be definite the contract is fair. When buying a house, we first put down earnest money as a pledge that we are definite about closing the deal. We like things that are definite.

In Luke 7, John the Baptist's disciples are confronted with something indefinite. Doubts have arisen as to whether or not Jesus is the Messiah. So John sends his disciples to Jesus with a pointed question: "Are You the one who is to come, or shall we look for another" (v. 19)? Whether these doubts concerning Jesus' identity originated in the minds of His disciples or in the mind of John himself we are not told, but this much is definite: some are indefinite as to whether or not Jesus is the Christ.

Jesus' answer to such indefiniteness is striking: "Go and tell John what you have seen and heard: the blind receive their sight, the lame walk, lepers are cleansed, and the deaf hear, the dead are raised up, the poor have good news preached to them" (v. 22). Jesus quotes Isaiah 35:5–6 and 61:1, both messianic prophecies, staking a definite claim to His status. "I am the Messiah!" Jesus says.

Interestingly, though the English Standard Version translates the definite article "the" in verse 22—"the blind receive their sight, the lame walk"—there is no definite article in Greek. Some take this as a reference to the fact that even though some lame are healed, not all the lame are healed. Although some dead are raised, not all the dead are raised. In other words, there is more to come. We continue to struggle with the indefiniteness that sin brings.

Even in a world of indefiniteness, we are promised that indefiniteness will not linger indefinitely! For when Christ returns, all the blind will receive their sight, all the lame will walk, all the lepers will be cleansed, all the deaf will hear, all the dead will be raised up, and all the poor will rejoice at God's good news. As Isaiah promises, "The Lord God will wipe away tears from all faces" (Isaiah 25:8). The definite article will be added once and for all. And of this promise, I am definite. For it is a promise of God.

WEDNESDAY—EASTER 3

Psalmody: Psalm 84:1–4
Additional Psalm: Psalm 23
Old Testament Reading: Exodus 34:29–35:21
Additional Reading: Exodus 35:22–38:20
New Testament Reading: Luke 7:36–50

Prayer of the Day

Almighty and everlasting God, increase in us Your gifts of faith, hope, and love that we may receive the forgiveness You have promised and love what You have commanded; through Jesus Christ, Your Son, our Lord, who lives and reigns with You and the Holy Spirit, one God, now and forever. (C64)

Meditation

When a group of scribes asked, "Which commandment is the most important of all?" Jesus replied, "You shall love the Lord your God with all your heart and with all your soul and with all your mind and with all your strength" (Mark 12:28, 30). When Jesus answered, "Love God," the scribes enthusiastically responded, "You are right, Teacher" (Mark 12:32). Indeed, this was the common consensus concerning which commandment was God's greatest.

In Luke 7, we meet a woman who believes this commandment well. In fact, Jesus says of her, "She loved much" (v. 47). As the story opens, Jesus is dining with a Pharisee named Simon when this woman enters to anoint Jesus. Luke is terse in his description of her: she is a sinner. Simon is appalled that Jesus would warmly welcome such a scandalous woman. "If this man were a prophet, He would have known who and what sort of woman this is who is touching Him, for she is a sinner" (v. 39). In the Greek, Simon's syntax betrays that he does not believe Jesus is a prophet. A

paraphrase might read, "If You were a prophet, Jesus, but You're not, then You would know that this is a sinful woman!"

In response to this attack on His identity, Jesus tells a parable: "A certain moneylender had two debtors. One owed five hundred denarii, and the other fifty" (v. 41). Such moneylenders were hard and unrelenting in their quests to call in loans. After all, it was their business. But this moneylender is different. For when his debtors "could not pay, he cancelled the debt of both" (v. 42). This moneylender is unexpectedly gracious! Jesus then reveals the intent of His parable with a question: "Now which of them will love him more" (v. 42)? Simon is forced to answer, "The one, I suppose, for whom he cancelled the larger debt" (v. 43). The lesson? Much forgiveness breeds much love. A person cannot believe the greatest commandment of loving God much without first being forgiven much by God.

Do you love the Lord your God with all your heart, soul, mind, and strength? If so, what a great sinner you must be! And what great forgiveness you must have been given by God! For he who loves much has been forgiven much. And being forgiven is God's good news.

THURSDAY—EASTER 3

Psalmody: Psalm 119:145–152
Additional Psalm: Psalm 20
Old Testament Reading:
Exodus 38:21–39:8, 22–23, 27–31
New Testament Reading: Luke 8:1–21

Prayer of the Day

Lord Jesus, Sower of the Seed, the women supported You from their own means during Your ministry of releasing creation from its bondage. Give us strength to support the work of sowing the seed of Your forgiveness in the world through our almsgiving as we embody in our lives Your mercy and charity; for You live and reign with the Father and the Holy Spirit, one God, now and forever. (1016)

Meditation

The great seventeenth-century English constitutional scholar John Seldon used a phrase in his Table Talk which has become commonplace: "Do as I say, not as I do." Interestingly, Seldon connects this phrase to pastors who preach one thing while living another.

In Luke 8, Jesus tells a parable about preaching and believing. "A sower went out to sow his seed," Jesus begins (v. 5). Later, Jesus reveals to His disciples, "The seed is the word of God" (v. 11). Thus, Jesus' parable is about a pastor, sowing the seed of God's Word through his preaching. And some believe this seed and some do not.

Christ is the Sower who scatters seed. He is the Pastor. But unlike Seldon's pastor, Christ does not adopt a "Do as I say, not as I do" attitude. Instead, He faithfully does as He says. Indeed, He does as He says even while He's still saying it.

After Jesus finishes preaching His parable, Luke includes this note: "As [Jesus] said these things, He called out, 'He who has ears to hear, let him hear' " (v. 8). The verbs are important. The phrase "as [Jesus] said" is a present tense participle, which can be translated, "While Jesus is saying these things . . . " The verb "called" is imperfect, denoting an ongoing action. In other words, it's not just that Jesus

"called out," it's that He "was calling out." "While Jesus is saying these things, He was calling out, 'He who has ears to hear, let him hear!' "

The sense is that Jesus' exhortation to "hear" is a refrain that He repeatedly calls out while saying the things of His parable. Thus, while Jesus is telling a parable about preaching and believing the Word of God, He is calling people, through His preaching, to believe the Word of God. Jesus does what He says even while He is saying it!

God's Word always does what it says. As God promises through His prophet Isaiah, "So shall My word be that goes out from My mouth; it shall not return to Me empty, but it shall accomplish that which I purpose, and shall succeed in the thing for which I sent it" (Isaiah 55:11). When the Word is preached, we can rejoice that it will always do as it says, even if we do not. By our ears of faith, may we always hear this Word, which not only speaks to us, but does for us everything it so preciously promises.

FRIDAY—EASTER 3

Psalmody: Psalm 107:23–32
Additional Psalm: Psalm 115
Old Testament Reading: Exodus 39:32–40:16
New Testament Reading: Luke 8:22–39

Prayer of the Day

O God, You have prepared for those who love You such good things as surpass our understanding. Cast out all sins and evil desires from us, and pour into our hearts Your Holy Spirit to guide us into all blessedness; through Jesus Christ, Your Son, our Lord, who lives and reigns with You and the Holy Spirit, one God, now and forever. (C65)

Meditation

In Luke 8, Jesus is at the height of His popularity. Indeed, we read that Jesus' own family "could not reach Him because of the crowd" (v. 19). Everyone wants to see Jesus. That is, everyone in Galilee wants to see Jesus. But then Jesus leaves His home turf and sails with His disciples "to the country of Gerasenes, which is opposite Galilee" (v. 26). Gerasenes is part of the Decapolis, a Gentile region known for its rank paganism. Where Jesus once had throngs of thousands clamoring to see Him in Galilee, only one man comes to meet Him in the Decapolis—a demon-possessed indigent. His demon possession is so ghastly that he has been exiled from his own people and forced to live not "in a house but among the tombs" (v. 27). But though these demons have wreaked havoc in this man, they are no match for Jesus. Jesus sends them into a nearby herd of pigs.

Understandably, the man who has been healed of such dreaded possession wants to follow Jesus: "The man from whom the demons had gone begged that he might be with Him" (v. 38). Jesus, however, demurs: "Return to your home, and declare how much God has done for you" (v. 39). This man, now able to rejoin society, is to be a witness for Jesus among his own people. This man wants to follow Jesus by being in close proximity with Jesus. Jesus wants this man to follow Him by being a witness for Jesus. And so this man witnesses.

Though we are never told specifically what happens to this formerly demon-possessed man, Mark offers a startling account of Jesus' next visit to the Decapolis: "Then [Jesus] returned from the region of Tyre and went through Sidon to the Sea of Galilee, in the region of the Decapolis . . . a great crowd gathered" (Mark 7:31, 8:1). When Jesus first visits the Decapolis, one man comes to greet him. Now, it is a "great crowd." Actually, it's

four thousand, whom Jesus then feeds with seven humble loaves of bread (cf. Mark 8:1–9). Perhaps that demon-possessed man told some people about Jesus after all. And perhaps four thousand believed as "the Lord added to their number day by day those who were being saved" (Acts 2:47). May God continue to add to His Kingdom as we continue to share His Gospel.

SATURDAY—EASTER 3

Psalmody: Psalm 41:1–3, 11–13
Additional Psalm: Psalm 76
Old Testament Reading: Exodus 40:17–38
Additional Reading: Leviticus 1:1–7:38
New Testament Reading: Luke 8:40–56

Prayer of the Day

Lord Jesus, You took our illnesses and bore our diseases, bringing hope to the sick and the dying. In Your death on the cross, You completed Your work of bearing all our burdens and on the third day showed us in Your resurrected body the firstfruits of the new creation. Heal us now by Your Word and Sacraments, and raise us up on the Last Day that we might live with You forever; for You live and reign with the Father and the Holy Spirit, one God, now and forever. (1017)

Meditation

Jairus's plight is desperate. His only daughter is on her deathbed. But Jairus believes that Jesus can heal her. And so, this stately synagogue ruler falls at Jesus' feet and begs Him to come and save his daughter's life. As Jesus is on His way to Jairus' house, a crowd of admirers almost crushes Him. In this crowd, there is a woman who has "had a discharge of blood for twelve years" (v. 43). But rather than boldly asking Jesus to heal her as Jairus does with his daughter, she covertly touches the fringe of Jesus' garment. Immediately, her bleeding stops.

Just when this woman thinks she can slip away unnoticed, Jesus notices. "Someone touched Me," He says, "for I perceive that power has gone out from Me" (v. 46). And so this woman must present herself, trembling with fear, to Jesus. Rather than scolding her, however, Jesus commends her: "Daughter, your faith has made you well; go in peace" (v. 48).

This doesn't make sense! Here is a woman whose faith is so timid that she tries to sneak a healing from Jesus. And she gets one. Not only that, but Jesus commends her faith! But then here is Jairus, a man who boldly implores Jesus to heal his daughter, and he's still waiting.

Tragically, things take a turn for the worse: "While [Jesus] was still speaking, someone from the ruler's house came and said, 'Your daughter is dead; do not trouble the Teacher any more'" (v. 49). A timid faith results in healing. A public faith leaves a man's daughter dead. How much more backward can this be?

In the end, Jesus travels to Jairus's home and raises his daughter from the dead. This story has a happy ending, but not every story does. Some sicknesses end in deaths that are not immediately thwarted. Some depression tightens rather than loosens its grip. Some emotional wounds never get healed in this life.

Although it might not immediately seem like it, the discontinuity between the boldness of faith and the severity of suffering is good news. This discontinuity means that we need not have superhero-like faith in order to receive God's blessings. For this bleeding woman's faith was anything but bold, yet it received healing from Jesus. That's because the blessings of faith are not the result of faith's intrinsic strength; rather, they are the result of the strength of the One to whom faith clings: Jesus Christ. And Jesus is always strong, even when our faith is weak.

FOURTH SUNDAY OF EASTER

Psalmody: Psalm 45:4–8a
Additional Psalm: Psalm 132
Old Testament Reading:
Leviticus 8:1–13, 30–36
New Testament Reading: Luke 9:1–17

Prayer of the Day

Almighty God, merciful Father, since You have wakened from death the Shepherd of Your sheep, grant us Your Holy Spirit that when we hear the voice of our Shepherd we may know Him who calls us each by name and follow where He leads; through the same Jesus Christ, Your Son, our Lord, who lives and reigns with You and the Holy Spirit, one God, now and forever. (L43)

Meditation

There is no rest for the weary. The Twelve have just returned from their inaugural tour of "preaching the Gospel and healing" (v. 6) and are understandably tired. Jesus, sympathetic to His disciples' plight, withdraws with them to Bethsaida. The problem is that, like a mob of rabid paparazzi, throngs of adorers pursue Jesus. But even when tired, Jesus' love for people never falters. Luke says, "He welcomed them" (v. 11). The Greek text denotes not only a welcome, but a friendly welcome. Jesus is glad to see these people! The disciples, however, want the evening to themselves. So they say to Jesus, "Send the crowd away to go into the surrounding villages and countryside to find lodging and get provisions, for we are here in a desolate place" (v. 12). But

Jesus will do no such thing. "You give them something to eat," Jesus says (v. 13). The "you" is emphatic. It is almost as if Jesus is wagging His finger at the Twelve, saying, "You! This is your job to provide food for these folks!" But this is a job the disciples cannot do: "We have no more than five loaves and two fish," they protest, "unless we are to go and buy food for all these people" (v. 13).

Luke says that there are about five thousand men in need of some supper—and these are just the men! By the time women and children are added, you're easily upward of twenty thousand mouths that need feeding. This is indeed a meal the disciples cannot provide. But Jesus can.

"Taking the five loaves and the two fish, [Jesus] looked up to heaven and said a blessing over them. Then He broke the loaves and gave them to the disciples to set before the crowd. And they all ate and were satisfied" (vv. 16–17). Jesus takes, blesses, breaks, and gives the loaves to the crowd even as He later takes, blesses, breaks, and gives Himself to us: "And as they were eating, [Jesus] took bread, and after blessing it broke it and gave it to [His disciples], and said, 'Take; this is my body' " (v. 22). Like the disciples at the feeding of the five thousand, Communion is a meal we cannot provide ourselves; it must be given to us by our Lord. And blessedly, He gives it. He gives to us His body and blood for our forgiveness. And we receive it with joyful hearts.

Monday—Easter 4

Psalmody: Psalm 119:129–138
Additional Psalm: Psalm 96
Old Testament Reading: Leviticus 9:1–24
New Testament Reading: Luke 9:18–36

Prayer of the Day

O God, in the glorious transfiguration of Your beloved Son You confirmed the mysteries of the faith by the testimony of Moses and Elijah. In the voice that came from the bright cloud You wonderfully foreshowed our adoption by grace. Mercifully make us co-heirs with the King in His glory and bring us to the fullness of our inheritance in heaven; through the same Jesus Christ, our Lord, who lives and reigns with You and the Holy Spirit, one God, now and forever. (L21)

Meditation

"[I believe] in one Lord Jesus Christ, the only-begotten Son of God." This is who we gladly confess Jesus to be in the Nicene Creed. Of course, there are other confessions of Jesus out there as well: "I believe Jesus was a good moral guide, but not eternally begotten from the Father." "I believe that Jesus showed us one path to God among many." "I believe Jesus, as He is presented in the Scriptures, never existed." These are just a few of the alternate confessions that vie for our attention and allegiance.

As it is today, so it was in the first century. In Luke 9, Jesus wants to know what confessions of Him are swirling around in the popular culture. And so He asks His disciples, "Who do the crowds say that I am?" They answer, "John the Baptist. But others say, Elijah, and others, that one of the prophets of old has risen" (vv. 18–19).

Sadly, even though many confessions grip the public's imagination, none of these confessions will do, for none of these confessions are correct. And so Jesus asks again, " 'But who do you say that I am?' And Peter answer[s], 'The Christ of God' " (v. 20).

Among much heresy, Peter's confession is correct. And so Jesus continues by explaining to His disciples exactly what such a confession of Jesus as "the Christ of God" entails: "The Son of Man must suffer many things and be rejected by the elders and chief priests and scribes, and be killed, and on the third day be raised" (v. 22).

The Son of Man must suffer many things? Says who? Says Scripture. Again, we confess in the Nicene Creed: "[Christ] was crucified also for us under Pontius Pilate. He suffered and was buried. And the third day He rose again according to the Scriptures." Jesus does all "according to the Scriptures."

To confess Jesus as "the Christ of God" means to confess that Jesus stared the "must" of Scriptural mandate in the face even when that "must" demanded His suffering and death. But make no mistake about it, Jesus did not suffer and die only out of bare necessity. No, He also suffered and died freely and willingly out of His love for you. Divine necessity was wedded with divine love on the cross. And from this comes our salvation. And it is this Jesus whom we gladly confess. Settle for no other confession than this.

TUESDAY—EASTER 4

Psalmody: Psalm 25:1–10
Additional Psalm: Psalm 141
Old Testament Reading: Leviticus 10:1–20
Additional Reading: Leviticus 11:1–15:33
New Testament Reading: Luke 9:37–62

Prayer of the Day

Lord of all power and might, author and giver of all good things, graft into our hearts the love of Your name and nourish us with all goodness that we may love and serve our neighbor; through Jesus Christ, Your Son, our Lord, who lives and reigns with You and the Holy Spirit, one God, now and forever. (C66)

Meditation

When Jesus makes up His mind to do something, His resolve is unflappable. For two years, Jesus has been teaching, healing, and ministering to those in His home of Galilee. But now, He has "set His face to go to Jerusalem" (v. 51), the place of His Passion. And He will not be deterred.

Three examples serve to illustrate Jesus' steely resolve. First, to one who says, "I will follow You wherever You go" (v. 57), Jesus responds, "Foxes have holes, and birds of the air have nests, but the Son of Man has nowhere to lay His head" (v. 58). The Greek word for "nests" can describe not only a bird's nest but also a human dwelling place (e.g., 2 Samuel 7:10 LXX). Thus, as Jesus heads toward Jerusalem, there will be no temporary residences along the way. He will find no nest for Himself. He must make it to His destination.

To another man who, before following Jesus, says, "Lord, let me first go and bury my father" (v. 59), Jesus replies, "Leave the dead to bury their own dead" (v. 60). At first, Jesus' response might sound harsh. But this is hardly the case. In the Ancient Near East, burials involved two stages: the initial burial where the body was placed in a tomb and then, approximately a year later, the removal of the deceased's bones to a permanent place of internment. Thus, this man could have been requesting a year's respite before following Jesus. Jesus, however, cannot dally for a year.

Finally, another man says to Jesus, "I will follow you, Lord, but let me first say farewell to those at my home" (v. 61). This man's "but" reveals his true allegiance—and it is not to His Lord. As Jesus says elsewhere, "Whoever loves his father or mother more than Me is not worthy of Me, and whoever loves his son or daughter more than Me is not worthy of Me" (Matthew 10:37). Family is important, but following Christ is preeminent.

Jesus has set His face for Jerusalem. And He will not stop for any man. But even though He will not stop for any man, He will die for every man. As Jesus says, "The Son of Man is about to be delivered into the hands of men" (v. 44). This is why Jesus will not be detoured. For Jesus is going to Jerusalem to be delivered and to die for you and me. Praise be to God that Jesus made it to His destination.

WEDNESDAY—EASTER 4

Psalmody: Psalm 19:7–14
Additional Psalm: Psalm 50
Old Testament Reading: Leviticus 16:1–24
New Testament Reading: Luke 10:1–22

Prayer of the Day

Almighty God, You have built Your Church on the foundation of the apostles and prophets with Christ Jesus Himself as the cornerstone. Continue to send Your messengers to preserve Your people in true peace that, by the preaching of Your Word, Your Church may be kept free from all harm and danger; through Jesus Christ, Your Son, our Lord, who lives and reigns with You and the Holy Spirit, one God, now and forever. (C67)

Meditation
"Familiarity breeds contempt." So says Aesop in "The Fox and the Lion." The first time the fox saw the lion, he was stricken with terror and ran to hide in the forest. The second time, he cautiously watched the lion from a safe distance. The third time, the fox leisurely approached the lion and struck up a conversation, not fearing him as the king of the jungle. Why did the fox become so at ease with the lion? Because he had become familiar with him. And familiarity breeds contempt.

"Familiarity breeds contempt." Such is the case with Jesus. Thus far, Jesus has done many "mighty works" (v. 13) in His home turf of Galilee. Yet, the people here have not believed in Him. As Jesus elsewhere says, "A prophet is not without honor except in his hometown and in his own household" (Matthew 13:57). Jesus' family and friends treat Him with contempt. Conversely, the pagan cities of Tyre and Sidon would have repented and believed had Jesus performed His signs there. And so, Jesus sends seventy-two disciples to these and other towns to preach His Gospel.

Before sending out His seventy-two, Jesus commissions them: "The harvest is plentiful, but the laborers are few. Therefore pray earnestly to the Lord of the harvest to send out laborers into this harvest" (Luke 10:2). Jesus' first instruction to His disciples is a mandate to pray for more disciples. Although Jesus' mission to the world begins with seventy-two, He does not intend it to end with seventy-two. Rather, He desires that more and more disciples be added to spread His Gospel. And blessedly, God has added heartily and mightily many more disciples. Millions now work in the Gospel's fields, sharing Christ's message.

You have been sent to share Jesus, but you are not the only one Jesus is calling. Jesus is calling many to share His message, some are those whose vocation is to be pastors, teachers, deaconesses, directors of Christian education, missionaries; others find opportunity to share the Good News of Jesus as they work in the myriad vocations outside of the Church. So share the Gospel and pray for God to raise up others to share it as well. For this is the blessed commission of our Savior.

Thursday—Easter 4

Psalmody: Psalm 17:7–15
Additional Psalm: Psalm 89
Old Testament Reading: Leviticus 17:1–16
New Testament Reading: Luke 10:23–42

Prayer of the Day

Lord Jesus Christ, in Your deep compassion You rescue us from whatever may hurt us. Teach us to love You above all things and to love our neighbors as ourselves; for You live and reign with the Father and the Holy Spirit, one God, now and forever. (C68)

Meditation

My mother used to tell me, "If you don't want the answer, don't ask the question." Apparently, a lawyer in Luke 10 learned no such lesson from his mother.

The text opens with the lawyer posing a question to Jesus: "Teacher, what shall I do to inherit eternal life?" Jesus immediately turns the man's question back on him: "What is written in the Law? How do you read it?" His answer is the standard one: "You shall love the Lord your God with all your heart and with all your soul and with all your strength and with all your mind, and your neighbor as yourself" (vv. 25–27). The Greek word for "neighbor" is *pleision*, meaning, "near one." Thus, loving your neighbor entails loving anyone near you, be they friend or foe.

But the lawyer is not sure he likes Jesus' answer to his question. After all, loving every pleision is hard! So, he tries to "justify himself" and his lack of love by looking for a loophole in the definition of "neighbor." "And who is my neighbor?" he asks Jesus (v. 29).

Jesus allows no loophole. He tells a parable about a wounded man, shunned by a priest and a Levite, but then helped by a Samaritan. Notably, Jews hated Samaritans (cf. John 4:9). Indeed, this lawyer must have been squirming at the thought of loving, or being loved by, the likes of a Samaritan. But Jesus will not allow this lawyer to escape the inevitable conclusion of what it means to love one's neighbor. And so He asks, "Which of these three, do you think, proved to be a neighbor to the man who fell among the robbers?" The lawyer must answer: "The one who showed him mercy" (Luke 10:36–37). The Samaritan.

God's Law leaves no room for self-justification. We cannot blast loopholes into Divine mandates, leaving us free to love one neighbor while hating another. No, we are called to love all people. And yet, we all fall short of this. We do not treat everyone as a "neighbor."

Mercifully, at the very crux of Christianity is the consoling canon that, because we cannot justify ourselves, we are justified by Christ. As Paul says, "We have now been justified by His blood" (Romans 5:9).

We do not have to justify ourselves. For we have already been justified by Christ—you and all your neighbors. Even the neighbors we don't like. This is the Gospel!

Friday—Easter 4

Psalmody: Psalm 119:1–8
Additional Psalm: Psalm 116
Old Testament Reading: Leviticus 18:1–7, 20—19:8
New Testament Reading: Luke 11:1–13

Prayer of the Day

O Lord, let Your merciful ears be attentive to the prayers of Your servants, and by Your Word and Spirit teach us how to pray that our petitions may be pleasing before You; through Jesus Christ, Your Son, our Lord, who lives and reigns with You and the Holy Spirit, one God, now and forever. (C70)

Meditation

When Jesus asks His disciples, "Which of you who has a friend will go to him at midnight and say to him, 'Friend, lend me three loaves'?" (v. 5), my answer probably would have been, "Not me." I don't know if I could make such a request of even a close friend. After all, this request seems awfully rude. Indeed, Jesus says as much: "I tell you, though he will not get up and give him anything because he is his friend, yet because of his impudence he will rise up and give him whatever he needs" (v. 8). The Greek word for "impudence" connotes persistence mixed with shamelessness. And this man is certainly shameless.

First, the timing of this man's request is shameless. To ask for food in the morning, afternoon, or evening is one thing, but to ask for food at midnight while the father is in bed with his children is downright brazen. After all, rousing the father would mean stirring his children as well.

Second, the amount of food for which this man asks is shameless. In a society where preservatives and refrigeration were not prevalent, and thus food was prepared only as needed so that it would not spoil, three loaves would have probably constituted all the food this family had prepared. To make such a demand means that the father's family would probably have nothing for breakfast the next morning!

And yet, this friend asks. And this father gives. And then comes Jesus' punch line: "If you then, who are evil, know how to give good gifts . . . how much more will the heavenly Father give the Holy Spirit to those who ask Him" (v. 13)! As the earthly father gives to his friend, so the heavenly Father gives to His children—except even more so. The heavenly Father is not evil and selfish as earthly fathers can sometimes be. No, the heavenly Father is generous and wants to give His good gifts. Even so, we are encouraged by the preacher of Hebrews: "Let us then with confidence draw near to the throne of grace, that we may receive mercy and find grace to help in time of need" (Hebrews 4:16).

So show a little bit of impudence as you approach your heavenly Father in prayer—not out of disrespect, but in glad faith and joyful assurance that God listens to your every care, concern, and need.

SATURDAY—EASTER 4

Psalmody: Psalm 36:7–12
Additional Psalm: Psalm 39
Old Testament Reading:
Leviticus 19:9–18, 26–37
New Testament Reading: Luke 11:14–36

Prayer of the Day

Lord Jesus, You are the Stronger Man who plundered Satan's house by casting out demons with Your finger and finishing him off by Your death on the cross. Blessed are those who hear Your Word and keep it by their works of mercy and charity as Satan falls like lightning from heaven when he sees You in us; for You live and reign with the Father and the Holy Spirit, one God, now and forever. (1018)

Meditation

It's exciting to watch the Lord grow His Church. In Luke 11, attendance at Jesus' church services is increasing exponentially: "When the crowds were increasing . . ." This says it all. People are packing the synagogue to hear Jesus preach. And so Jesus preaches. He begins His sermon: "This generation is an evil generation" (v. 29).

Maybe Jesus needs to take a remedial preaching course. Common wisdom would suggest that a sermon begin on a slightly more upbeat note. But Jesus, even in front of one of His largest crowds yet, wastes no time cutting the hearts of His hearers: "This generation is an evil generation. It seeks for a sign, but no sign will be given to it except the sign of Jonah" (v. 29).

With Jesus' ever-increasing crowds came the crowds' ever-increasing appetite for the miraculous. But while this crowd may hunger for impressive signs, they do not hunger to believe in Jesus. This is seen just verses earlier, as some accuse Jesus of casting "out demons by Beelzebul, the prince of demons" (v. 15). Beelzebul, whose name means "lord of the flies," is a play on the name of the Philistine god Baal-zebub, whose name means, "lord prince." Baal-zebub was so hated by the ancient Israelites that his name became associated with the devil. Thus, when some accuse Jesus of casting out demons by Beelzebul, they accuse Him of casting out demons by the power of Satan. They certainly do not believe in Jesus! And no miraculous sign—even that of exorcism—can change this crowd's opinion of Jesus. Rather, they're simply looking for the cheap chills and thrills that miracles inevitably generate.

But Jesus will not feed the crowd this kind of spiritual junk food. Instead of offering miraculous thrills, Jesus ominously states, "No sign will be given to [this wicked generation] except the sign of Jonah." (v. 29). In Matthew's parallel account, Jesus explains further: "For just as Jonah was three days and three nights in the belly of the great fish, so will the Son of Man be three days and three nights in the heart of the earth" (Matthew 12:40). Jesus will die and be buried. But He will not stay dead. For after three days, He will rise from death in triumphant vindication of His identity. And it is by this sign that we are called to believe in the One who gives it for us and for our salvation—Jesus Christ.

FIFTH SUNDAY OF EASTER

Psalmody: Psalm 37:1–9
Additional Psalm: Psalm 150
Old Testament Reading:
Leviticus 20:1–16, 22–27
New Testament Reading: Luke 11:37–54

Prayer of the Day

O God, You make the minds of Your faithful to be of one will. Grant that we may love what You have commanded and desire what You promise, that among the many changes of this world our hearts may be fixed where true joys are found; through Jesus Christ, Your Son, our Lord, who lives and reigns with You and the Holy Spirit, one God, now and forever. (L45)

Meditation

In Luke 11, Jesus is invited to a Pharisee's home. Almost immediately, things go downhill: "The Pharisee was astonished to see that [Jesus] did not first wash before dinner" (v. 38). Ritual washing before a meal was cumbersomely outlined in Jewish tradition. In one book of Jewish rituals, no fewer than twenty-six prayers are given to accompany ritual washings! The Jewish luminary Rabbi

Akiba is said to have died from dehydration because what he could have used for drinking water, he instead used for ritual washing. Thus was the importance of such washing. It was not prescribed in Mosaic Law, but by their traditions, the Pharisees had made it into a mountainous burden.

But Jesus overlooks all this when he begins His meal without washing. And the Pharisee who watches Jesus eat is astonished. But Jesus is incensed: "Now you Pharisees cleanse the outside of the cup and of the dish, but inside you are full of greed and wickedness" (v. 39). Jesus' language alludes to a debate between the two primary schools of Jewish theology in the first century: the Shammai school and the Hillel school. The Shammai school said the outside of a cup could be clean even if the inside was not while the Hillel school said a cup's interior must be cleaned first.

Jesus uses the language of this debate to talk not about the cleanliness of a cup, but about the cleanliness of a person. For the Pharisees are so rife with hypocrisy that they "are like unmarked graves, and people walk over them without knowing it" (v. 44). Again, Jewish tradition helps us understand Jesus' accusation. The Jews carefully marked all graves so that a person might not inadvertently walk over one and so become ritually unclean (cf. Numbers 19:11–13). Jesus calls the Pharisees "unmarked graves," thereby accusing them of being unclean themselves while also defiling others.

What is the solution to so much uncleanness? A different kind of washing; one that is a "washing with water with the Word" (Ephesians 5:26). What is needed is not ceremonial washing, but Baptism, which washes away our very sins according to Christ's promise. Interestingly, the Greek word for "wash" in v. 38 is *baptizo*. If only the Pharisees would have trusted in the baptizo done in the name of the Father, Son, and Holy Spirit rather than the baptizos done according to their traditions. For in God's baptizo, we are truly cleansed.

MONDAY—EASTER 5

Psalmody: Psalm 31:1–5
Additional Psalm: Psalm 25
Old Testament Reading: Leviticus 21:1–24
New Testament Reading: Luke 12:1–12

Prayer of the Day

Lord Jesus, by Your Spirit, You give us faith to cast out all fear of confessing the true faith; for we are helpless to save ourselves, and we must trust in You and You alone for our salvation. Keep us faithful to the end, that You will not be ashamed of us when You come in Your glory with Your Father and the holy angels; for You live and reign with the Father and the Holy Spirit, one God, now and forever. (1019)

Meditation
Leaven is not usually a positive in the Bible, and certainly not in this passage. The leaven of the Pharisees that our Lord warns against He identifies as hypocrisy. The hypocrite is a stage actor, playing a role. "All the world's a stage," says Shakespeare, but the Lord Jesus warns that this is a great danger to one's soul, for any playacting will be exposed and brought to light on the Day of Judgment. God is after truth—truth above all in the innermost being (Psalm 51:6). As Psalm 90 thunders at us: "You have set our iniquities before You, our secret sins in the light of Your presence" (v. 8). And what He even now sees—the whole truth about us—will be exposed for all to see on the Day of Judgment.

So fear. Don't fear people who try to impress with their playacting. Fear rather Him who cannot be fooled and who can kill not only the body but also cast your soul into the undying flame. Fear Him, indeed, but do not only fear Him. Above all, trust Him.

The little sparrows sold for pennies are all known, remembered, and loved by God. How much more you—you whose very hairs are numbered—are known, remembered, and loved by God. You whose value is revealed by the price that Christ willingly paid for you to have you as His own—His cross! No need to playact, then. You can't impress Him by your performance, but you can receive His love and purge out of your life entirely that pharisaical leaven of pretend religion.

And as you confess the One who has shown you your value to God, He rejoices to confess you as His very own before the angels. He delights to forgive you every sin and blasphemy, but He does warn against the final and most deadly hypocrisy—the sin against the Holy Spirit—where you are convicted of the truth of Jesus' claims and yet pretend that you are not. That's a sin without forgiveness.

Who is tempted to such blasphemy more than those afraid of what people in power will do to them if they confess the Christ? Rather than blaspheme the Spirit, Jesus urges you to rely upon Him. The Spirit will be your teacher; He will guide you in exactly what you ought to say as you confess your Savior before men. What do you have to lose? In Christ, you have been valued and loved with a life that no one can take from you. Ever.

TUESDAY—EASTER 5

Psalmody: Psalm 127
Additional Psalm: Psalm 92
Old Testament Reading: Leviticus 23:1–22
New Testament Reading: Luke 12:13–34

Prayer of the Day

O Lord, grant us wisdom to recognize the treasures You have stored up for us in heaven, that we may never despair but always rejoice and be thankful for the riches of Your grace; through Jesus Christ, Your Son, our Lord, who lives and reigns with You and the Holy Spirit, one God, now and forever. (C71)

Meditation

When you feel that you have been wronged, you long for the sort of Lord who might show up and take your side. "Teacher, tell my brother to divide the inheritance with me." But Jesus isn't that sort of Lord. That's not what He came for. "Who made me a judge or arbitrator over you?" And as is His way, He goes to the heart of the problem. The one who feels wronged and asks for help in obtaining the inheritance is focused on the passing stuff of this age and not the lasting treasures of eternity. Where are you focused? What do you give your fretting to?

Our Lord warns us to take care and to guard against all covetousness. That's thinking you can't be happy unless you have . . . whatever! "One's life does not consist in the abundance of his possessions." He who dies with the most toys still dies. And so the parable of the rich man—so focused on the stuff of this age and gathering it in, that he was a fool. He forgot all about the truth Job spoke: "Naked I came from my mother's womb, and naked shall I return" (Job 1:21). We can carry none of the stuff we call our own with us out of this world. But every last one of us is headed out of it, daily drawing closer to the Day of Judgment. If we are not fools, but wise, we will remember the lasting treasures—the deeds done in faith and love—that will accompany us on that day. Better than the money socked away for the rainy day, is the money given to the poor and needy.

And we're free to be generous with such earthly treasures, for in Jesus we've learned that we have a Father who clothes us, feeds us, shelters us, and keeps us. To focus on stuff is to serve up the liturgy of anxiety—constant fretting over what we're bound to lose. Instead of such liturgy, our Lord invites us into His liturgy of thanksgiving. The Father clothes us not just with earthly garments, but wraps us in the garment of His Son's holiness. We have a Father who feeds us not just earthly food, but who has provided a banquet table for us to feast from, giving us His Son's true body and blood, forgiveness, and life eternal. We have a Father who delights to lavish on us a Kingdom!

So our Lord invites us to toss the fear overboard; to dare to be kind and generous, giving and cheerful. We've got God's Kingdom as our dearest possession—and death cannot take it from us.

WEDNESDAY—EASTER 5

Psalmody: Psalm 116:12–19
Additional Psalm: Psalm 123
Old Testament Reading: Leviticus 23:23–44
New Testament Reading: Luke 12:35–53

Prayer of the Day

Merciful Lord, cleanse and defend Your Church by the sacrifice of Christ. United with Him in Holy Baptism, give us grace to receive with thanksgiving the fruits of His redeeming work and daily follow in His way; through the same Jesus Christ, Your Son, our Lord, who lives and reigns with You and the Holy Spirit, one God, now and forever. (C73)

Meditation

What kind of Master do we have in our Lord Jesus? He tells us to watch and wait for His coming with eager anticipation. The One we're waiting for is like no other master on earth. He's a Servant-King. He reigns by serving. And so when He shows up at the Last Day, He goes on doing what He's always done: serves! He will summon His own to His heavenly feast and He will wait on them.

It shouldn't surprise us. After all, didn't He say that He had come not to be served, but to serve? And does He not even to this day continue to serve His people in the Divine Service? He gathers us together to serve out on us promises of eternal life and forgiveness and to feed into us His undying body and blood.

Peter asks what seems a sensible question. "Are you talking to us or to all? Do you mean this just for us disciples, us apostles, us ministers? Or do you mean it for all who are Your followers?"

Peter and the others liked to think of themselves as important and great—and not in the way that our Lord spoke of greatness! So the Lord throws back to Peter and to anyone who would lord it over the Church a beatitude: "Blessed is that servant whom his master will find doing so—feeding the household their portion of food at the proper time—He will set him over all his possessions." The job of the ministry is to dish out the food, the food apportioned to each one according to his or her needs—Law served up to the hardened sinner; sweet Gospel set before the brokenhearted.

But if the servant forgets that he was set in position to serve, not to lord it over, let alone abuse, those in the household, a fearful judgment awaits. "Cut him into pieces and put him with the unfaithful." The Lord is after faithfulness; and so when much is entrusted, much will be required.

He wraps up a shocker: He comes to bring division. Families end up split down the middle. You either end up on His side or you end up fighting against Him. No earthly family ties may trump the relationship we have to Jesus and to one another in Him.

THURSDAY—EASTER 5

Psalmody: Psalm 52
Additional Psalm: Psalm 107
Old Testament Reading: Leviticus 24:1–23
Additional Reading: Leviticus 25:1–55
New Testament Reading: Luke 12:54–13:17

Prayer of the Day

O Jesus, Lord of the Sabbath, rescue us from our hypocrisy, which keeps us from seeing You as the center of all of Scripture and acknowledging the present time as the time of salvation. Call us to repent of our self-righteousness so that we might look to You alone as the source of our life; for You live and reign with the Father and the Holy Spirit, one God, now and forever. (1020)

Meditation

Our Lord desires our repentance. The signs of the times summon us to repentance. We're good at reading signs in nature: "Red sky at night, sailor's delight; red sky in morning, sailors take warning!" When we see the first robin, we know the worst of the winter is passed. Yet despite interpreting earth and sky, we fail miserably at reading the signs of the times, for everything cries out to us, "This life is not forever! You will die! You will go to stand before the Judge!"

So our Lord urges us to settle matters out of court—that is, before the Day of Judgment arrives. For the person who flees to the mercy of God and lives in repentance, who recognizes sin, asks forgiveness for it, turns from it, and by the Holy Spirit's power fights it—for such a person the Day of Judgment will not bring a sentence of condemnation, but of pardon.

How foolish we would be, then, to look at the catastrophes that befall others, and wonder what they did to deserve them; so the folks Pilate butchered; so the folks in Siloam who perished beneath the tower; so the folks in the last earthquake, tsunami, or wildfire. Our Lord would teach us, rather, that each horrific disaster invites us to pass judgment on ourselves. To remember that we, too, are poor sinners who deserve temporal and eternal punishment, and we are headed out of this age to the judgment seat of God at a time we do not know.

Our God is patient and loving. He doesn't immediately uproot the plant that doesn't bear the fruit it should. He tends and cares for it, does everything He can to coax it into bearing. But if in the end there is no fruit, no faith, no repentance, the ax will be laid to the tree and the tree placed in the fire.

In the bent woman, unable to stand straight up, we have a living picture of what sin does to us by nature. How it cripples us, bends us in ourselves. I, me, mine—the stuff of sin that we must repent of. But when our Lord invites to repentance, He also speaks a Gospel word that straightens us up and takes the focus off of me, myself, my pain, my sorrow, my boredom, my whatever! "Woman, man, you are freed from your disability!" And the result? "Immediately she was made straight and she glorified God." Such is the life of repentance and faith.

FRIDAY—EASTER 5

Psalmody: Psalm 119:33–40
Additional Psalm: Psalm 81
Old Testament Reading: Leviticus 26:1–20
New Testament Reading: Luke 13:18–35

Prayer of the Day

O Lord, You have called us to enter Your kingdom through the narrow door. Guide us by Your Word and Spirit, and lead us now and always into the feast of Your Son, Jesus Christ, who lives and reigns with You and the Holy Spirit, one God, now and forever. (C74)

Meditation

A little beginning with a huge result; so is the Kingdom. So is the mustard seed planted in a garden—and from the tiny seed, a great tree. So is leaven hidden in three measures of flour until it works its way through and raises the whole batch. The Kingdom starts little and grows big.

How little? A man dead on a tree, planted in the earth, raised to life. A little beginning from which nothing less than a new creation results. It starts in a corner of Judea and spreads its way across the whole world.

So is it many that are saved or few? The question is akin to the curiosity about whether those who suffer in mishaps are greater sinners. Your Lord doesn't deal in theoretical questions. He turns to you and says: "Strive to enter through the narrow door."

That door is so narrow that you cannot get through it carrying any of your own works. When those on the outside cry out about what they'd done, the Lord says: "I do not know where you come from." The Lord Jesus is the narrow door into the Kingdom. You cannot get in with any baggage of your own—any good deeds you think you've done for Him to reward with the Kingdom. The way into the narrow door is in confessing we have no claim on Him other than that He is merciful and kind.

People will come from all over—east, west, north, south—and join Him at His great feast in the Kingdom. They will all be those who enter by the narrow door of the cross: "Nothing in my hand I bring; Simply to Thy cross I cling" ("Rock of Ages, Cleft for Me"). They plead mercy, not their merit. Though they were last, they will be first. The Lord welcomes them into His eternal home.

The Lord's love for His people shines out in Jesus' lament over Jerusalem. Her rejection of those who speak in God's name to her and call her to repent and enter the narrow door will reach its climax in Jerusalem's rejection of the Lord Jesus. And yet He had come only to bring her blessing, only to gather her children together under His almighty protection. No one is lost because God chooses for them to be lost; the only way to be lost is to refuse the gift of entering the narrow door opened by the cross of Calvary.

SATURDAY—EASTER 5

Psalmody: Psalm 63:1–5, 8–11
Additional Psalm: Psalm 78
Old Testament Reading:
Leviticus 26:21–33, 39–44
Additional Reading: Numbers 1:1–2:34
New Testament Reading: Luke 14:1–24

Prayer of the Day

O Lord of grace and mercy, teach us by Your Holy Spirit to follow the example of Your Son in true humility, that we may withstand the temptations of the devil and with pure hearts and minds avoid ungodly pride; through the same Jesus Christ, our Lord, who lives and reigns with You and the Holy Spirit, one God, now and forever. (C75)

Meditation

Jesus, whose Law it is, knows that the heart of the Law is mercy—for mercy is His heart. So no Sabbath law can restrain Him from showing mercy. He heals the man of dropsy and sends him on his way.

And He who is merciful is likewise humble, and invites us to join Him in the way of humility. It is easy to miss that His words are a parable and to interpret them as rules of etiquette (though, they're not bad for that either). But they are first of all about Him. He is the One who took the lowest place from manger to cross, and because He did not exalt Himself, but entrusted Himself to the Father, His Father exalted Him to the highest place of all, honored Him with the name above all names (Philippians 2:5–11). Humbleness is near to the heart of God. For the shocking thing about our God is that He is Himself humble.

Focused then, not on the honor one accrues for one's self, but on the blessing one can be for others, His parable turns to speak of a great dinner or banquet at which not the rich and powerful, but the poor, crippled, lame, and blind are feasted—those who cannot repay. We cannot but think of His hosting such a table for us—His Holy Eucharist. Yet He does mean for us to be free to focus upon those in need, not worrying about what we get out of it. Our repayment will be the fullness of joy we will be given on the day of resurrection.

Thinking of the joyful day, one of His table companions exclaims: "Blessed is everyone who will eat bread in the kingdom of God!" Jesus is a bit skeptical whether he (or we) means it. "You think so?" He seems to say. "People sure don't act that way, because even now the Kingdom's banquet is spread and people are summoned to taste eternal life, and yet they come up with one excuse after another. And so they miss out on the joys."

O Lord, lift me up to humility and to mercy. Amen.

SIXTH SUNDAY OF EASTER

Psalmody: Psalm 135:13–21
Additional Psalm: Psalm 60
Old Testament Reading:
Numbers 3:1–16, 39–48
Additional Reading: Numbers 4:1–8:4
New Testament Reading: Luke 14:25–15:10

Prayer of the Day

O merciful Lord, You did not spare Your only Son but delivered Him up for us all. Grant us courage and strength to take up the cross and follow Him, who lives and reigns with You and the Holy Spirit, one God, now and forever. (C76)

Meditation

Can Love Incarnate actually command us to "hate" father, mother, brothers, sisters, spouse, children, and our own lives? The parallel text in Matthew 10:37 speaks of one who puts love of family ahead of love of Jesus. Clearly that is the sense here as well, not that we harbor resentment and bitterness toward our family, but that we do not put our family or even our own life above our Lord Jesus. He interposes Himself between every relationship—even our relationship to our own person.

There is a cost to discipleship, after all. Bonhoeffer stated it well: "When Christ calls a man, he bids him come and die." That is, to die to his own will and to live through the will of God. "Whoever does not bear his own cross and come after Me, cannot be My disciple," says the Lord. Our cross is wherever our will crosses the will of God. We pick it up and bear it after Christ by grace, learning to pray from and with our divine Master: "Thy will be done."

Part of learning to walk this path of the cross, following our Lord, is the renouncing of all that we have. That is, learning to confess and live in such a way that what we call "ours" is recognized as the Lord's and only under our management for a time, a management for which we will one day give account. We are but stewards.

As the tax collectors and notorious "sinners" gather to hear the Lord, the Pharisees begin their grumbling: "This man receives sinners and eats with them." They regard it as a disgrace; He, as a badge of honor.

Two stories unpack it: the man who leaves the ninety-nine sheep in the wilderness to search for the one lost—that one is Adam according to all the Church Fathers. And we are in him. So with the coin. We who were created in the image of God have been lost, and our Lord, like the woman, lights the lamp of His Word and sweeps and finds and celebrates the return of the lost.

Putting the Lord first is something that we find possible and joyous by grace as we remember how He has sought us, found us, and rejoiced over us.

MONDAY—EASTER 6

Psalmody: Psalm 103:6–14
Additional Psalm: Psalm 70
Old Testament Reading: Numbers 8:5–26
New Testament Reading: Luke 15:11–32

Prayer of the Day

Lord God, our heavenly Father, You stood afar off waiting to see Your prodigals appear at the gate. Then, running to us, You overwhelmed us with grace and invited us to sit at table, to rejoice at our homecoming. Help us to repent of our sins and strip us of every thought that we might merit Your salvation. Then bring us home to be with You at the marriage feast of the Lamb in His kingdom which has no end; through Your Son, Jesus Christ, our Lord. (1021)

Meditation

The Pharisees grumble over how Jesus receives sinners and eats with them. How can He help them understand what goes on in God's heart? So the parables of the lost: sheep, coin, and sons. Yes, sons. For both sons were lost—the one in the bondage of sin, the other in the bondage of legalism.

The surprise in the story is not to be found in how the father is overjoyed when the younger son comes home. Any parent whose child has wandered into the byways of sin knows the agony of waiting for the moment of the child's return. Any parent who knows that pain is not surprised by how the Father treated this prodigal: welcoming him with hugs, with kisses, with party and celebration.

No, the shocker is in the elder son—the one who had never left. The one who had stayed home, but suddenly the Father realizes has served without joy: "Look, these many years I have served you, and I never disobeyed your command, yet you never gave me a young goat, that I might celebrate with my friends." The older son thought it was about keeping the rules and he felt rather taken for granted. He couldn't understand the joy over his brother's return: "But when this son of yours came, who has devoured your property with prostitutes, you killed the fatted calf for him!"

And here's the surprise. The tenderness, the love with which the Father can speak to his oldest child: "Son, you are always with me, and all that is mine is yours. It was fitting to celebrate and be glad, for this your brother was dead and is alive; he was lost and is found."

"You are with me always." That's what it has been about. Not about keeping rules. Not about freedom to do whatever you want and ending up a slave to your own desires. No, it is about being with the Father, living in His company, feasting in His house.

No one could tell this parable except for Jesus. He alone can reveal the heart of the Father: "Child, you are with Me always. All I have is yours." Including my rejoicing over the brother who had been mired in sin and through repentance has come home. He gives the gift of our brother back to us. "This man receives sinners and eats with them." Indeed, for the Father's heart is His.

TUESDAY—EASTER 6

Psalmody: Psalm 85:1–7
Additional Psalm: Psalm 18
Old Testament Reading: Numbers 9:1–23
New Testament Reading: Luke 16:1–18

Prayer of the Day

O Lord, keep Your Church in Your perpetual mercy; and because without You we cannot but fall, preserve us from all things hurtful, and lead us to all things profitable to our salvation; through Jesus Christ, Your Son, our Lord, who lives and reigns with You and the Holy Spirit, one God, now and forever. (C78)

Meditation

Is our Lord praising dishonesty? No, He praises shrewdness. He praises the worldly smarts that can sum up a situation and provide a way out of a predicament. The dishonest manager realizes he's in a world of hurt: he's going to lose his job, he's too weak for manual labor, and too proud to hit the streets with a tin cup begging. So he decides what to do to assure that folks are in his debt when he's sent packing.

He will be very generous with his master's debtors—cuts this one's debt in half, that one's debt by 20 percent. The master is suitably impressed: That sly fox! He feathered his nest nicely after all, didn't he? Landed on his feet, he did!

Shrewdness is not a bad thing; it's a downright good thing. Jesus praises it, but laments its lack so often among His own children. "The sons of this world are more shrewd in dealing with their own generation than the sons of light."

So let's not be foolish! If you appraise our situation honestly, you will realize that your life in this age is not forever; that the goods you are blessed with in this life are not yours, but the Lord's; that you can't take a single one of them with you to the Day of Judgment, but that you can use them to be a blessing to others, others who on that day will be standing all around you.

No, you cannot serve both God and money. But if you serve God (by letting Him give to you His divine forgiveness and eternal life), you will be set free to use your wealth in blessed ways. You can make eternal friends by such charity and kindness. And when the world fails, as it will on the Day of Judgment, your friends will be there to welcome you to share with them the joys of heaven.

The Pharisees, lovers of money, thought this was all a bit much. But Jesus knows that what men praise is often an abomination in the eyes of God. Men praise the shrewdness that garners earthly goods. God praises the generosity that garners friends in this age and in the age to come. May the Lord help us to be generous and kind with His possessions, blessing the poor and needy, for we know this delights His heart!

WEDNESDAY—EASTER 6

Psalmody: Psalm 62:5–10
Additional Psalm: Psalm 19
Old Testament Reading: Numbers 10:11–36
New Testament Reading: Luke 16:19–31

O God, You are the strength of all who trust in You, and without Your aid we can do no good thing. Grant us the help of Your grace that we may please You in both will and deed; through Jesus Christ, Your Son, our Lord, who lives and reigns with You and the Holy Spirit, one God, now and forever. (C79)

Meditation

The rich man refers to Abraham as "father." What a marked difference between father and "son" here! For the rich man treated Lazarus like a piece of human garbage, ignored and allowed to suffer and die upon his own doorstep with only the dogs to show kindness.

But that doesn't reach the heart of the matter. Rather, mark the behavior of the rich man in Hades. When he can't persuade Abraham to send Lazarus to wait on him in the flames, he begs him to send Lazarus to his brothers "lest they also come into this place of torment."

Why Abraham's side? Why didn't Jesus say: "the angels carried him, Lazarus, to heaven?" Abraham is the key to unlocking this story. Think of Genesis 18 and what we know about how Abraham treated strangers who landed on his doorstep. Three strangers come his way and he rises up, welcomes and honors them, sets a veritable feast before them, and bids them eat. Abraham, who heard and heeded God's call in Ur of Chaldees; Abraham, who listened to the promises of God and by them came to believe the impossible; Abraham, who heeded the voice of God even when called upon to sacrifice his son, convinced that God would raise him from the dead to keep His Word; Abraham is amazed: "They have Moses and the Prophets [in other words, the Scriptures of the Old Testament]. Let them hear them."

The Word of God has the full power to keep them out of the flames and bring them to the banquet with Lazarus. The Word of God is powerful to produce and give repentance. The Word of God is powerful to impart the gift of faith. Hear and heed it!

But even in Hades' flames, the damned scorn the Word. "No, father Abraham, but if someone goes to them from the dead, they will repent." Abraham disagrees: "If they do not hear Moses and the Prophets, neither will they be convinced if someone should rise from the dead."

Why Abraham's side? He was the man who "believed the Lord, and He counted it to him as righteousness" (Genesis 15:6). Justified by faith, his life bore the fruits of love, welcoming the stranger and providing a feast. Abraham knew that the Word made all the difference. Lord, grant me a faith and love like Abraham's through Your Word! Amen.

THE ASCENSION OF OUR LORD

(Thursday—Easter 6)

Psalmody: Psalm 130
Additional Psalm: Psalm 47
Old Testament Reading:
Numbers 11:1–23, 31–35
New Testament Reading: Luke 17:1–19

Almighty God, as Your only-begotten Son, our Lord Jesus Christ, ascended into the heavens, so may we also ascend in heart and mind and continually dwell there with Him, who lives and reigns with You and the Holy Spirit, one God, now and forever. (L47)

The Ascension of Our Lord

Ascension Day is the coronation celebration of the Lord as He is proclaimed to be King of the universe. Jesus' ascension to the Father is His entrance to the greater existence beyond the confines of time and space, being no longer bound by the limitations of His state of humiliation. He now sits at the right hand of God, which Luther correctly taught is everywhere, having again taken up the power and authority which were His since before time. Yet our Lord is present with us who remain bound by time and space. He is with us as true God and true man, exercising His rulership in the Church through the means of grace which He established: His Word and His Sacraments. We mortals in those means of grace can grasp the King of the universe and receive a foretaste of the feast to come.

Meditation

Temptations to sin inevitably come along, but we should take care that they don't come through us, especially for the Lord's little ones. Nothing causes them to stumble so much as our refusal to forgive, our holding onto a grudge. So the Lord Jesus commands seven times in one day forgiving the brother who sins against you and then turns and says to you: "I repent." The disciples' jaws hit the floor. And as they think that through, they cry out: "Increase our faith!" Forgiveness flowing so richly and fully through them is something they're having a bit of a hard time imagining. What about you?

Jesus' answer is that it is not the size of faith that does it. The littlest faith will do. Tiny as a mustard seed! It's not a matter of how big or small your faith is; it's a matter of whom your faith is connecting you to. Connected to His mighty power there is no mulberry tree too big, no obstacle too grand, no task of forgiveness too heavy.

And such is our duty. It's not something we dare pride ourselves on. We who have been forgiven so lavishly in Christ are called to be forgivers. It's our vocation. St. John wrote, "we love because He first loved us" (1 John 4:19). It's also true that we forgive because He first forgave us. So St. Paul in Ephesians could write: "Be kind to one another, tenderhearted, forgiving one another, as God in Christ forgave you" (4:32). So when we have forgiven the repentant brother as we have been commanded to, we haven't done some grand work; we've just done our duty.

And not only is forgiving the repentant sinner our duty; thanksgiving is our duty too. "For all this it is our duty to thank and praise, serve and obey Him." So the one leper who asks for and receives mercy, who can't even think of going home without first returning and praising his Benefactor. "Were not ten cleansed? Where are the nine? Was none found to return and give praise to God except this foreigner?" His faith had made him well; had connected him to the Giver of every good gift, and so his life lit up with praise and glorifying God.

Your life has been cleansed as well. Your Savior has washed you in His font, put His righteousness upon you, and called you into a life of forgiving others and glorifying God in and through Him. This is your duty, your privilege, and your delight.

FRIDAY—EASTER 6

Psalmody: Psalm 77:11–15
Additional Psalm: Psalm 8
Old Testament Reading:
Numbers 11:24–29; 12:1–16
New Testament Reading: Luke 17:20–37

Prayer of the Day

Lord Jesus, Your kingdom continues to be in our midst as You come to us now through holy water, holy words, holy food. Help us to see that Your kingdom is a kingdom of suffering, but that through suffering, we will be prepared to enter into glory when You return on that final day; for You live and reign with the Father and the Holy Spirit, one God, now and forever. (1022)

Meditation

The Kingdom, God's gracious reign, is standing right there in the midst of them, yet they ask when it will come. Jesus, in effect, says: "Here I am! King of the Kingdom! The Kingdom is right under your noses if you but had the eyes to see it!"

And if the Kingdom was hidden from their eyes under the flesh and blood of the Man in front of them, how much more hidden would the Kingdom be after He had ascended (as we celebrated yesterday) and even His visible presence removed from them. "The days are coming when you will desire to see one of the days of the Son of Man, and you will not see it." From the moment of His ascension on, the Kingdom will not be found by sight, but by hearing. It will establish itself in the hearts of men by the hearing of God's Word and the faith that Word engenders. And all in whom that Kingdom is established will look forward with unspeakable joy to the day of its unveiling: the moment when the Lord Jesus appears in His glory, and His Kingdom will be manifest and shining, like the lightning in the sky.

Before that great and joyous unveiling of the Kingdom, though, He will first suffer and die and rise and ascend. And His people, who believe His coming, will wait and look toward that day. The world won't. The world will be like in Noah's time or Lot's. Busy with buying and selling, eating and drinking, marrying and being given in marriage. The world doesn't believe in this hidden Kingdom; it neither waits for it nor expects it. But the Kingdom will show up all the same. And when it does, a division will occur that will never be undone. "One will be taken and another left." Those who refused to believe and enter the Kingdom of grace will "be left."

The disciples ask: "Left where, Lord?" "Where the corpse is, there the vultures will gather." Left to death. Left to destruction. Left to hell. The subjects of the kingdom of grace will become the subjects of the kingdom of glory, and their joy will never end.

SATURDAY—EASTER 6

Psalmody: Psalm 119:97–104
Additional Psalm: Psalm 122
Old Testament Reading:
Numbers 13:1–3, 17–33
New Testament Reading: Luke 18:1–17

Prayer of the Day

O Lord, almighty and everlasting God, You have commanded us to pray and have promised to hear us. Mercifully grant that Your Holy Spirit may direct and govern our hearts in all things that we may persevere with steadfast faith in the confession of Your name; through Jesus Christ, Your Son, our Lord, who lives and reigns with You and the Holy Spirit, one God, now and forever. (C82)

Meditation

Our Lord would have us "always to pray and not lose heart." If the unrighteous judge will give justice in the end to the widow, who was merely being a pest, so that she leaves him alone, what do you think the heavenly Father will do for the elect, the chosen, the children that He loves when they cry to Him night and day? If pestering persistence works on a man who doesn't love the petitioner, how much more will it work on the Father who loves His children?

But will such faith be found on earth? When the Lord Jesus comes, will He find a community of faithful still asking, seeking, knocking, and waiting for the Father's gracious answer? Here He leaves the question hanging. In Matthew 16, he answers it with the promise that not even the gates of hell can prevail against His Church. In the Augsburg Confession we confess that the one Holy Church will be and remain forever (see Article VII).

This Church that will be forever is the Church of the tax collectors; the Church of those who beat their breast and ask for mercy. Mercy, though, is perhaps a bit weak of a translation. More literally: "be propitious to me" or "provide a sacrifice of atonement for me." The one telling the parable is the answer to the tax collector's prayer. Jesus is that sacrifice of atonement. He is the mercy of God. The proud, like the Pharisee, don't imagine they need Him. They are content with what they've done and parade that before God in prayer, not asking from Him but informing Him how fortunate He is to have such a devout servant.

The Church that will be forever is the Church of beggars only. They have nothing to give and can only receive. The little children that Jesus calls to Himself are the perfect picture. What can a baby do? Can it change its diaper? Feed itself? Clothe itself? Provide shelter? No. It can only be given these things. So the Lord extols the little ones as who are in a position only to receive, those whose only act is to plead for mercy. May the Lord lift us to the joy of being such a little one.

SEVENTH SUNDAY OF EASTER

Psalmody: Psalm 81:10–16
Additional Psalm: Psalm 9
Old Testament Reading: Numbers 14:1–25
New Testament Reading: Luke 18:18–34

Prayer of the Day

O King of glory, Lord of hosts, uplifted in triumph far above all heavens, leave us not without consolation but send us the Spirit of truth whom You promised from the Father; for You live and reign with Him and the Holy Spirit, one God, now and forever. (L48)

Meditation

Jesus asked the rich ruler why he called Him "Good Teacher." "No one is good except God alone." But the young man didn't know what to make of that. He thought he was rather good himself. Yet he must have known something was missing, something was wrong. So he asked, "What must I do to inherit eternal life?"

Jesus doesn't begin with the Gospel. He doesn't say a word about "believe in Me!" He takes in hand the Law. "You know the commandments," our Lord says as He rattles off the Second Table of the Law. The young man must have smiled a confused smile: "Oh, those. Not a problem. I've kept those from my youth." So Jesus gives him the full dose of Law: "One thing you lack. Sell all that you have and distribute to the poor, and you will have treasure in heaven; and come, follow Me."

How his face fell as Jesus spoke! A rich man attached to his riches, he turns away sad. No, he wasn't good after all. God wasn't good enough for him; he had to have his stuff. What about you? Jesus doesn't call him back. He lets him walk away and observes how hard it is for the rich to enter the Kingdom. Indeed, easier for a camel to pass through a needle's eye than for a wealthy person to enter the Kingdom. The disciples are shocked. "Who then can be saved?" Jesus says, "What is impossible with men is possible with God." Peter's face falls a bit. God will do the impossible and bring in those who haven't sacrificed as the disciples have? Jesus assures Peter and us that no one is a loser for sacrificing for the kingdom—they will end up with more than they gave up. And yet getting into the kingdom remains an impossibility for men, for anyone who asks: "what must I do to inherit eternal life?" It comes only as impossible gift from the Lord.

To make what is impossible for men possible, Jesus heads to Jerusalem where He will lose everything—including His life. That's how He will give to Peter as to the rich man and also to you, what no one could ever achieve. That's how Jesus shows us that He is the Good One come into our flesh and blood. And for that all glory to Him!

MONDAY—EASTER 7

Psalmody: Psalm 146:5–9
Additional Psalm: Psalm 142
Old Testament Reading: Numbers 14:26–45
Additional Reading: Numbers 15:1–41
New Testament Reading: Luke 18:35–19:10

Prayer of the Day

O Lord, stir up the hearts of Your faithful people to welcome and joyfully receive Your Son, our Savior, Jesus Christ, that He may find in us a fit dwelling place; who lives and reigns with You and the Holy Spirit, one God, now and forever. (C84)

Meditation

The blind man wouldn't be quieted, even when others told him to stop making a nuisance of himself. Faith cries for mercy to Jesus, and Jesus hears. On His triumphal way up to Jerusalem, He still has time to stop and answer the cry of mercy. Nothing delights Him more than to answer that cry, and indeed, it was to grant great mercy to the whole human race that He was on His way up to Jerusalem.

When the blind man is brought before the Lord, Jesus asks "What do you want me to do for you?" His request is simple and straightforward: "Lord, let me recover my sight." And then the Lord grants the request; he sees again. "Then the eyes of the blind shall be opened," Isaiah had foretold (35:5). When? When your God comes to save you! (35:4)

With eyes seeing, made well by his faith, by his faith's turning to Jesus and asking for mercy, the formerly blind man did two things. He began to follow Jesus and to give glory to God. So we, when our Lord opens our eyes blinded by nature (see 2 Corinthians 4:4) to see Him for who He is, we have the joy of following Him and singing His praises! Luke repeatedly teaches us that the result of meeting Jesus is to be brought into a life of praise and mercy.

And if the miracle of a blind man seeing were not enough, today we also get the miracle of a rich man freed from covetousness. Zacchaeus was small of stature, unable to see the Lord. So he climbed the tree to catch a glimpse of Him. But the Lord spies him in the tree, calls him by name, and invites Himself to Zacchaeus' house for dinner. The usual grumbling ensues about how Jesus eats with sinners. But that eating with sinners is the sinners' salvation! Jesus' love and mercy for Zacchaeus set him free. The money-grubbing tax collector is transformed into a generous benefactor. Money loses its hold over his heart, for Jesus has taken up residence with him, the Jesus who comes "to seek and to save the lost"—the Jesus who would climb a tree Himself to give to humanity the greatest treasure of all: forgiveness and eternal life.

Tuesday—Easter 7

Psalmody: Psalm 111
Additional Psalm: Psalm 45
Old Testament Reading: Numbers 16:1–22
New Testament Reading: Luke 19:11–28

Prayer of the Day

Lord God, heavenly Father, as we struggle here below with divisions among us, searching for peace among men, remind us daily of the peace of heaven purchased through the bloody death and triumphant resurrection of your Son, Jesus Christ, our Lord, who with you and the Holy Spirit are one God, now and forever. (1023)

Meditation
"They supposed that the kingdom of God was to appear immediately." They were thinking that's what the trip to Jerusalem was all about. But that's not how it was to be—not at all. So our Lord sets about preparing them for the interim: the time between His paschal victory and ascension to the Father's right hand and the time of His return when the Kingdom will make a visible appearance. The in-between time is a time for testing and learning faithfulness.

Before the nobleman departed to receive the kingdom, he gave gifts to three men and instructions to use them: "Engage in business until I come." One received 10 minas—30 months wages for a common laborer in those days, no little sum! Another received 5 minas—15 months wages; another but 1 mina—3 months wages. Each was charged to put the gifts they had been given to work so that the gifts might multiply.

When he returned, having received the kingdom, he asks for an accounting. The first has doubled what was entrusted to him. "Well done, good servant! Because you have been faithful in a very little, you shall have authority over ten cities." The second servant also doubled what was entrusted to him and received rule of five cities. But note the last servant: "Lord, here is your mina, which I kept laid away in a handkerchief; for I was afraid of you, because you are a severe man. You take what you did not deposit and reap what you did not sow." Afraid and paralyzed by his fear, he can only hand back what he received.

As the servant imagined the Lord to be, so the Lord was to him: hard and severe. How do you picture the Lord? Beware! He will be to you as you picture Him. But the first two servants saw the truth: the Lord Himself is generous and good and kind. He bestows gifts, and wants them used to the benefit and profit of His kingdom, so that others may share in its blessings. The gifts of the Kingdom are His Word and the Sacraments. Those who despise the gifs will end up losing everything. But those who faithfully use what God has entrusted to them will find that these produce abundant riches for the Kingdom, and they will receive far more from their faithful use of them than they ever imagined. Lord, help me to make faithful use of what you have given!

Wednesday—Easter 7

Psalmody: Psalm 118:19–25
Additional Psalm: Psalm 9
Old Testament Reading: Numbers 16:23–40
New Testament Reading: Luke 19:29–48

Prayer of the Day

O King who comes in the name of the Lord, through Your birth and death, earth and heaven were joined together in peace. May Your coming as King into Jerusalem in humility on the donkey help us to see that You continue to come to us as our King hidden in humble water, humble words, humble food; for You live and reign with the Father and the Holy Spirit, one God, now and forever. (1024)

Meditation

Four days before the Passover, the Law of Moses commands that the Passover lamb be taken and set aside (Exodus 12:3). So our Lord this day rides into Jerusalem to be that Lamb, the final Lamb and offering. And as He comes riding to Jerusalem the crowds break forth into wild rejoicing. At last, they think, He is claiming the kingship. There was no missing the fulfillment of Zechariah's prophesy (9:9) as Jesus rode down the Mount of Olives and up into the city on the borrowed burro.

But as the cries of "Blessed is the King!" and "Peace in heaven and glory in the highest" fill the air, as the clothes mark a royal pathway for the King, Jesus can restrain Himself no longer. He breaks into tears.

Jesus is not crying for Himself. He cries for this city He so loves; this city that will seal its earthly fate in its rejection of its true King, "because you did not know the time of your visitation." He cries for all who will finally reject the gift that He has come to give and to be for all people. He weeps for the needless destruction of those who will not have Him be their King.

Truly this was the moment of divine visitation: the King was entering His city to provide for her, for his people, and for all the people of the earth the final sacrifice for sin. The Roman guards at the Praetorian breathe easier as they watch the procession turn and head to the temple. It was never about earthly power and military might; it was a far greater struggle that was about to be waged. The one and only Lamb of God drives out all those who sold the sacrifices. You see, this Lamb is priceless, and yet He is free and no one can pay for Him. Rather, He is the payment for all.

As Jesus teaches this and treats the temple as His Father's own house, the plot thickens among the Jewish rulers. They look for some way, any way, to destroy Him. Yet it would have to be by stealth, under cover, for He had never been more popular among the people who "were hanging on His words"—words of the Lamb of God, who had come to His city to die for her and for all the people of the earth.

THURSDAY—EASTER 7

Psalmody: Psalm 80:14–19
Additional Psalm: Psalm 91
Old Testament Reading: Numbers 16:41–17:13
Additional Reading: Numbers 18:1–19:22
New Testament Reading: Luke 20:1–18

Prayer of the Day

Lord Jesus, You are the stone that the builders rejected. But on the third day, You became the cornerstone. By Your Word and Spirit, open our hearts to receive You as the beloved Son sent from the Father so that we might always embrace suffering as the means by which we enter into Your glory; for You live and reign with the Father and the Holy Spirit, one God, now and forever. (1025)

Meditation

By what authority was Jesus doing the things He was doing? You just didn't come into the temple and start to throw things in an uproar by tossing out those who sold the sacrifices and charging the temple authorities with having betrayed their trust by transforming God's house of prayer into a den of robbers! So they demand the proof from our Lord that He has authority to do such things.

The Lord won't answer their question until they answer one of His. He asks about John's Baptism, whether it was from God or from men. The leaders immediately sense a trap: "If we say, 'From heaven,' He will say, 'Why did you not believe him?' But if we say, 'From man,' all the people will stone us to death, for they are convinced that John was a prophet." Their solution to avoid giving an answer was to play the agnostic card. "We don't know." But our Lord's question wasn't a game. It was an invitation to repentance; an invitation that they refuse by not speaking the truth that they themselves knew. So Jesus Himself won't answer their question—for John's Baptism had already answered it for any who would not shut their hearts. John's Baptism had already revealed who Jesus was: the beloved Son of the Father, to whom heaven was open and the Spirit given.

This challenge to His authority leads our Lord to the parable of the wicked tenants. These tenants foolishly imagine they can keep the vineyard their own by killing the beloved Son—the title of Jesus from John's Baptism. Yet their complicity in murder does not win them the vineyard in the end, rather "He will destroy those tenants and give the vineyard to others."

Hearing this, they are shocked. "Surely not!" they cry. But Jesus is adamant. It will happen, for He is, after all, not only the beloved Son, but the stone that the builders rejected, only to find out that it was the cornerstone of the new temple God was building. So when our Lord was raised from the dead, He began to build His new temple—not like the one of old. This one built of living stones, of people who, being joined to Him by saving faith, grow up into a holy temple in the Lord. Yes, the vineyard is given over to others: to those who will build their hope upon the solid Rock of Jesus Christ.

FRIDAY—EASTER 7

Psalmody: Psalm 78:9–16
Additional Psalm: Psalm 110
Old Testament Reading: Numbers 20:1–21
New Testament Reading: Luke 20:19–44

Prayer of the Day

Living God, Your almighty power is made known chiefly in showing mercy and pity. Grant us the fullness of Your grace to lay hold of Your promises and live forever in Your presence; through Jesus Christ, Your Son, our Lord, who lives and reigns with You and the Holy Spirit, one God, now and forever. (C85)

Meditation

They were out to trap Him, but He was out to save them. "Is it lawful for us to give tribute to Caesar or not?" Surely, they think, if He says yes, then the people will turn on Him; if He says no, then we hand Him over as the rebel He is. But the Lord Jesus doesn't give a yes or no. He asks for the coin, and all attention is focused upon it. "Whose likeness and inscription does it have?" They smell a trap, but can't figure out where He's going. "Caesar's" is their tentative answer. "Then render to Caesar the things that are Caesar's, and to God the things that are God's." If Caesar gets his coin, God—who has stamped His image upon the human race and written His name upon us, He gets our lives.

Only we don't give Him our lives, and we have defaced His likeness in us. And that is why Jesus is there in Jerusalem that day. He is preparing to give us back the likeness—for He is the image of the invisible God—by giving the Father His all. And He is preparing a washing, Holy Baptism, through which the name of God will mark us as His own again.

The Sadducees, seeking to show the foolishness of the resurrection, come up with their story of the seven-times married woman. "In the resurrection, therefore, whose wife will she be?" Jesus' response shows that they understand nothing about the resurrection that they are mocking. In the resurrection marriage is no more—husband and wife will be there and together, but as brother and sister in the Lord. But the resurrection itself is shown in the way God identified Himself to Moses: "I am the God of Abraham and of Isaac and of Jacob." I am, not I was. "For all live to Him."

They are silenced by this, but as they think it over He has a question for them. He points to Psalm 110 and David's words about the Messiah being "my Lord." "David calls Him Lord, so how is He his Son?" Not fathoming the mystery of the incarnation they are left to wonder. He who is David's Lord and Son, He who is the Resurrection and the Life, He who is the Image and Likeness of God thus proceeds on His way toward Calvary where the folly of God makes foolish the wisdom of man.

SATURDAY—EASTER 7

Psalmody: Psalm 116:1–4, 16–19
Additional Psalm: Psalm 109
Old Testament Reading: Numbers 20:22–21:9
New Testament Reading: Luke 20:45–21:19

Prayer of the Day

Almighty and ever-living God, You fulfilled Your promise by sending the gift of the Holy Spirit to unite disciples of all nations in the cross and resurrection of Your Son, Jesus Christ. By the preaching of the Gospel spread this gift to the ends of the earth; through the same Jesus Christ, our Lord, who lives and reigns with You and the Holy Spirit, one God, now and forever. (L49)

Meditation

Human beings like to put on a show; Jesus looks beneath the show to the heart. Of the outward piety of the scribes, He warns us to beware; of the rich who ostentatiously dump in their contributions for all to see, He points rather to the poor widow who gave from her poverty all she had to live on and in so doing put in an offering far greater than their wealth.

The disciples of Jesus, too, are marveling at the outward beauty of the temple, the "noble stones and offerings." It was a sight to behold! But Jesus steers them away from what perishes to what lasts. "All these things that you see," He says will not endure. They, as good Jews, are shocked at the thought that there might be time when the temple of the Lord is destroyed. They want to know when.

Our Lord warns them not to be led astray. Deceivers will come in His name. They will say: "I am he! The time is at hand!" Don't buy it, He warns. There will be wars and upsets. Don't be terrified of that. These bad things must come first, but "the end will not come at once." The End, the conclusion, the final in-breaking of God's Kingdom, when what is seen perishes and what has been unseen appears as immovable.

And then Jesus brings it very personally home to them: amid all the upset, the nation rising against nation, the earthquakes, the famines and the disease—amid all the signs that cry out that this world is tottering toward its end, "they will lay hands on you." Arrested, hauled off before judges in synagogue and brought before kings, they will be given the joyful chance to witness to that which endures, to that which no trial and trouble of this world can take away, to the eternal life that they have tasted and known in Jesus of Nazareth. His name upon them marks them as hated by the world, because they stand as His witnesses that the world, with its show, is unstable and finally coming to its end. But in Jesus God has brought the gift of a world that does not come to an end.

"Not a hair of your head will perish." In Him they already share in the unshakable life that is currently unseen, but will shine on the day of the resurrection. You too. So your life is set free from pretense and show; You have in Jesus unshakable life.

The Day of Pentecost

Psalmody: Psalm 135:8–14
Additional Psalm: Psalm 58
Old Testament Reading: Numbers 21:10–35
New Testament Reading: Luke 21:20–38

Prayer of the Day

O God, on this day You once taught the hearts of Your faithful people by sending them the light of Your Holy Spirit. Grant us in our day by the same Spirit to have a right understanding in all things and evermore to rejoice in His holy consolation; through Jesus Christ, Your Son, our Lord, who lives and reigns with You and the Holy Spirit, one God, now and forever. (L50)

The Day of Pentecost

The Church lives and moves and has her being through the gracious inspiration of the Holy Spirit. Without God's Spirit, no one could come to Christ or believe in Him. The fifty-day celebration of Easter ends with this joyous festival. The risen and ascended Savior has sent the Holy Spirit to be our Sanctifier, entering our hearts at Holy Baptism, nurturing us through the Word, and enabling us to understand the Gospel and to live a life that honors God and serves our neighbor.

Meditation

The end of Jerusalem is not the end of the world, no matter what the disciples might be thinking as good Jews. There would be "a time of the Gentiles." A time when His word would go out among the nations and gather from them a people who trust in the promises, and who wait for the final promise to be fulfilled. It will be fulfilled that day when the visible world as we know it is shaken to the core and the Son of Man appears in a cloud with power and great glory. It's not a day to dread and fear, but to long and pray for. "Now when these things begin to take place, straighten up and raise your heads, because your redemption is drawing near."

Luther depicted it as a man in prison, captive to a foreign prince, and suddenly there is a boom, and the prison walls begin to shake. He looks out the window and sees his own prince there, knocking down the prison to rescue him and bring him home.

So the Lord uses the image of spring and summer—not of fall and winter with their death. God's eternal summer is what is breaking into this world at the appearing of our Lord Jesus. Gone will be all the old dreariness of the cold: our cold fickle hearts, our struggles and pains and sorrows. Death itself will be history. We'll discover on that day the truth that even though the present heaven and earth may pass away, the words of Jesus and what they promise us hold forever.

As a people whose destiny is the eternal Kingdom, where Love reigns over all, Jesus urges us to live here in this world toward that day. "Watch yourselves lest your hearts be weighed down with dissipation and drunkenness and the cares of this life." Instead, He calls us to a life of prayer, and eager watching, as we wait with bated breath for the unveiling of the Son of Man in His glory.

In the Nicene Creed we say: "And I look for the resurrection of the dead and the life of the world to come." Look for, that is, anticipate and eagerly expect it. And so we begin even here and now to live toward the joys of that day. We, who have been baptized into Christ, may face it without fear: for the One coming to judge is the One whose blood has blotted out our sin.

Monday after Pentecost

Psalmody: Psalm 128
Additional Psalm: Psalm 72
Old Testament Reading: Numbers 22:1–20
New Testament Reading: Luke 22:1–23

Prayer of the Day

O God, who gave Your Holy Spirit to the apostles, grant us that same Spirit that we may live in faith and abide in peace; through Jesus Christ, Your Son, our Lord, who lives and reigns with You and the Holy Spirit, one God, now and forever. (L51)

Meditation

Throughout Luke's Gospel we have been warned of the danger of loving money. Judas loved money, and so he consented to the plan of the Jewish leaders to do away with his master. "You cannot serve God and mammon."

But as Judas is fixated on money and the things below, our Lord is preparing a gift for His disciples that has been in His heart from before the ages began: a gift of heavenly treasure that the Church would prize as His greatest gift to her. Little did they know what Jesus was up to when He told them to "go and prepare the Passover for us, that we may eat it." His divinity again shines in His foretelling exactly who they would meet and where he would lead and how a guest room would be furnished for them. "And they went and found it exactly as He had told them." It always works that way. His words never fail.

And so at last the hour came. Gathered in that Upper Room, surrounded by His apostles, Jesus told them the secret of His heart: "I have earnestly desired to eat this Passover with you before I suffer." For this Passover would be unlike all the rest, the fulfillment of every Passover. This time, the Lamb would be a Man. "Behold, the Lamb of God!" John the Baptist had cried out. And this He manifests at the table.

The first cup shared: "I will not drink of the fruit of the vine until the kingdom of God comes." That would be upon a cross when sour wine would be pressed to His lips. The kingdom of God breaking into the world as forgiveness poured with His blood. Then the bread is blessed, broken, and given to them: "This is My body, which is given for you. Do this in remembrance of Me." Jesus instituted a new Passover meal—the body of the Lamb in and with the bread, given for them, that they might have life. Given for you, that you might have life. And at last the other cup, the cup that was the blood of the new covenant. Jeremiah 31 rings in with the promise that with the new covenant "I will forgive their iniquities and remember their sins no more."

And so with forgiveness offered in the Supper and yet rejected by Judas, the Passion itself is about to begin as the betrayer departs to his own endless sorrow.

TUESDAY AFTER PENTECOST

Psalmody: Psalm 94:8–14
Additional Psalm: Psalm 149
Old Testament Reading: Numbers 22:21–23:3
New Testament Reading: Luke 22:24–46

Prayer of the Day

Lord Jesus, the two swords of the disciples were enough to show themselves as sinners, fulfilling the prophecy of Isaiah that You would be numbered with transgressors. Yet You promised that they would eat and drink with You at Your table in Your kingdom, judging the twelve tribes of Israel. Help us to remember that You invite transgressors to Your Holy Supper where we are welcomed to receive the forgiveness of all our sins; for You live and reign with the Father and the Holy Spirit, one God, now and forever. (1026)

Meditation

Jesus had just given them the crown jewels of the Church: His very body and blood, given and poured out for the forgiveness of sins. And what are the disciples doing? They are arguing about which of them was the greatest. They're still getting it all wrong. Jesus, the greatest of all, is among them not to demand privilege and honor but to serve, to give up His body to the cross and to pour out His blood in order to serve them. Yes, He wants to lift them high—to give them nothing less than a Kingdom. But this King will wear a crown of thorns.

Who's the greatest? You can bet Simon was thinking he was pretty high on the list, if not at the top. Jesus lets him know that he's in for a rough time. "Simon, Simon, behold, Satan demanded to have you, that he might sift you like wheat." What will sustain Simon Peter? "But I have prayed for you that your faith may not fail."

Peter doesn't like the implications of this at all. He bursts out: "Lord, I am ready to go with You both to prison and to death." Peter's faith in Peter was stronger than his faith in Jesus' words. When will they learn that Jesus' words never fail? When will we? "I tell you the truth, Peter, the rooster will not crow this day, until you deny three times that you know Me."

As they head out of the Upper Room, our Lord reminds them that they lacked nothing when He sent them out. But a different time is at hand now—a time when He Himself will be numbered with transgressors. So they carry their swords. He carries His own sinlessness as His sole defense—that and His trust in the Father.

In the garden at the foot of the Mount of Olives, our Lord retreats to pray. The sands of time are running swiftly now. He knows how little time is left before the betrayal and all that follows. And so He does what He always did: He prayed. He tells the disciples to join Him: "Pray that you may not enter temptation." The sixth petition of the prayer He had given them earlier. His own prayer revolved around the third petition. If there is any other way, He asks for it, yet He submits to the will of the Father: "Nevertheless, not My will, but Yours, be done." Lo, how the Greatest prays! He will receive what the Father gives.

WEDNESDAY AFTER PENTECOST

Psalmody: Psalm 22:19–26
Additional Psalm: Psalm 102
Old Testament Reading: Numbers 23:4–28
New Testament Reading: Luke 22:47–71

Prayer of the Day

Almighty and ever-living God, You fulfilled Your promise by sending the gift of the Holy Spirit to unite disciples of all nations in the cross and resurrection of Your Son, Jesus Christ. By the preaching of the Gospel spread this gift to the ends of the earth; through the same Jesus Christ, our Lord, who lives and reigns with You and the Holy Spirit, one God, now and forever. (L49)

Meditation

A kiss isn't for this. "Judas, would you betray the Son of Man with a kiss?" Jesus had ever loved Judas, had ever striven for his salvation. And this is how he thanks the Lord? If Judas betrays one way, Peter betrays another. "Lord, shall we strike with the sword?" Jesus had told them to bring swords. Why, if not to use them? Whack, and off comes the ear of a servant of the high priest. "No more!" Jesus cries and heals the man. Then He challenges why they have come after Him as though He were some armed bandit. "But this is your hour and the power of darkness." Betrayal, violence, and injustice. Darkness indeed.

And the darkness grows. As Peter huddles about the fire, a servant girl begins to get suspicious: "This man also was with him," she says. Peter denies and denies and denies again. And then out in that black night, a rooster crows. As it does, Jesus turns to look upon His beloved Peter. That look reduced Peter to tears, brought him to repentance as he recalled the Lord's words, his own brash promise, his utter failure. He ran out weeping into the darkness of the night. It is painful beyond words to see yourself as you are; to know you can only live from forgiveness. Peter weeps, but does not despair of His Lord.

After Peter's departure, the violence escalated. Blindfolded, struck again and again. Voices raised in mockery and scorn.

At last they bring Him to the court: "If you are the Christ, tell us." His gentleness remains unshaken despite the abuse: "If I tell you, you will not believe, and if I ask you, you will not answer." He had come to bear witness to the truth, and it is for this truth that He is being abused and prepared for death. "But from now on the Son of Man shall be seated at the right hand of the power of God." Their eyes flash with glee. "Are you the Son of God, then?"

He will not lie. There is no falsehood in Him. He will speak the truth, though the truth brings Him to the tree: "You say that I am." They are finished. "What further testimony do we need?" What indeed? Our Lord is condemned for speaking truth, for being who He is: God's beloved and only-begotten Son. Behold what men do, when they get their hands on God.

THURSDAY AFTER PENTECOST

Psalmody: Psalm 1
Additional Psalm: Psalm 37
Old Testament Reading: Numbers 24:1–25
New Testament Reading: Luke 23:1–25

Prayer of the Day

Almighty and everlasting God and Father, You sent Your Son to take our nature upon Himself and to suffer death on the cross that all should follow the example of His great humility. Mercifully grant that we may both follow the example of our Savior, Jesus Christ, in His patience and also have our portion in His resurrection; through Jesus Christ, our Lord, who lives and reigns with You and the Holy Spirit, one God, now and forever. (1027)

Meditation

The "churchly" court had spoken; now it was time for the State to speak. The Jewish leaders haul Jesus off to Pilate. Charge after charge they lay against Him, but Pilate smells a rat. There's something off about this whole affair. He gets little enough out of the Man Himself: "You have said so." Pilate was no man of mercy, but he understood that this was gross injustice: "I find no guilt in this man." "He stirs up the people, teaching throughout all Judea, from Galilee even to this place."

Galilee gave him the out he needed. "Not my problem, then," Pilate thought, and shipped Jesus over to Herod, who happened to be in town for the big festival. Herod's delight in seeing Jesus turned sour when our Lord didn't do a circus trick or even talk. He stood there, sad and silent. And so the mockery continued. "He thinks He's a king!" Herod said, "so let's dress Him up pretty and send Him back." The odd thing is that Jesus brings reconciliation—even between His enemies. Pilate and Herod became good friends that very day.

When the apparently crazy king arrived back at his doorstep, Pilate was not amused. Again, the people demanded death. He pointed out that there was no reason for

that: "I did not find this man guilty," he says. "Neither did Herod." Pilate's solution was to appease the crowds with a bit of blood—but not enough to kill. "I will therefore punish and release Him."

The Jewish leaders were having none of that. They demanded instead that Pilate exchange prisoners, that he take Jesus and give them Barabbas—a murderer. The innocent for the guilty; the righteous for the unjust; the "Son of a Father" (which is what Barabbas means) for the Son of the Father. Their "Crucify! Crucify!" shouts prevailed. Neither for the first nor the last time did the government fail of its responsibility to justice due to pressure.

But here is divine justice—different from what anyone would ever imagine! Jesus stands silent against all the accusations, for He is prepared for them all to be true. He will bear in His body the sins of all, in fact, He will be made sin upon the tree, cursed and damned, in order to free from sin, from curse, from damnation the fallen race of man. "He delivered Jesus over to their will," yes, but it was also the will of His Father, as His prayer in the garden revealed.

FRIDAY AFTER PENTECOST

Psalmody: Psalm 132:8–12
Additional Psalm: Psalm 38
Old Testament Reading: Numbers 27:12–23
New Testament Reading: Luke 23:26–56

Prayer of the Day

Lord Jesus Christ, You reign among us by the preaching of Your cross. Forgive Your people their offenses that we, being governed by Your bountiful goodness, may enter at last into Your eternal paradise; for You live and reign with the Father and the Holy Spirit, one God, now and forever. (C87)

157

Meditation

Strange things happen when men kill their God. Strange was His prayer—as they are pounding in the nails, Jesus pleads, "Father, forgive them, for they know not what they do!" His whole life is wrapped up in that prayer, the sacrifice He is permitting Himself to become is but the plea: Father, forgive!

Horrible things happen in life. There is no getting around that. And death comes. How do we meet these? There are but two ways. We see them in the two thieves. Either we meet them railing in anger that our life is now up and cursing the God who won't save us from this horrible dying, as we cry out: "Not fair! It's not fair! I'm not supposed to die!" Or we meet them as the other thief, who confesses that he's but getting what his deeds have deserved, and yet who has the audacity of faith to turn to the One who knows the suffering and the pain and will shortly know the death, and to plead with Him: "Jesus, remember me when You come into Your kingdom!"

To the first thief, the Lord answers not a word. But to the second a most beautiful promise: "Amen, I say to you, today you will be with Me in Paradise." Though they met only as his earthly life was ending, the thief found a friend in the crucified Lord. They would never be parted.

And then the darkness, growing deep and deeper above the dreadful sacrifice, the curtain ripping in the temple, and the Lord upon the cross crying out: "Father, into Your hands I commit My spirit!" and suddenly breathing His last. Yes, strange things happen when men kill their God, or rather, when God in the flesh gives Himself into death to set us free.

But it is not only our death He shares; He even sanctifies our tombs. His precious body taken down from the cross by Joseph of Arimathea, tenderly laid in the bosom of the earth, as the women who had followed Him from Galilee look on. "Even though I walk through the valley of the shadow of death, I will fear no evil; for You are with me." How can I fear my grave when my Lord was laid there to bless it for me—to sanctify it and to make it be a place of slumber. Yes, I can go into that darkness with the thief's prayer on my lips and Jesus' promise in my heart: "today. . ."

Saturday after Pentecost

Psalmody: Psalm 97:6–12
Additional Psalm: Psalm 85
Old Testament Reading:
Numbers 32:1–6; 16–27
New Testament Reading: Luke 24:1–27

Prayer of the Day

Merciful Lord, through the angels You called the women at the tomb to remember that the Christ must be delivered into the hands of the sinful and be crucified and on the third day be raised from the dead. Help us to remember that it is only through suffering that we enter into glory and that in our sufferings we participate in the sufferings of Your Son, Jesus Christ, our Lord. (1028)

Meditation

The first day. And the light that shines that dawn is not only the light from the sun—it is the light that shines from the resurrected Lord. It is the first day of a new creation— forever beyond the darkness of the grave. It shines into this world a message of joy and hope that is downright unbelievable.

The women come to the tomb expecting a dead body; they meet two angels. The angels think they are silly to be looking for the Living One among the dead. They are shocked that the women did not remember the words of Jesus: "Remember how He told you . . . " Our struggle to believe the words of the Lord is always a wonder to the holy angels who have never known a single word of God to fail—well, neither have we. But we still stumble on in our doubt. The women have their doubt removed and they run to tell the others. Peter checks it out, verifies that the body is gone, and he marvels.

The two on the road epitomize how difficult it is for us to wrap our minds around the resurrection. They know the story. The women had even witnessed to them that angels said the Lord is alive. But folks don't come back from the dead, do they? Certainly, He had raised people from the dead before, but what now when He is dead? What hope remains? So their very sad "was"— "concerning Jesus of Nazareth, a man who was a mighty prophet." And in their distress they're saying: "we had hoped." They hoped no longer, though they didn't know what to make of the women's report.

The risen Christ, hidden before their eyes, listening to their tale of woe, all the while brimming with the joy of a life that never ends. He would bring them into His joy: "O foolish ones, and slow of heart to believe all that the prophets have spoken!" And He begins the Bible study of a lifetime. As they walk along, He romps with them through all the prophesies in Moses and the Prophets and shows them how it was all about Him. All foretold the suffering before the glory; the dead before the life; the agony before the peace. Later they will note that their very

hearts burned within them as He opened to them the Scriptures. He, the Crucified yet risen Lord, is the very key to unlocking the joy of the Word of God.

THE HOLY TRINITY

Psalmody: Psalm 46:1–7
Additional Psalm: Psalm 46
Old Testament Reading: Numbers 35:9–30
Additional Reading: Acts 1:1–7:60
New Testament Reading: Luke 24:28–53

Prayer of the Day

Almighty and everlasting God, You have given us grace to acknowledge the glory of the eternal Trinity by the confession of a true faith and to worship the Unity in the power of the Divine Majesty. Keep us steadfast in this faith and defend us from all adversities; for You, O Father, Son, and Holy Spirit, live and reign, one God, now and forever. (L52)

The Holy Trinity

Having celebrated the greatest event in God's history of salvation, the death and resurrection of the Son of God, we pause a bit at the Feast of the Holy Trinity to consider the essence of God. Certainly the essence of God is beyond our weak comprehension, but that He has graciously revealed Himself to us as Father, Son, and Holy Spirit. When we want to summarize all the Holy Scripture says about God as our Creator, Redeemer, and Sanctifier, we call Him the Holy Trinity. Even beyond the glorious summary of the persons and work of God found in the Creeds, to speak of God as the Holy Trinity says at one time all the many things that the Scriptures say about God. Our worship never ceases confessing our faith in the triune God and giving glory to the Father and to the Son and to the Holy Spirit; as it was in the beginning, is now, and will be forever. Amen.

Meditation

"Stay with us." They didn't know who He was yet, but they knew already that they hungered for His teaching. And so He stayed. He then did the truly odd thing: He acted not as guest, but as host. He took the bread as though it were His, He blessed it, He broke it, and then . . . they saw! They saw what was before their eyes the whole time but that they had not recognized. It was Jesus, their Lord and their Master, not dead, but living. And still teaching and guiding them toward the words of God, and toward the bread.

They run back with their joyful news only to find out that the Lord had been busy that day not just with them. Simon Peter had also seen Jeus. Scripture never recounts what happened in that first meeting between the denier and the Forgiver. The Emmaus disciples add some more to the story: they let the others know the strange way in which the Lord chose to reveal Himself, breaking the bread. Their minds went back, no doubt, to the strange meal on the day before His suffering.

And even as they wonder and marvel together, there He is. Standing among them, speaking His peace to their fearful and astonished hearts. Out of nowhere! No wonder they thought, "Ghost!" He disabuses them of that notion right away. No ghost. He invites them to check out His resurrected body, hands and feet, touchable. Not a phantom. And yet He does things with that risen body of His that defy our understanding entirely. We, with them, bow before the mystery of the resurrection with joy and awe.

Once again, He directs back to the writings of the Old Testament and to His own words spoken to them. "Thus it is written, that the Christ should suffer and on the third day rise from the dead, and that repentance and forgiveness of sins should be proclaimed in His name to all nations, beginning from Jerusalem." From suffering and death, foretold and accomplished, to His risen life, we see that it was for giving the gift of repentance and forgiveness of sins. A gift He intends for all people, all nations. This is what they witness as they go forth: Your sins have been forgiven; your death has been destroyed; God in Christ gives to you an unending life!

Luke's Gospel wraps up where it began—in the temple and with great joy, the apostles continually blessing God, and we with them.

The Time of the Church

18 MAY

Psalmody: Psalm 86:6–13
Additional Psalm: Psalm 86
Old Testament Reading:
Song of Solomon 1:1–2:7
New Testament Reading: John 5:1–18

Prayer of the Day

O God, the giver of all that is good,
by Your holy inspiration grant that
we may think those things that are
right and by Your merciful guiding
accomplish them; through Jesus Christ,
Your Son, our Lord, who lives and
reigns with You and the Holy Spirit,
one God, now and forever. (L46)

Meditation

Jesus is always working, and so is His
Father (John 5:17). That's why Jesus healed
on the Sabbath. There was work to be done.
The invalid of thirty-eight years needed to be
healed. And healed he was: "Get up, take up
your bed, and walk."

By healing on the Sabbath, Jesus angered the
religious authorities. Because He called God
His Father, they sought to kill Him. In their
minds, it was a sin for the man to carry his
bed and for Jesus to heal on the Sabbath. For
Jesus to call God His Father was blasphemy,
and thus worthy of death.

Always working. Does this describe you? Do
commitments with work, family, and church
quickly fill up your days? Do you wonder how
you are going to get everything done? Do you
stay up at night worried about all you have to
do the next day? Do you spread yourself so thin
that your relationships suffer—including your
relationship with your Lord? God commands
you to rest, but you conclude that there's just
not enough time in your busy schedule.

Jesus is always working. During His earthly
ministry, Jesus was always working to bring
healing and restoration to soul and body. He
was working to seek and save the lost. He
was working to proclaim the gospel of the
kingdom. On Good Friday, He was working to
accomplish your salvation and atone for your
sins and for the sins of all people.

Jesus is always working, and He is working
on you. He, who came not to be served but to
serve, now serves you as your living Savior.
The Lord of the Sabbath desires to give you
His rest. He is the Great Physician who heals
your infirmities. He is the only Son of the
Father, true God and true man, who is always
working to forgive, strengthen, and comfort
you. He is working on you, in you, and
through you.

Jesus is always working. This is the reason
He wants you to take some time every day to
stop working—stop so that He can work on
you. Stop so that He can speak to you through
His Word. Stop so that He can help and
strengthen you. Stop so that He can apply the
healing medicine of His forgiveness. In this
way, every day becomes a Sabbath day, a day
that is holy and consecrated to the Lord.

19 MAY

Psalmody: Psalm 43
Additional Psalm: Psalm 9
Old Testament Reading:
Song of Solomon 2:8–3:11
New Testament Reading: John 5:19–29

Prayer of the Day

Lord God, heavenly Father, You sent
Your Son, Jesus Christ, to give life to
the world. Make us hearers of Your
Word that we may share in His divine
life, be partakers of all its gifts, and
receive the fullness of that life in the
heavenly places; through Your Son,
Jesus Christ. (1029)

Meditation

You have already died. That's what Jesus says: "You have passed from death to life." A resurrection has already happened in your life. Although every day you are one day closer to death, you have already passed from death to life. This resurrection occurred at your Baptism. For there to be a resurrection, there must be death. At the font, this death occurred as your sinful nature was crucified and put to death, and the new nature was raised to life. Death no longer has mastery over you; through Baptism, you have passed from death to life.

Thus, eternal life is already your possession. It is not a matter of "I will be saved," because you are already saved. It is not "I will have eternal life"; you have already passed from death to life. Jesus states, "Whoever hears My word and believes Him who sent Me has eternal life" (John 5:24). You don't have to wait until you die for eternal life; this life is already yours through God's Son. The Son does what the Father does. The Father raises the dead and so does the Son. The Father gives life and so, too, does the Son, and you have received this life.

Those who refuse to believe in the One sent from the Father remain dead—spiritually dead in their trespasses and sins. Although their bodies will be raised at the second coming, it will not be a resurrection to life but a resurrection to judgment. Without faith, even their best deeds are evil, and so they are condemned. Since they reject Christ, the resurrection and the life, they will not experience this second resurrection.

Your first resurrection is the guarantee of your second resurrection on the Last Day. Both resurrections are connected to Christ's resurrection. You were raised to new life at your Baptism because through this sacrament, you were joined to Christ's death and resurrection. Because Jesus rose from the dead, you can be certain that your body will be raised on the Last Day. As Jesus says, "Because I live, you will live also" (John 14:19). Regardless of whether you have been in the grave for ten years or 10,000 years, when Christ comes again, your lifeless and decayed body will hear the voice of the Son of Man and live. On that great and glorious day, you will dwell with your living Lord in life and joy forever.

20 MAY

Psalmody: Psalm 119:105–112
Additional Psalm: Psalm 75
Old Testament Reading:
Song of Solomon 4:1–5:1
New Testament Reading: John 5:30–47

Prayer of the Day

Almighty and everlasting God, give us an increase of faith, hope, and love that we may trust the testimony of Scripture concerning You and obtain what You have promised; through Jesus Christ, Your Son, our Lord. (1030)

Meditation

To the religious leaders who are questioning His divine identity, Jesus provides three witnesses. First, John the Baptist. Previously, the religious leaders had sent representatives to John the Baptist to ask him if he was the Christ (John 1:19–28). This John denied; instead, he announced the coming of the One whose sandals he was not worthy to untie.

Jesus' second witness is a greater witness than John the Baptist—it's Jesus' own Father. The Father sent His Son to accomplish His will. Jesus speaks and acts according to His Father's desire. His miracles, His authoritative teaching, and His power over demons all testify that He is from the Father.

Jesus provides a third witness—the Scriptures. The Old Testament Scriptures that these religious leaders had learned, studied, and memorized are the very words that testify about Christ. The Hebrew Scriptures are not merely laws and regulations; they are not merely a historical record of an ancient nation. They are all about Christ. They testify to Him. Old Testament laws, commandments, prophecies, sacrifices, feasts, and worship all find their fulfillment in Christ.

"Only on the evidence of two witnesses or of three witnesses shall a charge be established" (Deuteronomy 19:15). The truth about Jesus is established on the basis on these three witnesses, but the Jews refused to believe in Him. They refused to listen to John the Baptist's testimony, and their hardened hearts kept them from seeing the very Scriptures that were been fulfilled before them. By rejecting Christ, they were rejecting Moses and the entire testimony of the Old Testament, for all these Scriptures testified to Christ.

The truth about Jesus has been established for us on the basis of these same witnesses. The Father's voice at Christ's Baptism and transfiguration confirms that Jesus is His beloved Son. The testimony of both prophets and apostles in the Scriptures testify that Jesus is both Lord and God and the Savior of the world. But doubts surface. Questions are raised. People attack the reliability of the Scriptures. The divinity of Christ and His authority are often denied even among those who claim to be Christian. The devil tempts us to believe that Jesus is someone other than who He says He is.

But the matter has been established on the basis of many witnesses. God's Word is truth, and these Scriptures bear witness of the One sent from the Father to give us eternal life.

21 MAY

Emperor Constantine, Christian Ruler, and Helena, Mother of Constantine

Psalmody: Psalm 132:8–18
Additional Psalm: Psalm 81
Old Testament Reading:
Song of Solomon 5:2–6:3
New Testament Reading: John 6:1–21

Prayer of the Day

Almighty God, through Your servant Constantine, Your Church flourished, and by his mother, Helena, the Church of the Holy Sepulchre in Jerusalem became a holy place for many pilgrims. Grant unto us this same zeal for Your Church and charity toward Your people, that we may be fruitful in good works and steadfast in faith. Keep us ever grateful for your abundant provision, with our eyes fixed, as Helena's were, on the highest and greatest treasure of all, the cross of Christ; through Jesus Christ, our Lord, who lives and reigns with You and the Holy Spirit, one God, now and forever. (1031)

Emperor Constantine, Christian Ruler, and Helena, Mother of Constantine

Constantine I served as Roman Emperor from AD 306 to 337. During his reign, the persecution of Christians was forbidden by the Edict of Milan in AD 313, and, ultimately, the faith gained full imperial support. Constantine took an active interest in the life and teachings of the Church and in AD 325 called the Council of Nicaea, at which orthodox Christianity was defined and defended. His mother, Helena (ca. AD 255–329), strongly influenced Constantine. Her great interest in locating the holy sites of the Christian faith led her to become one of the first Christian pilgrims to the Holy Land. Her research led to the identification of biblical locations in Jerusalem, Bethlehem, and beyond, which are still maintained as places of worship today.

Meditation

"Where are we to buy bread, so that these people may eat?" (John 6:5).

That is the question Jesus poses to Philip as people arrive by the thousands to the mountain where Jesus is with His disciples. Philip immediately responds that feeding such a crowd is financially impossible. It would take over a half-year's salary to feed so many, and then each person would only get just a little. Andrew takes it upon himself to discover how much food there is among the people. He only finds a boy with five barley loaves and two fish.

But this is all a test. Jesus already knows what He is going to do even before He asks the question. Philip and Andrew are right—they can't feed so many people. It's humanly impossible with their limited resources. What these two disciples fail to see is their most valuable resource is the One before them. Through Him all things were made (John 1:3). He who was present and active at creation can feed the people and still have leftovers. And that's what He does. From five loaves and two fish, He feeds the crowd of 5,000 men plus the women and children with twelve basketfuls to spare.

"Where are we to buy bread, so that these people may eat?" Jesus tested Philip with these words. Our possessions are often a test for us. In times of plenty, we assume it is because of our own hard work and dedication that we have abundance, forgetting that it is our Lord who blesses us with our talent and abilities and gives us the means to earn a living. In times of need, we wonder how we are going to provide for ourselves and our families, failing

to trust in Him who provides for all our needs of soul and body.

Plenty and need are both tests. Although this miracle reveals that Jesus is the Son of God, the crowd continues to follow Jesus only because they ate the loaves and had their fill (John 6:26). But Jesus provides. In times of plenty, He leads us to rejoice in what we have, for all comes from His gracious hand. In times of need, He leads us to trust that He will take care of all our needs, and He graciously and generously forgives us when we have worried about tomorrow or trusted in the things of this world rather than trusting in Him above all things.

22 MAY

Psalmody: Psalm 37:16–26
Additional Psalm: Psalm 78
Old Testament Reading:
Song of Solomon 6:4–7:5
New Testament Reading: John 6:22–40

Prayer of the Day

Merciful Father, You gave Your Son Jesus as the heavenly bread of life. Grant us faith to feast on Him in Your Word and Sacraments that we may be nourished unto life everlasting; through the same Jesus Christ, our Lord, who lives and reigns with You and the Holy Spirit, one God, now and forever. (B71)

Meditation

Jesus says that a wicked and adulterous generation always seeks a sign (Matthew 12:39). And here is no exception. The previous evening, the people were fed and filled from five loaves and two fish that were miraculously multiplied. Now they are demanding another sign so that they might believe in Jesus. After all, they point out, Moses not only gave the Israelites manna from heaven just once; there was manna six days a week for many years. Jesus quickly reveals the fallacy of the crowd's reasoning. First, it was not Moses that gave the people manna, but the Father in heaven. Second, in Jesus the people are receiving not only bread for their stomachs but also the true bread who has come down from heaven and gives life to the world.

The people demand signs, but Jesus gives Himself. They want Jesus to give them manna every day, but whoever comes to Jesus will neither hunger nor thirst. And this heavenly bread is received by faith. The same demands are placed on Jesus today: "If only I had a sign, then I would believe." Others expect Jesus to bless them with an abundance of material possessions. We, too, may seek Jesus for the wrong reasons, demanding that He give us the food that perishes rather than seeking the heavenly food that endures to eternal life.

Jesus is the bread that comes down from heaven. He satisfies our spiritual hunger and thirst. The people ask Jesus, "What must we do, to be doing the works of God?" The answer: "Believe in Him whom He has sent." And even faith is not a work that we do; it is a gift of God. Jesus, the Bread of Life, gives us the gift of faith by which we claim these blessings, and He accomplishes the Father's will by bestowing on us and all believers eternal life.

But where is the proof? Where is the sign? The proof is the cross where Jesus gives His life for the world. The sign is the Lord's Supper, where Jesus comes and feeds us with the Bread of Life, giving us His body to eat and His blood to drink. And in this way the Father's will is accomplished in us as by grace we are drawn to Christ in faith, receive His gifts, and are made heirs of eternal life.

23 May

Psalmody: Psalm 34:12–22
Additional Psalm: Psalm 34
Old Testament Reading:
Song of Solomon 7:6–8:14
New Testament Reading: John 6:41–59

Prayer of the Day

Gracious Father, Your blessed Son came down from heaven to be the true bread that gives life to the world. Grant that Christ, the bread of life, may live in us and we in Him, who lives and reigns with You and the Holy Spirit, one God, now and forever. (B72)

Meditation

The crowds love signs. They are quick to call Jesus the Prophet when He multiplies the loaves. They are eager to crown Him their Bread King. But when Jesus says that He is the bread that has come down from heaven, that's too much. After all, they know Jesus' father and mother. How can this native of Nazareth say that He is from heaven? The grumbling begins.

However, Jesus is not done speaking. He uses the miracle of the loaves and fish to teach about who He is and what He has come to do. His claims are many and direct: "I am the bread of life." "I am the living bread that came down from heaven." "I have seen the Father." "If anyone eats of this bread, he will live forever." "The bread that I will give for the life of the world is my flesh." "Unless you eat the flesh of the Son of Man and drink His blood, you have no life in you."

What started as grumbling ends in disputes and arguments among those in the crowd. The words of Jesus are difficult to accept. Two millennia later our Lord's words are still controversial, even for many believers. How can Jesus give us His flesh to eat and His blood to drink? Surely there must be additional paths to come to the Father other than the flesh of Christ. Why does Jesus speak in such a graphic and grotesque way?

The fact is our sinful nature would much rather prefer a bread king or miracle worker or even a great prophet than the Son of God who offers Himself on the cross and gives us His flesh to eat and His blood to drink. By nature we want a deity who provides for the here and now; who gives us what we want, when we want it, and in the way that we want it.

Although these words of Christ continue to confront and challenge the faithful, they are precisely the words we need to hear. Jesus is our living bread. He is the means by which we come to the Father. His flesh was offered for our life and for the life of the world. And in His Word and in His Supper, we feast on His flesh and blood as He nourishes us with His heavenly food. As a result of this spiritual eating and drinking, we will live forever.

24 MAY

Esther

Psalmody: Psalm 39:4–11
Additional Psalm: Psalm 39
Old Testament Reading: Ecclesiastes 1:1–18
Additional Reading: Esther 1:1–10:3
New Testament Reading: John 6:60–71

Prayer of the Day

O God, You graced Your servant Queen Esther not only with beauty and elegance but also with faith and wisdom. Grant that we, too, might use the qualities that You have generously bestowed on us for the glory of Your mighty name and for the good of Your people, that through Your work in us, we may be advocates of the oppressed and defenders of the weak, preserving our faith in the great High Priest who intercedes on our behalf, Jesus Christ, who lives and reigns with you and the Holy Spirit, one God, now and forever. (1032)

Esther

Esther is the heroine of the biblical book that bears her name. Her Jewish name was Hadassah, which means "myrtle." Her beauty, charm, and courage served her well as queen to King Ahasuerus. In that role, she was able to save her people from the mass extermination that Haman, the king's chief advisor, had planned (Esther 2:19–4:17). Esther's efforts to uncover the plot resulted in the hanging of Haman on the very same gallows that he had built for Mordecai, her uncle and guardian. Following this, the king named Mordecai minister of state in Haman's place. This story is an example of how God intervenes on behalf of His people to deliver them from evil, as here through Esther He preserved the Old Testament people through whom the Messiah would come.

Meditation

Jesus shouldn't have opened His mouth. After the miracles of the loaves, His following is more than 10,000. But then Jesus starts to preach, and the people quickly turn from Him. Many in the crowd began to dispute among themselves (John 6:52). Then even

His disciples begin to grumble. For them His words are too much. Many of His disciples turn away and follow Him no more.

So what about the Twelve? Will they follow the crowd and many of the other disciples? Will they also conclude that Jesus is out of His mind rather than the living bread that has come down from heaven? Jesus asks the question, "Do you want to go away as well?" Peter speaks on behalf of the others, "Lord, to whom shall we go? You have the words of eternal life, and we have believed, and have come to know, that You are the Holy One of God."

Do you want to go away as well? Your sinful flesh says, "Yes!" The flesh wants nothing to do with Christ. His words seem like foolishness. His sayings are too hard to accept. His claims about Himself are too unreasonable.

But the flesh is no help at all. It is the Spirit who gives life. On our own, we could never believe the words of Jesus. We, too, would grumble and walk away as some did that day when Jesus taught at Capernaum. What is impossible for our flesh to do, our triune God has done for us. God the Father by grace has drawn us to His Son, who offered His life on the cross. The Spirit has given us life through the words of Jesus, bestowing on us the gift of faith. With the Spirit, we confess with Peter that Jesus has the words of eternal life and that He is the Holy One of God.

Looking at the sixth chapter of John, it may appear that Jesus shouldn't have opened His mouth. His preaching led many to turn away from Him. But Christ is more concerned about truth than numbers. He doesn't preach to draw a crowd. His goal is not to give itching ears what they want to hear. This is preaching to the flesh. Instead, His proclaims Spirit-filled words of eternal life, a message that is rejected by many, but a message that is life and salvation for all who believe.

25 MAY

Bede the Venerable, Theologian

Psalmody: Psalm 110
Additional Psalm: Psalm 49
Old Testament Reading: Ecclesiastes 2:1–26
New Testament Reading: John 7:1–13

Prayer of the Day

Heavenly Father, when he was still a child You called Your servant Bede to devote his life to serve You in the venerable disciplines of religion and scholarship. As he labored in the Spirit to bring the riches of Your truth to his generation, grant that we may also strive to make You known in all the world in our various vocations; through Jesus Christ, our Lord, who lives and reigns with you and the Holy Spirit, one God, now and forever. (1033)

Bede the Venerable, Theologian

Bede (AD 673–735) was the last of the Early Church Fathers and the first to compile the history of the English church. Born in Northumbria, Bede was placed by his parents in a monastery in northern England at the age of seven. He rarely left the monastery and devoted the rest of his life to teaching and writing. The most learned man of his time, he was a prolific writer of history, whose careful use of sources provided a model for historians in the Middle Ages. Known best for his book *The Ecclesiastical History of the English People*, he was also a profound interpreter of Scripture; his commentaries are still fresh today. His most famous disciple, Cuthbert, reported that Bede was working on a translation of John's Gospel into English when death came and that he died with the words of the Gloria Patri on his lips. He received the title "Venerable" within two generations of his death and is buried in Durham Cathedral as one of England's greatest saints.

Meditation

Opinions abound. Some say Jesus is a good man. Others say that He is leading the people astray. His own brothers do not believe in Him and so they mock Him. The religious leaders want Him dead and seek to silence anyone who speaks about Him.

Opinions abound today. Some say Jesus is a good man. Some say He is a fraud. Many refuse to believe. Others are so bold in their unbelief that they mock Jesus. Still others, by ridicule and persecution, seek to silence any public discussion and confession of Christ.

And the reality is that we are often intimidated. Out of fear of the authorities, no one at the feast spoke openly of Jesus. Out of fear, we don't speak openly today. Our lives are not at risk for confessing Christ as is the case for other believers in the world, but when given the opportunity, we often say nothing. We cower in fear. We justify our silence. We think we won't say the right words. We worry about how our words will be received, so we say remain silent. Even when others mock Jesus or those who belong to Him, we are tempted to say nothing rather than defend the truth.

Jesus knows the heart of man. He knows He cannot openly go to the Feast, for His time had not yet fully come. It was not God's will for Jesus to offer His life for this evil world at this Feast of Booths. However, the hour would come for Jesus to do that which His Father had sent Him to do. He would give His life as the atoning sacrifice for all people, even people who mock and are reluctant to confess Him. Jesus' brothers were unbelievers at this time. We know that after the resurrection many of them did believe. James would later become the overseer of the Jerusalem Church and under the Spirit's inspiration pen the Epistle

that bears his name. Just as our Lord's brothers were not beyond the reach of our Lord's forgiving love, neither are we. Once unbelieving, we have received the gift of faith. For those times when we have been afraid and not confessed the truth, our Lord graciously forgives us. Through His Word, He empowers us to testify, to know that now is the time for us to confess His name, regardless of how it might be received by the world.

26 MAY

Psalmody: Psalm 56:1–4
Additional Psalm: Psalm 7
Old Testament Reading: Ecclesiastes 3:1–22
New Testament Reading: John 7:14–31

Prayer of the Day

Lord Jesus, You have come from the Father to do His will of suffering and dying on our behalf and thereby teaching us that the way of salvation is through the cross. Help us to understand that there is a time for everything under heaven, a time to be born and a time to die, and that our whole life, from birth to death, is according to Your good and gracious will; for You live and reign with the Father and the Holy Spirit, one God, now and forever. (1156)

Meditation

"None of you keeps the law" (John 7:19). These words sting; they hurt, especially for many of the Jewish authorities who prided themselves in their obedience. When it came to the Law, they believed they were perfect, or at least almost perfect.

But no one keeps the Law. By rejecting Jesus, they were breaking the Law. Their rejection of

Jesus and His teaching was a rejection of the Law, for the books of the Torah often testify of the coming Savior. Their condemnation of Jesus for healing on the Sabbath further reveals their hypocrisy. They circumcise on the Sabbath, but assume Jesus is sinning when He makes the lame walk on the same day. They seek to put Jesus to death, even though murder is forbidden.

"None of you keeps the law." How dare Jesus say this to us? We are not like the religious leaders who were seeking to kill Him. We aren't so consumed with the outward keeping of the Law that we harden our hearts to its message. We love Jesus. We worship Him. We try our best to do what He would have us do.

The judgment remains: "None of you keeps the law." We fall short; we sin daily. However, Jesus enters this world not as a second Moses, not as another rabbi who adds more laws and rules and regulations to the already hundreds of laws contained in the Old Testament. Instead, Jesus comes to fulfill the Law. He keeps the Law perfectly. What neither we nor the religious leaders of Jesus' day could do, Christ does for us. He perfectly obeys, and when His hour has come, He offers His life for every person, for every lawbreaker.

Sinful blindness prevented both the religious leaders and many of the people of Jerusalem from believing in Jesus. They sinned when they claimed Jesus had a demon and when others were plotting to kill Him. They were sinners, and so are we. However, Jesus is teaching the words of His Father. There is no falsehood or sin in Him. His word is truth and His ways are perfect. His words both convict and comfort, for He says to you again today, "You do not keep the Law, but I have kept the law for you. I have atoned for your sin and given you the faith to believe in Me and in the words I speak."

27 MAY

Psalmody: Psalm 27:4–10
Additional Psalm: Psalm 83
Old Testament Reading: Ecclesiastes 4:1–16
New Testament Reading: John 7:32–53

Prayer of the Day

O God, on this day You once taught the hearts of Your faithful people by sending them the light of Your Holy Spirit. Grant us in our day by the same Spirit to have a right understanding in all things and evermore to rejoice in His holy consolation; through Jesus Christ, Your Son, our Lord, who lives and reigns with You and the Holy Spirit, one God, now and forever. (L50)

Meditation

The Feast of Booths was one of three yearly feasts in which people traveled to Jerusalem. During the weeklong celebration, people would sleep in tents to commemorate the forty years of wilderness wanderings. This feast reminded the people that despite their sin, God provided for them in the wilderness, and at the end of the forty years He led them into the Promised Land.

By the first century, an additional ritual occurred during this Feast. Every day thousands of people would gather by the Pool of Siloam, the only source of fresh water for the city. The Jews compared the Pool of Siloam to the time when Moses struck the rock in the wilderness and water gushed forth. They called it living water. Just as the water from the rock sustained their ancestors in the wilderness, so the water of the Pool of Siloam was the water that sustained the people of Jerusalem.

Every day of the weeklong feast, a priest would fill a good vessel with water from the Pool of Siloam as the people sang these words from Isaiah: "With joy you will draw water from the wells of salvation" (12:3). On the last and thus the greatest day of the feast, as the people were gathered, Jesus cried out: "If anyone thirsts, let him come to Me and drink." In other words, if you want true living water, don't go to the Pool of Siloam, but come to Me, for I have the water that not only preserves life but gives life—eternal life. The water I give is the water of salvation. Drink of it, and you will live forever.

We need this living water. Without water, we die. Without living water, we are spiritually dead. And Jesus gives us this living water; it is His Spirit. It is the Spirit who gives life. At this time, the Spirit was not given in full measure, but would be when on Easter night Jesus breathed on His disciples and said, "Receive the Holy Spirit." Fifty days later the Spirit was powerfully bestowed on the disciples at Pentecost.

We also have received this Spirit-filled living water. At our Baptism, the Holy Spirit entered us. Our spiritual thirst has been satisfied. Not only have we received this living water, but through the Spirit's power, from our hearts now flow rivers of living water, as we offer that living water of salvation to others.

28 MAY

Psalmody: Psalm 32:1–5
Additional Psalm: Psalm 32
Old Testament Reading: Ecclesiastes 5:1–20
New Testament Reading: John 8:1–20

Prayer of the Day

Almighty God, whom to know is everlasting life, grant us to know Your Son, Jesus, to be the way, the truth, and the life, that we may steadfastly follow His steps in the way that leads to life eternal; through Jesus Christ, our Lord, who lives and reigns with You and the Holy Spirit, one God, now and forever. (B73)

Meditation

The adulteress woman was caught in sin. Both she and the man she was with deserved to die. The scribes and Pharisees saw this as an opportunity to test Jesus. Bring her to Jesus; maybe we can trap Him. If He says she should live, then He will be speaking against the Law, and we will have a basis for accusations against Him.

Jesus isn't fooled. The religious leaders wanted Him to judge, but He places the burden back on them, "Let him who is without sin among you be the first to throw a stone at her." What a hard word for these self-righteous religious leaders to hear. They prided themselves on their works. They boasted in the way they faithfully followed the Law. When forced to consider their own sinfulness, they had no choice but to put their stones down and walk away.

That day Jesus addressed both the sins of the religious leaders and those of the adulteress woman. He doesn't condemn the woman, but seeks to reveal her sin and the sin of those who wanted to stone her, so that they all might repent and live.

Like the woman, we, too, have sinned—sins for which we rightly deserve not only temporal death but also eternal damnation. Many of these are sins we hope that no one else discovers, sins of which we are ashamed, sins that fill us with guilt and remorse.

Like the religious leaders, we succumb to arrogant self-righteousness. Instead of empathizing and praying for the person trapped in sin, we are quick to condemn. Our words and attitudes reveal that we think ourselves to be above that particular sin, that we could never fall into such a terrible vice. Ironically, in our condemnation of the sins of others, we ultimately condemn ourselves. Instead of condemning, Jesus confronts for "God did not send His Son into the world to condemn the world, but in order that the world might be saved through Him" (John 3:17). He confronts so that He might save. He shows both the woman and the religious leaders their sin so that they might receive His forgiveness and salvation. He seeks to forgive so that by His power those entrapped in sin might turn from it and sin no more.

Our Lord's work of confronting and forgiving continues. Through His Word, He confronts every sin—our secret sins and our bold sins of pride and self-righteousness. He confronts so that He might save. He shows our sin; He brings us to repentance, and then He lovingly and graciously forgives.

29 MAY

Psalmody: Psalm 104:24–35
Additional Psalm: Psalm 104
Old Testament Reading: Ecclesiastes 6:1–7:10
New Testament Reading: John 8:21–38

Prayer of the Day

Almighty and gracious Lord, pour out Your Holy Spirit on Your faithful people. Keep us steadfast in Your grace and truth, protect and deliver us in times of temptation, defend us against all enemies, and grant to Your Church Your saving peace; through Jesus Christ, Your Son, our Lord, who lives and reigns with You and the Holy Spirit, one God, now and forever. (F33)

Meditation

"We are offspring of Abraham and have never been enslaved to anyone" (John 8:33). This would be true if the Israelites had not been enslaved to the Egyptians for 400 years, or if their land had not later come under control of the Babylonians, Persians, or Greeks. Even as those in the crowd spoke these words, they were enslaved, for the land had been under Roman occupation for nearly a century.

"Jesus," they thought, "we're not slaves, so You can't set us free." Misguided as they were regarding slavery, Jesus was speaking of a more significant slavery, a slavery from which no one can set himself free—the slavery to sin.

Just as Jesus' hearers balked at the notion of slavery, so His words still rub people the wrong way: I can do whatever I want. No one tells me how to live my life. It's my body, and it's my choice. This is the creed of many today. However, the irony is that the more a person exercises his or her imagined freedom, the more that person becomes entrapped by sin. Whether it's drugs, pornography, gambling, or sexual sins, a person continues on a downward spiral, unable to break free from sin.

You sin, and thus you are a slave to sin. That's the truth. But that's not the only truth Jesus spoke in the temple that day. Sin enslaves, but the Son sets you free. By His death and resurrection, you are free—free from sin, death, and the power of the devil. The price for your freedom has been paid. The cost was the perfect life and the terrible death of God's Son.

The Jews objected not only to the truth that they were slaves to sin but also that Jesus alone could set them free. They didn't believe they needed to be liberated from anything or anyone, and they certainly refused to believe that by abiding in Christ and His Word would they be set free. Ultimately, they concluded that Jesus was not the source of truth but a Samaritan who had a demon (John 8:48).

You have the words of Christ. The Scriptures reveal the truth. You are a slave to sin, but the Son has set you free. Abiding in the Word, you will remain in the freedom of Christ, both freed from your sin and, as a baptized child of God, free to serve others in His name.

30 May

Psalmody: Psalm 43
Additional Psalm: Psalm 111
Old Testament Reading: Ecclesiastes 7:11–29
New Testament Reading: John 8:39–59

Prayer of the Day

Almighty and everlasting God, You have given us grace to acknowledge the glory of the eternal Trinity by the confession of a true faith and to worship the Unity in the power of the Divine Majesty. Keep us steadfast in this faith and defend us from all adversities; for You, O Father, Son, and Holy Spirit, live and reign, one God, now and forever. (L52)

Meditation

The claims are bold: "If anyone keeps My word, he will never see death." "Abraham rejoiced that he would see My day. He saw it and was glad." "Before Abraham was, I am." Father Abraham was great, but Jesus makes the claim that He is greater. He is the great *I AM*, God Himself, the eternal Lord.

He must be silenced; He must be put to death. This is their conclusion. The Pharisees seek to stone Him, but His hour has not yet come. They cannot kill Him until the appointed time. Jesus hides Himself and then leaves the temple.

The claims are bold but true. Jesus is eternal. Jesus is Abraham's seed, the promised one through whom all nations would be blessed. He gives life, for He will taste death for all people so that those who believe in Him will not experience eternal death and condemnation.

To believe in Jesus is to be a child of Abraham, for Abraham believed the Lord, and it was counted to him as righteousness (Genesis 15:6). Regardless of their genealogy, believers are members of Abraham's family. Sadly, those in the temple rejected Jesus and in so doing rejected the Father. Their unbelief revealed that they were not children of Abraham.

Our politically correct world wants nothing to do with these words of Jesus. Absolutes have no place in the minds of many. Truth is not grounded in reality, but in what a person feels is true for them. The father of lies continues to convince many that Jesus is something less than the eternal Son of God and that there are many paths to glory other than through faith in Him. And so to this day, there are those who by dismissing the word of Christ reject Christ Himself, and in rejecting Christ also reject the Father.

The devil seeks to deceive you with his lies. He wants to convince you that Jesus is not who He says He is. He wants you to believe that He is not your Savior, God in human flesh who gives you life. He desires that you do his bidding rather than the will of your Father in heaven.

In contrast to the devil's lies, Jesus is the truth, and He speaks the truth. His claims are bold, but they can be completely trusted. Through Christ, your sins are forgiven and your eternal future is secure.

31 May

The Visitation (Three-Year Lectionary)

Psalmody: Psalm 146:5–10
Additional Psalm: Psalm 146
Old Testament Reading: Ecclesiastes 8:1–17
New Testament Reading: John 9:1–23

Prayer of the Day

Almighty God, You chose the virgin Mary to be the mother of Your Son and made known through her Your gracious regard for the poor and lowly and despised. Grant that we may receive Your Word in humility and faith, and so be made one with Jesus Christ, Your Son, our Lord, who lives and reigns with You and the Holy Spirit, one God, now and forever. (F18)

The Visitation

John the Baptizer and Jesus, the two great figures of salvation history, now come together in the visit to Elizabeth by the Virgin Mary (Luke 1:39–45), both of whom conceived their children under miraculous circumstances. Thus John is brought into the presence of Jesus while they are still in their mothers' wombs. This presence of the Lord causes a response by the child John as he leaps in Elizabeth's womb. John's response to the presence of Jesus, the Messiah, foreshadows John's own role as forerunner. Already now, a new creation is beginning, and a baby still in the womb hails the new creation's inception. Foreshadowed in John's leap are the miracles of Jesus, who will cause all creation to leap at His presence: "The blind receive their sight, the lame walk, lepers are cleansed, the deaf hear, the dead are raised up, the poor have good news preached to them" (Luke 7:22). The incarnate presence of the Messiah also evokes a response from Elizabeth, who proclaims Mary's blessedness. Mary's Magnificat (Luke 1:46–55) provides the theological significance of this meeting as Mary sums up her place in salvation history. Mary's song is a hymn to God for His gracious gifts to the least in this world, whom He has lifted up out of lowliness solely because of His grace and mercy.

Meditation

For every effect, there must be a cause. Things don't just happen. There has to be an explanation. That's what makes sense to us; it's what seems reasonable.

This is the disciples' thinking when they encounter this man born blind. He is blind; that's the effect. So what's the cause? Somebody must have sinned. So they conclude either this man sinned in the womb before he was born or his parents sinned. Something was the cause of this man's blindness.

So they ask Jesus, "Who sinned?" Their thinking though is misguided: "It was not that this man sinned, or his parents, but that the works of God might be displayed in him" (John 9:3). This man's blindness is not the punishment for his sin or the sin of his parents. Instead, his blindness is the means by which the works of God are revealed.

With these words, Jesus nullifies this type of cause and effect thinking when it comes to sickness and suffering; still, many today succumb to this line of reasoning. The televangelist announces to his worldwide audience that a recent natural disaster is a result of the nation's sin. The Christian wife and mother who is diagnosed with breast cancer assumes it was because of some past sin that she is now plagued with this terrible disease. The father whose teenage son dies in an automobile accident concludes that if he had been a better father, God would not have taken his son from him.

It's not someone's sin that resulted in the suffering and sorrow described above. We live in a world that is sinful where natural disasters, sickness, and death occur. However, God not only displays His works in miraculous events but also in the midst of suffering and sorrow. The man who was born blind had his sight restored. Without a doubt, God's work was displayed in him. However, God's works are also displayed when following natural disasters, God's people respond to serve those affected, providing for both physical and spiritual needs. God's work is displayed when those who are sick, instead of turning away from Him, are drawn closer to Him and strengthened in the faith. God's work is displayed when those who are grieving are filled with the hope of Jesus Christ, the resurrection and the life.

God's works were displayed in the man born blind, and God's works are constantly displayed in your life. Whether in prosperity or adversity, abundance or need, God is working to save, help, deliver, and strengthen you.

1 JUNE

Justin, Martyr

Psalmody: Psalm 97:4–12
Additional Psalm: Psalm 115
Old Testament Reading: Ecclesiastes 9:1–17
New Testament Reading: John 9:24–41

Prayer of the Day

Almighty and everlasting God, You found your martyr Justin wandering from teacher to teacher, searching for the true God. Grant that all who seek for a deeper knowledge of the sublime wisdom of Your eternal Word may be found by You who sent Your Son to seek and to save the lost; through Jesus Christ our Lord, who lives and reigns with You and the Holy Spirit, one God, now and forever. Amen. (1034)

Justin, Martyr

Born at the beginning of the second century, Justin was raised in a pagan family. He was a student of philosophy who converted to the Christian faith and became a teacher in Ephesus and Rome. After refusing to make pagan sacrifices, he was arrested, tried, and executed, along with six other believers. The official Roman court proceedings of his trial before Rusticius, a Roman prelate, document his confession of faith. The account of his martyrdom became a source of great encouragement to the early Christian community. Much of what we know of early liturgical practice comes from Justin.

Meditation

The blind man could see, but he still was not truly seeing. It's true, his sight was restored, but Jesus was not finished ministering to this man. There were more of God's works to be displayed in him (John 9:3). Jesus not only intended to remove his physical blindness, but also his spiritual blindness. He not only desired for this man to see the beauty of the world that surrounded him but also to see Jesus and believe in Him.

After the man's sight is restored, his neighbors take him to the Pharisees. Before the Pharisees, he confesses that Jesus is a prophet. He acknowledges that Jesus is from God, for only one sent from God could make the blind see. This confession is too much for the religious authorities, and the man is thrown out and excommunicated for speaking the truth. Although he no longer suffers from physical blindness, his suffering is not over. He now suffers for confessing Jesus.

However, Jesus wants this man to believe that He is more than just a prophet, and so Jesus searches for the man. After conversing with Jesus, the man confesses Jesus as the Son of Man and worships Him. Now He truly sees. God's works have been displayed in him. His eyes see, and He also sees with the eyes of faith.

God's works have been displayed in your life. You were born spiritually blind, unable to see, groping around in the darkness of sin and death. But now you do see. God was working for you at Calvary when Jesus closed His eyes in death to atone for your sinful blindness. God was displaying His works in you when at your Baptism He gave you spiritual sight by giving you the gift of faith. God continues to open your eyes through His Word to His life, truth, and forgiveness. When Christ comes again on the Last Day, your eyes will be opened once again and your lifeless body will be raised. You will see God face-to-face.

An amazing paradox: the blind see and the seeing become blind. The blind man receives both physical and spiritual sight while the Pharisees refuse to see what is clearly revealed. By their rejection, they become spiritually blind. Ultimately, this spiritual sight was the greatest work that Christ worked in the blind man, and there is no greater work that God has accomplished in our lives than when by His grace He made us, who were spiritually blind, see.

2 JUNE

Psalmody: Psalm 9:3–6, 13–14
Additional Psalm: Psalm 23
Old Testament Reading: Ecclesiastes 10:1–20
New Testament Reading: John 10:1–21

Prayer of the Day

Almighty God, merciful Father, since You have wakened from death the Shepherd of Your sheep, grant us Your Holy Spirit that when we hear the voice of our Shepherd we may know Him who calls us each by name and follow where He leads; through the same Jesus Christ, Your Son, our Lord, who lives and reigns with You and the Holy Spirit, one God, now and forever. (L43)

Meditation

Too familiar, overused, trite. These are some criticisms that people sometimes say about the imagery of Jesus, the Good Shepherd. They believe that this metaphor has been discussed so often, is focused on so many times, and is read at so many funerals that it has lost its meaning and significance.

But it's just the opposite. The imagery of Jesus the Good Shepherd hasn't become overused and too familiar for believers. It's used because this metaphor is filled with incredible comfort and strength for God's people. No husband would ever be rebuked as being trite for overusing the expression "I love you," if he said it every day to his wife. And when Jesus says, "I am the good shepherd," it is a message of love and care; He wants us to be constantly reminded of this.

Jesus is close to us. He knows us, His sheep, and He calls us by name. Jesus is also the door, the means by which we have entered into eternal life. Our Lord's love for us, His sheep, is so intense that He lays down His life to save us. It is an act that no hired hand would do. Jesus continues to seek and find additional sheep, uniting all believers as one flock under one shepherd.

Jesus calls us by name. Yet we sheep are tempted to listen to the voices of strangers who tell us that the Good Shepherd is not the only door that leads to life, but there are many gates leading to glory. Other strange voices deceitfully proclaim that the Good Shepherd's abundant life means that we will always be healthy, wealthy, and wise. We are led to believe that we can enter the sheepfold by climbing over the wall through our own good works rather than entering through the one gate, Christ. We easily wander and become lost; we are easy prey for our spiritual predators.

Despite our sheepish stupidity, Jesus is and remains our Good Shepherd. He, who laid down His life for us, forgives our sin. He calls us by name and draws us to Himself. He gathers us into His sheepfold, the Church. He leads us into green pastures and feeds us with His Word and Sacraments, and He will lead us into eternity, where we will dwell in the house of the Lord forever.

3 JUNE

Psalmody: Psalm 77:5–11, 14–15
Additional Psalm: Psalm 82
Old Testament Reading: Ecclesiastes 11:1–10
New Testament Reading: John 10:22–42

Prayer of the Day

Almighty and ever-living God, You fulfilled Your promise by sending the gift of the Holy Spirit to unite disciples of all nations in the cross and resurrection of Your Son, Jesus Christ. By the preaching of the Gospel spread this gift to the ends of the earth; through the same Jesus Christ, our Lord, who lives and reigns with You and the Holy Spirit, one God, now and forever. (L49)

Meditation

"If You are the Christ, tell us plainly." You should always be careful about what you ask for. Those gathered at the temple during Hanukkah demanded that Jesus confess who He truly was. They asked and they received: "I and the Father are one."

Although the crowd was ready to stone Jesus for blasphemy, His words should fill our hearts with great joy and move us to deepest reverence and devotion. If Jesus is not one with the Father, then He is not our Savior. If He is inferior to the Father, then His death on the cross did not atone for our sins. If Jesus

is not true God, then we have no hope for salvation.

Just as these words proved to be a stumbling block to the Jews that day, so Jesus' words continue to be a stumbling block to many today. False teachers and false churches make the claim that Jesus is not true God, that He is not one with the Father, and that He is at most "a" god. It's true that we cannot wrap our finite minds around the fact that Jesus is true God. How can God take on human flesh? How can God be lying in a manger? How can God suffer? How can God die?

But Jesus Christ, true God and true man, has done all these things. He does the Father's work because He is one with the Father. The good works He does further reveals that He is in the Father and the Father is in Him.

Because Jesus is one with the Father, He is the Good Shepherd who, by His grace, has made us part of His flock. No mere man or angel, no matter how powerful, could do this. As true God, He speaks, and His sheep hear His voice. Through the power of His Word, they follow Him. Because Jesus is true God, He gives eternal life, a gift only God could bestow. Because Jesus is one with the Father, no one can snatch any of those who belong to Him out of His hand, for He has chosen them, called them, and given them the gift of faith.

Jesus plainly tells us today who He is: "I and the Father are one." And because He has spoken plainly about Himself, we know who we are: His beloved sheep, those He knows by name and who follow Him, recipients of eternal life, and His chosen people whom He holds in the palm of His hand.

4 JUNE

Psalmody: Psalm 61
Additional Psalm: Psalm 27
Old Testament Reading: Ecclesiastes 12:1–14
New Testament Reading: John 11:1–16

Prayer of the Day

Almighty God, by Your great goodness mercifully look upon Your people that we may be governed and preserved evermore in body and soul; through Jesus Christ, Your Son, our Lord, who lives and reigns with You and the Holy Spirit, one God, now and forever. (L27)

Meditation

Jesus loves Lazarus. He loves Lazarus's sisters, Mary and Martha. They send word to Him: "Lord, he whom You love is ill." Instead of going to the family, Jesus, who loves them all, stays put. He doesn't immediately set out for Bethany; He remains where He is for two more days. When Jesus finally does arrive in Bethany, Martha's frustration is obvious, "Lord, if You had been here, my brother would not have died" (John 11:21). It is like she is saying, "Jesus, if You really loved us, You would have come right away."

Such is the devil's temptation. He loves to make us think, "Jesus, if You really loved me, You wouldn't have taken my loved one from me." "Jesus, if You truly cared, then I wouldn't be so sick." "Jesus, if You are always there for me, why am I feeling so lonely?"

Jesus loves Lazarus, and He loves Mary and Martha; that's why He waits. Although hard to comprehend, Jesus' inaction is the best action. Jesus knows what is going to happen—Lazarus will be raised from the dead, and the result of this miracle will be that Jesus will be glorified and many more will believe that He is the Son of God.

Because Jesus loves you, He often waits. He doesn't answer your prayer in the way or the time that you had hoped. He unexpectedly calls someone you love to her heavenly home. In the midst of trial, He appears to be slow to help or deliver. When this occurs, doubts arise, faith is shaken, and the believer might begin to question Christ's love.

"Be strong, and let your heart take courage; wait for the LORD!" (Psalm 27:14b). Waiting for the Lord is not easy. It wasn't easy for Mary and Martha, and it's not easy today. But our Lord will act, and it will be in the best way and in the best time. When He acts, He will bring glory to Himself, and when He acts on your behalf, it is always in love. Unlike Mary and Martha, He won't raise your loved one from the dead after four days in the grave, but Jesus, the resurrection and the life, will give you comfort and peace as you grieve. He may not heal your sickness or take away your cancer, but He will strengthen your faith through suffering and even use it as a witness to others. Because He loves you, your Lord will always do what is best for you.

5 JUNE

Boniface of Mainz, Missionary to the Germans

Psalmody: Psalm 72:12–19
Additional Psalm: Psalm 63
Old Testament Reading: Proverbs 1:8–33
New Testament Reading: John 11:17–37

Prayer of the Day

Almighty God, You called Boniface to be a witness and martyr in Germany, and by his labor and suffering You raised up a people for Your own possession. Pour out Your Holy Spirit upon Your Church in every land, that by the service and sacrifice of many Your holy Name may be glorified and Your kingdom enlarged; through Jesus Christ, our Lord, who lives and reigns with You and the Holy Spirit, one God, now and forever. Amen. (1035)

Boniface of Mainz

Boniface was born in the late seventh century in England. Though he was educated, became a monk, and was ordained as a presbyter in England, he was inspired by the example of others to become a missionary. Upon receiving a papal commission in 719 to work in Germany, Boniface devoted himself to planting, organizing, and reforming churches and monasteries in Hesse, Thuringia, and Bavaria. After becoming an archbishop, Boniface was assigned to the See of Mainz in 743. Ten years later, he resigned his position to engage in mission work in the Netherlands. On June 5, 754, while awaiting a group of converts for confirmation, Boniface and his companions were murdered by a band of pagans. Boniface is known as the apostle and missionary to the Germans.

Meditation

Jesus wept. It seemed strange to the grieving family and friends. They respond by saying: "Could not He who opened the eyes of the blind man also kept this man from dying?" (John 11:37). If Lazarus's death would make Jesus cry, why didn't He keep Lazarus from dying?

Jesus wept. It seems strange to us as well. Jesus purposely remained where He was for two days instead of going to Bethany. When He decided to make the journey to Bethany, Jesus told His disciples: "Our friend Lazarus has fallen asleep, but I go to awaken him" (John 11:11). Jesus knew what He was going to do in Bethany. He knew Lazarus had died. He knew He would raise him from the dead. He knew that through this miracle, many would believe in Him.

But Jesus wept. Jesus did not weep because Lazarus had died. He did not weep because He felt helpless. He did not weep because He was weak. Instead, He wept for Mary and Martha, their family and friends.

Jesus is the resurrection and the life. The one who believes in Jesus will live even though he dies, and the believer shall never experience eternal death. He who conquered death and the grave by His own death and resurrection gives life to all who believe now and also at the resurrection on the Last Day.

Jesus wept. And Jesus still weeps. As true man, He sympathizes with our weaknesses (Hebrews 4:15). In the Body of Christ, we rejoice with those who rejoice, and we weep with those who weep (Romans 12:15). And what is true of the body, is also true of Christ, the head of the Body. When a loved one dies, we can be certain that Jesus, the resurrection and the life, has given eternal life to our loved one who died in the faith. We can be confident the one we love will be raised again on the Last Day. We have that sure and certain hope, and yet we weep. We feel empty and lonely. Tears freely flow.

Jesus weeps too. He weeps for us. Even as He gives life to all who have departed in the faith, He weeps with those who continue their earthly pilgrimage. He not only weeps, but He also comforts, reminding us that He is the resurrection and the life, and by His word of promise, He strengthens us as we mourn.

6 JUNE

Psalmody: Psalm 119:169–176
Additional Psalm: Psalm 89:46–52
Old Testament Reading: Proverbs 3:5–24
New Testament Reading: John 11:38–57

Prayer of the Day

Heavenly Father, Your beloved Son befriended frail humans like us to make us Your own. Teach us to be like Jesus' dear friends from Bethany, that we might serve Him faithfully like Martha, learn from Him earnestly like Mary, and be raised by Him ultimately like Lazarus; through their Lord and ours, Jesus Christ, who lives and reigns with You and the Holy Spirit, one God, now and forever. (1036)

Meditation

Jesus reveals that He is the Son of God by raising Lazarus from the dead. Many believe in Him; others harden their hearts even more. They know the miracle happened; they know no mere man could raise to life a stinking and decaying body that had been in the tomb for four days, but this miracle only intensifies their desire to put Jesus to death. They fear the growing popularity of Jesus will ultimately result in the destruction of both the temple and Jerusalem. Their passion to destroy Jesus ultimately motivates them to begin plotting how they can also kill Lazarus (John 12:9–11).

Despite this miracle, the chief priests and Pharisees refuse to believe in Jesus and want Him eliminated. Their rejection of Christ motivates them to attempt to murder Lazarus as well.

Many today have hardened their hearts to the truth. The Scriptures bear witness to who Jesus is; over 500 people saw Him after He was raised from the dead, and other historical records and archaeological evidence validates the testimony of Scripture. Yet they refuse to believe. Their attitude is, "Don't confuse me with the facts!" Not only are there many who refuse to believe, there are some, such as the religious leaders, who vehemently seek to destroy Jesus. They hate Christ. They want His name and His Gospel not to be proclaimed outside of or inside the Church. And their hatred is directed to both Christ and His followers. The only reason they wanted Lazarus to die was because of his association with Christ. Today, Christians are ridiculed, slandered, impoverished, arrested, and even put to death for their connection to Christ. Because the world hates Christ, they hate those who belong to Him.

Despite his unbelief, God still speaks through His high priest. Caiaphas, not fully understanding what he was saying, had prophesied "Jesus would die for the nation, and not for the nation only, but also to gather into one the children of God who are scattered abroad" (John 11:51–52). Through the wicked scheme devised by Caiaphas and the other religious leaders, Christ did just that. He died for the nation and for all people. By His death and resurrection, He has gathered into one all the children of God, making them children of the heavenly Father through the waters of Holy Baptism. One did die for all, and because He died, though we might face ridicule and persecution for confessing Christ, we will not perish.

7 JUNE

Psalmody: Psalm 119:9–16
Additional Psalm: Psalm 118:22–29
Old Testament Reading: Proverbs 4:1–27
New Testament Reading: John 12:1–19

Prayer of the Day

Almighty God, grant that in the midst of our failures and weaknesses we may be restored through the passion and intercession of Your only-begotten Son, who lives and reigns with You and the Holy Spirit, one God, now and forever. (L29)

Meditation

In the Old Testament, anointing was the means by which prophets, priests, and kings were set apart for their special work. At Bethany, Mary anointed Jesus in her home. But this anointing was unusual. First, the perfume was expensive; it cost nearly a year's wages of a common worker. Second, she anointed Christ's feet and not His head, wiping His feet with her hair. Although this was an anointing much different that the anointing that occurred in the Old Testament, her actions revealed that she believed Jesus, who had raised her brother from the dead, was the Christ.

The next day, Jesus was welcomed into Jerusalem as a king. What Mary had confessed with oil, the crowds confess with palm branches. Their lips acknowledge that Jesus is king: "Hosanna! Blessed is He who comes in the name of the Lord, even the King of Israel!"

But there are those who object. Judas, in words that sound as pious as Mary's actions, argues that it would have been better for the perfume to be sold and the money given to the poor. On Palm Sunday, when the Pharisees see the crowd welcoming Jesus and receiving Him as king, they are discouraged and troubled by His multitude of followers.

Jesus is the Christ, the Anointed One. Although revered by Mary and the Palm Sunday pilgrims, He enters Jerusalem to die. The oil would prepare Jesus' body for burial six days later. The crowd's hosannas, a prayer for help and salvation, would be answered when Jesus was glorified by His death on the cross. On the cross, Jesus died for our sins of greed. He atoned for those times when our pious words and actions veil our sinful thoughts and intentions. He paid the price for the times when our hosannas of praise have been lacking. He gave His life for those times when we cower in fear rather than confess and praise Him.

The disciples did not understand these events. Later, it would all make sense to them. Mary's anointing, Judas' response, the palm branches, the young donkey, and the shouts of the crowd all occurred to fulfill prophecy and bring about the salvation of the world. We also, by God's grace, understand the significance of these events, and thus, when our glorified Savior comes to us with His body and blood in the Lord's Supper, we join with the Palm Sunday crowd in exclaiming: "Hosanna! Blessed is He who comes in the name of the Lord!"

8 JUNE

Psalmody: Psalm 36:7–12
Additional Psalm: Psalm 44:1–8
Old Testament Reading: Proverbs 5:1–23
Additional Reading: Proverbs 6:1–7:27
New Testament Reading: John 12:20–36a

Prayer of the Day

Merciful God, Your Son, Jesus Christ, was lifted high upon the cross that He might bear the sins of the world and draw all people to Himself. Grant that we who glory in His death for our redemption may faithfully heed His call to bear the cross and follow Him, who lives and reigns with You and the Holy Spirit, one God, now and forever. (F27)

Meditation

The hour has come. Jesus' hour had not come when He changed the water into wine (John 2:4) or when the religious leaders tried to arrest Him on two different occasions (John 7:30; 8:20). But now is the hour of His glorification, and He will be glorified through His death. Just as the grain of wheat must fall into the earth and die to bear fruit, so

Jesus must die in order to bear the fruits of salvation and life. The hour has come for the Son of Man to be glorified. The Father affirms this by speaking from heaven. The Father had glorified His Son through the signs and miracles, and He will glorify His Son again by Christ's death and resurrection.

The hour has come. "Now is the judgment of this world; now will the ruler of the world be cast out" (John 12:31). Not only has the hour come for Christ to be glorified as He is lifted upon the tree of the cross, but now is also the time for judgment. The cross appears to be the devil's greatest feat—darkness overtakes the light, evil overcomes good, and death suffocates life. Instead, the cross is Jesus' greatest victory. When Jesus breathes His last, the devil is cast out, the unbelieving world is judged, and at the cross Jesus gathers His people in every time and age to Himself.

Your hour has come. At the cross, Jesus gathered you to Himself. It was for your sin that He died. He offered His life in order to gather you into the family of His Father, the Church. This is what occurred at your Baptism. You became a child of God and a member of God's eternal family because on your Baptism day, you were crucified with Christ. You died with Him. Your unbelief, your doubts, your sin—it's all nailed to the cross of Christ. Since you are baptized, you have died with Christ.

But that's not the end of the story, for the hour of your glorification has come. You were glorified through your baptismal death, for you have not only been baptized into Christ's death but also into His resurrection. His death is your death, and His life is your life. You are the grain of wheat that has fallen to the ground and died, so that, raised with Christ, you now produce abundant fruit. And as one already raised to new life with Christ in Baptism, you can be certain that you will live forever with Him.

9 June

Psalmody: Psalm 77:10–15
Additional Psalm: Psalm 106
Old Testament Reading: Proverbs 8:1–21
New Testament Reading: John 12:36b–50

Prayer of the Day

Almighty God, grant that the birth of Your only-begotten Son in the flesh may set us free from the bondage of sin; through Jesus Christ, Your Son, our Lord, who lives and reigns with You and the Holy Spirit, one God, now and forever. (L08)

Meditation

Despite the signs, many refused to believe in Jesus. In the end, God hardened their hearts. Their unbelief fulfilled Isaiah's prophecy. But there were others, even some of the religious authorities, who did believe in Jesus, who saw the signs and heard Him preach and were convinced that Jesus was the Christ. Although they believed in their hearts, they refused to confess it with their mouths because they feared excommunication from the synagogue and scorn from their peers.

Although we are not numbered among those who have hardened their hearts to the saving Gospel, we can clearly identify ourselves as those who, loving the glory of men more than the glory of God, are too often afraid to confess Christ. We fear for our job, so we don't talk about Christ at work. We fear what will happen if we confront a friend who has fallen into sin, so we say nothing. We fear that there will be friction in the family if we talk to a family member who no longer attends church, so we're silent.

Despite our unwillingness to confess Christ, Jesus is still our Savior. He came not to save just a few people; He announces that He came to save the world (John 11:47). He is our advocate before the Father even when we are reluctant to speak of Him before others. His forgiving embrace covers all of our sins, even when we seek glory from others rather than from God. The Holy Spirit motivates us to confess Christ, regardless of the cost.

This is true of two of the religious authorities who believed in Jesus but were afraid to acknowledge Him before others. After Jesus died, Joseph of Arimathea, a member of the Council, asked Pilate for permission to bury the body of Jesus. He was assisted by Nicodemus, another member of the Sanhedrin, who had earlier spoken with Jesus at night. Although previously afraid to confess Christ, after His death, they were not afraid if others discovered their allegiance to Jesus.

The same Spirit that empowered Joseph and Nicodemus also empowers us to confess Christ, even if doing so may result in ridicule and rejection by family and friends. He removes our fears and He works through us so that we speak the truth in love. By confessing Christ, regardless of the outcome, we bring glory to God.

10 JUNE

Psalmody: Psalm 116:12–19
Additional Psalm: Psalm 132
Old Testament Reading: Proverbs 8:22–36
New Testament Reading: John 13:1–20

Prayer of the Day

Almighty and everlasting God, grant us by Your grace so to pass through this holy time of our Lord's passion that we may obtain the forgiveness of our sins; through Jesus Christ, Your Son, our Lord, who lives and reigns with You and the Holy Spirit, one God, now and forever. (L30)

Meditation

The disciples couldn't believe it. In the middle of supper, Jesus shed His outer garments and washed their feet. Although they respect their teacher, they would never have offered to do this for Him. This was menial labor, a task reserved for the lowest of slaves. Peter believed Christ's actions were so demeaning that He attempted to stop Jesus from washing his feet.

What the disciples viewed as demeaning and humiliating, Jesus saw as an opportunity to serve. True greatness is not being served; it's serving. True greatness is not found in considering yourself above others; it's sacrificially placing the needs of others before your own. True greatness is not arrogantly regarding yourself as too important or influential to help others; instead, true greatness is being the servant of all.

This lesson was not easy for the disciples to take to heart. Their world was one where the "haves" looked down on the "have-nots," where different social classes were clearly distinguished. Even among themselves, they had argued a number of times as to who was the greatest, including that night in the Upper Room (Luke 22:24). They desired honor and superiority, not humility and service.

We covet greatness and glory too. We invent countless excuses as to why we cannot serve. We exclude certain people from our love and concern. We think others are beneath us and certain tasks are too demeaning.

But not Jesus. He washed His disciples' feet, and He gave the example that they should follow. Thankfully, His humility and service did not stop in the Upper Room. The washing of the disciples' feet foreshadowed the ultimate act of sacrifice and service. The cross reveals that no act of love is too demeaning or humiliating for our Lord. He, who came to this world not to be served but to serve, served us and all humanity when He was lifted up on the cross. On the cross, Jesus wasn't just washing feet; He was cleansing us from all sin, even the sins of selfishness, prejudice, and pride. His desire to serve motivated Him to offer everything, including His own life.

Jesus' service to us didn't stop on Good Friday. As our risen and exalted Savior, He comes to serve us through the meal He instituted in the Upper Room, feeding us with His body and blood for the forgiveness of our sins. He serves us as He speaks His words of eternal life to us, and He serves as our mediator, offering our supplications before the throne of His Father.

11 JUNE

St. Barnabas, Apostle

Psalmody: Psalm 34:12–22
Additional Psalm: Psalm 109
Old Testament Reading: Proverbs 9:1–18
New Testament Reading: John 13:21–38

Prayer of the Day

Almighty God, Your faithful servant Barnabas sought not his own renown but gave generously of his life and substance for the encouragement of the apostles and their ministry. Grant that we may follow his example in lives given to charity and the proclamation of the Gospel; through Your Son, Jesus Christ, our Lord, who lives and reigns with You and the Holy Spirit, one God, now and forever. (F19)

Barnabas, Apostle

St. Barnabas was a Levite from Cyprus who sold some land and gave the proceeds to the early Christian community in Jerusalem (Acts 4:36–37). St. Paul informs us that he was a cousin of John Mark (Colossians 4:10).

Barnabas was sent by the Jerusalem Church to oversee the young Church in Antioch (Acts 11:22). While there he went to Tarsus and brought Paul back to Antioch to help him (11:25–26). It was this Church in Antioch that commissioned and sent Barnabas and Paul on the first missionary journey (13:2–3). When it was time for the second missionary journey, however, Barnabas and Paul got into a dispute over taking along John Mark. Barnabas took Mark and went to Cyprus; Paul took Silas and headed north through Syria and Cilicia (15:36–41). Nothing more is known of the activities of Barnabas, except that he was apparently known to the Corinthians (1 Corinthians 9:6). Tradition relates that Barnabas died a martyr's death in Cyprus by being stoned.

Meditation

It was the hour of darkness. Knowing what lies ahead, Jesus is troubled in spirit. He gives the morsel of bread to Judas, and Judas takes it and leaves to carry out the works of darkness. Peter boasts that his dedication of Christ is so great that he is willing to die for Him, but he speaks empty words. He will deny his Lord three times before the rooster crows.

And it was night. The powers of darkness were seeking to overcome the Light. Satan enters Judas to betray Jesus. By the next night, Jesus' lifeless body will be in the tomb. Where Jesus is going, the disciples cannot come. Jesus must contend with the powers of darkness alone. He must walk the way of suffering by Himself.

And it was night. The powers of darkness tempted Judas to betray Jesus and Peter to deny Him. The powers of darkness tempted the religious leaders to ask for Jesus' death and for the crowds to cry out, "Crucify Him!" As Jesus was crucified, an eerie and unexplainable darkness covered the land for three hours. And it was night. The powers of darkness seek to tempt us also. Their goal is for us to betray, deny, and turn away from our Lord. Darkness enters our lives through the death of loved ones, sickness, and other crosses we must bear in this life. As on Good Friday, it may appear that darkness will prevail. We sense that our faith is weak. We struggle to understand. We feel that God has forsaken us. It is as if the light of trust and hope is about to be snuffed out.

"In Him was life, and the life was the light of men. The light shines in the darkness, and the darkness has not overcome it" (John 1:4–5). It was night, but the darkness could never overcome Jesus, the Light of the world. Jesus took on the forces of darkness, and He overcame them, triumphing over them by the cross. Through His victory, we have been delivered from the dominion of darkness and brought into His kingdom. The light of Christ has shone upon our hearts, chasing away the darkness of sin, death, and the power of the devil. It is this light that shines on us that we now offer to a world in bondage to darkness. It is this light that motivates us to love others as Christ has loved us.

12 JUNE

The Ecumenical Council of Nicaea, AD 325

Psalmody: Psalm 37:1–7
Additional Psalm: Psalm 101
Old Testament Reading: Proverbs 10:1–23
Additional Reading: Proverbs 11:1–12:28
New Testament Reading: John 14:1–17

Prayer of the Day

Lord God, heavenly Father, at the first ecumenical council of Nicaea Your Church boldly confessed that it believed in one Lord Jesus Christ as being of one substance with the Father. Grant us courage to confess this saving faith with Your Church through all the ages; through Jesus Christ, our Lord. (1037)

The Ecumenical Council of Nicaea, AD 325

The first Council of Nicaea was convened in the early summer of 325 by the Roman Emperor Constantine at what is today Iznik, Turkey. The emperor presided at the opening of the council. The council ruled against the Arians, who taught that Jesus was not the eternal Son of God but was created by the Father and was called Son of God because of His righteousness. The chief opponents of the Arians were Alexander, bishop of Alexandria, and his deacon, Athanasius. The council confessed the eternal divinity of Jesus and adopted the earliest version of the Nicene Creed, which in its entirety was adopted at the Council of Constantinople in 381.

Meditation

"No one comes to the Father except through Me" (John 14:6b). Our politically correct world cannot tolerate such a claim. They contend that there must be many paths to glory, that truth is found in all religions, and that eternal life can be obtained through any number of belief systems.

Jesus is the way, the only way. These words of Jesus and this confession by the early Christians placed believers in opposition to both the Jews who had rejected Christ and the Gentiles who worshiped a plethora of gods. For all those who claim that there are many ways to paradise, all the other so-called ways are ultimately the way of works and self-centered individualism: Do your best. Live a good life. Try your hardest. Follow these principles. Obey these commandments. No matter what the religion or belief system is called, if it's not Christianity, the way to eternity is always focused on what the individual does or does not do.

And that's why Christ is the only way. Trying your hardest is never good enough. Even your good works are tainted by sin. That's why adherents of false religions are never certain if they have done enough to be saved. But you know that what you could never do, Christ has done for you. He lived the perfect life. He walked the way of the cross, and by His death and resurrection has opened the way for you to the Father.

Jesus is the truth. Some claim every religion has truth. Others go to the opposite extreme and say there is no such thing as absolute truth. There is truth, and Jesus embodies that truth. He can be completely trusted, for His words are truth. When He promises that He is preparing a place for you in the Father's house, you can be certain that there is a place waiting for you there. When He promises you the gift of the Holy Spirit, you can be certain that His Spirit dwells in you.

Jesus is the life. If Christ is the way, He must also be the life. Not only does He make this claim, He reveals its validity. Christ is your life, because He rose again on the third day. Death has no power over Him. And because He lives, you will live also. Because He lives, you will see the Father. Because He lives, you will dwell in the place of life and light prepared for you by Christ Himself.

13 June

Psalmody: Psalm 68:32–35
Additional Psalm: Psalm 85
Old Testament Reading: Proverbs 13:1–25
New Testament Reading: John 14:18–31

Prayer of the Day

O God, the giver of all that is good, by Your holy inspiration grant that we may think those things that are right and by Your merciful guiding accomplish them; through Jesus Christ, Your Son, our Lord, who lives and reigns with You and the Holy Spirit, one God, now and forever. (L46)

Meditation

Orphanages are heart wrenching. There are scores of children waiting for someone to love them, someone to welcome them into their home. Then there are other orphans, often older, who have all but given up any hope of ever being adopted.

The Church is not an orphanage. It's true that Christ did go away. He died, He rose, and He ascended into heaven. However, though we cannot see Him, that doesn't mean He's gone for good. He gives the promises that He dwells in us. We enjoy an intimate relationship with Him; He is with us always. Where two or three come together in His name, He is there to bless. He feeds us with His own body and blood to sustain and strengthen us in the faith until we see Him when He comes again in glory on the Last Day.

We are not orphans. The Father has sent the Holy Spirit in the Son's name. The Spirit is the Helper who teaches us all things. The Spirit leads us to remember all that Jesus has said and done, so we are centered and focused on Him.

We are not orphans, for Christ gives us His peace. His is a peace found nowhere else; no earthly peace can imitate it. It is a peace that comes from sin forgiven, a peace that is ours since we have been reconciled to the Father through His blood. It is a peace that calms our troubles and takes away our fears.

We are not orphans, yet we often act as though we are. It appears as though we believe that Christ is as far from us as the heavens are from the earth. We forget that Christ and His Spirit dwell within us. We spurn the presence of Christ and the gifts that He gives to us in the Divine Service. In times of need, we neglect the Sprit-filled words of Scripture, words that are given to comfort and encourage us. We allow our fears to get the best of us rather than clinging to the peace that Christ gives.

Despite our sin and our slowness of heart to believe, Christ refuses to abandon us. He does not sever the relationship but preserves it. He continues to come to us, dwell in us, and give us His peace. His Spirit continues to teach us all truth and to help us in our time of need.

14 JUNE

Elisha

Psalmody: Psalm 66:1–8
Additional Psalm: Psalm 66
Old Testament Reading: Proverbs 14:1–27
New Testament Reading: John 15:1–11

Prayer of the Day

Lord God, heavenly Father, through the prophet Elisha, You continued the prophetic pattern of teaching Your people the true faith and demonstrating through miracles Your presence in the creation to heal it of its brokenness. Grant that Your church may see in Your Son, our Lord Jesus Christ, the final end-times prophet whose teaching and miracles continue in Your Church through the healing medicine of the Gospel and the Sacraments; through Jesus Christ our Lord. (1038)

Elisha

Elisha, son of Shaphat of the tribe of Issachar, was the prophet of God to the Northern Kingdom of Israel ca. 849–786 BC. Upon seeing his mentor, Elijah, taken up into heaven, Elisha assumed the prophetic office and took up the mantle of his predecessor. Like Elijah, Elisha played an active role in political affairs. He also performed many miracles, such as curing the Syrian army commander Naaman of his leprosy (2 Kings 5)

and restoring life to the son of a Shunammite woman (2 Kings 4:8–37). A vocal opponent of Baal worship, Elisha lived up to his name, which means "my God is salvation."

Meditation

Jesus is the vine, and we are the branches. What a comforting illustration. We are connected to Christ. He is our source of life. Without Him we are dead and can do nothing, but connected to Him in faith, we are alive. We abide in Him, and we bear fruit.

Jesus is the vine, we are the branches, and the Father is the vinedresser. As the vinedresser, the Father cuts off those branches that bear no fruit, and those that bear fruit, He prunes so that they are even more fruitful. That's what the Father does—He either cuts off the dead branches, or He prunes the living branches. This metaphor may not seem so comforting to you anymore. After all, who wants to get pruned? Who wants to have our undying and unfruitful parts severed? If a grapevine could talk, it would not describe the process of having many of its branches clipped and shortened as joyful and comforting.

The Father prunes, and like a grapevine, we need pruning. This pruning process occurs through trials and adversity. To be pruned is painful; it hurts. We may be tempted to believe that if the Father truly loved us, He would not allow us to be pruned at all. In the midst of pruning, we may not understand how the trials and difficulties we are experiencing could ever be a blessing to us. We may think that the Father is attempting to destroy us.

However, this is not the case. Since the Father loves us, He prunes us. Although pruning hurts, it is necessary. The grapevine that isn't pruned will produce less fruit and eventually may not produce any fruit at all. Through pruning by trial and tribulation, we are led to see our absolute dependence upon our heavenly Father and are drawn to cling to Him in faith all the more. Through pruning, we are moved to repentance. Having confessed our sin, we are cleansed, and through the cleansing power of forgiveness, our connection to Christ, the true vine, is strengthened.

What is the result of this pruning? More fruit. Although pruning is never pleasant, in the end we are all the stronger for it. Through pruning, we abide in Christ and in His word and His love. Connected to the life that Christ gives, and routinely pruned by the Father, we produce fruit, abundant fruit through which the Father is glorified.

15 JUNE

Psalmody: Psalm 51:1–12
Additional Psalm: Psalm 10
Old Testament Reading: Proverbs 15:1–29
New Testament Reading: John 15:12–27

Prayer of the Day

O God, the giver of all that is good, by Your holy inspiration grant that we may think those things that are right and by Your merciful guiding accomplish them; through Jesus Christ, Your Son, our Lord, who lives and reigns with You and the Holy Spirit, one God, now and forever. (L46)

Meditation

Christ loves you. You can be certain of His love because He laid down His life for you. You are more than a servant; you are His friend. All that He has received from the Father He has made known to you. You did not initiate this relationship with Him; in love He chose you to be His own.

Since Christ loves you, you are to love others. Christ's love is the model for your love—unconditional, sacrificial, and selfless.

He loves you and now you love others. He chose you, and now you bear the fruit of love. Even when your love is lacking, when you selfishly turn in on yourself instead of reaching out in love to others, His love remains constant. He loves and He forgives, and this empowers you to love.

Just as you can be certain of Christ's love for you, you can also be confident of the world's hatred. The world hated Jesus; the world hates you. The world persecuted Christ; the world will persecute those who belong to Him. Believers are put to death every day because of their love for Jesus. The Christian who witnesses is labeled a religious fanatic. The follower of Jesus who speaks the truth in love is accused of trying to force her beliefs on everybody else.

You should not be surprised that the world hates you and all who confess Christ. It has been and will continue to be that way until Christ returns. But how do you respond to the hatred of the world? Love. Yes, love. In love, Jesus didn't just die for His friends; He died for His enemies (Romans 5:10). In fact, from the cross He prayed for His enemies.

Jesus loves. He loves those who hate Him, even those who persecute those who belong to Him. Jesus loves sinners, even a sinner like you. Because He loves you, He has chosen you as His own and calls you His friend despite your sin. And He who loves you, empowers you to love—to love those who love Jesus as you do and to also love those who hate Jesus. This is no easy command from the author of love. On your own, it's impossible. But you are not acting on your own. With the gift of the Holy Spirit and filled with the love of Christ, you now love as you have been loved.

16 JUNE

Psalmody: Psalm 147:1–11
Additional Psalm: Psalm 147
Old Testament Reading: Proverbs 16:1–24
New Testament Reading: John 16:1–16

Prayer of the Day

O God, You make the minds of Your faithful to be of one will. Grant that we may love what You have commanded and desire what You promise, that among the many changes of this world our hearts may be fixed where true joys are found; through Jesus Christ, Your Son, our Lord, who lives and reigns with You and the Holy Spirit, one God, now and forever. (L45)

Meditation

Jesus must go away. He must return to the Father. This should not move the disciples to sorrow and tears because it is for their benefit that Christ is returning to the Father. When Christ departs, the Sprit will be sent to them.

Jesus declares what the Spirit will do. He will convict the world of sin, righteousness, and judgment. The Spirit's work begins with convicting the world of sin. If a person does not recognize his sin, he will see no need for a Savior. If the Spirit does not hold up the mirror of the Law for us to see how we are held in bondage to sin and are unable to free ourselves, we will never be drawn to Christ. If the Spirit does not convict us our transgressions, we will never seek Christ's mercy and salvation. But the Spirit does convict us of sin. He convinces us that we cannot save ourselves.

Then the Spirit convinces the world of righteousness. This righteousness is not our own righteousness, for we are unrighteous. All our righteous acts are like filthy rags (Isaiah 64:6). Instead, that Spirit seeks to convince the world of Christ's righteousness. He seeks to reveal that Christ alone is righteous, that He is the only answer for our sin, and that He has perfectly fulfilled the Law in our place and thus is our substitute. Even as the Spirit convicts us of sin, He convinces us of who Christ is—the Righteous One who atoned for our iniquities.

And the Spirit convicts the world of judgment. However, the judgment here is not the judgment on the Last Day when Christ comes again. It's the judgment of the ruler of this world, the devil. The devil has been overcome; Christ has triumphed over Him by His death on the cross. He is condemned. One little word can fell him. Thus, those who reject Christ are condemned, for they are following the ruler of this world who has already been judged and condemned.

Jesus did go away and He did send the Spirit as He promised. Now the Spirit of truth leads us into all truth. He declares the truth that He has been given to speak. The Spirit has declared to us the truth about ourselves—we are sinners; the truth about Jesus—He is the righteous one; and the truth about the devil—he is judged and condemned.

17 JUNE

Psalmody: Psalm 107:1–9
Additional Psalm: Psalm 107
Old Testament Reading: Proverbs 17:1–28
Additional Reading: Proverbs 18:1–20:4
New Testament Reading: John 16:17–33

Prayer of the Day

O King of glory, Lord of hosts, uplifted in triumph far above all heavens, leave us not without consolation but send us the Spirit of truth whom You promised from the Father; for You live and reign with Him and the Holy Spirit, one God, now and forever. (L48)

Meditation

Jesus had much to say to His disciples in the Upper Room. He taught them about His imminent death and then His resurrection. He predicted Judas's betrayal and Peter's denial. He described the gift of the Spirit and how He would help the disciples. He said that His relationship with those who believe is like a vine to its branches. He spoke of the world's hatred and that He is the only way to the Father.

That's a lot to ponder. Yet when Jesus finishes His catechesis, the disciples claim they understand everything. They admit that they no longer need to ask Jesus any questions. What a boastful claim. Nearly two thousand years after Christ's death and resurrection, there are points of Jesus' Upper Room sermon that are still difficult to understand. But the disciples contend they have it all figured out. They know everything, no need for Jesus to keep talking, no need to ask Jesus any more questions.

We can fall prey to the same arrogance. The newly confirmed high schooler thinks he knows everything about the Scriptures and the doctrines of the Church and stops attending Bible classes. The young mother stops having daily devotions because she assumes there are more important tasks to do. The pastor announces the sermon on a familiar text and the church member zones out, assuming that he knows everything there is to know about this Scripture.

Even as the disciples boast about their great understanding, Jesus predicts that they will be scattered and desert Him. Jesus knows that they don't understand. He will die and they will be filled with sorrow. They will not remember His promise that He is only going to be gone a little while and then He will return to them. Instead of His peace, they will be troubled and afraid. They will doubt, and they will be slow to believe.

Like the disciples, it is unwise for us to boast about our spiritual knowledge or our unwavering faith. Boasting in ourselves is nothing more than sinful pride and results in our turning a deaf ear to Christ and His words. We think we know it all. We have it all figured out. Jesus, you don't need to teach us anymore.

Despite our sinful arrogance, Jesus goes to the cross. He overcomes the devil, and He overcomes the world. He blots out our iniquities, turns our sorrows into joy, and gives us His Holy Spirit who motivates us to hear the words of Christ and diligently search the Scriptures.

18 June

Psalmody: Psalm 86:9–17
Additional Psalm: Psalm 86
Old Testament Reading: Proverbs 20:5–25
Additional Reading: Proverbs 21:1–31
New Testament Reading: John 17:1–26

Prayer of the Day

O God, You make the minds of Your faithful to be of one will. Grant that we may love what You have commanded and desire what You promise, that among the many changes of this world our hearts may be fixed where true joys are found; through Jesus Christ, Your Son, our Lord, who lives and reigns with You and the Holy Spirit, one God, now and forever. (L45)

Meditation

Jesus prays that His Church be one as He and the Father are one. Yet this is not the case. Centuries after Christ's death and resurrection, Christians remain deeply divided. Churches act more like isolated islands rather than seeing themselves as one assembly of believers that comprise the Holy Christian Church on earth. Congregations increasingly keep more of their resources to serve their own members rather than supporting missionary work around the world. Fellow Christians view one another with distrust rather than as fellow brothers and sisters in Christ.

Often when unity is sought, the approach is misguided. Churches claim they are one even with serious theological differences. They agree to disagree. Unity is coerced by a powerful church hierarchy or through binding resolutions.

However, this is not the unity of which Jesus speaks. This is not the Church being one as the Father and the Son are one. True unity is always founded on the Word of God. It is not agreeing to disagree; it's not overlooking the truth so that churches can claim to be one when they really aren't. Instead, true unity is found as Christians confess the truths of Scripture together.

The result of this unity is that "the world may believe that You have sent Me" (John 17:21). True Christian unity gives a positive witness to the world. The Holy Spirit works faith through the Word, and Christians are united by and speak the word of truth to the unbelieving world. The Spirit is at work, working faith in the hearts of those who hear the Gospel.

By God's grace, you are a member of the one holy Christian and apostolic Church. You are united with every believer as one in every time and place. Sadly, serious divisions remain in the Church here on earth. Some of these divisions in church bodies and congregations are not founded on God's Word, but are petty disagreements or personality conflicts that are nothing more than temptations of the evil one to undermine the Gospel. However, there are legitimate divisions in the Church, when churches disagree on the truth of the Scripture. Our calling is not to pretend these divisions don't exist, but it is to speak the word of truth, to uncompromisingly hold to the infallible Word of God; it is only through this God-given means that Christian unity will be furthered. As we confess with one voice the one message, the world will hear and, by God's grace, be sanctified by the truth.

19 JUNE

Psalmody: Psalm 31:9–10, 14–19
Additional Psalm: Psalm 102
Old Testament Reading: Proverbs 22:1–21
New Testament Reading: John 18:1–14

Prayer of the Day

Almighty God, graciously behold this Your family for whom our Lord Jesus Christ was willing to be betrayed and delivered into the hands of sinful men to suffer death upon the cross; through the same Jesus Christ, Your Son, our Lord, who lives and reigns with You and the Holy Spirit, one God, now and forever. (L33)

Meditation

Yahweh—I Am Who I Am. This is the holy name of God as revealed to Moses. Moses was to tell the Israelites that "I AM has sent me to you" (Exodus 3:14). "I am" is how Jesus responds to the guards when they come to arrest Him. When He speaks these words, they immediately draw back and fall to the ground. They are in the presence of God Himself, and the powers of darkness are paralyzed before Him.

To the eye, it appears that Jesus is weak and defenseless. He is bound like a common criminal, but Jesus is not helpless as He is arrested, tried, and crucified. He knows exactly what will happen to Him (John 18:4). His power is such that simply by saying, "I am," the soldiers are not match for Him. Peter does not need to draw his sword and fight, for Jesus has all power and authority.

Although it seems as though the soldiers are the source of His pain and suffering, this is not the case. Ultimately, Christ suffers at His Father's hand. He drinks the cup the Father has given to Him. This cup is His Father's wrath and punishment over sin. He drinks the cup down to its very dregs. Although He has the power to overpower those who arrest Him, He allows Himself to be bound. He remains determined to fulfill the Father's will, and so He is led as a lamb to the slaughter.

Jesus is given the cup of wrath and suffering, and He drinks it. The Father desires His Son to drink this cup, but not because the Father is evil or punitive. He gives the cup to His Son because God is love. Jesus drinks the cup because God loves you.

This cup is rightly your cup. The wrath and punishment are rightly yours. You should be drinking it, not the perfect Son of God. But it is not given to you to drink. It is given to Jesus, and He drinks it for you.

Because Jesus drank the cup of God's wrath for you, you have been given another cup to drink—the cup of blessing—your Lord's blood given for you in the Lord's Supper. Because Christ drank the cup of wrath, He now gives you the cup that is filled with the blessings He won for you on the cross—filled to the brim with forgiveness, life, and salvation.

20 June

Psalmody: Psalm 45:6–12
Additional Psalm: Psalm 45
Old Testament Reading:
Proverbs 22:22–23:12
New Testament Reading: John 18:15–40

Prayer of the Day

Lord Jesus Christ, so govern our hearts and minds by Your Holy Spirit that, ever mindful of Your glorious return, we may persevere in both faith and holiness of living; for You live and reign with the Father and the Holy Spirit, one God, now and forever. (B87)

Meditation

What crime has Jesus committed? That's what Pilate wants to know. But even those accusing Jesus don't have an answer. They only assure Pilate that if Jesus had not done evil, they would not have brought Him to Pilate. Pilate must discern for Himself if Jesus deserves to die. Pilate asks Jesus if He is a king. A religious leader is no threat; he will not allow himself to be drawn into any religious controversy. But if Jesus is a political revolutionary and a threat to Roman rule, that's a different story.

Jesus affirms that He is a king, but Pilate has nothing to fear, for Christ's kingdom is not of this world. If it was, His followers would have fought for His release. Christ's kingdom knows no boundaries, no military, and no bureaucracy. Ultimately, Pilate doesn't see Jesus as a threat. He finds no guilt in Him. But the crowd doesn't want Him released. Instead, they demand freedom for the robber Barabbas.

Christ's kingdom is not of this world. His is not a kingdom founded on laws and statutes, but on grace and mercy. One is made a citizen of His kingdom by birth—by the birth of water and the Spirit in Baptism. Thus, Christ's kingdom knows no geographical borders, for it is found in the hearts of all believers; there Christ is reigning. As a citizen of this kingdom, Christ strengthens and blesses you through the Means of Grace, sustaining you in the faith until you dwell in the kingdom of glory.

Christ's kingdom is a kingdom founded on the truth. The religious leaders and Pilate rejected the truth that Jesus spoke, and, in so doing, rejected Christ who is the Truth. Those who belong to Christ have the truth, believe the truth, and bear witness to the truth. It is the truth that centers on the person and work of Christ. It is the truth about a King who by His death establishes an eternal kingdom. It is the truth about a king who is the servant of all. It is the truth revealed in the pages of Holy Scripture.

You, by God's grace, are a citizen of His kingdom. The truth has been revealed to you. Jesus, your crucified and glorified King, provides for all your needs of body and soul, protects and defends you, and promises to take you to be with Him in the kingdom of the Father.

21 JUNE

Psalmody: Psalm 22:22–27
Additional Psalm: Psalm 21
Old Testament Reading: Proverbs 24:1–22
New Testament Reading: John 19:1–22

Prayer of the Day

Lord Jesus, though ruthless Pontius Pilate declared Your innocence before the crowds, You who knew no sin became sin for us. May the shame You bore for us on the cross give us the greatest honor so that we might always see that only in suffering can we see who You truly are, our glorious King and Savior; for You live and reign with the Father and the Holy Spirit, one God, now and forever. (1039)

Meditation

Above Jesus' head is the inscription "Jesus of Nazareth, the King of the Jews." The chief priests protest. They want it to read, "This man said, 'I am the King of the Jews.' " But Pilate is unmoved, "What I have written I have written."

Pilate posted this sign on the cross so that all who passed by would know the charge against Jesus. It was intended as both a taunt and a mockery. What true king would be crucified as a common criminal? What legitimate king would meet such a terrible demise? What king would die alone, forsaken by almost all of His followers?

"What I have written I have written." Pilate intended it as a mockery, but what he ordered to be written was the truth. Jesus is the king of the Jews. He is the promised one, descended from Abraham, Isaac, and Jacob. He is the Suffering Servant who is fulfilling one prophecy after another as He is condemned and nailed to the cross. In fact, at the cross He is establishing His kingdom. He is defeating spiritual forces that seek His kingdom's demise. By His death, He is establishing a holy nation, a people cleansed by His blood, whose citizenship is in heaven. He is your king. Yes, behold your king on His throne. Behold, your king securing a place for you in His kingdom. Behold, your king not punishing you for your misdeeds but enduring in Himself what you rightfully deserved.

"What I have written I have written." These words were the truth, and they were written in three languages—Aramaic, Latin, and Greek. Although the sign read "The King of the Jews," Jesus was more than just the king for one nationality. He is the King of kings. He is Lord of all. After His resurrection and ascension, the message of Jesus the crucified King would be proclaimed in Aramaic, Latin, Greek, and many other languages throughout the Mediterranean world. Through this preaching, many believed in Jesus the crucified, and now glorified, King.

The preaching of Christ crucified continues to this day. As this message is heard, the Spirit works faith in those who do not believe and fortifies the faith of those who do believe. Through the proclamation of the crucified Christ, your sins are forgiven, and you have been brought to confess Jesus as your Savior and King.

22 JUNE

Psalmody: Psalm 22:12–21
Additional Psalm: Psalm 22
Old Testament Reading: Proverbs 25:1–22
Additional Reading: Proverbs 26:1–28
New Testament Reading: John 19:23–42

Prayer of the Day

Lord Jesus, our Savior and Lord, You declared that the work of bringing in a new creation was accomplished by Your declaration from the cross that "It is finished." Give us eyes to see the signs of the new creation in Your ongoing healing of our bodies and souls through Your Holy Sacraments, where You continue to come to us as our Creator who is bringing in the new creation; for You live and reign with the Father and the Holy Spirit, one God, now and forever. (1040)

Meditation

Finished is Jesus' saving work. Finished is the mission that the Father sent Jesus to this world to accomplish. Finished are the relentless attacks of the devil and his cohorts. Finished is the mockery and ridicule of those at the foot of the cross. Finished is the rejection by those He came to save. Finished is the pain and suffering. Finished is the bleeding and the dying.

"It is finished." When Satan heard these words, he knew that he was finished. On the cross, the devil thought he had Jesus right where he wanted Him. Satan had entered Judas and motivated him to betray Jesus. He had seized upon the religious authorities' rejection of Jesus to conspire to put Him to death. He had motivated the crowds on the morning of Good Friday to call for Jesus' execution. As Jesus hung on the cross, the devil thought he was victorious. How could Jesus save anyone in such a helpless state? If Jesus died, how could He possibly be the Savior? The ancient foe thought he was triumphant, that is, until he heard the words, "It is finished." Jesus was not a helpless man who was wrongly accused to die. He was not powerless as He hung on the cross. It was precisely through the weakness and humiliation of the cross that He won the victory. Through His death, Jesus triumphed over the devil. The devil cannot accuse those who belong to the Son. "It is finished." The prince of this world has been cast out. The devil struck Christ's heel, but in the end, Satan's head was crushed. Satan, you are finished!

"It is finished." You also are finished. Finished are your attempts to attain your salvation by your own good deeds or holy living, for your salvation has already been accomplished. Finished are your attempts to earn God's grace and favor by what you say and do, for the cross reveals that God is gracious to you and loves you beyond imagination. Finished are your doubts about where you will spend eternity. Since Christ's mission has been completed, the way to heaven is open for you.

It is finished. Rejoice in these words. Cling to these words. Trust in them. All that was needed to atone for your sins and secure your salvation has been accomplished. It is finished.

23 JUNE

Psalmody: Psalm 139:14–18, 23–24
Additional Psalm: Psalm 16
Old Testament Reading: Proverbs 27:1–24
Additional Reading: Proverbs 28:1–29:27
New Testament Reading: John 20:1–18

Prayer of the Day

Almighty God, through Your only-begotten Son, Jesus Christ, You overcame death and opened to us the gate of everlasting life. We humbly pray that we may live before You in righteousness and purity forever; through the same Jesus Christ, our Lord, who lives and reigns with You and the Holy Spirit, one God, now and forever. (L35)

Meditation

The tomb is empty. Although the disciples do not understand the significance of Christ's resurrection, they come to the conclusion that Jesus is alive. He is the resurrection and the life, as He said at the tomb of Lazarus. He called Lazarus forth from the grave, and now by His own authority and power He laid down His life, only to take it up again.

Jesus is the way, the truth, and the life, as He told His disciples in the Upper Room on the night before His death. He is life because death has no power over Him, and He is the way, for by His death and resurrection He has opened for us the way to eternal life.

Jesus is the light of the world. Early on the first day of the week, while it was still dark, the stone was rolled away, and as the sun rose over Jerusalem, Jesus revealed Himself to Mary Magdalene. Darkness could not overcome the Light. In the greatest battle ever waged, the Light has prevailed. The powers of darkness have no power over Him.

Jesus, the Good Shepherd, laid down His life for His sheep. On Easter morning, He called one of His sheep, Mary Magdalene, by name, and when He spoke her name, she realized that she was not speaking to the gardener but to Jesus. Mary recognized the voice of her Good Shepherd, and her tears immediately turned to joy. Risen from the dead, our Good Shepherd has called us by name in the waters of Baptism. We know His voice, and we follow Him. He leads us to the green pastures of His Word, and He will one day lead us through the valley of the shadow of death. We will dwell in the house of the Lord forever.

Jesus is the bread of life. When Jesus first spoke these words, His hearers objected to His claim that He is the living bread that came down from heaven. His resurrection proves His words are truth. He is sent by the Father. He is the Word made flesh. His flesh is the bread that He offered for the life of the world on the cross. Now glorified, He feeds His Church with the bread of life, His own flesh and blood in the Holy Supper.

Jesus is the great I AM. He was dead, but now He is alive. The tomb is empty. Mary has seen the Lord. Let us rejoice and be glad!

24 June

The Nativity of St. John the Baptist

Psalmody: Psalm 85:7–13
Additional Psalm: Psalm 85
Old Testament Reading:
Proverbs 30:1–9, 18–33
New Testament Reading: John 20:19–31

Prayer of the Day

Almighty God, through John the Baptist, the forerunner of Christ, You once proclaimed salvation. Now grant that we may know this salvation and serve You in holiness and righteousness all the days of our life; through our Lord Jesus Christ, Your Son, who lives and reigns with You and the Holy Spirit, one God, now and forever. (F20)

The Nativity of St. John the Baptist

St. John the Baptizer, the son of Zechariah and Elizabeth, was born into a priestly family. His birth was miraculously announced to his father by an angel of the Lord (Luke 1:5–23), and on the occasion of his birth, his aged father sang a hymn of praise (Luke 1:67–79). This hymn is entitled the Benedictus and serves as the traditional Gospel Canticle in the Church's Service of Morning Prayer. Events of John's life and his teaching are known from accounts in all four of the Gospels. In the wilderness of Judea, near the Jordan River, John began to preach a call to repentance and a baptismal washing (3:1ff), and he told the crowds, "Behold, the Lamb of God, who takes away the sin of the world!" (John 1:29). John denounced the immoral life of the Herodian rulers, with the result that Herod Antipas, the tetrarch of Galilee, had him arrested and imprisoned in the huge fortress of Machaerus near the Dead Sea. There Herod

had him beheaded (Mark 6:17–29). John is remembered and honored as the one who with his preaching pointed to "the Lamb of God" and "prepared the way" for the coming of the Messiah.

Meditation

The disciples blew it. In their sinful pride, they had vowed their allegiance to the Lord, but in the time of testing they had deserted Him. Most of them were nowhere to be found on Good Friday. They cowered in fear, horrified as the events of that dark day unfolded.

Three days later they were still afraid, gathered together behind locked doors. They knew the tomb was empty but did not understand the significance of the events of that day. Suddenly, an uninvited guest was in their midst. A stone could not keep Jesus in the tomb and a locked door would not stop Jesus from coming to His disciples. His disciples deserved a harsh rebuke. They had turned away. Instead of accusations, though, there is absolution. "Peace be with you." Sin is forgiven. Fears are removed. The relationship is restored. Unbelief dissipates.

Not only would the apostles be forgiven, they would be sent out as forgivers. As the Father sent the Son, so the Son now sends out those who belong to Him. He breathes on them, but this is no ordinary breath—this is the promised Holy Spirit, bestowed upon them for their calling. They were to go forth telling others about the events of the past three days. However, they were more than eyewitness reporters. Their calling was to distribute the benefits of Christ's death and resurrection. They were to proclaim repentance and forgiveness. To those who acknowledged their sin, they were under orders to forgive them. To those who refused to repent, they were to withhold forgiveness. As Christ's saving mission was coming to a close, their mission was just beginning. They were to speak

Christ's words. They were to forgive in Christ's name as they had been forgiven.

Through His Church, absolution is proclaimed to repentant sinners. The Church calls pastors to speak as Jesus spoke and to forgive as Jesus forgave. Since Christ has given this authority to His Church, you not only get to learn about what Jesus did some 2,000 years ago, you actually receive what He accomplished for you on the cross. You not only learn that Jesus died for your sins, but your sins are forgiven. You not only discover that through Christ's death and resurrection you are reconciled with the Father, but you receive that peace. You not only hear about who the Spirit is, but He comes and dwells in your heart.

You can be certain that your sins are forgiven. You have your risen Lord's word of absolution as a guarantee.

25 JUNE

Presentation of the Augsburg Confession

Psalmody: Psalm 119:41–48
Additional Psalm: Psalm 73
Old Testament Reading: Proverbs 31:10–31
New Testament Reading: John 21:1–25

Prayer of the Day

Lord God heavenly Father, You preserved the teaching of the apostolic Church through the confession of the true faith at Augsburg. Continue to cast the bright beams of Your light upon Your Church that we, being instructed by the doctrine of the blessed apostles, may walk in the light of Your truth and finally attain to the light of everlasting life; through Jesus Christ our Lord, who lives and reigns with you and the Holy Spirit, one God, now and forever. Amen. (1041)

Presentation of the Augsburg Confession

The Augsburg Confession, the principal doctrinal statement of the theology of Martin Luther and the Lutheran reformers, was written largely by Philip Melanchthon. At its heart, it confesses the justification of sinners by grace alone, through faith alone, for the sake of Christ alone. Signed by leaders of many German cities and regions, the confession was formally presented to the Holy Roman Emperor Charles V at Augsburg, Germany, on June 25, 1530. A few weeks later, Roman Catholic authorities rejected the Confession, which Melanchthon defended in the Apology of the Augsburg Confession (1531). In 1580, the Unaltered Augsburg Confession was included in the Book of Concord.

Meditation

In the time between Christ's resurrection and ascension, the disciples return home. For a while, instead of fishing for men they fish for fish. On this particular day, the disciples don't catch anything until Jesus appears on the scene. On the same lake where the disciples had a miraculous catch of fish three years earlier, history is repeated—153 fish in all. John recognizes Jesus, and Peter, who was in the boat at the last amazing catch, immediately swims to Jesus.

On the beach, there was a fire with bread and fish. On the shores of this lake where Jesus had miraculously fed more than five thousand people from a few loaves and a couple of small fish, He now provides a meal for His disciples. They eat and are satisfied, and more importantly, they know it is with their living Lord that they eat and drink.

Three years prior at the first miraculous catch of fish, Peter was terrified and pleaded with Jesus: "Depart from me, for I am a sinful man, O Lord" (Luke 5:8). This time, he swims toward Jesus, even though he had denied

Jesus only a few weeks earlier. What's the difference?

When God confronts us with our sin, there are ultimately only two options—we can either run away from Him or run toward Him. In the Garden of Eden, Adam and Eve hid when they sinned. Today, others run away from Jesus because they refuse to acknowledge their sin as sin. When Peter witnessed the first miraculous catch of fish, he knew he was in the presence of God and begged Jesus to leave. But this time is different. Peter is aware of his sin. He had wept over his sin. He knows that since he denied Christ, our Lord had every right to disown him. But Peter doesn't stay away. He doesn't make excuses for his actions. Instead, he swims toward Jesus.

And Peter is forgiven. Not only is he forgiven, his apostolic ministry is restored. He is to feed and tend the Lord's sheep. He will serve as an undershepherd of the Good Shepherd.

When we sin, the temptation is to flee from our Lord—to hide, to make excuses, to assume that our sin is too great to be forgiven. But there is a better way—not separating ourselves from our Lord but coming before Him, acknowledging our sin, with full confidence that in mercy He will forgive, renew, and restore us.

26 JUNE

Jeremiah

Psalmody: Psalm 31:19–24
Additional Psalm: Psalm 31
Old Testament Reading: Joshua 1:1–18
New Testament Reading: Acts 8:1–25

Prayer of the Day

Lord God heavenly Father, through the prophet Jeremiah, You continued the prophetic pattern of teaching Your people the true faith and demonstrating through miracles Your presence in creation to heal it of its brokenness. Grant that Your church may see in Your Son, our Lord Jesus Christ, the final end-times prophet whose teaching and miracles continue in Your Church through the healing medicine of the Gospel and the sacraments; through Jesus Christ our Lord. (1042)

Jeremiah

The prophet Jeremiah was active as God's prophet to the southern kingdom of Judah ca. 627 to 582 BC. As a prophet he predicted, witnessed, and lived through the Babylonian siege and eventual destruction of Jerusalem in 587 BC. In his preaching, he often used symbols, such as an almond rod and a boiling pot (Jeremiah 1:11–14), wine jars (13:12–14), and a potter at work (18:1–17). His entire prophetic ministry was a sermon, communicating through word and deed God's anger toward His rebellious people. Jeremiah suffered repeated rejection and persecution by his countrymen. As far as can be known, Jeremiah died in Egypt, having been taken there forcibly. He is remembered and honored for fearlessly calling God's people to repentance.

Meditation

"Who is this man?" It would seem that the answer to this question would depend upon who is doing the calling.

The Pharisees surely called Paul "the power of God that is called Great" for his efforts to persecute and eradicate the Church in Jerusalem and his efforts beyond Jerusalem.

The people of Samaria called Simon such a man for his continuous feats of magic with which he had amazed them.

While Simon may have thought Philip was such "power of God," he definitely believed Peter and John were. His offer of money to receive this power from them testifies to how great he thought they were with the power of God.

From God's perspective, surely those who continued to preach the Word when scattered by the persecution were "the power of God that is great." They were the power of God not because they preached the Word but because they continued to receive and thus believe the Word they preached.

Such was Philip, for apart from His God-given faith he would not have the power of God, and he would not have been preaching or driving out demons. All that the people of Samaria received from Philip's preaching was the power of God that Philip himself first received.

So also John and Peter would demonstrate the "power of God that was great" they had received through God-given faith, for apart from this faith the blessed Holy Spirit would not pass by their hands and their words to anyone.

It would be most rightly said that upon his conversion Simon had become the "power of God that is called great." Yes, Simon faltered in his infant faith as any believer does living as a sinner and a saint. What, but the power of God that is great, could have brought him to so quickly repent upon hearing the verdict of gall poisoning and what it would do to him. Jesus tells us how great when He said, "I tell you, there will be more joy in heaven over one sinner who repents than over ninety-nine righteous persons who need no repentance" (Luke 15:7).

The power of God that is great is rightly said of anyone who has received the Word, and by that Word been brought to repentance and faith in Jesus Christ. Even as Mary sang in her Magnificat, "He who is mighty has done great things for me" (Luke 1:49).

27 JUNE

Cyril of Alexandria, Pastor and Confessor

Psalmody: Psalm 51:1–9
Additional Psalm: Psalm 51
Old Testament Reading: Joshua 2:1–24
New Testament Reading: Acts 8:26–40

Prayer of the Day

Heavenly Father, Your servant Cyril steadfastly proclaimed Your Son Jesus Christ to be one person, fully God and fully man. By Your infinite mercy, keep us constant in faith and worship of Your Son, who lives and reigns with you and the Holy Spirit, one God, now and forever. Amen. (1043)

Cyril of Alexandria, Pastor and Confessor

Cyril (ca. AD 376–444) became archbishop of Alexandria, Egypt, in AD 412. Throughout his career, he defended a number of orthodox doctrines, among them the teaching that Mary, the mother of Jesus, is "rightly called and truly is the Mother of God"—*Theotokos*, "the God-bearer" (Formula of Concord VIII 12). In AD 431 the Council of Ephesus affirmed this teaching that the Son of Mary is also true God. The writings of Cyril on the doctrines of the Trinity and the person of Christ reveal him to be one of the most able theologians of his time. Cyril's Christology influenced subsequent Church councils and was a primary source for Lutheran confessional writings.

Meditation

"How can I, unless someone guides me?" Do you hear the unconditional surrender in this question?

How could Philip know that he should rise and go toward the south to the road that goes down from Jerusalem to Gaza unless the angel of the Lord guided him?

How could he know which chariot to go over to and join in its journey unless the Spirit guided him?

How could he know what to ask to the Ethiopian eunuch in the chariot unless the prophet Isaiah guided him as the eunuch read the Scriptures?

How could he know what to answer the eunuch unless he was guided by the good news about Jesus Christ?

How could the eunuch desire Baptism unless he was guided by the good news of Jesus Christ?

How could Philip baptize the eunuch unless he was guided by the Great Commission Jesus Christ gave to the Church?

How could Philip be carried away so that the eunuch saw him no more unless the Spirit guided him to Azotus?

How could the now wet eunuch go his way rejoicing unless he was guided by the grace of God in the good news of Jesus Christ?

How could Philip preach the Gospel to all the towns up the eastern coast of Israel to Caesarea unless the Spirit guided him?

Nothing in this text happens unless it is guided by the Lord. Whether it is the guidance of the angel of the Lord, the Holy Spirit, the Holy Scriptures, or the telling of the good news, all guidance is toward one end, the conversion and salvation of souls. In all the guidance given to Philip, it is given to put him in a place where he can teach and preach the Gospel and administer the sacrament of Baptism. This has one purpose, the salvation of the eunuch and all those from Azotus to Caesarea.

Doesn't this text speak to the Simons, to those caught in some temptation to pedal the Scriptures, the ministry, and even the Spirit of God for their own gain? Many are the spirits, not the Holy Spirit, that would guide even the elect of God. How shall I know if this is

the Spirit of the Lord, unless I know that the Spirit of God will only guide me by the Gospel and always bring me to Jesus Christ, and Him crucified, for my salvation?

How can I know the Spirit of God unless I listen to Him in the sacred guidance He speaks to me and all through Holy Scriptures?

28 June

Irenaeus of Lyons, Pastor

Psalmody: Psalm 89:24–29
Additional Psalm: Psalm 97
Old Testament Reading: Joshua 3:1–17
New Testament Reading: Acts 9:1–22

Prayer of the Day

Almighty God, You upheld Your servant Irenaeus with strength to confess the truth against every blast of vain doctrine. By Your mercy, keep us steadfast in the true faith, that in constancy we may walk in peace on the way that leads to eternal life through Jesus Christ our Lord, who lives and reigns with you and the Holy Spirit, one God, now and forever. Amen. (1044)

Irenaeus of Lyons, Pastor

Irenaeus (ca. AD 130–200), believed to be a native of Smyrna (modern Izmir, Turkey), studied in Rome and later became pastor in Lyons, France. Around AD 177, while Irenaeus was away from Lyons, a fierce persecution of Christians led to the martyrdom of his bishop. Upon Irenaeus's return, he became bishop of Lyons. Among his most famous writings is a work condemning heresies, especially Gnosticism, which denied the goodness of creation. In opposition, Irenaeus confessed that God has redeemed His creation through the incarnation of the Son. Irenaeus also affirmed the teachings of the Scriptures handed down to and through him as being normative for the Church.

Meditation

How many instruments does God take unto Himself for salvation of all people and the spreading of the Gospel?

The Lord clearly declares Saul to be His chosen instrument to carry His name into the presence of the Gentiles, kings, and the children of Israel. Inasmuch as God had chosen him before the foundation of the world (Ephesians 1:4), God also chose the events, activities, and even the people in Saul's life up to his conversion, as His instruments also.

How could Saul have a reason to go to Damascus without the Lord using the instrument of his hatred for the Way? How could Saul have been on the road to Damascus without the Lord using the instrument of high priest giving him letters of authorization to go and bind anyone belonging to the Way? How could Saul have been ready to listen without the Lord using the instrument of a light from heaven to knock him to the ground? How could Saul have been converted without the Lord's instrument of His spoken Word to Saul, declaring Himself to be Jesus, the object of his hatred and persecution?

Even after his conversion, the Lord chose many instruments by which He brought Saul to the point where he would proceed to be instrumental in bring God's name before the people. How could Saul begin to understand how blind he had been to the Christ that is proclaimed in the Old Testament Scriptures without the Lord's chosen instrument of blindness? How could Saul begin to grasp how misguided he was without the Lord's chosen instrument of Saul's servants to lead him into Damascus? How could Saul possibly regain

his sight without the Lord's chosen instrument Ananias, reluctant as he was, going to Saul, laying hands on him and proclaiming the good news to him through which he received the Holy Spirit? How could Saul be sealed in God's favor unless he received the Lord's chosen instrument of grace, Baptism? How could Saul be welcomed and encouraged in the communion of saints without the Lord's instrument of the disciples in Damascus?

How could those in the synagogue in Damascus begin to grasp the power of the gospel without Saul, the Lord's chosen instrument proclaiming, "Jesus is the Son of God"? Surely this is God working all things together for good (Romans 8:28), as we hear the Lord's chosen instrument proclaim in the synagogue and throughout the New Testament, "Jesus is the Son of God."

29 JUNE

St. Peter and St. Paul, Apostles

Psalmody: Psalm 103:1–12
Additional Psalm: Psalm 103
Old Testament Reading: Joshua 4:1–24
New Testament Reading: Acts 9:23–43

Prayer of the Day

Merciful and eternal God, Your holy apostles Peter and Paul received grace and strength to lay down their lives for the sake of Your Son. Strengthen us by Your Holy Spirit that we may confess Your truth and at all times be ready to lay down our lives for Him who laid down His life for us, even Jesus Christ, our Lord, who lives and reigns with You and the Holy Spirit, one God, now and forever. (F21)

St. Peter and St. Paul, Apostles

The festival of St. Peter and St. Paul is probably the oldest of the saints' observances (dating from about the middle of the third century). An early tradition held that these two pillars of the New Testament Church were martyred on the same day in Rome during the persecution under Nero. In addition to this joint commemoration of their deaths, both apostles are commemorated separately: Peter on January 18 for his confession of Jesus as the Christ (Matthew 16:13–16), and Paul on January 25 for his conversion (Acts 9:1–19).

The New Testament tells us much about both apostles. Peter was with Jesus from the beginning of His ministry and served as a leader among the disciples. Despite his steadfast faith, Scripture also records some of his failures, such as his rebuke of Jesus (Matthew 16:21–23) and his threefold denial of his Lord (26:69–75). Following Jesus' ascension, Peter continued as a leader in the Church (Acts 1:15; 2:14; 15:7).

Paul, a devout Jew also known as Saul, entered the scene as a persecutor of the Church. Following his miraculous conversion, in which the risen Christ Himself appeared to him, Paul became a powerful preacher of the grace of God. During his three missionary journeys (Acts 13–14; 16–18; 18–21) Paul traveled throughout modern-day Turkey and Greece. The New Testament account of his life ends with Paul under house arrest in Rome (28:16), though tradition holds that he went on to Spain before returning to Rome.

Meditation

Whenever a person comes to believe, that person has to be brought or delivered from their own unbelief. How often does the Lord deliver from unbelief in this text?

What was the plot of the Jews in Damascus built upon? What was the quest of the Hellenists Saul had disputed with driven by?

Yes, one could say hatred of Saul and what he was doing, but such hatred is nothing other than the rejection of belief. As Saul was delivered from his unbelief and all the deadly consequences of it, he was delivered again, but this time from the unbelief of the Jews and Hellenists and the consequences they both sought to bring upon him.

Arriving in Jerusalem, Saul attempts to join the disciples. however, they were afraid and thus rejected Saul because they did not believe he was a disciple. Although not the same unbelief of the Jews or Hellenists, it has the same roots of doubt in God's power to save. These disciples believed that God could save people like themselves, but someone as murderous as Saul, who likely killed people they love and were perhaps related to, was too much for their infant faith. Barnabas shares the testimony of what Christ did to and for Saul, and what Christ was now doing through him as he preached boldly in the name of Jesus. And Saul was delivered from the consequences of others' unbelief.

How does the Lord deliver the people in Lydda and Joppa from unbelief? The people are delivered from unbelief by Peter's speaking the Word of God upon those who were bound in the consequences of sin. In speaking God's Word, Peter delivered both Aeneas and Dorcas from the physical consequences of sin. As Aeneas was brought to wholeness of body and Dorcas was brought back to life in the body, people were delivered from their unbelief.

These acts of the apostles testify to the fact that deliverance from unbelief, whether it be personal unbelief or the unbelief of others and what they might do in that unbelief, is a completely passive deliverance born of the work and Word of God in Jesus Christ.

Even as Christ leaves Himself passively in the hands of His Father for deliverance from the work and words of unbelief that crucified Him, so is the way of deliverance for all who are brought to belief from unbelief, from death to life, from earth to heaven.

30 JUNE

Psalmody: Psalm 114
Additional Psalm: Psalm 144
Old Testament Reading: Joshua 5:1–6:5
New Testament Reading: Acts 10:1–17

Prayer of the Day

Lord God, Creator of heaven and earth, You opened Peter's eyes to see that all of creation is good and to be used by Your people for their delight and joy. Open our eyes to see that our bodies, restored by You in Holy Baptism, proclaim the goodness of Your creative will, that in paradise we will come to the fullness of what You created us to be; through Your Son, Jesus Christ, our Lord. (1045)

Meditation

Cornelius and Peter were both praying. That's what believers do. Cornelius prayed at three in the afternoon, the time of the evening sacrifice. The next day Peter was praying around noon as the midday meal was prepared.

Both were praying, and as they prayed, each received a vision. An angel told Cornelius to send for Peter, who was in the city of Joppa. In Peter's vision, he saw a sheet being let down from heaven, and the Lord instructed him to "Rise, Peter; kill and eat."

Both Cornelius and Peter were praying and both received a vision as they prayed. Both needed to hear the Gospel. Obviously, Cornelius needed the Gospel. He was a God-fearer, a Gentile who worshiped the true God, but he had not yet heard of Jesus the Messiah. He had not received the Good News that Jesus is the Savior from sin. He and his family had not been joined to Christ's death and resurrection through the saving waters of Baptism.

Peter also needed to hear the Gospel. Shocking as that may sound, it's true. It had been well over five years since Christ's resurrection and ascension, and Peter was still religiously following the dietary laws of the old covenant. During His ministry, Jesus had declared all foods to be clean (Mark 7:19). Before His ascension, Jesus commissioned Peter and the other apostles to make disciples of all nations. But Peter refused to leave behind the old customs. He only ate certain foods. He refused to visit with any Gentile (Acts 10:28). Peter needed the Gospel to transform his thinking and acting. He needed to be convinced that his righteousness before God did not depend on following these laws and that the Gospel of Jesus Christ is for all people.

Like Peter, we can fall into the trap of keeping the message of salvation to ourselves. We look down on those of a different nationality, race, age, or social class and invent countless reasons why we should not speak the Gospel to them. They are not like us, so we assume they won't be receptive. We conclude that they aren't "church people"; thus we refuse to witness to them.

Jesus forgave Peter's sin of partiality, and Jesus forgives our sin as well. His saving Gospel has reached our ears and our hearts, even though we do not deserve His salvation or any of His gifts. That same Gospel now motivates us to tell all, even those who may not be like us, the Good News about Jesus.

1 July

Psalmody: Psalm 47:1–7
Additional Psalm: Psalm 75
Old Testament Reading: Joshua 6:6–27
New Testament Reading: Acts 10:18–33

Prayer of the Day

Lord God heavenly Father, You called Cornelius the Gentile soldier to hear the Word proclaimed for his salvation and that of his household. As he responded to the hearing of Your Word with the giving of alms, so also may we be led to acts of mercy and charity as we embody Christ in our daily lives; through Your Son, Jesus Christ, our Lord. (1046)

Meditation

Peter refused to eat food regarded as unclean under the old covenant. He was reluctant to associate with Gentiles and to proclaim the Gospel to them. Cornelius, on the other hand, gathered his relatives and friends so that they, too, could hear the message when Peter arrives. He and his invited guests were eager to hear what Peter had to say.

As the Gospel is proclaimed, there are times when the message is ignored or rejected by those who hear. They want nothing to do with Christ and His salvation. Other times, as was the case with Cornelius and those gathered in his house, they were eager to hear what Peter had to say. They believed that they were in the presence of the Lord and that Peter spoke the Word of God.

God not only gives us faith to believe the Gospel, He also prepares our hearts to receive it. God worked in Peter's heart so that he was now willing to enter into a Gentile's home and proclaim the Good News. God gathered those in Cornelius's home and opened their hearts so that they were receptive to the proclamation of Christ crucified and risen. It is only by God's grace that we have received and now believe the Gospel. Cornelius knew he wasn't worthy to have Peter come into his house. That is why he bowed down before him. Likewise, we are not worthy of the blessings of the life and salvation we have received. God has brought us to faith through the Gospel word, and He sustains and strengthens us in the faith through that same word.

Throughout his ministry, there were occasions when Peter preached and many were brought to faith. In other instances, the vast majority of his hearers refused to believe the message. And so it is for us. By virtue of our Baptism, we are called to "proclaim the excellencies of Him who called you out of darkness into His marvelous light" (1 Peter 2:9). At times, this message will be received in faith with great joy. When this occurs, it is not a result of our charisma or presentation skills; it is the Holy Spirit working through our words. However, there will be other times when our words fall on deaf ears, when they are rejected and even spurned. However, the same God who has called us by the Gospel and made us His children now works through us to speak His Word to those He has placed in our midst, regardless of the outcome.

2 July

The Visitation (One-Year Lectionary)

Psalmody: Psalm 51:1–9
Additional Psalm: Psalm 60
Old Testament Reading: Joshua 7:1–26
New Testament Reading: Acts 10:34–48

Prayer of the Day

Almighty God, You chose the virgin Mary to be the mother of Your Son and made known through her Your gracious regard for the poor and lowly and despised. Grant that we may receive Your Word in humility and faith, and so be made one with Jesus Christ, Your Son, our Lord, who lives and reigns with You and the Holy Spirit, one God, now and forever. (F18)

The Visitation

John the Baptizer and Jesus, the two great figures of salvation history, now come together in the visit to Elizabeth by the Virgin Mary (Luke 1:39–45), both of whom conceived their children under miraculous circumstances. Thus John is brought into the presence of Jesus while they are still in their mothers' wombs. This presence of the Lord causes a response by the child John as he leaps in Elizabeth's womb. John's response to the presence of Jesus, the Messiah, foreshadows John's own role as forerunner. Already now, a new creation is beginning, and a baby still in the womb hails the new creation's inception. Foreshadowed in John's leap are the miracles of Jesus, who will cause all creation to leap at His presence: "The blind receive their sight, the lame walk, lepers are cleansed, the deaf hear, the dead are raised up, the poor have good news preached to them" (Luke 7:22). The incarnate presence of the Messiah also evokes a response from Elizabeth, who proclaims Mary's blessedness. Mary's Magnificat (Luke 1:46–55) provides the theological significance of this meeting as Mary sums up her place in salvation history. Mary's song is a hymn to God for His gracious gifts to the least in this world, whom He has lifted up out of lowliness solely because of His grace and mercy.

Meditation

Peter and his companions had previously shown partiality in their interactions with Gentiles, but God shows no partiality. Jesus died for all. The message of His suffering and resurrection is to be preached to all people. God wants all to be saved. There is no place for favoritism.

When those gathered in Cornelius's house heard the message, the Holy Spirit came upon them and they began speaking in tongues and extolling God. Ultimately, this sign was not for the benefit of these new Christians, but for Peter and his companions. They were shocked that these "unclean" Gentiles had received the Spirit just as they had. From their response, it appears as though they thought this was impossible.

If Gentiles have the Spirit, there is nothing to prevent their Baptism, for the Word, Spirit, and Baptism always belong together. Baptized into Christ, they were made members of His body, united with all believers in the family of God. Although they were uncircumcised Gentiles, their ethnicity was not a stumbling block to their incorporation into the family of God.

Through these events, Peter realized that one is clean before God not by what one does and does not eat, but by the cleansing power of Baptism. Cornelius, his relatives, and his friends believed and were saved, even though they were not circumcised. However, this would not be the last time Peter showed favoritism. Years later, at Galatia, he would fall into the sin of partiality again, preferring to eat and socialize with the Jewish Christians rather than the Gentile believers. His actions there led Paul to rebuke him harshly.

We are the Body of Christ. We are united by one Lord, one faith, and one Baptism. However, the sin of partiality can divide congregations. Cliques form, new members are not made to feel included, and visitors are not welcomed. The Church becomes an exclusive club rather than an assembly of a vast array of people receiving Christ's gifts and offering Him their praise.

Peter was forgiven for his sin, and so are we. We have received the Spirit who causes us to rejoice in our unity in Christ. The Spirit works in us so that we receive and welcome those whom the Lord has received and welcomed. The Spirit moves us from a sinful separatism to a desire to reach out in love and service to all our brothers and sisters in Christ.

3 JULY

Psalmody: Psalm 84:5–8
Additional Psalm: Psalm 45
Old Testament Reading: Joshua 8:1–28
New Testament Reading: Acts 11:1–18

Prayer of the Day

Lord God, the gift of Your Holy Spirit, the Spirit of Christ, was given to the Gentile Cornelius so that Christ dwelled in him and he dwelled in Christ. May that same Spirit of Jesus, which rested on us in Holy Baptism, give us courage to confess His holy name even in the face of the fiercest persecution, that we might receive the crown of everlasting life; through Your Son, Jesus Christ, our Lord. (1047)

Meditation

When Peter returns to Jerusalem, his reception is anything but warm. Those who insist on circumcision rebuke Peter for associating with and eating with the uncircumcised. They regard his actions as ungodly, and they reprimand him.

Peter responds to their objections with the facts. First, there was the vision of the clean and unclean animals, which was followed by the arrival of the Gentile men from Caesarea

and the Spirit's direction to go with them. Finally, the events that occurred at Cornelius's house where the Gentiles confessed Christ, received the Holy Spirit, and were baptized. Peter ends his defense by asking: "Who was I that I could stand in God's way?" (Acts 11:17).

Who was I that I could stand in God's way? These events were nothing short of miraculous; they had to be from God. Although the notion that both Jewish and Gentile believers are co-heirs of God's promises and are not bound by the laws of the Torah challenged Peter's own assumptions, he could not stand in God's way. After all, facts are facts.

Although Peter acknowledged that he could not stand in God's way, the reality is many in the Early Church did stand in the way of the Gentiles' incorporation into the Body of Christ. The circumcision party clung to the heresy that circumcision was necessary for salvation. In some churches, Gentile Christians were treated as second-class members. In other instances, those who defended the truth that the Gospel of Christ is for all people were regarded as false teachers.

Who was I that I could stand in God's way? People stood in God's way in the Early Church, and it happens today. God seeks to work through us to serve those who are already members of the Body of Christ and to extend His kingdom of grace to those who do not believe. Yet, we often stand in the way. We don't greet and welcome the new family sitting next to us in church. We invent a multitude of excuses as to why we shouldn't invite our unchurched neighbors to worship. Our own prejudices reveal that we don't treat others as God does, as those He loved so much that He sent His Son to die for them.

We stand in His way, but thankfully God has also granted us repentance unto life. He forgives our transgressions. He works in and through us so that we do not stand in His way but are the means through which His love, acceptance, and salvation are revealed, and His purposes are accomplished.

4 JULY

Psalmody: Psalm 50:1–6
Additional Psalm: Psalm 113
Old Testament Reading: Joshua 10:1–25
Additional Reading: Joshua 10:28–22:34
New Testament Reading: Acts 11:19–30

Prayer of the Day

Merciful Lord, Your Church expanded from Jerusalem to Antioch, where those who believed in Jesus were first called Christians. Through Your servants Barnabas and Paul, Gentiles were evangelized and now called by Your name. Give us courage to speak Your name even in the face of persecution, so that all might hear Your Holy Word and come to the knowledge of the truth; through Jesus Christ, our Lord. (1048)

Meditation

Christian. It is one of many titles that you bear. Other titles may include American, Lutheran, parent or child, employer or employee, teacher or student. Or you may be identified by where you live—if you're from Nebraska, you're a Cornhusker, or if you from Indiana, you're a Hoosier.

In Antioch, the believers were first identified as Christians. This was not a title they chose for themselves but what they were called by nonbelievers. To this day, millions of faithful people are known as Christians. For you, the title Christian is a constant reminder that you belong to Christ. He has joined you to Himself as a branch to the vine. He was made you a member of His body. He has joined you to His death and resurrection in Baptism, and He unites Himself with you as He feeds you with His own body and blood in the Sacrament. You belong to Christ; you are a Christian.

Paul and Barnabas's visit to the church in Antioch occurred almost ten years after Christ's resurrection and ascension. Until this time, the Church was almost entirely Jewish believers. In the decade following Christ's ascension, His disciples were reluctant to follow His command to make disciples of all nations. However, Antioch was the exception. Those from Cyprus and Cyrene spoke to both Jews and Greeks, and many believed. Paul and Barnabas remained in Antioch for one year teaching the people.

E pluribus unum means "Out of the many, one." This is the motto of the United States. Immigrants came from many lands and together became one nation. Beginning with Antioch, the same could be said of the Christian Church: out of the many, one. By God's grace, disciples have been made of all nations. The Church is fulfilling Christ's commission. In heaven, believers from all nations, tribes, people, and languages will be gathered before the throne of the Lamb. Out of the many, one. The Church is one, one in Christ.

Christians today are often also reluctant to speak God's Word to those of different nationalities or ethnicities. Maybe you find yourself with this same fear and apprehension. You are worried about how your words will be received; maybe you assume that they are unlikely to believe in Christ. Instead of making excuses, God calls you, and all who bear the name Christian, to confess Christ. Through your vocations, the various titles you have been given, you have the opportunity to speak God's Word and to sow the seeds of the Gospel.

5 JULY

Psalmody: Psalm 68:1–6
Additional Psalm: Psalm 149
Old Testament Reading: Joshua 23:1–16
New Testament Reading: Acts 12:1–25

Prayer of the Day

Heavenly Father, shepherd of Your people, You raised up James the Just, brother of our Lord, to lead and guide Your Church. Grant that we may follow his example of prayer and reconciliation and be strengthened by the witness of his death; through Jesus Christ, Your Son, our Lord, who lives and reigns with You and the Holy Spirit, one God, now and forever. (F31)

Meditation

Herod put James to death with the sword. He intended to do the same with Peter immediately after the Passover. However, God's people were praying for his deliverance, even gathering together to pray well into the night.

God's people were praying, and their supplications were granted. Although he was sleeping between two solders and bound by two chains, the angel brought Peter out of the prison, miraculously passing by the guards and through the iron gate.

Peter went to Mary's house where the disciples had gathered to pray. When the servant girl Rhoda reported who was at the gate, they thought she was crazy. Although they were praying for Peter's release, they weren't expecting God to do for them as they asked. Ironically, they were more inclined to believe that it was Peter's angel than Peter himself. But Rhoda was not out of her mind. God had answered their prayers. Peter was delivered from what appeared to be certain death.

Like the first disciples, we pray. We pray to God for our needs and the needs of others. However, when God answers prayer in a dramatic fashion, we are astonished. In joy we may exclaim, "I thought this would never happen!"

Why do we think this way? Do we assume that God is not going to hear our prayers? Do we feel that we have received so many "no" answers to our prayers, or that this particular request is so great that there is no way God will grant it? Do we question God's supreme power and authority? Do we doubt the wonderful promises that Christ has attached to prayer?

Prayers are offered, and often prayers are answered to the joy and surprise of God's people. Not every prayer is answered in the way we might desire, but when the answer is what we asked for, we should not be surprised. God is our Father. He wants to serve us; He wants to help us; He wants to do that which is best for us. Because He is our Father, He wants us to call on Him as His own dear children. Through Baptism, He has adopted us into His family and with full confidence we can speak to Him even as a child speaks to her own father. And when you pray, don't be surprised when you get what you pray for; don't be shocked when God does what would seem to be the impossible.

6 JULY

Isaiah

Psalmody: Psalm 100
Additional Psalm: Psalm 5:1–8
Old Testament Reading: Joshua 24:1–31
Additional Reading: Judges 1:1–36
New Testament Reading: Acts 13:1–12

Prayer of the Day

Lord God heavenly Father, through the prophet Isaiah You continued the prophetic pattern of teaching Your people the true faith and demonstrating through miracles Your presence in creation to heal it of its brokenness. Grant that Your church may see in Your Son, our Lord Jesus Christ, the final end-times prophet whose teaching and miracles continue in Your Church through the healing medicine of the Gospel and the sacraments; through Jesus Christ, our Lord. (1049)

Isaiah

Isaiah, the son of Amoz, is considered to be the greatest of the writing prophets and is quoted in the New Testament more than any other Old Testament prophet. His name means "Yahweh [the Lord] saves." Isaiah prophesied to the people of Jerusalem and Judah from about 740 BC to 700 BC and was a contemporary of the prophets Amos, Hosea, and Micah. Isaiah was a fierce preacher of God's Law, condemning the sin of idolatry. He was also a comforting proclaimer of the Gospel, repeatedly emphasizing God's grace and forgiveness. For this he is sometimes called the Evangelist of the Old Testament. No prophet more clearly prophesied about the coming Messiah and His saving kingdom. Isaiah foretold not only the Messiah's miraculous birth (Isaiah 7:14; 9:6), His endless reign (Isaiah 2:1–5; 11:1–16), and His public ministry (Isaiah 61:1–3), but most notably His Suffering Servant role and atoning death (52:13–53:12). The apostle John's description of Isaiah, that Isaiah saw Jesus' glory and spoke of him (John 12:41), is an apt summary of Isaiah's prophetic ministry.

Meditation

In 1908, English humorist Israel Zangwill staged a play titled *The Melting Pot*. It told the story of two Russian immigrants, David and Vera, who move to the United States, fall in love, and live happily ever after. This play's title became a rallying cry for the high aspiration that the United States would be a place of multiethnic assimilation. But long before the United States, the Church was history's original melting pot.

As Acts 13 opens, we meet a group of churchmen who come from notably disparate backgrounds: "Now there were in the church at Antioch prophets and teachers, Barnabas, Simeon who was called Niger, Lucius of Cyrene, Manaen a member of the court of Herod the tetrarch, and Saul" (v. 1).

Barnabas was a well-known Jewish teacher and cousin to Mark (cf. Colossians 4:10). Some believe that at one point he was better known than Paul, for early in Acts, his name is placed first when the two are paired (cf. Acts 11:30, 12:25, 13:7). Simeon and Lucius hailed from Africa. Niger, Simeon's surname, is a Latin word meaning "black," indicating possible African origins. Lucius is said to have come from Cyrene, a Roman province on the north coast of Africa. Manaen is "a member of the court of Herod the tetrarch," that is, Herod Antipas, the ruler who beheaded John the Baptist (cf. Matthew 14:1–12). The Greek word for "member of the court" is *syntrophos*, meaning, "brought up with." Thus, Manaen had probably known Herod all his life. Finally, there is Saul, the famed Jewish antagonist turned evangelist. These are the leaders of the church at Antioch. What a group!

And yet, for all their differences, they are united in Christ. Indeed, when the Spirit says, "Set apart for Me Barnabas and Saul for the work to which I called them" (Acts 13:2), there is no quibbling over the Spirit's appointments. No one protests, "But I wanted to be set apart!" Rather, they gladly lay their hands on these men, ordaining them into their appointed office (cf. 13:3).

Such is the Church: different people from different backgrounds doing different things under one Head, Who is Christ. The Church is a melting pot. But it is not a melting pot in which people's individual personalities and gifts are congealed into some bland soup. Rather, people's unique personalities and gifts are deployed according to the Spirit's purposes. And we, who are "from every tribe and language and people and nation" (Revelation 5:9), are part of this Church. What a glorious group we are in Christ!

7 JULY

Psalmody: Psalm 2:1–8
Additional Psalm: Psalm 78:56–72
Old Testament Reading: Judges 2:6–23
New Testament Reading: Acts 13:13–41

Prayer of the Day

Merciful Lord, You sent Paul and Barnabas to preach the Gospel in the synagogue of Pisidian Antioch and announce that Jesus is the Messiah, the Holy One whose resurrection shows us that He will not see corruption. May our union with Him in Holy Baptism give us peace and comfort in being incorruptible, even as He is incorruptible; through Jesus Christ our Lord. (1050)

Meditation

Encouragement is integral to a Christian's life. In the Greek text the word for "encouragement" is used in John 14:26 by Jesus to describe His Holy Spirit: "But the Helper, the Holy Spirit, whom the Father will send in My name, He will teach you all

things and bring to your remembrance all that I have said to you." The word *Helper* is related to that of encouragement. Jesus is devoted to encouraging His people by His Spirit.

In Acts 13, Paul and Barnabas are deployed from Antioch on a missionary jaunt. Upon arriving in Pisidia, they receive a request from the rulers of the local synagogue: "Brothers, if you have any word of encouragement for the people, say it" (v. 15).

This seems a suitable request for the synagogue rulers to make of Paul and Barnabas, especially since Barnabas's very name means "son of encouragement" (cf. Acts 4:36). And so Paul, along with his companion, the "son of encouragement," delivers a message of encouragement to those at the synagogue. What message of encouragement does he bring? The message of the Gospel, of course! Paul tells those gathered: "Let it be known to you therefore, brothers, that through this man [Jesus Christ] forgiveness of sins is proclaimed to you, and by Him everyone who believes is freed from everything from which you could not be freed by the Law of Moses" (13:38–39). The message of unmerited, undeserved, unearned salvation is Paul and Barnabas's message of encouragement.

One of my favorite pictures of Christian encouragement comes to us via the fourth century church father Gregory of Nyssa. In his mystical work, *The Life of Moses*, he opens with an analogy, using spectators at a horse race. The charioteers at the race, Gregory says, speed their horses with reigns and whips. The fans in the stands, on the other hand, speed the charioteers with their arms outstretched, cheering for the competitors. Gregory continues by saying that we, too, as Christians, cheer one another along the course of faith. And indeed we do. For we stretch out our arms to serve one another, fold our hands to pray for one another, and lift our voices to encourage one another with the precious Gospel of Christ even as we ourselves are encouraged by God's Spirit.

May you be encouraged with Christ's Gospel by Christ's Spirit. And may you encourage others just the same.

8 JULY

Psalmody: Psalm 16:5–11
Additional Psalm: Psalm 139:12–18
Old Testament Reading: Judges 3:7–31
New Testament Reading: Acts 13:42–52

Prayer of the Day

Almighty God, You brought joy to Gentiles and persecution to Paul and Barnabas through their proclamation that Jesus is a light to all nations to bring salvation to the ends of the earth. Give us courage to proclaim the Gospel throughout the world, even in the face of opposition, knowing that it is through suffering that we enter the kingdom of God; through Jesus Christ our Lord. (1051)

Meditation

Davy Crockett is not happy. The President of the United States, he laments, is drunk with power. Indeed, Crockett is so leery of this particular president that he calls him "the first king of this country," comparing him to King George III. Crockett's supposed tyrant is none other than Andrew Jackson. Crockett had liked him once upon a time—when he had some down home backwoods Tennessee sensibility. But now, Crockett says, Jackson has gotten "too big for his breeches."

Crockett's critique of President Jackson serves well as a general critique of the human condition. For we are all have a propensity to get "too big for our breeches." Such is the case with a group of Jews in Acts 13.

After Paul preaches a thrilling sermon at Pisidia, those who hear it beg him to stay and share his message again. Paul graciously obliges. But some Jews are filled with jealousy at Paul's popularity and try to discredit his ministry (cf. verses 42, 45). They think he has gotten "too big for his breeches."

But truth be told, it is not Paul who has gotten "too big for his breeches," it is his Jewish antagonists. After all, Paul encourages all who will listen "to continue in the grace of God" (Acts 13:43). In the Greek text the word for "continue" means "to remain at." Thus, Paul is encouraging his hearers to rely not on their own pious acts and good deeds for salvation, but to "remain at" the grace of God for their salvation, ever cognizant of their own unworthiness and sinfulness.

But Paul's Jewish antagonists will not listen to Paul's message of divine grace. For they do not want to "remain at" the grace of God, given through Christ. They would rather trumpet their own pious acts and good deeds. So Paul, along with his companion Barnabas, exclaims, "Behold, we are turning to the Gentiles" (13:46). And when they carry their message to the Gentiles, they receive it delightedly: "They began rejoicing and glorifying the word of the Lord, and as many as were *appointed* to eternal life believed" (13:48). Notice that it is God who appoints people unto eternal life. It is God's grace that marches on, electing people for salvation. Lest we get "too big for our breeches," we humbly believe, teach, and confess that it is not by our own pious deeds or good works that we are appointed unto salvation, but by the grace of God alone.

9 July

Psalmody: Psalm 138:1–6
Additional Psalm: Psalm 86:8–17
Old Testament Reading: Judges 4:1–24
Additional Reading: Judges 5:1–31
New Testament Reading: Acts 14:1–18

Prayer of the Day

Lord Jesus, in our bold proclamation of the Gospel, give us humility to know that those who hear us hear You, that those who preach and administer the Sacraments stand in Your stead and by Your command, and that whatever fruit is produced through our work comes from Your gracious hand; for You live and reign with the Father and the Holy Spirit, one God, now and forever. (1052)

Meditation

Idolatry is easy. It's so easy, in fact, that all of us sin in this way. Perhaps it's the god of money or the god of a career or another person whom we exalt as a god. Idolatry is easy. Just ask Paul and Barnabas as they arrive at Lystra in Acts 14.

Things begin innocently enough. Paul sees a man "crippled from birth" (v. 8) and heals him according to his faith in Christ. But those watching misinterpret Paul's actions. "The gods have come down to us in the likeness of men," they shout (v. 11). And they thus seek to worship Paul and Barnabas.

The crowd's bizarre actions seem to stem from an ancient legend, told by the Roman poet Ovid, that, once upon a time, Zeus and Hermes visited the Phrygian hill country, disguised as mortals, looking for a place to stay. After asking at a thousand homes, and being rejected by them all, they came to the shack of an elderly couple, Philemon and Baucis, who warmly welcomed them. In gratitude, Zeus and Hermes transformed their shack into a temple complete with a golden roof and marble columns. Lystra's residents seem intent on not missing another advent of their gods.

But Paul and Barnabas refuse to be idolized. They ask those in the crowd, "Men, why are you doing these things? We also are men, of like nature with you, and we bring you good news, that you should turn from these vain things to a living God" (v. 15). In the Greek text the word for "like nature" is *homoiopathes*—*homoio* meaning "like" and *pathes*, translated as "nature." Thus, Paul and Barnabas are saying, "We are not divine! We are *like* you: mere mortals."

Later, this word *homoio* was central in the Christological debates of the fourth century. When the Nicene Creed was being codified at the Council of Nicaea in AD 325, the Council declared Jesus to be "of one substance with the Father," the word for "one substance" being *homo'ousious*. The heretic Arius, however, who did not believe that Jesus was co-eternal with the Father, wanted to change the word to *homoiousious*, meaning, "of *like* substance" with the Father. Arius was eventually refuted and Jesus' divinity was upheld.

Paul and Barnabas confess themselves to be *homoiousious* with the people of Lystra. They are just *like* them. They thus refuse the worship of others. For worship belongs not to men who are *homoiousious* with men, but to Jesus, who is *homo'ousious* with His Father. By God's grace, may we worship Him alone.

10 July

Psalmody: Psalm 125
Additional Psalm: Psalm 7:1–8
Old Testament Reading: Judges 6:1–24
New Testament Reading: Acts 14:19–15:5

Prayer of the Day

Lord and Giver of all good things,
the same powers that crucified Jesus
persecuted Paul as he bore on his body
the marks of Jesus for preaching Christ
crucified. Give us faith to believe that no
matter what suffering we endure for the
sake of Christ, it is all gift and it is all
good, so that, with Paul, we may rejoice
in suffering as we bear on our bodies the
marks of Jesus; who lives and reigns with
the Father and the Holy Spirit, one God,
now and forever. (1053)

Meditation

Euclidian geometry teaches that the shortest
distance between two points is a straight line.
But Paul doesn't seem much concerned with
Euclidean geometry as he travels. In Acts 14,
Paul travels to Derbe, the farthest point of
his first missionary journey (cf. v. 20). The
account of his time here is brief, Luke saying
only that Paul and his companions "preached
the gospel to that city and . . . made many
disciples." But what Luke says next is striking:
"They returned to Lystra and to Iconium and
to Antioch" (v. 21). Isn't Lystra where Paul was
stoned so severely that the town's residents
thought he was dead (cf. v. 19)? Isn't Iconium
where Paul had to flee due to death threats (cf.
vv. 5–6)? Isn't Antioch where Paul suffered
persecution from jealous Jews (cf. Acts 13:50)?
Why would Paul, rather than traveling in
more or less a straight line from Derbe back to
his starting point of Syrian Antioch, 200 miles
to his southeast, choose to retrace his steps
through towns in which he had experienced
such violent opposition?

Acts 14:22 gives the answer: He returned
to strengthen "the souls of the disciples,
encouraging them to continue in the
faith." Paul's love for his congregations is
unmistakable and unshakable. He will risk
life and limb for them. Forget the straight line.

Paul goes back the way he came, even if the
way he came involved great pain.

The traditional route of our Lord's Via
Dolorosa, or "way of sorrows," is a crooked
one, with curves, turns, and even a couple of
places where our Lord backtracks as He makes
His way to the cross. But despite the curves,
turns, and backtracks, our Lord travels this
way of sorrows. Why? Because our Lord knows
that our salvation is riding on this route.

Isaiah prophesies that when the Lord comes,
"Every valley shall be lifted up, and every
mountain and hill be made low; the uneven
ground shall become level" (Isaiah 40:4). John
the Baptist quotes the Septuagint's translation
of this passage when he declares, "Every
valley shall be filled, and every mountain and
hill shall be made low, and the crooked shall
become straight" (Luke 3:5). Jesus, according
to the words of Isaiah, walks the winding
road to the cross so that our crooked paths of
sin might give way to God's straight way to
salvation. And what a blessed way this is. For
it is this way that leads us to, through, and
with our Savior.

11 JULY

Psalmody: Psalm 5:1–8
Additional Psalm: Psalm 5
Old Testament Reading: Judges 6:25–40
New Testament Reading: Acts 15:6–21

Prayer of the Day

O almighty and most merciful God,
at the apostolic council, You gave Peter
the courage to represent Paul and gave
James the wisdom to show from Scripture
that the Gentiles are also called by Your
name. May Your Church continue to
boldly proclaim that salvation is by grace
through faith and not by works of Law;
through Jesus Christ, our Lord. (1054)

Meditation

Christians do not always get along. An even cursory perusal of Christian denominations reveals disheartening disunity: Baptist, Presbyterian, Methodist, Roman Catholic, Episcopalian, Lutheran, and non-denominational. And, of course, denominational affiliations can be specified even further.

Christians do not always get along. This is nothing new, as can be seen from Acts 15. As the chapter opens, we are introduced to a faction of Christians who are teaching, "Unless you are circumcised according to the custom of Moses, you cannot be saved" (v. 1). This brings Paul and Barnabas into "no small dissension and debate with them" (v. 2). Indeed, this dissension and debate is so weighty, a church council is convened in Jerusalem at which there is "much debate" (v. 7) on the subject of circumcision.

There are some who believe that the cure for divisions among Christians is simply to gloss over differences and adopt a mushy consensus where pure doctrine and orthodox teaching are not well considered. But this is not the way the Jerusalem church handles their dispute. Rather, the leaders of the church have *much* debate over an issue that is of *no small* importance: the circumcision of Gentiles. In other words, even though these Christians are concerned about preserving unity, the importance of preserving *unity in doctrine* is never questioned. As it is with the Jerusalem church, so it should be with us.

Finally, James stands and announces, "My judgment is that we should not trouble those of the Gentiles who turn to God" (Acts 15:19). James sides with those who confess that Jews and Gentiles alike "will be saved through the grace of the Lord Jesus" (15:11). Interestingly, James could have easily sided with those who demanded Gentile circumcision, for he was well-known for his scrupulous adherence to the Law and his excellent Jewish piety. But

instead, he sides with the Gospel and promise of God that even the Gentiles "are called by My name" (15:17). And this, finally, is our call as well: to side with the Gospel of God as it is given to us in the Word of God. For the Gospel alone creates and sustains true unity. And so we pray like our Savior prayed: May we be kept in God's name as one, even as Christ and His Father are one (cf. John 17:11).

12 July

Psalmody: Psalm 118:10–18
Additional Psalm: Psalm 108
Old Testament Reading: Judges 7:1–23
Additional Reading: Judges 7:24–12:15
New Testament Reading: Galatians 1:1–24

Prayer of the Day

Lord God of Truth, You converted the apostle Paul from persecutor of the church to courageous preacher of the true Gospel that Jesus Christ gave Himself for our sins to deliver us from the present evil age. Deliver us from all false gospels, so that we remain faithful to Christ alone, whose death and resurrection are the source of our salvation; through Jesus Christ, our Lord. (1055)

Meditation

Paul writes, "As we have said before, so now I say again: If anyone is preaching to you a gospel contrary to the one you received, let him be accursed" (Galatians 1:9). When did Paul say this before? Only one verse earlier: "But even if we or an angel from heaven should preach to you a gospel contrary to the one we preached to you, let him be accursed" (1:8). In rapid-fire succession, Paul warns the Galatians against the dangers of departing from the Gospel: once in verse 8 and then again in verse 9.

Why is Paul so concerned that the Galatians are departing from the Gospel of Christ? Because he knows that they are being tempted by "a different gospel" (1:6), which is really no gospel at all (cf. 1:7).

Paul gives us a clue from his past as to what this "different gospel" might be: "For you have heard of my former life in Judaism, how I . . . was advancing in Judaism beyond many of my own age among my people, so extremely zealous was I for the traditions of my fathers" (1:13–14).

There seem to be some false teachers afoot who are tempting Galatia's congregants to supplement Christ's Gospel with extra rules and traditions borrowed from Judaism. In other words, there are some who are trying to sneak human works into Christ's all-sufficient work on the cross. But Paul knows that muddling up Christ's work with human works just *won't work*. And so Paul defends the work of Christ against the works of man. This is why Paul opens his letter: "Paul, an apostle—not from men nor through man, but through Jesus Christ and God the Father, who raised Him from the dead" (Galatians 1:1). For Paul, everything about him is thanks to Jesus and not to himself. It's all about Jesus' work and nothing about Paul's works.

Soli Deo Gloria. This old Latin phrase is often included as a postscript in theological works as a dedication of sorts, meaning that all scholarship, thought, and writing is to be to God's glory alone and not to the glory of any man. And this is Paul's admonition to the Galatians concerning the Gospel—that everything we are, everything we do, and everything we have is thanks to Christ and not to any man. *Soli Deo Gloria.* May we always glorify God.

13 JULY

Psalmody: Psalm 71:1–8
Additional Psalm: Psalm 71
Old Testament Reading: Judges 13:1–25
Additional Reading: Ruth 1:1–4:22
New Testament Reading: Galatians 2:1–21

Prayer of the Day

O Almighty God, Merciful Father, who in love has joined us to the precious body of your Son, Jesus Christ, in the water of Holy Baptism, grant that we may find peace and comfort in being incorruptible, even as He is incorruptible; through the same Jesus Christ, our Lord, who lives and reigns with you and the Holy Spirit, one God, now and forever. (1056)

Meditation

The Gospel is free, but it is also hard. For there are many people and philosophies that war against the true Gospel that "a person is not justified by works of the law but through faith in Jesus Christ" (Galatians 2:16). As such, it can be difficult to stand up for the true Gospel.

If you doubt the difficulty of standing up for the true Gospel, just ask Peter. In Galatians 2, we read that Peter *had* been eating with Gentiles, even though these Gentile converts to Christianity did not follow traditional Jewish dietary laws (cf. Leviticus 11). But eschewing Jewish culinary restrictions was no problem, for God had previously declared all foods "clean" (cf. Acts 10). But then, "certain men came from James" (Galatians 2:12), seeking to convince Peter to stop dining with his Gentile friends. And so, Peter drew back from eating with them in deference to these men from James.

For Peter, yielding to outside pressure is nothing new. During Jesus' trial before the high priest Caiaphas, when Peter is asked by a meager servant girl, "You also are not one of this man's disciples, are you?" (John 18:17), Peter persistently denies any association with his Master. Peter is worried what other people will think of him and, possibly, what they will do to him if he admits knowing Jesus.

How often do we fail to stand up for the Gospel because we fear what others might think of us or do to us? The Gospel is indeed free, for we can do nothing to earn or deserve it, but it is also hard to stand up for. Why is this the case? Because the Gospel destroys every human pretense that boasts, "I am *worthy* of God's love, forgiveness, and salvation because of what I have done." The Gospel declares that *no one* is worthy of such gifts from God. Rather, God freely gives His gifts to the undeserving and ill-deserving. This, of course, angers those who are so confident in their own piety that they try to coerce others into living up to their self-arbitrated standards of righteousness, as those who came from James tried to do with Peter and his Gentile companions.

Yet, even when we fail, as Peter failed, to stand up for the truth of the Gospel, the Gospel does not dissipate. Instead, it forgives us for our lack of boldness. Here, then, is the Gospel for the bold and timid alike: we are not justified by our boldness for the Gospel, but by Christ's boldness for us.

14 JULY

Psalmody: Psalm 119:1–8
Additional Psalm: Psalm 1
Old Testament Reading: Judges 14:1–20
New Testament Reading: Galatians 3:1–22

Prayer of the Day

Almighty and merciful God, by Your gift alone Your faithful people render true and laudable service. Help us steadfastly to live in this life according to Your promises and finally attain Your heavenly glory; through Jesus Christ, Your Son, our Lord, who lives and reigns with You and the Holy Spirit, one God, now and forever. (H72)

Meditation

There are some things that just don't mix: oil and water, a square peg and a round hole, morning people and night owls, works of the Law and righteousness by faith. Sadly, this final combination is precisely what the Galatians are trying to mix. They figure, having begun with God's Spirit and grace, they can now continue on with "works of the Law" (Galatians 3:2). But Paul flatly rejects this error and reminds the Galatians that no less than Abraham himself relied not on works of the Law, but "believed God, and it was counted to him as righteousness" (3:6). Works of the Law, Paul argues, were never meant to justify anyone in God's sight, but only to serve as an "intermediary" (3:19) between God's promise of blessing to Abraham and its fulfillment in Christ.

But by the first century, the Law had become much more than an "intermediary." It had become the path to righteousness before God. In the Mishnah, a codification of Jewish laws and traditions, Rabbi Phineas ben Jair predicates the reception of God's Spirit on being "saintly" according to the works of the Law! Paul quickly dispenses with such delusions. Indeed, he goes so far as to say, "All who rely on works of the law are under a curse" (Galatians 3:10).

In recent years, there has been much debate over the meaning of Paul's phrase, "works of the law." Some have asserted Paul never meant to imply that Jews believed they could be declared righteous in God's sight by rigid adherence to Mosaic Law. Rather, what Paul refutes here is the Jewish insistence that Gentiles must become circumcised so that they will be like Jews. Though it is true that Paul has circumcision front and center in his mind as a "work of the law" when he writes this epistle (cf. Galatians 5:6), this is not the only "work of the law" with which Paul is concerned. Notice that Paul speaks not of one *work* of the Law, but of many *works* of the Law. Thus, Paul is concerned with the whole corpus of Mosaic legislation and the arrogance of those who presume to follow it.

Finally, Paul's argument is that, while we have all become outlaws according to Mosaic Law because none of us can follow it perfectly, we have been "in-lawed" to Christ by faith! And because we have been in-lawed to Christ by faith, we are counted righteous. May we rest in Christ's pure righteousness alone, for it need not be mixed with anything else.

15 JULY

Psalmody: Psalm 33:13–22
Additional Psalm: Psalm 27
Old Testament Reading: Judges 15:1–16:3
New Testament Reading: Galatians 3:23–4:11

Prayer of the Day

Lord Jesus Christ, You came in humility and weakness to defeat the powers of sin, death, and the devil. Clothe our weakness with Your righteousness by Your baptismal grace that we might withstand the power of every adversary; for You live and reign with the Father and the Holy Spirit, one God, now and forever. (1057)

Meditation

A babysitter is necessary when you're young, but not when you're an adult. This is Paul's argument to the Galatians concerning their relationship to Mosaic Law.

It seems as though some within the Galatian church were seeking to "graduate" into spiritual maturity by rigidly following all sorts of Mosaic liturgical legislation concerning "days and months and seasons and years" (Galatians 4:10). They thought that spiritual maturity is to be found in the works of the Law that a person performs rather than in the faith in Christ that a person holds. Paul argues exactly the opposite: "The law was our guardian until Christ came, in order that we might be justified by faith. But now that faith has come, we are no longer under a guardian" (3:24–25). The Greek word for "guardian" is *paidagogos*, a word for "babysitter." Paul says that a person who believes he can follow the Law unto salvation is "enslaved" (4:3) to a babysitter.

A fascinating use of *paidagogos* comes in a dialogue between the great Greek philosopher Socrates and a son named Lysis. Socrates notes that this son has a pedagogue who watches over him. He finds it strange that a man who is a slave to the family, as was a pedagogue, would exert control over a son who is member of the family. So Socrates asks the son how this pedagogue controls him, to which the son answers, "He leads me to my teachers." According to Paul, this is precisely the function of the Mosaic Law. It was "our guardian until Christ came, in order that we might be justified by faith" (3:24). The Law, then, is not an end in itself nor is adhering to it a sign of spiritual maturity. Rather, the Law is only a babysitter to lead us to Christ. Seeking salvation by the Law is not a sign of spiritual maturity, but a sign of spiritual immaturity, as Paul says when he labels such an attempt as part of "the weak and worthless elementary principles of the world" (4:9).

What, then, is the hallmark of spiritual maturity? In a word, it is "faith." Not our own works. And so, as maturing sons of God, we bid adieu to the babysitter of the Law and gladly welcome our Savior in faith. For we can never outgrow or out-mature Him.

16 JULY

Ruth

Psalmody: Psalm 21:1–7
Additional Psalm: Psalm 21
Old Testament Reading: Judges 16:4–30
Additional Reading: Judges 17:1–21:25
New Testament Reading: Galatians 4:12–31

Prayer of the Day

Faithful God, You promised to preserve Your people and save Your inheritance, using unlikely and unexpected vessels in extending the genealogy that would bring about the birth of your blessed Son. Give us the loyalty of Ruth and her trust in the one true God, that we, too, might honor You through our submission and respect, and be counted among Your chosen people, by the grace of Jesus Christ, our Lord, and the Holy Spirit, who reign together with You, now and forever. (1058)

Ruth

Ruth of Moab, the subject of the biblical book that bears her name, is an inspiring example of God's grace. Although she was a Gentile, God made her the great-grandmother of King David (Ruth 4:17) and an ancestress of Jesus Himself (Matthew 1:5). A famine in Israel led Elimelech and Naomi of Bethlehem to immigrate to the neighboring nation of Moab with their two sons. The sons married Moabite women, Orpah and Ruth, but after about ten years, Elimelech and his sons died (Ruth 1:1–5). Naomi then decided to return to Bethlehem and urged her daughters-in-law to return to their families. Orpah listened to Naomi's advice, but Ruth refused, replying with the stirring words: "Where you go I will go, and where you lodge I will lodge. Your people shall be my people, and your God my God" (Ruth 1:16). After Ruth arrived in Bethlehem, Boaz, a close relative of Elimelech, agreed to be Ruth's "redeemer" (Ruth 3:7–13; 4:9–12). He took her as his wife, and Ruth gave birth to Obed, the grandfather of David (Ruth 4:13–17), thus preserving the messianic line. Ruth's kindness and selfless loyalty toward Naomi and her faith in Naomi's God have long endeared her to the faithful and redounded to God's praise for His merciful choice of one so unexpected.

Meditation

Allegorizing can be dangerous business. After all, in an allegory, a reader can interpret a text completely apart from an author's intent. By allegorizing, a reader can use a text as a pretext for whatever he wants to say or believe. For instance, how many sermons have been preached on Jesus' calming of a storm in Mark 4:35–41 comparing the storm on the Sea of Galilee to the storms in a person's life? Certainly Jesus can calm the storms of life, but this was not the evangelist's point when he wrote Mark 4. Rather, his intent was to confess Jesus' power over nature, even as the disciples ask, "Who then is this, that even the wind and the sea obey Him" (Mark 4:41)?

Martin Luther had little stomach for the allegorizing of Scripture, calling it "awkward and inept." But he makes an exception for Paul in Galatians 4.

It seems the Judaizers of Galatia, eager to coax the Gentile Christians into adhering to Mosaic Law, used the story of Hagar and Sarah as an allegory, comparing Hagar and her illegitimate son Ishmael to lawless, impious Gentiles. Sarah and her miraculous son Isaac, however, were compared to faithful, pious Jews. The Judaizers' argument likely went like this: Ishmael was an illegitimate son of Abraham—wild and uncouth, a desert wanderer, born not of Abraham's wife, but of Sarah's maidservant (cf. Genesis 16, 21:8–21). Isaac, on the other hand, was a true son of Abraham, the child of whom God had promised: "I will establish My covenant with him as an everlasting covenant for his offspring after him" (Genesis 17:19). The Judaizers then boastfully claimed that they were heirs of Isaac.

But one allegory deserves another. And so Paul proffers his own allegorical interpretation of this story, refuting the one put forth by the Judaizers. Paul says, "Now this may be interpreted allegorically: these women are two covenants. One is from Mount Sinai, bearing children for slavery; she is Hagar" (Galatians 4:24). Paul connects Hagar to the Mosaic Law from Sinai, the very thing the Judaizers boastfully claimed to keep! Thus, Paul says the Judaizers are slaves in the line of Hagar, while the Gentile believers at Galatia, "like Isaac, are children of the promise" (4:28). The Galatians are the true children of Abraham, not the Judaizers, for the Galatians belong to Christ. "And if you are Christ's, then you are Abraham's offspring, heirs according to the promise" (3:29). And that's not just an allegory, that's a promise.

17 JULY

Psalmody: Psalm 92:8–15
Additional Psalm: Psalm 92
Old Testament Reading: 1 Samuel 1:1–20
New Testament Reading: Galatians 5:1–26

Prayer of the Day

Merciful God, for freedom You have set us free through Christ's liberating death and resurrection. In this freedom teach us to live in the fruit of the Spirit given us in our Baptism that we may bear in our bodies the fulfillment of the Law as we love our neighbors as ourselves; through Jesus Christ, our Lord. (1059)

Meditation

Sin likes to hide. When God comes to Abraham and promises, "Sarah your wife shall have a son" (Genesis 18:10), Sarah laughs because she is well past childbearing age. When Abraham confronts her defiance of God's promise, she responds, "I did not laugh" (18:15). *She tries to hide her sin.* When David commits adultery with Bathsheba and she becomes pregnant, he calls in Bathsheba's husband from the battlefield and attempts to get him to sleep with his wife so that his affair might be covered. *He tries to hide his sin.* When Judas betrays Jesus for thirty pieces of silver, John adds this note to Judas's betrayal: "And it was night" (John 13:30). Under cover of darkness, *Judas tries to hide his sin.*

Sin likes to hide. And yet, sin can only hide for so long. As Paul warns, "Now the works of the flesh are evident: sexual immorality, impurity, sensuality, idolatry, sorcery, enmity, strife, jealousy, fits of anger, rivalries, dissensions, divisions, envy, drunkenness, orgies, and things like these" (Galatians 5:19–21). Sin, says Paul, becomes *evident*. It cannot hide forever. The Greek word for

219

"evident" is *phaneros*, from which we get the word *epiphany*. Indeed, in the Greek text, *phaneros* is the first word of Paul's sentence, making it emphatic. Paul does not want us to miss this: sinfulness always reveals itself! As Jesus warns, "Nothing is hidden that will not be made manifest, nor is anything secret that will not be known and come to light" (Luke 8:17). Again, the Greek word for "manifest" is *phaneros*.

Blessedly, not only is sin revealed according to God's judgment, our Savior is revealed according to God's promise. As Paul writes, "For the grace of God has appeared, bringing salvation for all people, training us to renounce ungodliness and worldly passions, and to live self-controlled, upright, and godly lives in the present age, waiting for our blessed hope, the appearing of the glory of our great God and Savior Jesus Christ" (Titus 2:11–13). In verses 11 and 13, the word for "appear" is *epiphaino*. Thus, though our sin may be made manifest, our Savior has also been made manifest in His birth, death, and resurrection and will be made manifest again on the Last Day. And His manifestation outshines and forgives any appearing of our sin. Christ's appearing, in turn, trains us to renounce ungodliness and reveals in us the fruit of Christ's Spirit: "Love, joy, peace, patience, kindness, goodness, faithfulness, gentleness, self-control" (Galatians 5:22–23). And so, we long for Christ's epiphany.

18 July

Psalmody: Psalm 20
Additional Psalm: Psalm 131
Old Testament Reading: 1 Samuel 1:21–2:17
New Testament Reading: Galatians 6:1–18

Prayer of the Day

O Lord, keep Your household, the Church, in continual godliness that through Your protection she may be free from all adversities and devoutly given to serve You in good works; through Jesus Christ, Your Son, our Lord, who lives and reigns with You and the Holy Spirit, one God, now and forever. (H81)

Meditation

It's more than karma. Sadly, Paul's words in Galatians 6:7 are often taken to be little more than a biblical recapitulation of the Eastern philosophical tenet. The apostle writes: "For whatever one sows, that will he also reap." Sounds like karma. Tit for tat. You do something good and get something good in return. You do something evil and get your just deserts. But Paul is speaking of something much weightier than crass karma. The apostle continues: "The one who sows to his own flesh will from the flesh reap corruption, but the one who sows to the Spirit will from the Spirit reap eternal life" (6:8). Paul speaks not of sowing things that are merely good or bad, but of sowing things that are of the flesh or of the Spirit. The things of the flesh yield only corruption, but the things of the Spirit yield eternal life.

What are the things of the flesh? Paul is referring here to circumcision: "For even those who are circumcised do not themselves keep the law, but they desire to have you circumcised that they may boast in your flesh" (6:13). Paul says that those who insist on following the rite of circumcision reap only damnation because a legalistic insistence on this rite leads to boasting in something other than the cross of Christ. And far be it from anyone "to boast except in the cross of our Lord Jesus Christ" (6:14).

Paul boasts in the cross. What a strange thing in which to boast! In the first century, a cross evoked not devotion and piety but disgust and repulsion. The first century BC Roman philosopher Cicero once remarked that a Roman citizen should not ever hear, see, or even think of a cross. Indeed, being crucified was considered so shameful that it was not permitted for a Roman citizen except by order of the emperor. But Jesus was no Roman citizen. And so Jesus is crucified. It's no wonder, then, that He was "One from whom men hide their faces" (Isaiah 53:3), so vile was His death. And yet, the cross is Paul's boast. He boasts in a shameful death, for he believes that through it, we reap eternal life. And no circumcision can reap this. And so in the cross of Christ we, too, boast. For this is sowing in the Spirit.

19 JULY

Psalmody: Psalm 82
Additional Psalm: Psalm 136
Old Testament Reading: 1 Samuel 2:18–36
New Testament Reading: Acts 15:22–41

Prayer of the Day

Our Lord Jesus, Your yoke is easy and Your burden is light. Keep us from becoming burdened by laws fulfilled in You, and help us to live lives sanctified by Your Spirit that we might bear witness that in You all things have been made new; for You live and reign with the Father and the Holy Spirit, one God, now and forever. (1060)

Meditation

"Can we all get along?" So asked Rodney King after three L.A.P.D. officers, accused of brutality against King, were acquitted. The acquittals provoked such terrible rioting in Los Angeles that King pleaded for peace with news cameras rolling: "Can we all get along?"

If we were to answer King's question honestly, our answer would have to be, "No. We cannot all get along." Children rebel against parents. Workers organize strikes against their corporate employers. Parishioners fight with their pastor. We cannot all get along. But this is nothing new. For even in the nascent days of the Christian Church, people were disputing, as we find with Paul and Barnabas in Acts 15.

Paul is preparing to embark on his second missionary journey. Barnabas, Paul's companion, wants to take John Mark with them, perhaps because the two men are cousins (cf. Colossians 4:10). Paul, however, does not. For "Paul thought best not to take with them one who had withdrawn from them in Pamphylia and had not gone with them to the work" (Acts 15:38). Apparently, Paul sees Mark as unreliable.

What comes of this difference between Paul and Barnabas? "There arose a sharp disagreement, so that they separated from each other" (Acts 15:39). In the Greek text the word for "sharp disagreement," *paraxusmos*, is itself a neutral term, denoting provocation. But this provocation leads to separation.

Can we all get along? Paul and Barnabas couldn't. And neither can we. Neither *do* we. For we dispute, fight, and provoke. We, like Paul and Barnabas, *paraxusmos*; nevertheless, there is hope.

As Paul pens 2 Timothy, he is imprisoned in Rome, nearing death. Indeed, some believe that this is Paul's final epistle, Luther calling it his "farewell letter." At the end of this very personal letter, we read this greeting: "Get Mark and bring him with you, for he is very useful to me for ministry" (2 Timothy 4:11). It appears that Paul now sees what Barnabas saw in Mark all along. For now, instead of disparaging Mark, Paul asks for Mark. Relationships that once were fissured are now mended. So it can be with us also.

We cannot always get along. But we can always mend, always heal, and always forgive, even as Christ has forgiven us. Rather than provoking one another to anger and dissension, we can "stir up one another to love and good works" (Hebrews 10:24), the Greek word for "stir up" being the same *paraxusmos*. May God grant us such sanctified unity and *paraxusmos* for Jesus' sake.

20 JULY

Elijah

Psalmody: Psalm 119:57–64
Additional Psalm: Psalm 115:9–18
Old Testament Reading: 1 Samuel 3:1–21
New Testament Reading: Acts 16:1–22

Prayer of the Day

Lord God heavenly Father, through the prophet Elijah, You continued the prophetic pattern of teaching Your people the true faith and demonstrating through miracles Your presence in creation to heal it of its brokenness. Grant that Your Church may see in Your Son, our Lord Jesus Christ, the final end-times prophet whose teaching and miracles continue in Your Church through the healing medicine of the Gospel and the Sacraments; through Jesus Christ, our Lord. (1061)

Elijah

The prophet Elijah, whose name means, "My God is Yahweh [the LORD]," prophesied in the Northern Kingdom of Israel primarily during the reign of Ahab (874–853 BC). Ahab, under the influence of his pagan wife Jezebel, had encouraged the worship of Baal throughout his kingdom, even as Jezebel sought to get rid of the worship of Yahweh. Elijah was called by God to denounce this idolatry and to call the people of Israel back to the worship of Yahweh as the only true God (as he did in 1 Kings 18:20–40). Elijah was a rugged and imposing figure, living in the wilderness and dressing in a garment of camel's hair and a leather belt (2 Kings 1:8). He was a prophet mighty in word and deed. Many miracles were done through Elijah, including the raising of the dead (1 Kings 17:17–24), and the effecting of a long drought in Israel (1 Kings 17:1). At the end of his ministry, he was taken up into heaven while Elisha, his successor, looked on (2 Kings 2:11). Later, the prophet Malachi proclaimed that Elijah would return before the coming of the Messiah (Malachi 4:5–6), a prophecy that was fulfilled in the prophetic ministry of John the Baptist (Matthew 11:14).

Meditation

"Mom! Look at me!" If you're a mother, you've probably heard these words from your daughter, insisting that you watch her as she performs some daring feat of defiance. But sometimes mothers get busy. They become engaged in conversation. They get working on a project. And they do not immediately snap to attention at the sound of their daughter's command. These moments of distraction rarely seem to deter a daughter, however. She'll just say it again: "Mom! Look at me!" And if mom doesn't look then, she'll say it again and again and again.

In Acts 16, Paul encounters someone more persistent than a grandstanding child. He meets "a slave girl who had a spirit of divination" (v. 16). The Greek for "a spirit of divination" reads literally, "a spirit, Python."

Python was a serpent in Greek mythology who guarded the oracle of her mother, Gaia, until she was slain by Apollo who subsequently made the oracle his own. This mythical serpent now shows up as a real demon in this young girl, who, like a little girl begging her mother to look at her, cries out again and again and again. The demon declares through the girl, "These men are servants of the Most High God, who proclaim to you the way of salvation" (v. 17). And talk about persistent! Luke continues, "And this she kept doing for many days" (v. 18).

After days and perhaps even weeks, Paul becomes annoyed and rebukes the demon: "I command you in the name of Jesus Christ to come out of her" (v. 18). And the demon obeys.

This girl's healing should have brought a sigh of relief to everyone involved. After all, she had finally quieted down. And more than that, she had finally been freed from her demon possession. But money talks. So when this young girl is no longer talking by means of her soothsaying spirit and "her owners [see] that their hope of gain [is] gone" (v. 19), they are not happy about it. So, "They [seize] Paul and Silas and [drag] them into the marketplace before the rulers" (v. 19).

Jesus asked, "What does it profit a man to gain the whole world and forfeit his soul" (Mark 8:36)? The owners of the demon-possessed girl are obsessed with the profits of this world. Paul, however, is not concerned with their profits, but with this girl's soul—something much more valuable than any profit margin. Indeed, it's so valuable that Jesus shed His blood for her soul—and for yours.

21 JULY

Ezekiel

Psalmody: Psalm 106:1–5
Additional Psalm: Psalm 106
Old Testament Reading: 1 Samuel 4:1–22
New Testament Reading: Acts 16:23–40

Prayer of the Day

Lord God heavenly Father, through the prophet Ezekiel, You continued the prophetic pattern of teaching Your people the true faith and demonstrating through miracles Your presence in creation to heal it of its brokenness. Grant that Your Church may see in Your Son, our Lord Jesus Christ, the final end-times prophet whose teaching and miracles continue in Your Church through the healing medicine of the Gospel and the Sacraments; through Jesus Christ, our Lord. (1062)

Ezekiel

Ezekiel, the son of Buzi, was a priest called by God to be a prophet to the exiles during the Babylonian captivity (Ezekiel 1:3). In 597 BC, King Nebuchadnezzar and the Babylonian army brought the king of Judah and thousands of the best citizens of Jerusalem—including Ezekiel—to Babylon (2 Kings 24:8–16). Ezekiel's priestly background profoundly stamped his prophecy, as the holiness of God and the temple figure prominently in his messages (for example, Ezekiel 9–10 and 40–48). From 593 BC to the destruction of Jerusalem and the temple in 586 BC, Ezekiel prophesied the inevitability of divine judgment on Jerusalem, on the exiles in Babylon, and on seven nations that surrounded Israel (Ezekiel 1–32). Jerusalem would fall, and the exiles would not quickly return, as a just consequence of their sin. Once word reached Ezekiel that Jerusalem and the temple were destroyed, his message became one of comfort and hope. Through him, God promised that His people would experience future restoration, renewal, and revival in the coming messianic kingdom (Ezekiel 33–48). Much of the strange symbolism of Ezekiel's prophecies was later employed in the Revelation to St. John.

Meditation

"Fathers, do not provoke your children to anger, but bring them up in the discipline and instruction of the Lord" (Ephesians 6:4). A humble jailer from Philippi modeled these words well.

We first meet this jailer in Acts 16 when his very livelihood and life hang in the balance. An earthquake has struck his correctional facility, decimating it. He thinks his prisoners have surely escaped. And since Roman law dictates that an officer be punished with the same penalty due his escaped inmate if he loses even one of his prisoners, the jailer prepares to fall on his sword (v. 27), knowing that he would soon be brutally executed if he did not execute himself. But then this despondent jailer hears a voice: "Do not harm yourself, for we are all here" (v. 28). As unbelievable as it seems, a prisoner named Paul has freely remained incarcerated and has encouraged his fellow inmates to do the same, even though the earthquake would have provided a prime opportunity for escape.

Such nobility on the part of Paul, coupled with this jailer's "near-death" experience, snaps his attention to eternal concerns. "Sirs, what must I do to be saved?" the jailer asks. Paul and his companions reply, "Believe in the Lord Jesus, and you will be saved" (vv. 30–31).

Upon believing, the jailer is marked by God's name in Baptism. But not only is the jailer baptized, "he and all his family" (v. 33)

are redeemed by water through the Word. The jailer, then, is concerned not only with his eternity, but with the eternity of his family as well. As Paul will write a decade later, the jailer wants to "bring them up in the discipline and instruction of the Lord" (Ephesians 6:4).

Just as the jailer presented his family for Baptism, we also are to present our families for Baptism. And we, too, are to raise them in the discipline and instruction of the Lord. For children are a precious trust from Him. If you have children, take a moment today to remind them of their Baptism and the faith that they have been given through the Holy Spirit. Take some time also to remember your own Baptism and thank those who have faithfully brought you up in the Lord. For when members of our families are baptized, they become members of a much larger family— God's family. And that is a family of which we can all be proud to be a part.

22 JULY

St. Mary Magdalene

Psalmody: Psalm 137:1–7
Additional Psalm: Psalm 56
Old Testament Reading:
1 Samuel 5:1–6:3, 10–16
New Testament Reading: Acts 18:1–11, 23–28

Prayer of the Day

Almighty God, Your Son, Jesus Christ, restored Mary Magdalene to health and called her to be the first witness of His resurrection. Heal us from all our infirmities, and call us to know You in the power of Your Son's unending life; through the same Jesus Christ, our Lord, who lives and reigns with You and the Holy Spirit, one God, now and forever. (F22)

St. Mary Magdalene

Whenever the New Testament Gospels name the women who were with Jesus, St. Mary Magdalene is listed first (John 19:25 is the only exception), perhaps because she was the first to see the risen Savior alive. Luke 8:2 reports that Jesus had cured her of being possessed by seven demons. Through the centuries, she has often been identified with the repentant "woman of the city" who anointed Jesus' feet as He sat at the table in the Pharisee's home (Luke 7:36–50). But there is no biblical basis for this identification of her with a penitent prostitute. Nor is she to be identified with Mary, the sister of Martha, in Bethany. According to the Gospels, Mary Magdalene saw Jesus die; she witnessed His burial; and, most important, she was the first to see Him alive again after His resurrection (John 20:11–18). It is for good reason that Bernard of Clairvaux calls her "the apostle to the apostles."

Meditation

From Athens to Corinth. The attempt to connect with the heathen by way of philosophy had not borne the fruit Paul had hoped for. He would later write the Corinthians that when he came among them, he really only had one message: Jesus Christ, and Him crucified. Not the wisdom of men, but the foolishness of God—a message strong to give faith, powered by the Spirit.

In Corinth, Paul meets up with Aquila and his wife Priscilla. Tent makers, as he, Paul stayed in their home and continued speaking in the synagogue each Sabbath. He sought from the Scriptures to prove to both native Jews and Gentile converts that Jesus really was the Christ long foretold and promised, that in Him was forgiveness and eternal life.

This message, though, is either believed and rejoiced in or hated and despised. No one remains neutral about Jesus and His claims.

So Paul is finally declared *persona non grata* at the synagogue, and he sets up shop right next door. The Lord continues to bless the Word and it reaps a harvest of faith: not only Titius Justus who opened his home for the gathering of the disciples, but also Crispus, the ruler of the synagogue himself, believes. Many, many of the Corinthians receive the Word and join Jesus in the waters of Baptism, having their sins washed away and being joined to the resurrection life that is in Him.

Evidently, not all the Christians were unwelcome in the synagogue, for Aquila and Priscilla continue to attend, and hearing an eloquent guest from Alexandria speak one day, they realize that he's a fellow Christian, though not quite informed fully. So they take him aside after service, and explain "the way of God to him more accurately" (Acts 18:26). Behold, the royal priesthood of the baptized at work! Friends explaining to one another the deep truths of Jesus and all that He is and gives. The result was to take an eloquent speaker and set him on fire for the Lord.

Apollos was eager to share the Good News in other places, and with joy. The Christians at Corinth wrote him a letter of recommendation and encouraged him as he went forth to preach. He was a great teacher and "greatly helped those who through grace had believed." But he would never have been such a blessing to the Church had not Aquila and Priscilla taken him aside to open up to him the full treasures of God in Jesus Christ. May we such witnesses be!

23 JULY

Psalmody: Psalm 119:113–120
Additional Psalm: Psalm 141
Old Testament Reading: 1 Samuel 6:19–7:17
New Testament Reading: Acts 19:1–22

Prayer of the Day

O Lord, since You never fail to help and govern those whom You nurture in Your steadfast fear and love, work in us a perpetual fear and love of Your holy name; through Jesus Christ, our Lord, who lives and reigns with You and the Holy Spirit, one God, now and forever. (H62)

Meditation

From Corinth to Ephesus. Here St. Paul encounters some leftovers from John the Baptist's ministry. They had received Baptism from John, but they didn't know of John's witness to the Lamb of God who takes away the sin of the world. Paul completes what is lacking in their instruction, much as Apollos had his knowledge deficit made up by Aquila and Priscilla. And so they receive Baptism and the laying on of hands, and the Spirit of God came upon them mightily.

Meanwhile in the synagogue, Paul follows his usual route. He attends, he speaks, he witnesses at every opportunity to how the Scriptures that are being read all have their fulfillment in Jesus of Nazareth, crucified and then risen and now reigning and soon to be returning. And as always, the message divides. Some accept, many reject. As in Corinth, Paul sets up shop at another place and continues to preach to those who will hear him.

What extraordinary signs the Lord gave to verify the preaching of His beloved apostle Paul! The Lord Himself so filled Paul, the grace of God so transformed him, that the Lord's miraculous healing power was at work in his body to the extent that it flowed out even in material things like the handkerchiefs and aprons that touched his skin. Remember how the Lord Jesus had foretold: "Truly, truly, I say to you, whoever believes in Me will also do the works that I do; and greater works than these will he do, because I am going to the Father" (John 14:12). The power of the Lord at work through the material of creation should not surprise us in the least. After all, it is by water He gives new birth and washes sins away. It is by bread and wine, joined to His very body and blood, that He gives us a share in His own divine life.

As word spreads of the miraculous powers at work in Paul, others try to cash in on it without the commitment to the Lord Jesus. The seven sons of Sceva dare to invoke the Lord's name and Paul's name. The words of the demon show that neither the Lord nor Paul can be magical amulets. The signs are signs to call to repentance and to faith.

Repentance and faith do blossom as the name of Jesus is extolled. Believers come, confessing their sins, turning their backs on magic arts and literally burning their secrets. So it is that the Word of the Lord conquers, increases, prevails.

24 JULY

Psalmody: Psalm 24:7–10
Additional Psalm: Psalm 24
Old Testament Reading: 1 Samuel 8:1–22
New Testament Reading: Acts 21:15–36

Prayer of the Day

Lord Jesus, with Your death, the temple curtain was torn from top to bottom, giving access to Your holy presence for all people. By the preaching of Your Gospel, may You be our peace, for You have made us one and have broken down in Your flesh the dividing wall of hostility by fulfilling the Law in Your death on the cross; for You live and reign with the Father and the Holy Spirit, one God, now and forever. (1063)

Meditation

What had our Lord said? "O Jerusalem, Jerusalem, the city that kills the prophets and stones those who are sent to it! How often would I have gathered your children together as a hen gathers her brood under her wings, and you would not!" (Matthew 23:37). So when the apostle Paul arrives in the city, despite every attempt by James and the brothers to shield him from malice, he is beaten and finally rescued by arrest.

James lays out the false charges against Paul: that he was seeking to turn Jewish believers in Jesus from practicing Jewish customs. You can see why they would think that. Paul did teach Gentiles that they didn't need to become Jews in order to believe in Jesus and be saved; they didn't need to keep that Law of Moses, which the Jews didn't actually keep either. It can't save a soul, for no one is capable of fulfilling its demands. The Law of Moses, rather, accuses us all. You too. It shows how you have failed to love God with your all and your neighbor as yourself. But it also points toward another who would come to crush the serpent's head, to become a curse by being hanged on a tree, and to bring to all people the gift of His perfect obedience, His unfailing love of God and the neighbor.

Paul had proclaimed this message throughout his journeys and as a result the Lord Jesus had gathered believers to Himself throughout the areas where the Good News went—but always, as we have seen, with opposition. So when some of the Jews from the Roman Province of Asia who had tangled with Paul and his message back home came to Jerusalem for the feast, they saw Paul in the temple and seized their chance—and him! They incited a riot as they charged him with bringing a Greek believer who had never been circumcised into that holy place—across that barrier wall that warned Gentiles not to trespass at the risk of death.

But it was all false. Paul had done nothing of the kind. Yet the Lord Jesus was preparing to reach Paul with a deeper share in His passion and His resurrection life. As the crowds had cried: "Away with Him! Crucify Him!" about our Lord, so now they cried "Away with him!" over Paul. Paul's drinking from the cup of our Lord's Passion was about to intensify, and as always, the Lord's grace would be made perfect through human weakness, and triumph!

25 JULY

St. James the Elder, Apostle

Psalmody: Psalm 63:1–8
Additional Psalm: Psalm 149
Old Testament Reading: 1 Samuel 9:1–27
New Testament Reading: Acts 21:37–22:16

Prayer of the Day

O gracious God, Your servant and apostle James was the first among the Twelve to suffer martyrdom for the name of Jesus Christ. Pour out upon the leaders of Your Church that spirit of self-denying service that they may forsake all false and passing allurements and follow Christ alone, who lives and reigns with You and the Holy Spirit, one God, now and forever. (F23)

St. James the Elder, Apostle

St. James with his brother John, sons of Zebedee and Salome (see Matthew 27:56 and Mark 15:40), were fishermen in the Sea of Galilee who were called with Peter and his brother Andrew to follow Jesus (Matthew 4:18–22). In the Gospel lists of Jesus' disciples, James is listed following Peter and preceding John. Together these three appear as leaders of the Twelve. Because James precedes John, it is reasoned that James is the elder of the brothers. The Book of Acts records that James was beheaded by Herod Agrippa I, probably between AD 42 and 44 (Acts 12:1–2). Thus James is the first of the Twelve to die a martyr.

Meditation

Zeal. Zeal for God and for His law and His ways. How can it be wrong? Paul stands before the multitude in the temple and begins his witness with zeal. Yes, he had been zealous for the Law of the God of Israel once too. His pedigree was impeccable. True, he had been born in Tarsus of Cilicia, but he had been brought up in the holy city. He had sat at the feet of the great Rabbi Gamaliel and had soaked up his wisdom. He lived his life according to the strictness of the Pharisees, and so yes, he was zealous for God and for the Law of God, just as that crowd before him was so worked up at the thought that a Gentile had entered the holy place. And his zeal for the Law led him to "persecute this Way to the death" (Acts 22:4). The Jewish officials could all bear witness of what he had gone to Damascus to do.

But as he was on his way and outside the city, He who is Light of light and very God of very God, revealed Himself to Saul. "Saul, Saul, why are you persecuting Me?" He is amazed and cries out: "Who are You, Lord?" The answer that he received shattered the man: "I am Jesus of Nazareth, whom you are persecuting" (Acts 22:7–8).

Paul had been so convinced the whole tale told by Jesus' followers was a dirty lie, a fabricated fiction, deadly and evil. And now he discovers that it was all true. He's left in the dark, blinded, but the light was beginning to dawn. "It's true? He's risen? What they say of Him is no lie?" His faith life in shambles, his zeal burned out to ash, he is led blinded into Damascus to wait.

And so Ananias comes to Paul. Another devout Jew who also believed and knew the truth that Jesus had risen from the dead, that

the sins of the world had been forgiven in Him, and who now learned that God's love embraced the most unlikely, rescued them, and put them to work. "Brother Saul, receive your sight." And with the sight came a clearer vision of God's plan for him. "The God of our fathers appointed you to know His will and to see the Righteous One; . . . you will be a witness for Him to everyone. . . . Rise and be baptized and wash away your sins" (Acts 22:13–16).

So Saul, the one-time zealous persecutor, was plucked up by Jesus to become Paul, the apostle of grace.

26 JULY

Psalmody: Psalm 69:30–35
Additional Psalm: Psalm 70
Old Testament Reading: 1 Samuel 10:1–27
New Testament Reading: Acts 22:17–29

Prayer of the Day

Lord Jesus, You promised that when we are dragged before kings and governors for the sake of Your name, You will give us a mouth of wisdom to bear witness to Your saving grace. Give us courage in these gray and latter days to proclaim the Gospel, even in the face of those who not accept our testimony of You; for You live and reign with the Father and the Holy Spirit, one God, now and forever. (1064)

Meditation

The Gentiles were the fly in the ointment. It was the notion that somehow the God of Israel would bring into His fold the Gentiles—but without them becoming Jews—that sent them round the bend. Remember that the Jewish people of that day were very evangelistic. Our Lord notes that they would cross "sea and land to make a single proselyte" (Matthew 23:15). They were not at all opposed to the Gentiles becoming Jews; they were deadly opposed to the notion that the Gentiles could become God's people in another way—through faith in Jesus.

So they listened to Paul and maybe even wondered about the truth of what he said, right up to the moment when he tells them that in the temple itself, Jesus had appeared to him and told him to flee the city because his witness would not be received. Paul was still ready to argue the point—thinking his own past opposition to the message of Christ would surely lend credibility. Had he not even stood by, watching and approving, when the holy martyr Stephen was killed?

Yet the Lord Jesus has other plans for Paul: "Go, for I will send you far away to the Gentiles" (Acts 22:21). And so the riot breaks out afresh, even worse than before. "Away with such a fellow from the earth! For he should not be allowed to live" (22:22). Why? Because he told the truth about Jesus: that whoever believes and is baptized into Him will be saved. That in Him one can be justified from all that the Law could demand, but not deliver.

Paul had found his Roman citizenship to be of use before this—recall the situation in the Roman colony of Philippi. He invokes it again as the torture is preparing to commence. "Is it lawful for you to flog a man who is a Roman citizen and uncondemned?" (22:25). Paul has shown repeatedly that he is neither afraid nor ashamed to suffer for the Lord, but when there is a way out, he takes it. Perhaps he already has an inkling of where this will lead: witnessing to Jesus before Caesar himself and then dying to seal his witness that Christ is victor over death and the grave.

The tribune backpedals mightily when he catches word that he's mishandled a Roman. "I bought this citizenship for a large sum" he tells Paul. "But I am a citizen by birth," the apostle answers (22:28). And so the

torture proposed comes to nothing, and the opportunity to witness from his long imprisonment begins.

27 JULY

Psalmody: Psalm 119:17–24
Additional Psalm: Psalm 141
Old Testament Reading: 1 Samuel 12:1–25
New Testament Reading: Acts 22:30–23:11

Prayer of the Day

Christ, our risen Lord, Your resurrection showed us what we will someday be and what we already are now through our Baptism into Your holy name. Give us courage to bear in our bodies Your resurrected life as we live out the fruits of Your victory over death through works of charity and mercy; for You live and reign with the Father and the Holy Spirit, one God, now and forever. (1065)

Meditation

That Paul was a Roman citizen, the tribune had already learned. What he didn't know was why on earth the man was at the center of riot. And so unbound he leads Paul into the Jewish council, sets him before them, and seeks to discover what it is that the man is guilty of that they would demand his death.

Paul begins his usual defense, appealing to his good conscience, but for this he receives a slap on the mouth, and he loses his temper a bit. One of the things that irritates him to no end, now that he has come to know the truth that is in Jesus, is how we human beings can sit in judgment on one another according to the Law and yet feel free to violate the Law when it suits our purposes. With the Law we condemn others; from the Law we excuse ourselves. He speaks of this in detail in Romans 2. But it was also wrong for him to call names, and he admits as much. "You shall not speak evil of a ruler of your people" (Acts 23:5).

Realizing the composite nature of the council, Paul proceeds to divide and conquer. Jews they all were, but some were the rationalistic Sadducees, denying resurrection, angels, spirits; some were believing Pharisees who confessed all of these as Scripture teaches. "Brothers, I am a Pharisee" (23:6). Note that Paul said "I *am*," not "I *was*." The essential truth that the Pharisees held to in the matters in dispute with the Sadducees is something they share with all Christians. "It is with respect to the hope and the resurrection of the dead that I am on trial" (23:6).

The hope of the resurrection goes to the heart of it. That a man who once died should be raised in a body incorruptible and made the source of everlasting salvation to all who believe in Him—this is the beating heart of Paul's proclamation. And as he shouts it out, the house does indeed divide. "We find nothing wrong in this man" the Pharisees began to shout out. Soon the place was in an uproar.

The tribune saw again that whatever Paul said seemed to incite riot, so he took him by force and locked him up again. It wasn't a failure. The Lord Jesus stood by him again with the promise: "Take courage, for as you have testified to the facts about Me in Jerusalem, so you must testify also in Rome" (Acts 23:11). Facts! The truth that seems so unbelievable, but that is, well, true.

28 July

Johann Sebastian Bach, Kantor

Psalmody: Psalm 59:1–5
Additional Psalm: Psalm 57
Old Testament Reading: 1 Samuel 13:1–18
New Testament Reading: Acts 23:12–35

Prayer of the Day

Almighty God, beautiful in majesty and majestic in holiness, You have taught us in Holy Scripture to sing Your praises and given to Your servant Johann Sebastian Bach grace to show forth Your glory in his music. Continue to grant this gift of inspiration to all Your servants who write and make music for Your people, that with joy we on earth may glimpse Your beauty and at length know the inexhaustible richness of Your new creation in Jesus Christ, our Lord, who lives and reigns with you and the Holy Spirit, one God, now and forever. Amen. (1066)

Johann Sebastian Bach, Kantor

Johann Sebastian Bach (1685–1750) is acknowledged as one of the most famous and gifted composers in the Western world. Orphaned at age ten, Bach was mostly self-taught in music. His professional life as conductor, performer, composer, teacher, and organ consultant began at age nineteen in the town of Arnstadt and ended in Leipzig, where for the last twenty-seven years of his life he was responsible for all the music in the city's four Lutheran churches. In addition to being a superb keyboard artist, the genius and bulk of Bach's vocal and instrumental compositions remain overwhelming. A devout and devoted Lutheran, he is especially honored in Christendom for his lifelong insistence that his music was written primarily for the liturgical life of the Church to glorify God and edify His people.

Meditation

As zealous as Saul had been to destroy and punish all the witnesses of Jesus and His resurrection, so now a crowd of Jewish zealots are eager to do away with Saul turned Paul, the apostle, because of his witness to our Lord. They want that witness silenced, no matter what the cost. So they bind themselves by an oath. Think of it! An oath taken to the God of Israel, in whose honor they presume to do this deed of murder. They are as mistaken in their zeal as Saul had been in his. The God of Israel, after all, raised His Son from the dead and sent Him to give repentance and forgiveness first to His own people and then also to the Gentiles. Their false oath was seeking to silence those who bore witness to the truth! When word of the planned lynching leaked out, Paul's nephew hears about the proposed attack and scurries to warn his uncle, heeding well the Fifth Commandment to "help and support [our neighbor] in every physical need." Paul has the lad repeat the story to the tribune, who decides quickly that the situation has gotten out of hand. The tribune orders a secret mission to the Roman Governor Felix to head out in the dead of that very night, delivering Paul from their insidious plot. Instructive is the letter that Claudius Lysias, the tribune, wrote to Felix. As you read over it, you no doubt notice what people today call "spin." Claudius appears in the guise of a hero almost—rescuing Paul from the Jewish mob because he learned that he was a Roman citizen, and seeking to give him a fair trial. But, of course, that is not quite how it happened, is it? How often is it the case that when you recount a story, you do the same? How often do you portray yourself in a better light than you know have a right to? Repent. The same apostle Paul would later urge the Ephesians to speak the truth to one another. Truth speaking is a mark of Jesus' disciples.

Felix reads the letter and looks over his new problem. He tells Paul "I will give you a hearing when your accusers arrive" and commanded him to be guarded (Acts 23:35). So Paul is moved one step closer to the fulfillment of our Lord's words to him, that he would witness also for the Savior in the city of Rome.

29 JULY

Mary, Martha, and Lazarus of Bethany

Psalmody: Psalm 119:41–48
Additional Psalm: Psalm 13
Old Testament Reading: 1 Samuel 14:47–15:9
New Testament Reading: Acts 24:1–23

Prayer of the Day

Heavenly Father, Your beloved Son befriended frail humans like us to make us Your own. Teach us to be like Jesus' dear friends from Bethany, that we might serve Him faithfully like Martha, learn from Him earnestly like Mary, and be raised by Him ultimately like Lazarus. Through their Lord and ours, Jesus Christ, who lives and reigns with You and the Holy Spirit, one God, now and forever. (1067)

Mary, Martha, and Lazarus of Bethany
Mary, Martha, and Lazarus of Bethany were disciples with whom Jesus had a special bond of love and friendship. John's Gospel records that "Jesus loved Martha and her sister and Lazarus" (John 11:15). On one occasion, Martha welcomed Jesus into their home for a meal. While Martha did all the work, Mary sat at Jesus' feet, listening to His Word, and was commended by Jesus for choosing the "good portion which will not be taken away from her" (Luke 10:38–42). When their brother Lazarus died, Jesus spoke to Martha this beautiful Gospel promise: "I am the resurrection and the life. Whoever believes in Me, though he die, yet shall he live" (John 11:25). Ironically, when Jesus raised Lazarus from the dead, the Jews became more determined than ever to kill Jesus (John 11:39–54). Six days before Jesus was crucified,

Mary anointed His feet with a very expensive fragrant oil and wiped them with her hair, not knowing at the time that she was doing it in preparation for Jesus' burial (John 12:1–8; Matthew 26:6–13).

Meditation

What a contrast between the professional orator and the plain-speaking apostle! The orator seeks first to win the good will of the governor by flattery. When he thinks he has obtained this, he proceeds to offer a most general reason for Paul's arrest, amounting to little more than: "we think he's a troublemaker." Particularly insidious is the suggestion that Felix should "examine him" to find out from him about the things he is accused of. "Examine" here means investigate under torture—precisely what the tribune Lysias had been preparing to do to Paul when Paul inquired whether it was legal to torture a Roman citizen, uncondemned.

In utter contrast to their vagaries and flattery, Paul is happy to make his defense before a man who certainly must know some of what has happened in his territory in the past several years. "You can verify," Paul begins. Check out the truth of what I'm telling you. He makes it plain that he hasn't even been two weeks in the city, that he wasn't stirring up trouble in the temple or in any synagogue, and so they can't prove any of their charges. Except for this one: "But this I confess to you, that according to the Way, which they call a sect, I worship the God of our fathers, believing everything laid down by the Law and written in the Prophets, having a hope in God, which these men themselves accept, that there will be a resurrection of both the just and the unjust" (Acts 24:14–15).

Paul is not the least bit ashamed either to be a Christian or to be known as one. He boldly confesses that he worships Israel's God according to the Way. And it was moved by that worship of the God of mercy, that he had

come to Jerusalem on a mission of mercy, bringing alms for the poor of his people—alms that had been gathered from the little communities of the Way scattered throughout the Roman provinces of the east. If Paul is guilty of stirring up the crowd, the only thing he can think of that fits the description is when he cried out in the Jewish Council: "It is with respect to the resurrection of the dead that I am on trial before you this day."

The hope of the resurrection was always at the center of Paul's joyful witness—for it is the center of the Law and the Prophets and it is the center of the Way, the Christian faith.

30 JULY

Robert Barnes, Confessor and Martyr

Psalmody: Psalm 50:1–6
Additional Psalm: Psalm 130
Old Testament Reading: 1 Samuel 15:10–35
New Testament Reading: Acts 24:24–25:12

Prayer of the Day

Almighty God, heavenly Father, You gave courage to Your servant Robert Barnes to give up his life for confessing the true faith during the Reformation. May we continue steadfast in our confession of the apostolic faith and suffer all, even death, rather than fall away from it; through Jesus Christ, our Lord. (1068)

Robert Barnes, Confessor and Martyr
Remembered as a devoted disciple of Martin Luther, Robert Barnes is considered to be among the first Lutheran martyrs. Born in 1495, Barnes became the prior of the Augustinian monastery at Cambridge, England. Converted to Lutheran teaching, he shared his insights with many English scholars through writings and personal

contacts. During a time of exile to Germany, he became friends with Luther and later wrote a Latin summary of the main doctrines of the Augsburg Confession titled *Sententiae*. Upon his return to England, Barnes shared his Lutheran doctrines and views in person with King Henry VIII and initially had a positive reception. In 1529, Barnes was named royal chaplain. The changing political and ecclesiastical climate in his native country, however, claimed him as a victim; he was burned at the stake in Smithfield in 1540. His final confession of faith was published by Luther, who called his friend Barnes "our good, pious dinner guest and houseguest . . . this holy martyr, St. Robert Barnes."

Meditation

Drawn and repulsed. So men often find their experience of God's Word. Drawn to it, inexplicably, and yet scared by it, and so fleeing it. Again and again, Felix called for Paul and listened to his teaching. Paul spoke the Law in its full severity. He told the Roman Governor plainly about righteousness, self-control, and how all people—even Roman governors—would have to stand in the end before a Judge who would not play favorites, hold out for bribes, or permit spin and half-truths. All people in the end will stand before a Judge "to whom all hearts are open, all desires known, and from whom no secrets are hid." None. Alarmed, Felix sent the apostle away, but the words and their power remained. "When I get an opportunity I will summon you" (Acts 24:25). Time after time, the Governor would listen to this strange prisoner of his, and then shoo him away again when the message struck too close to home.

Finally, forgetting about righteousness and self-control and the certainty of coming judgment and whatever else of God's Word Paul had shared with him, the Governor, when he moved on, decided to do the Jews a favor and leave the apostle sitting in prison. How often must Paul have wondered in those days: How can I be Your witness in Rome if I sit here in a Roman prison in Palestine? The new governor is not much better. Festus wants to hit it off right with the local politicians and leaders, so he asks Paul about going up to Jerusalem to be tried on the charges that the Jews continued to level against him. Paul was not having any of it. "I am standing before Caesar's tribunal, where I ought to be tried" (Acts 25:10). He knew that the Jews had no case against him, but he remembered well the plot to take his life in Jerusalem. So he invokes the final right of every Roman citizen: "I appeal to Caesar!" (25:11).

Amazed, Festus and his council consult and decree: "To Caesar you have appealed; to Caesar you shall go" (Acts 25:12). The tone, perhaps, suggested to the apostle that it was a fool's path he had chosen; Caesar was not known for mercy.

So it was, though, that the words of the Lord Jesus to Paul earlier began to be fulfilled: "As you have testified to the facts about Me in Jerusalem, so you must testify also in Rome." (Acts 23:11) All things work together for the good of those who love Christ Jesus (cf. Romans 8:28).

31 JULY

Joseph of Arimathea

Psalmody: Psalm 80:14–19
Additional Psalm: Psalm 80
Old Testament Reading: 1 Samuel 16:1–23
New Testament Reading: Acts 25:13–27

Joseph of Arimathea

This Joseph, mentioned in all four Gospels, came from a small village called Arimathea in the hill country of Judea. He was a respected member of the Sanhedrin, the Jewish religious council in Jerusalem. He was presumably wealthy, since he owned his own unused tomb in a garden not far from the site of Jesus' crucifixion (Matthew 27:60). Joseph, a man waiting expectantly for the kingdom of God, went to Pontius Pilate after the death of Jesus and asked for Jesus' body (Mark 15:43). Along with Nicodemus, Joseph removed the body and placed it in the tomb (John 19:38–39). Their public devotion contrasted greatly to the fearfulness of the disciples who had abandoned Jesus.

Meditation

The perplexed Governor Festus is happy that a man so experienced with the Jews as King Agrippa has arrived in town. As he lays the matter before him for counsel, Festus reveals how confounded he is. He expected the prisoner to be charged with serious crime since the Jewish leaders sought his death, but the best he could figure out, their complaint against Paul was points of dispute about their religion. Above all, it was about a "certain Jesus, who was dead, but whom Paul asserted to be alive" (Acts 25:19).

And there is the heart of the faith and the supreme point of contention between the followers of the Way and other Jews. They all agreed that the man Jesus had been killed by crucifixion. But the dispute began when Paul and the others insisted with vigor that the Crucified One had been raised from the dead. That though He *was* dead, He *is* alive— alive forevermore as the sign, guarantee, and promise of the general resurrection of the dead. Alive as the firstfruits and the firstborn of a new creation.

Agrippa and Bernice listened as Festus laid out the problem. The man had done nothing deserving of imprisonment, but rather than face his accusers in Jerusalem, the prisoner had appealed to Rome, to Caesar himself! But what on earth was Festus to write? How could he begin to explain the charges against Paul in a way that would even make sense? When was asserting that a dead man was raised into life a crime? Agrippa listens and says: "I would like to hear the man myself" (Acts 25:22). And so it is arranged.

With great pomp and earthly display the King and his Queen enter, together with the Roman Governor and his military officials, and the court sits. And then the lowly prisoner is brought before the assembled powers. What does he think as he looks them over? He is a man whose conscience is clear, who knows his imprisonment is unjust. Yet he is not about to whine or complain. Rather, he sizes up an opportunity to do exactly what he is called to do, what he loves to do: to witness to one and all about the resurrection.

So in every circumstance that meets us, particularly in adversity, God likewise is providing an opportunity for us to witness to the resurrection of Jesus Christ, His Son. Though we may not be dragged before temporal authorities, countless are the opportunities God arranges for us to witness to the life we have known in His Son.

1 AUGUST

Psalmody: Psalm 70
Additional Psalm: Psalm 75
Old Testament Reading: 1 Samuel 17:1–19
New Testament Reading: Acts 26:1–23

Prayer of the Day

Gracious Lord of all, You turned the apostle Paul from a persecutor of the Church to the apostle to the Gentiles. By Your Holy Word, turn our hearts from darkness to light, from the power of Satan to God, that we might receive the forgiveness of our sins and a place among those who are sanctified by faith in Your Son, Jesus Christ, our Lord, who lives and reigns with You and the Holy Spirit, one God, now and forever. (1070)

Meditation

Agrippa is no stranger to some of Paul's tidings. Such miracles as our Lord did and as His apostles continued to do could not be kept hidden. But what did they mean? What did such power at work among men portend? Paul asks for a patient hearing as he begins to explain.

Paul was well-known for his manner of life. As a Pharisee he had hope in the resurrection of the dead, and he daily joined in worshiping the God of the Living. Why should any rational being stumble at the notion of the almighty, living God raising the dead to life?

What he had stumbled over were the claims that God had raised this Jesus of Nazareth as the firstfruits of the dead. He was convinced it was a lie, a fraud, a satanic deception. He fought it with might and main. He lays his shame out before Agrippa and Festus: "when they were put to death I cast my vote against them." Stephen loomed large in Paul's memory. And yet it all changed on that day outside Damascus, when the Resurrected One appeared to Paul in light brighter than the sun and asked Paul why he was persecuting Him. Note that. To touch the saints of God is to touch the Lord Jesus—to persecute them is to persecute Him, for He is one body with them. Our Lord, in His outrageous grace, had a plan and purpose for His erstwhile persecutor. Paul reveals here more of the words of the Lord to him than at any other point. The Lord Jesus appoints him as servant and witness of what he has seen. He is being sent to the Gentiles, to open their blind eyes, to turn them from darkness to light, and to bring them from the domain of Satan to the joyous kingdom of God, by preaching to them forgiveness, giving them a place among the sanctified—those made holy—by their faith in the Lord Jesus.

And that, says Paul, is what he's been doing. Traveling hither and yon, summoning all into repentance, and for this they seek his death. And yet he still stands and testifies to the small and to the great that what Moses and the prophets foretold has come to pass: the Christ had to suffer, be raised, and be given as light to Jew and Gentile.

2 AUGUST

Psalmody: Psalm 71:1–8
Additional Psalm: Psalm 98
Old Testament Reading: 1 Samuel 17:20–47
New Testament Reading: Acts 26:24–27:8

Prayer of the Day

Lord Jesus Christ, before whom all in heaven and earth shall bow, grant courage that Your children may confess Your saving name in the face of any opposition from a world hostile to the Gospel. Help them to remember Your faithful people who sacrificed much and even faced death rather than dishonor You when called upon to deny the faith. By Your Spirit, strengthen them to be faithful and to confess You boldly, knowing that You will confess Your own before the Father in heaven, with whom You and the Holy Spirit live and reign, one God, now and forever. (111)

Meditation

The Roman Governor Festus had listened with increasing incredulity. "Paul, you are out of your mind; your great learning is driving you out of your mind." The Gospel appeared foolish to him, as it does to every man by nature. "The natural person does not accept the things of the Spirit of God, for they are folly to him, and he is not able to understand them because they are spiritually discerned," Paul wrote to the Corinthians (1 Corinthians 2:14). But even if they appear folly, Paul argues that they are anything but: "I am speaking true and rational words."

So Paul had laid before Agrippa the appeal to verify the facts. Festus, newly arrived, may well be hearing these things for the first time. Agrippa, long a resident of the area, knew that the story was too well founded to be mere rumor, myth, or someone's imagination. "The king knows about these things, and to him I speak boldly. For I am persuaded that none of these things has escaped his notice, for this has not been done in a corner." The miracles testify by themselves that something extraordinary and unknown in the history of mankind was at work—and so did the fervor of these witnesses of the resurrection.

Paul presses Agrippa hard. "King Agrippa, do you believe the prophets? I know that you believe." There is no denying that Isaiah's words had come to life under Agrippa's nose. The blind had seen, the deaf heard, the dead were raised up, and good news was being preached throughout the length and breadth of Palestine.

Whose trial is it? Paul's or Agrippa's? Suddenly the judge and jury are in the dock. "Do you believe?" Paul asks and suddenly he is presiding at court. Agrippa is astonished: "In a short time would you persuade me to be a Christian?" Note the use of the word *Christian*. Already the name that the Way was given in Antioch has become common parlance. To belong to Christ is to be a Christian. Agrippa's question doesn't answer Paul's question to him. Yet Paul responds and says his heart's desire: "I would to God that not only you but also all who hear me this day might become such as I am" and then he looks down at the chains and adds "except for these chains."

As the court recesses, Agrippa agrees with Festus. Paul doesn't deserve imprisonment let alone death. So the journey begins that will land him before Caesar to witness, to seek, and to persuade him too.

3 AUGUST

Joanna, Mary, and Salome, Myrrhbearers

Psalmody: Psalm 68:4–10
Additional Psalm: Psalm 68
Old Testament Reading: 1 Samuel 17:48–18:9
New Testament Reading: Acts 27:9–26

Prayer of the Day

Mighty God, Your crucified and buried Son did not remain in the tomb for long. Give us joy in the tasks set before us, that we might carry out faithful acts of service as did Joanna, Mary, and Salome, offering to You the sweet perfume of our grateful hearts, so that we, too, may see the glory of Your resurrection and proclaim the Good News with unrestrained eagerness and fervor worked in us through our Lord Jesus Christ, who rose and reigns with You and the Holy Spirit, one God, now and forever. (1071)

Joanna, Mary, and Salome, Myrrhbearers

Known in some traditions as "the faithful women," the visit of these three persons and other women to the tomb of Jesus on the first Easter morning is noted in the Gospel records of Matthew (28:1), Mark (16:1), and Luke (24:10). Joanna was the wife of Chuza, a steward in Herod's household (Luke 8:3). Mary, the mother of James (the son of Alphaeus), was another of the women who faithfully provided care for Jesus and His disciples from the time of His Galilean ministry through His burial after the crucifixion. Salome, the mother of the sons of Zebedee (Matthew 27:56), joined with the women both at the cross and in bringing the spices to the garden tomb. These faithful women have been honored in the Church through the centuries as examples of humble and devoted service to the Lord.

Meditation

What does a wandering apostle know about sailing? So Julius, the centurion, decides to go with the advice of the sailors rather than the advice of this strange man he is charged with delivering to Rome. It was, of course, a fateful decision.

The storm struck fiercely and they were driven to their wit's end. It looked very, very bad.

When even seasoned sailors are frightened enough to pitch overboard the ship's tackle, the fear of death is just around the corner. In the midst of such great anxiety, Paul received a visitor. An angel of God appeared and spoke to him: "Do not be afraid, Paul; you must stand before Caesar. And behold, God has granted you all those who sail with you."

Peace, then. Whatever form Paul's death would come in, it would not be death at sea. At least not before he'd spoken to Caesar about the hope of the resurrection. As the storm raged on and the anxiety on the ship increased, Paul sought to bring them into his peace.

"You should have listened to me" he begins, for then there would not have been this great loss of property and danger to life. "Yet now I urge you to take heart, for there will be no loss of life among you, but only of the ship." You can imagine the incredulous looks that Paul received as he stated this so calmly and so certainly. As their faces clearly asked: "How do you know?" he told them. He had learned it from "an angel of the God to whom I belong and whom I worship."

And that God happened to be the Lord of the sea as well as of the dry land. Did Paul remember and pray Psalm 107 during those long hours of waiting? "For He commanded and raised up the stormy wind, which lifted up the waves of the sea. . . . He made the storm be still . . . He brought them to their desired haven. Let them thank the Lord for His steadfast love, for His wondrous works to the children of man" (Psalm 107:25, 29, 30–31).

"So take heart, men, for I have faith that in God that it will be exactly as I have been told." Paul had long since learned the truth that there is nothing in this world more certain than a promise from the God of Israel. He summoned his fellow travelers into the peace of God's promise, and he knew it would open the door to faith in God's even greater promise in Jesus Christ.

4 AUGUST

Psalmody: Psalm 56:1–4
Additional Psalm: Psalm 56
Old Testament Reading: 1 Samuel 18:10–30
New Testament Reading: Acts 27:27–44

Prayer of the Day

Almighty God, by Your great goodness mercifully look upon Your people that we may be governed and preserved evermore in body and soul; through Jesus Christ, Your Son, our Lord, who lives and reigns with You and the Holy Spirit, one God, now and forever. (L27)

Meditation

Paul continues his mission of directing a safe shipwreck. When the sailors, sensing the approach of land and taking their sounding, realize that shipwreck is imminent, they prepare to escape the ship in the smaller boat. Paul discloses their plot to the soldiers. The sailors are kept on board as the ship's boat is cut and drifts away, and the ship draws closer to land.

Before the day dawned when the ship would wreck, Paul urges the 276 passengers to eat. They'll need the strength given them by the food for the swim ahead. He assures them one more time that none of them will die. His trust in God's promise is unshakable. He takes bread, gives thanks to God before them all, broke it, and began to eat. Encouraged by his confidence, they follow his example. And when they'd eaten, they threw the rest of the wheat out into the sea to lighten the ship still more. Come what may, they knew their journey was near its end.

As the sun rose, they saw land before them and a bay. The sailors try to make for the bay but run into a reef and the ship is stuck. Just as Paul had foretold, the pound of the surf begins to break up the ship.

Roman soldiers guarded their prisoners well, for they knew that their lives were forfeit should the prisoners escape. Think of the Philippian jailer's despair in Acts 16 when he thought that he had lost his prisoners. So, for the Roman soldiers, the logical thing to do is to kill Paul and the other prisoners.

But Julius, the centurion, will not hear of it. He wants to save Paul, a man whose peace and calm in this disaster had surely weighed on his own heart. He must have wondered time and again: "What makes that man tick? What makes him so peaceful and calm? Rumor is that he's not even guilty of anything, and yet he's a cheerful prisoner and lives as though he's king of the world? What gives?" So under Julius's direction, the prisoners are allowed to attempt the swim toward shore. And Julius no doubt hopes fervently that Paul's prescience would come through for them all one more time.

As God had promised Paul, every one of the 276 passengers make it safely to land. You can imagine how, after catching their breath and feeling solid ground under their feet again, they must have gathered around that odd wandering preacher to hear more about this God he worshiped and served.

5 AUGUST

Psalmody: Psalm 21:1–7
Additional Psalm: Psalm 21
Old Testament Reading: 1 Samuel 19:1–24
New Testament Reading: Acts 28:1–15

Prayer of the Day

Lord God, heavenly Father, You delivered us from the enemy through the death of Your Son, Jesus Christ, our Lord, with whom we are united in Holy Baptism. Continue to deliver us, we pray, from our diseases and afflictions by Your merciful gift of healing as You feed us holy food and give us the cup of everlasting life to drink; through Jesus Christ, our Lord. (1072)

Meditation

What had our Lord promised? "They will pick up serpents with their hands; and if they drink any deadly poison, it will not hurt them; they will lay their hands on the sick, and they will recover" (Mark 16:18). So the signs marking the apostle are fulfilled in Paul after the shipwreck on Malta.

Because of the rain and cold, the natives of the island had started a fire for the victims of the shipwreck. Paul was seeking to help out, gathering a bundle of sticks to put on the fire. But as he drew near the fire to put it on, a viper, escaping the heat, latched onto his hand. The natives rapidly conclude that justice is being done; though the man escaped the shipwreck, he obviously was one deserving of death. Imagine their shock when Paul shakes the serpent off and goes about his business, none the worse. How could it be? How could it possibly be?

They draw another erroneous conclusion: he must be a god visiting them. Recall the people of Lystra (Acts 14:11) had made a similar wrong conclusion. It is true that through the apostle miraculous powers were at work, but he was not divine himself; through Jesus, though, he had been restored to communion with God and to verify the truth of his message, these signs were granted. This is how the apostle would express it to the Church at Corinth: "The signs of a true apostle were performed among you with utmost patience, with signs and wonders and mighty works" (2 Corinthians 12:12).

Paul was not only unharmed by the viper's poison, but he also healed Publius's father with prayer and the laying on of hands. Soon all the sick around Malta were descending on Publius's estate to be healed. And through Paul, they all were. The miracles proclaimed with a loud voice that God loves us, that He hates death and all that attends it, and that He has come to save and rescue us from it through the gift of His Son.

Luke's story is wending to its close. He moves rapidly from Malta to Syracuse, from Syracuse to Rhegium and Puteoli, and finally, "so we came to Rome." Even before they reach the city, brothers in Christ come to greet the holy apostle. Well might the centurion have wondered: "If I am delivering a prisoner, why does it feel like I'm attending a conquering hero instead?"

6 AUGUST

Psalmody: Psalm 92:1–9
Additional Psalm: Psalm 92
Old Testament Reading: 1 Samuel 20:1–23
New Testament Reading: Acts 28:16–31

Prayer of the Day

Lord Jesus, Paul, Your apostle to the Gentiles, proclaimed the kingdom of God and taught about the Lord Jesus Christ while in prison in Rome. In our freedom to worship You rightly, give us burning hearts when we hear Moses and the Prophets expounded before us, and open our eyes in the breaking of the bread to see You as our Savior and Lord; for You live and reign with the Father and the Holy Spirit, one God, now and forever. (1073)

Meditation

How utterly unsatisfying is the ending of Acts! We want to know: What happened to Paul? We've been following his story so closely it seems intolerable for Luke to break it off as he does. But, of course, Luke was not chronicling Paul's life. Luke was chronicling the progress of the Word of God as it moved out from Jerusalem to Judea and Samaria and to the ends of the earth (Acts 1:8).

So Luke's account ends with Paul gathering the Jews together and following the exact same pattern we've seen him use from the beginning.

He sought to persuade them from Moses and the Prophets, using the sacred writings of the Old Testament, that Jesus of Nazareth was "the real deal"—that He was in fact the promised Messiah and had been raised from the dead.

As always the message divides the house. Some believe and rejoice in the tidings Paul brings; for others it just seems too good to possibly be true. They reject it. In so doing, they fulfill the words of Isaiah's prophesy about the fate of God's Good News among His ancient people: "You will indeed hear but never understand . . . lest they should see with their eyes and hear with their ears and understand with their heart and turn, and I would heal them." They judge themselves unworthy of eternal life.

Paul is saddened but not cast down. "Therefore let it be known to you that this salvation of God has been sent to the Gentiles; they will listen." And so they have. Most of you who are reading this are proof of that; you are Gentiles who have been brought to faith through the Holy Spirit in the Messiah long promised to the Jewish people, but rejected by so many of them.

Paul continued to live at the center of the empire for the next two years at his own expense, though under house arrest. He wasn't free to go out, but he was free to receive visitors, and he gladly welcomed all who came to him, for that gave him the opportunity to speak about the Kingdom of God, God's gracious reign through Jesus in the forgiveness of sins. He was free to preach and teach without anyone hindering him, and he did so with great boldness.

Here Luke ends the story: the good news about Jesus being proclaimed by the Lord's apostle in the very heart of the Roman Empire. The Word of the Lord had indeed grown and triumphed!

7 AUGUST

Psalmody: Psalm 144:3–10
Additional Psalm: Psalm 144
Old Testament Reading: 1 Samuel 20:24–42
Additional Reading: 1 Samuel 21:1–23:29
New Testament Reading: 1 Corinthians 1:1–25

Prayer of the Day

O God, whose infinite love restores to the right way those who err, gathers the scattered, and preserves those whom You have gathered, of Your tender mercy pour out on Your Christian people the grace of unity that, all schisms being healed, Your flock, gathered to the true Shepherd of Your Church, may serve You in all faithfulness; through Jesus Christ, our Lord. (1155)

Meditation

Society, generally speaking, is not interested in the shocking truth of the necessity for judgment and grace—the plain truth of sin and mercy. Our culture is not interested in the greatness and glory of God. Folks run to Him in times of danger and tragedy, as in the aftermath of 9/11. Or beg Him to heal them when they are sick.

The world wants God on its terms. Christians, at times, have similar thoughts, but these thoughts must give way to faith.

It's natural to want God on our terms, to fit Him to our ideas of what God should be. The Jews demanded of Jesus a sign from heaven to prove His deity. If He did not oblige them, they would not believe He was true God.

The sophisticated Greeks demanded wisdom. They believed in an intellectual approach to help understand God's existence. Paul faced these intellectuals at Athens when he spoke of the nature of the true God and His Son, Jesus, the Christ. Most of them mocked his message as foolishness.

Our generation hardly demands miracles or wisdom. We want success. We demand success from God. Some of the megachurches on television preach the "gospel of success and wealth," not the gospel of sin and grace. We, at times, believe that God exists only for us, to do our bidding.

It must break God's heart when He sees our stupid and ridiculous efforts to understand Him or have Him come to us on our terms. It should be obvious to everyone that it is against God's nature for Him to demonstrate Himself to us, His creation. It is about as ridiculous as making a carpenter responsible and answerable to the house he has just built.

If God is required to identify Himself with our success, then we have things turned around. God is not answerable to us! If we can comprehend and control God, then God is not God anymore. Maybe this is what we intend.

God scoffs at human wisdom as foolishness, confusion, and failure. Instead, He lets the world see what it considers foolishness—Jesus, the Christ, on the cross. Christ crucified was a stumbling block to the Jews and utter stupidity for the Greeks. His foolishness was too wise for them.

For those seeking success, Christ crucified is beyond their reach. God can only be grasped by faith "through the folly of what we preach to save those who believe." All us foolish ones are saved through the preaching of the cross.

8 AUGUST

Psalmody: Psalm 62:1–7
Additional Psalm: Psalm 62
Old Testament Reading: 1 Samuel 24:1–22
New Testament Reading:
1 Corinthians 1:26–2:16

Prayer of the Day

O God, whose strength is made perfect in weakness, grant us humility and child-like faith that we may please You in both will and deed; through Jesus Christ, Your Son, our Lord, who lives and reigns with You and the Holy Spirit, one God, now and forever. (B78)

Meditation
People in third-world countries are very poor compared to our standard of living. In Madagascar, Lutheran pastors receive a monthly salary of $50.00. They are able to sustain their families because the cost of food and shelter is comparably low.

Even though we think they are poor in worldly goods, they know they are very rich in spiritual treasures that far exceed earthly items. Most members of the Malagasy Lutheran Church do not own cars and walk several miles to worship.

Together with them, we also know God in His wonderful mercy. Our loving heavenly Father has made us extremely rich in Christ, our blessed Savior. Paul confirms this as he tells us "And because of Him you are in Christ Jesus, who became to us wisdom from God, righteousness and sanctification and redemption . . ."

God has chosen the foolish, the weak, and despised things to eliminate any boasting in God's presence. God is the only source of life in Christ. Since New Testament times Christians have been despised and scorned. Yet they have displayed a power and endurance that cannot be explained by reason.

We are rich in wisdom, for we know the only way of salvation is through faith in Jesus' death for our sins, and His resurrection to eternal life.

But this would not be possible if Christ had not become our righteousness. We are extremely rich in righteousness before the holy God. There is no need to fear His wrath, which we deserve because of our sins. Jesus kept God's law perfectly. His righteousness and perfect fulfillment of God's law has been applied to us. Therefore, our whole life is consecrated to God.

Christ is also our sanctification, and this makes us rich. Out of love for Him we daily strive to lead a life pleasing to Him. But we know we fall short, realizing our own righteousness and holiness are like filthy rags before our holy God. But Jesus steps in, taking our place, covering us with His righteousness purchased with His blood.

Those great blessings are ours by faith because faith accepts the promise that God, for Jesus' sake, is gracious to us.

Though we must all through much tribulation enter the kingdom of God, yet how rich we are! As our redemption, Christ will deliver us from all evil and take us through a blessed death to rest in His arms. There He will wipe away all tears.

9 AUGUST

Psalmody: Psalm 94:8–15
Additional Psalm: Psalm 94
Old Testament Reading: 1 Samuel 25:1–22
New Testament Reading:
1 Corinthians 3:1–23

Prayer of the Day

Lord Jesus, You have joined us to Yourself in Holy Baptism and made our bodies a temple of Your Holy Spirit. May the fruit of the Spirit be born in our bodies as we show forth in the world Your love, joy, peace, patience, kindness, goodness, faithfulness, gentleness, and self-control, for against such things there is no law; for You live and reign with the Father and the Holy Spirit, one God, now and forever. (1074)

Meditation

There had to be a very powerful incentive for God to become man, to leave behind the glory of heaven. It had to be love! His name is Savior. Salvation was on His mind. He came to save us from all that is rotten and evil in the world, from all that our sins have brought us.

For what, however, did He save us? Heaven, we usually say. But if heaven is what God has saved us for, why isn't heaven ours right now? Why doesn't He just whisk us away to our prepared mansions and save us the grief of the world?

Heaven is the crowning climax of His saving purpose, but it is not the purpose. The word *salvation* means to be rescued from destruction. *Salvage* has the same root. It means to take something that is worthless from the arena of nothingness and reclaim it. Salvation involves reclaiming us, redeeming us from the realm of nothingness, and putting us into the realm of "somethingness," to be utilized. God's purpose in our salvation is to put us to new use in the world, to draw others into the fellowship of the Savior, and finally to bring us into heaven through His Gospel.

A Christian's life of service involves getting our hands dirty, our brows sweaty and our muscles achy. Our calling might be compared to building a structure. We are called to be the raw building materials; God's love is the motivating impetus; and His Spirit is the power that restructures our lives into a structurally sound building. Our lives should not be something to be looked at, but exist for a function and purpose. We have been called to serve.

This structure is a place where God's Spirit lives and works. The structure of our life is a salvaged structure in a slum, a place of love in a world of hate, and a place of life in a world of death. It has life. It was salvaged in order to salvage.

It has love that it might love. It has life in Christ to give life through His Gospel. It is a marketplace, not a showplace. Paul wants us to learn why in the world we are in the world. Christian involvement means taking risks. We do not retreat from responsibility for fear of failure. God's mercy in Christ covers our failures, His love resolves our messes, and His grace is for us as we seek to do His will and to proclaim His grace to the world. God help us.

10 August

Lawrence, Deacon and Martyr

Psalmody: Psalm 14
Additional Psalm: Psalm 53
Old Testament Reading: 1 Samuel 25:23–44
New Testament Reading:
1 Corinthians 4:1–21

Prayer of the Day

Almighty God, You called Lawrence to be a deacon in Your church to serve Your saints with deeds of love, and You gave him the crown of martyrdom. Give us the same charity of heart that we may fulfill Your love by defending and supporting the poor, that by loving them we may love You with all our hearts; through Jesus Christ our Lord, who lives and reigns with You and the Holy Spirit, one God, now and forever. Amen. (1075)

Lawrence, Deacon and Martyr

Early in the third century AD, Lawrence, most likely born in Spain, made his way to Rome. There he was appointed chief of the seven deacons and was given the responsibility to manage Church property and finances. The emperor at the time, who thought that the church had valuable things worth confiscating, ordered Lawrence to produce the "treasures of the church." Lawrence brought before the emperor the poor whose lives had been touched by Christian charity. He was then jailed and eventually executed in the year AD 258 by being roasted on a gridiron. His martyrdom left a deep impression on the young Church. Almost immediately, the date of his death, August 10, became a permanent fixture on the early commemorative calendar of the Church.

Meditation

There is much confusion regarding the term "minister," especially its definition. For hundreds of years it referred to the Office of the Holy Ministry, the pastoral office. The definition has been changed by many in the last few decades to include all the members of a Christian congregation. A parish now has a "ministry or ministries." A recent church bulletin listed them as our Sunday school "ministry," our youth "ministry," our music "ministry," our teaching "ministry," our worship "ministry," and the list goes on.

The Scriptures speak of the Office of the Holy Ministry, and Paul gives very good instruction how Christians are to regard their pastors and other ministers of the Word. In these days of false prophets we should be thankful if we have a faithful pastor who teaches and preaches God's Word in its purity, and who, by his conduct, knows his highest purpose is to save his own soul and the souls entrusted to his care.

However, for some church members this is not good enough. They believe they have the right to make other demands on the pastor, such as requiring him to be an inspiring speaker, a witty conversationalist, or a good social mixer. Others try to "run" the congregation through the pastoral office by expecting him to do their bidding.

The conduct of the Corinthian congregation members suggested that they did not think that only preaching the Gospel was sufficient. They thought their ideas of community improvement were also necessary. This would make them seem important in the community.

Jesus said to those He sent out to preach, "The one who hears you hears Me, and the one who rejects you rejects Me, and the one who rejects Me rejects Him who sent Me" (Luke 10:16). The pastor represents his Savior and is responsible for his stewardship of God's mysteries. He is in charge of and responsible to God for administering the Word and the Sacraments—Holy Baptism and Holy Communion. Through these Means of Grace God reveals and imparts to sinners the riches of His grace through Christ's blood that covers all our sins.

Therefore, the pastor's work includes calling sinners to repentance, denying forgiveness to hardened sinners that refuse to repent, and rejecting all slick programs that offer him and the congregation cheap popularity. He should follow the lost lambs and sheep of Christ's flock, holding all the members in his heart, and remembering them in his prayers.

We want our pastors to pray for us. Let us not forget to pray for them.

11 August

Psalmody: Psalm 51:10–13
Additional Psalm: Psalm 51
Old Testament Reading: 1 Samuel 26:1–25
Additional Reading: 1 Samuel 27:1–28:2
New Testament Reading:
1 Corinthians 5:1–13

Prayer of the Day

O Lord, so rule and govern our hearts and minds by Your Holy Spirit that, ever mindful of the end of all things and the day of Your just judgment, we may be stirred up to holiness of living here and dwell with You forever hereafter; through Jesus Christ, Your Son, our Lord, who lives and reigns with You and the Holy Spirit, one God, now and forever. (H86)

Meditation

"Do you not know that a little leaven leavens the whole lump? Cleanse out the old leaven that you may be a new lump, as you really are unleavened. For Christ, our Passover lamb, has been sacrificed."

Paul leads us back to that frightful night in Egypt when the angel of the Lord killed every firstborn son in the land of Pharaoh, but passed over the homes whose doors were marked with the blood of the Passover lamb. The hour of freedom had struck for the captive children of Israel, who had been held in slavery for four hundred years. Pharaoh had released them, and with songs of rejoicing they went forth from their houses of bondage. The saving of Israel through the paschal lamb was prophetic of the greater redemption that came to God's people when Christ, our Passover Lamb, was sacrificed for us.

From that time forward, in preparation of the Passover, the Jews were advised to thoroughly search every corner of the house and scrape out carefully any leaven (yeast) so that it may not spoil the festival of the Passover. If any remained, even the smallest portion would penetrate and taint the new dough. In the same way, the Corinthians were to clean out the open sexual corruption that infected the congregation so the sin would not spread.

Christians at all times are to clean out the old leaven of sin in them by daily contrition and repentance. The object of such purging is that you may be new, unleavened dough, a holy lump governed by God's Spirit. This is based on God's gift of grace, the fact that believers are looked upon as unleavened, clean and pure for the sake of Christ's sacrifice for our sins. "Let us therefore celebrate the festival, not with the old leaven, the leaven of malice and evil, but with the unleavened bread of sincerity and truth."

May each day be a holy, blessed Easter! When sickness strikes, we may rejoice that we have Christ our Paschal Lamb who bore our griefs, carried our sorrows, and still bears them with us. When our sins accuse us and our conscience weeps, we have Christ our Paschal Lamb who was the chastisement of our peace and with whose stripes we are healed.

When sorrow fills us over our departed dear ones, we can find heavenly comfort in the resurrection. With them we shall stand before the throne of the Lamb, rejoicing in our heavenly rest of eternal life.

12 AUGUST

Psalmody: Psalm 99:1–5
Additional Psalm: Psalm 99
Old Testament Reading: 1 Samuel 28:3–25
Additional Reading: 1 Samuel 29:1–30:31
New Testament Reading:
1 Corinthians 6:1–20

Prayer of the Day

Almighty God, unto whom all hearts are open, all desires known, and from whom no secrets are hidden, cleanse the thoughts of our hearts by the inspiration of Your Holy Spirit that we may perfectly love You and worthily magnify Your holy name; through Jesus Christ, our Lord. (211)

Meditation

Christian liberty is often abused. A Christian may have the right to do something, but it is not always prudent to do it. Paul wanted to clarify this to the Corinthians by saying " 'All things are lawful for me,' but not all things are helpful. 'All things are lawful for me,' but I will not be enslaved by anything."

Christian liberty does not include freedom to do as you please. It is incompatible with the license of our sinful nature. Christ's love must regulate my Christian liberty so that my deeds, over which I have power, are to help and ben-

efit my neighbor. On the other hand, someone else may not use their Christian liberty to take me captive.

As in the Corinthian congregation, people today try to excuse their moral failings by claiming they have "the right." The most extreme example of this today is legalized abortion, which may be lawful but certainly is not morally right.

The apostle tells us that eating is morally neutral. But, if you become a slave of your stomach and indulge in gluttony, it is obviously an abuse of the power given you by God. He also tells us that fornication is a perversion of the legitimate uses of the body.

The body belongs to the Lord, and it should be used in His service. The Lord will, in turn, live in the body. "Abide in Me, and I in you" (John 15:4). This is strongly emphasized because the final goal of the body is eternal life. It will be raised from the grave and fashioned like Christ's immortal body.

It is quite apparent that Satan has much influence on television today with its many lascivious programs. History has shown a culture that revels in lewdness is sinking towards its own destruction.

Paul speaks to the Christian in order to help us realize that each of us, together with all Christians, are one in Christ. Each of us, and all of us, are the temple of the Holy Spirit who descends to take up His dwelling place in our hearts and bodies.

We all have sinned. It is necessary to come to the Savior, with heartfelt contrition and repentance, begging His forgiveness He offers by grace through His blood.

We glorify God in our body by letting it serve as a temple in which each of us serves as a priest to the Most High God.

13 AUGUST

Psalmody: Psalm 68:1–6
Additional Psalm: Psalm 68
Old Testament Reading: 1 Samuel 31:1–13
New Testament Reading:
1 Corinthians 7:1–24

Prayer of the Day

Most gracious God, we give thanks for the joy and blessings that You grant to husbands and wives. Assist them always by Your grace that with true fidelity and steadfast love they may honor and keep their marriage vows, grow in love toward You and for each other, and come at last to the eternal joys that You have promised; through Jesus Christ, our Lord. (243)

Meditation

The apostle instructs that the principles of a Christian marriage should be applied in other areas of Christian living. He was uncompromising in using any aspect of the law for salvation. Now that Christ had come, circumcision was no longer a sacrament but only a custom without any religious or moral value.

God looks upon the heart. Where living faith is found, all are one in Christ. Accordingly, it is not necessary to change our nationality or occupation to be acceptable to the Lord. We can joyfully serve the Lord in whatever station in life we occupy.

Paul points out that even a slave is still the Lord's free man. Similarly, a person that is called, while he is free in Christ, is Christ's servant. This is a paradox but also a beautiful way of describing the relation of both the slave and the free. This freedom is spiritual freedom from the power of sin, and this freedom has been accomplished by Jesus and offered in the gospel. By faith this freedom gives us the strength to serve the Lord with all our heart, soul, and mind.

The price of redemption that has been paid to deliver us from the slavery of sin and Satan keeps us from abandoning the truth of the Scriptures and falling victim to man-made doctrines.

The purpose of Christian living (our vocation) is to love and serve the people whom God has set before us. Luther said our vocations are "masks of God." God is hidden in contractors, mechanics, and teachers—those who build our houses, fix our cars, and instruct us. Vocation is part of how God governs the world.

God does not need our good works, but our neighbors do. Our relationship to God is based on His work for us in Christ Jesus. We have been redeemed and grafted into Christ through Word and Sacraments. God sends us into the world for our faith to bear fruit in acts of love to our neighbors.

What we do to make a living is also a vocation. Our talents and abilities open up avenues of service. Our labor, when done in faith, can be an expression of love and service to our neighbors as they benefit from what we do. We fail to love and serve our neighbors as we should. We bring the sins done in our vocations to the Lord where we receive forgiveness. Refreshed and built up in faith, we return to our various callings.

14 AUGUST

Psalmody: Psalm 33:13–21
Additional Psalm: Psalm 33
Old Testament Reading: 2 Samuel 1:1–27
New Testament Reading:
1 Corinthians 7:25–40

Prayer of the Day

O Lord, keep Your Church with Your perpetual mercy; and because of our frailty we cannot but fall, keep us ever by Your help from all things hurtful and lead us to all things profitable to our salvation; through Jesus Christ, Your Son, our Lord, who lives and reigns with You and the Holy Spirit, one God, now and forever. (H74)

Meditation

The institution of holy matrimony generally has been denigrated. For many, marriage has lost the sacredness of its obligations. Mass media presents the most distorted views of the relationship between husband and wife, the main one being the satisfaction of sexual desires.

Christians must remember what the Bible says of holy wedlock. God, in His wisdom, instituted marriage creating Eve and giving her to Adam as his wife. Holy matrimony between a man and a woman, together with its family life, is the foundation of true soundness and stability in society.

The Bible speaks of marriage with the highest respect, and the sins committed against it are condemned with righteous wrath. This leaves no doubt concerning the meaning of God's will.

The Lord Himself stated the purpose of marriage, "It is not good that the man should be alone; I will make him a helper fit for him" (Genesis 2:18). A wife is the husband's faithful companion, helper, and partner. Marriage is a partnership of mutual love and helpfulness. The Lord also stated that children are to be conceived and born through marriage.

With the institution and blessing of God, a husband will consider his wife as a gift of God. He will give her honor, love her, and treat her with the respect that the Lord demands. He will fulfill his role as the head of the house, acting not as a tyrant, but in a true evangelical manner. He is to love his wife as Christ loved the Church, His Bride.

A wife, in return, will love and respect her husband, giving him honor, and recognizing his headship. This is not disgraceful or degrading but done gladly and willingly, flowing from mutual agreement according to God's will. She will be a true helper and, if their marriage is blessed with children, a happy mother. She will accept the praise that the Bible grants the diligent, gracious, and virtuous woman. She will know as a wife and mother that she is serving the Lord in marriage, realizing that it is very pleasing to Him.

Being a husband or wife is a calling. In the vocation of marriage we have one neighbor we are to love and serve. Wives love and serve their husbands by submitting themselves to Christ. Husbands are to love and serve their wives by giving themselves up for her, as Christ did for the Church. Christ is always hidden in a Christian marriage with His blessings.

15 AUGUST

St. Mary, Mother of Our Lord

Psalmody: Psalm 132:11–18
Additional Psalm: Psalm 132
Old Testament Reading: 2 Samuel 5:1–25
New Testament Reading:
1 Corinthians 8:1–13

Prayer of the Day

Almighty God, You chose the virgin Mary to be the mother of Your only Son. Grant that we, who are redeemed by His blood, may share with her in the glory of Your eternal kingdom; through Jesus Christ, Your Son, our Lord, who lives and reigns with You and the Holy Spirit, one God, now and forever. (F24)

St. Mary, Mother of Our Lord

St. Mary, the mother of Jesus, is mentioned repeatedly in the Gospels and the Book of Acts, with nearly a dozen specific incidents in her life being recorded: her betrothal to Joseph; the annunciation by the angel Gabriel that she was to be the mother of the Messiah; her visitation to Elizabeth, the mother of John the Baptizer; the nativity of our Lord; the visits of the shepherds and the Wise Men; the presentation of the infant Jesus in the temple; the flight into Egypt; the Passover visit to Jerusalem when Jesus was twelve; the wedding at Cana in Galilee; her presence at the crucifixion when her Son commended her to the care of His disciple John; and her gathering with the apostles in the Upper Room after the ascension, waiting for the promised Holy Spirit. Thus she is present at most of the important events in her Son's life. She is especially remembered and honored for her unconditional obedience to the will of God ("Let it be with me according to Your word" [Luke 1:38]); for her loyalty to her Son even when she did not understand Him ("Do whatever He tells you" [John 2:1–11]); and above all for the highest honor that heaven bestowed on her of being the mother of our Lord ("Blessed are you among women" [Luke 1:42]). According to tradition, Mary went with the apostle John to Ephesus, where she died.

Meditation

Paul was asked if it was right for Christians to eat meat that had been offered to idols. The crux of the matter was that if one ate this meat, did it not imply that they recognized the validity of the false idols? Some Corinthians may have thought so.

Eating this meat was not sinful in itself. Christians stronger in faith would have no problem in doing so. Christians weaker in faith may have believed it was wrong and against their conscience. Out of Christian love and concern for the weaker in faith, those who believed it was permissible would voluntarily refrain from eating this meat.

In this regard a person does not insist on expressing his right. To know God in Christ is the childlike knowledge that does not puff itself up; it is the incentive for us to imitate the great love God has showered upon us in our misery and wretchedness and brought us salvation.

We should always be aware of the consequences of exercising our right to do something. Your right may be an obstacle to someone who is weak. If it gives offense, then it is no longer a matter of Christian liberty. If you know a guest in your home is an alcoholic, would you deliberately exercise your right to drink in front of him? Of course not.

We must remember that we sin against a fellow Christian by offending their weak conscience. And this is the greater wrong. When we strike a blow to the conscience of the weaker Christian that brings harm to his faith, we sin against Christ. In repentance, we then ask His forgiveness.

It is our duty to strengthen weaker Christians for whom Christ also died—Christ's love compels us. This is the strongest incentive to express brotherly concern through which we show love to Christ. We should be aware that a brother in Christ cannot be strengthened by inconsiderate behavior. By thoughtless behavior the weaker brother is frustrated.

Christ's salvation is for all people. When a Christian chooses to insist on exercising his liberty, a weaker Christian may be tempted to do something he regards as sinful and thereby corrupt his conscience; it could endanger his faith.

The apostle uses the term "my brother" with special emphasis. For the sake of brotherly love and in the interest of weaker Christians, the principle that must regulate the use of all liberty is love.

16 AUGUST

Isaac

Psalmody: Psalm 11
Additional Psalm: Psalm 84
Old Testament Reading: 2 Samuel 6:1–19
New Testament Reading:
1 Corinthians 9:1–23

Prayer of the Day

Almighty God, heavenly Father, through the patriarch Isaac You preserved the seed of the Messiah and brought forth the new creation. Continue to preserve the Church as the Israel of God as she manifests the glory of Your holy name by continuing to worship Your Son, the child of Mary; through Jesus Christ, our Lord. (1076)

Isaac

Isaac, the long promised and awaited son of Abraham and Sarah, was born when his father was one hundred years old and his mother was ninety-one years old. The announcement of his birth brought both joy and laughter to his aged parents (thus the name Isaac, which means "laughter"). As a young man, Isaac accompanied his father to Mount Moriah, where Abraham, in obedience to God's command, prepared to sacrifice him as a burnt offering. But God intervened, sparing Isaac's life and providing a ram as a substitute offering (Genesis 22:1–14), thus pointing to the substitutionary sacrifice of Christ for the sins of the world. Isaac was given in marriage to Rebekah (Genesis 24:67), and they had twin sons, Esau and Jacob (Genesis 25:19–26). In his old age, Isaac, blind and feeble, wanted to give his blessing and chief inheritance to his favorite—and eldest—son, Esau. But through deception Rebekah had Jacob receive them instead, resulting in years of family enmity. Isaac died at the age

of 180 and was buried in the family burial cave of Machpelah by his sons, who by then had become reconciled (Genesis 35:28–29).

Meditation

Christ gave the Office of the Keys to Christian congregations to exercise publicly. The congregation has the authority that works like a key to open heaven by forgiving sins, or to close heaven by not forgiving them. This God-given way of applying the Gospel is publicly carried out by the congregation through preaching the Gospel, through Holy Baptism and through the Sacrament of the Altar. By the command of Christ the congregation calls a pastor to fulfill its responsibilities in this regard. Pastors therefore speak in Christ's name and on behalf of the congregation.

The congregation and the pastor take care together that the Gospel is purely preached and taught, and the Sacraments are administered according to God's Word. This is more difficult in church circles today due to the influence of other "gospels."

Another such "gospel" is called American Evangelism. American Evangelicalism has its roots in the sovereignty of God. This dominating doctrine distorts the biblical understanding of salvation. It spawned the false teaching that God from eternity, through a sovereign (absolute) degree elected certain people to go to heaven and certain people to go to hell. It postulated there was no sense in Christ spilling precious blood on those who were not going to heaven. And as the Gospel was powerful only for those whom God had predetermined would be saved, there was no sense wasting evangelical power on those destined for hell.

From its beginnings, the key central teaching of American Evangelicalism is the idea that grace is something that must be felt and experienced. Therefore, the primary need of Christians has come to be the emotional or psychological evidence of God's presence within the heart.

An example of this is the conclusion of the prayer at President Obama's inauguration ceremony that focused on the central teaching of American Evangelicalism. Rev. Rick Warren prayed, "In the name of the one who changed my life." Jesus has no objectivity—it was all about the relationship.

The apostle Paul said, "Woe to me if I do not preach the gospel!" Give eternal praise to God if you hold membership in a congregation that maintains and supports the true preaching of the Gospel.

17 August

Johann Gerhard, Theologian

Psalmody: Psalm 24:1–6
Additional Psalm: Psalm 24
Old Testament Reading: 2 Samuel 7:1–17
New Testament Reading:
1 Corinthians 9:24–10:22

Prayer of the Day

Most High God, we owe You great thanks that in the sacred mystery of the Supper You feed us with the body and blood of Your Son. May we approach this heavenly meal with true faith, firmly convinced that the body we eat is the one given into death for us that the blood we drink is the blood shed for our sins; through Jesus Christ, our Lord. (1077)

Johann Gerhard, Theologian

Johann Gerhard (1582–1637) was a great Lutheran theologian in the tradition of Martin Luther (1483–1546) and Martin Chemnitz (1522–86) and the most influential of the seventeenth-century dogmaticians. His monu-

mental *Loci Theologici* (twenty-three large volumes) is still considered by many to be a definitive statement of Lutheran orthodoxy. Gerhard was born in Quedlinburg, Germany. At the age of fifteen he was stricken with a life-threatening illness. This experience, along with guidance from his pastor, Johann Arndt, marked a turning point in his life. He devoted the rest of his life to theology. He became a professor at the University of Jena and served many years as the superintendent of Heldburg. Gerhard was a man of deep evangelical piety and love for Jesus. He wrote numerous books on exegesis, theology, devotional literature, history, and polemics. His sermons continue to be widely published and read.

Meditation

God has called Christians to a wonderful goal, the inheritance of heaven. However, it is not a matter of course; it is not automatic that we reach that inheritance.
Sadly, a person that has been called into God's kingdom can willfully reject God's grace and be cast out of His kingdom. Some denominations teach this is not possible. They say "once saved, always saved" no matter what a person does. This is contrary to Scripture, reason, and experience.

In reference to the people of Israel during their forty years of pilgrimage in the wilderness, Paul gives a strong warning. God had delivered them from bondage and protected them. He led them with a cloud by day and with fire by night. Bread and water were in rich supply. One would assume that they stood strong as a rock in faithfulness to God. But Paul says, "Nevertheless, with most of them God was not pleased, for they were overthrown in the wilderness."

This should cause us to consider whether we will remain faithful to the Lord, no matter what spiritual gifts, possessions, or high status we have.

The Israelites soon tired of the bread (manna) from heaven and complained they had no meat. God answered their cravings and sent quail in great numbers. They greedily ate them till they were stuffed. In response to their greed God sent a plague, causing many people to die. Moses called the place "the graves of the lusters."

Today, overindulgence in food and drink is a huge health issue physically and spiritually. Many people gluttonize and guzzle to the point of making their belly their god.

While Moses was in the mountain with God, the Israelites were dancing in wild worship before an idol, relishing sensual lust. God's wrath burned against them and twenty-three thousand souls went to hell.

Dancing around the altar of idol worship has never ceased. The golden calves of today are molded into more subtle forms such as money, fashionable clothes, sensual pleasures, and self-admiration. These can easily become one's heart desires.

The warning given by Paul is for us today and calls us to repent of our spiritual idolatry. Christ is the Rock from which flows the true Water of Life, the forgiveness of sins given to us through His blood. May we take delight in the true Bread of Life that gives us everlasting food that carries us to our eternal home.

18 AUGUST

Psalmody: Psalm 107:1–9
Additional Psalm: Psalm 106:1–5
Old Testament Reading: 2 Samuel 7:18–29
New Testament Reading:
1 Corinthians 10:23–11:16

Prayer of the Day

O God, by the patient suffering of Your only-begotten Son, You have beaten down the pride of the old enemy. Now help us, we humbly pray, to imitate all that our Lord has of His goodness borne for our sake, that after His example, we may bear with patience all that is adverse to us; through Jesus Christ, our Lord. (1078)

Meditation

Most people want the best of both worlds. If Christians join in the wild celebrating of our culture, they are just as guilty as were the boastful Corinthians in their day. The Corinthian Christians were a privileged people who had been touched by God's grace. Yet, they had taken God's grace lightly. Paul shows one sin after another: adultery, incest, drunkenness, lawsuits, choosing favorites among pastors, and a whole parade of foolishness masquerading as freedom. Many in the churches of Corinth were living as though God had never come to stay with them.

Paul appeals to the hearts of these Christians by calling them brothers. And he connects them (the New Testament Church) with the Israelites. Both are God's chosen people. God's people passed through the Red Sea, bound to their leader Moses. Christians are also privileged people, touched by God's grace. We have received Baptism in which God brought forgiveness and adoption into our lives. We were baptized into the name of our leader, Jesus Christ, and are bound to Him.

Israel had the Son of God walking with them, supplying all their physical and spiritual needs. It is the same way for us when our Savior gives us His grace and goodness. We have the privilege of eating and drinking spiritual food again and again—the very body and blood in Holy Communion that God Himself offered and poured out to place us into

His family. Our needs have been supplied by a merciful Savior for time and eternity.

God's warning is never to be taken lightly. The children of Israel tired of waiting for Moses to come down from his meeting with the Lord on Mount Sinai. So they made up their own kind of god.

How easy it is for us to get tired of waiting for Jesus to come, as though He is never going to show up again. To say that "none of these things could happen to me" is dangerous. We must humble ourselves under God and repent. God is faithful. The sweet Gospel pours out forgiveness. He dresses us in the purity of His Son. And when we resist temptation and sin, God provides a way to escape.

19 August

Bernard of Clairvaux, Hymnwriter and Theologian

Psalmody: Psalm 12
Additional Psalm: Psalm 22:14–21
Old Testament Reading: 2 Samuel 11:1–27
New Testament Reading:
1 Corinthians 11:17–34

Prayer of the Day

O God, enkindled with the fire of Your love, Your servant Bernard of Clairvaux became a burning and a shining light in Your Church. By Your mercy, grant that we also may be aflame with the spirit of love and discipline and may ever walk in Your presence as children of light; through Jesus Christ, our Lord, who lives and reigns with You and the Holy Spirit, one God, now and forever. Amen. (1079)

Bernard of Clairvaux, Hymnwriter and Theologian

A leader in Christian Europe in the first half of the twelfth century AD, Bernard is honored in his native France and around the world. Born into a noble family in Burgundy in 1090, Bernard left the affluence of his heritage and entered the monastery of Citeaux at the age of twenty-two. After two years, he was sent to start a new monastic house at Clairvaux. His work there was blessed in many ways. The monastery at Clairvaux grew in mission and service, eventually establishing some sixty-eight daughter houses. Bernard is remembered for his charity and political abilities, but especially for his preaching and hymn composition. The hymn texts "O Jesus, King Most Wonderful" and "O Sacred Head, Now Wounded" are part of the heritage of the faith left by St. Bernard.

Meditation

It is usually given to the pastor to preach the sermon. But the entire congregation preaches a mighty sermon when it eats the bread and drinks the cup. It proclaims the Lord's death. The Sacrament conveys the great truth of salvation that our Lord died, that He gave His body and poured out His blood to satisfy God's wrath for the sins of all.

Holy Communion proclaims Christ. This is what Jesus intended. At no time was Jesus as conspicuous as in His death. To know Him you must see Him on Calvary, bruised for our iniquities and wounded for our transgressions. Jesus' death is the climax of the life He lived for sinful people. When we proclaim Christ who died, it includes all He said and did: feeding, comforting, healing, raising the dead, rising from His tomb, and ascending to God's right hand.

When Christ's Gospel is preached, Christ is proclaimed because He is the Gospel. Sometimes Jesus is overlooked and another "gospel" is substituted that promises to help do great things for individuals or congregations. We might say Christ fades into the background; His face is veiled.

Then the Lord's Supper speaks. It boldly says Christ shed His blood to buy us out of the bondage of sin. It brings us face-to-face with Him who is meant to be the object of our love and center of our life.

The day may come when the Church fails to focus its preaching and teaching around Christ. The Church may succumb to the programs and ways of the world and lose sight of its glorious purpose. But as long as the Lord's Supper is faithfully observed, so long will the Sacrament proclaim Christ and the forgiveness of sins, and the faithful remnant will be preserved.

We often compromise with sin. We think it is just a little mistake. We even believe that God will look the other way when we sin. Then Law of God screams out against sin. It declares that sin is a deadly rebellion against God; that sin destroys, kills, and takes hope away.

To know the terrible cost and result of sin we must go to Golgotha and see Jesus sink into death. The bread and the cup are born out of tragedy, of suffering made necessary by sin. Justice requires payment for sin. Therefore, proclaiming Christ's death is to acknowledge the need for a Savior and to rejoice that He is found in Jesus Christ alone. The Holy Sacrament then loudly preaches victory! Jesus lives! His victory is our victory. We live in Him forever.

20 AUGUST

Samuel

Psalmody: Psalm 51:1–8
Additional Psalm: Psalm 51
Old Testament Reading: 2 Samuel 12:1–25
Additional Reading: 2 Samuel 13:1–19:43
New Testament Reading: 1 Corinthians 12:1–13

Prayer of the Day

Almighty God, in Your mercy You gave Samuel courage to call Israel to repentance and to renew their dedication to the Lord. Call us to repentance as Nathan called David to repentance, so by the blood of Jesus, the Son of David, we may receive the forgiveness of all our sins; through Jesus Christ, our Lord. (1080)

Samuel

Samuel, last of the Old Testament judges and first of the prophets (after Moses), lived during the eleventh century BC. The child of Elkanah, an Ephraimite, and his wife Hannah, Samuel was from early on consecrated by his parents for sacred service and trained in the house of the Lord at Shiloh by Eli the priest. Samuel's authority as a prophet was established by God (1 Samuel 3:20). He anointed Saul to be Israel's first king (1 Samuel 10:1). Later, as a result of Saul's disobedience to God, Samuel repudiated Saul's leadership and then anointed David to be king in place of Saul (1 Samuel 16:13). Samuel's loyalty to God, his spiritual insight, and his ability to inspire others made him one of Israel's great leaders.

Meditation

The Christians at Corinth had received a variety of gifts given by the Holy Spirit. Instead of being built together on the foundation of Christ and bound by the Spirit's love, the members were envious over spiritual gifts. Gifts are meant to serve the Church and each other; gifts that were meant to promote unity were instead promoting discord.

If God wanted us to be united with one another, He might have made us all the same, using one big heavenly cookie cutter. The Church would consist of one enormous mass of look-alike, think-alike people.

Paul reminds us "There are varieties of gifts, but the same Spirit." We are diverse and gifted in various ways, but these gifts should never be used for personal glory, thereby shattering the unity that God desires. Our different gifts, strengths, and abilities are for building up one another and thus the Church. This is the key to understanding the diverse gifts found in the Church and the potential to show God's love. We are not cookie-cutter Christians, but gifted Christians committed to use our gifts.

This is at the very point that our sinful nature attacks. The genius of sin is not that it destroys God's gifts; its genius lies in its ability to twist and pervert them. Sin tempts us to turn our gifts inward—to twist love and acts for others into love for self. This is always the underlying sin. Misuse of God's gifts is the symptom, but the disease is selfishness. Satan's finest hour occurs when selfish individualism results in strife among God's people, when God's gifts become opportunities for personal glorification.

Paul calls all Christians to unity under the true Shepherd, Jesus. He took the form of a servant, bore the price of our sin, and offers us righteousness founded in His death on the cross. His triumph over sin, death, and the grave compels us to confess, "He is my Lord and my God," and therefore give all glory to God and not to ourselves. We see this in the loving acts of the gifted people in the Church. Gifted and guided by the Holy Spirit, the works of our hands further true unity; the works done for others demonstrate the love of our Savior active among us. To Him be the glory and the power!

Being recipients of God's gifts calls us to service. As the Lord served us we are led by the Spirit to serve. The sick and suffering are not burdens, but kings and queens in Christ; the elderly are not to be considered undesirable, but objects of our love and prayers.

Christ died because He loved us with a burning love in order for us to love one another as we walk together in faith.

21 AUGUST

Psalmody: Psalm 139:13–16, 23–24
Additional Psalm: Psalm 139
Old Testament Reading: 1 Kings 1:1–4, 15–35
New Testament Reading:
1 Corinthians 12:14–31

Prayer of the Day

Lord God Almighty, even as You bless Your servants with various and unique gifts of the Holy Spirit, continue to grant us the grace to use them always to Your honor and glory; through Jesus Christ, our Lord. (192)

Meditation

Paul had previously discussed the problem of divisions in the Church. He continues to emphasize congregational unity because the Corinthian Christians could do nothing about their other problems until they came together as a congregation.

Paul uses the analogy of a human body to aid understanding. The parts of the body fit together and function perfectly. Each part is useful. Just as the body is united, so is Christ's Body, the Church. Faction and division have no place in the Church, as they have no place in the body.

As the human body has many parts, so does the Body of Christ; there is great diversity in the Church. Problems arise in the Church because there is a failure to recognize legitimate differences. It is absurd to think of competition between body parts. Feet do not covet the function of the hands, and ears do not covet the role of the eyes. Even if they could covet each other's gifts, nothing would change. They would still be part of the body.

The hard feelings and factionalism seen in Corinth are still seen in Christian parishes today. The results are seen as people quit coming to worship, stop financial contributions, or leave the congregation altogether because they did not get their way on some issue. They do not care for what the majority may have decided and remove themselves from the source of their frustration, or seek in some way to punish those with whom they disagree.

Paul reminds us that it is absurd to think that each one should have similar gifts. "If the whole body were an eye, where would be the sense of hearing?"

Certainly some gifts are to be desired, even prized, in a congregation, but if everyone had the same gift, the congregation could not function. Leaders and followers are both necessary. Just as the human body was put together with a plan, so also the Holy Spirit has assembled the Body of Christ. God gives specific talents to the Church so that it may grow and prosper. The Corinthian congregation was blessed with spiritual gifts like, perhaps, no congregation in history. However, unless they worked together, they would fail.

No matter what a person's role is in the congregation, everyone is needed: pastors and Sunday school teachers, council presidents and youth leaders, organists and choir members, custodians, ushers, encouragers, and faithful worshipers.

No Christian is an island. When one suffers, all suffer; when one Christian rejoices, all rejoice. We are baptized into one Body in Christ for remission of all sins. Everything comes together in Him. We are in this together.

22 AUGUST

Psalmody: Psalm 97:6–12
Additional Psalm: Psalm 97
Old Testament Reading: 1 Kings 2:1–27
New Testament Reading:
1 Corinthians 13:1–13

Prayer of the Day

Almighty and everlasting God, give us an increase of faith, hope, and charity; and that we may obtain what You have promised, make us love what You have commanded; through Jesus Christ, Your Son, our Lord, who lives and reigns with You and the Holy Spirit, one God, now and forever. (H73)

Meditation

The Corinthian Christians reflected their wealthy and talented city. After Paul left they argued, sued one another, tolerated open immorality, questioned the value of marriage, and offended each other in matters of conscience.

However, they were blessed with many wonderful spiritual gifts. Some could speak in languages they had not known; others had the gift of healing; some the gifts of knowledge and wisdom; and other gifts.

Even though they had these great gifts, they showed by their quarreling they had overlooked the greatest gift—Christian love.

No spiritual gift has any value if it is used without love. Others may benefit from one's charitable contributions, but the one giving the gift gains nothing without love. The lack of love leaves only selfishness and pride as the motivation for the giver.

Christian love is the greatest virtue. Love is action. Like an angel of mercy it moves among the suffering, relieving pain, drying tears, sheltering the homeless, poor and social outcasts, and taking care of the elderly.

All the other gifts are temporary. A time will come when they will have served their purpose, and they will be abolished. Love never ends. It never drops out of existence. Like the eternal God who gives it, it lasts forever.

No one can see if we have saving faith in our hearts, but everyone can see from our words and actions whether or not we love other people. That is the love of which Paul speaks. It is not the love we owe God because He gave His Son for our sins, but the unselfish love we ought to show in all our actions.

The apostle's meaning for love can be grossly misinterpreted when it is used to support the false belief that we are made acceptable before God by our deeds of love and not by unquestioning faith in Christ, our Redeemer.

Our works of mercy are the fruit of faith, which is love. Where there is no love, faith cannot exist. True faith always works by love.

In heaven we will still have faith—completely and fully realized. In heaven we will still have hope; we will never think there is nothing more to see or do or enjoy. In heaven we will still have love, the greatest of these three.

23 AUGUST

Psalmody: Psalm 111:1–3, 9–10
Additional Psalm: Psalm 49
Old Testament Reading: 1 Kings 3:1–15
Additional Reading: 1 Kings 3:16–4:34
New Testament Reading:
2 Corinthians 1:1–22

Prayer of the Day

O Lord, Father of all mercy and God of all comfort, You always go before and follow after us. Grant that we may rejoice in Your gracious presence and continually be given to all good works; through Jesus Christ, Your Son, our Lord, who lives and reigns with You and the Holy Spirit, one God, now and forever. (C63)

Meditation

We cool and heat our homes, medicate our bodies, and even pad our pews. How important it seems to be comfortable. But what an important difference there is between com-fortableness and comfort. We can be snug in our physical environment but still suffer deep spiritual pain. Without genuine comfort, life would be a continuously dreadful experience. True comfort only comes from the true God, so we join Paul in saying, "Blessed be the God and Father of our Lord Jesus Christ, the Father of mercies and God of all comfort."

The afflictions for which we need God's true comfort are many and varied. Yes, there are the physical and relational burdens of living in a fallen world—illness, disappointment, estrangement. Paul knew discomfort of every sort. He experienced a thorn in the flesh as well as the painful agony of so much dysfunction in the Corinthian Church. Our loving Lord is concerned about all of these hurts and always intervenes to help. However, the deepest wounds and the most intense hurts are those in our relationship with Him. He has not caused that pain; we have. An honest assessment of our spiritual condition apart from Him could leave us disconsolate. What can I do to make it better? What can I do to take away the anguish and anger I have caused by my sins and failure? What can I do to be reconciled to Him? On all counts, the answer is nothing.

That is where the comfort lies. Paul understands this when he says in verse 9, "Indeed, we felt that we had received the sentence of death. But that was to make us rely not on ourselves but on God who raises the dead." The pains of body, heart, and soul point us to the cross and the empty tomb. Our Savior suffered the agony of scourging, mocking, crucifixion, and the rejection of His own Father, so that we would have salvation. In His death we have life; in His wounds we are healed; in His pain we have comfort. This life-giving comfort is more than just a temporary analgesic; it is a permanent cure. When hope for a recovery is lost, medical caregivers strive to make the patient as comfortable as possible. The care given by our Great Physician ultimately results in total recovery and enduring comfort, which cannot be kept to ourselves. As conduits for Christ, the comfort we have received flows from Him to us and into the lives of others.

24 AUGUST

St Bartholomew, Apostle

Psalmody: Psalm 27:1, 7–11
Additional Psalm: Psalm 27
Old Testament Reading: 1 Kings 5:1–18
Additional Reading: 1 Kings 6:1–7:50
New Testament Reading:
2 Corinthians 1:23–2:17

Prayer of the Day

Almighty God, Your Son, Jesus Christ, chose Bartholomew to be an apostle to preach the blessed Gospel. Grant that Your Church may love what he believed and preach what he taught; through Jesus Christ, our Lord, who lives and reigns with You and the Holy Spirit, one God, now and forever. (F25)

St Bartholomew, Apostle

St. Bartholomew (or Nathanael, as he is called in St. John's Gospel) was one of the first of Jesus' twelve disciples. His home was in the town of Cana, in Galilee (John 21:2), where Jesus performed His first miracle. He was invited to become one of the Twelve by Philip, who told him that they had found the Messiah in the person of Jesus of Nazareth (John 1:45). Bartholomew's initial hesitation to believe, because of Jesus' Nazareth background, was quickly replaced by a clear, unequivocal declaration of faith, "You are the Son of God! You are the King of Israel!" (John 1:49). He was present with the other disciples (John 21:1–13) when they were privileged to see and con-

verse and eat with their risen Lord and Savior. According to some Early Church Fathers, Bartholomew brought the Gospel to Armenia, where he was martyred by being flayed alive.

Meditation

To say that restoring broken relationships is a difficult task is a vast understatement. It is an excruciatingly exhausting task of extraordinary proportions. It is more accurate to say that it is a humanly impossible task. That is not to assert that human energy should not be expended in the effort. Individuals who are at odds with each other should work tirelessly to rectify the problem. The solution to broken human relationships, however, comes only with divine intervention.

Paul forthrightly addresses the situation at Corinth in today's reading. Something serious has happened. A public sin of such magnitude has occurred that it has caused pain not only to Paul, but to the entire congregation (v. 5). In all likelihood, the perpetrator of the sin has been excommunicated. Those offended might have uttered, "Goodbye and good riddance to the troublemaker."

It would be easy for the congregation to think that was the end of the matter. But that was certainly not the end of the matter. The apostle, inspired by the Holy Spirit, speaks words to the Corinthians asserting that the sinner should be forgiven and restored. He writes, "I beg you to reaffirm your love for him."

Nearly two millennia later, the human and ecclesiastical situation has not changed. Unresolved quarrels, arguments, and jealousies still divide individuals; conflicts, dissent, and schisms still divide congregations. Our human reactions to the situations remain sinful and inadequate—avoidance, anger, a quick and convenient transfer to another congregation—with no meaningful reconciliation. Then and now, the only solution is the powerful God-given tool of forgiveness.

To avoid or withhold forgiveness when sin is confessed and forgiveness is desired plays into the hand of Satan. It is his desire that individual Christians as well as the Body of Christ refuse to forgive by seeking vengeance or holding long-lasting grudges. A bitter, angry heart is his goal.

To extend forgiveness is a work of God, who has freely forgiven us through the shed blood of Christ Jesus. Our Savior, who loves us and gave Himself for us, has taught us to pray, "Forgive us our trespasses as we forgive those who trespass against us." This is not a mechanical, impersonal task, performed out of obligation on our part. It is a product of His transformation of our lives. Luther's explanation of the Fifth Petition reminds us that, by God's grace, we will "sincerely forgive and gladly do good to those who sin against us." "Conflict Resolution" is not an oxymoron. It is a reality because of the forgiveness God gives through Christ.

25 AUGUST

Psalmody: Psalm 32:1–7
Additional Psalm: Psalm 32
Old Testament Reading: 1 Kings 7:51–8:21
New Testament Reading: 2 Corinthians 3:1–18

Prayer of the Day

O God, You resist the proud and give grace to the humble. Grant us true humility after the likeness of Your only Son that we may never be arrogant and prideful and thus provoke Your wrath but in all lowliness be made partakers of the gifts of Your grace; through Jesus Christ, our Lord. (216)

Meditation

Biblical literacy involves more than just quoting words from Holy Scripture. It is also important to apply those words in the way they were intended by God, the author of Scripture. The words of Paul in verse six, "For the letter kills, but the Spirit gives life," have been used in a variety of ways, not all of which correctly relate to the context of the words within this epistle and their relationship to the message of Scripture as a whole.

These words have been bandied about with regard to the relationship between Law and Gospel. Is it wrong for the Church and pastors to focus so much attention on issues the Bible addresses as sin (the letter which kills), or should they expend more efforts on non-judgmentally accepting the sinner (the Spirit which gives life)? Should we see the Bible as flexible, so that what was condemned in the ancient world should now be condoned in the modern world? Doesn't "love cover a multitude of sins" (1 Peter 4:8)? Jesus Himself seems to argue against the letter of the Law when He asserted that it was "lawful to do good on the Sabbath" (Matthew 12:12). Is the passage here before us a rejection of the Law?

Paul is not rejecting the Law in its entirety; he is only rejecting the Law as a means of salvation. We need the Law to curb evil behavior, to identify our sin, and—for the Christian—to guide us in holy living. The freedom which Paul talks about (v. 17) does not mean that we may do as we please in an antinomian frenzy; it means that we are now liberated from the Law's accusing, condemning power.

It is for our spiritual benefit that "the letter kills." Had the Law not shown us our sin, we in faith could never have seen our need for a Savior. It was necessary for our Lord Jesus to live under the letter of the Law for us. His obedience to the Law paid the price of our disobedience and rebellion. It was the Law that killed Him, when we deserved that fate. If the Law was the instrument of our salvation, we would always have to worry what God thinks of us, wonder if we had done enough to earn His favor, and then wait for His judgment. Because of Jesus, the matter is settled, and the verdict is pronounced. The Spirit writes Christ's name on our hearts, and we are letters from Him to the world.

26 AUGUST

Psalmody: Psalm 36:7–12
Additional Psalm: Psalm 36
Old Testament Reading:
1 Kings 8:22–30, 46–63
New Testament Reading:
2 Corinthians 4:1–18

Prayer of the Day

Almighty and everlasting God, always more ready to hear than we to pray and to give more than we either desire or deserve, pour down upon us the abundance of Your mercy, forgiving those things of which our conscience is afraid and giving us those good things that we are not worthy to ask, except through the merits and mediation of Christ, our Lord, who lives and reigns with You and the Holy Spirit, one God, now and forever. (H71)

Meditation

We've seen the markings on some of the packages delivered to us: "Fragile. Handle with Care." While that label can't be permanently affixed to us, it probably should be. People may have deteriorating physical health, and their emotional health might be equally delicate. But when it comes to our spiritual condition, those adjectives also apply. Paul equates us with "jars of clay." We are common, ordinary vessels holding an uncommon, extraordinary treasure. There are moments when it might seem like Jesus—who certainly should know what we are made of—seems unaware of our vulner-

ability. It is as if He needed the warning label to be reminded of how fragile we are. Life as a Christian can be difficult. Like Paul, we can be afflicted, perplexed, persecuted, and struck down. Whatever the unique manifestation of these conditions might be for us personally, however, they do not destroy us. The clay of our life may be cracked, but the vessel itself is never destroyed as long as Jesus, the Treasure, remains in it. In fact, the cracks that result from the traumatic outward events of our life only serve to expose the valuable contents on the inside of our life—faith in Him.

The promises of God are present in stunning paradoxes here. The only Son from heaven came to live in an imperfect world. The Son of God chose to take on human flesh and become a "jar of clay," like us. He had the power and capacity to be invincible and unbreakable, but He chose not to exercise it. His body was broken as He experienced the unjust, sinful inhumanity of man and the abandonment of His own Father. His pierced body was put in a container of its own and sealed shut. But that vessel could not contain Him. It was cracked open on the dawn of the third day, and its valuable contents spilled out for the world to see. Because of the resurrected Jesus, we who are clay pots will eventually be reconstituted and resurrected by our powerful, victorious Lord in a new and glorious way. The afflictions that rattle us in this world are but momentary nuisances that move us to joyfully anticipate the unending joy of the perfect, resurrected life with Him. So, "we look not to the things that are seen but to the things that are unseen." Because of the cross and the empty tomb, the cracks in the vessel of life help us to focus on the crown of everlasting life.

27 AUGUST

Monica, Mother of Augustine

Psalmody: Psalm 72:1–7
Additional Psalm: Psalm 72
Old Testament Reading:
1 Kings 9:1–9; 10:1–13
New Testament Reading:
2 Corinthians 5:1–21

Prayer of the Day

O Lord, You strengthened Your patient servant Monica through spiritual discipline to persevere in offering her love, her prayers, and her tears for the conversion of her husband and of Augustine, their son. Deepen our devotion to bring others, even our own family, to acknowledge Jesus Christ as Savior and Lord, who with You and the Holy Spirit lives and reigns, one God, now and forever. (1081)

Monica, Mother of Augustine

A native of North Africa, Monica (AD 333–387) was the devoted mother of St. Augustine. Throughout her life, she sought the spiritual welfare of her children, especially that of her brilliant son Augustine. Widowed at a young age, she devoted herself to her family, praying many years for Augustine's conversion. When Augustine left North Africa to go to Italy, she followed him to Rome and then to Milan. There she had the joy of witnessing her son's conversion to the Christian faith. Weakened by her travels, Monica died at Ostia, Italy, on the journey she had hoped would take her back to her native Africa. On some Church Year calendars, Monica is remembered on May 4.

Meditation

There is no mistaking the sound of a groan. It is not a cheer of victory or even the neutral noise of mindless busyness. A groan is the voice of desperation. Paul says that while we live in the tent of this body we groan. The frail nature of earthly life leaves us susceptible to all the ailments of body and soul that this fallen creation can offer. Our groaning verbalizes the often unspoken fact that we are weak and powerless. We do not have the ability to care for ourselves, comfort ourselves, or cure ourselves of any temporal or spiritual problem, including our estrangement from God. Groaning reminds us that this earthly tent we live in will be destroyed.

For the Christian, groaning also serves an anticipatory purpose. Paul says, "But we ourselves, who have the firstfruits of the Spirit, groan inwardly as we wait eagerly for adoption as sons, the redemption of our bodies" (Romans 8:23). Our present lamentations remind us that when the travails of this life are over, we have a new, eternal, groan-free life forever with the Lord. Our hopes are more than just futile wishes or vain dreams. We can be of good courage, walking by faith, not by sight (verse 7).

But as we walk by faith, we remember the sound of One who groans with us. His cry of dereliction on the cross was louder and more anguished than any we could ever utter. He lovingly chose to abandon life in this world for us. Yet, because He was and is the very Son of God in addition to our brother in the flesh, He had the power and ability to resurrect the tent of His body into a glorified, eternal house.

Because of this work on our behalf, even now our groans can be transformed to shouts of alleluia. The new creation is at work. Unless He returns first, our existence in this world will grind and groan to a halt, but it is not really the end. We will live with Him in the heavenly home He has prepared for us, first with our soul, then, at the day of resurrection, with our new, glorified body.

As we wait for that day, we do not pass our time in idle resignation. The Gospel's power makes us ministers of reconciliation as we respond as agents of Jesus to the groans of those around us who do still not know Him.

28 AUGUST

Augustine of Hippo, Pastor and Theologian

Psalmody: Psalm 48:1–8
Additional Psalm: Psalm 48
Old Testament Reading: 1 Kings 11:1–26
New Testament Reading:
2 Corinthians 6:1–18

Prayer of the Day

O Lord God, the light of the minds that know You, the life of the souls that love You, and the strength of the hearts that serve You, give us strength to follow the example of Your servant Augustine of Hippo, so that knowing You we may truly love You and loving You we may fully serve You—for to serve You is perfect freedom; through Jesus Christ, our Lord, who lives and reigns with You and the Holy Spirit, one God, now and forever. (1082)

Augustine of Hippo, Pastor and Theologian
Augustine was one of the greatest of the Latin Church Fathers and a significant influence in the formation of Western Christianity, including Lutheranism. Born in AD 354 in North Africa, Augustine's early life was distinguished by exceptional advancement as a teacher of rhetoric. In his *Confessions* he describes his life before his conversion to Christianity, when he was drawn into the moral laxity of the day and fathered an illegitimate son. Through the devotion of his sainted mother, Monica, and the preaching of Ambrose, bishop of Milan (339–97), Augustine was converted to the Christian faith. During the great Pelagian controversies of the fifth century, Augustine

emphasized the unilateral grace of God in the salvation of mankind. Bishop and theologian at Hippo in North Africa from AD 395 until his death in AD 430, Augustine was a man of great intelligence, a fierce defender of the orthodox faith, and a prolific writer. In addition to *Confessions*, Augustine's book *City of God* had a great impact upon the Church throughout the Middle Ages and Renaissance.

Meditation
It is often easier to talk about spiritual issues to a complete stranger than to one who is close to us. We know that faith in Jesus is absolutely the most important possession a person can have, and yet we often hesitate to discuss it with those who are most important to us. We don't want to risk saying something offensive; we don't want to be perceived as overbearing or quarrelsome. So we let the person slip away from faith rather than risk an encouraging word that could be used by the Lord for their spiritual good. Father, forgive us.

Throughout his correspondences with the Church at Corinth, Paul has given us a model in this regard. He obviously had a deep concern for the people of God there. He speaks to them out of a genuine love for their spiritual well-being. There is no beating around the bush in this passage. Instead, he speaks directly and forthrightly, appealing to them "not to receive the grace of God in vain."

The people at Corinth are in spiritual jeopardy and seem to be unconcerned about their situation and uninformed about the urgency of the matter. We can almost hear the vehemence in Paul's voice as he says, "Behold, now is the favorable time; behold, now is the day of salvation." The apostle attempts to rouse the Corinthians from their lethargy, reciting how God worked through Paul's ministry among them. Yet Paul was only a messenger and instrument; the message and means of salvation were God's through Christ.

The Corinthians should consider their past relationship with Paul as well as their present relationship with others, and how both affect their ongoing relationship with Jesus. Their present company was drawing them away from the message of the Gospel. Again, Paul does not hesitate to address the situation. He renders more than mere advice or a gentle opinion. He boldly tells them not to be "unequally yoked with unbelievers."

As Christians who are yoked to Christ, we do not shun the world or the people in it. We joyfully and willingly become involved in the lives of others, including those who have known the Savior but appear to be on the brink of falling away. We cannot stand by idly. Yet, with a God-empowered vigilance, we are always watchful of our own spiritual condition. Instead of becoming casualties of the world, we are empowered by God to be witnesses to the world.

29 AUGUST

The Martyrdom of St. John the Baptist

Psalmody: Psalm 17:6–14
Additional Psalm: Psalm 17
Old Testament Reading: 1 Kings 11:42–12:19
New Testament Reading: 2 Corinthians 7:1–16

Prayer of the Day

Almighty God, You gave Your servant John the Baptist to be forerunner of Your Son, Jesus Christ, in both his preaching of repentance and his innocent death. Grant that we, who have died and risen with Christ in Holy Baptism, may daily repent of our sins, patiently suffer for the sake of the truth, and fearlessly bear witness to His victory over death; through the same Jesus Christ, our Lord, who lives and reigns with You and the Holy Spirit, one God, now and forever. (F26)

The Martyrdom of St. John the Baptist

In contrast to the Nativity of St. John the Baptist (observed on June 24), this festival commemorates his beheading by the tetrach Herod Antipas (Mark 6:14–29). From the perspective of the world, it was an ignominious end to John the Baptist's life. Yet it was in fact a noble participation in the cross of Christ, which was John's greatest glory of all. Christ Himself said that there had arisen none greater than John the Baptist (Matthew 11:11). He was the last of the Old Testament prophets and also the herald of the New Testament. As the forerunner of Christ, John fulfilled the prophecy that the great Prophet Elijah would return before the great and terrible Day of the Lord (Malachi 4:5; Matthew 17:10–13). By his preaching and Baptism of repentance, John turned "the hearts of fathers to their children and the hearts of children to their fathers" (Malachi 4:6). And in the footsteps of the prophets who had gone before him—in anticipation of the Christ whose way he prepared—this servant of the Lord manifested the cross by the witness of his death.

Meditation

This passage is a high point in the epistle. Titus has reported that problems in the Corinthian congregation were abating. Who was responsible for this positive outcome? A worldly maxim says, "Success has many fathers, but failure is an orphan." It might appear as if Paul's continued emphasis on the legitimacy of his ministry is his way of claiming credit for the Corinthian turnaround. This would be a false reading of the text. Rather, he rejoices that God's Word has accomplished such wonderful results. To be sure, the apostle's God-inspired admonitions were a tool in the process, but the sole factor in bringing about this improvement was a "godly grief" which "produces a repentance that leads to salvation." This was a divine work, not a human one.

Like Paul, we Christians today rejoice in seeing positive results in the spiritual realm. Yet the danger—indeed, the sin—that confronts us is the tendency to transfer credit for success to ourselves. Whether it is a program or activity of the corporate church or a circumstance or struggle that affects us personally, we often evaluate results on the basis of our performance rather than on God's work, as though He would be impotent without our assistance. Furthermore, our measure of success is often aberrant, based more on empirical evidence than on a spiritual perspective.

This is but one manifestation of our tendency to long for a theology of glory rather than a theology of the cross. From a critical perspective, the life of our Lord Jesus was not a rousing success. He neither commanded any large armies nor led any massive empire. The numbers of those who initially followed Him dwindled with the passing of time. His closest disciples did not always remain devoted to Him, and in the end He died the death of a common criminal. His last words were, "It is finished" (John 19:30).

Paul speaks of "dying together" and "living together" with the Corinthians. This is more than just another sentimental display of his affection. It is the womb from which all spiritual transformation, change, and success is given birth, both for the Corinthians and for us.

Faith in Jesus unites Christians with the Savior in His death and resurrection and works in our life everything that God intends to accomplish. Success does not have many fathers. All victories are given by God the Father through the work of His Son by the power of the Spirit.

30 AUGUST

Psalmody: Psalm 29:1–4, 10–11
Additional Psalm: Psalm 75
Old Testament Reading:
1 Kings 12:20–13:5, 33–34
Additional Reading: 1 Kings 14:1–16:28
New Testament Reading:
2 Corinthians 8:1–24

Prayer of the Day

Almighty God, heavenly Father, You have called us to be Your children and heirs of Your gracious promises in Christ Jesus. Grant us Your Holy Spirit that we may forsake all covetous desires and the inordinate love of riches. Deliver us from the pursuit of passing things that we may seek the kingdom of Your Son and trust in His righteousness and so find blessedness and peace; through Jesus Christ, our Lord. (195)

Meditation

We often hear about the unique ability certain people have to compartmentalize life, separating and isolating different aspects of their daily routine. Some individuals are able to avoid taking the frustrations of work home; for them, family matters are never revealed or discussed with coworkers. Celebrities are occasionally described as being able to maintain a line of division between their public and private lives.

This sort of compartmentalization is not a virtue when it comes to the Christian life. All the aspects of discipleship are interlocking and overlapping. A follower of Jesus cannot pick and choose if he will be a worshipper, a learner, a servant, a witness, or a steward. A disciple is all of these and more.

Talk about the stewardship of material resources particularly rankles some people today. Pastors shy away from sermons on the topic because they do not want to be accused of "always asking for money." People in the pew take offense because they consider it a personal matter. It is almost as if we allow faith in Jesus to touch every aspect of life but our bank account.

Our sinful hesitancy to avoid this topic and share the resources God has given us may be due to the fact that we find unwarranted comfort in financial security. In reality, there is no such thing. Life's circumstances can change at a moment's notice. The billionaire can suffer a business reversal and be a pauper. The frugal person who devotes decades accumulating a large reservoir of financial resources can become impoverished in a much smaller span of time due to unexpected medical bills or other exigencies of life. In this regard Paul alludes to the children of Israel in the wilderness as they collected manna, saying, "Whoever gathered much had nothing left over, and whoever gathered little had no lack."

Money matters are a concern for the child of God. In his correspondences with the Corinthian congregation, Paul discusses financial stewardship in a very open and Gospel-centered manner. He reminds them and us that possessions are gifts from God, and God's gifts are always given for the good of others. The Macedonian Christians were eager to share their bounty from the Lord, and we can be too. Giving is an act of grace, which flows from God's greatest act of grace—the gift of Jesus. Our Savior is both the greatest treasure and the surest security that we will ever have.

31 AUGUST

Psalmody: Psalm 68:15–20
Additional Psalm: Psalm 70
Old Testament Reading: 1 Kings 16:29–17:24
New Testament Reading:
2 Corinthians 9:1–15

Prayer of the Day

O God, the source of all that is just and good, nourish in us every virtue and bring to completion every good intent that we may grow in grace and bring forth the fruit of good works; through Jesus Christ, Your Son, our Lord, who lives and reigns with You and the Holy Spirit, one God, now and forever. (B75)

Meditation

Occasionally, those who raise funds for a particular cause in today's world resort to using the phrase, "give until it hurts." From a biblical point of view, this is a foreign and erroneous way of encouraging generosity. This tactic might generate short-term results, but it is totally wrong.

In chapters eight and nine of 2 Corinthians, Paul has been dealing with the Judean relief fund. Earlier, his readers had expressed their intent to participate in this philanthropic effort, and now he gives them a kindly reminder that representatives will soon be coming to receive the monetary gift which has been offered.

Giving of our material resources back to the Lord is, indeed, an important act. Yet, the act of giving can never be separated from the attitude that stimulates the giving in the first place. Paul describes the Corinthians as "ready" and "zealous." They truly desired to be involved in this effort; no coercion or slick public relations pitch was necessary. Their giving did not cause pain; it was a pleasure and a privilege. Their attitudes and actions were consistent. Paul gives affirmation of this fact when he says in verse seven, "God loves a cheerful giver."

Christian giving as God intends and Paul describes is not done out of a feeling of guilt over past transgressions; neither is it offered in the hope of gaining a reward or recognition from others or from God. When the apostle here talks about sowing and reaping (verse 6), he is not issuing a threat or suggesting a business transaction but describing the promises of God. Genuine, large-hearted benevolence is a work inspired by the Heavenly Father. When we give cheerfully, we are mirroring what He has already done for us in Christ Jesus. This is a fruit of the Gospel, not a product of the Law.

The message of the Gospel tells us that Christ is the only One who could truly "give until it hurts." Yet He suffered the agony of Calvary without compulsion. As the great hymn says, He was the Lamb who went "uncomplaining forth." Scripture tells us that He endured the cross "for the joy that was set before Him" (Hebrews 12:2). When confronted with an opportunity to give as with the Corinthians, we don't need to ask, "What would Jesus do?" as the expression goes. Rather, we can ask, "What did Jesus do?" God loves cheerful givers because that is precisely what His Son was for us, and what we now are because of Him.

1 SEPTEMBER

Joshua

Psalmody: Psalm 47
Additional Psalm: Psalm 8
Old Testament Reading: 1 Kings 18:1–19
New Testament Reading: Ephesians 1:1–23

Prayer of the Day

Lord Jesus Christ, Your servant Joshua led the children of Israel through the waters of the Jordan River into a land flowing with milk and honey. As our Joshua, lead us, we pray, through the waters of our Baptism into the promised land of our eternal home, where You live and reign with the Father and the Holy Spirit, one God, now and forever. (1083)

Joshua

Joshua, the son of Nun, of the tribe of Ephraim, is first mentioned in Exodus 17 when he was chosen by Moses to fight the Amalekites, whom he defeated in a brilliant military victory. He was placed in charge of the tent of meeting (Exodus 33:11) and was a member of the tribal representatives sent to survey the land of Canaan (Numbers 13:8). Later, he was appointed by God to succeed Moses as Israel's commander-in-chief. Joshua eventually led the Israelites across the Jordan River into the Promised Land and directed the Israelites' capture of Jericho. He is remembered especially for his final address to the Israelites, in which he challenged them to serve God faithfully (Joshua 24:1–27), concluding with the memorable words, "As for me and my household, we will serve the Lord" (24:15).

Meditation

As you read Ephesians, underline or note how often the phrase "in Christ" occurs. In many ways it is the key to this entire glorious epistle. Paul starts blessing God. How many times in Acts did he not speak of the God whom he worshiped? What better way to begin a letter than giving praise, glory, and thanks to God? But note how it is all "in Christ."

"In Christ" we are blessed with every spiritual blessing in the heavenly places; God has held nothing back from us in His Son.

"In Christ" He chose us before the world's foundation was laid down in order that we should be His holy, blameless people. Me? Holy and blameless? Yes, you! "In Christ." You have been lovingly predestined for adoption as God's own beloved child in Jesus Christ. That was God's will—and it overflows to the praise of His grace!

"In Christ" you have redemption through His blood. Your trespasses are forgiven, wiped out in the blood of the Lamb.

"In Christ" you have been included in God's great purpose in these last times. Christ is to be the new Adam, and God will "re-head" the race in Him. When you're connected via faith to Christ, you've been made part of God's new humanity.

"In Christ" you have an inheritance—He came to our earth to open to us His heaven.

"In Christ" God has a plan for your life. He intends for you to be to the praise of His glory. You have been summoned into a life of doxology, of praise and thanksgiving to God.

"In Christ" when you heard the word of God's truth, you were given a seal—the promised Holy Spirit. The Holy Spirit is God's guarantee, His down payment, on your full inheritance until you take possession of it.

And so Paul prays for his beloved Ephesian Christians (and for you) that God would open wide your eyes, enlightening them by that same Holy Spirit, so that you may begin understand the riches that are yours with all God's people, and how great His power is at work in you who believe. Why, it's the very same power that raised Jesus Christ up from the dead, seated Him at the Father's side, and gave Him the name above every name. Everything is under His feet—and when you are "in Christ," then everything that is His is yours.

2 September

Hannah

Psalmody: Psalm 138
Additional Psalm: Psalm 135
Old Testament Reading: 1 Kings 18:20–40
New Testament Reading: Ephesians 2:1–22

Prayer of the Day

God the Father Almighty, maker of all things, You looked on the affliction of Your barren servant Hannah and did not forget her but answered her prayers with the gift of a son. So hear our supplications and petitions and fill our emptiness, granting us trust in Your provision, so that we, like Hannah, might render unto You all thankfulness and praise, and delight in the miraculous birth of Your Son, Jesus Christ, who lives and reigns with You and the Holy Spirit, one God, now and forever. (1084)

Hannah

Hannah was the favored wife of Elkanah, the Ephraimite, and the devout mother of the prophet Samuel. He was born to her after years of bitter barrenness (1 Samuel 1:6–8) and fervent prayers for a son (1 Samuel 1:9–18). After she weaned her son, Hannah expressed her gratitude by returning him for service in the house of the Lord at Shiloh (1 Samuel 1:24–28). Her prayer (psalm) of thanksgiving (1 Samuel 2:1–10) begins with the words, "My heart exults in Lord; my strength is exalted in the Lord." This song foreshadows the Magnificat, the Song of Mary centuries later (Luke 1:46–55). The name *Hannah* derives from the Hebrew word for "grace." She is remembered and honored for joyfully having kept the vow she made before her son's birth and offering him for lifelong service to God.

Meditation

Everything that is Christ's is yours. But before you can appreciate the depth of that, you have to realize what you had on your own. What were you apart from Christ, not in Him, just yourself? Paul's words aren't flattering.

You were dead. You see, He alone is life, and not one of us was born connected to His life. We were all born in "trespasses and sins." Original sin is what Paul is talking about here. From the very first moments of our existence we've rebelled against God, insisting on our own way. And in that rebellion, we were following Satan's lead. He's the one Paul calls "the prince of the power of the air, the spirit that is now at work in the sons of disobedience."

That was us and that is us—apart from Christ. Without Christ we live out the passions of our flesh and carry out the sinful desires of our corrupt body and mind. "I want to do what I want to do when I want to do it!" And so we did. How does the apostle characterize us? He says that we are "by nature children of wrath." That's how we're born: dead to all that's good and alive to all that's evil.

"But!" That's a glorious word that changes everything. But God, rich in mercy, loving us with an inexplicable and great love, even when we were dead as doornails in our trespasses and sins, made us alive together with Christ! He did it as a totally free gift to us undeserving sinners. He made us alive with Christ. He raised us up with Him. He even made us to sit in the heavenly places with Christ. Because He is the new head of the race, all that happens to Him happens to anyone who is joined to Him by faith.

By grace—free, undeserved mercy—we have been saved through faith. Even faith isn't something we come up with on our own. It's a gift God gives us. There is no room for boasting here. Dead men don't bring themselves back to life, but in Christ God has raised us from our death and given us a brand new life—a life full of good works that He prepares and sets before us for us to receive and do.

Remember, Paul writes to us Gentiles, what life was like outside of Christ. And give thanks to Him who brings us near through the blood of Christ and makes Jews and Gentiles together by faith one family.

3 SEPTEMBER

Gregory the Great, Pastor

Psalmody: Psalm 119:57–64
Additional Psalm: Psalm 108
Old Testament Reading: 1 Kings 19:1–21
Additional Reading: 1 Kings 20:1–22:53
New Testament Reading: Ephesians 3:1–21

Prayer of the Day

Almighty and merciful God, You raised up Gregory of Rome to be a pastor to those who shepherd God's flock and inspired him to send missionaries to preach the Gospel to the English people. Preserve in Your Church the catholic and apostolic faith that Your people may continue to be fruitful in every good work and receive the crown of glory that never fades away; through Jesus Christ, our Lord, who lives and reigns with You and the Holy Spirit, one God, now and forever. (1085)

Gregory the Great, Pastor

One of the great leaders in Europe at the close of the sixth century, Gregory served in both the secular and sacred arenas of his era. As mayor of Rome, he restored economic vitality to his native city, which had been weakened by enemy invasions, pillage, and plague. After he sold his extensive properties and donated the proceeds to help the poor, he entered into full-time service in the Church. On September 3, 590, Gregory was elected to lead the Church in Rome. As bishop of Rome, he oversaw changes and growth in the areas of church music and liturgical development, missionary outreach to northern Europe, and the establishment of a Church Year calendar still used by many church bodies in the Western world today. His book on pastoral care became a standard until the twentieth century.

Meditation

Mystery in the Bible doesn't mean an enigma you can't solve. Mystery means a truth that human wisdom could never have arrived at on its own; it takes a revelation from God. And when God reveals a mystery, it doesn't cease to be mysterious; it continues to move us to awe, praise, and adoration.

The mystery to end all mysteries is what Paul calls "the mystery of Christ." In former ages it was hinted at, but now it has been unveiled fully. Through God's apostles and prophets the Holy Spirit unpacks the secret plan of God: in Jesus Christ, all people—whether Jew or Gentile—get to be fellow heirs with the divine Son, members of His one body, and partakers of the promise of forgiveness and eternal life in Him.

This mystery has another name: the Gospel, the Good News. The crucified yet risen Lord appointed Paul to be a minister of this Gospel as a free gift of His grace. He gave to Paul—yes, the same one who had persecuted this faith—the grace to preach among the Gentiles the unsearchable riches that God has for them in Jesus Christ. He gets to let everyone in on God's secret plan: the re-heading of our race in Jesus Christ, the opportunity for every single human being to receive pardon, forgiveness, and life unending.

As the Church makes this mystery known, as she shares this good news in a bad news world, even the angels look on in awe and wonder at what God has done and promised through His Son. In Jesus every single human being has the gift of access with boldness and confidence to God the Father. Paul gladly suffers for the privilege of sharing that good news with every single human being.

And so the apostle's prayer is rather straightforward. He prays to the Father to grant Christians to be strengthened by the Holy Spirit in their true and inner life so that, with Christ dwelling in their hearts by faith, they may comprehend with all God's holy ones the breadth, length, height, and depth of the all surpassing love given in Christ so that each of us may be filled up with all the fullness of God.

He prays to the One who is able to do more than we could ever dream through His power—His Spirit—at work in us, and whose glory the Church praises forever.

4 SEPTEMBER

Moses

Psalmody: Psalm 90:13–17
Additional Psalm: Psalm 107
Old Testament Reading: 2 Kings 2:1–18
New Testament Reading: Ephesians 4:1–24

Prayer of the Day

Lord God, heavenly Father, through the prophet Moses, You began the prophetic pattern of teaching Your people the true faith and demonstrating through miracles Your presence in the creation to heal it of its brokenness. Grant that Your Church may see in Your Son, our Lord Jesus Christ, the final end-times prophet whose teaching and miracles continue in Your Church through the healing medicine of the Gospel and the Sacraments; through Jesus Christ, our Lord. (1086)

Moses

Moses was born in Egypt several generations after Joseph brought his father, Jacob, and his brothers there to escape a famine in the land of Canaan. The descendants of Jacob had been enslaved by the Egyptians and were ordered to kill all their male children. When Moses was born, his mother put him in a basket and set it afloat in the Nile River. He was found by Pharaoh's daughter and raised by her as her son (Exodus 2:1–10). At age forty, Moses killed an Egyptian taskmaster and fled to the land of Midian, where he worked as a shepherd for forty years. Then the Lord called him to return to Egypt and tell Pharaoh, "Let My people go, that they may hold a feast to Me in the wilderness" (Exodus 5:1). Eventually Pharaoh gave in, and after the Israelites celebrated the first Passover, Moses led them out. At the Red Sea the Egyptian army was destroyed, and the Israelites passed to safety on dry land (Exodus 12–15). At Mount Sinai, they were given the Law and erected the tabernacle (Exodus 19–40). But because of disobedience, they had to wander in the wilderness for forty years. Moses himself was not allowed to enter the Promised Land, although God allowed him to view it (Deuteronomy 34). In the New Testament, Moses is referred to as lawgiver and prophet. The first five books of the Bible are attributed to him.

Meditation

You have received a noble calling. God has summoned you into His Son to become His beloved child and heir. Now, Paul urges, live as one who has that high calling. Live here in this age, which is corrupt and dying, the undying love and life of the age that has become your true home.

What does that love look like? Humility, gentleness, patience, bearing with each other in love, being zealous to maintain the unity that the Holy Spirit gave you when He joined you to the one Body of Christ. If fallen humanity tends towards splitting and division, fighting and faction, the Spirit of Christ tugs in the other direction: toward oneness. Note all the "ones": one Body (the Church), one Spirit, one hope (eternal life), one Lord (Jesus), one faith (His trust in the Father), one Baptism, one God and Father of all. Oneness flows from the one Father, who sent the one Son to pour out on us the one Spirit, who brings us to faith in the one Son, who presents us with joy to the one Father.

And for all of this to happen, our Lord descended to the depths and ascended to the heights of heaven in order to bring back with Him an army of those who had been captive to the devil and death. For this work, He appoints the ministry: apostles, prophets, evangelists, pastors, and teachers. As they speak the truth in love, they build up the Body of Christ. And the members of that Body, speaking God's truth to each other, too, makes the Body grow as it builds itself up in love.

So with this new life before us and the call to unity and truth with each other, no room exists for the old way, the futile way of the Gentiles who think that life is given for you to please yourself: eat, drink, and be merry. Alienated from God, they miss out on the purpose of life. And the sad thing is that all who chase down that pleasure road daily end up worse. That's not how we learned to live in Christ.

The truth with which we are confronted in Christ shows us that that way of living was just corrupt from the beginning. We need to ditch it, like taking off dirty clothes, and receive instead a brand new mind, a new way of looking at life and the world, through Christ, who is the likeness of the Father.

5 SEPTEMBER

Zacharias and Elizabeth

Psalmody: Psalm 56:8–13
Additional Psalm: Psalm 56
Old Testament Reading:
2 Kings 2:19–25; 4:1–7
New Testament Reading:
Ephesians 4:25–5:14

Prayer of the Day

O God, who alone knits all infants in the womb, You chose improbable servants—old and childless—to conceive and parent the forerunner of Christ and, in so doing, demonstrated again Your strength in weakness. Grant us, who are as unlikely and unworthy as Zacharias and Elizabeth, the opportunity to love and serve You according to Your good and gracious will; through Jesus Christ, our Lord, who lives and reigns with You and the Holy Spirit, now and forever. (1087)

Zacharias and Elizabeth

Zacharias and Elizabeth were "righteous before God, walking blamelessly in the commandments and statutes of the Lord" (Luke 1:6). Zacharias, a priest in the Jerusalem temple, was greeted by the angel Gabriel, who announced that Zacharias and Elizabeth would become parents of a son. Initially, Zacharias did not believe Gabriel's announcement because of their old age. For his disbelief, Zacharias became unable to speak. After their son was born, Elizabeth named their son John. Zacharias confirmed his wife's choice, and his ability to speak was restored. In response, he sang the Benedictus, a magnificent summary of God's promises in the Old Testament and a prediction of John's work as forerunner to Jesus (Luke 1:68–79). Zacharias and Elizabeth are remembered as examples of faithfulness and piety.

Meditation

What does it look like when you begin to live in Christ, toward the age to come, instead of in the corruption you inherited from Adam? Paul gives some very clear pictures of the things that you leave behind and the new gifts that replace them.

Lies of every sort get left behind; they are replaced with straight speaking, speaking the truth with each other in love. Anger doesn't entirely get left behind, but it's not allowed to turn into bitterness; before the sun sets each day, the Christian makes peace as far as he or she can. Thievery goes—including the subtle thievery of taking pay for shoddy or no work; what comes instead is honest industry, motivated by a desire to give to those in need, a desire to share. Worthless talk gets buried, the sort that leads others into sin; what comes instead is using speech to build up other people. What is abandoned is that grieving of the Holy Spirit when we insist "my will be done"; what comes instead is seeking the will of God, knowing that we are people who belong already to the day of redemption. Out go bitterness, wrath, anger, clamor, slander, and every form of malice; in come kindness and a tender heart that forgives even as we have been forgiven. In short, the new life is about God's children imitating Him, learning to walk in love together with the One who loved us and gave Himself up for us.

It should go without saying that you cannot live the new life and at the same time indulge the flesh. There is no way to be a member of God's eternal family, rejoicing in forgiveness and eternal life, and yet persist in sexual immorality. Anyone who tells you that you can have that cake and eat it, too, is simply lying. God's wrath comes upon those who persist in such disobedience.

Paul urges us not to fall into that trap but to see that as our past has no power to destroy our present or future life in Christ. When we live in the light of Christ, we turn our backs on the darkness in which we once reveled. When we live in the light of Christ, we rejoice in everything that is good, right, and true, and we seek in all things to do what pleases the Lord, who in Baptism raised us from death and gave us life.

6 September

Psalmody: Psalm 127
Additional Psalm: Psalm 128
Old Testament Reading: 2 Kings 4:8–22, 32–37
New Testament Reading: Ephesians 5:15–33

Prayer of the Day

O Lord, we implore You, let Your continual pity cleanse and defend Your Church; and because she cannot continue in safety without Your aid, preserve her evermore by Your help and goodness; through Jesus Christ, Your Son, our Lord, who lives and reigns with You and the Holy Spirit, one God, now and forever. (H75)

Meditation

What does the life of the coming age look like? How does it shape our life even here as we await its coming fullness? It teaches us to use our time well, to redeem that time, to buy it back. How? By letting the Spirit fill us (instead of being drunk with pleasures of this world) and so move us to join even now in the endless doxologies that are the joys of the age to which we are headed. What is life for? For singing praises to God! Psalms, hymns, spiritual songs are to replace all the grumbling, the griping, the moaning and groaning, the unkind and bitter words that would fill our mouths. By psalms, hymns, and spiritual songs, we can be lifted to a life of thanksgiving "always and for everything" to God the Father. No, we'll not live it perfectly, but we see that is the goal, where we are headed in Christ Jesus.

The gift of the Church's song isn't intended to stay between the covers of a hymnal. The Spirit has given it to the Church so that her Te Deum and Magnificat, her Psalms and her "Mighty Fortress," might fill your heart and overflow your mouth. Take out that hymnal today and

sing some. Do it every day. That's how you practice for the coming age.

A truly profound feature of this new life is that in it there is no playing "who's the boss." That's something on which the old Adam and the old life thrived. You get to die to it. You are called to submit to each other, to see and serve Christ in one another.

The apostle turns to marriage. He sees something beautiful about the marriage relationship: it's an enactment of the love between Christ and His bride, the Church. What does a Christlike marriage look like? The new husband, crowned the servant-king of a new family, treasures and loves his bride. The new wife, crowned the servant-queen of a new family, submits to her husband as the Church submits to Christ and receives the gifts that He gives her.

When a marriage is Christlike, it is a living icon of Christ and the Church, and the children, the fruit of the marriage, will see that icon up close.

7 September

Psalmody: Psalm 131
Additional Psalm: Psalm 77
Old Testament Reading: 2 Kings 4:38–5:8
New Testament Reading: Ephesians 6:1–24

Prayer of the Day

Grant to us, Lord, the Spirit to think and do always such things as are right, that we, who cannot do anything that is good without You, may be enabled by You to live according to Your will; through Jesus Christ, Your Son, our Lord, who lives and reigns with You and the Holy Spirit, one God, now and forever. (H68)

Meditation

The new life in Christ transforms not only the relationship of husbands and wives, but also that of parents and children, slaves and masters (or, as we'd likely put it today, employers and employees). Children are to honor their parents as the Fourth Commandment teaches and to trust that God will bless such honoring as the Law promises. Fathers (or perhaps, parents—the Greek is a little ambiguous) are not to provoke or exasperate their children—loading them down with criticisms and burdens—but instead to bring them up in the discipline and the instruction of the Lord. Day in and day out, the Word of God is to resound throughout the Christian home, filling it with the wisdom of God in Christ.

But even outside the home, relationships are transfigured by Christ. Slaves or employees who live the joy of the age to come can never forget whose eyes are upon them and who is the ultimate recipient of their diligent work: the Lord Himself, who takes every good deed done as done to Him. Similarly, employers are to do the same, realizing that they have a Master in heaven to whom even they must answer. So the old ways of laziness on the part of workers or harshness on the part of employers is set aside for the joys of the new life in Christ. Imagine how workplaces would be completely transformed if we each served in such a way.

As the capstone of the whole epistle, the apostle urges us to be strong in the Lord—that is, to be clothed with His strength, not our own. He uses the image of a soldier, for Baptism has us enlisted into the *militia Christi*, Christ's army, to engage in warfare—only we're not battling "flesh and blood." Other people are never the ultimate problem. The ultimate problem is the devil and his angels, "the cosmic powers over this present darkness." They are the ones we're really fighting.

But since they are spirit beings and the fight is a spiritual battle, we need spiritual armor in order to stand firm against them: truth, righteousness, the readiness to spread the Gospel of peace, faith to quench the devil's flaming arrows, salvation to guard our head, and the Spirit's sword, the Word of God, in our hand. All of these gifts from the Lord we take up, "praying at all times in the Spirit." So dressed for battle, we can triumph indeed in the Lord's own strength.

8 SEPTEMBER

Psalmody: Psalm 71:12–16
Additional Psalm: Psalm 69
Old Testament Reading: 2 Kings 5:9–27
New Testament Reading: Philippians 1:1–20

Prayer of the Day

Lord Jesus Christ, the giver of all good gifts, our thanksgiving overflows for the life You created in us and the new life we now have in You through Holy Baptism. Continue to shower us with Your gifts as we offer thanksgiving for our ongoing communion with You in Your body and blood; for You live and reign with the Father and the Holy Spirit, one God, now and forever. (1088)

Meditation

Our Lord applied the words "out of the abundance of the heart the mouth speaks" (Matthew 12:34) to the Pharisees to uncover their hypocrisy. He branded their prayers as pretense and as polluted streams springing from evil hearts.

If we apply these words to Paul, however, we see his sincerity in his prayer of gratitude to God on behalf of his beloved Philippians, who were especially dear to Paul. He says, "I hold you in my heart."

What gave Paul particular cause for rejoicing was the Philippians' partnership in the Gospel. They were partners with him in preaching and teaching the Gospel that proclaims to all that they are sinners and that Christ atoned for their sins by pouring out His blood. It was not just good news in general, but through faith they could say, "This Good News is for me." This was the good work God had begun in them.

It is also the good work God has begun in us. From pure grace, for Jesus' sake, without seeing anything good in us, our heavenly Father has brought us to faith in our Savior. What great joy to know we are God's dear children and all our sins are forgiven.

Do we give thanks for our fellow believers as Paul did? It is easy to find things to criticize in them. We live so closely with them that we see their faults and shortcomings. And if that were not enough, Satan and our sinful nature enjoy making great mountains of evil out of the faults of others. That way they seem so much worse than our own. This robs us of the joy we could have in seeing the great things God, by His grace, can do in the lives of His people. This was Paul's joy.

When I understand that Jesus has forgiven my sins, then I want others to know the One who died for me and for all. We hold this work in common with other Christians of telling the Good News to all, just as the Gospel is our common possession. That is real partnership in the Gospel.

When we pray for and with each other, we are not just wishing we will somehow muddle through life to Judgment Day with our faith intact. Prayer is not wishing; it is an expression of our absolute trust and confidence in God. We are completely confident, as was Paul, that we will greet the Lord with joy at His return.

9 SEPTEMBER

Psalmody: Psalm 61
Additional Psalm: Psalm 59
Old Testament Reading: 2 Kings 6:1–23
Additional Reading: 2 Kings 6:24–8:29
New Testament Reading: Philippians 1:21–2:11

Prayer of the Day

Merciful Lord, You sent Your Son, Jesus, into our world to humble Himself by becoming obedient unto death, even death on a cross. Teach us to be obedient so that we might declare with St. Paul that "for me to live is Christ, and to die is gain" (Philippians 1:21) and that our lives may be worthy of the Gospel of Christ; through Jesus Christ, our Lord. (1089)

Meditation

On Palm Sunday we see Jesus enter Jerusalem as a humble, meek, lowly king, not mounted on a royal thoroughbred, but on a donkey. On the other hand, the glorification of this king is suggested by the garments and branches that His followers scattered in His path and the shouts of "Hosanna to the Son of David."

More than any other New Testament passage, Philippians 2:1–11 demonstrates how the great prophecy of Isaiah 53 was fulfilled in the suffering and glorification of Christ. The apostle asks us to follow Jesus into His humiliation.

To follow Christ into His humiliation, we must get rid of all selfishness that is so prevalent among us. Family life is often ruined because one member places self-interest above family welfare. Employers and workers frequently are locked in labor disputes because each side contends the other is unreasonable. It seems that most political and economic arenas of life are saturated with the lust for self-advancement.

From the common citizen to the highest head of state, the triumph over self is the crying need of our time. Paul suggests that this can only be achieved one way. "Let each of you look not only to his own interests, but also to the interests of others. Have this mind among yourselves, which is yours in Christ Jesus."

Christ's mind was completely different from the mind of mankind. People often exploit every opportunity to squeeze out each advantage for their benefit—but not Christ. He did not abuse His divinity. He was characterized by a willingness to set aside His divine glory.

As Christians, to have a Christlike mind, we put aside the world's pomp and glory. To have a mind like Christ, it is essential to have a mind in Christ. To effect a change from selfishness to selflessness requires a change motivated by Jesus. Our thinking must be released from sin; our mind is rendered contrite and penitent; and our soul is impelled to bless the Lord in gratitude for all the benefits it has received.

Christ laid aside His divine glory and humbled Himself, becoming obedient unto death for our sins. This is our greatest blessing. What joy it is to bask in the forgiveness of sins.

Inasmuch as Christ humbled Himself, the Father also glorified Him, giving Him the highest name of all—Jesus.

Our names also reflect the glory of Christ given us through faith. We are sons of the living God and saints of the Most High—we are the beloved of God.

10 September

Psalmody: Psalm 58:1–8
Additional Psalm: Psalm 53
Old Testament Reading:
2 Kings 9:1–13; 10:18–29
Additional Reading: 2 Kings 13:1–18:8
New Testament Reading: Philippians 2:12–30

Prayer of the Day

Lord Jesus, light of the world, You shine with the brightness of the sun in the darkness of our crooked and twisted generation. Give us strength to shine as lights in the world as we live out our baptismal life by serving our neighbors with thanksgiving and joy as sacrificial offerings of mercy and love; for You live and reign with the Father and the Holy Spirit, one God, now and forever. (1090)

Meditation

It is easy to speak in generalities and fancy-sounding words about the Church. We can sit and pat it on the back, or slap it in the face, without realizing what we are really doing. We are the Church. The Church needs ongoing reformation because we need to be constantly reformed and renewed in heart and mind by ongoing repentance.

The Church cannot be the Church unless it exists in the person and work of Jesus. If we are to be what is required of the Church, we must be bound closely to Christ and no longer expressing ourselves. What He did flowed out of His inner being. Jesus came to be God-for-us.

Our Savior, now and always, comes through His Word, not just to be God-for-us, but also to be God-with-us and God-in-us. We cannot know God as He is. We can only know Him as He comes in Jesus. We can see His heart only as He reveals it in Christ.

To know God we must make the journey to a stable in Bethlehem. We can enter only if we leave behind our own ideas of spirituality and kneel before the baby who is God. We see God on the dusty roads of Palestine as the man of Nazareth, despised and rejected, caring for the hungry and lonely, expressing Himself in our terms and on our level.

Many folks stop here, but we must continue and stand at Calvary. We will not worship God if we do not worship the Crucified One. We will never know God unless we hear His Son cry out that He was forsaken by His Father. Only then could He proclaim, "It is finished" (John 19:30). We will only know God's grace through faith in Jesus' blood payment for our sins.

As Jesus is God-for-us, just as surely do we exist as the Church under God's grace. Christ, as Lord, has made Himself fully responsible for us. He exercises lordship over our sins, misery, hopelessness, and anything that would drag us away from God's love.

In our standing before God, our appeal is always to God's mercy. This is what makes the Church—this conglomeration of sinners we are, the harassed and anxious people we are—stand together under the forgiveness of sins.

Our faith alone makes us the Church and renews us daily through Christ's love to live Christlike lives.

11 SEPTEMBER

Psalmody: Psalm 44:1–8
Additional Psalm: Psalm 100
Old Testament Reading: 2 Chronicles 29:1–24
New Testament Reading: Philippians 3:1–21

Prayer of the Day

Most merciful Father, with compassion You hear the cries of Your people in great distress. Be with all who now endure affliction and calamity, bless the work of those who bring rescue and relief, and enable us to aid and comfort those who are suffering that they may find renewed hope and purpose; through Jesus Christ, our Lord, who lives and reigns with You and the Holy Spirit, one God, now and forever. (F41)

Meditation

Paul's encourages Christians to "rejoice in the Lord." We are to find true joy and hope of salvation through faith in Jesus Christ alone and not through any works we do.

Often we are satisfied to just get by. We do our tasks in an easygoing manner with the minimum of effort. We excuse our mistakes with the old cliché, "After all, I am only human."

This attitude often carries over into our spiritual thinking. Even though we strive to do Christian works of love, we should never get the notion that we have "arrived" at being perfect Christians. However, it is something toward which we should keep pressing "on toward the goal for the prize of the upward call of God in Christ Jesus." This takes more than anything and everything we have in us. Our perfection is in Christ, nowhere else. Only when we accept the perfect holiness of Christ in humble faith, only when we believe we are justified by faith in Christ's blood payment for sin, only then can we have peace with God. Only Christ's righteousness with which He covers us is perfect.

Not only is our perfection in Christ, but Christ's perfection also will grow in us. To live our Christian faith is not easy. It requires more than what we have in us. It requires the help and strength of the Holy Spirit as He feeds our faith with God's Word.

Our life in Christ is not a part-time vocation. The shaping of our Christian character in Christ is our life's work. Are we up to it? Or are we content to treat it as a hobby? For many people, faith is a Sunday exercise with no relevance to the big issues of life.

Christian living involves always pressing and constantly fighting on in the Spirit's power until the last enemy is routed and we stand with the palm of victory before God's throne. Our last great goal is the perfection of eternal life, which lies ahead.

God has set that goal before us, the perfect glory of heaven, won and paid for by Christ's perfect righteousness. We eagerly look forward to it. Yet it is necessary to crucify the sinful nature in order not to lose the prize. We focus on heaven and strive toward spiritual maturity until we finally take full possession of the eternal prize.

12 September

Psalmody: Psalm 94:12–15
Additional Psalm: Psalm 94
Old Testament Reading: 2 Chronicles 31:1–21
New Testament Reading: Philippians 4:1–23

Prayer of the Day

O God, You have prepared for those who love You good things that surpass all understanding. Pour into our hearts such love toward You that we, loving You above all things, may obtain Your promises, which exceed all that we can desire; through Jesus Christ, Your Son, our Lord, who lives and reigns with You and the Holy Spirit, one God, now and forever. (H65)

Meditation

On his second missionary journey Paul stopped in Philippi with Silas. For proclaiming Christ they were imprisoned in the filth and stench of the local dungeon. After being beaten, with their feet in stocks, and during an earthquake, these men were heard singing joyful psalms of thanksgiving.

The reason for their hymns are given by these words, "My God will supply every need of yours according to His riches in glory in Christ Jesus." In spite of one of the worst scenarios that life could bring, their hearts were overflowing in praise to God.

It sounds almost trite to say it, but God has been abundantly good to us and provided everything we need to support our physical needs. This past harvest produced another record corn crop in the Midwest and helps feed the hungry. We have access to the best health care system in the world. Truly, this is a tremendous blessing for which to give thanks. Despite economic stress and false starts of recovery, the Lord still provides a goodly percentage of folks with employment to take care of their families.

Due to the vast improvements in mass communication, the Gospel of Christ's mission is being proclaimed as never before. If Paul and our ancestors could see it, they would be amazed and shout with joy.

It is a challenge for us to be thankful when life is hard and heartaches cross our path. Each of us can recall many examples, such as long periods of unemployment, debilitating or terminal illness, a tragic accident, or a devastating family crisis. At times such as these, the riches of God become obscured by our personal problems. We tend to forget that God is the author of this inexhaustible supply of riches. God wants us to remember His promises that He will be with us, will strengthen and comfort us, and will supply all our needs.

God's ultimate gift was announced by angels singing, a star pointing the way, and men on their knees before the manger of God in the flesh. The Father was saying, "There is nothing more I can give—My only Son—the proof of My love."

Then on a black Friday afternoon we see the God-Man suffering the agony of hell, the separation from His Father for our iniquities. Three days later an angel declares, "He is not here, for He has risen" (Matthew 28:6). This guarantees our resurrection. This is what is meant by God supplying all our needs.

13 September

Psalmody: Psalm 27:7–13
Additional Psalm: Psalm 31
Old Testament Reading: 2 Chronicles 32:1–21
Additional Reading: Hosea 1:1–14:9
New Testament Reading: Colossians 1:1–23

Prayer of the Day

Stir up, O Lord, the wills of Your faithful people that they, plenteously bringing forth the fruit of good works, may by You be plenteously rewarded; through Jesus Christ, Your Son, our Lord, who lives and reigns with You and the Holy Spirit, one God, now and forever. (H84)

Meditation

False teachers who professed Christianity were spreading false doctrines in Colossae. They spouted a dangerous mixture of Jewish ceremonial laws, Greek concepts of the spirit world, and Christian terminology. They said a higher wisdom than that of simple Christianity was needed, which they were prepared to furnish. By their speculations, human doctrines, and commandments, they placed themselves in opposition to Christ and His death for us.

This posed a serious threat to the people's faith. Paul wished to bolster the confidence of the Colossian Christians and Christians of all time in the all-sufficiency of Christ. He also gave instruction in Christian morality.

False teachers like to use catchwords such as "fullness," "thorough knowledge," and "wisdom" to spice up their message. They claim that newborn Christians have only taken a few baby steps; but if they want full knowledge in wisdom and spiritual things, they need to follow these teachers. Claims are made today that there are different levels of Christianity; that to be a "full Christian," one must be able to speak in tongues.

False teaching robs people of the certainty of a close relationship with God, and it robs people of a desire and power to do God's will. The antidote for false teaching is a thorough knowledge of Christian doctrine and fervent prayer that the Gospel would fill a person with knowledge of God's will.

Doctrinal error makes for emptiness, not fullness; ignorance, not knowledge; and foolishness, not wisdom. Only God's Word (Law and Gospel) gives us what we need. Once the Gospel takes root in a person's heart, it continues to water, fertilize, and shine the light of God's love so that it produces fruit in our life.

What happens when a fruit tree has fruitless branches? It is pruned and fertilized so that it will bear fruit. A Christian needs to make consistent use of God's Word so the Law can cut away attitudes and actions that are not according to God's will. This prepares the way for the Gospel to bear fruit.

As we learn more about living according to God's desires, we increase in strength, patience, and endurance given by God. Trees need to stand strong amidst wind and hail. When the storms of family problems, illness, and job stress strike us, we need strength from God to bear up under pressure.

God has rescued us from Satan's dungeon and holds us in the kingdom of His Son. He has done the impossible. We have the continuing blessing of the forgiveness of sins.

14 September

Holy Cross Day

Psalmody: Psalm 38:6–16
Additional Psalm: Psalm 38
Old Testament Reading:
2 Chronicles 33:1–25
Jonah 1:1–4:11
New Testament Reading: Colossians 1:24–2:7

Prayer of the Day

Merciful God, Your Son, Jesus Christ, was lifted high upon the cross that He might bear the sins of the world and draw all people to Himself. Grant that we who glory in His death for our redemption may faithfully heed His call to bear the cross and follow Him, who lives and reigns with You and the Holy Spirit, one God, now and forever. (F27)

Holy Cross Day

One of the earliest annual celebrations of the Church, Holy Cross Day traditionally commemorated the discovery of the original cross of Jesus on September 14, 320, in Jerusalem. The cross was found by Helena, mother of Roman Emperor Constantine the Great. In conjunction with the dedication of a basilica at the site of Jesus' crucifixion and resurrection, the festival day was made official by order of Constantine in AD 355. A devout Christian, Helena helped locate and authenticate many sites related to the life, ministry, death, and resurrection of Jesus throughout biblical lands. Holy Cross Day has remained popular in both Eastern and Western Christianity. Many Lutheran parishes have chosen to use "Holy Cross" as the name of their congregation.

Meditation

The only-begotten Son of God was made flesh and earned a full reconciliation between the righteous God and the sinful world through His sacrificial death. He bore the curse of being forsaken by God and of being condemned to the fires of eternal death. He paid our debt and delivered us from sin, death, and the devil.

Do you believe this reconciliation is yours as a free gift of God's love? Do you believe His purpose was to present us before Him as holy people, cleansed from sin and consecrated to God? Did He intend to free us from the stains of sin so that no one could accuse us? Yes, indeed!

We certainly will continue in this relationship as we remain firmly grounded through faith and firm in the hope of the Gospel, which we have heard. Faith is the means by which salvation is accepted. With faith in redemption through Christ's death and resurrection, we have the certain foundation throughout life and in the hour of death.

Paul's marvelous attitude was one of joy—joy in suffering for the Colossian parish and joy in serving the congregation with the Word of God's grace.

Fellowship with Christ brings with it fellowship in His sufferings. Jesus said, "If anyone would come after Me, let him deny himself and take up his cross daily and follow Me" (Luke 9:23). There is no pattern for these sufferings regarding their severity or where they strike.

Paul's sufferings advanced the interests of Christ's Church, the whole body receiving benefit from one member. The afflictions of an individual member of the Body of Christ, we must remember, benefit the whole congregation. They make the Christian fellowship more intimate and equalizes joys and sorrows.

Christians endure suffering and persecution because that is the way Satan and his evil forces strike out against Christ. On the Last Day the great cup of this suffering will be filled and complete.

The Church will suffer under the devil's attacks because it has been entrusted with the Office of the Keys, the commission to preach the Word of God to the whole world, and to faithfully administer the sacraments. Christ and the glory of the Gospel, the certainty of salvation, is to be proclaimed without apology to this heathen world.

It is God's will that each believer is presented as perfect before Christ, instructed in all the wisdom that the Word of God offers. This perfection is possible only in Christ, in knowledge of Him and fellowship with Him.

15 September

Psalmody: Psalm 1
Additional Psalm: Psalm 4
Old Testament Reading:
2 Chronicles 34:1–4, 8–11, 14–33
Additional Reading: Nahum 1:1–3:19
New Testament Reading: Colossians 2:8–23

Prayer of the Day

O God, because without You we are not able to please You, mercifully grant that Your Holy Spirit may in all things direct and rule our hearts; through Jesus Christ, Your Son, our Lord, who lives and reigns with You and the Holy Spirit, one God, now and forever. (H78)

Meditation

The congregation at Colossae was struggling with teachers who wanted to bypass Christ. There were angel or spirit worshipers giving the impression that such worship was the way to greater spiritual knowledge. Paul counters this heresy by pointing to the completed work of Christ, sufficient for all people.

Paul tells Christians that we are plants firmly rooted in Jesus; we are buildings rising on Christ, the solid foundation; our faith has been strengthened. This is the result of all we have learned, giving reason for joyful thanksgiving.

The warning is that there are slave raiders always attacking us. They use human philosophy—a façade with nothing behind it—to spiritually enslave us. This philosophy teaches that mankind can summon the ability from within to save.

Paul slams the door on this false teaching. Christ is more than a fine Jewish teacher. He is everything that man needs—the real force for salvation. He is true man and true God. In Christ we are completely fulfilled. The fullness of the Godhead took on human flesh in the person, in the body of Jesus.

How does the fullness of Christ come to us? In Christ believers reach their full life, and in fellowship with Him through faith, we are filled with all the fullness of God. We have divine life, abundant, active, and fruitful life in Him. Filled with God's fullness, we should fear no power on earth.

In addressing a congregation chiefly of Gentiles, Paul compares the Sacrament of Baptism, by which they were received into God's kingdom, with that of circumcision. By circumcision the Jews were made members of the outward people of God. This Sacrament of Baptism, "made without hands," is a sacrament in which the sinful nature of man is laid aside like a filthy garment.

This circumcision by Christ, the stripping off of our sinful nature, is Holy Baptism. Our sinful nature was killed when our Lord received us as His own in Baptism, the visible means by which the Lord works rebirth in our hearts. Buried with Christ and dead to sin, we, through the effective working of the Word in Baptism, become partakers also of Christ's resurrection.

The blessings of Christ, forgiveness of sins, are given through faith, which the Gospel has worked in our hearts. This was a proof of the same divine power by which God raised Jesus from the dead.

There is no more guilt to condemn us; the Law no longer has power over us. Christ's death has brought us eternal life.

16 September

Cyprian of Carthage, Pastor and Martyr

Psalmody: Psalm 108:1–6
Additional Psalm: Psalm 108
Old Testament Reading:
2 Chronicles 35:1–7, 16–25
Additional Reading: Zephaniah 1:1–3:20
New Testament Reading: Colossians 3:1–25

Prayer of the Day

Almighty God, You gave Your servant Cyprian boldness to confess the name of our Savior, Jesus Christ, before the rulers of this world and courage to die for the faith he proclaimed. Give us strength always to be ready to give a reason for the hope that is in us and to suffer gladly for the sake of our Lord Jesus Christ, who lives and reigns with You and the Holy Spirit, one God, now and forever. (1091)

Cyprian of Carthage, Pastor and Martyr

Cyprian (ca. AD 200–258), was acclaimed bishop of the North African city of Carthage around AD 248. During the persecution of the Roman Emperor Decius, Cyprian fled Carthage but returned two years later. He was then forced to deal with the problem of Christians who had lapsed from their faith under persecution and now wanted to return to the Church. It was decided that these lapsed Christians could be restored, but that their restoration could take place only after a period of penance that demonstrated their faithfulness. During the persecution under Emperor Valerian, Cyprian at first went into hiding but later gave himself up to the authorities. He was beheaded for the faith in Carthage in AD 258.

Meditation

Corporations pay big money for motivational speakers to inspire employees to be more productive. Their main theme is usually centered on setting higher goals, emphasizing the thought that by setting goals, practices and ways of thinking are constructed that make the goal achievable.

Paul pointed to where Christians should set their minds, saying, "Set your minds on things that are above, not on things that are on earth." He was not calling Christians to hate this world, to reject the earth. Instead he was attacking a heresy that was flourishing in Colossae. Today we would call it fatalism.

Many Colossians (and apparently some Christians) came to believe the world was controlled by a series of great powers that Paul called "elemental spirits" (Colossians 2:20). They believed God had created the world, but great powers had somehow come to dominate it. God was far away, and these powers did with you as they pleased. If you wanted to become attuned to them, you had to practice rigid religious rituals that might help you discover their secrets. Then you could harness your powers with theirs.

Most heathen religions today have rigid religious rituals carried out by their followers, i.e., suicide bombers. In their thinking, the forces of the universe have replaced the elemental spirits. Many feel trapped by the "blind laws" of nature.

Some folks sit and wait for what they think of as a generic god who will solve their problems. They do not know anything about him, but somehow, someway, things will turn out okay. We would call this fatalistic thinking.

Paul calls this earthly thinking. By commending us to think on higher things, he was not referring to space travel, but he asks us to fasten our minds on Christ who ascended to His Father and rules over all.

No matter what lofty ideals we set for life on earth, we shall return to dust. Paul vividly reminds us of this by listing various ugly sinful behaviors that we should kill. But this is not easy. It is hard to put to death the self-demanding part of our natures. We lust, covet, slander, and speak foul words. We are wretched folks.

The secret is that "your life is hidden with Christ in God." Through Baptism our life is "hid" with Christ. Through Baptism we died to all sins and evil lusts, and through the Holy Spirit's power we begin to leave those things behind. By faith we are called to humility, compassion, and love.

17 September

Psalmody: Psalm 130
Additional Psalm: Psalm 143
Old Testament Reading: 2 Chronicles 36:1–23
New Testament Reading: Colossians 4:1–18
Additional Reading: Philemon 1–25

Prayer of the Day

Let Your merciful ears, O Lord, be open to the prayers of Your humble servants; and that they may obtain their petitions, make them to ask such things as shall please You; through Jesus Christ, Your Son, our Lord, who lives and reigns with You and the Holy Spirit, one God, now and forever. (H69)

Meditation

It is not easy to live your Christian faith in a turbulent world. At times we are inclined to anger and bitterness over the pessimism and apathy that we observe. Though the Lord prophesied faith would fail and love would grow cold in the latter days, we have difficulty accepting His prophecy.

Standing up for Christ is very hard in a world that looks to the heavens and sees what a writer described as a "transitory and senseless contortion upon the idiotic face of infinite matter" and looks to human life and sees a "story that will come to nothing."

Christians have a wonderful opportunity to show Christ's love toward non-Christians. The children of the world are watching Christians for any evidence of behavior that contradicts the dictates of their faith. Paul reminds us to "let your speech always be gracious, seasoned with salt." We should take great care to use tact and wisdom so that our conduct advertises Christ's love and its blessings and promotes the spread of the Good News of salvation through Christ.

Faith in Christ and His love causes us to want others to also know Him. Faith is the motivating power for Christian living. Christian faith is a special miracle. It must be handled with great and tender care. Faith in Jesus' payment for sin through His crucifixion is what brings us salvation—everlasting life now and in eternity.

We believe we also come to our Father in prayer. It is part of our life. In fervent prayer we bring our petitions before Him at all times in full trust and confidence, realizing that without His help we can do nothing.

We also include thanksgiving with our prayer, for we know that God hears every cry of His children in His own way and His own time, but always for our benefit, and so we give Him thanks.

Even though living according to our Christian faith is difficult and at times seemingly impossible, it is an ongoing process. The progress is never smooth, and often we stumble and fall. But, as God restores and empowers us by the Gospel of forgiveness, His image will become more and more vivid in our lives.

May we by Christ's grace learn to bear with each other in love during these troubled times. We need one another for support as we look forward to Him who will appear in glory. Set your mind on that, and take heart in Jesus.

18 September

Psalmody: Psalm 118:5–14
Additional Psalm: Psalm 118
Old Testament Reading: Nehemiah 1:1–2:10
Additional Reading: Haggai 1:1–2:23
New Testament Reading: 1 Timothy 1:1–20

Prayer of the Day

Almighty God, our heavenly Father, whose nature it is always to have mercy, visit with Your fatherly correction all who have erred and gone astray from the truth of Your holy Word, and bring them to a true sense of their error that they may again receive and hold fast Your unchangeable truth; through Jesus Christ, our Lord. (114)

Meditation

A carpenter's power drill should never be wielded as a dental tool. This is not its intended use. If employed in this way, it would only bring destruction. Similarly, God's Law should be utilized only according to His design. Paul says, "Now we know that the law is good, if one uses it lawfully." In Paul's age, just as in ours, there are those who wish to implement the Law in ways for which it was not intended. This is why the apostle charged Timothy to be vigilant to correct those who teach a "different doctrine."

Some false teachers attempt to make the Law do the work of the Gospel, emphasizing the importance of an individual's attitudes, actions, and behavior as the avenue to salvation. If these are only ordered in a proper way, the implied message says, one will have reconciliation with God and a blessed life. Nothing could be further from the truth. Although humans sometimes find comfort in knowing exactly what is required of them so they know if their performance matches predetermined expectations, there is absolutely no solace in attempting to achieve salvation by our own efforts. The Law will only destroy us and drive us to despair by reminding us of our failure.

Another misuse of the law is nonuse of the Law. Some try to remove the crushing burden of condemnation by falsely asserting that there is no moral code, that God has no standards of right or wrong. Rather, they say, He allows individuals to set norms of thought and conduct based on their personal experiences and lifestyle choices. In our present, tolerant, libertine world, perhaps this is the heterodoxy that is most prevalent and dangerous.

The Law had worked its intended use on Paul. It opened his eyes to the reality of his true condition apart from Christ, crushed him with the burden of his guilt, and moved him to confess that he was the "foremost" of sinners. Only then could the Gospel bear its fruit, instilling faith in the merciful work of Jesus Christ, who "came into the world to save sinners."

"Sound doctrine" is important both for Christ's Church as a whole and for us as individual members of it. The adjective here implies health and vigor; literally, the Law is "hygienic." Sound health is not achieved when a disease is denied or mistreated. Thankfully, in the proper distinction of Law and Gospel, we know both our ailment and the cure.

19 SEPTEMBER

Psalmody: Psalm 136:1–9
Additional Psalm: Psalm 136
Old Testament Reading:
Nehemiah 2:11–20; 4:1–6
New Testament Reading: 1 Timothy 2:1–15

Prayer of the Day

O Lord, grant that the course of this world may be so peaceably ordered by Your governance that Your Church may joyfully serve You in all godly quietness; through Jesus Christ, our Lord, who lives and reigns with You and the Holy Spirit, one God, now and forever. (H64)

Meditation

The peaceful and quiet life for which we pray in today's collect and read about in this passage of Scripture is a great and underappreciated gift. Consider again the sobering reality that this is a fallen, depraved world. Without the intervention of a loving, caring God there would certainly be anarchy and public turmoil of an unimaginable degree. Yet He rules within the realm of His lefthand kingdom to establish governments for the good of His Church and the blessing of His people. Even cruel and despotic rulers can serve as His instruments. This is why there is no qualification attached to the exhortation to pray for "kings and all who are in high positions." We do not simply pray for those public figures that hold to policies and viewpoints we espouse; rather, we intercede for all of them, unequivocally.

God's works and ways are far beyond our limited ability to comprehend. He sees not only the present but also the future. What we might regard as a catastrophic political development, He might see merely as a short prelude to a divine irony of dramatic proportions, resulting in enduring, beneficial results. He is in control of all history and is directing it toward the ultimate conclusion.

Paul has this end in mind when he says that God "desires all people to be saved and to come to the knowledge of the truth." The day will come when earthly governments and rulers will be forever abolished, having become superfluous in the perfection of the new heavens and earth where the triumphant Lamb is reigning from His heavenly throne.

In order to populate that realm with more individuals then, God establishes earthly governments now and bids us to pray. It is difficult to imagine the government as an ally in evangelism efforts, but it is. To the extent that political authorities maintain civil order and grant us freedom to openly witness to our Savior and speak of His redemptive work on our behalf, they are partners—albeit passive ones—in the spreading of the Gospel.

This desire for a peaceful and quiet life also impacts our existence in the Church. We are not to clamor for positions of power and authority. As we live and serve within the vocations and stations of life where He has placed us, we can find great satisfaction and joy. Hands uplifted in prayer or engaged in loving service are more pleasing to Him than angry voices and clenched fists recruited for conflict and rivalry.

20 SEPTEMBER

Psalmody: Psalm 46
Additional Psalm: Psalm 54
Old Testament Reading: Nehemiah 4:7–23
New Testament Reading: 1 Timothy 3:1–16

Prayer of the Day

O God, You led Your holy apostles to ordain pastors in every place. Grant that Your flock, under the guidance of Your Holy Spirit, may choose suitable men for the ministry of Word and Sacrament and may uphold them in their work for the extension of Your kingdom; through Him who is the chief Shepherd of our souls, Jesus Christ, our Lord. (121)

Meditation

It is difficult to imagine that any corporate human resources department would craft a list of expectations and requirements for a position that would be as rigorous as those given here by the apostle. In the business world results are emphasized, and therefore candidates for employment must possess abilities that will contribute to the success of the enterprise. It is desirable to find workers who are aggressive and goal driven.

In the Church a different set of priorities exists. What matters more than human aptitude is God-given attitude. Certainly, one must possess gifts for ministry. Workers in the Lord's vineyard are equipped for their tasks by Him.

The requisite abilities are present in each of them in one degree or another. He gives, forms, and refines the talents necessary for service. Nevertheless, the emphasis is not on effectiveness but on character. A man may possess extraordinary speaking abilities, highly efficient administrative skills, wonderful personal charisma, and other earthly gifts, but if he is quarrelsome, undisciplined, inhospitable, and adulterous, he is disqualified from consideration as a public servant of the Church.

Being an overseer, a deacon, or holding any other office in the Lord's Church is more than a mere job. It is a high and holy calling; not a right to be demanded by those seeking the office, but a privilege to be granted by the Lord who established the office. These qualifications are different because the Church is different than secular organizations—it is holy and set apart. It is not run by a chief executive officer concerned only with the bottom line; it is led by a gentle, caring Shepherd who forgives and empowers imperfect people to represent Him to others. Servants of the Church are gifts from the Lord of the Church. Therefore, we thank Him for them, pray for them, and do what we can to support and encourage them, so that their service among us is a blessing and not a burden.

From his discussion about qualifications for ministry, Paul concludes this section by writing about the "mystery of godliness." The Church's confession of faith is an objective reality focused on the life and ministry of Jesus. Officeholders in the Church, as well as all members of the Church, are only qualified for ministry and membership because He makes us so. The Church is a "household of God," where the living, life-changing Lord calls us His own sons and daughters and equips us for service.

21 SEPTEMBER

St. Matthew, Apostle and Evangelist

Psalmody: Psalm 55:12–19
Additional Psalm: Psalm 119:89–96
Old Testament Reading:
Nehemiah 5:1–16; 6:1–9, 15–16
New Testament Reading: 1 Timothy 4:1–16

Prayer of the Day

O Son of God, our blessed Savior Jesus Christ, You called Matthew the tax collector to be an apostle and evangelist. Through his faithful and inspired witness, grant that we also may follow You, leaving behind all covetous desires and love of riches; for You live and reign with the Father and the Holy Spirit, one God, now and forever. (F28)

St. Matthew, Apostle and Evangelist

St. Matthew, also known as Levi, identifies himself as a former tax collector, one who was therefore considered unclean, a public sinner, outcast from the Jews. Yet, it was such a one as this whom the Lord Jesus called away from his occupation and wealth to become a disciple (Matthew 9:9–13). Not only did Matthew become a disciple of Jesus, he was also called and sent as one of the Lord's twelve apostles (Matthew 10:2–4). In time, he became the evangelist whose inspired record of the Gospel was granted first place in the ordering of the New Testament. Among the four Gospels, Matthew's portrays Christ especially as the new and greater Moses, who graciously fulfills the Law and the Prophets (Matthew 5:17) and establishes a new covenant of salvation in and with His own blood (Matthew 26:27–28). Matthew's Gospel is also well-known and beloved for its record of the visit of the Magi (Matthew 2:1–12); for the Sermon on the Mount, including the Beatitudes and the Our Father (Matthew 5–7); for the institution of Holy Baptism and the most explicit revelation of the Holy Trinity (Matthew 28:16–20). Tradition is uncertain where his final field of labor was and whether Matthew died naturally or a martyr's death. In celebrating this festival, we therefore give thanks to God that He has mightily governed and protected His Holy Church through this man who was called and sent by Christ to serve the sheep of His pastures with the Holy Gospel.

Meditation

Satisfaction with the status quo in spiritual affairs is always a hidden danger because there is no such thing. To be sure, faith in the Lord Jesus does need to be sustained, but this does not mean that faith remains static. On the contrary, a faith that is nurtured through the means of grace God gives is a growing faith; a faith that is not constantly receiving this sustenance is dying and will eventually be lost entirely.

Paul tells young pastor Timothy the sobering news that there will be people who "will depart from the faith." Jesus also spoke of apostasy when He described the signs of the close of the age (Matthew 24:10–11). Clergy and laity today see this sad reality in the life of their own congregations. Some who formerly seemed to have such a deep love for the Lord and a commitment to His Church reach the point where neither love nor commitment are present in their lives. Why is this so?

Paul identifies the root cause of this sad phenomenon to be false teaching. This reminds us how important it is for the Church to confess the truth of God's Word in every age. We realize, too, that the last days are now and that the spiritual dangers facing the Church as well as individual Christians are lethal and real.

Doctrine does affect the ongoing life of God's people. Faith and practice cannot be separated. While the fellowship of believers with one another is of primary importance in the estimation of many people, that fellowship must be based on Scriptural truths, not on tolerance of error or merely the joy of being together. The Church is more than a social club; the Church believes, teaches, and confesses the message of Law and Gospel. Conviction, catechesis, and confession can never be separated. A true disciple of Jesus is one who is continually following Him and learning from Him.

We take heart from the commendation Paul gave to his beloved spiritual son, as he talks about Timothy's progress. Yet Timothy was not to become satisfied with the status quo or become complacent in his present situation. It was necessary for him—as it is for us now—to be diligent and alert, to "keep a close watch on yourself and on the teaching." Because the words of Jesus are life-giving and life-sustaining (John 20:31), their work in our lives will have the same results.

22 SEPTEMBER

Jonah

Psalmody: Psalm 133
Additional Psalm: Psalm 119:97–104
Old Testament Reading:
Nehemiah 7:1–4; 8:1–18
Additional Reading: Ezra 1:1–10:19
New Testament Reading: 1 Timothy 5:1–16

Prayer of the Day

Lord God, heavenly Father, through the prophet Jonah, You continued the prophetic pattern of teaching Your people the true faith and demonstrating through miracles Your presence in creation to heal it of its brokenness. Grant that Your Church may see in Your Son, our Lord Jesus Christ, the final end-times prophet whose teaching and miracles continue in Your Church through the healing medicine of the Gospel and the Sacraments; through Jesus Christ, our Lord. (1092)

Jonah

A singular prophet among the many in the Old Testament, Jonah the son of Amittai was born about an hour's walk from the town of Nazareth. The focus of his prophetic ministry was the call to preach at Nineveh, the capital of pagan Assyria (Jonah 1:2). His reluctance to respond and God's insistence that His call be heeded is the story of the book that bears Jonah's name. Although the swallowing and disgorging of Jonah by the great fish is the most remembered detail of his life, it is addressed in only three verses of the book (Jonah 1:17; 2:1, 10). Throughout the book, the important theme is how God deals compassionately with sinners. Jonah's three-day sojourn in the belly of the fish is mentioned by Jesus as a sign of His own death, burial, and resurrection (Matthew 12:39–41).

Meditation

The human heart yearns for love, respect, support, and acceptance. A biological family that functions according to God's design provides all this and more. So does the Church for it, too, is a family, albeit a spiritual one.

Timothy is instructed here to treat the body of believers as his own kin. We are mistaken if we perceive the imperative mood of the verbs to imply the tone of a strong mandate—as if the apostle were forcefully demanding that Timothy behave in this manner. Rather, the tone is more benign, if not benevolent. These instructions are descriptive not of how believers must act, but of how believers naturally will act in relationship to others in the household of faith. The apostolic exhortation is not to be regarded by the Christian as mere rules that are slavishly followed, but as a way of life that is willingly led. In a happy family, members do not need to be told to love and care for one another; the innate desire to do exactly that is always present, without a sense of coercion. To do so is not a duty but a delight.

The thought of the Church as a family helps us more fully appreciate the corporate nature of the Body of Christ. One of the dangers of life in every age is spiritual isolationism. Our sinful inclination is to be concerned only about our own well-being. We selfishly hesitate to become involved in the life of a congregation on more than a superficial level, lest we find ourselves involved in messy and unpleasant relationships with people who might make demands upon us. We come to Church to be fed by the Word of God, and then we go home, falsely thinking this is all that matters.

While we, indeed, do need the nourishment that is given in the public assembly of believers, our life of faith is not meant to be quarantined in that way. We are fed so that we can be fueled for service in the Savior's name. The Body of Christ suffers as a whole when any part of it suffers, so we take action. Christian deeds of mercy flow from a life of faith in our Brother, Jesus. We help without hesitation because that is what He did for us.

Shed blood produces shared blood. The suffering, death, and resurrection of Jesus on our behalf mean that, as believers in Him, we are all part of one family; we have a common bloodline with all who profess His name.

23 SEPTEMBER

Psalmody: Psalm 51:5–13
Additional Psalm: Psalm 12
Old Testament Reading: Nehemiah 9:1–21
New Testament Reading: 1 Timothy 5:17—6:2

Prayer of the Day

Lord of all power and might, author and giver of all good things, graft into our hearts the love of Your name, increase in us true religion, nourish us with all goodness, and of Your great mercy keep us in the same; through Jesus Christ, Your Son, our Lord, who lives and reigns with You and the Holy Spirit, one God, now and forever. (H66)

Meditation

Being members of the kingdom of God does not exempt us from the concerns of the world. Even in the noble task of ministry one must be able to earn a living. Paul begins this section of the epistle by giving specific instructions about compensation for "the elders who rule well." The "double honor" he speaks about certainly encompasses the joy and privilege of serving God's people and the resultant respect that comes from such a position of spiritual leadership, but that alone does not put food on the table or provide for one's family. The other dimension of this twofold gift to worthy elders undoubtedly alludes provision for their earthly lives.

When Paul refers to the words of Moses that "the laborer deserves his wages," he is putting forward a truth that applies to all of us, regardless of whether we are full-time servants of the Lord or laypeople. It is just and right that an individual be compensated for his work. We need never feel guilty about earning a fair and equitable salary, whatever our chosen vocation. Yet we must not forget the source of that blessing. Our ability to earn a living and the earthly rewards we receive for using the talents and abilities with which we are endowed are gifts of God. As such, they are really not our possessions but His, and they are to be used in His service.

Just as an "elder who rules well" uses the "double honor" he receives to continue his task of preaching and teaching, so also those who serve in other vocations use the wages they are given to provide for their families and extend the kingdom of God through their life and witness at home and in the workplace. These are the "good works" to which Paul refers. Some of these works are visible now and bear immediate fruit; others are not visible now but are equally important and will come to fruition at a later date.

Thoughts of labor and livelihood ultimately turn our attention to the Lord. He received not double honor, but double rejection—first, despised by the world and then even abandoned by His Father for a time as He hung on the cross. Yet His work on our behalf compensated the Father for the debt of our sins and frees us to be His people who joyfully live for Him in this world.

24 SEPTEMBER

Psalmody: Psalm 123
Additional Psalm: Psalm 99
Old Testament Reading: Nehemiah 9:22–38
Additional Reading: Nehemiah 10:1–13:31
New Testament Reading: 1 Timothy 6:3–21

Prayer of the Day

O God, our refuge and strength, the author of all godliness, by Your grace hear the prayers of Your Church. Grant that those things which we ask in faith we may receive through Your bountiful mercy; through Jesus Christ, Your Son, our Lord, who lives and reigns with You and the Holy Spirit, one God, now and forever. (C80)

Meditation

Perhaps contentment is so difficult to attain and keep because we do not fully understand what it really is. Does a quest for contentment mean that I give up all ambition and desire to improve myself and my lot in life? Does it mean that I renounce the material possessions I already have and lead a life of asceticism? Is it to be sought only by those of greater means and not by those in the middle or lower classes of life? Can contentment be enjoyed, or is it simply meant to be endured?

By equating this characteristic with godliness, Paul is asserting that Christian contentment is vastly different than any other kind of philosophical ideal. This is not merely a revision of Stoicism, where man depends on himself for self-sufficiency; neither is it simply a renunciation of want and craving, as the "Noble Truths" of Buddhism teach.

Christian contentment is unique because of its source. It comes not from the mind of man but from the all-providing hand of God. It is bestowed, not achieved; it is a product of divine grace, not individual effort. Christian contentment means not only that we quit paging through the catalog of earthly wants, but that we focus on what God has already provided. It is not just an elimination of desires, but a redirection of desires toward our Savior. The First Article God who "richly and daily provides me with all that I need to support this body and life" is also the Second and Third Article God who provides and keeps me in faith directed toward His Son. Jesus was content to live a life devoid of earthly luxury and wants. He went about as an itinerant preacher, with no permanent place to lay His head. After He gave His life for us, His body was even laid in a borrowed tomb.

But in Jesus I have God's greatest and most necessary gift; nothing is better. The appreciative heart of the believer says, "It is enough. Because God has given me salvation through the life and work of my Savior, I really have everything I need."

With the divine gift of contentment, earthly possessions become no longer an impediment to faith but instruments through which faith can be shared and God's kingdom expanded. While the love of money is the "root of all evil," money itself is not. It is a gift of God that can serve both as a blessing to us and to the others with whom we share it.

25 September

Psalmody: Psalm 51:5–13
Additional Psalm: Psalm 12
Old Testament Reading: Malachi 1:1–14
New Testament Reading: Matthew 3:1–17

Prayer of the Day

Father in heaven, at the Baptism of Jesus in the Jordan River You proclaimed Him Your beloved Son and anointed Him with the Holy Spirit. Make all who are baptized in His name faithful in their calling as Your children and inheritors with Him of everlasting life; through the same Jesus Christ, our Lord, who lives and reigns with You and the Holy Spirit, one God, now and forever. (L12)

Meditation

In each generation you often hear older folks say the younger set is "going to the dogs." However, we are all born in sin and by nature are the children of wrath. This sinful nature shows itself generation after generation.

Christ's herald and forerunner, John the Baptist, broke into the complacent life of the Israelites to denounce the sins of his age. He blasted forth the powerfully challenging message, "Repent, for the kingdom of heaven is at hand." He preached the Law in all its cutting and damning forcefulness. He was not concerned about hurting people's feelings. He emphasized that the Jews were not saved because they were descendants of Abraham. They needed to repent, turn to God, and to Him who was sent by God, His Lamb slain for sinners. The hour had struck, Scripture was being fulfilled, and the Messiah had come. John pointed to Jesus saying, "Behold, the Lamb of God, who takes away the sin of the world" (John 1:29). But the Jews turned a deaf ear, continuing in their unrepentant ways.

In our modern high tech generation it is no secret that many, including Christians, have become callous and unconcerned about sins simply because we do not want God interfering in our lives. We chase after our own gods, believing we are only responsible to ourselves. We attach ourselves to many gods of this world, such as the cares and pleasures of life and chasing after happiness that we believe money can buy. We may be so in love with our own sinful, blotched self-righteousness that we think we don't need repentance. Whenever we think we are not "real bad" sinners and have no need for repentance, we nullify our need for Christ's forgiveness through His sacrifice for sin.

John, however, not only came preaching repentance, but he also came baptizing "with water for repentance." Those baptized by John did not need to be re-baptized after Jesus instituted the Sacrament of Baptism. John's baptism was a ceremonial cleansing of the Old Testament dispensation to which Jesus submitted to fulfill all Law. Jesus, born under the Law, began to fulfill it. God the Father gave His approval of Jesus as the heavens opened.

Holy Baptism—what a great saving mystery given us by Christ with simple water and God's Word. Through Baptism God claims us. He has made a covenant of grace with us that we are His children and He is our heavenly Father. God never breaks this agreement.

26 SEPTEMBER

Psalmody: Psalm 16
Additional Psalm: Psalm 32
Old Testament Reading: Malachi 2:1–3:5
New Testament Reading: Matthew 4:1–11

Prayer of the Day

O Lord God, You led Your ancient people through the wilderness and brought them to the promised land. Guide the people of Your Church that following our Savior we may walk through the wilderness of this world toward the glory of the world to come; through Jesus Christ, Your Son, our Lord, who lives and reigns with You and the Holy Spirit, one God, now and forever. (L23)

Meditation

After His Baptism Jesus was "led up by the Spirit into the wilderness to be tempted by the devil." The Father permitted His Son to be subjected to the temptations of the evil one. Christ had to pay for Adam and Eve's failure and for our failure to resist temptation. His Anointed One also taught us how to fight against temptation and win.

In the Garden of Eden Satan was successful in appealing to hunger, and he thought it would also work with Jesus. After all, Jesus had fasted forty days. But Jesus refused to turn stones into bread to satisfy His hunger. He declared that bread is not the most important issue of life. We depend on food for physical life, but the highest priority for people should be to feed on the Bread of Life, Christ, the Savior of the world.

After he failed to tempt Jesus with food, sneaky Satan invited Him to jump off the top of the temple in Jerusalem. The deceiver wanted to test God's protective hand by referring to God's protecting angels. The master of deception and half-truth misquoted God's Word, omitting the important words that God would protect "in all your ways" (Psalm 91:11). When Jesus refused to jump, He emphasized that people should not throw caution to the wind. God's promises do not guarantee safety if we act foolishly. Foolish acts only provoke God's wrath and tempt Him.

Losing two battles, the great liar was persistent and resorted to a bribe, as he often does today. If Jesus had given in to share with Satan the glories of the world without dying for the sins of all, He would have renounced Himself as the Savior. But He resisted and strongly proclaimed that there can be no allegiance or compromise with evil and sin.

He commanded Satan to "get out of My sight; get out of My mind." Then Satan must go into everlasting fire. Christ must drink the cup of suffering and shed His blood for our transgressions. Jesus went uncomplaining to Golgotha to redeem us from sin, Satan, and eternal death.

In each temptation, Jesus wielded the mighty sword of the Spirit to overcome Satan. When succumbing to sinful temptation, let us bow our head in repentance, asking God's forgiveness, and rise up, bathed in His forgiveness, which was won through Christ's shed blood. We should also boldly remember to say Christ's words, "Get out of my sight, get out of my mind," to drive away the father of lies.

27 SEPTEMBER

Psalmody: Psalm 91:9–16
Additional Psalm: Psalm 91
Old Testament Reading: Malachi 3:6–4:6
New Testament Reading: Matthew 4:12–25

Prayer of the Day

Almighty and everlasting God, mercifully look upon our infirmities and stretch forth the hand of Your majesty to heal and defend us; through Jesus Christ, Your Son, our Lord, who lives and reigns with You and the Holy Spirit, one God, now and forever. (L15)

Meditation
Jesus demanded that we love God above everything else. He came teaching that we should love our neighbor as ourselves. He taught that we must obey more than the letter of the Law; that hate is a form of murder; that lust is adultery in the heart; and that coveting is sinful wanting, all of which makes us transgressors of the divine will. He opened our eyes to see sin in its ugliness and inhuman brutality. And above all, He taught that sin, until it is removed, removes us from God's kingdom.

As John preached, so also Jesus came preaching, "Repent, for the kingdom of heaven is at hand." He explained that He was the One whom the prophets and Moses spoke. He was the Light to banish the blindness and darkness of sin. He preached that "God so loved the world, that He gave His only Son, that whoever believes in Him should not perish but have eternal life" (John 3:16).

The Savior came calling people from every walk of life to follow Him and serve Him. This would not mean a life of easy living in the comfort of luxurious homes, but rather a cross-bearing life of suffering as He suffered. However, in the end, it would mean finding life and salvation.

Jesus came healing all types of diseased folks, even some possessed of the devil. He healed them of bodily sickness and also the leprosy of sin. This made Him popular and great numbers of people followed Him. He was their answer to life's questions and problems.

The weary, the depressed, the troubled, the sin-sick, and the dying still come to Jesus to find rest for their distressed lives, peace of mind, healing for their body, and salvation for their soul. Graciously and tenderly Jesus is also calling us. Whatever our problem, heartache, or disappointment, in Him we can find comfort, strength, and guidance. He loves us, has redeemed us, and knows our name.

When we weep and mourn, He tells us "I am the resurrection and the life" (John 11:25). When we doubt, He promises, "Fear not, for I am with you; be not dismayed, for I am your God; I will strengthen you, I will help you" (Isaiah 41:10). If we have denied Him and been ashamed of Him, He says "Take heart, My son; your sins are forgiven" (Matthew 9:2).

He calls us today. His love and compassion stretch forth in His pierced hands, and He pleads with us to come. What foolishness it is to turn away from such a love.

28 SEPTEMBER

Psalmody: Psalm 145:17–21
Additional Psalm: Psalm 145
Old Testament Reading: Deuteronomy 1:1–18
New Testament Reading: Matthew 5:1–20

Prayer of the Day

Almighty God, You know we live in the midst of so many dangers that in our frailty we cannot stand upright. Grant strength and protection to support us in all dangers and carry us through all temptations; through Jesus Christ, Your Son, our Lord, who lives and reigns with You and the Holy Spirit, one God, now and forever. (L16)

Meditation

Jesus' great sermon to His followers has a twofold purpose. First, He clarifies the meaning of the Law in view of the shallow interpretation given by the world. Doing what is moral is necessary, but Christ looks at the heart, one's attitude. For example, if we are kind to our neighbor because we want him to be kind to us, then we are being selfish.

The Law is not fulfilled by keeping yourself respectable. You have not kept the commandment only if you have not killed your neighbor. If we have not loved others as much as ourselves, we have broken the Law and are condemned. Therefore no one is good enough in God's perception to save his own soul.

Second, Christ tells believers how we are to live and please God. Because we have been saved by God's grace in Christ, we desire to serve Him. The Law then serves as a road map for Christian living.

Qualifications for membership in God's kingdom are unique by worldly standards. Money, power, or success do not count. "Whoever seeks to preserve his life will lose it" (Luke 17:33).

Jesus tells us that His kingdom includes:
• The poor in spirit, who know their spiritual uncleanness and that salvation cannot be earned but is theirs only by grace.
• Those who mourn over their sins and are comforted that Christ's blood cleanses them from all sin.
• The meek, the humble, who do not boast of their own salvation but are called through the Gospel and kept in faith by God's grace to enjoy God's richness.
• Those who hunger and thirst for righteousness, who desire to please God in appreciation of His love in Christ. Their satisfaction comes in finding great joy in serving God.
• The merciful, who are kind, patient, thoughtful, and sympathize with the suffering. As they do good works from their renewed hearts, mercy is shown them.
• The pure in heart in whom no guile or deceit or lip service is found. They shall see God.

• The peacemakers, who lubricate life, keeping friction to a minimum. How they are needed! They keep things running smoothly at home, in the church, and nation.

• The persecuted, who, because they confess Christ as Savior are hated. Lies and false accusations are their lot. Life is hard, bitter, and dangerous.

However, we can rejoice with all these, for their names and our names are written in the Book of Life. "Beloved, we are God's children now . . . we shall see Him as He is" (1 John 3:2).

29 SEPTEMBER

St. Michael and All Angels

Psalmody: Psalm 19:7–14
Additional Psalm: Psalm 34
Old Testament Reading:
Deuteronomy 1:19–36
New Testament Reading: Matthew 5:21–48

Prayer of the Day

Everlasting God, You have ordained and constituted the service of angels and men in a wonderful order. Mercifully grant that, as Your holy angels always serve and worship You in heaven, so by Your appointment they may also help and defend us here on earth; through Your Son, Jesus Christ, our Lord, who lives and reigns with You and the Holy Spirit, one God, now and forever. (F29)

St. Michael and All Angels

The name of the archangel St. Michael means "Who is like God?" Michael is mentioned in the Book of Daniel (12:1), as well as in Jude (v. 9) and Revelation (12:7). Daniel portrays Michael as the angelic helper of Israel who leads in battle against the forces of evil. In Revelation, Michael and his angels fight against and defeat Satan and the evil angels, driving them from heaven. Their victory is made possible by Christ's own victory over Satan in His death and resurrection, a victory announced by the voice in heaven: "Now the salvation and power and the kingdom of our God and the authority of His Christ have come" (Revelation 7:10). Michael is often associated with Gabriel and Raphael, the other chief angels or archangels who surround the throne of God. Tradition names Michael as the patron and protector of the Church, especially as the protector of Christians at the hour of death.

Meditation

Many Americans believe occasional church attendance and giving a little left-over money constitutes being a Christian. Some believe this "easy-going religion" is free from the Law. They see no contradiction between professing Christ and following the pursuits of their sinful nature. In the midst of this shallow superficiality about religion, few really care about offending God.

People rebel against the Law because it tears away our self-righteous clothing and reveals the nakedness of our sin. Jesus did not come to nullify the stern commands of God's justice, but to make them crystal clear so sinful humans could see their desperate condition and seek the mercy of God.

The scribes (lawyers and judges) and the Pharisees (a strict religious sect) kept the outward forms of the Law. They did so especially by prohibitions, for example, not cursing or not working on the Sabbath. They gave large gifts to the temple funds instead of taking care of their needy parents. They were spiritually arrogant as they thought their self-determined standard of conduct was superior to others. Jesus plainly called them hypocrites.

As we renounce such practices as unworthy of Christians, we must remember that an external and negative religion is not satisfactory. God-pleasing righteousness proceeds from our relationship to Christ and emphasizes what is useful. Godly righteousness has its source in faith in the Redeemer, and it centers in love for God and people. It is guided not by a book of rules, but by a sympathetic concern for the sufferings and problems of people.

The righteousness of people is uprightness and goodness that makes us respected in the world. This uprightness of character, kindheartedness, and virtuous living is found even among non-Christians. In Christians, this is the fruit of faith as we walk in Christ's light. But this righteousness does not save, for it is not perfect. "All our righteous deeds are like a polluted garment" (Isaiah 64:6).

The highest form of righteousness in believers is the righteousness of Christ, received by faith. "Abraham believed God, and it was counted to him as righteousness" (Romans 4:3).

For us and in our place Christ Jesus kept the Law perfectly. This perfect Christ assumed our sins and took them to the cross to make complete payment for our transgressions, thus satisfying God's wrath. "The blood of Jesus His Son cleanses us from all sin" (1 John 1:7). The Law is upheld, justice is executed, and we are redeemed and saved through Christ.

30 SEPTEMBER

Jerome, Translator of Holy Scripture

Psalmody: Psalm 119:161–168
Additional Psalm: Psalm 63
Old Testament Reading:
Deuteronomy 1:37–2:15
New Testament Reading: Matthew 6:1–15

Prayer of the Day

O Lord, God of truth, Your Word is a lamp to our feet and a light on our path. You gave Your servant Jerome delight in his study of Holy Scripture. May those who continue to read, mark, and inwardly digest Your Word find in it the food of salvation and the fountain of life; through Jesus Christ, our Lord, who lives and reigns with You and the Holy Spirit, one God, now and forever. (1093)

Jerome, Translator of Holy Scripture
Jerome was born in a little village on the Adriatic Sea around AD 345. At a young age, he went to study in Rome, where he was baptized. After extensive travels, he chose the life of a monk and spent five years in the Syrian desert. There he learned Hebrew, the language of the Old Testament. After ordination at Antioch and visits to Rome and Constantinople, Jerome settled in Bethlehem. From the original Hebrew, Aramaic, and Greek, he used his ability with languages to translate the Bible into Latin, the common language of his time. This translation, called the Vulgate, was the authoritative version of the Bible in the Western Church world for more than a thousand years. Considered one of the great scholars of the Early Church, Jerome died on September 30, 420. He was originally interred at Bethlehem, but his remains were eventually taken to Rome.

Meditation
As God's people, we worship Him because love for God compels us. God sent His Son to buy us back from the guilt of sin and the terrors of death. Then by His grace He called us into His kingdom through faith. Worship must not consist of going through the motions but must be done in truth and sincerity of spirit. "The sacrifices of God are a broken spirit; a broken and contrite heart, O God, You will not despise" (Psalm 51:17).

Prayer is one of the richest forms of worship. This royal privilege of approaching our just and holy God is ours because Jesus opened the way by reconciling us to God when we were yet sinners. Jesus gave us His blessed prayer. How rich and blessed the Lord's Prayer will make us if we truly pray it and not merely say it.

Our Father who art in heaven—God, our Father, adopted us as His children through Christ and reconciled us to Himself with Christ's blood.

Hallowed be Thy name—His name is holy to us as we teach and believe His Word in all truth and lead Christian lives to glorify His name.

Thy Kingdom come—His kingdom, the kingdom of heaven, comes to sin-troubled souls through preaching the Gospel.

Thy will be done on earth as it is in heaven—May the wickedness of the world and Satan's cunning tricks be restrained by God's holy will. May His gracious will be accomplished in bringing souls to faith and salvation.

Give us this day our daily bread—We ask for all people that God would open His hand in goodness and grace to supply all we need for this life.

And forgive us our trespasses, as we forgive those who trespass against us—Please Lord, cancel our sins with Your precious blood, and help us be forgiving to those who sin against us.

And lead us not into temptation—Keep from us the temptations of the devil, the world, and our own sinful flesh. When such temptations come, give us grace and strength to overcome them through victorious faith.

But deliver us from evil—May the troubles and sins of body and soul never snatch us out of our Father's hand.

For Thine is the kingdom and the power and the glory forever and ever. Amen—All things belong to God, and through His power He can grant our prayers. To Him be honor and glory.

1 OCTOBER

Psalmody: Psalm 130
Additional Psalm: Psalm 51
Old Testament Reading:
Deuteronomy 2:16–37
New Testament Reading: Matthew 6:16–34

Prayer of the Day

Eternal God, You counsel us not to be anxious about earthly things. Keep alive in us a proper yearning for those heavenly treasures awaiting all who trust in Your mercy, that we may daily rejoice in Your salvation and serve You with constant devotion; through Jesus Christ, Your Son, our Lord, who lives and reigns with You and the Holy Spirit, one God, now and forever. (A61)

Meditation

Generations past were often in need of the necessities of life—they were in want, as are many today in all countries. People worried. Today, few in America are in great want. Our greatest concerns usually center on our possessions.

These earthly possessions bring worry and anxiety. Will our stocks and bonds lose their value? Will the equity in our house fall as the housing market takes a big hit? They can be lost; thieves and scammers can take them from us, money is devalued, and at last death pulls them out of our trembling hands.

Possessions can easily become idols that cause us to make a choice. Which shall I love—God or money, including everything that money can buy?

Worshiping the treasures of this life comes naturally. They seem more real than the spiritual things of God. For example, if we have been restored to health, we are more thankful for the medicine God has provided than for the Giver.

Sometimes Christians act like unbelievers, being more concerned about bread for the body than food for the soul. This attitude is expressed when we do not have time for devotions, for corporate worship, or to teach the Christian faith and values to our children. We fail to conduct our business and daily living from a foundation of love for God and our neighbor. When this happens, God is shuffled to the background of our lives and possibly forgotten in the end.

Jesus tells us "Do not be anxious about tomorrow. . . . Sufficient for the day is its own trouble" (Matthew 6:34). He wants us to live one day at a time. He reminds us that birds do not fret about food for God feeds them, and flowers do not work but are beautifully clothed by the heavenly Father.

Then our Lord reaches down, reminding us "will He [your heavenly Father] not much more clothe you, O you of little faith?" If God gave such beauty to the flowers, will He forget us for whom His Son died? This would be utter foolishness.

We have a much greater priority in life. Jesus lovingly directs us to put first the kingdom of God and His own righteousness. When through faith we are clothed in His righteousness, we bask in the forgiveness of sins. His Gospel and Sacraments are far more important than the physical things we need for this present time. Our Savior promises all these things to those who love and serve Him.

2 OCTOBER

Psalmody: Psalm 3
Additional Psalm: Psalm 2
Old Testament Reading: Deuteronomy 3:1–29
New Testament Reading: Matthew 7:1–12

Prayer of the Day

Merciful God, in Your Son, Jesus Christ, our Lord, You give good gifts to Your children, the gifts of forgiveness, life, and salvation. Teach us to give the gift of love and mercy to our neighbors so that we may do unto others as we wish them to do unto us; through Jesus Christ, our Lord. (1094)

Meditation

The Golden Rule is the most quoted sentence in the Bible. "So whatever you wish that others would do to you, do also to them" (Matthew 7:12). We insist that others do this, but too often neglect to follow it ourselves.

As we use this standard to judge the actions of others, we often condemn them and their sins as unworthy of Christians. At the same time, we excuse our sinful behavior by rationalizing and calling it just a "mistake." Somehow our sins appear less sinful than the sins of others.

Jesus was a realist and put it most succinctly. He described these actions of enlarging our neighbor's faults. We make them look like a six-foot-long two-by-four while making our own faults seem like a small sliver. We must confess that we are often guilty of thinking we are such "nice people," while complaining about others.

On the other hand, Jesus did not mean that we cannot judge or call immoral acts sinful. If so, then the Ten Commandments would be negated.

Faultfinding gives evidence of a loveless heart where Christ cannot make His abode. When we do this, may we hang our heads in shame and repentance, begging our Lord's forgiveness. Remember, He already paid for this sin and all our sins.

Instead of being critical and finding fault with everybody, He instructs us to pray. We may raise our eyebrows and ask, "But what good does it do to pray?" James answers, "You do not have, because you do not ask. You ask and do not receive, because you ask wrongly" (James 4:2–3).

Perhaps we have not been persistent in prayer. Jesus tells us not to give up if there is no answer after the first attempt. If sinful parents give good things to their children, how much more will God, who loves us in Christ, give good things to those who ask?

Our loving heavenly Father does not answer prayer according to our desires but according to His gracious will. If we could dictate to Him how to answer prayer, He would not be God but an extension of our will. God forbid! Remember, when we forget to pray, Jesus is praying for us.

We can be certain that God will answer our cry before His throne of grace in our best interests. Our security for this is Jesus, who killed death for us that we might live eternally as God's reconciled children and members of His household.

3 OCTOBER

Psalmody: Psalm 119:9–16
Additional Psalm: Psalm 125
Old Testament Reading: Deuteronomy 4:1–20
New Testament Reading: Matthew 7:13–29

Prayer of the Day

Lord of all power and might, author and giver of all good things, instill in our hearts the love of Your name, impress on our minds the teachings of Your Word, and increase in our lives all that is holy and just; through Jesus Christ, Your Son, our Lord, who lives and reigns with You and the Holy Spirit, one God, now and forever. (A62)

Meditation

It is apparent that we live in the "state of ambiguity." Moral confusion is rampant, caused by the notion that there is no absolute objective truth. Postmoderns insist that reality is only a construct of our culture. Everything is relative. Postmoderns reject the possibility of objective morality. They say what is right or wrong varies according to the culture or the individual. A person may choose the values that he believes are right for him. In this kind of thinking, nothing is morally right or wrong—everything is just there.

Moral thinking and behavior require an objective standard against which it is measured. If there is no standard—no absolute—then moral behavior can be whatever you wish.

Spiritual confusion results from the same notion that there is no God, who alone is the only true and absolute Supreme Being. Religion and theology today are characterized by vagueness and indecisiveness that only breed confusion and doubt. In many ecumenical worship services all deities are considered equal. All prayers offered are valid.

Because many believe there is no such thing as truth, it is not popular to accuse a church body of false teaching. However, when Christ warns against false teachers, we must also do so. He often took the false teachers to task. He warns, near the end of His Sermon on the Mount, against great dangers that easily confuse Christians.

"Beware of false prophets, who come to you in sheep's clothing." Counterfeit teachings are offered in God's name. They appeal to itching ears and the fleshly mind but slowly poison the soul.

Fraudulent teachers can be judged by their insincere lives. "You will recognize them by their fruits." Counterfeit lives betray them and their teachings.

Jesus also warns against lip service to the Lord. Simply repeating the Lord's name is not enough. Empty words reveal an empty heart.

Beware of counterfeit worship. When we sin, we confess to Him and plead for mercy. Jesus will receive us, wash and cleanse us from all sin, and by His grace give us peace and eternal life.

We remain loyal to Christ and His Gospel as we firmly stand on the Word of God and the Lutheran Confessions. These are the standards by which false teachings are measured. God help us do so.

4 OCTOBER

Psalmody: Psalm 80:1–7
Additional Psalm: Psalm 80
Old Testament Reading:
Deuteronomy 4:21–40
New Testament Reading: Matthew 8:1–17

Prayer of the Day

O Lord, grant to Your faithful people pardon and peace that they may be cleansed from all their sins and serve You with a quiet mind; through Jesus Christ, Your Son, our Lord, who lives and reigns with You and the Holy Spirit, one God, now and forever. (H80)

Meditation

Sin has caused us much pain and suffering. Our blood is tainted from the time of our conception. "Behold, I was brought forth in iniquity, and in sin did my mother conceive me" (Psalm 51:5).

Suffering may be the result of personal transgression of God's Law, as was the death of David's son. It was the consequence of David and Bathsheba's adultery (2 Samuel 12:14). However, not all suffering can be traced to personal sins. In John 9 the disciples thought the man born blind was guilty of a special sin, and if not he, then at least his parents. Jesus told them, "It was not that this man sinned, or

his parents, but that the works of God might be displayed in him" (John 9:3).

Others, from whom we catch sickness of sins or who inflict pain in the natural course of events, can also bring on our suffering. But no matter how sufferings come, be they physical, mental, or moral ills, Jesus promises to help with His healing touch. It is shown in His mercy.

We may lament, "Why do Christians have to suffer?" If we went through life without suffering and pain, we would soon think we did not need God, that we could deal with life and all its problems. Suffering brings us to Jesus; it makes us realize how much we are dependent on the Lord.

We have a sickness worse than leprosy and more incurable than pancreatic cancer; one that stalks us day and night unto death. Wonder drugs will not help. Our natural mind and will is enslaved to Satan and hates God.

God has blessed us with the greatest advances in medicine and health care—hospitals, doctors, specialists, surgical procedures, and great medicines to help cure diseases and alleviate pain and suffering. However, sin is our monster illness. Sin closes heaven for us. Sin kills us. "For the wages of sin is death" (Romans 6:23). There is no hope, and there is no help we can supply. There is no vaccine or new wonder drug for the punishment and misery caused by sin. We must turn for mercy to Christ.

As we turn to Him, we discover Jesus who, in His mercy, wisely deals with us, blesses us, and saves us. His primary mission was to extend mercy to lost sinners. He came to cancel all our sins, to offer His life as the supreme payment, to suffer and die, and to effect the final and complete cure for sin. His miracles of healing are proof of His power to heal and forgive sins.

5 October

Psalmody: Psalm 86:1–10
Additional Psalm: Psalm 86
Old Testament Reading: Deuteronomy 5:1–21
New Testament Reading: Matthew 8:18–34

Prayer of the Day

Lord Jesus, Creator and Redeemer, You have power over the demons and over all of creation so that even the winds and waves obey You. Give us faith to leave everything behind to follow You in the way of suffering as You feed us along the way with Your very body and blood; for You live and reign with the Father and the Holy Spirit, one God, now and forever. (1095)

Meditation

Many people want to follow Jesus without counting the cost. "Teacher, I will follow You wherever You go." Jesus reminded those who wanted to follow Him that if God's Son does not have a pillow, you may not even have that. "Foxes have holes, and birds of the air have nests, but the Son of Man has nowhere to lay His head."

Others think the cost is unreasonable. "Lord, let me first go and bury my father." Christ's answer appears insensitive when He tells the young man to forget about burying his father and follow Jesus. There will be times when Christians will have to break human ties for the sake of Jesus.

Joseph in Kenya had been a Muslim. He described how, after hearing about Jesus, he professed Christ. His tribe severely beat him, trying to beat Jesus out of him, but he would not renounce his Savior. He was thrown out, and his father told him that if he ever came home, he would kill him. He gave up parents, family, and friends—all human ties—for Christ.

Jesus also came to a city that "threw Him out" as it begged Him to leave. The apostle reminds us "He came to His own, and His own people did not receive Him" (John 1:11). Ever since Jesus was born, many have rejected Him and chosen to serve Satan and sin.

Why do many "throw Him out" of their lives? His presence greatly upsets them because His Word tells them not to lie, lust, cheat, steal, and kill. They want to live as they wish, not as God wants. They do not care about truth, are deaf to their conscience, and block the gospel from their ears.

Sin and Satan always wreak havoc, robbing us of our health and poisoning our minds. They are out to destroy our souls by taking saving faith from us. Sin makes us immoral, hating God.

Christ, our Savior, restores us. He came to destroy the works of the devil. He gave us His Word as the sword with which to kill Satan and conquer the forces of hell. With His power we can resist temptation.

Our mind is only at peace through Christ and through knowing we are washed from sin through His blood. May we never "vote Jesus out of our lives" but walk with Him in joy, standing boldly in the face of death and rising to join the saints around His banquet table.

6 October

Psalmody: Psalm 91:9–16
Additional Psalm: Psalm 97
Old Testament Reading:
Deuteronomy 5:22–6:9
New Testament Reading: Matthew 9:1–17

Prayer of the Day

Almighty and most merciful God, You sent Your Son, Jesus Christ, to seek and to save the lost. Graciously open our ears and our hearts to hear His call and to follow Him by faith that we may feast with Him forever in His kingdom; through the same Jesus Christ, our Lord, who lives and reigns with You and the Holy Spirit, one God, now and forever. (A63)

Meditation

The Pharisees thought that by patching some good actions on to their reputation, they would be eligible for heaven. They criticized Jesus for eating with tax collectors and sinners. This violated the outward tenets of Judaism, which they went great lengths to observe. Their desire to keep the law was ultimately based on how they looked, rather than acknowledging their attitude was the most important aspect of keeping God's laws.

Jesus explained what true religion is. Christ did this by taking the Pharisees to task, implying they were the sinners and not the folks with whom He was eating. "Go and learn what this means, 'I desire mercy, and not sacrifice.' For I came not to call the righteous, but sinners" (Matthew 9:13). This was a difficult lesson for them to learn, as it is for people today.

When you ask people on what basis do they hope to be saved, most will mention good things they have done. They say, "I tried my best to be a good parent, faithful to my spouse, helping my neighbors, supporting the community, and giving to my church and charities." For salvation, Jesus wants transformed hearts. Clean patches of outward goodness do not make a clean heart. Anyone can fast and diet and appear religious without being a Christian. Patches of outward, nice-looking acts are as ineffective as a patch that is not preshrunk and tears away at the first washing. We must be clothed in Christ's righteous acts to be acceptable to God.

The old covenant was one of promise with rules, procedures, symbols, and sacrifices. These served as reminders of the promise of salvation in Christ, the Messiah. Many man-made rules were added. Believing in the promise of salvation saved the children of Israel. The new covenant in Christ became the fulfillment of the promise. He fulfilled the Law of God in every detail and also deleted the man-made rules.

Matthew, the tax collector, had broken with the past. He knew he could not save himself. We also should be alert that we do not depend on our virtues to make us pleasing before God. No matter how good they look to us, these patches of our goodness do not make us acceptable to God. We must be washed by Christ's forgiveness of sins, which is given us through His shed blood. Then we look forward with hope beyond old age and death. Through Christ and His cross we see beyond this life—heaven and God.

7 OCTOBER

Henry Melchior Muhlenberg, Pastor

Psalmody: Psalm 121
Additional Psalm: Psalm 131
Old Testament Reading:
Deuteronomy 6:10–25
New Testament Reading: Matthew 9:18–38

Prayer of the Day

Lord Jesus Christ, the Good Shepherd of Your people, we give You thanks for Your servant Henry Melchior Muhlenberg, who was faithful in the care and nurture of the flock entrusted to his care. So they may follow his example and the teaching of his holy life, give strength to pastors today who shepherd Your flock so that, by Your grace, Your people may grow into the fullness of life intended for them in paradise; for You live and reign with the Father and the Holy Spirit, one God, now and forever. Amen. (1096)

Henry Melchior Muhlenberg, Pastor

Moving from the Old World to the New, Henry Melchior Muhlenberg established the shape of Lutheran parishes for North America during a forty-five-year ministry in Pennsylvania. Born at Einbeck, Germany, in 1711, he came to the American colonies in 1742. A tireless traveler, Muhlenberg helped to found many Lutheran congregations and was the guiding force behind the first Lutheran synod in North America, the Ministerium of Pennsylvania, founded in 1748. He valued the role of music in Lutheran worship (often serving as his own organist) and was also the guiding force in preparing the first American Lutheran liturgy (also in 1748). Muhlenberg is remembered as a church leader, a journalist, a liturgist, and—above all—a pastor to the congregation in his charge. He died in 1787, leaving behind a large extended family and a lasting heritage: American Lutheranism.

Meditation

Dr. Luther called experiencing life on this earth as going through a "vale of tears." It certainly is with its myriad of sorrows, pain, heartaches, and death. During the bubonic plague in Germany, Pastor Philip Nicolai bur-

ied fourteen hundred members of his parish in one year, having as many as thirty funerals in one day. Truly those days were evil. Strife, misery, despair, sickness were all around, and the smell of death was in the air.

Everywhere Jesus journeyed in Israel, He found illness, misery, and strife. Jesus saw the whole world of humanity straying and losing itself in the grief of sorrow and death. People were scattered by doubt, unbelief, and apathy. They were lost in fear, self-pity, and the stress of daily living. No one cared for their souls.

The Lord came with a heart of compassion. As He walked the streets and lanes of the villages, He looked on the people with sympathetic eyes and reached out His hand to help. He gave sight to the blind, new life to a dead girl, and delivered a demon-possessed man from the devil's tyranny. No matter the sickness, He was ready to touch the hurting with His healing hand.

Then Jesus went to Calvary to give His life as a payment for the world's sins that we might be gathered into His sheepfold. Only in Christ can one find healing from the pain of sin and His protection against the evil foe. He laid down His life for the souls of all people that they might be redeemed from the guilt of sin and the fear of death. Our sins made Calvary a necessity.

The situation has not changed today. Sheep are still scattered. People are without hope, trying to make themselves look good before God by self-appointed acts of mercy that will induce God to grant them salvation.

Jesus is still compassionate today. He offers Himself in the Scriptures and the Sacrament as the Light, Hope, and the Savior of the world. We know how much He loves us.

The search for scattered sheep is limitless. The blessed Savior asks that our eyes behold this tragic scene. He asks that we pray He will send workers to proclaim His mission of salvation through the cross. May our compassion for lost souls be followed by our prayers and support for those laboring in the harvest field for the sake of the Gospel.

8 OCTOBER

Psalmody: Psalm 126
Additional Psalm: Psalm 141
Old Testament Reading: Deuteronomy 7:1–19
New Testament Reading: Matthew 10:1–23

Prayer of the Day

Almighty, eternal God, in the Word of Your apostles and prophets You have proclaimed to us Your saving will. Grant us faith to believe Your promises that we may receive eternal salvation; through Jesus Christ, our Lord, who lives and reigns with You and the Holy Spirit, one God, now and forever. (A64)

Meditation

It is noteworthy that Jesus chose His twelve apostles from the common people. They were not men of influence, not men of financial means, and not even religious leaders. However, they turned the world upside down by preaching Christ crucified and risen from the dead. They accomplished this as Jesus gave them power from on high through His Holy Spirit.

He commissioned them to preach the saving news that unto us is born a Savior, who is Christ, the Lord. Jesus gave them power for miraculous physical healing and by the Word to bring forgiveness of sins for spiritual healing.

We are confronted with a suffering and sin-sick world to which we are to give witness to Christ, the great Physician of souls, and tell of the hope within us. Jesus, the Christ, is the bread of life. He healed our souls by giving the extreme payment for sin—His very life into death. He frees and gives peace to our con-

science through faith—the true spiritual bread.

From the world's point of view it does not appear that the Savior, the Prince of Peace, has brought peace to the earth. Nations war against other nations as the blood of millions is poured out on battlefields. Years of peace are only short interludes between bloody conflicts. How can we say Jesus brought peace?

Families have their quarrels and sometimes bitter fighting. Siblings refuse to speak to one another and harbor long-standing grudges. Children and parents refuse to visit one another, and divorce causes untold heartache. Did Jesus truly bring peace?

Even the Christian Church is torn apart by false teachers and false doctrine. There are those bent on building their own little kingdoms instead of Christ's kingdom. Did Christ really bring peace?

It may seem almost unbelievable, but the Prince of Peace predicted all this would happen. Hatred and contention exists between God and the devil. God told the tempter, "I will put enmity between you and the woman, and between your offspring and her offspring" (Genesis 3:15).

The world may hate us and battles still rage. Nevertheless, there can be peace in our heart that the world cannot give. Nothing in this life can separate us from God's love that is ours through Christ. Our sins are forgiven, our mind is at peace, salvation is our promise, and heaven is our eternal home. Christ did bring peace on earth, a glorious peace with God in heaven that no enemy can take from us.

9 OCTOBER

Abraham

Psalmody: Psalm 103:1–10
Additional Psalm: Psalm 103
Old Testament Reading: Deuteronomy 8:1–20
New Testament Reading: Matthew 10:24–42

Prayer of the Day

Lord God, heavenly Father, You promised Abraham that he would be the father of many nations, You led him to the land of Canaan, and You sealed Your covenant with him by the shedding of blood. May we see in Jesus, the Seed of Abraham, the promise of the new covenant of Your holy Church, sealed with Jesus' blood on the cross and given to us now in the cup of the new testament; through the same Jesus Christ, our Lord, who lives and reigns with You and the Holy Spirit, one God, now and forever. (1097)

Abraham

Abraham (known early in his life as Abram) was called by God to become the father of a great nation (Genesis 12). At age seventy-five and in obedience to God's command, he, his wife, Sarah, and his nephew Lot moved southwest from the town of Haran to the land of Canaan. There God established a covenant with Abraham (15:18), promising the land of Canaan to his descendants. When Abraham was one hundred and Sarah was ninety, they were blessed with Isaac, the son long promised to them by God. Abraham demonstrated supreme obedience when God commanded him to offer Isaac as a burnt offering. God spared the young man's life only at the last moment and provided a ram as a substitute offering (Genesis 22:1–19). Abraham died at age 175 and was buried in the cave of Machpelah, which he had purchased earlier as a burial site for Sarah. He is especially honored as the first of the three great Old Testament patriarchs—and for his righteousness before God through faith (Romans 4:1–12).

Meditation

We often complain about the high cost of living. Someone has suggested that the high cost of living is not our problem, but rather, it is the cost of high living.

Jesus talked with His disciples, however, and pointed out a higher priority—the high cost of discipleship. What does it cost to be a believer? It will cost you nothing, and yet it will cost you everything.

It costs us nothing to be a disciple of Jesus because He already paid the price in full, that is, with His holy blood He covered our sins. This Gospel the Holy Spirit uses to bring us to faith, by which we are justified.

Yet, there are consequences to following Christ. In a certain sense it will cost us everything. Jesus wants us to know this up front so we do not complain about paying the price for confessing Him as Savior. We cannot remain secret Christians. He says, "I chose you out of the world, therefore the world hates you. . . . If they persecuted Me, they will also persecute you" (John 15:19–20). Confessing Christ often brings persecution and resentment.

The high price of discipleship includes fighting for Christ. "Do not think that I have come to bring peace to the earth. I have not come to bring peace, but a sword." Christianity is not an "easy chair" religion. Where there is evil, impenitence or blasphemy, we should be willing to testify against it. It is not easy to help others see their sins. They often resent it with anger.

This is fighting the good fight of faith. It is bearing witness of the sacrifice Christ made for us. It is part of the price one must pay.

Jesus now gets to the core of the cost of discipleship by asking if we really love Him. "Whoever loves father or mother . . . [or] son or daughter more than Me is not worthy of Me." It is easy to deceive oneself into thinking you are a fine Christian. Christ is not suggesting we neglect our families, but He is suggesting that He should always be our first love.

Now Jesus cuts to the chase, so to speak. "Whoever does not take his cross and follow Me is not worthy of Me." We want the soft life, not hardships, contention, and ridicule. But we are to bear our crosses as crosses that discipline and stabilize us.

Losing our lives in service to Christ brings us lasting treasures, such as forgiveness, peace, salvation, and heaven.

10 OCTOBER

Psalmody: Psalm 106:1–12
Additional Psalm: Psalm 106
Old Testament Reading: Deuteronomy 9:1–22
New Testament Reading: Matthew 11:1–19

Prayer of the Day

Gracious God, our heavenly Father, Your mercy attends us all our days. Be our strength and support amid the wearisome changes of this world, and at life's end grant us Your promised rest and the full joys of Your salvation; through Jesus Christ, Your Son, our Lord, who lives and reigns with You and the Holy Spirit, one God, now and forever. (A67)

Meditation

Who was the greatest person that ever lived? Historians speak of Alexander the Great, Julius Caesar, Abraham Lincoln, but none even mention John the Baptist. Jesus must have a different standard for measuring the worth of a man for He said, "Among those born of women there has arisen no one greater than John the Baptist."

What makes a person great? John was great because he forgot himself and pointed to Jesus as the Lamb of God. He said he was not even worthy to untie Christ's sandal. He refused all honors. And what was his reward? King Herod had him thrown into a dungeon because John had condemned Herod's sinful marriage. John was a faithful preacher. He believed that Jesus was the Messiah, the Lamb slain for sinners, and the Savior.

Faith in the Gospel, the forgiveness of sins, makes us great. Our greatness consists of our names being written in the Book of Life; heaven is ours.

Even though Jesus appeared to have failed John, John was not offended. He was in prison, and Jesus did not help to get him out. John enthusiastically proclaimed Christ's cause. He gave witness to Jesus without counting the cost. No matter what happened to him, Jesus was his Savior. This is why Jesus said no one ever born is greater.

As Jesus comes to us, He is not always "nice." He tells us about our sins; He points out our faults. He tells us how filthy our righteousness is. That hurts. That offends.

Yet we know we cannot save ourselves. We have failed God miserably. But we come, believing that Jesus has paid for our sins. He removes our guilt, heals our grief and sorrows, and makes our hearts clean. Humbly coming to Him in this fashion makes us great.

However, too often we think greatness consists of power and authority. We want to control people and even wish to control God to do our bidding. This is similar to Satan's tactics in the wilderness when He tempted Jesus. Even in the church we "play games" with God. We want sin condemned, but not ours; we want an easy do-what-I-want Christianity. That is why many today come to church to be entertained. But no matter, critics of Jesus and His Church do not harm Him or the Gospel that remains the power of salvation.

11 OCTOBER

Philip, Deacon

Psalmody: Psalm 23
Additional Psalm: Psalm 114
Old Testament Reading:
Deuteronomy 9:23–10:22
New Testament Reading: Matthew 11:20–30

Prayer of the Day

Almighty and everlasting God, we give thanks to You for Your servant Philip the Deacon. You called him to preach the Gospel to the peoples of Samaria and Ethiopia. Raise up in this and every land messengers of Your kingdom, that Your Church may proclaim the immeasurable riches of our Savior, Jesus Christ, who lives and reigns with You and the Holy Spirit, now and forever. (1098)

Philip, Deacon

Philip, also called the evangelist (Acts 21:8), was one of the seven men appointed to assist in the work of the twelve apostles and of the rapidly growing Early Church by overseeing the distribution of food to the poor (Acts 6:1–6). Following the martyrdom of Stephen, Philip proclaimed the Gospel in Samaria and led Simon the sorcerer to become a believer in Christ (Acts 8:4–13). He was also instrumental in bringing about the conversion of the Ethiopian eunuch (Acts 8:26–39), through whom Philip became indirectly responsible for bringing the Good News of Jesus to the people on the continent of Africa. In the town of Caesarea, he was host for several days to the apostle Paul, who stopped there on his last journey to Jerusalem (Acts 21:8–15).

Meditation

On the north shore of the Sea of Galilee once stood three flourishing cities, Chorazin, Bethsaida, and Capernaum. Together they had a population of one million people. Today, there is not even a trace. What happened to them?

In their glory days Jesus did many of His mighty works among them, performing miracle after miracle. He preached many of His greatest sermons to them, but they rejected Him as the promised Messiah. Therefore, He pronounced misery, wretchedness, and judgment on them because they refused to repent. They rejected His invitation to come to Him. He said, "It will be more tolerable on the day of judgment for the land of Sodom than for you."

God's Law has called people to repentance, and the Gospel has proclaimed the forgiveness of sins through Christ's blood. It has been preached, taught, written, and broadcast on radio and television worldwide. Yet, the majority of people have flaunted and rejected the message of salvation in favor of false religions, some even pretending to be Christian. Sadly, they call on others to court God's favor through human reason instead of relying on Christ's work of salvation.

No matter how often the masses turn their faces from Christ's love, Christ still asks them to come. "Come to Me, all who labor and are heavy laden, and I will give you rest."

Finding rest in Jesus does not mean He will remove and shield us from all pain and sorrow, or lift each heavy agony of life. That is not His promise. His promise is that He will be with us in our pain and suffering and see us through; that He will lighten every heavy load; and that He will take the cutting edge off the crosses (yokes) He allows us to carry. At the end of each day we have comfort as we place ourselves in His care.

Rest in Christ implies certainty and reconciliation. In Him we are sure of forgiveness. Through His cross we are reconciled with our heavenly Father; His wrath has been sated. Sin is removed. Peace is restored because of the Messiah's blood payment.

The forgiveness of sins opens the door to the throne of prayer. We repent of the times we have pushed Jesus aside. We turn to His grace. In His grace our past sins are canceled; our life is changed. Burdens are lifted, and we find rest for our weary souls.

12 OCTOBER

Psalmody: Psalm 119:97–104
Additional Psalm: Psalm 146
Old Testament Reading:
Deuteronomy 11:1–25
New Testament Reading: Matthew 12:1–21

Prayer of the Day

Lord of the Sabbath, You gave Your servant David the bread of the Presence on the Sabbath to teach him that You desire mercy and not sacrifice. Be merciful to us by healing us from all our sins and diseases, that we may be merciful to others as You have been merciful to us; for You live and reign with the Father and the Holy Spirit, one God, now and forever. (1099)

Meditation

The Sabbath question had been a burning issue, whether it was Saturday, the Old Testament Sabbath, or Sunday, the New Testament Sabbath.

Long before Christ there were bitter controversies among the Jews concerning what was permissible on the holy day. The Matthew reading clearly shows the question had not been settled when Christ came.

Some debates at the time of Christ are laughable, such as whether it was lawful to eat an egg that was laid on the Sabbath because the chicken worked to lay the egg. This seems ridiculous. It is not that much different than when the Pharisees charged the disciples with breaking the Sabbath because they picked a few heads of wheat to eat. The disciples had rubbed the kernels out in their hands.

What about us as individuals? Are we sure of our understanding of the Sabbath and our observance? The Lord's Day can be observed in a way similar to that of the Pharisees, only concerned with keeping the letter of the law; or kept in the spirit of Christ with Christian love.

It is possible to obey the letter of the law and at the same time grossly break the spirit of the same precept. We can hide behind outward observances of the commandments to excuse our neglect, as the Pharisees did. They hid behind the strict letter of the Third Commandment to excuse themselves from any acts of mercy on the Sabbath.

Jesus defended the disciples because the rules of love apply in observing the Ten Commandments. Jesus healed a man on the Sabbath and reminded the people it was proper to save a sheep that had fallen into a pit. People are more important than sheep because people have souls. A soul that has fallen into the pits of Satan has been redeemed from sin through God's Son. Jesus gave His life as our ransom for sin. Then God gave His Word to all His redeemed; the Law to help us see ourselves as sinners, and also the Gospel, the message of salvation for the forgiveness of sins.

As Christians living under grace, we are motivated to live as God's redeemed people and at all times to show mercy as Jesus did.

The right observance of the Lord's Day depends on the rightness of our heart with Christ in faith. The Sabbath, as a day of rest, is a gift of God, and as such we shall endeavor to use it in His service and to His praise.

13 OCTOBER

Psalmody: Psalm 111
Additional Psalm: Psalm 115
Old Testament Reading:
Deuteronomy 11:26–12:12
New Testament Reading: Matthew 12:22–37

Prayer of the Day

O God, the protector of all who trust in You, without whom nothing is strong and nothing is holy, multiply Your mercy on us that, with You as our ruler and guide, we may so pass through things temporal that we lose not the things eternal; through Jesus Christ, our Lord, who lives and reigns with You and the Holy Spirit, one God, now and forever. (H63)

Meditation

Jesus lamented over Jerusalem because the people rejected Him. He said, "How often would I have gathered your children together as a hen gathers her brood under her wings, and you would not" (Matthew 23:37)! Since that time most people have rejected Christ.

Christianity is not limited to any age group, race, or language. It offers to each generation the only satisfying solution for sin and casts no one out of the circle of God's love in Jesus. Yet, at the same time, it is very narrow. It teaches there is no other way to eternal life except by God's Son made flesh. Jesus said to Thomas, "I am the way, the truth, and the life. No one comes to the Father except through Me" (John 14:6).

The Christian religion does not permit any divided loyalty, no serving two masters at the same time. You either trust the one true God, or you do not. The claim is made that one god is as good as another, such as Allah, Buddha, the gods of Hinduism, and human reason, and that there is not just one true God. We know there is no other God but the triune God who has revealed Himself in Scripture; there is not another Savior but Jesus; there is no other true revelation but the Holy Scriptures; and there is no other way to eternal life but by faith in the blood of Christ for all sin.

The Pharisees hated Jesus and accused Him of doing miracles by the power of Beelzebub (Satan), the prince of demons. They were extremely persistent in their unbelief. Jesus then explained the unforgivable sin, which is blasphemy against the Holy Spirit. He said, "I tell you, every sin and blasphemy will be forgiven people, but the blasphemy against the Spirit will not be forgiven."

The sin against the Holy Spirit is the stubborn unbelief that refuses to accept Jesus as the Savior from sin. Unbelief closes the door of heaven because a person cannot refuse and accept Jesus at the same time. Faith in Christ is enlivened in us by the Holy Spirit. "No one can say 'Jesus is Lord' except in the Holy Spirit" (1 Corinthians 12:3). We can resist the working of the Holy Spirit in us through the Gospel and thereby close the only door to the glories of heaven.

The multitudes gathered in heaven who praise the Lamb come from every nation and every language. Each one has been washed white in the blood of the Lamb. We pray God to keep us in the faith and our allegiance to the Lamb of God.

14 OCTOBER

Psalmody: Psalm 114
Additional Psalm: Psalm 124
Old Testament Reading: Deuteronomy 12:13–32
New Testament Reading: Matthew 12:38–50

Prayer of the Day

Blessed Lord, since You have caused all Holy Scriptures to be written for our learning, grant that we may so hear them, read, mark, learn, and inwardly digest them that we may embrace and ever hold fast the blessed hope of everlasting life; through Jesus Christ, Your Son, our Lord, who lives and reigns with You and the Holy Spirit, one God, now and forever. (A68)

Meditation

Scripture clearly states that without faith in Christ as the Savior from sin, it is not possible to be saved unto eternal life. In spite of the clarity of the Scriptures, some people offer excuses for unbelievers, like "If they never had the chance to hear the message of salvation, how could God, in His mercy, condemn them?"

This is faulty thinking. First, in Romans it clearly states, "For what can be known about God is plain to them [unbelievers], because God has shown it to them. For His invisible attributes, namely, His eternal power and divine nature, have been clearly perceived, ever since the creation of the world, in the things that have been made. *So they are without excuse*" (Romans 1:19–20, emphasis added). Second, it confuses Law and Gospel. The unbelievers are not judged according to God's mercy but according to God's wrath. Only believers are judged under God's mercy.

The scribes and Pharisees, the skeptics in the New Testament, wanted a sign from Jesus that proved He was the promised Messiah. He told them He would accomplish the greatest miracle of all time that would prove beyond all doubt that He was the promised Christ, the Savior of the world.

The sign would be that of the prophet Jonah who was in the belly of the fish for three days and lived. So also would He, the Son of Man, be crucified, placed in a grave, and after three days be raised alive from the tomb.

But they paid no attention to the greatest miracle of miracles that gave undeniable proof that Jesus was God. He had fulfilled His Father's will and accomplished His mission of redeeming the souls of mankind from the deadly consequences of sin—eternal death.

Since Christ's resurrection, unbelievers have no excuse. He showed beyond all doubt that He is God of God and Savior of all. Those who reject Him today have nothing to support claim of inexcusable unbelief.

How does one explain this stubborn pigheadedness that refuses to accept the risen Christ? The devil has taken over their empty hearts. He allows them to be religious and good in the eyes of society. He doesn't care how religious you are. The devil does not want you to come to Christ and look to His holy blood poured out for your salvation.

Many have ears but do not hear. Blessed are those who do hear the message of salvation and believe it. Peace floods into their hearts through the risen Savior. May we be counted among them.

15 OCTOBER

Psalmody: Psalm 119:33–40
Additional Psalm: Psalm 34:8–18
Old Testament Reading:
Deuteronomy 13:1–18
New Testament Reading: Matthew 13:1–23

Prayer of the Day

O God, so rule and govern our hearts and minds by Your Holy Spirit that, ever mindful of Your final judgment, we may be stirred up to holiness of living here and dwell with You in perfect joy hereafter; through Jesus Christ, Your Son, our Lord, who lives and reigns with You and the Holy Spirit, one God, now and forever. (A69)

Meditation

Jesus knew our puny little minds could not comprehend the mysteries of God's kingdom. To help us understand, He often took the ordinary things of life and gave them spiritual significance in what we call parables. The simple act of planting seeds is given a heavenly interpretation. The lilies were as common as dandelions, but Jesus tells us that Solomon never looked so magnificent in all his kingly robes.

The farmer scatters the seed. The birds quickly eat it; or it dies before the grain ripens; or the weeds choke it and kill it; or due to the lack of moisture the plant dries up.

Our Lord does not always explain His parables, but He explains here with such poignant meaning. He says, "He who has ears, let him hear."

Satan, the great slanderer, goes to Church but not to hear. In worship Satan helps us think about other things so that we do not hear God's Word that strengthens our faith. How often we daydream, and the Word does not take root. Someone hurts our feelings by saying something offensive. Maybe we were offended when the pastor preached to us the Law. As a result we leave worship with a chip on our shoulder, and the Word finds no room in our heart.

Who among us has not let every day problems take over our thinking while we should be meditating on God's Word? A child is having problems in school, another is misbehaving, another is causing great trouble at home, and expenses seem to be greater than our income. We worry and worry. It does not help but only closes our heart to God's Word. We go back home to our problems without finding comfort in God's gracious promises.

Our sinful nature hates God. It does not wish to listen to Him but would rather listen to the devil's lies that tell us we do not need God.

We are amazed when we see a tree growing out of rocky ledge. A seed found a small bit of good soil in a crack. It is the same with us. In a Christian's heart the seed of God's Law has worked repentance, causing us to express sorrow over negligence of the Word. The saving seed of His message of salvation from sin, death, and the power of Satan has planted faith unto eternal life. To God be the glory.

16 OCTOBER

Psalmody: Psalm 37:3–11
Additional Psalm: Psalm 37
Old Testament Reading:
Deuteronomy 14:1–2, 22–23; 14:28–15:15
New Testament Reading:
Matthew 13:24–43

Prayer of the Day

Almighty and everlasting God, give us an increase of faith, hope, and love, that, receiving what You have promised, we may love what You have commanded; through Jesus Christ, Your Son, our Lord, who lives and reigns with You and the Holy Spirit, one God, now and forever. (A70)

Meditation

What is the kingdom of God? More thought on God's kingdom would help the kingdoms of the world live in peace. God's kingdom is the only thing that lifts people from the level of beasts.

The kingdom of God sometimes refers to the heavenly arena where, with the saints and angels, God has His throne. However, the kingdom Jesus speaks of is present in our world. So what is it?

It is the holy Christian Church, the communion of saints that we confess in the Apostles' Creed. It has no territorial limits, is not identical with any denomination, but it is the total of all people who trust in Christ as Savior.

Even though only the heavenly Father knows who is in His kingdom, it is present in our world wherever the message of salvation through faith in Christ is proclaimed. Its citizens are the real, blessed people and are a real blessing to their communities.

What are the facts of this kingdom? It has a difficult time in this world. Many are so occupied with the pleasures of life that nothing else finds room in their mind. They are not interested in God or things spiritual. They believe if they have enough money, investments, and real estate holdings, they may eat, drink, and enjoy life.

If the Gospel, the message of Christ's mission, is not appreciated, it will be taken and given to others. If we persistently close our ears and eyes, we may hear but not understand; we may see but not recognize.

That is why sermons often fail. Our mind is closed to spiritual truths and our interests lie in other places. Our Savior pleads with us to hear properly and adds, "Blessed are your eyes, for they see, and your ears, for they hear" (Matthew 13:16).

Christians, even though tempted by the glitz and glitter of the world, recognize the importance of their responsibility of proclaiming Christ's salvation to the world.

The kingdom of God is hated by the world. It has been ridiculed and cursed. It has done more for humanity than all other political institutions combined. It has lifted the morals of the world and elevated the life of society because of its leavening effect.

The Good News of the Gospel penetrates hearts with the message of God's forgiveness and cleanses from the filth of sin. It causes faith and trust to grow to replace doubt and skepticism. As Christ's new creatures, we have that inward peace and hope that makes heaven our home.

17 OCTOBER

Ignatius of Antioch, Pastor and Martyr

Psalmody: Psalm 39:4–7, 12–13
Additional Psalm: Psalm 38
Old Testament Reading:
Deuteronomy 15:19–16:22
New Testament Reading: Matthew 13:44–58

Prayer of the Day

Almighty God, we praise Your name for Ignatius of Antioch, bishop and martyr. He offered himself as grain to be ground by the teeth of wild beasts that he might present to You the pure bread of sacrifice. Accept the willing tribute of our all that we are and all that we have, and give us a portion in the pure and unspotted offering of Your Son, Jesus Christ, who lives and reigns with You and the Holy Spirit, one God, now and forever. (1100)

Ignatius of Antioch, Pastor and Martyr

Ignatius was the bishop of Antioch in Syria at the beginning of the second century AD and an early Christian martyr. Near the end of the reign of the Roman emperor Trajan (AD 98–117), Ignatius was arrested, taken in chains to Rome, and eventually thrown to the wild beasts in the arena. On the way to Rome, he wrote letters to the Christians at Ephesus, Magnesia, Tralles, Rome, Philadelphia, and Smyrna, as well as to Polycarp, bishop of Smyrna. In the letters, which are beautifully pastoral in tone, Ignatius warned against certain heresies (false teachings). He also repeatedly stressed the full humanity and deity of Christ, the reality of Christ's bodily presence in the Lord's Supper, the supreme authority of the bishop, and the unity of the Church found in her bishops. Ignatius was the first to use the word catholic to describe the universality of the Church. His Christ-centeredness, his courage in the face of martyrdom, and his zeal for the truth over against false doctrine are a lasting legacy to the Church.

Meditation

Parables—earthly stories with heavenly meanings—have always been accepted by Christians as good teaching tools. However, some modern theologians are casting doubt on historical accounts and even the truthfulness of the Bible by misusing the word "parable." They use "parable" to mean fictional stories.

Modern theologians tell us that the explanation of the creation of the world is a parable, or that Adam and Eve were not real people. The fall into sin never really happened, but it is a parable; or the account of the flood is a parable. The Biblical account of the prophet Jonah and the big fish is a parable. They claim these historical events are just fictional stories. This is a diabolical way of undermining the truthfulness of the Scriptures.

The two parables speak of a treasure that is worth more than anything else. This treasure is the kingdom of heaven.

By our sinful nature we are born into the kingdom of darkness. Whether we realize it or not, the devil controls our lives and destinies. But through Holy Baptism we are born from above through faith in Jesus, who has destroyed the works of the devil. Christ makes us His children and brings us into His kingdom. God then controls our lives and destinies, and we strive to live under Him.

Some modern theologians insist the kingdom of God has nothing to do with heaven, but consists only of a perfect social order in which there is no poverty or conflict or injustice. But Jesus clearly said that His kingdom is not of this world even though it is in this world. We know there will never be a perfect social order.

When we correctly understand that the kingdom of God is the greatest treasure a person can possess, then we will know the truth Jesus taught when He asked, "What does it profit a man to gain the whole world and forfeit his soul" (Mark 8:36)?

Jesus is our treasure; Jesus is our pearl. He assumed our sins; He killed death with His death, and through the Gospel offers us His forgiveness, His righteousness.

It is said that a person finds the grace of God when the grace of God finds him. God's grace is given through His Word and the Sacraments—Holy Baptism and Holy Communion.

18 OCTOBER

St. Luke, Evangelist

Psalmody: Psalm 75
Additional Psalm: Psalm 77
Old Testament Reading:
Deuteronomy 17:1–20
New Testament Reading: Matthew 14:1–21

Prayer of the Day

Almighty God, our Father, Your blessed Son called Luke the physician to be an evangelist and physician of the soul. Grant that the healing medicine of the Gospel and the Sacraments may put to flight the diseases of our souls that with willing hearts we may ever love and serve You; through Jesus Christ, Your Son, our Lord, who lives and reigns with You and the Holy Spirit, one God, now and forever. (F30)

St. Luke, Evangelist

St. Luke, the beloved physician referred to by St. Paul (Colossians 4:14), presents us with Jesus, whose blood provides the medicine of immortality. As his traveling companion, Paul claims Luke's Gospel as his own for its healing of souls (Eusebius). Luke traveled with Paul during the second missionary journey, joining him after Paul received his Macedonian call to bring the Gospel to Europe (Acts 16:10–17). Luke most likely stayed behind in Philippi for seven years, rejoining Paul at the end of the third missionary journey in Macedonia. He traveled with Paul to Troas, Jerusalem, and Caesarea, where Paul was imprisoned for two years (Acts 20:5–21:18). While in Caesarea, Luke may have researched material that he used in his Gospel. Afterward, Luke accompanied Paul on his journey to Rome (Acts 27:1–28:16). Especially beloved in Luke's Gospel are the stories of the Good Samaritan (Luke

10:29–37), the prodigal son (Luke 15:11–32), the rich man and Lazarus (Luke 16:19–31), and the Pharisee and the tax collector (Luke 18:9–14). Only Luke provides a detailed account of Christ's birth (Luke 2:1–20) and the canticles of Mary (Luke 1:46–55), of Zechariah (Luke 1:68–79), and of Simeon (Luke 2:29–32). To show how Christ continued His work in the Early Church through the apostles, Luke also penned the Acts of the Apostles. More than one-third of the New Testament comes from the hand of the evangelist Luke.

Meditation

The tragic, tangled web of sin is described in the Bible, not in abstract principles, but in concrete and colorful examples from life. Furthermore, the central teaching of Scripture, that we are justified before God only by faith in Christ's sacrifice for sin and not by our own righteousness, is vividly demonstrated and made very clear.

The moral principles of Christianity are also illustrated in the Scripture by examples of living personalities, ranging from royal princes to the lowest forms of humanity. The sixth commandment, "You shall not commit adultery," is no exception.

King David's transgression of the sixth commandment with Uriah's wife, Bathsheba, and King Herod with his unlawful wife, Herodias, serve as vivid examples of the sin of adultery and its tragic results.

Sinful acts always come back to torment. Sin gets us into deep water and finally drowns us in the sea of despair and guilt, unless we are rescued by our Savior. The history of Herod's family is an example of God "punishing the children for the sin of the fathers to the third and fourth generation" (The Close of the Commandments).

Because Herod lusted after his brother's wife, he divorced his wife and unlawfully married his brother's wife, Herodias. John the Baptizer

did not worry about hurting the king's feelings and plainly told him he was living in incestuous adultery. "It is not lawful for you to have her." This condemnation irritated the royal couple in their self-righteous hypocrisy, and Herodias got her revenge. When the opportunity arose, she was responsible for having John beheaded.

It is easy to condemn Herod and Herodias. But can we say we have never lusted, told smutty sexual jokes, looked at filthy pictures, or read a trashy paperback? How easy the trap is set that drags us into the depths of iniquity and sin.

Herod broke his first wife's heart, broke up his brother's marriage, and broke God's commandment. Then he refused to break a foolish oath that resulted in John's death. The adulterer became a murderer.

Our adulterous society constantly glorifies illicit sex and portrays it without consequences. When we succumb to temptation, we usually do not think of the consequences. But we can keenly remember the bitter payback of our sins—our burning conscience and the hurt caused to loved ones.

May we always seek cleansing through daily contrition and repentance and turn to Christ's shed blood that covers all our sins and grants us forgiveness.

19 OCTOBER

Psalmody: Psalm 80:14–19
Additional Psalm: Psalm 80
Old Testament Reading:
Deuteronomy 18:1–22
New Testament Reading: Matthew 14:22–36

Prayer of the Day

Almighty and most merciful God, preserve us from all harm and danger that we, being ready in both body and soul, may cheerfully accomplish what You want done; through Jesus Christ, Your Son, our Lord, who lives and reigns with You and the Holy Spirit, one God, now and forever. (A72)

Meditation

Our failure as followers of Christ is partly our inability to perceive our Savior as being interested in helping us in the small ordinary situations of life. Oh yes, we easily see Him stretched in agony on the cross for our sins, but do we readily see Him concerned about paying the bills, over an argument with our neighbor, or about a marital disagreement?

The greatness of God consists in this: that He is concerned about our minor problems. He knows our weaknesses and sympathizes with us. We often fail to find help from God because of our little faith, not God's inability to help.

We can learn this from looking to the Sea of Galilee and see how Jesus showed, in a miraculous act, that He is victorious over human inabilities. Suddenly a violent windstorm swept down on the ship with the disciples. Jesus comes to them, walking on the water, climbs into the ship, and the stormy winds calm down.

This is a parable of life. An auto accident sweeps into our lives causing severe injuries, or a heart attack or stroke strikes. Then Jesus comes and "climbs into our boat" with His outstretched hands of mercy and healing. Once again we find hope in His promises and strength in His Word.

The stormy winds of life vary. They come as doubt when we question the mercies of God. Or some forgotten sin comes back to haunt us and we question God's love. Yes, even sickness and death sweeps into our home and we sorrowfully cry, "Why us?" We lose our job in a depressed economic time; frustration and disappointment help make the future look dismal.

Unless Jesus comes into our dark nights with His comfort and hope, we wallow in bitterness, hopelessness, and despair. He removes fear, anxiety, and uncertainty. He tells us, "Take heart, it is I. Do not be afraid."

When the apostle Peter was walking to Jesus on the water and started to sink in the large waves, he panicked and cried to Jesus for help. Jesus reached out and grabbed him. How often we despair, certain that we are sinking in the pressures of life or that the overpowering forces of sin are closing in on us. Then let us hear Jesus reach out to us and say, "Take heart, it is I." The forgiven soul is released from sin's bondage. This fills our hearts with unending joy.

20 October

Psalmody: Psalm 138
Additional Psalm: Psalm 140
Old Testament Reading:
Deuteronomy 19:1–20
New Testament Reading: Matthew 15:1–20

Prayer of the Day

We pray You, O Lord, to keep our tongues from evil and our lips from speaking deceit, that as Your holy angels continuously sing praises to You in heaven, so may we at all times glorify You on earth; through Jesus Christ, our Lord. (210)

Meditation

Man has always wanted to replace God's revelations with his own natural religion. This makes man appear supremely important, as having accomplished the ultimate. A person does not want to admit he cannot save his own soul.

But more importantly, Jesus is the most concerned. He has information about our heart that is not perceived by the stethoscope or that can be revealed by an electrocardiogram or stress test. He knows our heart is spiritually sick with sin. He knows that "what comes out of the mouth proceeds from the heart, and this defiles a person. For out of the heart come evil thoughts, murder, adultery, sexual immorality, theft, false witness, slander." These destroy not only the body but also the soul. These are the things that defile a person.

The Pharisees were not concerned with the spiritual condition of their hearts. Instead, they focused on those items that people noticed, such as not eating unclean food or washing themselves when returning from the market. They wanted people to think they were the most holy people.

But Jesus saw through such hypocrisy and veneer. He let them know in no uncertain terms, which, of course, highly offended them. By nature we prefer the outward observances of rituals to genuine worship of the heart. We can drift through an entire worship service because we may know it by rote.

When we think about Cain's murder of his brother, we probably pat ourselves on the back, thankful we have never done such a horrific crime. But make no mistake, by nature our heart is just as corrupt and capable of carrying out any sin. Jeremiah gives us a most humiliating appraisal of our heart when he says, "The heart is deceitful above all things, and desperately sick; who can understand it?" (Jeremiah 17:9).

What can I do about my sinful heart? How can I change it? There is absolutely nothing I, nor anyone else, can do. But God can. He has the solution.

From eternity God recognized man's problem and decided on redemption through the blood of His Son. He foresaw Adam and Eve's sin, and He promised them a Savior. God knew that for people to have peaceful hearts, they would first need forgiveness of sins. He would supply this forgiveness through His Son's sacrifice.

21 OCTOBER

Psalmody: Psalm 142
Additional Psalm: Psalm 91
Old Testament Reading:
Deuteronomy 20:1–20
New Testament Reading: Matthew 15:21–39

Prayer of the Day

Almighty and everlasting Father, You give Your children many blessings even though we are undeserving. In every trial and temptation grant us steadfast confidence in Your loving-kindness and mercy; through Jesus Christ, Your Son, our Lord, who lives and reigns with You and the Holy Spirit, one God, now and forever. (A73)

Meditation

The greatest victories are not won on the field of battle, on the high seas, or in the air. They are won in people's hearts and lives. They are the victories over sin and temptation, and they are victories dealing with suffering and the trials of life. These victories are important because of eternal issues and also on account of the great power of those forces against whom these victories must be won.

We all face suffering and pain. Some people have great staying power when disaster strikes. Their sufferings and setbacks do not crush them, but rather serve as opportunities to prove their faith, as with the Canaanite woman whose daughter was severely oppressed by a demon.

This mother's faith faced the test of extreme hardship. She knew she needed help. Her faith gave her the courage to go to Jesus, even though she was a Gentile, a stranger. She faced the test of silence. Jesus seemed not to pay any attention to her pleading and was in no hurry to help. She even faced the test of rebuke as Jesus compared her to dogs that only get the crumbs.

But her faith did not waver—it won! Her daughter was healed. Jesus pointed out the heroic faith in her heart that is an example to all of us who become discouraged.

We can become downhearted because we did not receive relief from our troubles at our first prayer for help. Our faith is often tested by obstacles in our path, such as sinful living. We want to follow our sinful nature on the one hand, and on the other, we covet God's great blessings given through His Son. We may have misgivings about Jesus, about whether He really does offer and forgive our grossest sins. And it certainly is not logical that we cannot do anything to make God love us.

Suffering is worldwide. Sufferings that test our faith are endurable if we come to the great Physician asking for help.

God sends us through the clinic of suffering, where pain is often acute. By His grace we come through as heroes of faith. We can face life's trials with great confidence and courage knowing "I can do all things through Him who strengthens me" (Philippians 4:13).

Our greatest victory of faith is when we kneel before our gracious Father, knowing we have been bought and won from our sins by Christ's suffering and death. We know we are His. He will never leave or forsake us. This brings the peace that passes all understanding.

22 OCTOBER

Psalmody: Psalm 62
Additional Psalm: Psalm 119:137–144
Old Testament Reading:
Deuteronomy 21:1–23
Additional Reading: Deuteronomy 22:1–24:9
New Testament Reading: Matthew 16:1–12

Prayer of the Day

Almighty God, whom to know is everlasting life, grant us to know Your Son, Jesus, to be the way, the truth, and the life that we may boldly confess Him to be the Christ and steadfastly walk in the way that leads to life eternal; through the same Jesus Christ, our Lord, who lives and reigns with You and the Holy Spirit, one God, now and forever. (A74)

Meditation

We often focus on the misguided nature of the plea made by the adversaries of Jesus rather than the request itself. The Pharisees and Sadducees were not interested in giving Jesus a fair hearing, even if the Lord had presented them with a sign from heaven. These antagonists were not on the verge of belief; they were entrenched in unbelief. Theirs was not simply a request but a demand, not a search for more information but an attempt to ensnare.

They were engaged in the most primal of sins—reversing roles with the Lord. Adam and Eve had done the same in Eden. They desired to assume God's position and have Him be in theirs. Satan used the identical ploy in the Judean wilderness. His requests for Jesus to turn the stones into bread, to throw Himself down from the pinnacle of the temple, and to claim the kingdoms of the world in exchange for idolizing Satan were all sinfully audacious, not only because of their content, but merely because they were made.

When we understand this, the accusing nature of the Law strikes us with full force, for we have done likewise. We are also members of the "evil and adulterous generation" of which our Lord speaks. True, we are usually not filled with such malice; we might have no overt intention of conducting a spiritual ambush for our Savior. Our requests are much more innocent and benign. Yet we derive a measure of perverse pleasure in giving God orders. This is why the Lord previously instructed us to pray according to His will (Matthew 6:10). That little phrase attached to every request, plea, or entreaty for any earthly matter reminds us of our role as well as His. He is the Creator; we are the creatures. He is the Giver; we are the recipients. He is the Lord and Master; we are the subjects and servants.

Because of our rebellious tendency to reverse roles with Him, our Lord—moved by love, not spite—did the same to us. His Son took the role of a servant and creature to bring us the salvation we could never accomplish on our own. His death and resurrection—the sign of Jonah—is the only evidence we need, for it shows us our standing as God's own sons and daughters.

23 OCTOBER

St. James of Jerusalem, Brother of Jesus and Martyr

Psalmody: Psalm 107:10–16
Additional Psalm: Psalm 107
Old Testament Reading:
Deuteronomy 24:10–25:10
New Testament Reading: Matthew 16:13–28

Prayer of the Day

Heavenly Father, shepherd of Your people, You raised up James the Just, brother of our Lord, to lead and guide Your Church. Grant that we may follow his example of prayer and reconciliation and be strengthened by the witness of his death; through Jesus Christ, Your Son, our Lord, who lives and reigns with You and the Holy Spirit, one God, now and forever. (F31)

St. James of Jerusalem, Brother of Jesus and Martyr

St. James of Jerusalem (or "James the Just") is referred to by St. Paul as "the Lord's brother" (Galatians 1:19). Some modern theologians believe that James was a son of Joseph and Mary, and therefore a biological brother of Jesus. But throughout most of the Church (historically, and even today), Paul's term "brother" is understood as "cousin" or "kinsman," and James is thought to be the son of a sister of Joseph or Mary who was widowed and had come to live with them. Along with other relatives of our Lord (except His mother), James did not believe in Jesus until after His resurrection (John 7:3–5; 1 Corinthians 15:7). After becoming a Christian, James was elevated to a position of leadership within the earliest Christian community. Especially following St. Peter's departure from Jerusalem, James was recognized as the bishop of the Church in that holy city (Acts 12:17; 15:12ff.). According to the historian Josephus, James was martyred in AD 62 by being stoned to death by the Sadducees. James authored the Epistle in the New Testament that bears his name. In it, he exhorts his readers to remain steadfast in the one true faith, even in the face of suffering and temptation, and to live by faith the life that is in Christ Jesus. Such a faith, he makes clear, is a busy and active thing, which never ceases to do good, to confess the Gospel by words and actions, and to stake its life, both now and forever, on the cross.

Meditation

One of the most disconcerting aspects of this passage is the contrasting reactions Peter receives from our Lord. Initially Peter is commended on account of his bold and correct confession of Christ. However, when he then objects to the disclosure of Jesus regarding the events of the Passion about to occur, Peter is named "Satan" and called a hindrance to the Lord's ministry. What a sudden and dramatic change of tone and events!

We have here a sobering and dramatic picture of human inconsistency—an object lesson in the sinner/saint dichotomy that each of us possess. We are engaged in a struggle. On the one hand, we profess to be followers of Jesus and delight in confessing Him, but on the other, we struggle and fail, sometimes to a miserable, shameful degree. Our Lord had every right to react in this way to Peter. Jesus is not unpredictable or temperamental; Peter was the fickle, capricious one who deserved this severe rebuke.

Jesus identifies the cause of this condition when He tells Peter, "For you are not setting your mind on the things of God, but on the things of man." An anthropocentric focus will naturally concentrate its attention on whatever appears to be easy and comfortable. It focuses only on the moment at hand and rebels against the idea of taking up a cross and following Jesus. It is the result of sin. A God-centered mindset does the opposite. It focuses not on self but on the Savior, not on glory but the cross. It is not a product of one's own effort, but a divine gift, the result of faith in the One whom Peter rightly confessed.

The stinging indictment of the Law, which shows us our sinful inconsistency, is indeed disconcerting. It should sadden us to ponder the fact that we have been "hindrances" to the Lord. But we are not left in this condition. The message of the Gospel is both encouraging and empowering. Jesus is our equal, possessing a human nature like us. But He is also our opposite, possessing none of our shortcomings and sins. He shows His disciples that He "must go" to Jerusalem in order to suffer, die, and rise again. He will not waver or hesitate. He will not be deterred, because He is determined to win our salvation. He faithfully and consistently carried out His mission as the Savior of the world so that we sinner/saints might confess and serve Him in the world with ever-increased faithfulness and consistency.

24 OCTOBER

Psalmody: Psalm 99
Additional Psalm: Psalm 97
Old Testament Reading:
Deuteronomy 25:17–26:19
New Testament Reading: Matthew 17:1–13

Prayer of the Day

O God, in the glorious transfiguration of Your beloved Son You confirmed the mysteries of the faith by the testimony of Moses and Elijah. In the voice that came from the bright cloud You wonderfully foreshowed our adoption by grace. Mercifully make us co-heirs with the King in His glory and bring us to the fullness of our inheritance in heaven; through the same Jesus Christ, our Lord, who lives and reigns with You and the Holy Spirit, one God, now and forever. (L21)

Meditation

Few of us are in the habit of reading the last chapter of a book first or viewing the climax of a movie before the rest. Yet that, in essence, is the significance of the transfiguration. The Lord gives His closest disciples a foretaste of the future glory that will be both His and theirs, in order to fortify them for the difficult days they will soon encounter.

This spectacular event was for the benefit of these disciples as well as us. Jesus did not experience it by Himself and then relate the incident to them verbally; rather, Scripture very deliberately says He was transfigured "before them," in their very presence. They needed this confirmation and reassurance. Six days earlier Jesus had spoken to them about losing their lives for His sake. He had warned them that some of them would taste death. Morose thoughts related to this conversation undoubtedly were still lingering in Peter's mind, motivating him to suggest the erection of three tents to house the glorious Lord and His attendants, in order that this miraculous moment on the mountain could endure. Before Peter could finish this foolish suggestion, the divine voice caused even further trepidation, and he and the other disciples fell to the ground paralyzed with fear. The words, the sight, and the touch of Jesus changed that.

The situation for us is stunningly similar. We are satisfied with being a Christian when life is trouble-free. But when difficulties, challenges, and heartaches come, our faith is tested, perhaps even rendered inert. As we journey though the valleys and deserts of life seemingly far from the mountaintops, we long for a dazzling display of this sort and crave a foretaste of future glory.

How foolish we are to forget that we already have it. The touch of Jesus given to us by water and the Word foreshows the day when we will gather at the river with all the saints of God (Revelation 22:1). The very body and blood of the Lord we receive in, with, and under the bread and wine presage the bounty of the messianic banquet. The forgiveness we receive in Absolution points forward to the white robes of righteousness that we will wear in eternity. True, this world is not heaven. But knowing where we are going and glimpsing a preview of the final destination won for us by the Lord at the cross and the empty tomb gives us strength and joy for the journey.

25 OCTOBER

Dorcas (Tabitha), Lydia, and Phoebe, Faithful Women

Psalmody: Psalm 93
Additional Psalm: Psalm 87
Old Testament Reading:
Deuteronomy 27:1–26
New Testament Reading: Matthew 17:14–27

Prayer of the Day

Almighty God, You stirred to compassion the hearts of Your dear servants Dorcas, Lydia, and Phoebe to uphold and sustain Your Church by their devoted and charitable deeds. Give us the same will to love You, open our eyes to see You in the least ones, and strengthen our hands to serve You in others, for the sake of Your Son, Jesus Christ, our Lord, who lives and reigns with You and the Holy Spirit, one God, now and forever. (1101)

Dorcas (Tabitha), Lydia, and Phoebe, Faithful Women

These women were exemplary Christians who demonstrated their faith by their material support of the Church. Dorcas (also known as Tabitha) was well-known and much loved for her acts of charity in the city of Joppa, especially for her making clothes for the poor. When Dorcas died suddenly, the members of her congregation sent to the neighboring city of Lydda for the apostle Peter, who came and raised her from the dead (Acts 9:36–41). Lydia was a woman of Thyatira, who worked at Philippi selling a famous purple dye that was much in demand in the ancient world. She was also a "worshiper of God" at the local synagogue (Acts 16:14). When the apostle Paul encountered her in prayer among other proselyte women, his preaching of the Word brought Lydia to faith in Christ. She and her friends thus became the nucleus of the Christian community in Philippi (Acts 16:13–15, 40). Phoebe was another faithful woman associated with the apostle Paul. She was a deaconess from Cenchreae (the port of Corinth) whom Paul sent to the Church in Rome with his Epistle to the Romans. In it, he writes of her support for the work of the Early Church (Romans 16:1–2).

Meditation

Quality and quantity need not always be pitted against each other. Often these two characteristics are intertwined, as in today's text. Jesus rebukes the disciples for their inability to cure an epileptic boy. When our Lord had earlier sent the twelve into the world as His representatives, He gave them explicit instructions to "heal the sick, raise the dead, cleanse lepers, cast out demons" (Matthew 10:8). Miracles such as these would give visible substantiation to their preaching about Him. Now when the need arose, they were unable to do as they had been told. This caused them consternation, so they sought a diagnosis from Jesus.

With a brutal but loving honesty our Lord said the reason for their failure was "because of your little faith." Yet, this wasn't just a deficient faith; it was a faith that was essentially non-existent. Both its quality and its quantity were lacking. The "faithless and twisted generation" about which the Lord speaks included also these close—but erring—followers.

In contrast, Jesus speaks about faith as small as a mustard seed that is able to move mountains. Here again, quality and quantity are not exclusive but overlapping. It is not the size of the faith that matters but its foundation and focus. People today may profess to have "a lot of faith" in themselves, their president, their physician, their plumber, or a plethora of other people or objects. The degree of this sentiment is totally irrelevant, for this "faith" signifies nothing more than hopeful anticipation of a desired result. It is merely a feeling.

For the Christian, however, faith is more than a personal sensation or opinion; it is a God-given trust in the fact of our Lord's redemptive work on our behalf. It is the instrument God uses to bring the results of the salvation, which He accomplished through His Son, to each of us individually. This is the reason Jesus repeatedly points to His Passion, reiterating to His disciples that He will suffer, die, and rise again.

We sometimes speculate if our faith will be "strong enough" to withstand certain tests that may come our way. This is a misdirected analysis. Instead, we should be concerned with faith's focus. When our gaze of trust is directed toward the cross and the empty tomb, this is the quality of faith God gives and desires. Therefore, its quantity will always be pleasing to Him as well.

26 OCTOBER

Philipp Nicolai, Johann Heermann, and Paul Gerhardt, Hymnwriters

Psalmody: Psalm 12
Additional Psalm: Psalm 9
Old Testament Reading: Deuteronomy 28:1–22
New Testament Reading: Matthew 18:1–20

Prayer of the Day

Almighty God, the apostle Paul taught us to praise You in psalms and hymns and spiritual songs. We thank You this day for those who have given to Your Church great hymns, especially Your servants Philipp Nicolai, Johann Heermann, and Paul Gerhardt. May Your Church never lack hymn writers who through their words and music give You praise. Fill us with the desire to praise and thank You for Your great goodness; through Jesus Christ, our Lord, who lives and reigns with You and the Holy Spirit, one God, now and forever. (1102)

Philipp Nicolai, Johann Heermann, and Paul Gerhardt, Hymnwriters

Philipp Nicolai (1556–1608) was a pastor in Germany during the Great Plague, which took the lives of thirteen hundred of his parishioners during a sixth-month period. In addition to his heroic pastoral ministry during that time of stress and sorrow, he wrote the texts for "Wake, Awake, for Night Is Flying" and "O Morning Star, How Fair and Bright," known, respectively, as the king and queen of the Lutheran chorales. Johann Heermann (1585–1647), also a German pastor, suffered from poor health as well as from the ravages of the Thirty Years' War (1618–48). His hymn texts are noted for their tenderness and depth of feeling. Paul Gerhardt (1607–76) was another Lutheran pastor who endured the horrors of the Thirty Years' War. By 1668, he lost his pastoral position in Berlin (for refusing to compromise his Lutheran convictions) and endured the death of four of his five children and his wife. He nevertheless managed to write 133 hymns, all of which reflect his firm faith. Along with Martin Luther, he is regarded as one of Lutheranism's finest hymnwriters.

Meditation

Our faith in Jesus never exists in isolation from others. As much as we might seek solitude on occasion, the fact remains that we live in community and daily interact with people God puts into our lives. Therefore, human relationships are a concern for the child of God. Because we communicate with and live among both believers and nonbelievers, our personal associations give us opportunity not only to show our Christianity but also to share our Christianity. There are some individuals within our sphere of influence who are a joy to be near. Our interaction with them is relatively easy and spiritually edifying. There are others, however, who present challenges to us and our faith. Perhaps—it must be noted—we present the same dilemma for them.

This section of Matthew's Gospel describes our life with others. The phenomena described here are as true now as when they were originally written. Sinful human nature with its

character flaws persists through the centuries. One of these blemishes is our propensity for rivalry. The disciples experienced this, too. Their question to Jesus about greatness in the kingdom of heaven shows an unhealthy competitiveness and an over-eagerness to get ahead of others. They, like us, would rather be lords than servants, the VIP rather than the ordinary man or woman in the crowd.

Our selfish pride is difficult to contain. Genuine humility does not come naturally or easily. We want to be noticed and appreciated. This warped sense of self can also do spiritual damage, not only to our self, but to others as well. Scripture here warns us about the danger of being a stumbling block to someone else's faith. When relationships are so skewed that they become broken, we are to seek reconciliation. This begins on a personal level (verse 15), even if we are not the one who has caused the problem.

It is vitally important that this section of Matthew's Gospel is not merely considered a "how-to" guide to relationships, with a law-oriented approach regarding what we must do and not do. Rather, it is a vivid description of the way life works when the Gospel of Christ is the operating principle. Verse 20 is the key. Our Lord says, "For where two or three are gathered in My name, there am I among them." Our Savior, who came to this world to be among us, not apart from us, brings peace between God and us. A natural result of this reconciliation is that we live in peace with others.

27 OCTOBER

Psalmody: Psalm 20
Additional Psalm: Psalm 25
Old Testament Reading:
Deuteronomy 29:1–29
New Testament Reading: Matthew 18:21–35

Prayer of the Day

O God, our refuge and strength, the author of all godliness, hear the devout prayers of Your Church, especially in times of persecution, and grant that what we ask in faith we may obtain; through Jesus Christ, our Lord, who lives and reigns with You and the Holy Spirit, one God, now and forever. (A77)

Meditation

We are accustomed to the idea that certain commodities are limited. We are told the world's natural resources are limited; we know from experience that our personal resources are limited also, both tangible goods like money as well as intangible attributes like patience and creativity. Yet Jesus tells us that one dimension of our life is not. Our Lord's answer to Peter's question shows us that forgiveness is boundless.

It is necessary for the supply of forgiveness to be inexhaustible because it is greatly needed. As yesterday's text reminded us, our relationships are not always problem-free. We sin against one another, and as Peter implies here by his inquiry about a "brother" who sins, this happens even between those who are bound together by the love of Christ. Strained and broken relationships in the Church should especially receive urgent attention.

The parable of the unforgiving servant gives us a proper perspective on the matter. The enormity of the servant's debt to his master compared to the almost microscopically insignificant debt this same man owed to a fellow servant is meant to strike us in the mind, heart, and conscience by its dramatic contrast.

For the redeemed child of God the message is clear: we have been forgiven much by an abundant and gracious Lord; therefore, the forgiveness we give in turn should never be considered impossible or even merely inconvenient. The master in the parable did not refinance the loan, extend its terms, or force the debtor to declare bankruptcy with a restructuring of the obligation to be paid later. Instead, in an almost unimaginable act of magnanimous generosity, he simply forgave it without qualification of any sort. To an even greater degree, this is what God does for each of us in Christ Jesus. There is no transgression too huge that cannot be erased by the sacrifice our Savior made on our behalf.

This Gospel truth then motivates us to be quick and eager to act in the same way to those indebted to us. We pray the Fifth Petition of the Lord's Prayer with regularity as a reminder of this divine transaction. Leaving forgiveness in arrears only moves us to spiritual insolvency. On the other hand, passing on a small portion of the unencumbered, generous grace we have received becomes for us a satisfying and joyous privilege. God's forgiveness in Christ comes to us and then naturally flows through us.

28 OCTOBER

St. Simon and St. Jude, Apostles

Psalmody: Psalm 127
Additional Psalm: Psalm 132
Old Testament Reading:
Deuteronomy 30:1–20
New Testament Reading: Matthew 19:1–15

Prayer of the Day

Almighty God, You chose Your servants Simon and Jude to be numbered among the glorious company of the apostles. As they were faithful and zealous in their mission, so may we with ardent devotion make known the love and mercy of our Lord and Savior Jesus Christ, who lives and reigns with You and the Holy Spirit, one God, now and forever. (F32)

St. Simon and St. Jude, Apostles

In the lists of the twelve apostles (Matthew 10:2–4; Mark 3:16–19; Luke 6:14–16; Acts 1:13), the tenth and eleventh places are occupied by Simon the Zealot (or "Cananaean") and by Jude (or "Judas," not Iscariot but "of James"), who was apparently known also as Thaddaeus. According to early Christian tradition, Simon and Jude journeyed together as missionaries to Persia, where they were martyred. It is likely for this reason, at least in part, that these two apostles are commemorated on the same day. Simon is not mentioned in the New Testament apart from the lists of the twelve apostles. Thus he is remembered and honored for the sake of his office, and thereby stands before us—in eternity, as in his life and ministry on earth— in the name and stead of Christ Jesus, our Lord. We give thanks to God for calling and sending Simon, along with Jude and all of the apostles, to preach and teach the Holy Gospel, to proclaim repentance and forgiveness, and to baptize in the name of the Father and of the Son and of the Holy Spirit (John 4:1–2; Matthew 10; 28:16–20; Luke 24:46–49).

Jude appears in John's Gospel (14:22) on the night of our Lord's betrayal and the beginning of His Passion, asking Jesus how it is that He will manifest Himself to the disciples but not to the world. The answer that Jesus gives to this question is a pertinent emphasis for this festival day: "If anyone loves Me, he will keep My Word, and My Father will love him, and We will come to him and make Our home with him" (John 14:23). Surely both Jude and Simon exemplified, in life and death, their love for Jesus and their faith in His Word. Not only are we thus strengthened in our Christian faith and life by their example, but, above all, we are encouraged by the faithfulness of the Lord in keeping His promise to them to bring them home to Himself in heaven. There they live with Him forever, where we shall someday join them.

Meditation

The attack on marriage is not a new phenomenon. Christians of every age need to be vigilant lest they disregard or distort this holy institution of God and follow a contemporary, worldly view of marriage rather than the scriptural understanding of this estate. The influence of Darwinian evolution has done more damage than we might concede. If God Himself did not create the universe by His divine word and if the Genesis account is to be regarded as a myth or parable, then Adam and Eve are no longer real, historical people, and marriage becomes a cultural convenience rather than a divine institution. Furthermore, if life itself evolved, as this worldview teaches, then marriage does, too, and we can be free to adjust it to meet the needs of individuals or society at large.

This is not the biblical understanding. In today's passage, our Lord refers to both the origins of the world and the origins of marriage, "Have you not read that He who created them from the beginning made them male and female?"

God established marriage as part of His created order. Not only does it benefit those who enter into it (and Jesus does concede that not all people will have a vocational calling to married life), but it also benefits society at large. This is the divine plan, not a cosmic accident or a human invention that can be altered or redefined.

God intended marriage to be a blessing to the world and especially to a husband and wife who are united in Him. The dialogue with the Pharisees shows us how sin has tainted this good gift. In asking about the permissibility of divorce, they display their evil intent to incriminate the Lord; but they also manifest a sinful understanding of marriage that is common to our day, showing that some do enter into it "inadvisedly or lightly," rather than "reverently, deliberately, and in accordance with the purposes for which it was instituted by God" (*LSB*, p. 275).

Marriage is, indeed, a sacred institution; it is a visible display of scriptural truths. Failed marriages point out the reality of sin. Successful marriages are a foretaste of the wedding feast of heaven. Divorce is tragic whenever it occurs, but it should not be stigmatized as an unforgivable sin. Our Savior always remains faithful to us, despite our unfaithfulness to Him. Marriage is a covenant of commitment pointing to the greatest love of all—that which Christ, the heavenly Bridegroom, has for His bride, the Church.

29 OCTOBER

Psalmody: Psalm 56
Additional Psalm: Psalm 58
Old Testament Reading:
Deuteronomy 31:1–29
New Testament Reading: Matthew 19:16–30

Prayer of the Day

O God, from whom all good proceeds, grant to us, Your humble servants, Your holy inspiration, that we may set our minds on the things that are right and, by Your merciful guiding, accomplish them; through Jesus Christ, Your Son, our Lord, who lives and reigns with You and the Holy Spirit, one God, now and forever. (A76)

Meditation

The grasp of greed is powerful and potentially deadly. It skews perspectives, misdirects priorities, and distorts relationships. Look at the man in this text. What arrogance it must take to approach the Savior of the world and say, "What good deed must I do to have eternal life?" This rich young man was so accustomed to achieving what he regarded as worldly se-

curity by his own efforts that it was natural for him to assume that he could do the same with his eternal security.

After hearing Jesus summarize the demands of the Law, the rich young man's question, "What do I still lack?" shows that he was beginning to understand his own deficiency. His foolish sense of self-sufficiency was now waning. Jesus delivered the knockout blow when He told the man to liquidate his assets for the benefit of the poor. This he obviously could not do. All ideas of saving himself were now totally obliterated. He "went away sorrowful." The Law had accused him, as it does us.

Like the disciples, this exchange makes us uncomfortable. Why? Because we also have "great possessions." Materialism has made its mark on our life. Even those of us with a modest lifestyle by current standards still have an abundance of worldly blessings when compared to most people of the world. We fall far short even of these disciples who left family, friends, and fishing nets for Jesus. Are we ready to renounce the entirety of our worldly goods and live in abject poverty? No. We are neither ready nor willing to do that, but one day we will. Death will ultimately leave us as beggars. St. Paul reminds us, "For we brought nothing into the world, and we cannot take anything out of the world" (1 Timothy 6:7).

The comforting assurance is that we are saved not because of our poverty but because of Christ's. No sacrifice we could ever make for anyone would be sufficient to earn our salvation, but the sacrifice He made for all people was fully adequate to win the world's salvation. Faith is the gift that grasps that sacrifice and makes it our own. Faith removes us from the stranglehold of greed and every other sin and puts us into the arms of Jesus. The disciples understood correctly when they asked, "Who then can be saved?" We fall far short of every demand of the Law, but the Good News of the Gospel is the treasure of our salvation.

30 OCTOBER

Psalmody: Psalm 90:7–17
Additional Psalm: Psalm 90
Old Testament Reading:
Deuteronomy 31:30–32:37
New Testament Reading: Matthew 20:1–16

Prayer of the Day

Lord God, heavenly Father, since we cannot stand before You relying on anything we have done, help us trust in Your abiding grace and live according to Your Word; through Jesus Christ, Your Son, our Lord, who lives and reigns with You and the Holy Spirit, one God, now and forever. (A78)

Meditation

Employers today would never follow the tactic of the owner of the vineyard in this parable. If they did not intend to give compensation that was commensurate to work, they certainly would be more discreet than this. Perhaps the wages would be placed in a sealed envelope and distributed without fanfare, and certainly the longest working would be paid first so they would be on their homeward way without knowing what the latecomers received. But this parable is not about fairness; it is about grace, and grace is not doled out clandestinely. It is lavishly given for the entire world to see.

Satan and our sinful flesh team up to cause us to grumble in a similar manner to the workers who went out early in the morning. As we consider our years as Christians or the extent of our service in the Church, it might be easy for us to pharisaically wonder how much better our congregation or community would be if everyone were like us. We resent that others don't seem to do their part or contribute their fair share. We self-righteously long for recognition or reward, as our inner self all the while becomes more agitated and wants to cry out,

"It's not fair!" Sentiments such as these betray a grave problem. Envy and resentment mean that we regard serving the Lord as a chore rather than a privilege.

Imagine the bitterness Jesus could have experienced, the grumbling He could have uttered. He left the Father's throne in heaven to come to earth. He kept God's laws perfectly in thought, word, and deed. Not once did He sin. He went about healing, preaching, and teaching the kingdom of God, showing kindness and love to all. What reward did He receive for His efforts? He was sentenced in a parody of justice and died the death of a common criminal. Yet He never uttered a word of complaint despite all the injustice and unfairness that were imposed upon Him.

Were it not for God's unfairness to Jesus, we would never have His grace. The injustice that the heavenly Father showed toward His own Son resulted in our salvation. Faith in the crucified and resurrected Savior gives us a new perspective. We are grateful for the joy and satisfaction of each day that He gives us to live under His grace and serve Him in the world. And we rejoice that others also receive this grace before it is too late.

31 OCTOBER

Reformation Day

Psalmody: Psalm 46
Additional Psalm: Psalm 115
Old Testament Reading:
Deuteronomy 32:28–52
Additional Reading: Deuteronomy 33:1–29
New Testament Reading: Matthew 20:17–34

Prayer of the Day

Almighty and gracious Lord, pour out Your Holy Spirit on Your faithful people. Keep us steadfast in Your grace and truth, protect and deliver us in times of temptation, defend us against all enemies, and grant to Your Church Your saving peace; through Jesus Christ, Your Son, our Lord, who lives and reigns with You and the Holy Spirit, one God, now and forever. (F33)

Reformation Day

On October 31, 1517, an Augustinian monk posted ninety-five statements for discussion on the door of the Castle Church door in Wittenberg, Germany. Dr. Martin Luther hoped that posting his theses would bring about an academic debate regarding repentance, the sale of indulgences, and other matters of concern within the Roman Catholic Church. However, Rome eventually excommunicated Luther, judging him to be a heretic. Luther's reforms, centered on the teaching that a believer is justified by grace through faith in Jesus Christ, sparked religious reforms not only in the German states but also in many European countries. In 1667, Elector John George II of Saxony standardized the custom of observing Luther's October 31 posting of the Ninety-five Theses.

Meditation

Perhaps we should hesitate a moment before we point an accusing finger at the mother of James and John. On the surface her request seems rather presumptuous and egotistic. But might not we do the same? Who could fault any father or mother for seeking the best for their children? The reason for her request, however, should rouse our suspicion and move us to search our consciences.

Granted, this mother came with at least a measure of humility. She did kneel in the pres-ence of Jesus and preface her request with a question regarding its permissibility. But that may have been the full extent of her modesty. The plea coming from her lips—but which the prompting of her two sons undoubtedly also fueled—was based on the pretentious and false assumption that James and John had earned this potential honor. Present in their minds might have been a list of the brothers' sacrifices for the Savior: they were among the first to be called as disciples; they left their former way of life; and they were always among the closest confidants of Jesus. Through it all, they had a reversed perspective. The matter of the utmost importance was not what they had done for Him, but what He was about to do for them.

An old adage warns, "Be careful what you ask for, because you might get it." The disciples asked to be near the Lord, not fully realizing that His kingdom comes only through the cross. They, like us, were enamored with glory, honor, and power. They wanted easy adulation and painless prestige; they were eager to share in Christ's realm, but oblivious to the suffering He repeatedly told them He would endure. They would drink His cup and suffer for His sake before glory came.

Here is the irony of salvation: the earthly mother who wanted the best for her sons did not understand that the divine Son to whom she was speaking had a heavenly Father who was willing to give His Son the worst. Jesus suffered the abandonment of His Father on the cross so that we might have the honor of God's favor. There may be moments in our lives when it seems that God does not favor us. Yet we need not despair. God wants the best for us. Because of Christ's redemptive work we will conquer in all trials and one day be seated with Him in the glory of His everlasting kingdom.

1 November

All Saints' Day

Psalmody: Psalm 150
Additional Psalm: Psalm 147
Old Testament Reading:
Deuteronomy 34:1–12
New Testament Reading: Matthew 21:1–22

Prayer of the Day

Almighty and everlasting God, You knit together Your faithful people of all times and places into one holy communion, the mystical body of Your Son, Jesus Christ. Grant us so to follow Your blessed saints in all virtuous and godly living that, together with them, we may come to the unspeakable joys You have prepared for those who love You; through Jesus Christ, our Lord, who lives and reigns with You and the Holy Spirit, one God, now and forever. (F34)

All Saints' Day

This feast is the most comprehensive of commemoration, encompassing the entire scope of that great cloud of witnesses with which we are surrounded (Hebrews 12:1). It holds before the eyes of faith that great multitude which no man can number: all the saints of God in Christ—from every nation, race, culture, and language—who have come "out of the great tribulation . . . who have washed their robes and made them white in the blood of the Lamb" (Revelation 7:9, 14). As such, it sets before us the full height and depth and breadth and length of our dear Lord's gracious salvation (Ephesians 3:17–19). It shares with Easter a celebration of the resurrection, since all those who have died with Christ Jesus have also been raised with Him (Romans 6:3–8). It shares with Pentecost a celebration of the ingathering of the entire Church catholic—in heaven and on earth, in all times and places—in the one Body of Christ, in the unity of the Spirit in the bond of peace. Just as we have all been called to the one hope that belongs to our call, "one Lord, one faith, one baptism, one God and Father of us all, who is over all and through all and in all" (Ephesians 4:4–6). And the Feast of All Saints shares with the final Sundays of the Church Year an eschatological focus on the life everlasting and a confession that "the sufferings of this present time are not worth comparing with the glory that is to be revealed to us" (Romans 8:18). In all of these emphases, the purpose of this feast is to fix our eyes upon Jesus, the author and perfecter of our faith, that we might not grow weary or fainthearted (Hebrews 12:2–3).

Meditation

Appearances can be deceiving. This section of Matthew's Gospel is labeled "The Triumphal Entry," but what really is triumphant about it? Had we been an uninformed bystander on the day of these events, we might have noticed the gathering of people and the ensuing commotion, yet what unfolded would seem odd in so many ways. The one being celebrated was not adorned in any special uniform with ribbons or medals indicating His rank or accomplishments. His mode of transport was not a stunning white steed but an ordinary beast of burden. He was not accompanied by an honor guard or a security detail. He was not insulated from the people, observing the proceedings from a distance; He was in the midst of the crowd, totally accessible to the ones acclaiming Him. Those who had come to pay homage were not dignitaries with special invitations but common Passover pilgrims from throughout the land.

The events that that followed Christ's triumphal entry would undoubtedly raise more questions about the peculiarity of these proceedings. This hero who was hailed with hosannas would soon be considered a criminal and be condemned to crucifixion. Where exactly is the majesty, the splendor, the pomp, the celebration, the triumph in all of this? We are, of course, not uninformed bystanders. We evaluate this event from a post-Easter perspective. Yet the strains and pains we experience as God's people in this world often distort or mask this perspective for our life. Personal circumstances might lead us to doubt the fact that we are the chosen and elect of God. "If I am really His child," we say, "why is He allowing this to happen to me?" Intellectually we know we are saints of God, yet when we don't experience triumphant lives, our faith is tested.

Scripture reminds us "through many tribulations we must enter the kingdom of God." The great All Saints' Day hymn asserts that we "feebly struggle" in the church militant. Life's circumstances for the Christian may have difficulties and sorrows, but there is always cause for thankfulness and celebration. The juxtaposition of All Saints' Day with this Holy Week reading holds before us the certainty that, because of Jesus, we will one day be among those "standing before the throne and before the Lamb, clothed in white robes, with palm branches in their hands" (Revelation 7:9). There is always triumph in Him—even now, but especially then. Appearances may be deceptive, but God's promises in Jesus never are.

2 November

Psalmody: Psalm 118:22–24
Additional Psalm: Psalm 118
Old Testament Reading: Jeremiah 1:1–19
New Testament Reading: Matthew 21:23–46

Prayer of the Day

Gracious God, You gave Your Son into the hands of sinful men who killed Him. Forgive us when we reject Your unfailing love, and grant us the fullness of Your salvation; through Jesus Christ, Your Son, our Lord, who lives and reigns with You and the Holy Spirit, one God, now and forever. (A80)

Meditation

Do actions (or inactions) really speak louder than words? Such is the case with the characters in our Lord's parable of the two sons. The first son disregarded his father's authority and abruptly told him that he would not work in his father's vineyard. Later, however, he had a change of heart and did serve his father. His actions spoke louder than his words. This was a picture of the tax collectors, prostitutes, and other despised members of society whom the religious authorities thought had no place in the kingdom of heaven.

We also see ourselves in that first son. The message from Jesus is that no person is ever too bad to be loved and forgiven. More important than the terrible things we may have done in the past is the forgiveness we now have in the present. Sin is not to be celebrated, continued, or ignored; it is to be acknowledged, addressed, and forsaken. The Holy Spirit does this by working contrition and repentance in our lives so that a spiritual U-turn takes place.

The second son took a U-turn also, but headed in the wrong direction. He promised obedience but failed to deliver it. Jesus used him to represent the religious authorities who were challenging His authority. They were smug and comfortable in their positions, thinking they already possessed Fatherly favor by their own merit. They honored God with their lips, but their hearts were far from Him.

We share the familial traits of that second son as well. The faith we confess is not always evident in our daily conduct. While piously promising faithfulness to God, we do not follow through with total consistency. In the Divine Service we ask God to "forgive us, renew us, and lead us, so that we may delight in Your will and walk in Your ways" (*LSB*, p. 151), but our sinful misdeeds translate this as, "Forget us, release us, and leave us, so that we may delight in our will and walk in our ways." Our inactions speak louder than our words. Whether we are disobedient and then pious, or pious and then disobedient, whether a tax collector or a temple official, we all need rescue from our sinful situation. That is given to us by a third Son, not explicitly mentioned in the parable, but the One speaking the parable. There were no second thoughts, U-turns, or inconsistencies on His part. Both the words and actions of Jesus speak loudly to us of God's love and salvation.

3 NOVEMBER

Psalmody: Psalm 15
Additional Psalm: Psalm 26
Old Testament Reading: Jeremiah 3:6–4:2
New Testament Reading: Matthew 22:1–22

Prayer of the Day

Almighty God, You invite us to trust in You for our salvation. Deal with us not in the severity of Your judgment but by the greatness of Your mercy; through Jesus Christ, Your Son, our Lord, who lives and reigns with You and the Holy Spirit, one God, now and forever. (A81)

Meditation

An invitation to a wedding rarely leaves us apathetic. Either it arouses great eagerness as we joyfully anticipate joining the celebration, or else it evokes a dreaded frustration about how to tactfully excuse ourselves from the event. Our Lord's parable of the wedding feast demonstrates that there were these antithetical reactions to Him. At this point in the Gospels opposition to Jesus was mounting. So, too, were the pressures on those who followed Him.

This teaching moves us to examine our spiritual condition and confront the obstacles to faith in our Savior that have been erected by Satan, the world, and our sinful flesh. The verb in verse five is an especially harsh, but true, indictment of the Law upon us. The original Greek text is translated as "they paid no attention," but this is more than just a lack of focus and concentration; there are strong overtones of neglect and even disdain implicit in this word as well.

Does that describe our life as a Christian on occasion? Regrettably, it does. Like those who spurned the invitation and went off to their farms, businesses, and daily routines, we sometimes separate discipleship from our everyday tasks. The hurry and flurry of worldly responsibilities rob us of the joy of belonging to the heavenly Bridegroom. We think that there are more urgent needs than worshiping and serving Him, reasoning that we can do it later. We become so concerned about daily life that we lose our focus on the One who gives it to us. Procrastination on spiritual matters leads to the absence of Jesus from our lives—by our neglect, not His.

The discussion of the wedding garment restores our focus and refreshes us with Gospel promise. We have this garment already now by virtue of our Baptism. The king in the parable announced that the wedding feast was fully prepared. Christ fulfilled these hosting responsibilities by His life and work on our behalf. He adorns us for the feast and makes us His honored guests. He "has clothed me with the garments of salvation; He has covered me with the robe of righteousness" (Isaiah 61:10). "For as many of you as were baptized into Christ have put on Christ" (Galatians 3:27). This baptismal garment serves as our "wedding clothes," but also as our "work clothes." We never take it off, for we can never truly separate our lives in Christ and our lives in the world. Our entire lives are joyfully lived as His children.

4 NOVEMBER

Psalmody: Psalm 110
Additional Psalm: Psalm 108
Old Testament Reading: Jeremiah 5:1–19
New Testament Reading: Matthew 22:23–46

Prayer of the Day

O God, You have commanded us to love You above all things and our neighbors as ourselves. Grant us the Spirit to think and do what is pleasing in Your sight, that our faith in You may never waver and our love for one another may not falter; through Jesus Christ, Your Son, our Lord, who lives and reigns with You and the Holy Spirit, one God, now and forever. (A83)

Meditation
Not every question is asked merely to gather information. Whether the setting is a classroom, a press conference, or the family table, the intent of some inquiries is to make a statement, challenge authority, or voice hostile disagreement. Such conversation is grounded in malice rather than innocence.

The adversaries of Jesus launched their pointed and deceptive questions in a continuous barrage on Tuesday of Holy Week in the temple courts of Jerusalem. This vigorous exchange was not a dialogue at all. The Herodians, Pharisees, and Sadducees were not seeking greater theological insight on questions

of taxes, the resurrection, or the Law; their purpose was to uphold their point of view and prove Jesus wrong.

As we face the varied challenges of life in this world, questions arise in our hearts and minds. We look to the Lord. We come to His Word for answers. This is right and proper. But as we look and come, we must examine our motives and properly discern the spirit that is at work within us. As sinful human beings we are prone to come like these adversaries—not truly seeking guidance and truth; rather, we inquire with the desire to ensnare the Lord in an error or contradiction. We approach with preconceived answers already formulated, foolishly hoping to prove Him wrong. We are blindly and erroneously confident of personally possessing the correct understanding and interpretation; He is the one who needs to be informed, not us.

This is the spirit of the latter days. We come not to receive His teaching, but to challenge it or ultimately reject it in favor of our own interpretation of the matter. Questioning Jesus thus becomes a scoff at the truth rather than a search for the truth. We deserve to hear the same harsh rebuke that Jesus uttered on this day, "You are wrong, because you know neither the Scriptures nor the power of God."

Such an approach is doomed to futility. The authority of our Lord's Word and the veracity of His teaching may be challenged, but it will always prevail. His victory in this verbal battle was so stunning that the text says no one dared to ask Him any more questions.

Our Lord still invites questions, so let them come. But let the questions come in sincerity rather than hypocrisy; let them be asked in a spirit of genuine humility and faith as we learn from Him and grow in His Word. He is ready to answer because He is the answer.

5 November

Psalmody: Psalm 38:9–22
Additional Psalm: Psalm 38
Old Testament Reading: Jeremiah 7:1–29
New Testament Reading: Matthew 23:1–12

Prayer of the Day

Merciful and gracious Lord, You cause Your Word to be proclaimed in every generation. Stir up our hearts and minds by Your Holy Spirit that we may receive this proclamation with humility and finally be exalted at the coming of Your Son, our Savior, Jesus Christ, who lives and reigns with You and the Holy Spirit, one God, now and forever. (A84)

Meditation

Hypocrisy is universally detested. People may shrug their shoulders with resigned disappointment or indifference when a celebrity or political leader engages in sinful behavior. But when that same celebrity or political leader has previously pontificated against the very sin they have committed, the reaction of the public when the false piety is uncovered turns to angry disgust. It is not easy to tolerate a person who fails to practice what he preaches.

Our Lord, too, detests hypocrisy. In today's reading we have the beginning of an extended commentary on the matter. In these verses our Lord speaks to His disciples as well as to a larger gathering of people about the pretentiousness of the scribes and Pharisees. In tomorrow's reading He will use stronger and more pointed language. He is not hesitant to indict these charlatans for this loathsome and grievous sin. Earlier in the Gospel He had linked them with the prophecy of Isaiah, "These people honor Me with their lips, but their heart is far from Me" (Matthew 15:8). The negative example of the scribes and Phari-

sees can instruct us, for the abhorrent sin of hypocrisy frequently plagues our walk of faith. Regrettably, the actions of our lives do not always harmonize with the profession of our lips. We have unsuccessfully tried to live a double life. The lie will always be exposed. We might dupe others and even ourselves, but we will never deceive our perceptive Lord. The hoax of hypocrisy is both delusional and destructive. It lulls us into a false and distorted sense of self-righteousness that—left unchecked—forfeits faith in the righteousness won for us by Christ.

Christ is everything that pharisaical hypocrites (including us) are not. They "tie heavy burdens"; His yoke is easy because He bears our burden (Matthew 11:28). They do their deeds to be seen by others; He shunned the spotlight, often telling the beneficiaries of His miracles to be quiet about what He had done. They love the places of honor; He was "numbered with the transgressors" (Isaiah 53:12). They strive for exaltation; He came as a humble servant.

While our Savior detests hypocrisy, He never detests us. Instead, His forgiving grace aligns the disparities in our lives. While the watching world waits for inconsistent Christians to give another example of hypocrisy, Jesus empowers us both to confess confidently His name and to live boldly before all people as His disciples.

6 November

Psalmody: Psalm 118:25–29
Additional Psalm: Psalm 118
Old Testament Reading: Jeremiah 8:18–9:12
New Testament Reading: Matthew 23:13–39

Prayer of the Day

Lord God, heavenly Father, the holy city of Jerusalem rejected the prophets and stoned those who were sent to her, killing Your Son, the final prophet sent to redeem her and the whole world from their sins. Through His innocent suffering and death, gather Your Church into His loving embrace that we may truly be the Body of Christ; through Jesus Christ, our Lord. (1103)

Meditation

In addition to the words, the pitch, tone, and inflection of a person's voice are all immediate indications of the gravity of the message that is being conveyed. Nonverbal cues also amplify a communication. Even without audio or video footage of this encounter, we are aware that this is a strong and impassioned message from Jesus. If we could listen to it, we would undoubtedly detect the intensity in His voice. If we could see the exchange, the gestures and body language of our Lord would also certainly convey the measure of His emotions.

Yet it is also abundantly clear from the words of Holy Scripture alone that Jesus is not speaking these words with delight. They serve as a stern, but compassionate warning, a final effort to call sinners to repentance. They are truthful but not hateful. Jesus speaks them not out of delight but with great sadness. Even with such a long laundry list of transgressions, the Son of God stands ready to forgive and restore the scribes and Pharisees. After all, He has been sending them "prophets and wise men and scribes." His intent was not to write them off as unworthy of salvation. These people, too, were offered His redeeming grace, but they rejected it. This moves the Lord to deep and profound lament.

The woes Jesus pronounced on the scribes and the Pharisees stand in great contrast to the beatitudes spoken to the disciples earlier in the Gospel. In this juxtaposition we see the same Lord but two different groups of people. Those who receive His benediction delight in following Him because they understand by faith that He has rescued them from a hopeless condition on account of their sins. Those who receive His warning find perverted joy in following their own selfish desires without any recognition of their need for repentance and forgiveness. They will bring upon themselves the judgment He was hoping they would avert.

So we insert ourselves into this drama. Jesus desires to gather us under the wings of His mercy as a hen gathers its brood. We may stubbornly shun His advances, but He persists with the desire to reach us. In this world we read and apply His words from the pages of Holy Scripture. But one day we will see His face, hear the tone of His voice, and see the nonverbal communication He uses. It behooves us to take seriously the woes now so we will receive the beatitudes then.

7 NOVEMBER

Psalmody: Psalm 121
Additional Psalm: Psalm 135
Old Testament Reading: Jeremiah 11:1–23
Additional Reading: Jeremiah 12:1–19:15
New Testament Reading: Matthew 24:1–28

Prayer of the Day

Lord Jesus, as You were lifted up on the cross, the entire world experienced birth pains as the cosmos was rocked as Your death gave birth to a new creation. Focus our eyes on Your holy cross that we may see it as a tree of life preparing us for Your final coming in judgment as the Son of Man; for You live and reign with the Holy Spirit, one God, now and forever. (1104)

Meditation

Forecasting is not the exclusive of domain of meteorologists. Economists, politicians, and others all attempt to predict the future. Christians certainly should have an interest in mankind's unfolding destiny from a spiritual perspective. Scripture teaches us much about the end times, giving us a proper mindset as we explore these questions. God's Word shows us that we are in the end times already now. In this section of Matthew's Gospel Christ uses the impending judgment of Jerusalem as a telescoping frame of reference for the events that will occur immediately prior to His second coming. While we might like more specificity, we can be satisfied and comforted with the information He does give us. His words are not merely an educated guess or a likely probability. This is direct information from the Son of God. It can be trusted as the truth.

Jesus reminds us that the future will bring a time of great distress. The deceitful presumptions of Darwinian evolutionary philosophy have convinced us that our world is on an upward climb, not a downward spiral as Jesus describes here. But while standards of living, life expectancy, and new scientific discoveries may be accelerating and improving life around the world, the spiritual condition of mankind is not improving. The Lord gives us sobering information that in the last days many will turn away from the faith. Those who remain faithful, He says, will face persecution and even death on account of Him.

These grim thoughts certainly shake us from spiritual complacency. Jesus gives us this forecast so we can know where to find help, hope, and strength. His account of unfolding events not only includes a prediction of days of great trial and affliction, but also the promise of great relief. This unprecedented time of distress will be "cut short" for the sake of the elect. While God's people will not be immune from present and future tribulations, they will always be shielded in every tribulation. Ultimately the news for us is good, not glum. Our Savior always has the best interest of His people in mind. He is the God-man who entered this fallen world, which is sputtering toward finality. He promises "the one who endures to the end will be saved." He has already done that for us. Salvation and endurance both come from Him. He faithfully endured temptations, injustices, and suffering, so that with faith in Him we might do the same.

8 NOVEMBER

Johannes von Staupitz, Luther's Father Confessor

Psalmody: Psalm 143
Additional Psalm: Psalm 144
Old Testament Reading: Jeremiah 20:1–18
New Testament Reading: Matthew 24:29–51

Prayer of the Day

Almighty, everlasting God, for our many sins we justly deserve eternal condemnation. In Your mercy, You sent Your dear Son, our Lord Jesus Christ, who won for us forgiveness of sins and everlasting salvation. Grant us a true confession that, dead to sin, we may hear the sweet words of Absolution from our confessor as Luther heard them from his pastor, Johannes von Staupitz, and be released from all our sin; through Jesus Christ our Lord, who lives and reigns with You and the Holy Spirit, one God, now and forever. (1105)

Johann von Staupitz, Luther's Father Confessor

Johann von Staupitz (ca. 1469–1524), vicar-general of the Augustinian Order in Germany and friend of Martin Luther, was born in

Saxony. He studied at the universities in Leipzig and Cologne and served on the faculty at Cologne. In 1503, he was called by Frederick the Wise to serve as dean of the theological faculty at the newly founded University of Wittenberg. There Staupitz encouraged Luther to attain a doctorate in theology and appointed Luther as his successor as professor of Bible at the university. During Luther's early struggles to understand God's grace, it was Staupitz who counseled Luther to focus on Christ and not on himself.

Meditation

The phrase "business as usual" can be complimentary or critical. In the former case it refers to a person with such a high degree of discipline and motivation that nothing deters him or her from the task at hand. In the latter case, it refers to a person who continues down a tired, worn, inefficient, or unethical path and lacks either the desire or the ability to change. The determining factors for whether "business as usual" is used as praise or condemnation are the nature of the "business" that is being done and the mindset of the person doing it.

When talking about the coming of the Son of Man, Jesus references the days of Noah, describing people who were "eating and drinking, marrying and giving in marriage." These activities are not intrinsically evil; however, the mindset that accompanied them was. Wicked people of the antediluvian era were so tyrannized by sin that they focused on worldly pursuits to the exclusion of repentance and faith, thus failing to understand the coming wrath of God. For them, "business as usual" was spiritually fatal. But during these same years Noah had his own daily routine for building the ark. For him, however, "business as usual" was salvific, not condemnatory. Likewise, Jesus goes on to describe two men in the field and two women at the mill. Both of the men and both of the women were going about their regular activities and vocations, but one of each pair

was included in the kingdom while the other of each pair was excluded.

The lesson for us here is that when Christ's "business" is our "business," we will never be caught unawares by His coming. Faith in Him is not a commodity that can be separated into "sacred" or "secular" realms; it permeates our entire existence. More important than knowing the exact day and hour of His return is having a continuous habit of faithful readiness that is integrated into our daily life. We are not called upon to sell our earthly possessions and await His return while clad in white sheets on mountaintops. We can be vigilant even as we pursue our earthly roles and schedules. Our vocation is to be His disciple within the station of life where He places us. We live in a state of grace, and as our Savior nurtures our faith through His means of grace, we are ready for anything. It's all part of the routine.

9 NOVEMBER

Martin Chemnitz (birth), Pastor and Confessor

Psalmody: Psalm 147:1–11
Additional Psalm: Psalm 147
Old Testament Reading: Jeremiah 22:1–23
New Testament Reading: Matthew 25:1–13

Prayer of the Day

Lord God, heavenly Father, through the teaching of Martin Chemnitz, You prepare us for the coming of Your Son to lead home His Bride, the Church, that with all the company of the redeemed we may finally enter into His eternal wedding feast; through the same Jesus Christ, our Lord, who lives and reigns with You and the Holy Spirit, one God, now and forever. (1106)

Martin Chemnitz, Pastor and Confessor

Aside from Martin Luther, Martin Chemnitz (1522–1586) is regarded as the most important theologian in the history of the Lutheran Church. Chemnitz combined a penetrating intellect and an almost encyclopedic knowledge of Scripture and the Church Fathers with a genuine love for the Church. When various doctrinal disagreements broke out after Luther's death in 1546, Chemnitz determined to give himself fully to the restoration of unity in the Lutheran Church. He became the leading spirit and principal author of the 1577 Formula of Concord, which settled the doctrinal disputes on the basis of Scripture and largely succeeded in restoring unity among Lutherans. Chemnitz also authored the four-volume *Examination of the Council of Trent* (1565–73), in which he rigorously subjected the teachings of this Roman Catholic council to the judgment of Scripture and the ancient Church Fathers. The Examination became the definitive Lutheran answer to the Council of Trent, as well as a thorough exposition of the faith of the Augsburg Confession. A theologian and a churchman, Chemnitz was truly a gift of God to the Church.

Meditation

"The door was shut." There is such a sense of emphatic finality in that statement and in the mental image it evokes. The words of the text literally convey a stern message of permanence, "The door was shut and would stay that way." Open doors are a picture of invitation and new possibilities; closed doors are emblematic of squandered opportunities and irreversible rejection.

The rejection implicit in the image of the closed door in this parable does not originate from the One who speaks these words, who called Himself "the door" (John 10:9); rather, such rejection is exercised by those who foolishly fail to heed these words. The midnight cry to meet the bridegroom would be heard by all. Sound waves do not discriminate—neither does the Savior. He desires that everyone have a place at His banquet celebration.

Just as the Savior does not exclude any in His call to the wedding banquet, neither does the devil, the world, and the sinful flesh insulate anyone from their desire that people spurn the wedding call. Both the wise and foolish virgins "became drowsy and slept." This can be seen as a description of the danger facing humans on this side of eternity rather than an indictment of any potential wedding participants. That indictment, judgment, and sentence comes in the image of the closed door. The fact that distinguished the two groups of virgins was their lack of preparation.

This text has an eschatological emphasis. We must remember, however, that end time consequences are shaped by present time beliefs and practices. The lack of preparation demonstrated by the foolish virgins portrays the procrastinating neglect some people in this world have toward the Lord of all times. While our temporal life endures, He gives us countless opportunities to turn to Him. There will be some who gain entrance into His kingdom "just in the nick of time," like the contrite thief on the cross or the workers who were enlisted for labor late in the day. But ultimately the day of salvation will dawn, and then there will be no extension of grace. Even though the heavenly Bridegroom exercises extreme patience in allowing all people the opportunity to repent of their sinful errors, the time will come when the banquet must proceed. When the kingdom is consummated, the door will be shut. What a clarion call this is for us to constantly nurture the faith we have been given. Midnight is closer than we might think.

10 NOVEMBER

Psalmody: Psalm 24
Additional Psalm: Psalm 25:12–22
Old Testament Reading: Jeremiah 23:1–20
New Testament Reading: Matthew 25:14–30

Prayer of the Day

Almighty and ever-living God, You have given exceedingly great and precious promises to those who trust in You. Dispel from us the works of darkness and grant us to live in the light of Your Son, Jesus Christ, that our faith may never be found wanting; through the same Jesus Christ, our Lord, who lives and reigns with You and the Holy Spirit, one God, now and forever. (A86)

Meditation

Skills or abilities wane and deteriorate after prolonged periods of disuse. Financial wealth must also be invested wisely and put to work lest it depreciate. There is truth to the expression "use it or lose it." The talents described in today's parable are sums of money rather than particular proficiencies, but the principle still applies. Our heavenly Father desires that His resources be engaged for use, not shelved, hidden, or wasted.

As opposed to the parable of the minas in Luke 19, where all the servants are given responsibility for an equal amount of money, here the three servants are entrusted with varying quantities. Although one must be careful not to miss the central thought of a parable for the details, God's Holy Spirit reminds us through this apparent triviality that every person is uniquely gifted by Him. That is His design and desire. No two of us are exactly alike.

While God's gifts may be apportioned differently, the satisfaction that comes from using them in His service is not. It is uniform in its completeness and permeates every servant's life, whether he holds a position of prominence or performs a task that few desire and fewer still notice. Neither the five-talent nor the two-talent servant returned to the master with any suggestions or complaints. They did not bring along an agent to negotiate a profit sharing agreement or claim a percentage of the gain for themselves. Their total focus was on serving their benefactor faithfully. They were invited to "enter into the joy of your master," but joy had already been a benefit of their service. Now, however, their joy would be greater.

The third servant did not regard serving his master as a privilege and derived no joy from it. He described the master as "hard," showing that his perception of their relationship was distorted from its inception. Whenever we see our God as a tyrant that demands to be satisfied rather than a Father who desires our love, we fall into the sinful error of this servant.

Ultimately, the performance this parable emphasizes is not ours but Christ's. Because of Jesus, the "Good and Faithful Servant" par excellence, serving the Lord is for us a blessing rather than a burden. By the power of the Holy Spirit, our Savior transforms us from slaves or servants to sons and then to heirs (Galatians 4:1–7). "Use it or lose it?" God used His Son to serve us so that we would not be lost eternally.

11 NOVEMBER

Martin of Tours, Pastor

Psalmody: Psalm 143:1–10
Additional Psalm: Psalm 105:1–10
Old Testament Reading: Jeremiah 23:21–40
New Testament Reading: Matthew 25:31–46

Prayer of the Day

Lord God of hosts, Your servant Martin the soldier embodied the spirit of sacrifice. He became a bishop in Your Church to defend the catholic faith. Give us grace to follow in his steps so that when our Lord returns we may be clothed with the baptismal garment of righteousness and peace; through Jesus Christ, our Lord, who lives and reigns with You and the Holy Spirit, one God, now and for ever. (1107)

Martin of Tours, Pastor

Born into a pagan family in what is now Hungary around the year AD 316, Martin grew up in Lombardy (Italy). Coming to the Christian faith as a young person, he began a career in the Roman army. But sensing a call to a church vocation, Martin left the military and became a monk, affirming that he was "Christ's soldier." Eventually, Martin was named bishop of Tours in western Gaul (France). He is remembered for his simple lifestyle and his determination to share the Gospel throughout rural Gaul. Incidentally, on St. Martin's Day in 1483, the one-day-old son of Hans and Margarette Luther was baptized and given the name "Martin" Luther.

Meditation

Most people have an interest in—perhaps even a fascination with—the legal and judicial system. This text is a courtroom scene laden with high drama and all the elements associated with such a setting, yet containing remarkable variances from the usual process.

In the standard legal procedure of this world the outcome of a case rests on its merit, which is often a matter of intense and prolonged deliberation prior to the verdict being reached. Evidence needs to be examined, and questions need to be asked. Do the deeds committed by the accused merit an indictment or an acquittal?

Some non-Christians may take false comfort in this text by reasoning that, even though they do not believe in Jesus, they still perform deeds of mercy similar to those listed here. By all external appearances some unbelievers may, in fact, do just as much for those in need as any follower of Jesus. This, they hope, will be a factor in the determination of their fate on Judgment Day. But look closely at what happens in this court. The separation of the sheep and goats occurs before, not after, the listing of their deeds of mercy. Merit is not a consideration in this judicial decision. Here the order is reversed because questions about our worthiness have no role in the matter of salvation.

Merit is related to motive. The righteous ones were surprised when they were told by the Son of Man that they were really serving Him. Their motives were pure. They were not performing their acts for purposes of recognition or reward. They didn't say, "Yes, I was hoping You would notice." They were simply doing what they couldn't help but do.

This Judgment Day courtroom scene differs so much from worldly standards of jurisprudence because it is entirely framed by God's grace. Merit and motive are both tied to mercy, which is always the operating principle in the lives of God's people. We will show mercy because we have received it. We will reach out to the least, lost, and helpless of the world because that was our spiritual condition before we were rescued by our Savior. We are now and forever numbered with the sheep at God's right hand because He was the sacrificial lamb who offered His life in our place. Jesus stands the judicial system on its head. Through faith in Him our sins are forgiven, we are declared righteous, and our misdeeds are purged from the record. Only fruits of faith, empowered by Him, remain.

12 NOVEMBER

Psalmody: Psalm 137
Additional Psalm: Psalm 130
Old Testament Reading: Jeremiah 25:1–18
New Testament Reading: Matthew 26:1–19

Prayer of the Day

Eternal God, merciful Father, You have appointed Your Son as judge of the living and the dead. Enable us to wait for the day of His return with our eyes fixed on the kingdom prepared for Your own from the foundation of the world; through Jesus Christ, our Lord, who lives and reigns with You and the Holy Spirit, one God, now and forever. (A87)

Meditation

On the surface, today's reading contains what might appear to be four disparate incidents. The action in the Gospel is now accelerating at a rapid pace as its climax—the crucifixion and resurrection of Jesus—nears. The thematic element uniting these twenty verses is the concept of value and the process of appraisal that leads to an estimation of the worth of a person, a relationship, an object, or an event.

The chief priests and elders put a high value on their privileged position. They noticed the sense of expectation and fervor exhibited by the people regarding Jesus, and they considered Him a threat. They wanted to devalue Jesus in the eyes of His admirers as well as permanently removing Him as a future rival. They were savvy enough, however, to realize that this dastardly deed must be done later, lest the public uproar during the Feast disrupt their agenda. Judas Iscariot, whose name ever since has been synonymous with dishonor and betrayal, was enlisted in their wicked cause. In a candid picture of his crassness, this fallen disciple actually put a bounty on the life of Jesus. His former master was worth only thirty pieces of silver to him, little more than the wages of a day laborer for several months.

Interposed between these two sad scenes is the remarkable act of a woman who appraised Jesus as of much greater worth. She lavishly anointed Him with a flask of ointment that is described as "very expensive." In the parallel account related in John 12, Judas leads the outcry against this extraordinary act of devotion and generosity, but in his Gospel, Matthew hastens to add that the rest of the disciples also disapproved. Despite the indignation of His closest associates, Jesus praises the woman's action and uses it as an object lesson for His approaching Passion.

In the events of Christ's Passion all those who seek to devalue the Lord—including you and me—witness the high esteem He holds for us and the high price He is willing to pay for our redemption. As Peter and the Catechism declare, Jesus Christ has "purchased and won me from all sins, from death, and from the power of the devil; not with gold or silver, but with His holy, precious blood and with His innocent suffering and death" We who are spiritually bankrupt by ourselves have received the extravagance of God's grace in Him. God's high appraisal of sinful humanity is always evident at the cross.

13 NOVEMBER

Psalmody: Psalm 116:12–19
Additional Psalm: Psalm 50:7–15
Old Testament Reading: Jeremiah 26:1–19
New Testament Reading: Matthew 26:20–35
Additional Reading: Revelation 13:1–18

Prayer of the Day

O Lord, in this wondrous Sacrament You have left us a remembrance of Your passion. Grant that we may so receive the sacred mystery of Your body and blood that the fruits of Your redemption may continually be manifest in us; for You live and reign with the Father and the Holy Spirit, one God, now and forever. (L32)

Meditation

Understanding the context and setting of an event gives us additional insight into its nature and significance. Such is the case with the Lord's Supper. Jesus meets with His disciples on Thursday of Holy Week to celebrate the Passover at that place and time, transforming it into a sacrament for the Church of all places and times. The context and setting of this event is deliberate. Yes, there was the connection between this feast and His life. He would be the "Passover Lamb" who was sacrificed (1 Corinthians 5:7). But why this Passover and not one in an earlier year of our Lord's ministry?

The answer to that question is embedded in the *Verba*, literally, "the words," pronounced on every occasion the Supper is celebrated. The Words of Institution begin with this phrase, "Our Lord Jesus Christ, on the night when He was betrayed . . ." The Savior established this blessed meal of grace within the context of human sin. In the most sinister of those sins, Judas would betray Him. Peter would soon deny him, and the rest of the lot would be less than vigilant and faithful. All in all, their performance was dismal; it had to deeply disappoint and hurt Jesus. Yet, while most other people whose associates acted in such a manner might have shown their disgust and walked away, Jesus lovingly invites them to sit and dine with Him. This is fitting and proper because this supper is not an awards banquet recognizing human achievement, but a hospital meal given to patients who are critically ill and desperately need help.

The context of the Lord's Supper emphasizes human sin and divine compassion. We do not deserve the gifts He gives us here. In a stunning paradox, those who are worthy of receiving this life-giving meal are ones who recognize their sinful unworthiness to be in His presence. Because this very body and blood of the Savior is given "for the forgiveness of sins," we come, not to be rewarded for our successes, but to be pardoned for our failures. As we approach the table in humility, we are startled to see that our Host has humbled Himself for us. The Master becomes the servant, even washing the feet of those who come to Him. He sacrifices Himself, offering His true, physical body and blood as the food which passes over our lips, into our mouths, and out through our lives. Furthermore, He holds before us the certain hope of a future place at the everlasting banquet in the kingdom of heaven.

14 NOVEMBER

Emperor Justinian, Christian Ruler and Confessor of Christ

Psalmody: Psalm 53
Additional Psalm: Psalm 55:12–19
Old Testament Reading: Jeremiah 29:1–19
New Testament Reading: Matthew 26:36–56
Additional Reading: Revelation 14:1–20

Prayer of the Day

Lord God, heavenly Father, through the governance of Christian leaders like Emperor Justinian, Your name is freely confessed in our nation and throughout the world. Grant that we may continue to choose trustworthy leaders who serve You faithfully in our generation and make wise decisions that contribute to the general welfare of Your people; through Jesus Christ, our Lord. (1108)

Emperor Justinian, Christian Ruler and Confessor of Christ

Justinian was emperor of the East from AD 527 to 565, when the Roman Empire was in decline. With his beautiful and capable wife, Theodora, he restored splendor and majesty to the Byzantine court. During his reign, the empire experienced a renaissance, due in large part to his ambition, intelligence, and strong religious convictions. Justinian also attempted to bring unity to a divided Church. He was a champion of orthodox Christianity and sought agreement among the parties in the Christological controversies of the day as the groups disputed the relation between the divine and human natures in the person of Christ. The Fifth Ecumenical Council in Constantinople in AD 533 was held during his reign and addressed this dispute. Justinian died in his eighties without having accomplished his desire to forge an empire that was firmly Christian and orthodox.

Meditation

At critical junctures in life we often stop for moments of reflection before moving forward. On occasion the pause gives way to fearful hesitation, and initial plans are rejected in favor of the status quo. For the Christian these moments are always packaged in prayer as we look to our loving Father for guidance and direction.

To a certain extent the account of our Lord in Gethsemane seems out of character. Prior to this He had talked about His impending arrest and death with confidence and a courageous resignation. The picture that Scripture presents up until this moment is that of a person at peace with His coming fate. But now, the text says, Jesus "began to be sorrowful and troubled." His equanimity and resolve seem to have disappeared. What are we to make of the terrible anguish He experiences here? What does it mean when He says, "not as I will?" Is this an indication that He has hesitations about the task that God had called Him to perform and is looking for a way out? No, absolutely not.

It is vital to remember that this text shows us how the divine and human natures of Christ are united in one person. Moments of hesitation in our lives come because we are uncertain about what the future may bring. The God-man Jesus could look to the future and understand the full horror of what was about to happen. Rather than seeing His prayers in Gethsemane as a manifestation of indecisiveness, we need to understand them as part of the bitter woe He was to experience as our substitute. No mere mortal could have withstood this extreme test; had we been in this place, we would have run away in abject fear. But Jesus persevered and conquered with discipline, self-control, and obedience to His Father's will. Simply put, He suffered while His disciples slept.

That contrast between us continues. So, too, do His intercessions for us. We are sinners; He is the Savior. Because we are often weak, indecisive, and cowardly, especially in spiritual matters, we need the ongoing forgiveness and advocacy of the crucified, risen, and ascended Lord. His alertness and attention to the task continues. He drank from the cup of suffering so we could receive an overflowing cup of blessing. He anguished in the Garden of Gethsemane so we can rejoice forever in the restored Garden of Paradise. Because He fulfilled the Father's will, we can pray the same petition in our lives.

15 NOVEMBER

Psalmody: Psalm 51:10–19
Additional Psalm: Psalm 51
Old Testament Reading: Jeremiah 30:1–24
New Testament Reading: Matthew 26:57–75
Additional Reading: Revelation 15:1–8

Prayer of the Day

Lord Jesus Christ, the temple of Your body was destroyed on the cross and three days later raised from the dead and exalted to the right hand of the Father. Visit us now with this same body, that we may not deny that we know You but in faith hear in our ears Your life-giving voice and receive on our lips Your very body and blood to strengthen us in times of temptation; for You live and reign with the Father and the Holy Spirit, one God, now and forever. (1109)

Meditation

It is sometimes said that the only person who plans to fail is the person who fails to plan. Today's text shows the folly of that assertion. Neither careful preparations nor pious intentions guarantee results, especially in the spiritual realm. Our sinful weakness must be factored into the equation.

It would be interesting to know what the true intentions of Peter were as he made his way from Gethsemane to the courtyard of the high priest. After the arrest of Jesus on the Mount of Olives the rest of the disciples had deserted Him and fled for their lives. Peter, to his credit, showed at least limited courage in following the mob, albeit "at a distance." Perhaps he had hoped to implement a dramatic rescue if an opportunity presented itself. This would not be out of character for him, considering his impetuous behavior with the sword in the garden (John 18:10). Previously, after his bold confession of faith identifying Jesus as the Christ, Peter had insisted that the capture and crucifixion of Jesus would not occur (Matthew 16:22). Possibly even now at this late and desperate moment he could take action to avert that outcome. Whatever his intentions might have been, it is safe to assume that he never imagined his eventual actions would be

as shameful as they were. If he would not have the occasion to be the heroic rescuer, he could be just a benign bystander, but certainly not a despicable denier.

How dare we say that we would never do what Peter did! His performance is a somber reminder to us about our inability to predict a personal reaction to any situation. We might plan to have great faith in times of trial or temptation; we might sincerely want to be profound witnesses to the Lord in stressful and chaotic situations, but our desires do not—in and of themselves—produce results. Paul cautions us, "Therefore let anyone who thinks that he stands take heed lest he fall" (1 Corinthians 10:12).

Instead of looking to ourselves, we look to our steadfast and faithful Savior. His performance on our behalf is totally predictable. God had planned from eternity to rescue us from the folly of our sins; His Son was our designated hero. In times of test and temptation, the resolve of Jesus was unwavering. He has the strength and discipline we lack and the forgiveness we need. He gives us these gifts in abundant measure through His redeeming grace.

16 NOVEMBER

Psalmody: Psalm 54
Additional Psalm: Psalm 139:7–18
Old Testament Reading:
Jeremiah 31:1–17, 23–34
New Testament Reading: Matthew 27:1–10
Additional Reading: Revelation 16:1–21

Prayer of the Day

Almighty, everlasting God, through Your only Son, our blessed Lord, You commanded us to love our enemies, to do good to those who hate us, and to pray for those who persecute us. Therefore, we earnestly implore You that by Your gracious working our enemies may be led to true repentance, may have the same love toward us as we have toward them, and may be of one accord and of one mind and heart with us and with Your whole Church; through Jesus Christ, our Lord. (110)

Meditation

Two facts are remembered about Judas: he betrayed the Lord, and he killed himself. After the enumeration of those objective truths, the analysis of this disciple becomes more subjectively complex. Although we realize that only God can look into a person's heart at the time of death, Scripture gives us a frank assessment of Judas's eternal fate. While it says that Judas "changed his mind" about what he had done and even uttered the words, "I have sinned by betraying innocent blood," we should not understand this as a manifestation of true repentance. To be sure, he regretted what had happened. But this was sorrow for the consequences of sin, not for the sin itself. This is similar to the pseudo-confessions offered by public figures today who say, "I regret that people have been disappointed by my actions." Those carefully nuanced words are really an apology without an admission of guilt, remorse without real repentance. They speak more about the results of sin rather than the reason the sin occurred in the first place.

Note also that Judas spoke these words to the chief priests and elders. He did not return to his Lord with a broken and contrite heart, asking for pardon. In his moment of extreme desperation he did not come to the One who could have given him comfort and relief. His emotions might have changed since he first conspired to commit this act, but his true spiritual condition had not. Thus he was left without hope. That conclusion is substantiated in Luke's account of the elevation of Matthias "to take the place in this ministry and apostleship from which Judas turned aside to go to his own place" (Acts 1:25).

Paul says, "For godly grief produces a repentance that leads to salvation without regret, whereas worldly grief produces death" (2 Corinthians 7:10). We should be ever cognizant of this distinction. Our feelings about something should not be the sole test of the authenticity of our repentance. Genuine repentance consists of contrition and faith. The former affects our emotions; the latter affects our entire being. True repentance is more than situational remorse; it is a painful, penetrating acknowledgement of wrongdoing in the eyes of God, which—by the power of the Holy Spirit—also trusts in the powerful gift of forgiveness won for us by Jesus. The "blood money" returned by Judas was used to buy a burial place for the dead. The "blood money" shed by Jesus purchased forgiveness, life, and salvation.

17 November

Psalmody: Psalm 148:1–6
Additional Psalm: Psalm 148
Old Testament Reading: Jeremiah 33:1–22
Additional Reading:
Jeremiah 34:1–36:32; 45:1–51:64
New Testament Reading: Matthew 27:11–32

Prayer of the Day

Lord Jesus Christ, as the healer of nations, You released many from their bondage to sin, death, and the devil, but when it came time to release You, they chose a murderer instead. Through our co-crucifixion with You in the waters of our Baptism, may we continually be released from our sins as we confess You to be our everlasting King; for You live and reign with the Father and the Holy Spirit, one God, now and forever. (1110)

Meditation

Pontius Pilate faced a quandary of epic proportions. The dilemma was summed up in his question, "Then what shall I do with Jesus who is called Christ?" He encountered pressure from every direction. His wife begged, "Have nothing to do with that righteous man." The fevered crowds demanded, "Let Him be crucified!" But more exacting than either of these forces was the persistent gnaw of his conscience, convincing him that this "King of the Jews" was not deserving of death. In the end, Pilate ignored the still, small voice within and cowardly capitulated to the crowd's malevolent desires. His astoundingly contradictory actions of pronouncing Jesus innocent of any wrongdoing while simultaneously handing Him over for execution did not bring a satisfactory resolution. Despite his futile attempt to "wash his hands" of the matter, Pilate is remembered through the millennia by his inclusion in the Apostles' and Nicene Creeds.

Yet he is not the sole villain. We assume that role every time we succumb to temptation, every time expediency determines our actions, or every time loyalty to our Savior is trumped by personal convenience. The Lord is tried in our life and unjustly cast off when we, too, heed the clamoring call of sin rather than the guidance of His Word. The question, "Then what shall I do with Jesus who is called Christ?" is a daily indictment of our failures. We have often been sporadic in our worship, cowardly in our witness, cold in our love, miserly in our stewardship, and perfunctory in our prayer. When the selfish desires of our lives stand against the demands of His Law, we fail as miserably as did the governor in the Praetorium.

Our private infamy will not endure in the human record to the extent that Pilate's public infamy did. But we are assured that it will never endure in our Lord's memory. The Savior experienced no quandary about our fate. There was no compromise or cowardice on His part. He bravely faced the injustice of crucifixion so that our sins would never be recited, recalled, or retained in God's consciousness. While the crowds shouted to Pilate for His condemnation, Jesus would cry out to His Father in heaven for our forgiveness. Just as He gave no answer to the charges brought against Him then, so now He remains silent instead of bringing charges against us. He exchanges our guilt for His innocence. We are the "Barabbases" who gained released at His expense.

18 NOVEMBER

Psalmody: Psalm 22:1–5
Additional Psalm: Psalm 22:12–26
Old Testament Reading: Jeremiah 37:1–21
New Testament Reading: Matthew 27:33–56
Additional Reading: Revelation 17:1–18

Prayer of the Day

O God, creator of heaven and earth, grant that as the crucified body of Your dear Son was laid in the tomb and rested on this holy Sabbath, so we may await with Him the coming of the third day, and rise with Him to newness of life, who lives and reigns with You and the Holy Spirit, one God, now and forever. (L34)

Meditation

We know what it means to "add insult to injury." Those words describe an already bad situation that is made even worse, like a grieving widow who comes out of the funeral home to discover four flat tires on her car. With regard to the crucifixion of Jesus, the phrase applies in the highest degree. If the excruciating pain of crucifixion and all the torture inflicted upon Him before He was nailed to the cross were not enough, now we witness our Savior having to endure the taunts of two robbers crucified with Him (one, we know, would later repent) and the mockery of the chief priests, teachers of the Law, and the elders who said, "He saved others; He cannot save Himself." Insult added to injury, literally.

But the dramatic fact of the matter here is that even though these mockers meant their words to be demeaning, they were speaking the truth. Jesus absolutely could not save Himself. To withdraw from the pain and agony, even at this late moment, would have been to fail as the world's Savior. He could never do that. His love for sinful humanity was too great; it constrained Him from seeking relief.

The actions of those who taunted and mocked our suffering Lord cause us to recoil in disgust. We piously think, "I would never do that." Can we be so sure? Don't we mock Jesus and insult the sacrifice of His redemptive work on our behalf whenever we minimize our sins and maximize our self-righteousness? We compare ourselves to others and revel in our imagined "goodness," forgetting our own horrid transgressions of thought, word, and deed. It is beneficial to be reading the Passion account as the day of national Thanksgiving approaches, for we often fail to gratefully acknowledge each day what the Lord has done for us. How insulting it is when recipients do not recognize their Benefactor.

The Good News for us is that—despite the injury and the insult that we, too, inflict upon Him—our Lord endures, just as He did on Calvary. He does not abandon us or respond with condemnatory assaults of His own; rather, He turns to us in love. The death of Jesus is framed by two antithetical verbal events—the ridicule of His enemies and the respect of the centurion and those who were with him. Instead of adding insult to injury, may our Savior empower us to add increased daily commitment, fervor, and devotion to our confession of Him.

19 NOVEMBER

Elizabeth of Hungary

Psalmody: Psalm 20
Additional Psalm: Psalm 18:25–34
Old Testament Reading: Jeremiah 38:1–28
Additional Reading: Jeremiah 39:1–44:30
New Testament Reading: Matthew 27:57–66

Prayer of the Day

Mighty King, whose inheritance is not of this world, inspire in us the humility and benevolent charity of Elizabeth of Hungary. She scorned her bejeweled crown with thoughts of the thorned one her Savior donned for her sake and ours, that we, too, might live a life of sacrifice, pleasing in Your sight and worthy of the name of Your Son, Christ Jesus, who with the Holy Spirit reigns with You forever in an everlasting kingdom. (1111)

Elizabeth of Hungary

Born in Pressburg, Hungary, in 1207, Elizabeth was the daughter of King Andrew II and his wife, Gertrude. Given as a bride in an arranged political marriage, Elizabeth became the wife of Louis of Thuringia in Germany at age fourteen. She had a spirit of Christian generosity and charity, and the home she established for her husband and three children in the Wartburg Castle at Eisenach was known for its hospitality and family love. Elizabeth often supervised the care of the sick and needy and at one time even gave up her bed to a leper. Widowed at the age of twenty, she made provisions for her children and entered into an austere life as a nun in the Order of Saint Francis. Her self-denial led to failing health and an early death in 1231 at age twenty-four. Remembered for her self-sacrificing ways, Elizabeth is commemorated through the many hospitals named for her around the world.

Meditation

Our familiarity with the account of our Lord's burial is responsible for the muting of the element of surprise we might otherwise have if we were reading this narrative for the first time. Literary analysts could say that there is a dramatic plot development here. The care given to our Lord's body after His death is highly unusual given the preceding events of His life. After all, this was a man born in a stable; a man who lived for a time as a transient, saying that He had nowhere to lay His head. The culmination of this life of simplicity and poverty occurred when He was executed as a common criminal. One might expect, therefore, that He would be buried like a common criminal—having His body unceremoniously pulled off the cross by some slave assigned to the job, and who would then throw the corpse in a mass grave with others who had suffered the same fate.

But, of course, that is not what happened. Instead, Joseph of Arimathea, who is described as a rich man, gave the body of Jesus a decent burial. While all of this might have been unusual, it was not unpredictable. It was prophesied that the Messiah would be "with a rich man in His death" (Isaiah 53:9). What does this mean for us?

It means that in the burial of Jesus—a mundane, but necessary act—we see a glimpse of things to come. The burial of Christ is the hinge between His states of humiliation and exaltation. After He "suffered under Pontius Pilate, was crucified, died and was buried," then comes the exaltation. The Sabbath rest of our Lord's body was not spent idly. It began with His descent into Hell—not to suffer more, but to proclaim what He had already done.

What He has done most certainly affects us. "We were buried therefore with Him by baptism into death" (Romans 6:1). His life of poverty but burial with the rich reminds us again that salvation is complete and that Sabbath rest begins in Him. The next time you attend a committal at the graveside, listen for these words from the funeral liturgy, "O Lord Jesus, by Your three-day rest in the tomb You hallowed the graves of all who believe in You, promising resurrection to our mortal bodies." We wait now with patience, to celebrate that fact in all fullness and joy.

20 NOVEMBER

Psalmody: Psalm 118:19–29
Additional Psalm: Psalm 118:1–2, 15–24
Old Testament Reading: Daniel 1:1–21
New Testament Reading: Matthew 28:1–20

Prayer of the Day

O God, for our redemption You gave Your only-begotten Son to the death of the cross and by His glorious resurrection delivered us from the power of the enemy. Grant that all our sin may be drowned through daily repentance and that day by day we may arise to live before You in righteousness and purity forever; through Jesus Christ, our Lord, who lives and reigns with You and the Holy Spirit, one God, now and forever. (L37)

Meditation

Life transitions such as graduations, weddings, anniversaries, and even funerals bring a mixture of emotions—joy mingled with nostalgic sadness, satisfaction and relief over goals reached or challenges overcome interwoven with trepidation and uncertainty regarding what lies ahead. We understand and accept this phenomenon of ambivalence in certain circumstances. But doesn't such an amalgamation of competing emotions seem out of place on the morning of Christ's resurrection? Shouldn't this day of days be a time of unalloyed celebration?

Perhaps it should have been, but it wasn't. After the women had heard the announcement from the angel that Christ had risen, were invited to see His former resting place, and were given instructions regarding the transmission of this glorious message to the disciples, they departed with a disquieting mixture of "fear and great joy." Forty days later, after the living Lord had proved beyond a shadow of a doubt that His resurrection was no hoax and had given His disciples final earthly instructions, Matthew concludes his Gospel by saying, "They worshiped Him, but some doubted." Isn't there something wrong with that picture?

In view of this brutally honest picture of our feeble, struggling human nature, the reality of the resurrection and the promise of Christ to be with us always are all the more necessary and meaningful. We need the power of His conquest over sin, death, and the grave to constantly permeate our entire existence as we travel the pilgrim path through this world. We desire the assurance of His continual presence to strengthen and sustain us on the way. Spiritual ambivalence can be more than just a mixture of competing claims; it can also manifest itself as a fluctuation between the polar extremes of faith and unbelief. The crucified, risen, ascended, and reigning Lord is at work in our sinner-saint lives, pulling us away from sin and toward Him.

It is remarkable that there was not a trace of ambivalence in our Lord's Great Commission. He did not say, "Well, I'm happy you're going out in My name, but I really don't have much confidence in you." He did not submit the eleven to auditions, interviews, or proficiency examinations. He simply tells them, as He tells us, "Go therefore and make disciples." His unambivalent confidence in us is a reflection of the unconditional, unequivocal difference that His death and resurrection make in the course of our lives and in the course of history.

21 NOVEMBER

Psalmody: Psalm 114
Additional Psalm: Psalm 16
Old Testament Reading: Daniel 2:1–23
New Testament Reading: Revelation 18:1–24

Prayer of the Day

Lord Jesus, You call heaven and all the saints and apostles and prophets to rejoice when those who pretend to be the true Church are brought to judgment. Help us to discern between what is true and what is false, always knowing that Your kingdom comes through humility and suffering and that the truth of the Gospel is found in You alone; for You live and reign with the Father and the Holy Spirit, one God, now and forever. (1112)

Meditation

A lot can happen in a single day. We marry in a single day. We bear children—hopefully, at least—in a single day. And sadly, we die in a single day. Yes, a lot can happen in a single day.

Scripture regularly uses the phrase "single day" to describe the instantaneous and unexpected nature of God's judgment against sin. For instance, in Revelation 18 when Babylon is judged, a chorus sings: "Her plagues will come in a single day, death and mourning and famine, and she will be burned up with fire; for mighty is the Lord God who has judged her."

In Revelation, Babylon is a metaphor for Rome, whose emperors ruthlessly oppressed the Early Church. The Roman historian Tacitus tells how the emperor Nero would burn Christians, using them as torches in his palatial gardens. But John prophesies that Rome's reign of terror will soon come to an end. And it will end in a single day.

A single day. This seems awfully quick for a whole empire to crumble. But then John raises the stakes even further: "Alas! Alas! You great city, you mighty city Babylon! For in a single hour your judgment has come." Babylon's destruction will be so sudden that it will come not only in a single day but in a single hour.

Such a prophecy ought to serve as a warning for anyone who refuses to follow Christ. For Christ's return will be sudden and swift: "The day of the Lord will come like a thief in the night. While people are saying, 'There is peace and security,' then sudden destruction will come upon them as labor pains come upon a pregnant woman, and they will not escape" (1 Thessalonians 5:2–3). Babylon's fate is not only the fate of Rome, but the fate of all who do not believe in Christ. But for us who trust in the Lord, such a prophecy ought to offer comfort and hope. For the Last Day will be not only a day of judgment, but also a day of salvation, as God has promised: "I will remove the iniquity of this land in a single day" (Zechariah 3:9). And iniquity was indeed removed in a single day called Good Friday when Jesus died on a cross. Now, God promises to return on a single day, called the Last Day, when we will be taken to be with the Lord. And so we pray for that single day. We pray, "Come, Lord Jesus."

22 NOVEMBER

Psalmody: Psalm 111
Additional Psalm: Psalm 92:1–8
Old Testament Reading: Daniel 2:24–49
New Testament Reading: Revelation 19:1–21

Prayer of the Day

Lord God, heavenly Father, send forth Your Son, we pray, to lead home His bride, the Church, that with all the company of the redeemed we may finally enter into His eternal wedding feast; through Jesus Christ, our Lord, who lives and reigns with You and the Holy Spirit, one God, now and forever. (H88)

Meditation

In one of Grimm's most gory fairy tales, an evil stepmother convinces her husband to abandon his children in the forest. Hansel and Gretel try to find their way home via a trail of breadcrumbs they leave behind, but birds eat the crumbs. A woman invites the siblings into her house, only to try to cook them in her oven. But the children turn the tables on her and shove her in her own oven. The woman thought she had children on her dinner menu, but as it turns out, she winds up on the dinner menu instead.

Like Hansel and Gretel, Revelation 19 involves people who go from feasters to feasted upon. But unlike Hansel and Gretel, this is no fairy tale. Babylon, John's personification of all who persecute the Church, has been gorging herself on the blood of Christ's saints (Revelation 18:24). But when the Lord returns, the tables are turned. An angel invites a flock of birds, "Come, gather for the great supper of God, to eat the flesh of kings, the flesh of captains, the flesh of mighty men, the flesh of horses and their riders, and the flesh of all men, both free and slave, both small and great." So "all the birds were gorged with their flesh."

The Greek word for "gorged" is *chortazo*. These birds do not just fill themselves on the remains of Babylon, they stuff themselves.

As gruesome as this sight might seem, there is another feast. And this other feast invokes not a cry of pain but a cry of praise from a heavenly chorus: Hallelujah! For this other feast is none other than "the marriage supper of the Lamb." We, as those redeemed by Christ, are invited. We have received our invitation in the Gospel of Christ and are bidden even to come for a foretaste in the Sacrament of Jesus' body and blood.

In Revelation 19, the birds *chortazo* on the flesh of the demised. But we get to *chortazo* on something far finer, even as our Savior promises: "Blessed are those who hunger and thirst for righteousness, for they shall be satisfied" (Matthew 5:6). The Greek word for "satisfied," once again, is *chortazo*. Our feast is not the flesh of the damned but the righteousness of our Savior. And there's plenty of His righteousness to go around. Thanks be to God.

23 NOVEMBER

Clement of Rome, Pastor

Psalmody: Psalm 39:4–12
Additional Psalm: Psalm 38:12–22
Old Testament Reading: Daniel 3:1–30
New Testament Reading: Revelation 20:1–15

Prayer of the Day

Almighty God, Your servant Clement of Rome called the Church in Corinth to repentance and faith to unite them in Christian love. Grant that Your Church may be anchored in Your truth by the presence of the Holy Spirit and kept blameless in Your service until the coming of our Lord Jesus Christ, who lives and reigns with You and the Holy Spirit, one God, now and forever. (1113)

Clement of Rome, Pastor

Clement (ca. AD 35–100) is remembered for having established the pattern of apostolic authority that governed the Christian Church during the first and second centuries. He also insisted on keeping Christ at the center of the Church's worship and outreach. In a letter to the Christians at Corinth, he emphasized the centrality of Jesus' death and resurrection: "Let us fix our eyes on the blood of Christ, realizing how precious it is to His Father, since it was poured out for our salvation and brought the grace of repentance to the whole world" (1 Clement 6:31). Prior to suffering a martyr's death by drowning, Clement displayed a steadfast, Christlike love for God's redeemed people, serving as an inspiration to future generations to continue to build the Church on the foundation of the prophets and apostles, with Christ as the one and only cornerstone.

Meditation

In Revelation 20, John introduces a number: one thousand. Though it's only one number, this number has caused much confusion and debate in the Church. John writes: "Then I saw an angel coming down from heaven, holding in his hand the key to the bottomless pit and a great chain. And he seized the dragon, that ancient serpent, who is the devil and Satan, and bound him for a thousand years."

The "thousand years" to which John refers is best taken figuratively, even as it is used figuratively elsewhere (Psalm 90:4, 2 Peter 3:8), describing the period of the Church between Christ's first and second comings. Interestingly, at Christ's second coming, we are introduced to some books—and not the kind with numbers. Instead, these are books kept by God and used to judge the dead "according to what they had done." But not only are there books recording the works of humans, there is "another book . . . which is the book of life," containing the names of those washed by the blood of the Lamb.

John, then, presents us with two ways: the way of being judged by the books, which record every sin we commit, or the way of being found in the book, which is none other than the Book of Life, containing simply our names (verse 15). In other words, we can be judged either according to what we have done or according to what the Lamb has done.

Although I love having many books, there's only one book on which my salvation is founded. And it's not a book filled with my works, for apart from Christ my works are only shameful, embarrassing, and damning. No, my salvation is founded only in the book with my name in it, written in blood by the Lamb. For this book is my book of life. And it's yours too.

24 NOVEMBER

Psalmody: Psalm 41:7–12
Additional Psalm: Psalm 41
Old Testament Reading: Daniel 4:1–37
New Testament Reading: Revelation 21:1–8

Prayer of the Day

Lord Jesus, Alpha and Omega, in Your suffering and death You were making all things new, and from that tree You brought Your work of redemption to an end by declaring "It is finished." Be our beginning and our end, that our weeping now at Your table here below may prepare us to feast at Your heavenly banquet, where You will wipe every tear from our eyes and death will be no more; for You live and reign with the Father and the Holy Spirit, one God, now and forever. (1114)

Meditation

Occasionally, a lawyer will work on contingency. The principle of contingency is simple: a lawyer doesn't get paid unless his client wins.

Of course, the danger in such an arrangement is that if the lawyer loses the case, all his time and effort go uncompensated.

In grammar, a contingency is usually demarcated by two words: "if" and "then." "If" introduces the contingency itself. "Then" introduces the outcome of a contingency, if it indeed comes to pass.

We find an instance of such a contingency in Leviticus 26. God gives His people a contingent blessing: "If you walk in My statutes and observe My commandments and do them, then . . . I will walk among you and will be your God, and you shall be My people" (Leviticus 26:3–4, 12). God promises to dwell with His people and be their God. But only if the Israelites follow God's commands.

How well do the Israelites fare at following God's commands? Miserably. They sin again and again. And so God introduces another contingency clause—a contingency clause of punishment: "If you will not listen to Me and will not do all these commandments . . . then I will do this to you . . . I will set My face against you" (Leviticus 26:14, 16, 17). And indeed God does. He punishes the Israelites for their sins.

Truth be told, if God's favor on us and presence among us was contingent on our righteousness, all of us would receive nothing but divine wrath and damnation. For none of us follow God's ways and decrees. This is why Revelation 21 comes as such good news. For on the Last Day, God will declare: "Behold, the dwelling place of God is with man. He will dwell with them, and they will be His people, and God Himself will be with them as their God." In Revelation 21, God makes the same promise He makes in Leviticus 26 with one big difference: He does not begin with a contingency. Instead, He simply declares His presence as a fact.

This, then, is the fact of the matter: God dwells with us. He dwells with us through His Word. He dwells with us through His Sacraments. And He will dwell with us in His new creation. But His presence has nothing to do with our piety and righteousness. Rather, He dwells with us in spite of our sin and wickedness, for He loves us. And when it comes to God's love, there are no "ifs" about it.

25 NOVEMBER

Psalmody: Psalm 48:9–14
Additional Psalm: Psalm 48
Old Testament Reading: Daniel 5:1–30
Additional Reading: Daniel 7:1–8:27
New Testament Reading: Revelation 21:9–27

Prayer of the Day

Merciful God, You have promised to those whose names are written in the Lamb's Book of Life that they will dwell in the New Jerusalem, where the temple is the Lamb whose lamp lights the world. Prepare us to enter this heavenly city at the Supper You prepared for us here of the very body and blood of the Lamb, even as we participate now in the marriage feast of the Lamb in His kingdom, which has no end; through Jesus Christ, our Lord. (1115)

Meditation
In Revelation 21, we catch a glimpse of a cosmic city—God's new Jerusalem. In his description of this heavenly metropolis, John notes: "Its gates will never be shut by day—and there will be no night there."
Ancient cities would often shut their gates at night to keep out invaders. For instance, when the city of Jericho learns the Israelites are plotting an attack, Joshua records: "Now Jericho was shut up inside and outside because of the people of Israel. None went out, and none came in" (Joshua 6:1). Ancient cities shut their gates. The new Jerusalem will not.

Why is this? Because unlike the municipalities of antiquity, the new Jerusalem will have no foes of which to be afraid. For all the city's enemies will be conquered, even as John says: "But as for the cowardly, the faithless, the detestable, as for murderers, the sexually immoral, sorcerers, idolaters, and all liars, their portion will be in the lake that burns with fire and sulfur, which is the second death" (Revelation 21:8). The new Jerusalem's doors will remain forever open.

God is in the business of opening doors. Paul, after a mission tour through Iconium, Lystra, and Derbe, rejoices that God has "opened a door of faith to the Gentiles" (Acts 14:27). Paul later prays "that God may open to us a door for the word, to declare the mystery of Christ" (Colossians 4:3). Even at the beginning of Revelation, Jesus exclaims to the Church at Philadelphia, "Behold, I have set before you an open door, which no one is able to shut" (Revelation 3:8).

There's an oft-repeated cliché: "Whenever God closes one door, He always opens a window." This cliché's premise is that God will make a way, even when things don't turn out how we might expect or want. As much as I appreciate the sentiment, I'm not so sure that the imagery is accurate. For when it comes to doors, God is in the business of opening them. Thus, when we run up against roadblocks, before we accuse God of slamming doors in our faces, we should perhaps thank God for all the doors He has already opened, for they are many. He has opened the door to His wisdom through the pages of Scripture. He has opened the door to forgiveness through His Son, Jesus Christ. And He has opened the gates of His new Jerusalem so that we may enter.

26 November

Psalmody: Psalm 75
Additional Psalm: Psalm 108
Old Testament Reading: Daniel 6:1–28
Additional Reading: Daniel 9:1–27
New Testament Reading: Revelation 22:1–21

Prayer of the Day

Lord Jesus Christ, Alpha and Omega, bright Morning Star, You are the tree of life standing on each side of the river of the water of life, bringing healing to the nations. Prepare us for Your coming through the healing medicine of Your Word and Sacraments, putting to flight the diseases of our souls, that with willing hearts we may ever love and serve You; for You live and reign with the Father and the Holy Spirit, one God, now and forever. (1116)

Meditation

Fruit comes in and out of season. Though you may be able to buy strawberries all year, they're freshest, most succulent, and cheapest during the summer months when they're in season. The same is true of blueberries, raspberries, pineapples, and watermelon.

In the new Jerusalem there is a tree whose fruit never goes out of season. John explains: "Then the angel showed me . . . the tree of life with its twelve kinds of fruit, yielding its fruit each month." This tree, it seems, never has a month off.

Beyond the perpetual abundance in God's new creation illustrated by this tree, the reference to this tree's twelve kinds of fruit is also notable. Twelve is a principal number in biblical numerology. There were twelve apostles and twelve tribes of Israel. Indeed, we may find an allusion to Israel in this tree of life's twelve kinds of fruit.

In Isaiah 5, God sings a song for His beloved Israel, whom He dotingly calls His vineyard. He sings, "My beloved had a vineyard on a very fertile hill. He dug it and cleared it of stones, and planted it with choice vines; He built a watchtower in the midst of it, and hewed out a wine vat in it; and He looked for it to yield grapes, but it yielded wild grapes" (Isaiah 5:1–2). Whereas the tree of life in God's new Jerusalem is always in season, the tree of Israel in God's vineyard seems never to be in season. It yields only worthless fruit. So God declares, "I will make it a waste; it shall not be pruned or hoed, and briers and thorns shall grow up" (Isaiah 5:6). God's fruitless vineyard incurs God's terrible judgment. Jesus offers a similar warning when He says, "Every tree that does not bear good fruit is cut down and thrown into the fire" (Matthew 7:19).

In this world where the wild fruit of wickedness seems superabundant, it may be hard to imagine such a glorious tree as that of God's tree of life. Yet we are given a glimpse of this tree in the man who was crucified on the tree of the cross. For the tree of the cross is our tree of life. For through the tree of the cross death is conquered and salvation is procured. And through the tree of the cross we are given the assurance that we will one day be feasting on God's heavenly tree of life.

THE TIME OF CHRISTMAS

Advent Season

27 NOVEMBER

Psalmody: Psalm 66:16–19
Additional Psalm: Psalm 66
Old Testament Reading: Isaiah 1:1–28
New Testament Reading: 1 Peter 1:1–12

Prayer of the Day

Stir up Your power, O Lord, and come, that by Your protection we may be rescued from the threatening perils of our sins and saved by Your mighty deliverance; for You live and reign with the Father and the Holy Spirit, one God, now and forever. (L01)

Meditation

Peter's epistle is a pastoral treatise on Christian suffering. From the very first verse Peter sets his theme: "Peter, an apostle of Jesus Christ, to those who are elect exiles of the dispersion." Usually when we think of electing someone, we think of electing them to a position of honor and privilege. However when God elects a Christian, He often elects him not to honor and privilege but to "exile" and "dispersion."

In the original Greek text, "dispersion" is diaspora, a word denoting the scattering of the Jews throughout the world following their exile to Babylon in 586 BC. This word continued to be used into the first century to describe many persecutions, as in Acts 11:19: "Now those who were scattered because of the persecution that arose over Stephen traveled as far as Phoenicia and Cyprus and Antioch." The Greek word for "scattered" is diaspora. Thus, Peter addresses his letter to those who have been scattered by persecution.

Christians suffer. Indeed, the suffering of Christians is so common that Peter says, "Beloved, do not be surprised at the fiery trial when it comes upon you to test you" (1 Peter 4:12). Suffering is simply a part of following Christ. As Jesus says, "If anyone would come after Me, let him deny himself and take up his cross and follow Me" (Mark 8:34).

In his epistle, Peter wants to show his readers how to suffer well. Interestingly, the first pearl of wisdom that Peter proffers concerning suffering well is a blessing: "May grace and peace be multiplied to you." The word for "multiplied" literally means "filled." In the midst of multiple persecutions, scatterings, trials, and beatings, Peter wants to remind us that God's grace and peace can nevertheless fill us exponentially. For God's grace and peace can never be mitigated or muted by any amount of suffering or persecution. As the apostle Paul asks, "Who shall separate from the love of Christ? Shall tribulation, or distress, or persecution, or famine, or nakedness, or danger, or sword? . . . No, in all these things we are more than conquerors through Him who loved us" (Romans 8:35, 37).

Whatever trials or persecutions you may face, they cannot scatter you away from Christ's love. And so, while we suffer, we cling not only to God's love in times of trial, but we also cling to God's promise of "subsequent glories." For human suffering will soon melt away at the glory of God's appearing.

28 NOVEMBER

Psalmody: Psalm 102:13–17
Additional Psalm: Psalm 85
Old Testament Reading: Isaiah 2:1–22
Additional Reading: Isaiah 3:1–4:6
New Testament Reading: 1 Peter 1:13–25

Prayer of the Day

Stir up our hearts, O Lord, to make ready the way of Your only-begotten Son, that by His coming we may be enabled to serve You with pure minds; through the same Jesus Christ, our Lord, who lives and reigns with You and the Holy Spirit, one God, now and forever. (L02)

Meditation

Upon a person's death, his assets are generally divided among his family members. His spouse along with his children will receive certain portions of his estate as stipulated by his will. These portions are usually referred to as inheritances.

In 1 Peter, the apostle speaks not of a good inheritance but of a tragic one. Peter writes about "the futile ways inherited from [our] forefathers." Peter here is referring to the doctrine of original sin. Our forefather Adam has left us all an inheritance—not of blessing, but of slavery to the futile ways of wickedness.

But there is hope. For before there was Adam and his iniquitous inheritance, there was Jesus, who "was foreknown before the foundation of the world." And not only does Jesus come before us and all creation, He and His Word also remain long after us, as Peter quotes: "The Word of the Lord remains forever."

As the one who comes before us and remains after us, Christ redeems us so that we may remain with Him into all eternity. He ransoms us "from the futile ways inherited from [our] forefathers, not with perishable things such as silver or gold, but with [His] precious blood… like that of a lamb without blemish or spot."

When you buy a diamond, the jeweler will encourage you to consider three C's: color, clarity, and cost. Do you want your diamond to be perfectly colorless or is a little yellow okay? Must your diamond be flawless or are minor inclusions acceptable? And, of course, how much money would you like to spend?

When it comes to Jesus, He is "without blemish or spot." His life was perfectly uncolored by sin. His clarity of purpose was flawless as He carried out His Father's mission. And His value? Priceless. This is why He can ransom us from our futile ways. For no sin can accrue a debt larger than the value of the perfect and precious blood of Christ.

Peter concludes his thoughts on the infinite worth of Christ with a reminder: "And this word is the good news that was preached to you." The Greek noun for "word" is *rhema*, referring to a "spoken word." Hence this word of which Peter speaks is not just to be read, it is to be preached. It is to be proclaimed. It is to be shared. And so we continue to preach, proclaim, and share this word.

29 NOVEMBER

Noah

Psalmody: Psalm 118:19–24
Additional Psalm: Psalm 118
Old Testament Reading: Isaiah 5:1–25
Additional Reading: Amos 1:1–9:15
New Testament Reading: 1 Peter 2:1–12

Prayer of the Day

Almighty and eternal God, according to Your strict judgment You condemned the unbelieving world through the flood, yet according to Your great mercy You preserved believing Noah and his family, eight souls in all. Grant that we may be kept safe and secure in the holy ark of the Christian Church, so that with all believers in Your promise, we would be declared worthy of eternal life; through Jesus Christ, our Lord. (1117)

Noah

Noah, the son of Lamech (Genesis 5:30), was instructed by God to build an ark in which his family would find security from the destructive waters of a devastating flood that God warned would come. Noah built the ark, and the rains descended. The entire earth was flooded, destroying "every living thing that was on the face of the ground, man and animals" (Genesis

7:23). After the flood waters subsided, the ark came to rest on the mountains of Ararat. When Noah determined it was safe and God confirmed it, Noah, his family, and all the animals disembarked. Then Noah built an altar and offered a sacrifice of thanksgiving to God for having saved his family from destruction. A rainbow in the sky was declared by God to be a sign of His promise that never again would a similar flood destroy the entire earth (Genesis 8:20–22; 9:8–17). Noah is remembered and honored for his obedience, believing that God would do what He said He would.

Meditation

In 1857, Alice B. Haven, affectionately known to her readers as "Cousin Alice," published the book *A Place for Everything and Everything in Its Place.* Haven explained the purpose of her book was to cultivate "correct and diligent habits" and to stave off "evil and wrong." Of course, long before and long since Cousin Alice, this proverb was and remains a favorite among mothers who are trying to get their children to clean up their rooms. "Put things in their place!" these mothers say.

In 1 Peter 2, God speaks of a cornerstone which must be put in place: "Behold, I am laying in Zion a stone, a cornerstone chosen and precious, and whoever believes in Him will not be put to shame." This cornerstone is Christ. In the original text the word for "laying" is the Greek word *tithemi,* meaning "to put" or "to place." God has a specific place in mind for Jesus—the place of the cross. But not everyone appreciates God's place for Christ. For some, God's cornerstone becomes "a stone of stumbling, and a rock of offense." Or, as Paul writes, "We preach Christ crucified, a stumbling block" (1 Corinthians 1:23). Like a mother tripping over her child's toys in his bedroom, so there are those who trip on Christ's cross.

But why do some trip on Christ? Did God put His Son in a poor place? Hardly. For Christ's

place on the cross is the place of our salvation. But sadly, some people "stumble because they disobey the word, as they were destined to do." The Greek word for "destined" is again *tithemi.* Thus, these rebellious sinners who do not find their place on the cornerstone of Christ also have a place, but their place is hell.

It is important to note that Peter is not teaching double predestination when he speaks of those "destined" in disobedience. God is not predestining who will disobey. Rather, as Luther notes in his commentary on 1 Peter, God predestines the end of those who do not rest on the cornerstone of Christ, which is damnation. Thus, Peter presents us with two places: the place of Christ or the place of hell.

Blessedly, Peter declares that we are not consigned to the place of hell: "But you are a chosen race, a royal priesthood, a holy nation, a people for His own possession." We, as God's chosen people, have an eternal place on God's cornerstone of Christ.

30 NOVEMBER

St. Andrew, Apostle

Psalmody: Psalm 123:1–4
Additional Psalm: Psalm 7
Old Testament Reading: Isaiah 6:1–7:9
New Testament Reading: 1 Peter 2:13–25

Prayer of the Day

Almighty God, by Your grace the apostle Andrew obeyed the call of Your Son to be a disciple. Grant us also to follow the same Lord Jesus Christ in heart and life, who lives and reigns with You and the Holy Spirit, one God, now and forever. (F01)

St. Andrew, Apostle

St. Andrew, the brother of Simon Peter, was born in the Galilean village of Bethsaida. Originally a disciple of St. John the Baptist, Andrew then became the first of Jesus' disciples (John 1:35–40). His name regularly appears in the Gospels near the top of the lists of the Twelve. It was he who first introduced his brother Simon to Jesus (John 1:41–42). He was, in a real sense, the first home missionary, as well as the first foreign missionary (John 12:20–22). Tradition says Andrew was martyred by crucifixion on a cross in the form of an X. In AD 357, his body is said to have been taken to the Church of the Holy Apostles in Constantinople and later removed to the cathedral of Amalfi in Italy. Centuries later, Andrew became the patron saint of Scotland. St Andrew's Day determines the beginning of the Western Church Year, since the 1st Sunday in Advent is always the Sunday nearest to St Andrew's Day.

Meditation

Peter's death was a tragic one. Tradition says that he was crucified upside down by the Roman Emperor Nero. Peter's martyrdom was part of a campaign of persecution against Christians after a fire destroyed Rome. Nero found it convenient to blame the tragedy on the Christians and so persecuted them. It is no surprise, then, that Peter, at the end of this epistle, would refer to Rome as "Babylon" (1 Peter 5:13), a common biblical image for evil. After all, the Roman Empire was the archenemy of the Church.

It is against this historical backdrop that Peter writes: "Honor everyone. Love the brotherhood. Fear God. Honor the emperor." At first, it sounds as if Peter is serving up bland Christian niceties. "Honor everyone." Yes, it is good to respect others. "Love the brotherhood." Absolutely. Jesus Himself taught, "By this all people will know that you are My disciples, if you have love for one another" (John 13:35).

"Fear God." Of course! This is the First Commandment. "Honor the emperor." Now wait a minute. The emperor is Nero. The same Nero who kills Christians! Peter asks us to honor him? How can we honor such a diabolical despot?

Luther's exposition of the doctrine of the two kingdoms proves biblical and practical when confronted by a ruler like Nero. On the one hand, we are to honor secular rulers in the secular affairs of this world's kingdom, for God appoints these rulers to order such affairs (Romans 13:1). Thus, we pay our taxes and follow the laws of the land. However if a secular ruler tries to encroach on spiritual authority, we must resist, for this authority properly belongs to the kingdom of God. So when Peter says, "Honor the emperor," he encourages his readers to obey Nero insofar as his commands have to do with basic operations of the Empire. Yet, Peter can also call the Roman Empire "Babylon," for it is a heathen empire that seeks to encroach on spiritual matters and must be resisted when it does so.

And so, whether we love our rulers or desire to vote them out of office, to this we are called: we are to pray "for kings and all who are in high positions" (1 Timothy 2:2), for they are placed in their offices by God. And even if they, like Nero, might persecute us, we still have the assurance that, quite apart from their fleeting earthly kingdoms, we have received a "kingdom that cannot be shaken" (Hebrews 12:28).

1 December

Psalmody: Psalm 34:11–18
Additional Psalm: Psalm 50
Old Testament Reading: Isaiah 7:10–8:8
New Testament Reading: 1 Peter 3:1–22

Meditation

"Things can't get any worse," a man says after losing his job. But on the same day his wife also loses her job. "Computers can't get any smaller," I say after using my first laptop in college. But then computer companies market laptops with descriptors like "mini" and "air." How many times have we thought something has reached its superlative state only to be surprised by something even greater?

"There can never be a bigger flood than this," Noah must have thought after a catastrophic flood decimated the earth. And, in one sense, Noah was right. God promises, "Never again shall all flesh be cut off by the waters of the flood, and never again shall there be a flood to destroy the earth" (Genesis 9:11). God even offers a rainbow to seal the deal. But though there may never be another worldwide flood, that doesn't mean that there won't be a greater flood than even that of Noah's day. Indeed, this is Peter's argument when he references Noah's ark, in which "a few, that is, eight persons, were brought safely through water. Baptism, which corresponds to this, now saves you." In the original language text, the word for "correspond" is the Greek *antitypos*, meaning a "copy" or "type." Thus, Peter is arguing that the waters of Noah's flood, as mighty as they may have been, are no match for the waters of Baptism. Noah's flood is only an *antitypos*, or a "type," of the original and greatest flood of Baptism.

The preacher of Hebrews makes a similar argument when he says: "For Christ has entered, not into holy places made with hands, which are copies of the true things, but into heaven itself, now to appear in the presence of God on our behalf" (Hebrews 9:24). The Greek word for "copies" is *antitypos*. Thus, there is a heavenly temple and an earthly one; the earthly temple is only a dim copy of the glorious heavenly one.

As it is with the two temples, so it is with Noah's flood and Baptism. Noah's flood was only a dim copy of the glorious flood of Baptism. For the glorious flood of Baptism not only drowns our sins, it also saves our souls. It not only condemns and buries our old Adam, but it also raises us to life as new creations. Finally, the glorious flood of Baptism is done in the name of Jesus, and nothing is greater than Jesus. He is the superlative of which we can be sure.

2 DECEMBER

Psalmody: Psalm 119:105–112
Additional Psalm: Psalm 82
Old Testament Reading: Isaiah 8:9–9:7
New Testament Reading: 1 Peter 4:1–19

Meditation

In 1988, a former NASA engineer named Edgar Whisenant penned the book *88 Reasons Why the Rapture Will Be in 1988*. Not surprisingly, 1988 came and went without a rapture. But that did not detour Whisenant. The next year, he penned another book: *The Final Shout: Rapture Report 1989*. Apparently, if 1988 didn't work for Whisenant's rapture, he would simply move it to 1989.

Many Christians have fallen prey to apocalyptic crazes, convinced that the end is near. Even before Christ's first advent there were groups who stirred themselves into eschatological frenzies. The Essenes, for instance, lived in the desert at Qumran as they sought to prepare themselves for the Messiah's coming.

In 1 Peter 4, the apostle startlingly declares: "The end of all things is at hand." The phrase "is at hand" in Greek denotes an already completed action. Thus, Peter declares, "The end of all things has already drawn near."

The end is already upon us. So what are we to do? Hide in a cave? Stockpile supplies? Should we stand on a street corner and announce humanity's imminent doom? Peter presents a more modest option: "Therefore be self-controlled and sober-minded for the sake of your prayers. Above all, keep on loving one another earnestly, since love covers a multitude of sins." Instead of the bizarre behavior that regularly accompanies eschatological enthusiasm, Peter calls us simply to "keep on" doing what we have already been doing, which is "loving one another."

If there is one thing apocalyptic frenzy has bred, it is fear. The predictions proffered by self-styled latter day prophets arouse anxiety about being "left behind," or about multicolored horsemen who will gallop in from the sky to wreak worldwide annihilation. Thankfully, Jesus sooths our troubled souls when He says, "And you will hear of wars and rumors of wars. See that you are not alarmed, for this must take place, but the end is not yet" (Matthew 24:6).

There is no need to fear. While the world anxiously awaits the coming of tumult, war, and pestilence, we can keep on doing what we have always done. We can keep on loving each other, and we can keep on trusting in our Savior. For the end of the world is not about disaster coming, but it's about our Savior coming. And blessedly, this is a promise that strikes joy, not fear, into our hearts.

3 December

Psalmody: Psalm 55:16–23
Additional Psalm: Psalm 55
Old Testament Reading: Isaiah 9:8–10:11
New Testament Reading: 1 Peter 5:1–14

Prayer of the Day

Almighty and eternal God, Your Son, Jesus, triumphed over the prince of demons and freed us from bondage to sin. Help us to stand firm against every assault of Satan, and enable us always to do Your will; through Jesus Christ, our Lord, who lives and reigns with You and the Holy Spirit, one God, now and forever. (1118)

Meditation
Peter's readers must have felt like the apostle was consigning them to be doormats. While the Emperor Nero was fiercely persecuting Christians, Peter issues a call to humility in the face of suffering. "Clothe yourselves, all of you, with humility toward one another, for 'God opposes the proud but gives grace to the humble.'" The word for "clothe yourselves" is a word used to describe how slaves would put on aprons before serving. Thus, being clothed with humility means serving each other like slaves. This is not exactly dignified work.

But Peter is not finished. He continues saying, "Humble yourselves, therefore, under the mighty hand of God so that at the proper time He may exalt you, casting all your anxieties on Him, because He cares for you." Not only are we called to humble ourselves before each other, we are called to humble ourselves before God. Notably, Peter's example of how we humble ourselves before God is by "casting all [our] anxieties on Him." An anxious person is also often an arrogant person because he worries about things that he should trust God to oversee. In other words, an anxious person seeks to control things that properly belong under God's providence.

We are to humble ourselves before each other and humble ourselves before God. This is not an easy calling. For humbling ourselves, especially in the face of those like Nero, can be downright humiliating. It can make us feel like doormats.

So how are we to respond to those who exploit our humility to humiliate us? Peter answers: "After you have suffered a little while, the God of all grace, who has called you to His eternal glory in Christ, will Himself restore, confirm, strengthen, and establish you. To Him be the dominion forever and ever. Amen." Peter admits that we will suffer as humble servants of Christ. But he also promises that we will only suffer for "a little while." For while we might feel like doormats, we are finally under the loving care of the one who has dominion over all, and He will use His dominion not for our humiliation but for our salvation. So, as we suffer, we also long for Christ's appearing when we will receive our "unfading crown of glory." Humiliation at the whims of the wicked will not last forever. For Christ will return to lift us up (verse 6).

4 December

John of Damascus, Theologian and Hymnwriter

Psalmody: Psalm 145:1–9
Additional Psalm: Psalm 62
Old Testament Reading:
Isaiah 10:12–27a, 33–34
New Testament Reading: 2 Peter 1:1–21

Prayer of the Day

O Lord, through Your servant John of Damascus, You proclaimed with power the mysteries of the true faith. Confirm our faith so that we may confess Jesus to be true God and true man, singing the praises of the risen Lord, so that by the power of the resurrection we may also attain the joys of eternal life; through Jesus Christ, our Lord, who lives and reigns with You and the Holy Spirit, one God, now and forever. (1119)

John of Damascus, Theologian and Hymnwriter

John (ca. AD 675–749) is known as the great compiler and summarizer of the orthodox faith and the last great Greek theologian. Born in Damascus, John gave up an influential position in the Islamic court to devote himself to the Christian faith. Around AD 716, he entered a monastery outside of Jerusalem and was ordained a priest. When the Byzantine emperor Leo the Isaurian in AD 726 issued a decree forbidding images (icons), John forcefully resisted. In his Apostolic Discourses, he argued for the legitimacy of the veneration of images, which earned him the condemnation of the Iconoclast Council in AD 754. John also wrote defenses of the orthodox faith against contemporary heresies. In addition, he was a gifted hymnwriter ("Come, You Faithful, Raise the Strain") and contributed to the liturgy of the Byzantine churches. His greatest work was the *Fount of Wisdom*, which was a massive compendium of truth from previous Christian theologians, covering practically every conceivable doctrinal topic. John's summary of the orthodox faith left a lasting stamp on both the Eastern and Western churches.

Meditation

Signing a lease is never fun. After all, leases are long, boring, and written in incomprehensible legal language. You never sign just once. Instead, your leasing agent repeats ad nauseam: "Sign here. Initial here. Sign here. Date of birth here. Initial here. Sign here." As I sign and initial over and over again, I wonder to myself, "How many times do I have to sign and initial? Will this ever end?"

In 2 Peter 1, the apostle says that our lives are much like "signing and initialing here." He writes, "Therefore, brothers, be all the more diligent to make your calling and election sure." The Greek word for "sure" is *bebaios*, a legal term referring to a contract or agreement that a person would sign to make it official and binding. Peter uses this term to say, "You have been called by God. You have been elected by Christ. Live in a way that you sign on the dotted line of your already assured calling and election. Live like a called and elected child of God."

Our lives are our signatures. Thus, how we live reveals to others what we believe about our calling and election. Is our calling and election a precious document from God on which we joyfully write our names, or is it something that we treat as nothing but a hassle to sign and initial?

Beautifully, this Greek word *bebaios* is used not only of our election, but also of Jesus' electing. The preacher of Hebrews declares: "We have this as a sure and steadfast anchor of the soul, a hope that enters into the inner place behind the curtain, where Jesus has gone as a forerunner on our behalf" (Hebrews 6:19–20). The Greek word for "steadfast" is *bebaios*. Jesus has already entered the sanctuary of heaven by signing His life away on the cross for us. This gives us the steadfast, which is to say *bebaios*, hope that we will enter salvation. After all, Jesus' has signed His name, and His signature is sure.

We can do nothing to elect ourselves unto salvation. We are given the glorious privilege, however, of living out our election in Christ.

Jesus signed His name perfectly as He lived a perfect life, died a perfect death, and rose to eternal life. Although we do not sign our names perfectly because we are not perfect, we are still called to sign our names in righteousness, following Jesus' example. May God grant us His Spirit to sanctify our signatures.

5 DECEMBER

Psalmody: Psalm 49:5–12, 15
Additional Psalm: Psalm 49
Old Testament Reading: Isaiah 11:1–12:6
New Testament Reading: 2 Peter 2:1–22

Prayer of the Day

O God, who established Your Son as the Righteous Branch by which You would save Your people, grant that we who have been grafted into Christ through the waters of Holy Baptism may be preserved from every sin and evil and be borne secure in the ark of Your Church until we join the angels and the whole company of heaven to sing eternal praises to You, who with Jesus Christ, our Lord, and the Holy Spirit, is one God, now and forever. (1120)

Meditation

Jesus' mission for His disciples is wrapped in a promise to His disciples: "Follow Me, and I will make you fishers of men" (Matthew 4:19). Jesus wants us to fish for men with His Gospel. But we, as Christians, aren't the only ones who go fishing. Christ's enemies go fishing too. Peter talks about their evil angling when he writes, "They have eyes full of adultery, insatiable for sin. They entice unsteady souls." While we fish for men with Christ's Gospel, there are others who fish for us with their false and devious doctrines.

Even more disturbing is that these false teachers do their fishing under cover of darkness. Peter writes, "There will be false teachers among you, who will secretly bring in destructive heresies, even denying the Master who bought them, bringing upon themselves swift destruction." These false teachers are not readily apparent. They begin by introducing subtle lies, subsequently introducing larger and larger lies until those who listen to them are led away from Christ altogether. This is why Paul warns, "Keep a close watch on yourself and on the teaching" (1 Timothy 4:16). Paul knows that even an innocent doctrinal error can lead a person to eventually deny Christ. Indeed, Luther was so concerned with pure doctrine that he maintained that the tiniest doctrinal error could overthrow the whole Gospel.

So how are we to respond to our fishing foes? Peter answers this question, not with a battle plan against heresy, but with a promise. He writes, "If God did not spare angels when they sinned . . . if by turning the cities of Sodom and Gomorrah to ashes He condemned them to extinction . . . if He rescued righteous Lot . . . then the Lord knows how to rescue the godly from trials, and to keep the unrighteous under punishment until the day of judgment." "If God punishes evil and vindicates the righteous," Peter seems to say, "then God will certainly rescue us from meddling heretics." God will defeat false doctrine, and, even in this sinful world, He promises to keep it at bay (Revelation 20:1–3).

In this world, we are to boldly and fearlessly fight heresy. We, as Christians, are called to preach God's Word in its purity, and we are to rightly receive His Sacraments. And yet, despite our efforts, heresy remains. But it will not remain forever. God's truth will finally prevail, for God will finally prevail.

6 DECEMBER

Nicholas of Myra, Pastor

Psalmody: Psalm 56:1–2, 5–11, 13
Additional Psalm: Psalm 56
Old Testament Reading: Isaiah 14:1–23
New Testament Reading: 2 Peter 3:1–18

Prayer of the Day

Almighty God, You bestowed upon Your servant Nicholas of Myra the perpetual gift of charity. Grant Your Church the grace to deal in generosity and love with children and with all who are poor and distressed and to plead the cause of those who have no helper, especially those tossed by tempests of doubt or grief. We ask this for the sake of Him who gave His life for us, Your Son, our Savior, Jesus Christ, our Lord, who lives and reigns with You and the Holy Spirit, one God, now and forever. (1121)

Nicholas of Myra, Pastor

Of the many saints commemorated by the Christian Church, Nicholas (d. AD 342) is one of the best known. Very little is known historically of him, though there was a church of Saint Nicholas in Constantinople as early as the sixth century. Research has affirmed that there was a bishop by the name of Nicholas in the city of Myra in Lycia (part of modern Turkey) in the fourth century. From that coastal location, legends about Nicholas have traveled throughout time and space. He is associated with charitable giving in many countries around the world and is portrayed as the rescuer of sailors, the protector of children, and the friend of people in distress or need. In commemoration of *Sinte Klaas* (Dutch for "Saint Nicholas," in English "Santa Claus"), December 6 is a day for giving and receiving gifts in many parts of Europe.

Meditation

God's anger is fiery. It is called a "burning anger." In Exodus 32, when the Israelites fashion for themselves a golden calf and thereby prompting God's blistering wrath, Moses pleads with God, "Turn from Your burning anger and relent from this disaster against Your people" (Exodus 32:12). After the Israelite Achan steals plunder from Jericho against God's command, Joshua writes, "The anger of the LORD burned against the people of Israel" (Joshua 7:1). It's no wonder that the preacher of Hebrews declares, "Our God is a consuming fire" (Hebrews 12:29).

God's anger is fiery. But blessedly, it is kindled slowly. One of God's celebrated attributes is that He is "slow to anger and abounding in steadfast love" (Numbers 14:18). This "slow anger," as Moses calls it, is known in doctrinal parlance as "forbearance." Like a school loan in which payments can be deferred, God has deferred His immediate anger and consuming judgment out of His love. It is this doctrine that Peter celebrates in 2 Peter 3. The apostle writes, "The Lord is not slow to fulfill His promise as some count slowness, but is patient toward you, not wishing that any should perish, but that all should reach repentance." God wants to give people plenty of time to repent before He returns in judgment. His will for all is not instant judgment and damnation, but longsuffering and salvation.

Tragically, some mock God's forbearance. Peter laments, "Scoffers will come in the last days with scoffing, following their own sinful desires. They will say, 'Where is the promise of His coming?'" These people misinterpret God's patience as God's absence. But others do not mock God's forbearance. Instead, they believe in God's Son and are saved. This is why Peter can "count the patience of our Lord as salvation."

There will come a day when God's judgment will burn white hot and "the heavens will pass away with a roar, and the heavenly bodies will be burned up and dissolved, and the earth and the works that are done on it will be exposed." But until that day, our God waits. He waits for repentance, He waits for faith, and He gives salvation. Praise be to God that He remains patient with sinners like us. For because of God's patience, we have God's salvation.

7 DECEMBER

Ambrose of Milan, Pastor and Hymnwriter

Psalmody: Psalm 25:1–7
Additional Psalm: Psalm 73
Old Testament Reading: Isaiah 24:1–13
New Testament Reading: 1 John 1:1–2:14

Prayer of the Day

O God, You gave Your servant Ambrose grace to proclaim the Gospel with eloquence and power. As bishop of the great congregation of Milan, he fearlessly bore reproach for the honor of Your name. Mercifully grant to all bishops and pastors such excellence in preaching and fidelity in ministering Your Word that Your people shall be partakers of the divine nature; through Jesus Christ our Lord, who lives and reigns with You and the Holy Spirit, one God, now and forever. (1122)

Ambrose of Milan, Pastor and Hymnwriter

Born in Trier in AD 340, Ambrose was one of the four great Latin Doctors of the Church (with Augustine, Jerome, and Gregory the Great). He was a prolific author of hymns, the most common of which is *Veni, Redemptor Gentium* ("Savior of the Nations, Come"). His name is also associated with Ambrosian Chant, a style of chanting the ancient liturgy that took hold in the province of Milan. While serving as a civil governor, Ambrose sought to bring peace among Christians in Milan who were divided into quarreling factions. When a new bishop was to be elected in AD 374, Ambrose addressed the crowd, and someone cried out, "Ambrose, bishop!" The entire gathering gave their support. This acclaim of Ambrose, a thirty-four-year-old catechumen, led to his Baptism on December 7, after which he was consecrated bishop of Milan. A strong defender of the faith, Ambrose convinced the Roman emperor Gratian in 379 to forbid the Arian heresy in the West. At Ambrose's urging, Gratian's successor, Theodosius, also publicly opposed Arianism. Ambrose died on Good Friday, April 4, 397. As a courageous doctor and musician, he upheld the truth of God's Word.

Meditation

One would be challenged to find two metaphors more opposed than light and darkness. Hot and cold; good and evil; young and old are all antonyms of degree, and when left to subjective analysis, one might find only a small measure of distinction. But light and darkness leave little room for personal interpretation; they are absolutes, polar opposites. This is precisely the point the apostle strives to make. He asserts, "God is light, and in Him there is no darkness at all." The emphatic nature of that statement cannot be overemphasized. God has absolutely, positively, not a trace of darkness.

The introduction of this strong pronouncement at the beginning of John's first epistle is appropriate, for the apostle has serious matters to discuss. Dispensing with a formal greeting, he quickly gets down to business. False teachers threaten God's people. The light of Christ that those people had received is in danger of being eclipsed or dimmed, which—for all intents and purposes—meant that it would be extinguished. God forbid that this would happen lest they lose their faith and the gift of salvation. John bluntly speaks about the eventualities he hopes his listeners will avoid: "we deceive ourselves,

and the truth is not is us," and, "we make Him a liar, and His word is not in us."

Like John's original readers, our sin, too, is that we diminish the distinction between light and darkness, between Christ and the world. We attempt to hang a curtain separating faith and life, doctrine and practice. We profess the truth but make excuses and exceptions for our behavior, or as John says, "We say we have fellowship with Him while we walk in darkness." Since we dim our lights, shade our eyes, and shutter our windows, we think we can also compromise with false teaching and evil behavior. This is sinful folly. It will not stand.

The solution to this dire dilemma is found not in our feeble efforts to chase away the darkness; the metaphor here points to the reality of sin, far too powerful for us to subdue or control on our own—that was done by Christ. He truly cleanses us from all sin and serves as our advocate and propitiator because He bore the darkness for us. In Him was light, but on Him were our sins, suffered on a dark Friday that gave way to a luminous, joyous Sunday.

8 Dᴇᴄᴇᴍʙᴇʀ

Psalmody: Psalm 11
Additional Psalm: Psalm 142
Old Testament Reading: Isaiah 24:14–25:12
Additional Reading: Obadiah 1–21
New Testament Reading: 1 John 2:15–29

Prayer of the Day

Lord God, heavenly Father, in Holy Baptism You anointed us with holy chrism and healed us of all sin, making us little Christs who bear in our body Your Son, our Savior. Continue to strengthen us by Your Holy Spirit that we may embody Christ in the world through our words and in our actions; through Jesus Christ, our Lord. (1123)

Meditation

The opening words of today's reading are unsettling because they hit so close to home. Indeed, they hit squarely in the heart. The accusing power of the Law is in full assault mode. "Do not love the world or the things in the world." How can I find a way out of this? Perhaps there is escape in the word, love. If I give myself the benefit of the doubt, then I can say that even though I appreciate the comforts, amenities, and joys of temporal existence, I'm really not that attached to them. I may like the world, but I don't love it. Then I realize this ploy doesn't work. Holy Scripture reminds us elsewhere that even "friendship with the world is enmity with God" (James 4:4). Nuancing the word world to refer to opponents of God rather than the trappings of earthly life doesn't help either. In both ways I am still guilty. There is no escape there either.

Clearly, the demands of the Law are crushing. I sing the rhetorical question of the hymn, "What is the world to me?" and my conscience answers, "Quite a bit, actually." Where does that leave me? Is the only option to give away all my earthly goods, renounce family, enter a monastery, become an ascetic, and devote myself entirely to prayer and the study of God's Word? No, of course not.

It is precisely at this moment that the Good News steps in. In the most memorable verse of Scripture, this same holy writer has told us that God loves the world (John 3:16). Jesus gave His life for the world as a manifestation of the Father's love. I can now do the same. This is not to say, however, that Jesus is merely a model of good behavior. He is, indeed, my Savior. I can never duplicate His love, His sacrifice, His atonement for my sins. But since I share in His death and resurrection, I am empowered to be His person in the world. The blessings that do come into my life in the form of "worldly" goods come from Him; therefore, I use them for the glory of His name and the benefit of His

people. My life conforms to His will, as His will conformed to the Father's will. John reminds me that I "have been anointed by the Holy One" and "have knowledge." Because I am claimed by God as His child in the "last hour," the allurement of the world has been replaced by the yearning to love and serve Him.

9 DECEMBER

Psalmody: Psalm 17:6–15
Additional Psalm: Psalm 148
Old Testament Reading: Isaiah 26:1–19
New Testament Reading: 1 John 3:1–24

Prayer of the Day

Lord, we implore You, grant Your people grace to withstand the temptations of the devil and with pure hearts and minds to follow You, the only God; through Jesus Christ, Your Son, our Lord, who lives and reigns with You and the Holy Spirit, one God, now and forever. (H77)

Meditation

Families are complicated entities. They can be the source of considerable joy or places of profound heartache. We expect them to be sanctuaries of unconditional love, but on occasion they become the abode of great strife. Dysfunction can—and does—occur. Relationships become strained and severed.

John uses familial language to describe corporate life as the people of God. The Lord blesses our relationship with brothers and sisters in Christ, yet spiritual kinship does not cause automatic harmony. We must never underestimate our capacity to sin. The apostle gives a stern reminder of this reality when he recalls the dysfunctional relationship of Cain and Abel. The simple statement, "We should not be like Cain," refers to more than just the act of murder. The comprehensive nature of this demand of the Law is further explained by the apostle when he says, "Everyone who hates his brother is a murderer." Life in the family of God is governed by both actions and attitudes. Fratricide is terrible; but so, too, is neglecting a sister or brother suffering from destitution or fostering ill will toward them. If my heart does not feel affection for my brothers and sisters or compassion for their needs, then I need to change.

A God-pleasing change of heart can never come through exhortation or command. Simply telling me to love others might compel me with a sense of guilt, but this is not the proper motivation. Family members love not because they have to, but because they want to. John describes how this occurs, "We believe in the name of His Son Jesus Christ and love one another." Faith comes first; deeds of love follow. Our response to others is motivated by God's response to us. Rather than renouncing His ties with us and rejecting us from the family, our heavenly Father sent our faithful Brother Jesus to claim us back. We meet Him in the waters of baptism and need renewal from Him each day. We created the family discord and fractured the bonds of unity, but Jesus is the One who restored harmony and healed the wounds. We brought disgrace to the family, but He suffered disgrace on the cross so that we could remain members of God's family. Just as common traits are evidence of kinship, we now display the traits of His love, for He is constantly at work in our lives.

10 DECEMBER

Psalmody: Psalm 86:1–7
Additional Psalm: Psalm 130
Old Testament Reading: Isaiah 26:20–27:13
New Testament Reading: 1 John 4:1–21

Prayer of the Day

O God of love, those who abide in love abide in You, and You abide in them. Give us such perfect love of You and our neighbor that all fear may be cast out of our hearts and we may with confidence greet You on the Day of Judgment; through Jesus Christ, our Lord, who lives and reigns with You and the Holy Spirit, one God, now and forever. (1124)

Meditation

Discernment is a vital tool in nearly every earthly task. We must always be making judgments about the appropriateness of actions we take and words we speak lest there be serious repercussions. For example, if we speed on an icy road, injury or death could occur. How much more important is discernment in matters relating to our eternal life. John speaks of this when he tells us to "test the spirits."

John's readers may have let their guard down. They had become vulnerable to the destructive intents of false prophets, who are also labeled as liars. These charlatans had the spirit of the Antichrist because they robbed Jesus of His honor and glory as the God-man who saves the world. In doing so, they also robbed unsuspecting Christians of their salvation. Their falsehoods were seductive, deceitful, and deadly; those who were not firmly grounded in God's Word were easy prey.

The task of discerning truth from error is no less challenging today. A worldview which understands truth as relative and denies the unchanging truth of divine revelation will always views those who test claims and assertions against God's Word as old-fashioned, intolerant, unloving troublemakers. But it is never charitable to allow heresy to persist; salvation is at stake. We must always be vigilant, constantly "testing the spirits," especially as the time of our Lord's return nears and error intensifies.

This is not an issue solely for the theological elite. While we certainly pray that our pastors and teachers are so familiar with God's Word that they can detect any falsehood, each of us needs to be equipped for this task. Theological error never comes with a warning label. It is often wrapped in an attractive package by the devil and his allies, who hope that it will be widely spread and eagerly consumed.

Discernment is a sister to confession. John says, "Whoever confesses that Jesus is the Son of God, God abides in him, and he in God." To confess is to say the same things as God, to echo back to Him the truths He has spoken to us. Confession accepts no substitutes or counterfeits. It focuses on the One who first loved us so that we can then love others by sharing the truth of His Word with our mouths and our lives.

11 December

Psalmody: Psalm 5:1–8
Additional Psalm: Psalm 142
Old Testament Reading: Isaiah 28:14–29
New Testament Reading: 1 John 5:1–21
Additional Reading: 2 John 1–13
Additional Reading: 3 John 1–15

Prayer of the Day

Lord God heavenly Father, Your Son, Jesus Christ, began His ministry through a water Baptism in the Jordan River that lead Him to a bloody baptism on the cross. Even now, He saves us through the water of Holy Baptism and the blood of the cup of the new testament. Grant us steadfastness to trust in water and blood as the means by which He continues to offer us His gracious presence; for He lives and reigns with You and the Holy Spirit, one God, now and forever. (1125)

Meditation

If "beauty is in the eye of the beholder," as the old expression goes, then certainly burdens can also be a matter of perspective. A husband who cares for his mentally and physically incapacitated wife of many years regards it as a joyous privilege, while detached onlookers would regard tasks as an oppressive chore. The differences in the "eye of the beholder" reflect the relationship of the parties involved. The husband has a long, established union of love with his spouse; the unrelated bystander does not.

This analogy helps us understand the assertion that we love God by keeping His commandments, which are not "burdensome." There is no confusion about the doctrine of justification here. This is our salvation at work. God, who brought us to faith in Christ and established a relationship with us, causes us to delight in keeping His commandments.

All those who reject or misunderstand the profound truth that we are saved by God's grace through faith in Christ alone will never comprehend this. To them the commandments of God are threatening and onerous. To be sure, the Law of God expressed in His commandments accuses us of our sins and points to the condemnation we deserve. It circumscribes our behavior by showing us what is and what is not in accordance with the will of God. But because of the forgiveness we have through the Savior, Christ Jesus, we are now liberated to live a life that conforms to God's will. Our joy is not to live for ourselves but for Him. While we will only do that imperfectly on this side of eternity, everyone who is born of God by the water, blood, and Spirit of Christ "does not keep on sinning." Rather than continuously and impenitently disobeying the will of God, we truly desire to serve the Savior.

The view of the commandments as a joy rather than a burden is more than mere personal perception. It is based on the reality of

Christ's redemptive work. He is the one who promised us that His "yoke is easy" and His "burden is light" (Matthew 11:30). He is the one who has "borne our griefs and carried our sorrows" (Isaiah 53:4). He did the heavy lifting so that we could be God's unencumbered people, empowered by the Gospel to joyfully follow His commandments.

12 DECEMBER

Psalmody: Psalm 106:1–5
Additional Psalm: Psalm 106
Old Testament Reading: Isaiah 29:1–14
New Testament Reading: Jude 1–25

Prayer of the Day

Almighty God, we implore You, show Your mercy to Your humble servants that we, who put no trust in our own merits, may not be dealt with after the severity of Your judgment but according to Your mercy; through Jesus Christ, Your Son, our Lord, who lives and reigns with You and the Holy Spirit, one God, now and forever. (H85)

Meditation

What degree of intensity does God intend for Jude's mandate to "contend for the faith"? One could contend like an amateur sportsman, with a small amount of interest but no genuine zeal. On the other hand, one could contend as a combatant in battle with much more effort, concentration, and fervor. After all, life itself is at stake in such a struggle. This sort of contending is more than a hobby or momentary diversion; it is a matter of survival. Clearly, the Scripture describes the latter scenario. Contending for the faith consists of earnest and impassioned involvement from those who follow Christ.

This, however, is where our shortcomings become most evident. A self-examination of our will and desires shows that we would rather not be committed to such a degree. We prefer to be a spectator instead of a participant in the event. Avoiding controversy is always more comfortable than engaging in it. To expose, confront, and resist any deviation from God's Word is complex, arduous work that none of us relishes.

Recognition of our sinful hesitancy and failure to speak the truth sounds a warning cry, waking us to the reality that our life is at stake in this struggle. Certainly God does not need us to defend the truth of the Gospel against the false teachers around us. He can do that Himself without our feeble efforts. With one fell swoop of plague or catastrophe He could destroy His enemies. Rather, He engages us in the task of contending for the faith, not for His sake but for ours.

By enlisting us in this effort, He reminds us of the danger presented by false teachers of every era so that we might be increasingly vigilant for the treacherous spiritual threats that face us in this era. If we are not constantly contending for the truth "once for all delivered to the saints," we are tacitly consenting to the errors of the moment. This is why contending for the faith leads to a "building up" of the faith, because it moves us to continually focus on the object of our faith—our Lord Jesus. He contended for us by leaving His throne in heaven to assume human flesh, by engaging the devil in the Judean wilderness, and by facing His adversaries all the way to the cross. He was not satisfied with minimal involvement or effort. He gave His all. At His return, all contending will cease; His victory will be complete.

13 DECEMBER

Lucia, Martyr
Psalmody: Psalm 89:20–29
Additional Psalm: Psalm 143
Old Testament Reading: Isaiah 29:15–30:14
New Testament Reading: Revelation 1:1–20

Prayer of the Day

O Almighty God, by whose grace and power Your holy martyr Lucia triumphed over suffering and remained ever faithful unto death, grant us, who now remember her with thanksgiving, to be so true in our witness to You in this world that we may receive, with her, new eyes without tears and the crown of light and life; through Jesus Christ, our Lord, who lives and reigns with You and the Holy Spirit, one God, now and forever. (1126)

Lucia, Martyr

One of the victims of the great persecution of Christians under the Roman emperor Diocletian, Lucia met her death at Syracuse on the island of Sicily in AD 304. Known for her charity, "Santa Lucia" (as she is called in Italy) gave away her dowry and remained a virgin until her execution by the sword. The name Lucia means "light," and, because of that, festivals of light commemorating her became popular throughout Europe, especially in the Scandinavian countries. There her feast day corresponds with the time of year when there is the least amount of daylight. In artistic expression, she is often portrayed in a white baptismal gown, wearing a wreath of candles on her head.

Meditation

The seven churches to which the book of Revelation is addressed were facing intense persecution. The apostle John was himself exiled on the island of Patmos for confessing Christ. These struggling congregations, many of them small, were all facing tremendous hardships.

Persecution continues against Christ's Church to this very day. In some lands, the Church has all but been driven underground. Somewhere in the world today, someone will die for confessing Christ. Even in countries that grant religious liberty, the Church is losing its influence in culture and society. Many congregations are declining in size, and in a desperate but ungodly attempt to remain "relevant," some churches have watered down or compromised God's Word.

Whether the first century or the twenty-first century, it's easy for God's people to become discouraged. Our enemies are great, and we appear to be weak and small. When we observe our world, we may even wonder if Jesus still cares for us and for His Church. We wonder if He has abandoned His people.

In Revelation 1:19–20, Jesus identifies the seven stars that He is holding in His right hand and the seven lampstands that surround Him. The seven stars are the angels of the seven churches, and the seven lampstands are the seven churches addressed in Revelation. Has Jesus abandoned His people? Does He no longer care for His Church? Are the forces of evil going to triumph over Christ's Church? The answer to all these questions is a resounding no. Jesus stands in the midst of the churches. He is truly present among them. He sends His angels to guard and protect the churches. Think of your own church—St. Paul, Zion, Faith, Peace, Christ; Jesus is in the midst of your congregation. He holds it in His right hand. He cares for your congregation. He is deeply concerned about you and those who worship with you. He is not far removed from your congregation; He is present as you gather in His name.

Even though the Church may appear weak or insignificant, this is certainly not the case. Jesus is Lord of the Church, and He is in the midst of His Church. Not even the gates of hell can prevail against Christ's Church. He will not forsake His Church or His people but will continue, through His Word and Supper, to feed and nourish, strengthen, and sustain those He has freed from their sins through His blood.

14 DECEMBER

Psalmody: Psalm 27:1, 4–5, 11–14
Additional Psalm: Psalm 24
Old Testament Reading: Isaiah 30:15–26
New Testament Reading: Revelation 2:1–29

Prayer of the Day

Lord Jesus, You sent Your angels to the churches of Asia Minor to announce to them either their fidelity to the Gospel or their departure from the true faith. By the preaching of today's pastors, continue to bring to our churches the Good News of Your liberating death and resurrection by calling us to repentance and faith; for You live and reign with the Father and the Holy Spirit, one God, now and forever. (1127)

Meditation

Christ is in the midst of His churches. This is a great comfort for believers. However, this also means that Christ sees and hears everything that occurs in every congregation—the good, the bad, and the ugly. In the second and third chapters of Revelation, we are given a picture of what Christ saw when He looked at these seven churches and hear His words of rebuke and encouragement to these congregations, both pastors and people.

What would Christ say about your congregation? Would He commend you for your church's faithfulness to His Word, or would He accuse you of watering down or compromising the truth? Would He commend you for godly living and for your courageous witness, or would He condemn your congregation for not calling sin a sin and for not confessing Him before others? What would He say about your worship services? Would He praise you for services that are focused on Him, His cross and empty tomb, His Word and Sacraments, or would He rebuke you for services that seek to appease itching ears? What would Jesus say about your board meetings and voters' assemblies? Would what was said and done please Him?

These are important questions to ask. When Jesus addresses the Church in Ephesus, He warns the congregation that if they do not repent, He will remove their lampstand from its place. The lampstand represents the Ephesian congregation. In other words, if the Christians at Ephesus don't change, they run the danger of no longer being a Christian Church. Their lampstand will be removed. Christ will no longer be in their midst to strengthen and bless them.

What we say and do in the Church matters. It matters for us individually; it matters for our families, our fellow church members, and for those who do not yet believe. It also matters to Christ. If we wander too far from Christ and His Word, we may lose everything. However, as you read the letters to each of the seven churches, the message is the same: Repent. Examine your life and the life of your congregation on the basis of God's Word. Acknowledge your sin. Receive the forgiveness that Christ won for you on Calvary's cross, and then, by God's help, seek to turn from your sin. The Church ultimately is not our Church. It is Christ's Church. And thank God it is. Through His Church Christ comes to us, His people, to call us to repentance and to give us His forgiveness and life.

15 December

Psalmody: Psalm 146:1–7
Additional Psalm: Psalm 80
Old Testament Reading: Isaiah 30:27–31:9
New Testament Reading: Revelation 3:1–22

Prayer of the Day

Lord Jesus, You sent Your angels to the churches of Asia Minor to announce to them either their fidelity to the Gospel or their departure from the true faith. May Your flock today hear the call of these angels to repent and believe in the Gospel, turn from their sins to the only true God, and show forth works of mercy and charity to those who are broken by the fallenness of this world; for You live and reign with the Father and the Holy Spirit, one God, now and forever. (1128)

Meditation

Lukewarm. That's what Jesus says the Church in Laodicea is. They are neither hot nor cold. Outwardly things may have seemed fine. They gather for worship, receive the Lord's Supper, and enjoy Christian fellowship, but inwardly they had become apathetic and indifferent. This attitude was only furthered by the abundance of the material possessions that many of the members of this congregation enjoyed.

Lukewarm. That's what our world wants Christians to be—neither cold nor hot. You can believe what you want to believe about Jesus; just don't try to "force" your beliefs on anyone else. You can speak freely about your faith at church or home, but it would be politically incorrect of you to speak about it at work or school. You can follow the Ten Commandments, but don't even think about lovingly confronting someone who lives an ungodly life.

And we become lukewarm. We are content to worship when there's nothing "better" to do, study the Scriptures once in a while, pray when we feel like it or only if we have a special need, and think that our faith and Christian life is what it should be. We don't witness. We don't stand up for the truth. We buy into the devil's lie that our faith and our confession should go no further than the four walls of our church.

"I will spit you out of my mouth." That's what Jesus says will happen to the lukewarm Laodiceans if they do not repent, and this is what will happen to us as well if we continue in our smug lukewarmness. Jesus tells the Laodicean Christians, "I stand at the door and knock." Even though they believe in Jesus, He is standing at the door and knocking: "Hey, remember Me? I'm the one who you pushed out. I desire to be the center of your congregation and the center of your life. Through repentance, open the door for Me to come back into your midst."

Being lukewarm pushes Christ away. No one can serve two masters. Eventually we may even push Christ out the door of our church or the door of our hearts and slam it in His face. But Christ keeps knocking. He keeps calling us to repentance. He seeks to warm our cold and lukewarm hearts by His Gospel, so that we might desire to receive His gifts, walk in His ways, and confess His saving name to others.

16 December

Psalmody: Psalm 149
Additional Psalm: Psalm 61
Old Testament Reading: Isaiah 32:1–20
New Testament Reading: Revelation 4:1–11

Prayer of the Day

Worthy are You, our Lord and God, to receive glory and honor and power, for You created all things, and by Your will they existed and were created. Give us the faith to behold the majesty of Your presence in simple words, simple water, and simple bread and wine, as You come to us in the very body of Your Son, Jesus Christ, our Lord, who lives and reigns with You and the Holy Spirit, now and forever. (1129)

Meditation

The door to heaven is open, and John is allowed to enter. He experiences heaven even before he dies. He sees the Lord seated on the throne. He enjoys the beauty and bliss of paradise. He is permitted to hear the angels sing their unending hymn of praise. He watches as God's saints, believers from both the Old and New Testament eras, cast down their crowns before the throne of God and offer Him their worship and adoration.

We may envy the apostle John. How great it would be to experience such a magnificent revelation. How comforting it was for him and the many other Christians who were enduring persecution for the sake of the Gospel. See what lies ahead! Look what the future holds for those who belong to Christ. Remain faithful, for one day we will be with the Lord.

Although we will never receive a revelation like that of John, the door into God's presence is open for us also. It is the door to God's house. In the Divine Service, we are invited to come before God. In worship, God is present, and we join in that unending hymn of praise as we sing "holy, holy, holy" with the angels, archangels, and all the company of heaven. Like the saints in glory, we bow down before our Creator and offer Him our praise. We gather around the Lord's Table to receive heavenly food, the body and blood of Christ, which is a foretaste of the feast to come.

The Divine Service is as close as we will ever be to heaven until we die. It is truly heaven on earth. Yet, we invent excuses as to why we cannot attend church. When we do come, the knowledge that we are in the presence of our holy God and worshipping with His holy angels doesn't transform our thoughts and attitudes. We put in our time, thinking that God needs an hour a week from us rather than believing that we need this time for God to serve and help us.

The door remains open. Jesus invites us to come to Him with all our sins and burdens and to receive His rest. He invites us into His presence, into His Father's house, so that we are forgiven and strengthened for our earthly pilgrimage. Until He brings us to that eternal paradise He has prepared for us, He brings that paradise to us in His Word and Supper.

17 DECEMBER

Daniel the Prophet and the Three Young Men

Psalmody: Psalm 40:1–5, 16–17
Additional Psalm: Psalm 20
Old Testament Reading: Isaiah 33:1–24
New Testament Reading: Revelation 5:1–14

Prayer of the Day

Lord God heavenly Father, You rescued Daniel from the lion's den and the three young men from the fiery furnace through the miraculous intervention of an angel. Save us now through the presence of Jesus, the Lion of Judah, who has conquered all our enemies through His blood and taken away all our sins as the Lamb of God, who now reigns from His heavenly throne with You and the Holy Spirit, one God, now and forever. (1130)

Daniel the Prophet and the Three Young Men

Daniel the prophet and the three young men—Shadrach, Meshach, and Abednego—were among the leaders of the people of Judah who were taken into captivity in Babylon. Even in that foreign land, they remained faithful to the one true God in their piety, prayer, and life. On account of such steadfast faithfulness in the face of pagan idolatry, the three young men were thrown into a fiery furnace, from which they were saved by the Lord and emerged unharmed (Daniel 3). Similarly, Daniel was thrown into a pit of lions, from which he also was saved (Daniel 6). Blessed in all their endeavors by the Lord—and despite of the hostility of some—Daniel and the three young men were promoted to positions of leadership among the Babylonians (Daniel 2:48–49; 3:30; 6:28). To Daniel in particular the Lord revealed the interpretation of dreams and signs that were given to King Nebuchadnezzar and King Belshazzar (Daniel 2, 4, 5). To Daniel himself, the Lord gave visions of the end times.

Meditation

No one is worthy to open the seals. Sinners cannot. The saints in glory cannot. Even the powerful angels are not able to open the seals. There is only one who can open the seven seals, and He has. He is the Lamb who was slain on the altar of the cross. His blood paid the ransom so that we now are the people of God, gathered from every tribe and language, people and nation. He is not only the Lamb; He is also the Lion of the tribe of Judah. As David's Seed and David's Lord, He has conquered. Sin and death have no power over Him. He is alive, and He is seated on the throne. Exalted and victorious He is worthy to receive worship and honor both on earth and in heaven.

Christ is worthy to open the seals, and His worthiness is for our benefit. Christ is our only hope for salvation. If He had not conquered by His death, we would be forever dead in our trespasses and sins. Had He not been the perfect Lamb of God, we would never be perfected and glorified in eternity. Had He not ransomed us, we would not be the people of God.

Christ has died. He is victorious. He is our exalted Lord and Savior. He is worthy to receive power and might. Furthermore, He uses His power and might to serve us. Since He has made us people of God by His blood, we are a kingdom—His kingdom. Through the waters of Baptism, we were made citizens of His kingdom of grace, and one day we will dwell in His kingdom of glory and join in the heavenly song of the saints and angels.

We are a kingdom, and we are priests. Priests serve. They serve God. Only because of Christ can we serve God. Through Jesus Christ, our great High Priest, we are now priests. The One who alone is worthy has elevated us by His grace and made us worthy to be priests of God. Priests not only serve God; they also serve for God. They are His representatives. They pray for others. They speak God's Word to others. They serve others in the Lord's name.

Christ, the Lion and the Lamb, is worthy to open the seals. Since He has ransomed you by His blood, you are a citizen of God's kingdom and His priest as, through your vocation, you serve God by serving others.

18 December

Psalmody: Psalm 119:81–88
Additional Psalm: Psalm 145
Old Testament Reading:
Isaiah 34:1–2, 8–35:10
Additional Reading: Micah 1:1–7:20
New Testament Reading: Revelation 6:1–17

Prayer of the Day

Merciful and everlasting God, You did not spare Your only Son but delivered Him up for us all to bear our sins on the cross. Grant that our hearts may be so fixed with steadfast faith in Him that we fear not the power of sin, death, and the devil; through the same Jesus Christ, our Lord, who lives and reigns with You and the Holy Spirit, one God, now and forever. (L31)

Meditation

Things may be bad now, but they are going to be worse. Jesus had predicted that, before the end, there would be signs in nature, famine, pestilences, and increased tribulation and persecution. As Jesus opens each of these seals, His words are fulfilled. The time is short; the end is near.

Perhaps you may struggle with the idea that Jesus is opening these seals that result in so much death and destruction. Why does Jesus do this? These disasters and tribulations not only affect unbelievers; the faithful must also suffer as well. Jesus knows what is going to occur as He opens the seals, so why does He do it?

Christ's motivation for opening the seals that bring disaster and devastation is ultimately repentance. Often in the Old Testament God worked through natural disasters and invading armies to lead errant Israel to acknowledge their sin and return to Him. Before the Last Day, this will occur on a greater scale than ever before. The disasters and tribulations described as the seals are opened cannot be compared to the fires of hell and an eternity separated from God. Thus Jesus, desiring that many would repent and be saved on the day of His coming, opens the seals allowing these disasters to strike the earth, allowing the powers of death and Hades to inflict great pain and suffering.

Believers often question why there is so much evil and suffering in this world. Those in the seven churches of Revelation also had these questions as they were persecuted for confessing Christ. The opening of the seven seals reminds us and all believers in all times that God is in control. Evil is not unchecked in this world. The devil doesn't have free rein. Through His death, Christ has conquered death and hell. God works through the troubles and tribulations of this world to accomplish His purposes—to lead unbelievers to repentance and life and to strengthen the faith of those who do believe.

In the face of your own adversities and tragedies, you also may have questions. Even though you will never have all the answers to the questions of why you must endure this trouble or bear that cross, you can be certain that God is faithful. He is in control. He is always at work—even through the evil and suffering that comes into your life—to lead you to repentance, strengthen you, and keep you faithful to the end.

19 December

Adam and Eve

Psalmody: Psalm 103:11–18
Additional Psalm: Psalm 19
Old Testament Reading: Isaiah 40:1–17
New Testament Reading: Revelation 7:1–17

Prayer of the Day

Lord God, heavenly Father, You created Adam in Your image and gave him Eve as his helpmate, and after their fall into sin, You promised them a Savior who would crush the devil's might. By Your mercy, number us among those who have come out of the great tribulation with the seal of the living God on our foreheads and whose robes have been made white in the blood of the Lamb; through Jesus Christ, our Lord. (1131)

Adam and Eve

Adam was the first man, made in the image of God and given dominion over all the earth (Genesis 1:26). Eve was the first woman, formed from one of Adam's ribs to be his companion and helper (Genesis 2:18–24). God placed them in the Garden of Eden to take care of the creation as His representatives. But they forsook God's Word and plunged the world into sin (Genesis 3:1–7). For this disobedience, God drove them from the garden. Eve would suffer pain in childbirth and would chafe at her subjection to Adam; Adam would toil amid thorns and thistles and return to the dust of the ground. Yet God promised that the woman's Seed would crush the serpent's head (Genesis 3:8–24). Sin had entered God's perfect creation and changed it until God would restore it again through Christ. Eve is the mother of the human race, while Adam is representative of all humanity and the fall, as the apostle Paul writes, "For in Adam all die, so also in Christ shall all be made alive" (1 Corinthians 15:22).

Meditation

The angel seals God's people. They bear the seal on their foreheads. They are marked as those belonging to Christ. The number sealed is 144,000, a symbolic number representing the full number of believers from the Old and New Testament eras.

You are sealed. You are included in the 144,000. You are numbered among those who belong to the living Lord. At your Baptism, you received the sign of the cross upon your forehead and upon your heart, a visible reminder of how you were sealed with the promised Holy Spirit through this Sacrament. You did not choose the seal; you did not earn this seal; the seal was placed upon you.

Not only have you been sealed, you have also been clothed—clothed with the white robe that has been washed in the blood of the Lamb. It's a paradox. Blood is one of the most difficult stains to remove from clothes. However, washing these robes in the blood of Christ has made them pure white. It's the cleansing power of His blood. Since you are baptized, you are clothed with a blood-washed white robe.

Since you are sealed and clothed with your blood-washed white robe, you will stand before the throne of God. What John witnesses in his vision is your future. You will be numbered among that great multitude from every nation. You will be in the presence of God. You will never hunger or thirst. Jesus, both the Lamb who was slain for you and your Good Shepherd, will lead you to springs of living water, and God will wipe every tear from your eyes.

Our Lord saves and seals His people. He clothes them and brings them into His glorious presence, and those who are before Him worship Him. With palm branches, symbols of victory in hand, they praise God and the Lamb for their salvation.

You do not need to wait until you stand before the throne of God to participate in this heavenly worship. You are sealed and clothed with Christ. You are numbered with those who have inherited life. You have received the salvation won for you by the Lamb who was slain. The response of the Church on earth is the same as that of the Church in heaven—worship. Salvation is yours; heaven is your future, and with the angels and the saints in glory, you gladly join in their unending hymn of praise.

20 DECEMBER

Katharina von Bora Luther

Psalmody: Psalm 119:25–32
Additional Psalm: Psalm 141
Old Testament Reading: Isaiah 40:18–41:10
New Testament Reading: Revelation 8:1–13

Prayer of the Day

O God, our refuge and our strength, You raised up Your servant Katharina to support her husband in the task to reform and renew your Church in the light of Your Word. Defend and purify the Church today and grant that, through faith, we may boldly support and encourage our pastors and teachers of the faith as they and proclaim and administer the riches of Your grace made known in Jesus Christ, our Lord, who lives and reigns with You and the Holy Spirit, one God, now and forever. (1132)

Katharina von Bora Luther

Katharina von Bora (1499–1552) was placed in a convent while still a child and became a nun in 1515. In April 1523, she and eight other nuns were rescued from the convent and brought to Wittenberg. There Martin Luther helped return some of the women to their former homes and placed the rest in good families. Katharina and Martin were married on June 13, 1525. Their marriage was a happy one and was blessed with six children. Katharina skillfully managed the Luther household, which always seemed to grow because of the reformer's generous hospitality. After Luther's death in 1546, Katharina remained in Wittenberg but lived much of the time in poverty. She died in an accident while traveling with her children to Torgau in order to escape the plague.

Meditation

During Advent the Church remembers not only the first coming of Christ at Christmas but also His glorious return on the Last Day. Old Testament readings during Advent often speak of the day of the Lord when God will come to judge His people. John the Baptist's wilderness preaching calls us to repentance with the warning that judgment awaits those who do not heed this call.

The opening of the seven seals is followed by the blowing of the seven trumpets. Each of these trumpets unleashes even more death and destruction upon the earth. The seven trumpets parallel many of the plagues that God visited upon Egypt. The first trumpet results in fire and hail. The second and third trumpets, where the water is turned to blood and made bitter, recall when Moses changed the waters of the Nile into blood. The fourth trumpet brings to mind the plague of darkness.

The plagues caused great devastation in Egypt, and the destruction right before the end of the world will be greater. Instead of one lone voice in the wilderness calling people to repentance, creation itself will dramatically warn people of the coming wrath for those who refuse to repent and believe. God doesn't want anyone to perish, so through sign after sign, He will give people the opportunity to repent and believe.

The events described are frightful. They are even more frightful when we consider our sin, for we rightly deserve all of this and even more—an eternity separated from God. Although we must endure much tribulation before entering the kingdom of God, through Christ, we are reconciled to the Father. Because of Jesus we do not receive what we rightly deserve for our sins. The struggle against sin and evil in this world is fierce. The battle against the devil and his minions is intense, but the victory is ours. Christ will keep those who belong to Him until the end. The prayers of the saints on earth will continue to rise as incense to the throne of the Father. As God's people of old were delivered from slavery to Pharaoh through the plagues, so also, after these signs have been fulfilled, our final deliverance will come, and we will be forever free from sin, death, and trouble.

Even as we celebrate our Lord's coming at Christmas, we also look forward with joy and anticipation to His second coming on the Last

Day. Though the foundations of the earth give away, we will remain firm on Christ, the solid rock.

21 December

St. Thomas, Apostle

Psalmody: Psalm 102:24–28
Additional Psalm: Psalm 102
Old Testament Reading: Isaiah 42:1–25
New Testament Reading: Revelation 9:1–12

Prayer of the Day

Almighty and ever-living God, You strengthened Your apostle Thomas with firm and certain faith in the resurrection of Your Son. Grant us such faith in Jesus Christ, our Lord and our God, that we may never be found wanting in Your sight; through the same Jesus Christ, who lives and reigns with You and the Holy Spirit, one God, now and forever. (F02)

St. Thomas, Apostle

All four Gospels mention St. Thomas as one of the twelve disciples of Jesus. John's Gospel, which names him "the Twin," uses Thomas's questions to reveal truths about Jesus. It is Thomas who says, "Lord, we do not know where You are going. How can we know the way?" To this question Jesus replies, "I am the way, and the truth, and the life" (John 14:5–6). John's Gospel also tells how Thomas, on the evening of the day of Jesus' Resurrection, doubts the report of the disciples' that they had seen Jesus. Later, "doubting Thomas" becomes "believing Thomas" when he confesses Jesus as "my Lord and my God" (John 20:24–29). According to tradition, Thomas traveled eastward after Pentecost, eventually reaching India, where still today a group of people call themselves "Chris-tians of St. Thomas." Thomas was martyred for the faith by being speared to death.

Meditation

The devil is a fallen angel. He was cast out of heaven, and he has the key to the bottomless pit. From the pit he unleashes yet another plague upon the earth—locusts. Unlike the previous trumpets, these demonic locusts can harm neither creation nor God's people. Instead, they are only allowed to attack unbelievers.

The devil does have the key to hell, and he wants to populate it. He knows his eternal fate, and his desire is to bring as many mortals with him as possible. To achieve this goal, he sends calamities and disasters. He tempts and lures people into sin. He leads young and old to doubt and to disregard the truth. Often the devil is successful in his endeavors. People refuse to believe or forsake the faith they once confessed. It may appear that the devil's control and influence only increases.

The devil has the key to the bottomless pit, but he does not have the key to heaven. He cannot lock anyone out of glory. He can harm the body, but he cannot destroy the soul. Even though his names Abaddon and Apollyon mean destroyer, he has already been crushed by the cross of Christ. Even when he desires to inflict suffering on many, God determines the limits of Satan's destruction. Although he wishes to attack the faithful with locusts, he is not permitted. By God's command only unbelievers can be attacked, and so the devil attacks even though he doesn't realize his folly. By allowing the devil to do this, God desires to bring the unbelievers to repentance and faith. The goal is to snatch them from the devil's power and unlock and open the door to heaven for them. But the devil cannot resist doing evil, and so he attacks with a vengeance.

The devil does not have the key to heaven. Jesus does. By His death, He destroyed death and the devil, and by His coming to life, He has opened the door of heaven for you and for all believers. He has now given the keys of heaven to His Church so that, as people are forgiven, the door to heaven is opened for them. As you are absolved, the heavenly door stands wide open for you, and even though the devil often attacks and harms you, he can never lock you out of the paradise your Lord has prepared for you.

22 DECEMBER

Psalmody: Psalm 115:1–8, 11
Additional Psalm: Psalm 125
Old Testament Reading: Isaiah 43:1–24
New Testament Reading:
Revelation 9:13–10:11

Prayer of the Day

Almighty and ever-living God, You have given exceedingly great and precious promises to those who trust in You. Grant us so firmly to believe in Your Son Jesus that our faith may never be found wanting; through the same Jesus Christ, our Lord, who lives and reigns with You and the Holy Spirit, one God, now and forever. (B85)

Meditation

When John eats the scroll, it is both sweet and bitter; it tastes sweet as honey in his mouth, and once it enters his stomach, it is bitter. Bitter. There are many bitter words in Revelation. John has recorded many terrible events that will occur before the end of the world. With the opening of the seals and the sounding of the trumpets, one catastrophic event after another will occur. There will be massive devastation; people will perish; and Satan will be unleashed for a time. God allows all this bitterness to happen to lead people to repentance. However, what's even bitterer than all these events is the fact that people will not repent of their sin or forsake the worship of idols. Instead, they will persist in their sin and unbelief all the more.

The scroll that John eats is also sweet as honey. John must proclaim the terrible events that will occur before the end. He must proclaim the Law and the wrath of God, but as the prophets before him, he also proclaims the grace and mercy of God. He declares that God will sustain His people and His Church through the impending trials and tribulations. He has the privilege of entering the throne room of heaven and conveying the beauty and joy of the world to come. His visions offer assurance that Jesus is not only the Lord of the Church but Lord of all things, and He acts in human history for the benefit and blessing of His people and to extend His kingdom. This is truly the Gospel in all its sweetness.

It is often around this point in Revelation that many people stop reading. Plague after plague, natural disaster after disaster, trial after trial—it seems as though it will never end. It's too depressing, too devastating, and too difficult to comprehend, and so they give up. Many words in Revelation are bitter, but bitterness is not the only message. Neither is bitterness the final message. God's saints will triumph. He will keep them faithful unto the end. Christ will come again and bring His own into the presence of His Father. All believers will dwell in the new heaven and new earth for all eternity. We will take our place at the marriage feast of the Lamb in the Father's kingdom that will never end. How sweet indeed this Gospel word is for us.

23 December

Psalmody: Psalm 39:4–8
Additional Psalm: Psalm 144
Old Testament Reading: Isaiah 43:25–44:20
New Testament Reading: Revelation 11:1–19

Prayer of the Day

O God, Your divine wisdom sets in order all things in heaven and on earth. Put away from us all things hurtful and give us those things that are beneficial for us; through Jesus Christ, Your Son, our Lord, who lives and reigns with You and the Holy Spirit, one God, now and forever. (B82)

Meditation

In the next couple of days, many gifts will be exchanged and many presents opened. Some people exchange presents to remember the greatest gift the Father gave us in His Son on the first Christmas. Others exchange gifts as a cultural or family tradition, while still others, even though they may exchange presents, passionately desire to remove Christ from Christmas altogether.

In today's Scripture, God sends two witnesses to prophesy for three and a half years. They wear sackcloth, for their message is one of judgment and repentance. They preach, and in the end, they are put to death. Instead mourning their demise, people rejoice and even exchange presents, for they are glad that they no longer have to endure the witnesses' tormenting message.

For many people today, Christmas would be much better if presents were exchanged without mention of the gift of the Christ Child. In many minds, Christmas would be better if everyone talked about peace on earth, but no one mentioned the Prince of Peace. For many, the joy of the season is found in the presents under the tree rather than the joy that comes from the baby wrapped in swaddling cloths and lying in a manger.

Beginning with Herod, who attempted to kill this newborn king, many sought the demise of Jesus, and many were glad when He was crucified. To this day, many rejoice at the death of Christians and aggressively seek their demise, and many more seek to silence the Gospel of Jesus Christ. On Good Friday, it appeared that the forces of evil had silenced Christ, but this only lasted three short days since He rose victoriously from the grave. In the reading, the two witnesses were put to death only to be raised again to life after three and a half days.

The enemies of Christ and His Church will not overcome. On the Last Day the kingdom of this world will become the kingdom of our Lord and of His Christ, and He will reign forever. No longer will there be anyone who rejects the kingdom, who persecutes the citizens of God's kingdom, or who seeks to stifle the good news of the kingdom. Those who reject Christ and His kingdom will be condemned forever. You, however, will be welcomed into God's presence where you will rejoice with all the saints in His heavenly temple forever.

THE TIME OF CHRISTMAS

Christmas Season

24 December

The Nativity of Our Lord—Christmas Eve

Psalmody: Psalm 98:1–6, 9
Additional Psalm: Psalm 2
Old Testament Reading:
Isaiah 44:21–45:13, 20–25
Additional Reading: Daniel 10:1–12:13
Additional Reading: Isaiah 48:1–22
New Testament Reading: Revelation 12:1–17

Prayer of the Day

O God, You make us glad with the yearly remembrance of the birth of Your only-begotten Son, Jesus Christ. Grant that as we joyfully receive Him as our Redeemer, we may with sure confidence behold Him when He comes to be our Judge; through the same Jesus Christ, our Lord, who lives and reigns with You and the Holy Spirit, one God, now and forever. (L05)

The Nativity of Our Lord—Christmas Eve

The exact date of the birth of Jesus is not known, and during the earliest centuries of the Church it seemed to have little significance. This followed the Early Church's tradition of honoring and celebrating a Christian's death as his or her birth date into eternity and the ongoing presence of Jesus. Likewise the life, work, death, and resurrection of the Christ was of much greater importance to early Christians than the earthly details of His life. The earliest nativity feast, Epiphany (January 6), celebrated both the birth and Baptism of Christ. However, in the fourth century, great Christological controversies that questioned Christ's divinity and humanity raced through Christianity. By AD 336, December 25 had been established in Rome as the celebration of Christ's birth, a festival welcomed particularly by orthodox Christians in the West. From Rome, Christ's natal festival spread throughout the Western Church. In Eastern traditions of the Church, Epiphany remains the principal celebration of the birth of Jesus.

Meditation

Tonight in worship we will again hear the Christmas Gospel. Mary and Joseph, the baby in the manger, shepherds watching their flocks by night, the heavenly host—it's all so familiar to us. Revelation 12 is not an appointed Scripture reading for any Christmas service but could be, for it reminds us of the unseen realities of Christ's birth. As soon as Christ was born, the devil sought to destroy Him. On this holy night, the Son of God entered the battlefield. Mary holds her baby in her arms; the scene appears peaceful and serene, but the greatest battle ever has begun.

It wouldn't take long for Satan to strike. He used King Herod to attempt to kill this newborn King. God hid Jesus and His earthly family in Egypt until Herod died. This struggle would continue throughout our Lord's life and ministry and reach its climax on the cross. On Mount Calvary, Jesus conquered the devil. He prevailed by His death. The result is that Satan has been cast out of heaven.

This is good news for you. Since Satan has been thrown down from heaven, he can no longer accuse you before God. In the Old Testament era, Satan was allowed into God's presence, but that changed at the cross. He has been hurled down from heaven. Additionally, since Christ conquered the devil, we, too, conquer him. The strength to conquer is not from within, for by ourselves we would surely fail. Instead, we overcome the devil by the blood of the Lamb and by the word of the testimony. Through Christ and His Word, the victory is ours.

But there's also some bad news. The devil knows he's defeated. He has no doubt what his future holds. He knows his time is short, so he now pursues the woman. He goes after the

Church, believers, you! Until the end, the devil will pursue those who belong to the Lamb. He will tempt you. He will attack you. He will seek to destroy your faith.

"For unto you is born this day in the city of David a Savior . . ." (Luke 2:11). Even at His birth, Jesus is your Savior. He has rescued you from sin, death, and the power of the devil. Even though the devil will attack you, you are a conqueror through Christ, and because of the baby lying in the manger, your eternal future is secure.

25 DECEMBER

The Nativity of Our Lord—Christmas Day

Psalmody: Psalm 96:1–5, 11–13
Additional Psalm: Psalm 150
Old Testament Reading: Isaiah 49:1–18
New Testament Reading: Matthew 1:1–17

Prayer of the Day

Most merciful God, You gave Your eternal Word to become incarnate of the pure Virgin. Grant Your people grace to put away fleshly lusts, that they may be ready for Your visitation; through Jesus Christ, our Lord, who lives and reigns with You and the Holy Spirit, one God, now and forever. (L07)

The Nativity of Our Lord—Christmas Day

Advent prepared us for the coming of the Savior, the fulfillment of the promise first made in the Garden of Eden in response to the sin of Adam and Eve. Christmas is the day we celebrate that hope fulfilled. Jesus is the only hope of the world, because Jesus is the only one who could set us free from our sins. The commemoration of the Nativity of Our Lord puts before us once again the story of the long-awaited King who left His heavenly throne to enter time and become human like one of us. When God wanted to save you from your sins, He did not send a prophet or even an angel: He sent His own Son into human flesh just like ours.

Meditation

On this joyful day of the Lord's Nativity, we read a long list of names that show the descent of our Lord from Abraham, to whom the promise had been given that from his seed would come the One who would bring blessing to every nation and every family of the earth. When we read the list attentively, we notice what sinners from whom the Lord chose to descend. How could it be otherwise, when He had come to rescue us from our sin?

Not too far down the list is Tamar. You can read her story in Genesis 38 where it sticks out like a sore thumb in the Joseph cycle. Her father-in-law, Judah, was ready to burn her for playing the part of a harlot when she reveals to him who the true father of her child is, and he must confess, "She is more righteous than I" (Genesis 38:26). From Judah and Tamar, our Lord descends.

Rahab sticks out next. The spies had been sent into the land and a prostitute who lived on Jericho's wall had received them and protected them. Through her faith she was commended, and not only was her life spared, but she became an ancestress to the One who would later show kindness and forgiveness to a woman caught in the very act of adultery (John 8).

Then there is Ruth, a Moabite. She was not one of God's chosen people at all but from a nation that had begun through Lot's incest with his daughters. Her kindness to her mother-in-law, Naomi, showed that she had embraced the faith of the God of Israel. She would became the great-grandmother of Israel's greatest king—David—and thus also ancestress to the Savior.

David brings us to Bathsheba. She is not named in the list, but spoken of rather as "the wife of Uriah" so that we might not forget David's sin: the lust, the adultery, the lying, the murder, and the attempted cover-up. Behold, then, the ancestors of the Lord Jesus. Sinners like us, and yet from them, born of such blood, came the One who was without sin. Son of the pure Virgin, He came to shed His blood to atone for a race gone wrong. He belongs to us sinners. Since he had no sin of His own, He was free to take our sin upon Himself. He became a child of sinful men to bring us the blessing of becoming the children of God.

26 DECEMBER

St. Stephen, Martyr

Psalmody: Psalm 34:4–10, 19
Additional Psalm: Psalm 60
Old Testament Reading:
Isaiah 49:22–26; 50:4–51:8, 12–16
New Testament Reading: Matthew 1:18–25

Prayer of the Day

Heavenly Father, in the midst of our sufferings for the sake of Christ grant us grace to follow the example of the first martyr, Stephen, that we also may look to the One who suffered and was crucified on our behalf and pray for those who do us wrong; through Jesus Christ, our Lord, who lives and reigns with You and the Holy Spirit, one God, now and forever. (F03)

St. Stephen, Martyr

St. Stephen, "a man full of faith and the Holy Spirit" (Acts 6:5), was one of the Church's first seven deacons. He was appointed by the leaders of the Church to distribute food and other necessities to the poor in the growing Christian community in Jerusalem, thereby giving the apostles more time for their public ministry of proclamation (Acts 6:2–5). He and the other deacons apparently were expected not only to wait on tables but also to teach and preach. When some became jealous of him, they brought Stephen to the Sanhedrin and falsely charged him with blaspheming against Moses (Acts 6:9–14). Stephen's confession of faith, along with his rebuke of the members of the Sanhedrin for having rejected their Messiah and being responsible for His death, so infuriated them that they dragged him out of the city and stoned him to death. Stephen is honored as the Church's first martyr and for his words of commendation and forgiveness as he lay dying: "Lord Jesus, receive my spirit" and "Lord, do not hold this sin against them" (Acts 7:59–60).

Meditation

Joseph was a just man—that is, a justified man, a man whose faith in the Lord had been accounted to him as righteousness. As such, he loved the Law of God and strove to obey it by the Holy Spirit's power. He had chosen a wife whom, he believed, loved and cherished that Law in the same way. But then she became pregnant.

As a justified man, a sinner who knew that he stood before God only by the gift of God's forgiveness, Joseph did not desire to shame Mary. No doubt deeply saddened and hurt, he had decided to divorce in a quiet way. He could not share his life with someone who thought so lightly of God's holy laws.

While he was planning on this, he had a dream. Just as God had spoken to the patriarch Joseph in the Old Testament through dreams, so now He speaks to this Joseph through His holy angel. "Joseph, Son of David, do not fear to take Mary as your wife, for that which is conceived in her is from the Holy Spirit." We are never told if Mary tried to explain this to Joseph, or if she simply thought it would be impossible to convince anyone. Either way,

Joseph's heart now melts, and he feels himself an even greater sinner than before. He had doubted his beloved Mary and had imputed to her sins that she had never committed.

"She will bear a son, and you shall call His name Jesus, for He will save His people from their sins." Joseph listened with growing awe. For sinners such as himself, the little One had come. He had come to be the sin bearer for the whole human race. It was exactly as the prophet had said years and years before: "Behold, the virgin shall conceive and bear a son, and they shall call His name Immanuel."

"The God who is with us," Joseph said to himself as he woke from his sleep and did as the angel told him. He went and took Mary and brought her into his home. And he did not touch her in the way of a husband until she had given birth, for she was carrying within her body the God who is with us. When the child was born, Joseph stared at the promise of the ages, and then joyfully gave Him the appointed name: Jesus.

27 DECEMBER

St. John, Apostle and Evangelist

Psalmody: Psalm 72:1, 4, 10–15, 18–19
Additional Psalm: Psalm 92
Old Testament Reading: Isaiah 51:17–52:12
New Testament Reading: Matthew 2:1–12

Prayer of the Day

Merciful Lord, cast the bright beams of Your light upon Your Church that we, being instructed in the doctrine of Your blessed apostle and evangelist John, may come to the light of everlasting life; for You live and reign with the Father and the Holy Spirit, one God, now and forever. (F04)

St. John, Apostle and Evangelist

St. John was a son of Zebedee and brother of James the Elder (whose festival day is July 25). John was among the first disciples to be called by Jesus (Matthew 4:18–22) and became known as "the disciple whom Jesus loved," as he refers to himself in the Gospel that bears his name (e.g., John 21:20). Of the twelve, John alone did not forsake Jesus in the hours of His suffering and death. With the faithful women, he stood at the cross, where our Lord made him the guardian of His mother. After Pentecost, John spent his ministry in Jerusalem and at Ephesus, where tradition says he was bishop. He wrote the fourth Gospel, the three Epistles that bear his name, and the Book of Revelation. Especially memorable in his Gospel are the account of the wedding at Cana (John 2:1–12), the "Gospel in a nutshell" (John 3:16), Jesus' saying about the Good Shepherd (John 10:11–16), the raising of Lazarus from the dead (John 11), and Jesus' meeting of Mary Magdalene on Easter morning (John 20:11–18). According to tradition, John was banished to the island of Patmos (off the coast of Asia Minor) by the Roman emperor Domitian. John lived to a very old age, surviving all the apostles, and died at Ephesus about the year AD 100.

Meditation

They arrive in Jerusalem excited and ready to honor the newborn king. Yet they find no celebrations, no party, just business as usual. Perplexed, they inquire where the newborn King may be found. Such an inquiry troubles Jerusalem, for Herod soon hears of it. He suffered no rivals. He'd already butchered family members whom he feared wanted his throne. When Herod was troubled, all Jerusalem was set trembling. As far as Herod was concerned, there was only one king in Judah, Herod the Great, and any other who wished to be king would soon find himself dead.

But Herod knows what to do. He calls the Bible scholars to inquire where that supposed

Messiah of theirs was to be born. They recite immediately from Micah: "Bethlehem, in the land of Judah." Off he sends the wise men to find the child and then bring him word: "that I too may come and worship Him." Bloody worship that is.

We are not told how the star had first communicated to the wise men that a king had been borne to the Jews, but we are told that after they learned from God's Word where to find the Child they sought, the star blazed again before them and led them on their way. With great joy, they enter the house, behold the mother and the child, and offer their gifts: gold, frankincense, and myrrh.

Long has the Church seen in the gifts a mystical confession of the child's true identity. Gold to crown the King of kings, for the child is truly the everlasting King and the long-awaited One who would sit on David's throne and rule through endless days. Frankincense, for the child is not only Son of David but also Son of God—Immanuel, God in our flesh—to whom divine worship is due. Myrrh is most mysterious of all, like giving a child the gift of embalming fluid. It pointed to what this Son of David and Son of God had come to do: to render His life a sacrifice for your sins and the sins of the whole world. He was born to die that, in His death, sin might be forgiven and death itself destroyed.

The wise men do not return to the murderous king, but warned in a dream, they take another route home. Their lives were forever changed by what they had experienced, though—ours too. The bright star of the Word of God still leads us to where we find the Christ and offer to Him our worship.

28 DECEMBER

The Holy Innocents, Martyrs

Psalmody: Psalm 9:11–14
Additional Psalm: Psalm 31
Old Testament Reading: Isaiah 52:13–54:10
New Testament Reading: Matthew 2:13–23

Prayer of the Day

Almighty God, the martyred innocents of Bethlehem showed forth Your praise not by speaking but by dying. Put to death in us all that is in conflict with Your will that our lives may bear witness to the faith we profess with our lips; through Jesus Christ, our Lord, who lives and reigns with You and the Holy Spirit, one God, now and forever. (F05)

The Holy Innocents, Martyrs

Matthew's Gospel tells of King Herod's vicious plot against the infant Jesus after being "tricked" by the Wise Men. Threatened by the one "born King of the Jews," Herod murdered all the children in and around Bethlehem who were two years old or younger (Matthew 2:16–18). These "innocents," commemorated just three days after the celebration of Jesus' birth, remind us not only of the terrible brutality of which human beings are capable but more significantly of the persecution Jesus endured from the beginning of His earthly life. Although Jesus' life was providentially spared at this time, many years later, another ruler, Pontius Pilate, would sentence the innocent Jesus to death.

Meditation

In Jesus, the whole history of Israel is reenacted. Abraham went to Egypt, and of course, so did the children of Israel. "Out of Egypt I called my son," the prophet Hosea said. He was describing the Exodus, but his words held a greater import than even he knew. Jesus is Israel reduced to one, the perfect Son of the Father.

Joseph, however, is likely not thinking of how he is fulfilling prophecy by carrying away the blessed Virgin and her holy Child. He is thinking only of keeping them alive, keeping them safe. Herod has them in his sights. As the miles grow between the holy family and the wicked king, Joseph breathes easier.

Herod, realizing that the wise men had betrayed him, decided that a shotgun method of dealing with the problem might work. He ordered all the male children in Bethlehem, and—to play it safe—in the surrounding regions, to be killed. Any male two years old or under was butchered. This is how unbelief deals with the gift of God's Son: it seeks His death, because it fears His reign. For indeed, as we sing, "for He who offers heavenly birth seeks not the kingdoms of the earth" (*LSB* 399:2).

Unspeakable grief comes as Rachel weeps for her children who are no more, fulfilling the sad words of Jeremiah 31. Homes were shattered by the senseless fear of a man whose real enemy was already closing in on to take his throne, his kingdom, his very life despite his attempts to preserve it. Death would come for Herod. Again, the angel appears to Joseph in Egypt in a dream to let him know that he can now return; Herod has died.

Yet at the very borders he heard word that Archelaus, Herod's son, was now upon the throne, and he judged Judea not a safe place yet for his family. He headed north, up to Nazareth, where there was plenty of work for a carpenter. Unwittingly, this fulfilled another passage of Scripture—the Child would be called a Nazarene, a play on the word for "branch." The *nazar* (Hebrew) is the branch from David's house, in whom the promise of an everlasting kingdom would be fulfilled. It would not be the sort of king or kingdom that Herod feared, but rather a kingdom in the hearts of human beings.

29 DECEMBER

David

Psalmody: Psalm 78:1–7
Additional Psalm: Psalm 93
Old Testament Reading: Isaiah 55:1–13
New Testament Reading: Luke 1:1–25

Prayer of the Day

God of majesty, whom saints and angels delight to worship in heaven, we give You thanks for David who, through the Psalter, gave Your people hymns to sing with joy in our worship on earth so that we may glimpse Your beauty. Bring us to the fulfillment of that hope of perfection that will be ours as we stand before Your unveiled glory; through Jesus Christ, our Lord, who lives and reigns with You and the Holy Spirit, one God, now and forever. (1133)

David

David, the greatest of Israel's kings, ruled from about 1010 to 970 BC. The events of his life are found in 1 Samuel 16 through 1 Kings 2 and in 1 Chronicles 10–29. David was also gifted musically. He was skilled in playing the lyre and the author of no fewer than seventy-three psalms, including the beloved Psalm 23. His public and private character displayed a mixture of good (for example, his defeat of the giant Goliath [1 Samuel 17]) and evil (as in his adultery with Uriah's wife, followed by his murder of Uriah [2 Samuel 11]). David's greatness lay in his fierce loyalty to God as Israel's military and political leader, coupled with his willingness to acknowledge his sins and ask for

God's forgiveness (2 Samuel 12; see also Psalm 51). It was under David's leadership that the people of Israel were united into a single nation with Jerusalem as its capital city.

Meditation

Luke begins his account of the life of our Lord where none of the other evangelists begin: in the temple. He will end his account there too (see Luke 24:43). Zechariah, faithful priest of the Lord offering incense in the Holy Place, is startled by an angel. Their images are before him on the curtain that separated the Holy Place from the most holy place, but there stood beside him the reality, not the image.

And what news the angel brought! His prayer had been heard, and his wife would conceive. Surely, Zechariah must have thought: that prayer was rather long ago, wasn't it? The Lord's timing is not ours. Zechariah and Elizabeth had waited and prayed and had long since resigned themselves to childlessness. But God had other plans.

"You shall call his name John. And you will have joy and gladness, and many will rejoice at his birth, for he will be great before the Lord. . . . and he will go before Him in the power and spirit of Elijah . . . to make ready for the Lord a people prepared." The angel delivered the message so calmly and certainly. All the while, Zechariah's mind is spinning: "but, but, but."

At last he bursts out, "How shall I know this? For I am an old man, and my wife is advanced in years." Unbelief staggers before the astonishing promises of God. And nothing seems to rile an angel so much as our foolish doubting. You see, they've never known a single word of God to fail, and they know we haven't either. They don't understand how we could possibly doubt.

Gabriel gives Zechariah a sign—a sign of silence. He will be silent as he watches the promise of God take shape and grow before his eyes. Then the angel was gone. Zechariah must have waited a bit in stunned silence

before walking out. The people were wondering why he delayed, and why he wasn't giving them the blessing. He began to motion with his hands, and they realized that something had happened in the temple, something to strike silence into the old priest.

It was Abraham and Sarah all over again, an old woman beyond the years of childbearing conceiving and carrying a child. The Lord seems to delight in doing what we think is impossible. Would Zechariah lay his hand upon her swelling womb and weep in silence over the surpassing goodness of God? The time long promised was now at hand.

30 DECEMBER

Psalmody: Psalm 89:1–4, 14–18
Additional Psalm: Psalm 132
Old Testament Reading:
Isaiah 58:1–59:3, 14–21
New Testament Reading: Luke 1:26–38

Prayer of the Day

Almighty God, grant that the birth of Your only-begotten Son in the flesh may set us free from the bondage of sin; through Jesus Christ, Your Son, our Lord, who lives and reigns with You and the Holy Spirit, one God, now and forever. (L08)

Meditation

How striking the contrast between Zechariah and the Blessed Virgin Mary. When the angel appeared to Zechariah, we are told that he was troubled and afraid. Mary is not afraid at the angel's appearing but she is troubled at the greeting he gave her: "Greetings (or, perhaps better rendered, "Rejoice"—the Greek can be translated either way), O favored one, the Lord is with you!" Humble Mary wonders what such a greeting can possibly mean; the sudden appearing of the angel doesn't seem to surprise her in the least.

Gabriel tells her not to fear for she has found favor with God. She will conceive and bear a Son, a Son who will be named Jesus. We can well imagine the angel staring in awe at her as he continues his message: "He will be great and will be called the Son of the Most High. And the Lord God will give Him the throne of His father David, and He will reign over the house of Jacob forever, and of His kingdom there will be no end."

All of this means that Gabriel knows he is standing before the woman who will be mother of God. The Child born of this woman will be the One he delights to serve and honor and has since his creation. The Creator born of a creature. The Maker conceived and carried in the womb of one He made. If the news to Zechariah was staggering, how much more the news to the blessed Virgin.

Unlike Zechariah, Mary does not say: "How shall I know this?" She simply asks for more information: "How will this be, since I am a virgin?" There is no doubt in her words. The angel tells her that this miracle beyond all miracles will be performed within her by the power of the Holy Spirit who will overshadow her and bring forth in her body the Son of God. Truly, her Son, sharing fully her humanity, and yet at the same time the only Son of the Father who was before the ages began.

The angel lets her in on Elizabeth's secret, too, and then adds: "For nothing will be impossible with God." He is the master of bringing the impossible to pass. Mary humbly bows before the weight that has been laid on her: "Behold, I am the servant of the Lord; let it be to me according to your word." And so began the fulfillment of all of God's promises, taking shape in the Virgin's womb.

31 DECEMBER

Psalmody: Psalm 111:1–6, 10
Additional Psalm: Psalm 8
Old Testament Reading: Isaiah 60:1–22
New Testament Reading: Luke 1:39–56

Prayer of the Day

Eternal God, we commit to Your mercy and forgiveness the year now ending and commend to Your blessing and love the times yet to come. In the new year, abide among us with Your Holy Spirit that we may always trust in the saving name of our Lord Jesus Christ, who lives and reigns with You and the Holy Spirit, one God, now and forever. (F06)

Meditation

How terrifying it must have been for Mary after the angel departed. Who could possibly believe the news that had been told her? Another explanation of her pregnancy would leap to the mind of sinful men—and even her espoused Joseph. But the angel had told her that Elizabeth was carrying a miracle baby too, and so Mary heads down to Judea to find her kinswoman.

As the voice of Mary's greeting reaches Elizabeth's ears, John does a somersault of joy in her aged womb. Suddenly Elizabeth understands. The Holy Spirit tells her the secret of the ages, and she stands and stares in wonder at the young woman before her.

"Blessed are you among women," she cries out. "And blessed is the fruit of your womb!" Indeed, the One foretold to Abraham, who would bring blessing to every family of the earth, was literally in front of her. "Why is this granted to me that the mother of my Lord should come to me?"

At this point, one can imagine the blessed Virgin's relief and joy. She's not the only one who knows this secret. Elizabeth knows, and even better, believes. Elizabeth cries out, "And blessed is she who believed that there would be a fulfillment of what was spoken to her from the Lord."

So Elizabeth teaches us the true blessedness of the blessed Virgin. She is blessed in being mother of the Blessed One, but she is also blessed in believing the astonishing promise of God to her. Mary can keep it in no longer. She bursts forth into a song of praise that the Church has delighted to sing with her for century upon century: "My soul magnifies the Lord, and my spirit rejoices in God my Savior." Yes, all generations from that time forward have and will call Mary "blessed."

Though Luke does not explicitly say so, it is suggestive that Mary remained three months. It is likely that she stayed through to John's birth. The last trimester can be difficult for any woman, let alone an old one. Mary was there to serve and help, even as her Son came not to be served but to serve and to give His life as the ransom for many.